# Syria
# Jordan

MICHELIN

Travel Publications

Syr./Jor. ang. 1

## Note to readers

The history, archeology and people of Syria and Jordan have many points in common, and for this reason a general introduction, entitled "Eastern Promise" deals with these subjects.

To understand how the guide is organised, turn to the contents list on page 4.

The countries are presented by region. The tour itineraries described and shown on the maps give ideas for excursions off the beaten track; ■ indicates possible overnight halts.

Just one point here about the practical information. The chapters entitled "Practical Information" give general information to help you prepare your trip and get along once there. In the chapters "Exploring Syria" and "Exploring Jordan", after each description of a town or tour itinerary there is a practical section (eg page 133 "Making the most of Damascus") giving all the information about the place in question: access, useful addresses, accommodation, eating out, other things to do, shopping guide, etc.

Hotels and restaurants are classed by price category (in US dollars) to help you plan your budget. However, we are obliged to point out that living costs vary constantly and opening hours may change, so that prices and practical information may have changed since publication.

Michelin Travel Publications
Published in 2000

# NEOS

N ew – In the NEOS guides emphasis is placed on the discovery and enjoyment of a new destination through meeting the people, tasting the food and absorbing the exotic atmosphere. In addition to recommendations on which sights to see, we give details on the most suitable places to stay and eat, on what to look out for in traditional markets and where to go in search of the hidden character of the region, its crafts and its dancing rhythms. For those keen to explore places on foot, we provide guidelines and useful addresses in order to help organise walks to suit all tastes.

E xpert – The NEOS guides are written by people who have travelled in the country and researched the sites before recommending them by the allocation of stars. Accommodation and restaurants are similarly recommended by a 😊 on the grounds of quality and value for money. Cartographers have drawn easy-to-use maps with clearly marked itineraries, as well as detailed plans of towns, archeological sites and large museums.

O pen to all cultures, the NEOS guides provide an insight into the daily lives of the local people. In a world that is becoming ever more accessible, it is vital that religious practices, regional etiquette, traditional customs and languages be understood and respected by all travellers. Equipped with this knowledge, visitors can seek to share and enjoy with confidence the best of the local cuisine, musical harmonies and the skills involved in the production of arts and crafts.

S ensitive to the atmosphere and heritage of a foreign land, the NEOS guides encourage travellers to see, hear, smell and feel a country, through words and images. Take inspiration from the enthusiasm of our experienced travel writers and make this a journey full of discovery and enchantment.

# EASTERN PROMISE

# SYRIA

P. Meunier

# JORDAN

## Exploring Jordan      308

# EASTERN
# PROMISE

# Setting the scene

P. Meunier

Tile decoration
from the Darwish
Pasha Mosque
in Damascus

| Dates BC | Events | Sites |
|---|---|---|
| 8500-4500 | Neolithic revolution: settlement, the development of agriculture and villages. | *Aïn Ghazal, Beidah Mureybet, Tell Halaf.* |
| 4500-3200 | Copper Age: spread of settlement on the Mesopotamian model. Traditional date of Creation according to Jewish calendar. | *Habuba Kabira.* |
| 3200-1200 | Bronze age: development of city-states, the invention of writing | *Mari, Ebla.* |
| 1500 | The Canaanites on the Mediterranean coast. | *Ugarit.* |
| 1200 | Invasions by the Sea Peoples. | |
| 1200-539 | Iron Age: exodus of the Israelites. The kingdoms of Edom, Moab and Ammon. Aramean, Phoenician and Neo-Hittite principalities in northern Syria. | *Aïn Dara, Arwad.* |
| 900-539 | Assyrian, then Babylonian domination. | |
| 539-332 | Persian domination. | |
| 332-63 | Conquest by Alexander the Great. Rivalry between the Seleucids and the Lagids. | *Doura Europos, Iraq al-Amir.* |
| 63 | Conquest by Pompey. Syria made into a Roman Province. Expansion and prosperity. | *Apamea, Bosra, Decapolis, Jarash.* |

| Dates AD | Events | Sites |
|---|---|---|
| 46-58 | St Paul evangelises. The rise of Christianity. | |
| 106 | Annexation of the Nabataean kingdom by the Roman Empire. | *Petra.* |
| 272 | Aurelian conquers Palmyra. | *Palmyra.* |
| 324-630 | Disintegration of the Roman Empire; establishment of the Byzantine Empire. | *Madaba, Rassafa, St-Siméon, the Dead Cities.* |
| 570-661 | Muhammad. The Arab conquest and rise of Islam. | |
| 661-750 | Damascus established as the capital of the Umayyad Empire. | *Amman, desert castles, Damascus.* |
| 750-1171 | Arab dynasties (Abbasids, Fatimids). | *Raqqa.* |
| 1071-1263 | First foreign dynasties (Seljuk, Zengid, Ayyubids). | *Aleppo citadel.* |
| 1096-1291 | The Crusades followed by Muslim reconquest under Nur al-Din, Saladin and Baybars. | *Kérak, Krak des Chevaliers, Marqab, Saône.* |
| 1250-1516 | The Mamelukes. | |
| 1400 | Mongol invasion led by Tamerlane. | |
| 1453 | Constantinople falls into the hands of the Ottoman Turks. | |
| 1516-1918 | The Ottoman provinces of Syria. and Palestine governed by Turkish pashas. | *Salt, Aleppo, Damascus.* |
| 1914-1918 | First World War: Arab revolt against the Turks. | |
| 1922 | Institution of the British and French mandates; delimitation of modern frontiers. | |

# HISTORICAL MILESTONES

The history of both Syria and Jordan is a disruptive one largely as a result of their positions at the intersection of the African, Asian and European continents, and at the crossroads of the great empires of Mesopotamia, Egypt and Anatolia. Many of the peoples inhabiting these lands migrated from Arabia in successive waves as it was subjugated by powerful dynasties. In time, these tribal people were to form independent kingdoms – often highly original and innovative – based on their direct experiences of weak government and feeble leaders. This complex evolution is reflected in the extraordinarily diverse and remarkably intact architectural fragments that survive scattered there. Having said this, both states preserve another legacy that has yet to be reconstructed by archeological teams, often from abroad, who continue to provide an ever more precise insight into long vanished civilisations.

## Cradle of Civilisation

### Neolithic revolution (9th-5th millennia BC)

Prior to the Ice Age, man had subsisted from hunting, fishing and gathering for more than a million years, content to live in caves or as nomads. But the climatic changes at the end of the Ice Age revolutionised this way of life. As water supplies dwindled and disappeared, wild animals and plants became scarce and the hunter-gatherer was constrained to discovering how to grow sufficient food to satisfy his needs. Having to maintain and watch over his crops until harvest, man was forced to settle and adapt to living in village communities. He learnt to domesticate small animals (sheep and goats), and realised the benefits of animal husbandry. By 10 000 BC sedentary life was well established, with several settlements dotting the region between the Tigris and the Euphrates (Mesopotamia). This so-called Neolithic revolution, although hesitant at first, was to have far-reaching consequences for the course of human history over succeeding millennia, with this new style of life spreading quickly to neighbouring continents. Sites both at **Aïn Ghazal** in Amman and **Mureybet** in Syria have revealed the existence of houses with several rooms, making them among the earliest known villages in human history. The remains of these houses show that various forms of religious worship were practised there, involving the worship of the Earth Mother, the bull and ancestors.

### Emergence of city-states (4th millennium BC)

Between 6000 and 4000 BC, Neolithic developments became widespread: village settlements spread throughout the region and clay became used in making pottery. This invention paved the way for other essential discoveries, such as the smelting of metals (copper) and the use of dry brick in

Statuette from Aïn Ghazal (Amman Museum)

C. Pavard

construction. At the same time, growers were diversifying from wheat and barley into dates, olives and lentils. Before long it was necessary to fortify the small hamlets and growing villages. During the 4th millennium BC different types of buildings came to be developed at **Uruk** in the south of Mesopotamia (now in Iraq). In this **Sumerian** town we find a house for the figure of authority (which came to be known as a "palace"), and one for God (the precursor of the temple). As the cities grew in size and consequence they emerged as separate entities or "states" with control over outlying villages; citizens migrated to found new colonies as at **Habuba Kabira** on the banks of the Syrian Euphrates. The wheel, the plough and bronze appeared. Eventually, in circa 3100 BC, little cuneiform symbols appeared inscribed in clay tablets heralding the advent of writing.

### City-states to empire (3rd millennium BC)

Ebla and Mari, two Syrian sites dating from the third millennium, have provided a great deal of information regarding the functioning of the cities. Their organisation centred around the temple and the palace, where successive dynasties of princes ruled. **Ebla**, 60km south of Aleppo, controlled a territory stretching from Hama to the Taurus Mountains. It had its own language and profited from a network of alliances formed by dynastic marriages. The kingdom of **Mari** controlled river traffic on the Euphrates. The king launched a project to build a 120km canal, which involved considerable expertise and technical skill. These city-states established strong – and highly lucrative – commercial links with neighbouring empires, providing the means for their citizens to enjoy a wonderful quality of life, as the fabulous artistry and exquisite workmanship displayed today in museums testifies (figurative statuary, jewellery, cylinder seals used to endorse contracts). As the rival states vied for control over ever larger territories, conflicts broke out leading occasionally to war. Towards 2300 BC, King Sargon of Akkad finally managed to unify the cities of southern Mesopotamia to form an aggressive empire intent on conquering the West. Mari and Ebla both succumbed to the **Akkadian** onslaught. They were not the only ones: in the north of Syria, hundreds of such tells – artificial hills formed by successive occupations accumulated over the millennia – bear witness to the upheavals occasioned by the birth of empires.

### Turbulent times (2nd millennium BC)

The end of the third millennium was disrupted by the arrival of the Semitic tribes known as the **Amorites**. It was in this context, sometime in the 19C BC, that Abraham left his native city of Ur to cross Syria and Palestine where he lead a nomadic existence. Eventually his Hebrew clan, comprising the 12 tribes of Israel born of Jacob, established themselves in Egypt. **Ebla** and **Mari** enjoyed a brief renaissance under the Amorite dynasties before being overcome and absorbed by the neighbouring empires: Mari by the Babylonians under Hammurabi; Ebla by Hittites from the north. In 1287 BC, the Hittite army clashed with the troops of the Egyptian Pharaoh Ramses II in the battle of **Qadesh** (south of Homs). Both neighbours withdrew their forces and local leaders resumed control. At **Ugarit** on the Mediterranean coast, an inventive society developed and perfected an alphabet which was to have major repercussions on language as a whole and on Arabic, Hebrew, Greek and Latin in particular. It is generally agreed that the Exodus described in the Old Testament of the Bible, when the Hebrews were led out of Egypt by Moses, took place during the 13C BC. After wandering for 40 years in the desert, they travelled the length of Jordan from south to north to reach Canaan, which they regarded as the Promised Land. On their way they encountered the Edomites, Moabites and the Ammonites, Semitic peoples living on the Transjordanian plateau. At the same time, the mysterious **Sea Peoples** invaded the coastal plains stretching from the north of Syria to Egypt, and settled there. The Hittite Empire, the kingdom of Ugarit and most of the coastal towns were destroyed.

## Sons of Aram (1st millennium BC)

At the beginning of the 10C, a new Semitic people – the **Aramaeans** – entered the fray. After the devastating passage of the Sea Peoples, these semi-nomads beset the little **neo-Hittite** kingdoms: namely Aleppo, Hama, Gozan (Tell Halaf), Hadatu (Arslan Tash), Tell Barsip (Tell Ahmar), Arpad (Tell Refad) to mention but the most famous. In Palestine, King David slowly gained control of all Israel and then attacked his neighbours (Aramaeans in Damascus and Ammonites in Amman). With the death of Solomon, the 12 tribes of Israel formed two kingdoms (Israel to the north and Judah to the south) that stretched across the whole of southern Syria and Jordan. In the 8C BC, the area was captured by yet another Eastern power, the **Assyrians**. Innumerable towns were destroyed and populations deported. Their successors, the **neo-Babylonians**, defeated the Egyptians at Karkemish in 605 BC and extended their control over the whole of the Fertile Crescent (the Jews were kept in captivity in Babylon between 587-538 BC). They, in turn, were overthrown by the **Persian Achaemenids**. King Darius I, the builder of Persepolis, pushed as far as Macedonia whilst his son, Xerxes I, occupied Athens. This dynasty ruled over an immense empire of satrapies, allowing each the freedom to preserve their religions and customs. Aramaic, that last relic of the independent kingdoms and result of tribal intermixing during the millennium, became the official language of the Persian Empire. During the early part of the millennium, the **Phoenicians** returned to continue the work of their Canaanite ancestors on the coasts before they were interrupted by the invasions of the Sea Peoples. They developed and expanded trading relations with the whole Mediterranean basin, founding trading posts where required – including Carthage (Tunisia). In this way, they gradually managed to create a unified territory of their own.

# Western domination

## Alexander, Seleucus and Ptolemy (333-64 BC)

By cutting the famous Gordian knot, **Alexander the Great** fulfilled the oracle's prophecy that whosoever untied the knot would win control of Asia. In 333 BC he marched into Syria, at the start of an epic journey that was to lead him to the banks of the Indus and what was then considered to be the edge of the world. In the course of the next decade he built up a vast empire that he never had the opportunity of governing. For he died ten years later and the empire that he had hoped would accommodate both the conquered and conquerors side by side as a single people, was immediately dismantled and shared out among his generals. The **Ptolemies** reigned over Egypt, Palestine and Transjordan; the **Seleucids** took possession of Mesopotamia and northern Syria. The colonies that were established constituted living centres of Greek culture (Hellenism). Ten influential cities established a league called the Decapolis. Alas, Jarash, Pella, Damascus, Aleppo and Latakia preserve scant remains of their Hellenistic heritage, as these were largely obliterated and replaced by the

S. Grandadin/HOA QUI

The barley-sugar columns at Amapea

Romans. In Judea, to where the Jews had returned from Babylon, a movement emerged to resist Hellenism. In 167 BC Antiochus marched on Palestine and outlawed Judaism. The **Hasmonean** dynasty, founded by Judas Maccabeus, promptly reacted by seizing control of the cities in Jordan.

## Pompey and the Roman Empire (64 BC-330 AD)

In 64 BC the Roman general **Pompey** conquered Asia Minor, Syria and Palestine. Only one community – the **Nabataeans** – showed any serious resistance to being ruled by the Roman Empire. These were nomadic people originally from northern Arabia who traded along the caravan routes between Hauran and the Red Sea. Sometime in the 4C BC they had formed a kingdom of their own and established **Petra** as their capital. It was not until 106 AD that **Trajan** was finally able to secure Nabataea as a Roman province. Throughout the 1C AD, the **Pax Romana** ensured that peace and stability reigned across the whole Mediterranean Basin. Meanwhile, the Hellenistic cities continued to expand. The extant remains of sumptuous architecture at Jarash, Palmyra and Bosra bear witness to the great wealth accumulated in the eastern provinces of the Empire. Trade, encouraged by the proliferation of caravan routes, provided the provinces with increasing amounts of power. The Latin poet Juvenal exclaimed indignantly: "For a long time now, the Syrian Orontes has been flowing into the Tiber". But the trend was irreversible. A century later, Syria installed two of its progeny on the Roman Imperial throne – the young **Elagabalus** (218-222) followed by **Philip the Arab** (244-249). In 272 **Queen Zenobia** attempted to free the East from Roman domination. This prompted Aurelian to retaliate and the Palmyran Queen's army was defeated. Then, in this vast empire where the worship of the Graeco-Roman pantheon prevailed, a new religion began to emerge in Jewish circles. Not only did Jesus of Nazareth preach in the land of Palestine, he continued to the River Jordan where he was baptised by John the Baptist. He crossed Lake Tiberias and visited the Decapolis. **St Paul**, who was converted at Damascus, became one of the leading exponents of the new Church journeying across to Ephesus and on to Rome. At his death in about 64, Christian churches had been instituted in all the great centres of the Roman

Empire. A little less than 300 years elapsed between Christ's Crucifixion and the promulgation of the Edict of Milan (313) authorising Christian worship. Throughout these years, the faith had spread first through Jewish enclaves, then among the gentiles, who ranked as the lower classes of the Roman provinces. The ensuing decades are marked by alternating periods of persecution and tolerance. The East had its share of martyrs: St Serge at Rasssafa, St Elian at Homs as well as a host of others across the Roman Empire now forgotten in the annals of history.

## Constantine and the Byzantine Empire (330-636 AD)

In 330, the Emperor **Constantine** transferred the capital of the Roman Empire to Byzantium, which he renamed Constantinople. Throughout his reign, Constantine remained sympathetic to the new faith and converted to Christianity on his deathbed. Countless centres of pilgrimage evolved: the foremost being Jerusalem of course, but people also flocked to places associated with martyrs and ascetics in and around **Madaba** and **St Simeon**. In 392 all pagan cults were outlawed. Three years later the Roman Empire was subdivided into the Eastern Roman Empire (Byzantine) and the Western Roman Empire, which was under serious threat from invading Barbarians. In the 6C the Emperor Justinian attempted to reunify the factions into a single whole, but this was short lived. Following a gloomy and despondent 3C came prosperity: wealthy villages mushroomed everywhere, the most notable being the **Dead Cities** in northern Syria. A succession of religious crises shook the Empire, provoked in part by the disparity between the Hellenised elite and the various Aramaic-speaking Semitic peoples in Byzantine society. The threat of invasion, which hitherto had been contained, exacerbated the tension further. In the wake of countless devastating raids during the 6-7C, the Sassanid Persians occupied Syria, Palestine and Jordan.

# Rise of Islam and an Arab identity

## Umayyad Caliphate at Damascus (636-750)

The enfeebled Byzantine and Persian Empires were easy targets for the Arabs who had rallied in Mecca and Medina in the wake of the **Prophet Muhammad**'s Koranic revelations. The Arab armies advanced through Jordan and Syria (Battle of Yarmuk 636) conquering lands that were to extend from the Atlantic to the Indus. Meanwhile, the Byzantine Empire contracted to the confines of Asia Minor. The new masters had little trouble in instituting their authority because much of the populace was disenchanted with Byzantine policies. The people even tolerated their property being requisitioned; Christian Churches continued to be embellished with beautiful mosaics, especially those in the Madaba region. **Damascus** was designated the capital of this empire, which was renamed after the ruling dynasty – the Umayyads. The Umayyads were wealthy and generous patrons, and all forms of art flourished with new-found brilliance. Furthermore, they did not hesitate to assimilate influences from both Byzantine and Sassanid art into their own culture. This fertile exchange of taste and tradition shines through in such singular masterpieces as the gold-spangled mosaics of the Umayyad Mosque in Damascus, the **desert castles** and the bronze objects recovered from Mafraq in Jordan. Damascus court culture became increasingly sophisticated. But serious tension was brewing over who should be regarded as Muhammad's first successor. The ensuing schism precipitated the birth of **Shiah** – the sect that rejects the first three Sunnite Caliphs in favour of the Prophet's son-in-law Ali – and provoked the downfall of the Umayyad dynasty.

## Transfer of power to other Arab and foreign dynasties (750-1260)

In 750 the **Abbasids** – a rival dynasty – eliminated the Umayyads and transferred their capital to Baghdad. Abd al-Rahman I, the only member of the Umayyads to escape massacre, established himself in Cordova where he founded the brilliant Umayyad Caliphate in Spain. The Abbasid Empire reached its peak under the great caliph **Haroun al-Rachid**, a contemporary of Charlemagne and a character in the *Thousand and One Nights*. The empire declined with the emergence of Persian and then Turkish dynasties. Syria was relegated to the rank of a province, although **Raqqa** was at one time chosen as summer capital. In 1058, the **Seljuks** (Turkish converts to Islam) swept in from Central Asia and seized power. Further west, the Shiite **Fatimids** flooded in from Tunisia to establish themselves in Egypt. Squeezed between the two, Syria and Palestine became a bloody battlefield, conquered at last by the Seljuks. In the 10C, an Arab principality was formed in northern Syria, centred around Aleppo, which strove to check the advance of the Byzantine armies. At their court, the **Hamdanid** rulers entertained the great poets al-Mutanabbi and Abu Firas.

## The Crusades (1098-1302)

In 1095, Pope Urban II launched an appeal for a crusade to conquer Jerusalem. His call had a great success and the first wave of crusaders took the Holy City by assault in 1099 after terrible suffering. Thanks to successive crusades, the territories of the Latins grew and stretched from Edessa in Turkey to Aqaba. From their impregnable fortresses **(Krak des Chevaliers, Karak)** the crusaders kept watch over the territory between the Mediterranean coast and their lands stretching up to beyond the River Jordan. The Frankish states that formed were ruled by feudal lords. The Orders of Knights **(Hospitallers and Templars)** were instituted to ensure the safety of the conquered lands. The Muslim camp was very divided and slow to react. In 1171, **Saladin** deposed the Fatimid caliph and so united Syria and Egypt. In 1187, at the Battle of Hattin (near Lake Tiberias), he inflicted the first severe blow on the crusaders. But the Franks were able to maintain themselves for nearly another 100 years.

Krak des Chevaliers

J. F. Galmiche

## Egyptian Mamelukes in Palestine (1260-1516)

At the end of the 13C, the Mamelukes, a new Turkish dynasty, succeeded in expelling the Franks once and for all, thanks to the intervention of **Baybars** and his successor **Qalawun**. The Mamelukes formed a completely new kind of military class that selected its leader (Sultan) from among its peers, many of whom had been slaves from the steppes of southern Russia. They remained in power until the Ottomans arrived, overseeing a sultanate that stretched from northern Syria down into Egypt. At the same time, the **Mongols**, a race made up of nomadic horsemen, swept across the heart of Central Asia, mounting several incursions into Mameluke territory. The most momentous ended in the sack of Damascus (1400) and the deportation of the labour force to Samarkand, Tamerlane's great capital. Damascus enjoyed a new golden age under the Mamelukes, even if its supreme masters resided in Egypt.

## Four centuries of Turkish Ottoman rule (1516-1918)

The Ottoman Turks had established themselves in Anatolia in the 14C and had already encroached upon Byzantine territories when they seized Constantinople (1453). In so doing, they gained a foothold in Europe and quickly set about establishing Muslim colonies in Bosnia, Serbia, Bulgaria and Greece. The last Byzantine Emperor fell in battle defending his people. The Ottomans turned towards the south defeating the Mamelukes in 1517. When Suleiman the Magnificent was enthroned, their empire stretched to the gates of Morocco. It was not long before this vast and unwieldy Empire showed signs of slowing down, and found itsself unable to compete with Europe's economic, technological and military progress. Eventually, France succeeded in forcing the Ottomans to capitulate on several fronts: securing exclusive terms of trading for French merchants and the right to open a consulate in **Aleppo**. Before long, the French authorities had taken charge of the Christian minorities scattered across the Ottoman provinces under pasha rule. Meanwhile, the *millet* system allowed communities to be officially recognised and administered by their own religious hierarchies. At the end of the 19C, after centuries of Turkish domination, Arab nationalism swept through the Empire. When in the First World War, the Sublime Porte sided with Germany it also signed its death warrant: Faisal, son of Sahrif Husein the Emir of Mecca, rallied the Arabs with the support of Colonel T E Lawrence and the British army. They revolted in 1916, stormed Aqaba and marched triumphant into Damascus. The Turks retreated behind the frontiers of present-day Turkey. The leader of the Arab Revolt, having been promised the creation of an independent Arab kingdom, travelled to Paris in all confidence only to discover the true terms of the Sykes-Picot pact: Syria and the Lebanon would be ruled by the French; Palestine, Transjordan and Iraq by the British. The Sharifan Prince Faisal was to be a pawn in the grand scheme, responsible for overseeing a series of Arab governors and the Arab administration. Syria would fly an Arab flag, but her finances and policies were to be directed by France. Faisal and Lawrence had been betrayed. The frontiers of today's states had been defined and were confirmed by the League of Nations in 1920.

*For more information on the history of Syria and Jordan since the First World War, see p 74 for Syria and p 287 for Jordan.*

# ART AND ARCHITECTURE

## In the beginning

One can but speculate as to how the art of building evolved in the Ancient Near East over the long period between the 4th-1st millennia BC, and give but a general outline of the principal features. For a reconstructed picture of architecture shows that there were numerous regional styles at play.

### Building materials

Raw **clay**, which is readily available across the whole of Mesopotamia, provided the main building material. Depending on the region, the mud was mixed with straw, gravel or ash and then moulded into **bricks** that were dried in the sun. Once hard, these were laid in layers to build walls. Given the scarcity of fuel, the bricks were rarely fired unless it was to face an important building, or line water conduits.

The only trees available were palms, but their trunks are fibrous and unsuited for use as timber rafters and roof beams. **Wood** was hard to come by, but nonetheless was imported by the Mespotamians. Cedar – so prized for its durability and natural scent – was transported from the mountains of Lebanon to the southern areas of the Fertile Crescent by water.

### Living quarters

The earliest **houses** were circular, and only became orthogonal in the 8th millennium so as to accommodate additional rooms. They could be built on several levels, providing shelter for the whole family and storage space for food supplies. Differences only became apparent with the advent of towns, the larger buildings being occupied by the community leaders and the smaller ones by tradesmen or set aside for the gods.

When grouped together, these residential quarters became veritable rabbit-warrens of mud-brick houses organised around **narrow alleyways**. Structural walls were often party walls, pierced in the upper sections to provide light and ventilation. The larger houses were centrally planned around a courtyard, surrounded by a string of rooms furnished with a bread oven, a few rugs and small chests. The roof would be flat.

### Monumental architecture

During the 5th millennium, the different styles of house show that a social hierarchy existed within these early urban communities.

The temples and palaces were normally situated on an **acropolis**, the most elevated part of the city. The **palace**, which played the leading role in political life, comprised a multitude of rooms (sometimes more than a hundred) for staff, and for use as kitchens and archives. The king's living quarters were normally situated above on the first floor. The **temple** was designed as the god's house and it was occupied by special retainers and orderlies – termed as "temple servants". Only the initiated were allowed within. Inside was the inner sanctum: a square or rectangular sacred chamber containing the god's effigy and deemed as the divinity's official seat. To one side stood the **ziggurat**, a tall tapering edifice modelled on the Tower of Babel, comprising several superimposed galleries. Little is known about this feature, although every Mesopotamian town would have had one. Great staircases provided access to the top where there was probably a second sacred chamber. From the 4th millennium BC, all the cities in the Ancient East would have been fortified with walls punctuated by gateways and towers.

## Outstanding examples

Two remarkable Syrian sites convey some idea of the extraordinary architecture in the Ancient East between the 2nd-3rd millennia BC. The vast palaces and temples at **Mari** and **Ebla** are an indication of the splendours achieved by the first dynasties. Behind the flourishing harbour of **Ugarit** on the Syrian coast stood a substantial city: the base of walls map out the bare outlines of what were substantial villas with several rooms, centred around a courtyard. Rather than the actual sites, which have suffered the ravages of time and can be confusing to the uninitiated visitor, it is the treasures contained in the museums of Aleppo, Damascus and Amman that reveal the true artistic wealth of these vanished civilisations.

# Classical Antiquity

*See the architectural illustrations on p 32*

Most modern travellers will be struck by the sheer number of Greco-Roman architectural fragments encountered on their journeys through the Mediterranean basin. Whether in Rome, Volubilis, Jarash or Palmyra, the same familiar elements recur time and again: the fallen temple columns, broken vaults of thermal baths, or the exuberant leaf decoration of a Corinthian capital survive remarkably intact. All conform to the same rules of proportion and aesthetics prescribed by the planners of Antiquity in the building of cities throughout their vast empire.

## Town planning

The cities designed by both the Ancient Greeks and the Romans were laid out according to standard criteria set by Hippodamus of Miletus in the 5C BC. In essence, the straight streets were arranged in a rectilinear grid-pattern around **blocks** of building (*insulae*). The main street, lined with **colonnades**, bisected the city on an east-west axis (*decumanus maximus*) and grouped together the town's municipal buildings. Pride of place was allocated to the **forum**, the town's central square where markets and public meetings were held with, to one side, a **council room** for local government officials. Additional buildings might include a **nymphaeum** – a small sanctuary with a fountain dedicated to the nymphs, the **public baths** equipped with swimming pools, one or more **temples** and a **theatre**. The intersections along the "high" street with the major lateral streets (*cardo*) were often marked with a **tetrapylon**. The colonnades would have been adorned with statues representing illustrious men associated with the city or Empire. The four main axes of the city would often extend beyond four monumental **gateways** in the enclosing **walls**, along paved roads heading out towards other cities of the Roman Empire. Monumental **arches** were erected in memory of triumphant military campaigns or in honour of a particular individual.

## Religious buildings

In each and every province, the foreign conquerors endeavoured to match local deities with the gods of the Greco-Roman pantheon. The mighty Zeus (Roman Jupiter) was identified with the Syrian Hadad and the Nabataean Dushara. Where no equivalent could be devised, a foreign god might be added to the pantheon, as in the case of the Sumero-Akkadian Tammuz and Phoenician Adoni who became known to the Greeks and Romans as Adonis. If possible, the **temples** were built high above the city so that the gods might protect it. These **shrines** comprised a cella into which only initiates were admitted. The sacred area of the **temenos** was surrounded by the **peribolos** and accessed by means of a **propylaeum**. The decoration was in strict accordance with the three orders of architecture: Doric, Ionic and Corinthian.

## Public entertainment

The **theatre** was semicircular in shape and comprised three parts: the auditorium with tiered seating, the orchestra reserved for prominent persons and members of the cast, and the actual stage which was above the orchestra. The stage backdrop was a permanent stone frieze with columns, niches and statues fashioned to look like a palace façade. The **odeon**, built on similar lines to an amphitheatre, was reserved for musical entertainment, while the **hippodrome** was used exclusively for chariot racing.

## Domestic quarters

The Roman home – a **domus** (modest home), **insula** (multi-storey apartment block) or **villa** (a sumptuous residence on the outskirts of town) was designed to reflect the status of its owner. The most elegant were built of stone or brick, in marked contrast with the mud-brick dwellings of the lower classes.

## Outstanding examples

**Doura Europos** and **Iraq al-Amir** are two rare examples of Greek architecture blended with regional influences that survived the Roman period intact. **Apamea** and **Bosra**, as well as **Palmyra** and **Jarash,** preserve enough ruins of temples, forums, baths and theatres to show the magnificent splendour and sophistication achieved by the Roman occupiers. **Petra**, which stands in a category of its own, was carved out of the rose-red rock by the Nabateans out of pride in their Semitic origins and respect for a Classical canon of beauty.

Oval forum, Jarash (Jordan)

# Byzantium

*See the architectural illustrations on p 32.*

Byzantine architecture had little impact on Syria and Jordan after the 8C. For the Christian communities preferred to consolidate and turn in upon themselves after witnessing the rapid spread of Islam, developing their own art in the form of manuscripts, ceramics and frescos now preserved in museums. Elsewhere, people continued to live in the great Roman cities that changed little over time.

## Christian churches

The greatest Byzantine innovations were made during the construction of religious buildings. Christians chose not to adapt pagan temples to their needs because these monuments were too powerful a reminder of ancient practices. Furthermore, the temples were ill-suited to Christian rituals as the internal space was exclusively reserved for a statue of the divinity rather than a congregation of believers. Instead, the early Christians opted for the **basilica** – a public meeting hall or occasional courtroom – with a central nave terminating in an apse and flanked by aisles that could be converted into a church. Ideally, the church would be orientated towards the east so that the light of the rising sun could flood through an opening into the apse and sanctuary. The east end was flanked by two sacristies: the **diaconicon** on the right and the **prothesis** on the left. In the middle stood the **bema** or lectern from where the gospels were read.

J.-L. Dugast/HOA QUI

Y. Traynard

Basilica of St Simeon Stylite

In the 6C, a vastly different type of church emerged, of a kind perfected at St Sophia in Constantinople but pioneered at Bosra. In this case, the building was **centrally planned** around an octagonal space surmounted by a dome; recessed exedras filled the supporting piers. In either case, builders were always ready to reuse blocks of cut stone pillaged from ancient sites.

## Mosaic

Mosaic reigned supreme over the fine and decorative arts under Roman and Byzantine patronage. Specialised teams were required to undertake huge schemes – covering floors, walls and ceilings – that cost considerably more than any painting. In the 1C BC, artists learnt how to use the **tesserae** (stone or glass pieces) to define graduated features, shading and perspective that brought the technique ever closer to painting. Splendid mosaics adorned the Byzantine churches of the Madaba region *(see p 360)*.

## Dead Cities

Nearly 700 **Dead Cities** dating from Byzantine times have been identified in the range of limestone hills west of Aleppo. Founded in part by the Romans, these communities were particularly prosperous in the Byzantine era (4C-6C). The villages, for these small towns comprising some 20-50 farms could not properly be termed "cities", often had a church and, in some cases, a monastery on site. The walls of the houses were constructed of large quadrangular blocks arranged in regular rows. The ground floor and maybe the basement were dedicated to some agricultural use (furnished with a press, storage racks or animal stalls) while the raised floors were used for human habitation. Other buildings were sometimes arranged around the courtyard, complete with a cistern and garden, surrounded by a wall. The prime concern was the cultivation of olives and fruit trees (and in some places the vine as well) so well suited to the local limestone soil. For the most part, presses were used to make oil.

## Outstanding examples

The somewhat haunting ruins of the **Dead Cities** north of Aleppo are highly evocative tokens of a great legacy: the jewel being the Basilica of **St Simeon**, which, with **Rassafa**, constituted one of the main centres of Christian pilgrimage. The mosaics of **Madaba** in Jordan are some indication even further afield of the power and fervour of Eastern arm of the early Christian Church.

# The Crusades

In the 12C and 13C, the crusaders built a string of castles stretching from Cilicia to the Red Sea, the lofty silhouettes of which still dominate the high relief of Jordan and Syria.

## Fortified castles

The castles were carefully positioned along the main access routes, ready and waiting for any incursion, thereby making up for their manpower deficiency in spite of the reinforcements recruited among native mercenaries (of Turkic origin). In this way, an armed band could be quickly despatched from the inviolable fortress to contain an enemy raid. In the event of a siege, the defenders were able to retract behind the fortifications and await the arrival of reinforcements stationed further along the line. When the Crusaders set out from Europe in the early 12C the design of fortified castles there was still very rudimentary. Their first attempts were modelled on the square Byzantine forts, but by the mid-12C they had perfected a prototype and erected a series of castles – the most famous being at **Saône**, **Krak des Chevaliers** and **Marqab**. Having been designed to endure armed attack and the ravages of time, many of these complexes survive surprisingly intact. Essential elements included a number of **circular towers** linked by **curtain walls** that offered few blind spots to an attacker, and an outer **concentric wall** that continued the line and angle of the natural escarpment making it difficult to see where the ground ended and the masonry began. A less fortified **outer bailey** provided shelter for the civilians employed in service and maintenance of the castle. Life revolved around the **inner bailey** that was overlooked and defended by a **keep**, off which stood the **chapel** for celebrating mass. Carefully constructed **ramps** allowed access to be monitored. **Storerooms** were accommodated within the ramparts on various levels to contain the provisions required in case of siege, and a sophisticated system of conduits collected rainwater from the battlements and conveyed it to a large underground cistern. Machicolations, arrow slits, portcullises, murderholes and other such classic defensive devices were also incorporated.

In addition to these impregnable fortresses built high up on inaccessible rocky spurs, or separated from the mountainside by a deep ditch, the Crusaders constructed a series of secondary castles to watch over the harbours on the Mediterranean coast.

## Knightly orders

Before long, it became evident that the burden of financing these huge enterprises could no longer be entirely borne by the Frankish nobility empowered at that time in Europe by the feudal system. Instead, it was decided that the highly organised religious military orders with large revenues at their disposal should oversee the construction of the Crusader fortresses and take charge of the defence of the Latin states. The oldest and most important of these bodies was the **Knights Hospitallers**: who under the auspices of St John of Jerusalem devoted themselves to tending the sick, often in conjunction with the pilgrim hostels managed by Benedictine monks. During the Crusades they assumed a military role wearing the black habit of the Benedictines inscribed with the eight-pointed cross; in 1142 they were assigned Krak des Chevaliers. The **Knights Templars** started out as a civilian organisation in 1118 to ensure the safe passage of pilgrims to and from Jerusalem. During the Crusades, dressed in their distinctive mantles with a red cross on the shoulder, they showed great devotion and courage in fighting the cause and were allocated the citadel of Tartus to defend. Before long, the military operation depended almost entirely on the Hospitallers, Templars and German knights of the Teutonic Order. Meanwhile, sponsorship depended on the generous contributions of Christians everywhere eager that Jerusalem be defended from the Infidels, and so each order accumulated great wealth. The Templars, who by this time had superseded the Hospitallers, established numerous religious houses in various parts of Europe soliciting jealousy from both popes and ruling monarchs - in 1308 Edward II confiscated all properties belonging to the English Templars; in 1312 the Order was abolished by Pope Clement V and suppressed by Philip the Fair of France.

## Outstanding examples

At one time, a string of Crusader castles stretched from Turkey to Egypt, defending the Christian Lands from the Infidels. Today the best preserved include **Krak des Chevaliers**, **Margat**, **Saône**, **Karak** and **Shobak**. Among the citadels built at the same time by the opposing Muslims, fine examples survive at **Harim**, **Sheizar**, **Rabadh** and **Missiaf**.

# Islam

*See the architectural illustrations on p 32*

## Towns

The ancient cities built along Roman lines – like Damascus and Aleppo - changed quite considerably with the advent of Islam. The large open public areas disappeared beneath private dwellings and shops. Residents – be they Muslim, Christian or Jewish – organised themselves in residential quarters that could be defended from raids and incursions, especially at nightfall.

A whole new range of functional religious buildings made their appearance such as the **mosque**, **bimaristan** (hospital), **mausoleum**, sometimes with a **madrasa** (religious school) attached. The **souk** grew up around a network of alleyways crammed with shops and workshops, alongside the **khans** (Arab inns or caravanserai). The **hammam**, however, was modelled on the Roman baths. Together they formed the **medinas**, the hearts of the great Islamic cities of today.

## Mosques

The main mosque (Grand Mosque or *jami*), which provided the Muslim community with a regular meeting place – at least once a week usually for the Friday prayers – was often constructed on the site of an ancient temple (Damascus, Aleppo). Smaller mosques *(masjid)* were built in the various quarters to meet daily needs. While Islam outlawed the use of naturalistic figurative representation in favour of stylised calligraphy, geometry and organic decoration, it allowed monuments to be built on a variety of plans that range from the great basilica at Damascus to the domed mosques of the Ottomans.

## Covered markets

The **souk** is the main commercial area at the heart of the medina. It is perhaps the most evocatively oriental component of any Middle Eastern town. The complex is permeated with narrow alleyways – often roofed over – lined with countless little booths, and divided up into quarters according to trade: textiles, herbs and spices, perfumes, leather goods, gold and silver merchants and such like. On the periphery, the booths comprise a practical workshop where brass, copper and tin can be seen being worked. Each souk will have several old **khans** (caravanserais) where merchants and their caravans from India and China could be accommodated: these consist of a courtyard in which the animals were kept, a series of storerooms for the merchandise and then, on the floors above, a series of dormitories. Here the merchants could recover from their arduous journeys, relax in the hammam nearby and dispose of their merchandise as required.

J. F. Galmiche

Umayyad Mosque, Damascus

## Living quarters

Traditionally, the Arab house was built around a courtyard planted with sweet-smelling flowering trees (usually oranges) where the family could enjoy the open air and the refreshing sound of a playful fountain. The larger, wealthier households might have two such courtyards: one for private use **(haremlik)**, the other for receiving guests **(salemlik)**. The **iwan** *(see illustration on p 416)*, an open seating area on the south side of the courtyard, allowed residents to enjoy the oblique rays of the winter sun. The external appearance counted for little. The walls giving onto the street were usually windowless, or otherwise furnished with projecting bow-windows screened off with wooden lattice-work **(mashrabiya)**. By contrast, the interior was richly decorated with marble, stucco, wood and carpets.

## Desert outposts

With the rise of the Umayyad dynasty, a broad variety of constructions began to be built miles out of town. The "desert castles" commissioned by the new princes were splendid **residences** equipped with their own **hammam**, and comprised apartments *(bayt)* arranged around a central courtyard, with rooms disposed in the same way on the ground and first floors. Along the caravan routes, **caravanserais** were built to provide travelling traders and their retinues with food and shelter in remote parts of the desert. Unlike the urban khans, these single-storey hostels were usually spread over a wide area, had designated pens for stabling the camels and other animals overnight, and provided guests no facilities for off-loading their merchandise.

## Outstanding examples

Eight centuries separate the building of the **Umayyad Grand Mosque** from that of the **Takiya Soulaymania** in Damascus: time enough for Muslim art to undergo profound changes. The sober lines and basic forms of the Grand Mosque look back to Roman and Byzantine traditions and continue to articulate the desert castles (as at **Qusayr Amra**) and Seljuk culture; however these dissolve away and are replaced by exuberant colour under the Mamelukes. The Ottomans perfected the dome and used it to cover mosques, baths and khans; their minarets, meanwhile, became increasingly tapered and delicate. The best examples of this magnificent period survive in the old quarters of **Salt**, **Damascus** and **Aleppo** in particular.

*Terms illustrated in the architectural illustrations are not repeated here*

### Greek, Roman and Byzantine buildings

| | |
|---|---|
| Acanthus | Artichoke-like plant with scalloped leaves carved to decorate the Corinthian capital. |
| Acropolis | Citadel built on the highest point above Greek cities – enclosing main temples and public buildings. |
| Adobe | Sun-dried mud brick |
| Adytum | Inner sanctuary of a Greek temple reserved for priests. |
| Agora | Open space in Greek cities used for public meetings and market; often surrounded by a portico as in a Roman forum. |
| Ambo | Raised stand from which the Gospels and Epistles were read: replaced in the 14C by the pulpit. |
| Anastylose | Reconstruction of a ruined building using the original materials. |
| Andron | Meeting place for men in the Greek, Roman and Byzantine worlds. |
| Anta | Corner (in antis) pilaster of a different order from the rest of the building. |
| Archivolt | Continuous architrave moulding on the extrados of an arch. |
| Arrow slit | Loophole, or narrow opening in a wall used by archers |
| Attic storey | Storey above the main entablature; upper storey of a building. |
| Basilica | Rectangular civil building with a central nave terminating in an apse, flanked by one or more aisles, used by the Romans for public meetings and tribunals and adapted the early Christians for use as a church. |
| Bema | Greek word for a speaker's tribune or platform; raised stage in the apse of Orthodox churches used by the clergy; raised areas containing the altar and Bishop's throne screened off by the iconostasis in an Eastern church. |
| Betyl | Sacred stone used by the Nabataeans to represent the presence of god. |
| Cardo | Street running on a north-south axis across a Roman city, parallel to the main thoroughfare known as the cardo maximus and perpendicular to the decumanus. |
| Cella | Main chamber in a classical temple containing the cult image (naos). |
| Chancel | East end of a church containing the main altar, used by the clergy and choir. From the Latin cancellus, low balustrade dividing the choir from the nave. |
| Cryptoporticus | Semi-subterranean chamber surrounded by a portico. |
| Decumanus | Street running east-west across a Roman city. |
| Diaconicon | Sacristy in Byzantine churches, where the clergy kept their vessels and vestments. |
| Exedra | Semicircular or rectangular recess with raised seats. Also used to denote the stone bench of the same shape, a niche for statuary or an apse. |
| Forum | See "agora". |
| High place | Nabataean place of worship built on a mound or high ground. |
| Hypogeum | Underground funerary chamber. |
| Hypostyle | Classical temple or palace with a roof supported by columns (form the Greek "stylos" meaning column). |
| Iconostasis | Screen inset with icons, separating the nave from the choir of Orthodox churches. |
| Impost | Stone, usually projecting from wall, from which an arch springs. |

| | |
|---|---|
| Insula | A residential quarter or block in an ancient city, delimited by streets. |
| Intrados | Lower or inner curve of arch or vault. |
| Limes | Frontier zone fortified by the Romans. |
| Loculus | A long recess in which a dead body is laid (loculi). |
| Macellum | Covered food market. |
| Martyrium | Monument erected over a site of Christian importance, such as a martyr's tomb. |
| Merlon | Raised section or crenellation of battlemented parapet. |
| Mosaic | Assembly of coloured tesserae for decorative effect, applied to floors and walls in early buildings. |
| Narthex | Vestibule or western porch before the main body of a church used by women, penitents and catechumens before baptism. |
| Necropolis | Burial site or cemetery in Antiquity. |
| Nefesh | Nabataean funerary stela representing the soul of the deceased person. |
| Nymphaeum | Natural spring or artificial fountain dedicated to the nymphs. In Roman cities, the monumental fountain might honour an emperor and symbolise the power of the Empire. |
| Odeon | Small theatre, usually covered, for concerts and public readings. |
| Opus | See "bond". |
| Order | Classical style of architecture defined by a system of proportion, and distinguished by the ornament applied to the capital of a column and the treatment of the entablature. |
| Orthostate | From the Greek meaning "standing stone": carved and cut upright block of stone used to form the base of a wall and support a bas-relief panel. |
| Parascenium | The wings extending to either side of the stage in a theatre. |
| Peribole | Closed garden surrounding a temple, containing votive monuments. |
| Peripteral | Of a building surrounded on all sides by a colonnade. |
| Peristyle | Gallery ("stoa" in Greek), or colonnaded portico surrounding a temple or courtyard. |
| Pilaster | A shallow pier or rectangular column, protruding from the wall. |
| Portico | Covered gallery supported by a colonnade. |
| Praetorium | Residence of a Roman governor, or barracks. |
| Propylaeum | Monumental gateway to an important public building, sanctuary, sacred precinct, or a citadel. |
| Proskenion | Flat area before the front of the stage in a Roman theatre. |
| Prothesis | Sacristy located to the left of the main apse, opposite the diaconicon (see above) where the Holy Sacraments were prepared prior to consecration. |
| Pulpitum | Front wall of stage or proskenion in Roman theatre, ornamented with bas-reliefs and niches. Stone screen in a large church, between nave and choir. |
| Redan | Small raveline, or outwork projecting from the curtain wall over the main ditch, in military architecture. |
| Stucco | Plaster (gypsum), used for surface mouldings, and carved wall and ceiling decoration. |
| Synthronon | Bench or benches reserved for the clergy arranged around the apse or in rows on either side of the bema (see above) in Early Christian and Byzantine churches. |
| Tell | Artificial mound formed by accumulated remains of ancient settlements. |

| | |
|---|---|
| Temenos | A sacred precinct around a sanctuary, bounded by the peribole, where the faithful assemble. Sacred esplanade of an acropolis. |
| Tessella | Small cube of stone or coloured glass used in the making of mosaics. |
| Tessera | Token (metal, ivory or earthenware) used to cast a vote in an election or to obtain right of entry. |
| Tetrapylon | From the Greek "tetra" meaning "four". Monument comprising four piers marking the intersection of two Roman thoroughfares. |
| Tholos | Circular temple with a conical roof or dome. |
| Triclinium | Roman dining room or table with couches on three sides. |
| Vomitorium | Passageway allowing entry to or exit from an ancient (amphi)theatre. |
| Ziggurat | Pyramidal tower in ancient Mesopotamia, surmounted by a temple from which the stars were observed. |

## Islamic buildings

| | |
|---|---|
| Bayt | Apartment; later used to denote an Ottoman dwelling. |
| Bimaristan | Hospital and school of medicine in the Arab World. |
| Caravanserai | See khan. |
| Hammam | Turkish steam baths found across the Muslim world, adapted from Roman prototypes, although with no actual pool as, in accordance with Muslim ideology, water should run freely and liberally (through a fountain or "sebil"). |
| Haremlik | Private apartments in Ottoman palaces and homes. |
| Iwan | Small room opening out onto a courtyard, enclosed on three sides, found in secular and religious Muslim complexes. |
| Khan | Fortified hostelry built along the principle trade routes across the Middle and Far East where caravan travellers could stop and rest, unload their cargo into secure warehouses and stable their animals; usually located at 25km intervals or a day's ride. |
| Khanqah | Sufi monastery. |
| Madrasa | Koranic school, equivalent to a medersa in the Maghreb. |
| Mihrab | Niche in a mosque indicating the direction of Mecca. |
| Minbar | Raised pulpit in a mosque with a flight of steps, from which Friday prayers are addressed. |
| Mashrabiya | Window or balcony of a traditional Muslim house. screened off with wooden or stone lattice-work allowing the women to see out without being seen. |
| Muqarnas | Stalactite decoration in stone, brick or stucco. |
| Noria | Large water wheel with buckets. |
| Qibla | Mosque wall oriented towards Mecca. |
| Salemlik | Apartments in Ottoman houses used to entertain guests. |
| Serail | Ottoman palace, then a seat of administration. |
| Takiya | Sufi monastery, dervishes' convent (tekke in Turkish). |

Lexicon of architectural terms

# ARCHITECTURE OF ANTIQUITY

## TEMPLE

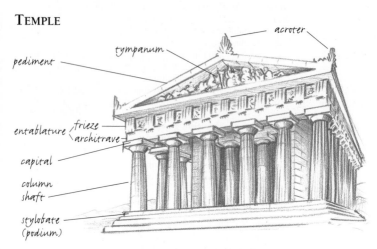

acroter

tympanum

pediment

entablature
frieze
architrave

capital

column
shaft

stylobate
(podium)

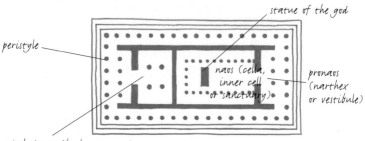

statue of the god

peristyle

naos (cella,
inner cell
or sanctuary)

pronaos
(narthex
or vestibule)

opisthodomos (back-room used as a
treasury accessible only to priests)

## THREE CLASSICAL ORDERS

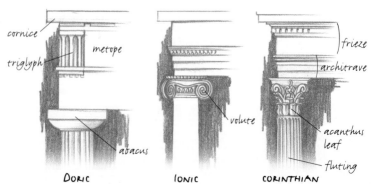

cornice

triglyph

metope

abacus

DORIC

volute

IONIC

frieze

architrave

acanthus
leaf

fluting

CORINTHIAN

H. Choimet

# ROMAN AMPHITHEATRE

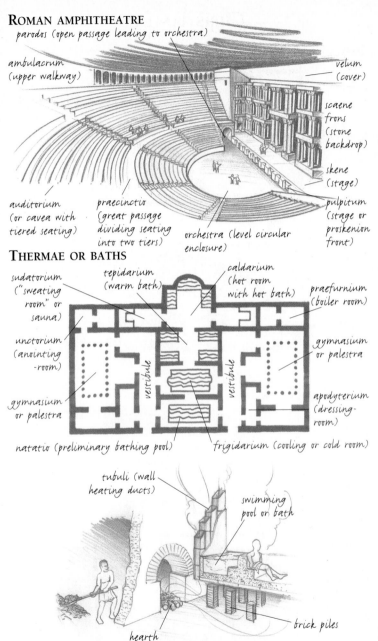

parodos (open passage leading to orchestra)

ambulacrum (upper walkway)

velum (cover)

scaene frons (stone backdrop)

skene (stage)

pulpitum (stage or proskenion front)

auditorium (or cavea with tiered seating)

praecinctio (great passage dividing seating into two tiers)

orchestra (level circular enclosure)

# THERMAE OR BATHS

sudatorium ("sweating room" or sauna)

tepidarium (warm bath)

caldarium (hot room with hot bath)

praefurnium (boiler room)

unctorium (anointing-room)

gymnasium or palestra

vestibule

vestibule

gymnasium or palestra

apodyterium (dressing-room)

natatio (preliminary bathing pool)

frigidarium (cooling or cold room)

tubuli (wall heating ducts)

swimming pool or bath

gymnasium or palestra

brick piles

hearth

HYPOCAUST HEATING SYSTEM

H. Choimet

# CHRISTIAN ERA

## ROMAN BASILICA

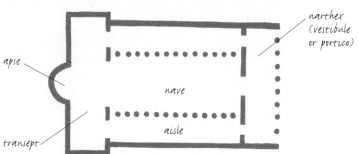

narthex (vestibule or portico)

apse

nave

aisle

transept

## BYZANTINE CHURCH

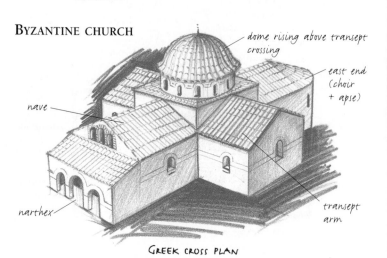

dome rising above transept crossing

east end (choir + apse)

nave

narthex

transept arm

GREEK CROSS PLAN

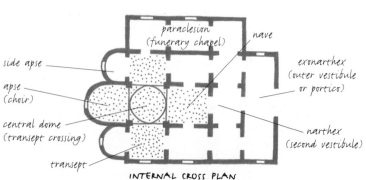

paraclesion (funerary chapel)

nave

side apse

exonarthex (outer vestibule or portico)

apse (choir)

central dome (transept crossing)

narthex (second vestibule)

transept

INTERNAL CROSS PLAN

# DOMES

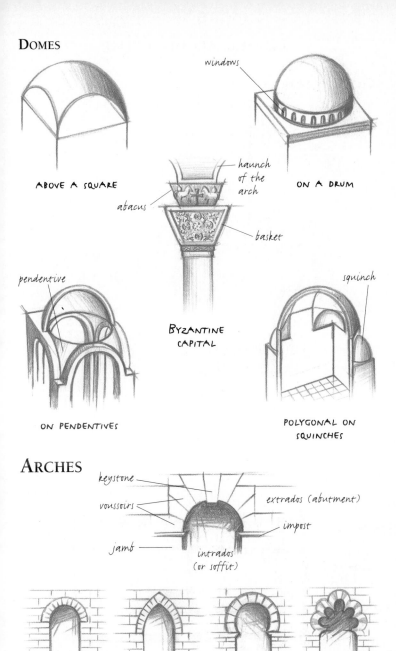

ABOVE A SQUARE

windows

ON A DRUM

haunch of the arch

abacus

basket

BYZANTINE CAPITAL

pendentive

ON PENDENTIVES

squinch

POLYGONAL ON SQUINCHES

# ARCHES

keystone

voussoirs

extrados (abutment)

impost

jamb

intrados (or soffit)

ROUND-HEADED (ROMAN)

POINTED (LANCET OR GOTHIC)

HORSESHOE

MULTIPOIL

H. Choimet

35

# ISLAMIC ARCHITECTURE

## OTTOMAN MOSQUE

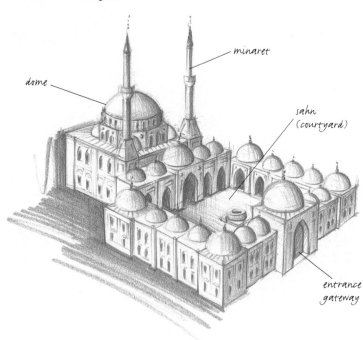

minaret

dome

sahn
(courtyard)

entrance
gateway

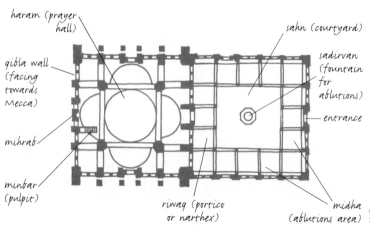

haram (prayer
hall)

sahn (courtyard)

qibla wall
(facing
towards
Mecca)

sadirvan
(fountain
for
ablutions)

entrance

mihrab

minbar
(pulpit)

riwaq (portico
or narthex)

midha
(ablutions area)

H. Choimet

# MINARETS

lantern

balcony

MUQARNAS
("STALACTITES")

MAMELUKE (MIDDLE EAST)

OTTOMAN (TURKEY)

# FURNISHINGS

dikka
(tribune)

mihrab

minbar (pulpit)

kursi (lutrin)

H. Choimet

# Meeting the people

Syrian girls

# LAND OF A THOUSAND SMILES

## Ahlan wa sahlan – Welcome!

Arab hospitality is renowned worldwide. So lone travellers should be prepared to be greeted with sympathy from everyone: Jordanians and Syrians enjoy company too much to imagine that anyone might want to spend their free time far from friends and family. Indeed one Arab proverb states that, "Where there is nobody, there is the Devil" and solitude is synonymous with poverty. People go to the souk *en famille* or with friends (in the latter case always of the same sex), ambling along arm in arm, browsing in the shops and discussing prices, chattering away about everything and nothing – just for the pleasure of being together.

Furthermore, when a stranger stops off in a remote part of the country, instead of being shunned as a foreigner, he will be accosted by curious locals eager to ascertain the nature of his business and whether they can be of service. Nothing is so important as to take precedence over tea with a newcomer, even if the parties are unable to understand each other's language. For in this land, everyone takes pleasure in entertaining a guest, asking after their family, their journey from home and their occupation. A warm-hearted and excited group often gathers around the guest: children, overcome with shyness, remain speechless while news of an *ajnabi* (foreigner) spreads to close relatives and neighbours. Initial greetings are formally exchanged, but before long everyone is on first-name terms. This same scenario recurs time and again in the course of a journey, but the welcome never palls or appears burdensome.

Sociability here is a way of life: relatives and friends drop in on someone at the slightest excuse. The simple act of passing in front of a door will bring a flood of invitations, cries of *"Tfaddal!"* which may be construed as "Please, do come in!". This welcome is then followed up by a standard ritual: a glass of cool water, for example, is offered while Arab coffee is prepared, conversation is engaged with the uttering of *"Ahlan wa sahlan"* (You are welcome) being repeated at regular intervals as sweetmeats and other tit-bits are brought in. Note: it is impolite to turn down or refuse any such displays of hospitality, just as it may be unseemly to get down to the subject of a visit too quickly. There will be family news to inquire after and many anodyne remarks to be made before the real aim of the visit can be broached almost shamefacedly.

## Arab hospitality

Irrespective of social or religious background, people form relationships in a very straightforward and easy way. The waiter will sit for a few minutes to chat; passengers will sit to the right of a taxi driver; both artist and member of parliament will frequent the same popular cafés. People address each other as "my brother", "my sister", even *"habibi"* (my dearest) and the more familiar forms of address are widely used. For everyone is equal in the desert because everyone needs water, food and rest when they are completing an arduous journey. Anonymity is shunned because everyone is everyone else's brother and friendships are founded on trust; furthermore it is likely that two "brothers" will share mutual friends and acquaintants.

Central to this complex social structure is the family, and the image of this group must be immaculate. Offspring – even when adult – may be rejected if they tarnish family honour or cause loss of face (with delinquency, adultery, criminal acts), and retribution is to be expected. On the other hand, the family ensures emotional and economic security, so it is rare to see destitution and homelessness on a scale found in cities in the Western world. Family members, however remote they might be, can always take shelter in the family home, and seek help in finding employment from the patriarch. In this way, it is unusual for a Syrian or Jordanian to seek complete independence from the family, and it is rare for a son not to call on his parents several times a week, for their authority does not weaken with age – even after he is married. It is a question of respect. Siblings will often live close by, often in the same building, which will have been bought as a joint purchase with each family occupying a floor. There are no old people's homes, for when the parents become old, it is expected that they will be cared for by the children. The father acts as the family's moral adjudicator; should he be absent or dead, the eldest son assumes that responsibility. Within this framework, couples rarely find themselves alone and so are unlikely to be able to indulge in any intimacy. A marriage not swiftly blessed with the birth of a child will be suspect, and when the children are born, it is difficult for people to imagine themselves separating from them. Offspring are smothered with attention and love largely because they perpetuate the family line and, as such, are a cause for pride. Despite appreciable changes, a traditional wife will be content to remain in the family home, reigning unchallenged over her domain and setting the pace of daily life. The husband's duty is to bring in the family's income.

The family can also act as a visiting card. The greatest have made a name for themselves as landowners, traders or industrialists through alliances that cover the whole of the Near East. The recent frontiers have never formed a real obstacle, for the common language of Arabic has facilitated alliances. Moreover, the Bedouin have long ignored frontiers, which have no physical reality in the desert. However, technical progress and western mores transmitted by satellite – hence the proliferation of receivers along the rooftops – are beginning to challenge traditional values and practices. Many people (predominantly men) have travelled afar to Saudi Arabia, the Gulf States, the Lebanon, the United States, Canada and the EU to try their luck at making their fortune. Expatriate Jordanians and Syrians form discreet communities that always maintain strong ties with the family back home.

Economic uncertainty is also having an impact. Poor income levels are delaying the onset of marriage and a shortage of housing is slowing the birthrate. Over recent years, the average family that once comprised seven children is now finding itself limited to two or three. These behavioural traits depend, of course, on the social milieu in which the individual has grown up. The middle classes often adopt habits acquired abroad. But behind the modernism, the taste for novelties (cars, tape recorders, private parties, the Internet, western music) is all show, for the heart and mind remain Levantine. The "eccentricities" adopted when in Europe and tolerated from a foreigner, are diplomatically curbed when back on home ground.

## A sense of belonging

Before being Jordanian or Syrian, a Levantine defines himself by the community to which his family is attached. The community could be religious (Sunni, Alawite, Druze, Greek Orthodox...), ethnic (Arab, Kurdish, Circassian), national (Palestinian) or linked to a way of life (Bedouin). People are proud of their special characteristics and inter-communal marriages are rare, even if everyone has dealings with and respects each other in daily life. Each community lives in its particular quarter where its traditions are perpetuated. This is one of the great differences with the West.

## Mahmud the Sunni, Agop the Armenian...

A Jordanian or Syrian is quick to identify the origin of a new interlocutor. More than clothing or features, it is nowadays the first name, the patronymic or accent that denotes a person's status. With the exception of Palestinians, identity cards bear no mention of ethnic community. In Syria, there is no attempt to identify the distinctive minorities so it is often hard to determine the type and size of ethnic communities.

## Sedentary Sunni Arabs

These form the most important group in both Syria and Jordan, where they constitute the traditional population of the towns and villages. As Sunni Muslims they belong to what is by far the largest Islamic community (see p 46).

## Bedouin

The Arab nomads (Bedouin), who took part in the revolt against the Ottoman regime during the First World War, are becoming fewer and fewer (10 000 in Jordan, 300 000 in Syria).

Generally, a distinction is made between sheep-rearing tribes and camel-rearing tribes. Ruwala and Sihran to the north of Amman, Bani Sakhr, Bani Attiyat, Hajaya and Howeitat to the south are the most important tribe confederations. All are Sunni Muslims and epitomise the ideal of Arab life: honour, simplicity and magnanimity, even if the city dwellers who suffered from their raids in the past are still distrustful of them. When they do in fact settle, nostalgia will sometimes lead them to put up a tent beside their house.

In Jordan, the Bedouin constitute one of the pillars of the regime and are the emblematic image of the Jordanian kingdom, even if most of them live settled lives in villages on the Transjordanian plateau. In Syria, almost half the Bedouin live semi-nomadic existences, based in villages along the banks of the Euphrates.

## Druze

The Jordanian and Syrian Druze migrated across the Lebanese mountains in the 19C and have now installed themselves in the south of Syria (where they represent 3% of the population), with a few in the north of Jordan.

The origins of the sect go back to the Egyptian Caliphate of Hakim, in 10C AD. His followers were quick to establish themselves in Syria where they took refuge in the mountains and developed a very particular form of Islam, the knowledge of which is reserved for the initiates alone (the *uqqal*). Their faith is based on the association of a number of religious texts among which are the Koran, the Bible and Plato. They have renounced the five pillars of Islam, they have no mosques and celebrate only the festivals of the Sacrifice and of Ashura. The largest community continues to reside in southern Lebanon, although a small group has taken root in the north of Israel. These Arabs enjoy very strong community ties: marriage outside the community is forbidden, and they are known to have a strong propensity to revolt against authority and be fearless fighters. The French at the time of the mandate learned this to their cost in 1925.

A Jordanian wearing the keffieh

The older generation still wear their distinctive form of dress: a *sarwal* (ample trousers that narrow at the ankle – said to be so devised so that the next messiah, when he is born to a man, will be caught safely in the folds), a black jacket and white turban. The young of both sexes tend to follow a western role model more obviously than Sunnis do: the women do not wear the veil, and men drink alcohol. The community continues to be headed by an Emir: the Joumblatts (in the Lebanon) and the Atrash dynasties (in Syria) are the best known.

## Christian Arabs

It is not unusual to meet Christians in Jordan (5 % of the population) and Syria (10 % of the population) because both countries neighbour the region known as the Holy Land. Even in ancient times, this region welcomed early Christian converts: after all, the New Testament documents Christ visiting the Jordanian Decapolis and the conversion of St Paul at Damascus.

The majority of the population was converted during the Byzantine era and embraced Islam only when ruled by Muslim dynasties from the 7C. Indeed there have only been a few periods of unrest when conversions were enforced and when discriminatory measures were imposed (such as the wearing of distinctive clothes, certain proscriptions, taxes). Otherwise Islam has shown itself tolerant of "the People of the Book" (Christians and Jews) on its territory. The Christians are, in the large majority, Arabs and they are divided into a dozen different confessions *(see p 48)*. There is also an important Armenian community.

## Armenians

The history of the Armenian people is said to date back to the 7C BC, and can be traced to a specific geographical area in northeastern Anatolia, centred around Mount Ararat. Armenia was the first nation to make Christianity the official religion in the early part of the 3C, largely as a result of St Gregory the Illuminator whose church was granted independence in the 5C by the Council of Chalcedon. The Armenian people have been able to develop their own identity in the national, linguistic, cultural and religious spheres and this has enabled them to survive numerous periods of occupation.

The terrible genocide of 1915, with its million victims, led to the exodus of the Armenians from Turkey, where they had formed a large minority. Many survivors at that time found refuge in Syria, especially in Aleppo, over the Turkish frontier.

Nowadays, the seven million Armenians are divided in equal parts between the Republic of Armenia, which has been free from the Soviet yoke since 1991, and a diaspora of which more than one million members live in the United States. Aleppo and Beirut are home for a large part of the 300 000 Armenians in the Middle East. In Aleppo they are mainly professional people. The signs outside their places of business are written with the tall cursive letters of a 38-letter alphabet especially designed for the Armenian language in the 5C AD.

## Alawites

They are also known by the name of the Nusayris and were originally concentrated in the Jebel Ansariya, which dominates the Mediterranean coast in northern Syria. They constitute about 13 % of the Syrian population, but are practically non-existent in Jordan. Their sect, which is of Shiite origin, established itself in northern Syria during the 10C AD. At that time, the sect's members settled in the mountains – the traditional refuge of minorities –

where they scraped a living in isolation, until the French mandate. The elite that emerged in the Alawite state, set up by France in 1922, progressively played an ever greater role in the nationalist struggle and then in the Baath Party and the army. President Hafiz al-Asad and several senior Syrian officials are of Alawite origin. The Alawite religion is only known to initiates and its practice is not over-demanding.

## Ismailis
They are members of a Shiite sect that recognises Ismail as the seventh and last imam. They form a small community established in Salemiye to the east of Hama. Some of them recognise the authority of the Agha Khan.

## Jews
They form a very ancient community in Syria (the synagogue of Doura Europos, which dates from the 3C AD, bears witness to this fact) and they have practically all left Syria and Jordan. There are said to be a little more than 300, mainly living in Damascus, since having received permission to emigrate in 1992. At that date, there were about 5 000.

## Kurds
They represent perhaps 6 % of the Syrian population. They are Sunni Muslims and set themselves apart from the Arabs by their language, which belongs to the group of Iranian languages, and their strong nationalist aspirations. This people, which is formed of tribes originating in the mountains and reckoned to exceed 20 million in number, is split between Turkey, Iran, Iraq and Syria. In the latter country, they traditionally occupy the Kurd-Dagh massif to the northwest of Aleppo and more especially the upper regions of the Jazira along the Turkish border (the Qamishli region). The city of Aleppo has a large Kurdish community.

## Circassians
These Caucasians became Muslims in the 16C and 17C and are also known (in Arabic) as Shirkass. They were expelled by the Imperial Russian army in the 19C and found refuge in the Ottoman Empire. The 25 000 members of the community have acquired considerable weight in Jordan where they form the king's guard of honour. They have preserved their language and their customs. Chechens and Turcomans from Caucasia have also found refuge in the kingdon. Small communities also exist in Syria.

## Palestinians
The Palestinians – Arabs who are in the majority Muslims but who can also be Christians – feel strongly attached to lands situated to the west of the River Jordan. The refugees of the Israeli-Arab wars of 1948 and 1967 have settled temporarily in camps in Jordan and, to a lesser extent, in Syria. With the hope of a return fading, the camps, which were originally of tents, have evolved into modest residential quarters. In both cases, the influx of a close-knit community has caused some upset to the local people. In Jordan, they represent perhaps 60 % of the inhabitants of the country and have a very considerable socio-economic weight. They have been educated in the UNWRA schools put in place by the United Nations and often have a higher than average educational level. Despite the closure of the frontiers, they have maintained contact with their families scattered across the globe.

# FAITH AND CREED

The Middle East was the birthplace of three great monotheistic religions: Judaism, Christianity and Islam. It was also the crucible for currents of thought which have diversified and enriched beliefs. The schisms that have shaken the three religions have given birth to communities which have maintained themselves until today. Muslims form the majority of the population and the different Christian communities are still very much in evidence, but very few of the Jews have remained on Syrian and Jordanian territory (*see p 45*).

## Islam

Islam is the name given by Muslims to their religion and it means: submission to the will of God. There is only one God. A Muslim's profession of faith runs: "There is no God but Allah and Muhammad is his prophet".
Apart from the orthodox branch of the **Sunni**, which is far and away the most important, Syria and Jordan have also a number of **Shiites** and some small minorities such as the **Alawites** and **Druze**.

### Origins

**Muhammad** was born in Mecca in about 570 AD. He was a shepherd in his childhood and later accompanied caravans. He had his first prophetic visions at the age of 40. For about ten years, he preached at **Mecca**, but his revelations were ill received and he had to flee to **Medina**. This emigration, the **Hijra**, marks the beginning of the Muslim era. Muhammad claimed to transmit the word of God just as Abraham, Moses and Jesus, whom he revered as having brought the first gleam of true light, had done before him. His teaching spread rapidly, and at his death in 632, the progress achieved by Islam was already considerable. Tradition relates that in the course of one of his journeys he entered Bosra, but not Damascus, "for one does not enter Paradise twice".
The actual words of Allah, as revealed to the Prophet, were set down verse by verse in the **Koran**. These revelations were collected together by the faithful and put into chapters or **suras**. The memorisation of the 114 suras constitutes the basis of Koranic teaching. The **Sunna**, or tradition, is a series of narratives **(hadith)** – sometimes legendary – of the life of Muhammad and serves to elucidate certain obscure points of the Koran, amplifies the precepts in the book and deals with questions of daily life.

### The "Five Pillars" of Islam

The Koran lays down five essential obligations:
- **the profession of faith** (*Shahada*), which is the main act denoting conversion to Islam;
- **prayer** (*Salat*), which is to be repeated five times a day;
- **the Ramadan fast** (*Sawm*);
- **legal alms** (*zakat*);
- **the pilgrimage to Mecca** (*Haj*), which every believer must make at least once in a lifetime.

Besides these five fundamental injunctions, the Islamic religion proscribes alcoholic drinks, the meat of the pig and animals not emptied of their blood (including game); it also forbids games of chance, usury and murder. Islam also has precepts concerning, for example, charity or the despicable nature of certain goods.

## Prayer

It consists of a series of prostrations, during which the Muslim will recite certain verses of the Koran. It can be said anywhere as long as it is said in the direction of Mecca. The solemn prayer on Friday includes a sermon and Muslims attend in large numbers. Sunni Islam has neither clergy nor sacraments. A particularly knowledgeable Muslim, the **Imam**, leads the prayers, which are not accompanied by any music or singing. The prayer must be said in a state of purity, which explains the custom of removing shoes at the entrance of a mosque and the presence of a fountain or pool of water for ablutions in the courtyard: bodily cleanliness reflects that of the soul.

### The Adhan

The Adhan can be heard five times a day. It is the call to prayer given from the top of a minaret by the muezzin (replaced in fact more and more often by a recorded tape). It begins with the formula "Allah Akbar" ("God is Great") repeated twice or four times in different modes: "I testify that there is but one God! I testify that Muhammad is the Messenger of God! Come to prayer! Come to the good! Prayer has begun! God is Great!"

Finally the uniqueness of God is proclaimed a final time: "There is no God but Allah!" The muezzins are chosen for the power and beauty of their voices; the grand muezzin of Aleppo (Sabri Mudallal) has even made several recordings.

## Ramadan

The most spectacular manifestation of religious life is Ramadan or the month of fasting. During the ninth month of the Muslim lunar year, fasting is obligatory for every Muslim adult, who is responsible and capable of bearing it, with the exception of the sick, pregnant women and those on a long journey. There is abstention from eating, drinking and having sexual relations from sunrise to sunset. The whole life of a country follows this month's rhythm of prayer and devotion. The night of the 26th of Ramadan is the "night of destiny". It commemorates Muhammad's first revelation.

## Religious festivals

Everyday life in Jordan or Syria is governed by the Gregorian calendar, but religious life is regulated according to the **Islamic calendar**. This has its start date on 16 July 622. The Hijri year, which is a lunar year, consists of 12 months, each being of 29 or 30 days. It is therefore shorter than the solar year and gains about 10 days a year. This is why the month of Ramadan and the great religious feasts are moveable in relation to our calendar.

**1 Muharram** is New Year's Day in the Islamic calendar.

**Mawlid al-Nabi**, which was instituted in the 6C of the Hijra, commemorates the birth of Muhammad.

**Id al-Fitr** marks the end of Ramadan. This day is an occasion for family celebrations and children are given new clothes. Giving alms is part of the enjoined duties of the festival.

The **Id al-Kabir** commemorates the sacrifice of Abraham. It is traditional for each family to sacrifice a sheep. The festival can be compared in importance to that of Christmas for Christians. The Id al-Kabir also marks the period of the pilgrimage to Mecca.

| Calendar of Islamics Festivals | | | | |
|---|---|---|---|---|
| Hijra Year | **1421** | **1422** | **1423** | **1424** |
| New Year | 5 Apr 2000 | 25 Mar 2001 | 14 Mar 2002 | 3 Mar 2003 |
| Prophet's Birthday | 14 June 2000 | 3 June 2001 | 23 May 2002 | 12 May 2003 |
| Ramadan begins | 27 Nov 2000 | 16 Nov 2001 | 5 Nov 2002 | 25 Oct 2003 |
| Id al-Fitr (end Ramadan) | 27 Dec 2000 | 16 Dec 2001 | 5 Dec 2002 | 24 Nov 2003 |
| Id al-Kabir | 5 Mar 2001 | 22 Feb 2002 | 11 Feb 2003 | 31 Jan 2004 |

NB. The difficulty in calculating precisely the beginnings of lunar months can make these dates vary by one or two days.

## Sufism

Sufism is far from being limited to the spellbinding dances of whirling dervishes presented nowadays by certain restaurants. This mystical branch of Islam has developed a large number of varied practices, ranging from living as hermits to living in monasteries. In this last form (the *tariqa*), which has been the most widespread since the 12C AD, Sufis place themselves under the authority of a spiritual master (*Sheikh*) in monasteries called, according to the region, *zawiya*, *ribat*, *khanqa* or *tekkiya*. Each congregation has its own ritual and its own liturgy, such as recitations (*dhikr*) or dances (in the case of whirling dervishes) with the ultimate aim of growing nearer to God. In contrast with monasticism, Sufism does not demand detachment from temporal life, nor does it require celibacy. The social role of Sufis was often important, to the point that they have sometimes been termed the Freemasons of Islam. Rumi, the great poet of Konya; Hallaj, condemned to death for having proclaimed: "I am the Truth, that is to say God"; Al-Rifa'i, the founder of the *rifayya*; Ibn al-Arabi and the Persian poets Hafiz and Attar are counted among the greatest Sufis.

## Shiites: Ali's partisans

The Shiites believe that the descendants of Ali, the son-in-law of the Prophet by virtue of his having married the Prophet's daughter, Fatima, should have succeeded Muhammad. They accused the Umayyads of usurpation. Hussein, Ali's son, resolved to avenge his father, who had been removed from power, but was killed in battle at Kerbela in 680 (modern day Iraq). According to the Shiites, the divine light was transmitted from Muhammad to all the imams descended from Ali up to the last called the *mahdi*. The Shiites of Iran count 12 imams since Ali and they are called in consequence "**twelvers**". The **Ismailis** diverge from this line of succession at the seventh Imam. These two Shiite branches of Islam are opposed to the much larger orthodox branch called **Sunni**.

The **Druze** (see p 42) and **Alawites** are also of Shiite origin.

# Christianity

## A dozen churches

Eastern Christians, the inhabitants of the region that witnessed the birth and passion of Christ, are split into a dozen communities. The first differences to arise within the ranks of Christians concerned the nature of Christ's godliness (divine or not) and can be described as "Byzantine" because of the extent to which its meaning and implications escaped the grasp of ordinary mortals. The points at issue lay elsewhere. The doctrinal debate was not an adequate mask for the desire for independence felt by the populations of the provinces faced with the hegemony of Constantinople. The first break came at the Council of Nicaea (325 AD) which condemned **Arianism**. In 431 AD, the Council of Ephesus was marked by the birth of **Nestorianism** (adopted by the Assyrians). It was followed 20 years later by the Council of Chalcedon, which condemned Monophysitism and saw the birth of three distinct churches: the **Jacobite** in Syria, the **Coptic** in Egypt and Ethiopia, and the **Armenian**. The other faithful remained in the Greek Orthodox Church, as later, at the time of the Eastern schism of 1054. A second bout of fragmentation occurred between the 16C and the 19C AD. Each church developed a so-called uniate branch, that is to say, one that recognised the authority of the Pope. Since then, there has been a **Chaldean Church** (Assyrian Catholics), a **Syrian Catholic** (Jacobite uniates), **Coptic Catholic**, **Armenian Catholic** and **Melchite** (Greek Catholics).

What is left today of the incredible diversity of Eastern Christianity? Christians represent 10 % of the Syrian population and nearly 5 % of that of Jordan. Of the whole, the **Greek Orthodox** are in a large majority (with perhaps 450 000 in Syria and 80 000 in Jordan). Because of their economic weight and their traditional links with the West, the importance of Eastern Christians is, however, greater than would be suggested by stark demographical statistics.

## Preserving identity

Eastern Christians retain a certain autonomy. They have to follow the rules of their church as regards personal status. In contrast to a Muslim, a Greek Catholic cannot take several wives. Christian shopkeepers usually close their shops on Sundays, whilst their Muslim counterparts take their rest on Fridays. The date of Easter for the Orthodox is calculated on the basis of the Julian calendar and is therefore later than the Catholic festival.

Inside St George's Church, a Greek Orthodox Church at Izraa

P. Meunier

# DAILY LIFE

As a consequence of the diversity of communities and social differences, daily life is very different from one milieu to another. It tends to approximate to the western model in the great cities, especially Amman, whilst in the desert it retains the rhythm of the true nomads.

## Family Portraits

### On the hills of Amman

The Ruba'is work in the import business. This well-to-do family lives in a beautiful villa, a brilliant alliance of modernity and tradition, in the smart Abdun quarter. Muhammad, the head of the family, divides his time between Jordan and the United States, where his son is studying at university. The mobile telephone and the computer jar a little among the rich furnishings, which betray a clear leaning towards tradition. Part of the sitting room, of an original design, whose vaulting imitates the roof of a tent, reminds visitors that the family is of Bedouin origin. Suha, the mother, is a member of the management board of an American style project, the aim of which is to aid women from modest backgrounds. This is an activity which, alongside bringing up her children, takes up a great deal of her time. The winter holidays are spent in Aqaba, whilst in summer, the whole family takes off for Europe or the United States.

### In Damascus

The Sabbagh family lives in a modest residential quarter. On the balconies are rose bushes growing from large metal *ghee* containers (the universally-used cooking butter). The concrete buildings are identical to each other in this urban scene, where the electric wires weave an immense web. The little courtyard from which one enters the street is scented with jasmine, whilst in the middle there grows a large medlar tree. The large sitting room is stuffed full of imposing settees and low furniture. Also in the room are the yellowing photos of grandparents, artificial flowers on the television, mats, boards with Arabic calligraphy, a reproduction of a painting by a European master. Maher, the head of the family, is a civil servant. He works from 8am until 2pm. His salary is very modest, a few thousand (Syrian) pounds a month, which is not enough to feed his family but which gives him the right to draw social security payments. After the midday meal, which is taken with the whole family, he starts a second, more lucrative, day. With his brother, he has launched a small typesetting business. This leaves little time for holidays, all the more so as there is only one weekly day of rest.

### In a Palestinian camp

The Mawaid family has been living in the Palestinian camp of Wahda since 1968. This is a true town within the city of Amman and no longer bears any resemblance to the crowded tents or the shanty towns hastily erected after the Israeli-Arab wars of 1948 and 1967. Over the years, the Mawaids have recreated the world of a Palestinian village, whilst the infrastructure has been slowly developing. The children go to schools run by UNWRA (the agency which cares for the Palestinian refugees) before entering Jordanian society. The mother is glad to wear the traditional, embroidered costume of her native village. In the camp, the streets bear the names of villages in Palestine. Very often, the young have known nothing else but the camp and dream of a better life, whilst their elders follow the progress of the peace process, in the hope of a return to Palestine.

## In the country

Life is hard in the country, where material conditions are less comfortable than in the towns. In their house of breeze-blocks, which has replaced the traditional beehive-shaped mud-brick construction, the Mudir family strives for protection against the extremes of heat and cold. The floor of the house is covered by carpets of felt or woven wool in order to reduce the cold. Furniture is scanty. There are various attractive embroideries, some brightly coloured patchworks and a clock to decorate the walls. The mattresses used at night are heaped in a corner of the room. Work in the fields is completed by men, women and even children outside school terms. The old people take care of the youngest children before they too join the work in the fields. Every week, the big expedition of the Mudir family is to the market, which is held in the nearest town. There they sell the produce of their farm: the vegetables, the dairy products, the eggs, the chickens and the sheep. The cereals go to the co-operative. With the money they earn from trading, the family buys what is necessary to the life of the farm, before taking the bus at the end of the morning in order to return to the village.

## In the desert

The daily life of Muhammad Huwaytat, a slender Bedouin with a hatchet-like face, centres around his tent, which, according to the season, will be put up in a place forming part of the tribal area. Usually, there are no more than a few tents together belonging to the same clan. The tent is made up of long strips of cloth woven out of goat's hair for the roof, as this is the most waterproof material against the winter rains. The shape given to the tent by changing the positioning of its wooden poles depends on the weather. In summer, the

A Bedouin family

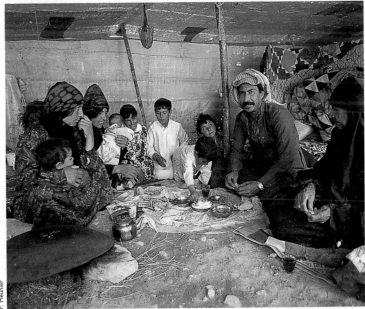

P. Meunier

movement of air will be welcomed, whilst in winter or on a rainy day, the elements will be shut out. Inside the tent, the sexes are separated by means of a curtain. The side reserved for the men is the one mainly used for welcoming visitors. Carpets and cushions are arranged around the fireplace where the hot embers are used for the preparation of tea and coffee served in beautiful copper utensils. On the women's side, provisions are heaped up next to the blankets used during the night. Kitchen utensils are kept alongside the cradles. The traditional food of the Huwaytats is simple, consisting of flat cakes of bread, dates and milk. A lamb might be roasted (*mashwi*) and on days when there is a big celebration, a **mensef** will be cooked. For travel, the dromedary has been replaced by the four-wheel drive vehicle, which has become the essential tool for the Bedouin nowadays. The flocks are watched over at a distance from the tent by child shepherds or women. Women look after the children, do the cooking and weave on long looms set up outside. The men have charge of the flocks and are responsible for dealing with the outside world.

## Public Places

### The coffee house

The traditional café is flourishing in Syria, since the younger generations continue to gather in the cafés alongside the older customers. Under the trellises of jasmine and honeysuckle, the wooden chairs arranged side by side seem very welcoming. In an Arab café, tea, coffee and fizzy drinks are served, but never alcohol. It is the games, more than the drinking, which draw in the clientele. There are games of cards, the only music in the café being the movement of the **tric-trac** (variant of backgammon) counters on the fine boards of well-worn wood along with the gurgling of the **narghile**. Even now customers might occasionally be entertained by a storyteller. This is a magical spectacle during which the audience will repeat in chorus the best known lines. Arab women are rarely to be seen in a café, but foreign female travellers are welcome.

### In the hammam

Jordan no longer has traditional hammams, but in Syria cafés and hammams are the two main places for social life. It is said that women meet there to choose their sons' future wives in the light of qualities that are often other than intellectual! Men never mix with women in a hammam. Some establishments are reserved for men, whilst others have different hours for the two sexes. At the entrance, clients specify what they want: just a bath, a sauna, a rub-down, a massage, some soap.

### The narghile

It would be a pity to miss trying this strange water pipe. Both elegant and clumsy, the smoker holds it by its long, flexible pipe for a seemingly endless session of smoking. The smoke has been cooled and filtered by its brief passage through the water and tastes bitter or perfumed according to the quality of the tobacco. The preferred tobacco is not the "tombac", which is plain and strong, but rather the "asal" (with honey fragrance), the "tuffah" (apple flavour) or the "fawakih" (fruit mixture). When the glow of the coals begins to die, the attendant will rush round: "naraya, naraya" ("fire, fire"). From his metal coal carrier he will extract a glowing piece of charcoal with his pincers and place it delicately on the tobacco. This procedure might be repeated two or three times before the narghile is abandoned.

P. Meunier

In the hammam, Damascus

Customers are given one or more wristbands representing the service(s) requested. Wallets, watches and jewellery are left in the attractive wooden lockers: the key to the locker will be attached to another wristband. In the main room, which is usually surmounted by a dome, clients undress completely and will be supplied with a towel to knot round the waist. The towel should be kept in position in the baths (it is not the custom to be naked in the hammam). Wooden shoes are provided when going to the other rooms in the baths. If there are a lot of people around, clients might have to wait to be rubbed down with a horsehair glove (beware of patches of sunburn) and to have a massage. In the small rooms, which are either hot or tepid, there are marble slabs to stretch out on. The water basins contain either hot or cold water for splashing over yourself. Once out of the bath, clients can relax, wrapped from head to toe in fresh towels, and drink tea in peace.

## In the souk

The souk evokes all the magic and the mystery surrounding the East. There are tangled alleyways, welcoming shopkeepers, marvels of handicraft, the scents of spices, the memories of distant lands... The souk is an experience, not only for the senses, but also in trading customs. Rarely do visitors not take to the business of haggling in a big way, even after the occasional hesitation – the absence of fixed prices can be somewhat inhibiting at first. But beware! Far from being a mere shop assistant, a trader in the souk is, above all, a profound psychologist. He will be quick to analyse the very least of a prospective buyer's reactions. A mere look, either of approbation or of distaste, and the trader will have discovered all he needs to know and will suggest things to tempt the buyer. A touch of over-enthusiasm for that carpet – the one of your dreams – and that is it! And even if he asserts the contrary, his price will be yours.

# Rites of Passage

## Circumcision

This was a custom already in use among the Ancient Egyptians and is still practised among Ethiopians, Copts, Jews and Muslims. Although it is by tradition rather than by Koranic prescription, the removal of a boy's foreskin takes place at about seven years old. Previously, circumcision was an occasion for rejoicing, but more discretion is exercised nowadays. The circumciser or barber is present at all the ceremonies relating to the operation.

## Marriage

This is the most important stage of life and those who escape it are rare indeed. To be over 30 (often much less in country districts) and unmarried is considered to be a sign of poverty or of a defect. A marital partner is often suggested rather than imposed and marriages are arranged by the parents, sometimes a long time ahead. But many are refused their heart's desire by parents anxious to observe tradition. The choice is often dictated by social considerations. The proposed partner must share the same religious or ethnic milieu. Within the framework of a marriage entered into more for practical reasons than for passion, affection between the couple is centred on the bringing up of the children. The wedding is paid for by the family of the husband and is very expensive, since normally there are many guests and the celebrations last several days. There are musicians (*munshid*) to entertain during the evening. In traditional Muslim families, men and women are kept separate; the Shaikh comes to seal the union before God by reading the first sura of the Koran (the *fatiha*).

# TRADITIONAL ARTS

## Costumes

The diversity of traditional costumes in Jordan or Syria can best be seen in the souks of the cities or in the villages. For centuries, men and women in rural areas bought their clothes from travelling traders. Nowadays, as a consequence of better transport, they buy their clothing in the specialised areas of the souks. The materials, which in the past were suited to the heat or the cold, have today been replaced by synthetic materials that do not always have the same qualities. Clothing is increasingly modelled on fashion in the West. For a long time now, the man in the street has been wearing trousers, western-style shirts, jeans and T-shirts.

### Male dress

Up to the middle of the century, the Bedouin used to wear traditional costume. Over the long, white or coloured robe (*jellaba*) with the tight collar (*thawb*), they would throw a sort of sleeveless cape (*abaya*). In winter, they would wrap themselves in a warm, fur-lined coat with long sleeves (*farwa*). Nowadays, they wear a European style jacket or anorak over the *jellaba*. The *keffieh*, the head-dress popularised by Yasser Arafat, a large square of material kept in place by black cords (*aqal*), remains the distinctive garb of Palestinians, Jordanians and Syrians from the country districts. The decoration of small squares (red or black on white background) is the most commonly encountered, although plain ones also exist. The *keffieh* is even worn in town, where it can accompany otherwise western dress. The *tarbush*, a stiff, dark red cylindrical hat made of felt (Moroccan fez), which was the fashion under the Ottomans, has practically disappeared. The ordinary man in the street always has his hair done properly and is closely shaved, though mostly with a moustache. He is frequently to be seen in western clothes (jacket, jeans). His shirt will often be brightly coloured and have striking designs on it.

### Female dress

Women are more traditional in their dress than men, though it is true that the infamous robe comprising three metres of material, which served at one and the same time as dress, undergarment and veil (*thob'ob* or *khalagah*), disappeared in the 1940s. It gave way to long dresses of satin or synthetic fibres. Their black colour serves to enhance the delicate cross-stitching of the embroidery. The decoration is always geometric and usually red, being used to set off the neckline, the sleeves and the hem. This type of dress is worn from northern Syria to the Negev, but with perceptible differences in the motifs used to denote a particular village or tribe. In the larger cities like Damascus and Amman, traditional dress is being progressively replaced by western fashions with a clear preference for frilly dresses adorned with beading, sequins and gold or silver appliqué panels. This does not rule out the wearing of the headscarf, which could be a sign of renewed fervour or be a political statement.

In the street, women usually wear long coats of beige, grey or light-green poplin, covering the ankle. But this "uniform" worn by women between the ages of 20 to 40 does not exclude a certain coquetry. Their make-up can sometimes look a bit over the top, jeans are often worn, and the blouse with its chaste neckline

is adorned with multicoloured, golden or silver beads. When hair is worn loose, it is always long and very often hennaed. The khaki uniform, which is obligatory at school, is sometimes worn with the veil, this being an attempt to satisfy the demands of the party and at the same time to silence wagging tongues. The peasant women are the ones who add a splash of colour to the pavements of the cities. Their brightly-coloured costumes and head dresses are different depending on the village or tribe.

## Jewellery

For a Bedouin woman, jewels are not only her finery but also her capital. Jewels received as dowry form part of the transaction that precedes marriage. They become the property of the married woman, who does with them what she will. **Amulets** are associated with popular beliefs: a white stone will encourage milk production in the young mother, whilst a blue pearl will afford protection from the evil eye. They are often to be found in the shape of small cylindrical boxes or as fish worn round the neck.

The most impressive **necklaces** (*kirdan*) are those in the form of chokers. They are fixed to a textile backing and are formed of multiple pendants to which are hung Ottoman coins.

**Bracelets** (*asawira*) are worn in pairs, one on each arm. The simplest model is formed of semicircles of twisted metal with large bulbs fixed to each end. Large, smooth, circular bracelets, closed with a pin, and decorated with niello date from the 1930s onwards.

**Rings** are worn on four fingers and are sometimes set with a stone. Bedouin women, traditionally, only wore stones set in silver. Nowadays, mass-produced gold jewellery, widely available from the souk (priced by weight), is the preferred choice for all be they living in the city or in the desert. As a consequence, goldsmiths have practically disappeared. Silver jewellery has become the prerogative of souvenir shops or antique dealers. As for men, they occasionally slip a large ring onto one of their fingers.

## Decorative and applied arts

A visit to the Azem palaces of Damascus or Hama, the Historical Museum of Old Damascus, or several other "bayt" in the old quarters will highlight the sumptuousness of the architecture (*see p 26*) and of the traditional decorative arts.

The **cedar chests** incrusted with mother-of-pearl stand out against the beautifully painted **wood panelling** adorning the walls and ceilings. The technique of *al-ajami* uses a synthetic resin to mould decoration that is subsequently painted and gilded. Shelving, set into the panelling, gleams with beautiful examples of glazed earthenware, graceful ewers and silver objects. **Lamps** of enamelled glass decorated with calligraphy hang from the ceiling.

**Kilims** (woven carpets) with delicate geometrical motifs serve as wall coverings or cover the divans placed around the room along the walls. In the richest palaces, kilims are replaced by brocade and damask. The dishes of food or mezze are set out on small tables with inlaid legs and topped with a magnificent **chased brass** or **copper tray**, a traditional speciality associated with Damascus.

The Hamadiyyeh Souk, Damascus

P. Meunier

Inlaid woodwork, Historical Museum of Old Damascus

## Calligraphy

Calligraphy has become one of the most characteristic forms of Islamic decoration as figurative representations are forbidden. It has gone far beyond the confines of books and has extended to objects, furniture and monuments. Two main styles can be distinguished: the angular, sober and monumental *kufi* used in the early days of Islam; the *naskhi*, which is more supple and fluid for transcribing religious texts.

# Handicrafts today

Jordan and Syria are rightly renowned for the quality of their handicrafts, but traditional trades are tending to disappear and the techniques have vastly changed. In Damascus, the pieces of wood and mother-of-pearl used for inlaid furniture were at one time individually shaped. Nowadays, they are mass-produced in the workshops of Bab Sharqi and plastic has replaced the mother-of-pearl. There are still some glass-blowers blowing their hearts out round the hearths and producing glasswork without great originality in ochre, green or blue. The copper is rather clumsily incised. The producers of ceramics and weapons, who in the past made the Syrian capital famous, have nearly all disappeared. There are still some old looms for weaving brocade where the shuttle will move backwards and forwards to produce delicate patterns through the criss-crossing of precious threads of silk at the rate of a few inches a day.

## Copper

The damascening of copper, a process by which another metal of a different colour is introduced into the copper, can still produce some attractive pieces. Other less inspiring objects have been merely chased (engraved).

## Marquetry

This is a speciality of Damascus that has spread throughout the Levant. It seems to have taken over the decoration of furniture such as chests, armchairs, small tables and card tables, but also small boxes, lecterns (for the Koran) and tric-trac boards... Yet it is necessary to distinguish two qualities. The first, in the tradition of the 19C, was made of non-synthetic materials, such as mother-of-pearl and bone assembled into rather large patterns, either of geometric or floral inspiration (cypress trees or petals) and sometimes underlined with an inlaid strip of metal. The other quality, which is less generous and is generally used for small boxes, employs quantities of synthetic materials and its purely geometric design seems to repeat itself into infinity.

## Basketwork

Baskets and round trays, on which meals were served, are made from coloured wheat straw. They are woven in Jebel al-Arab. The geometric patterns form stars or spirals. Some trays can measure more than a metre across.

## Marble

This is the traditional facing for more expensive houses and is much used for the decoration of restaurants, big hotels, fountains and paved areas. It is put together according to the *opus sectile* technique: small plaques of different coloured marbles are cut, so that geometric and floral patterns can be produced.

## Carpets

The hand-knotted carpets that are on sale in Syria are not usually of local manufacture. However, the Bedouin women maintain their long tradition of weaving. Outside in the open air, they make enormous floor coverings and brightly-coloured cushions to furnish the tents. They also make the bags with their geometric designs in white and red on black background, which are used for storage and the transporting of merchandise. A very rudimentary, horizontal loom is placed on the ground in front of the tent. Two women can work there side by side. In the towns, a less clumsy vertical loom is used. The wool normally comes from goat, sheep or camel hair.

In Jordan, the women of the settled Bani Hamida tribe, continue the tradition of the **woven carpet** whilst adapting it to modern tastes. The patterns used are still geometric but they have abandoned bright colours in favour of pastel shades such as mauve, beige, orange and bottle green.

# MUSIC AND DANCE

Music is everywhere and its forms are varied, diffused via cheap, pirated cassettes (recordings of classical Arab music as well as the latest western hits) and traditional ensembles hired to entertain people at parties and festivals, and to provide accompaniments to highly structured dances.

## Musical instruments

Arab folklore has its very own set of traditional instruments. In the desert, the Bedouin play very expressive music on simple instruments: the **reed flute** (nay), sometimes double, produces a high-pitched tone. The **Arab rebec** (rababa) comprises a primitive trapezoidal soundbox with a single string and emits what seems to be a series of long wails. The **tabla**, a Bedouin percussion instrument, consists of a simple skin stretched on a frame. In the cities and towns, the **lute** – which was first used by the Umayyads – is regarded as the king of all instruments: this is played on its own or to accompany a singer. It has four to six double strings attached to a neck. The soundbox is often lavishly decorated with delicate marquetry in the damascene tradition. The favourite instrument for the more highbrow type of music is the **flat zither** (qanun) which is played by plucking the strings with a metal plectrum. **Tambourines** are mounted on a frame that sometimes has a set of small cymbals (duff or riqq) attached. Another percussion instrument is the **drum** (dirbakka), which is often shaped like a big vase.

## Popular music

Religious music does not employ instruments, except on very rare occasions. Only the chanting of the human voice is accepted for the reading of the Koran or the call to prayer. Otherwise orchestras comprise four to five musicians and are often brought in for celebrations. Restaurants sometimes employ an orchestra: this can be a great introduction to the popular music of the region with the locals often joining in. The repertory has been interpreted by many great and enduring Arab singers such as the Egyptian **Umm Kalthum**, **Farid al-Atrash**, a Druze from Suwaida (in southern Syria) and a great charmer in Egyptian musical comedies and **Fayruz**, the famous Lebanese female vocalist. The repertory also includes popular songs, whose composers are often unknown. Among the great voices of Syria, the following should be mentioned: **Sabah Fakhri**, **Sabri Mudallal**, **Hamza Shakkur**, **Adib Dayère** and **Mayad al-Hennawi**.

## Dance

The **belly dance** is rarely performed in Syria and Jordan, at least in public. It tends to be restricted to seedy casinos. The **dabke** is less lascivious and so popularly performed in groups at festivals. The participants hold hands and form circles in the manner of certain European folklore dances. Then you have the highly dramatic **sword dance** which sometimes verges on being dangerous. In some ways it is more of a symbolic joust than a dance and should be performed by skilled practitioners, often to the astonishment of the audience. Finally, there are the **whirling dervishes** who practise the liturgical dance of the disciples of Jalal al-Din al-Rumi (d 1273). This famous whirling dance is extremely symbolic (performances in Syrian restaurants are mostly toned-down versions). The white costume of the dervishes represents the shroud, their high hats the gravestone. The black cloak represents the tomb and the fact of their taking it off before greeting people symbolises the rebirth. The dervishes take short rhythmic steps in time to a tambourine. They turn with arms extended, the right hand reaches to heaven, from which it receives grace, whilst the left is stretched towards the ground to spread the received grace. The dance can go on and on, sometimes for hours, and is thought to encourage the mastery of self and the fusion of the dancer with God.

J.-F. Galmiche

Musicians in the
Aboul-Ezz Restaurant
in Damascus

# SOCIAL ETIQUETTE

Attentive and sociable foreigners travelling in ones and twos will have no difficulty in making friends. The Jordanians, like the Syrians, hold to their traditional reputation for generosity and hospitality – which if anything is sometimes understated. Small demonstrations of human warmth are frequent. Smiles, the offer of a glass of tea, help with directions, a seat on public transport: these are all gestures which help to foster good relations. Visitors would do well to interest themselves in their host's way of life and to listen to his point of view: he will be just as interested in hearing about life in the West. Try to introduce a certain degree of flexibility into any itinerary to allow for unexpected encounters.

• A family photo is the ideal prop for a conversation. People from the East love to see pictures of partners, parents, brothers and sisters. In the same way, showing a postcard of your locality or your town will help communication despite the language barrier.

• In traditional families, a female traveller will often be separated from a male companion and shown into the room reserved for women, the man remaining with the other males. Two different experiences of the Arab family to compare when it is time to say goodbye!

• A visit to the cultural institute serving your home country is an ideal meeting place for a conversation in your mother tongue during an art exhibition or a theatrical event.

• It is not uncommon for travellers to be invited home by a family. They might even offer board and lodging, sometimes for several days. But be careful! Although hospitality is a duty for everyone, whether rich or poor, and it brings with it protection and comfort, it does impose certain obligations on the guest. Understandably, visitors will have to respect the way of life of the host family and give the right impression at every occasion. The family will wish to introduce their guest to all the neighbours, and maybe even to the authorities. It would be impolite to avoid these visits, the meaning of which might not be immediately apparent, but they must be taken for what they are: an honour. It might mean always being accompanied by a member of the family and perhaps cancelling plans. If that is impossible, it would be best to refuse the invitation on the spot rather than suddenly slip away. But by doing this, travellers will miss out on so much by not making personal contact with the inhabitants of the country.

## Forewarned is forearmed

At all times, remain calm and smile. This is the best way to go about getting accepted. Everything can be arranged with a little patience. The key to that little church that you had hoped to visit will be found in the end. Avoid broaching a contentious issue with the authorities or with a trader until after you have made some "small talk": politics, business, the weather even! What is important is the fact you are seen to make an effort to socialise, especially if you are from a strange land. On entering a shop, greet the people, say a few words, even if it is in English. This is a far cry from a hypermarket in the West and the trader will appreciate the gesture of goodwill and common courtesy. Better still: learn a few words of Arabic *(see lexicon p 104).*

## Gifts

Should you be invited to stay in the family home, do not worry about being unable to reciprocate. The only things expected of you are your presence and your well-being. A gift is always welcome as a memory of your visit. Do not, at all costs, offer food or alcohol: a small souvenir of your country (*see p 81*), or even flowers are a better choice of present. Avoid distributing sweets, pens or money to the children.

# Mixing with the locals

• At the mosque: shoes should be removed before entering; women should wear something over bare arms and shoulders (a shawl is fine) and cover their heads with a scarf.
• Children and men are willing to pose for photographs. On the other hand, it is advisable to ask for permission before aiming a camera at a woman (*suura* means "photo"). It is quite likely that permission will be granted.
• If you promise to send a print, do not forget to take down the address. Get them to note the address in Arabic straight onto an envelope.
• Tuck cameras out of sight when passing before frontier posts, military bases or civil engineering structures.
• Politeness takes different forms: do not expect people to utter profuse thanks over a gift. Even if they make no mention of it, the gesture will be appreciated even if they do not actually open the present until after you have left.
• At a restaurant, lone women and couples should eat in the area set aside for families, often on the first floor, from which single men are excluded. The atmosphere is calmer and more relaxed there and lone women travellers will be completely safe.
• Do not go behind the iconostasis in Eastern churches (the decorated screen separating the nave from the sanctuary, with icons often covered with curtains).
• Do not discuss political subjects. The King of Jordan, the Syrian president and Israel are delicate subjects that are best tactfully avoided lest they cause embarrassment. To avoid saying something that might compromise friends, it is as well not to report remarks to a third person.
• Do not indulge in heavy petting. It soon becomes apparent that couples do not give public signs of tenderness. However, men will hold hands, or take each other by the arm or around the neck, and kissing is quite natural. Do not take this as a sign of loose morals. Clearly observable signs of homosexuality are not appreciated.
• Do not ask questions about the women of the family, if male.
• Do not make advances to the beautiful but wary Jordanian or Syrian women.
• Do not flatter children. People will suspect you of putting the evil eye on them.
• Do not speak cynically of serious matters. People do not joke about poverty, sickness or death.
• Do not waste water. It is scarce in these arid countries.
• Do not attempt to bribe a Jordanian policeman if you have broken the law. That could land you straight in jail! Try to smile and explain your point of view.
• Do not eat or receive a present with your left hand.
In spite of these recommendations, fear of committing a faux-pas should not put you off: you can always apologise and use the fact you are a foreigner as an excuse. Remember, as contact with the West increases, the importance attached to traditions tends to recede: city folk are well acquainted with the behaviour of westerners.

# TASTES AND FLAVOURS

Levantine cuisine hinges on its small bite-size *meze*. Most of these morsels of food involve elaborate preparation, something that is often overlooked when a plate of exquisitely uniform bundles arrive on the table of a popular Lebanese restaurant. Their infinite variety is a strong indication of the munificence of a people and of a land. When choosing à la carte or (still better) at a buffet, be sure to take a good selection and do not hesitate to be adventurous. In contrast, the main dishes featured on a restaurant menu can be rather uninteresting and often a poor representation of a rich and varied culinary tradition alive and well in the family home. For a start, desserts are rarely listed: but it would be a pity not to taste the delicious *baklava* or locally grown fresh fruit. Travellers with a sensitive palate need not worry: with the exception of certain dishes from Aleppo, the local specialities are full of flavour but never too spicy.

## Meze

When eating out, the table is quickly laden with little dishes. And what a surprise! A standard staple is the famous **tabouleh**, only here, this tends to be made with large quantities of chopped parsley and lemon juice, lesser amounts of onion and tomato, and a small pinch of cracked wheat *(burghul)*. Others include the deliciously creamy **hummus**, a fine purée of chickpeas with sesame oil (tahina); **kibbeh** – a deep-fried egg-shaped meatball made of minced lamb and *burghul*. Caution is required here! **Kibbeh niyya** is made with the same ingredients, only it is eaten uncooked. **Waraq inab** are vine leaves stuffed with rice and are served warm or cold. There are two delicious aubergine/egg-plant purées with a delicately smoked flavour: **baba ghanuuj** (with pomegranate juice) and **mutabbal** (with tahina). **Muhammara** is a purée of tomatoes and peppers with varying amounts of hot spices. Broad beans are served warm with a dash of lemon **(fuul)**. Look out for the delicious, spicy olives known as **Zaytuun**. The best known salad is probably **fattuush**, made of chopped lettuce, tomatoes, cucumbers and radishes with croutons of Arab bread. **Khiyaar ma' laban** is a very refreshing salad of cucumbers and yoghurt. In winter, **shuurbat 'adas** (lentil soup) is a must. **Shiish burek** are savoury pasties of puff pastry with cheese or meat and **fataayer** are hot fritters with spinach. These hors-d'œuvres are accompanied with **pickled vegetables**, a cos-lettuce salad, chopped herbs and flat bread *(hubz)* – quite irresistible when served hot. Cheese (either cream cheese or hard cheese) is often served at breakfast along with olives, hard-boiled eggs, butter and jam *(murabba)*.

## Meat courses

Grilled chicken **(farruuj)**, brochettes of lamb **(kebaab)** or chicken **(shiish tauuk)** are the most common meat dishes listed on restaurant menus, and they usually come with rice or fried potatoes. An excellent Bedouin dish to look out for is **mensef**, which consists of lamb boiled in curdled milk and served on a bed of saffron rice. **Musakhkhan** is chicken in an onion sauce wrapped in a slice of bread. Restaurants on the Mediterranean coast and on the Gulf of Aqaba serve **fish**, usually fried or grilled. Less well known is **maqluuba**, which consists of chicken (sometimes replaced by lamb) accompanied by aubergines and rice. **Kofta** are meatballs made with bread. Accompaniments to main dishes include rice *(ruzz)*, French fries *(bataata)*, and possibly **maluukhiyya** - a kind of spinach, **baamia** (known in Europe as *okra*), or **fasuulya** (haricots).

## On the hoof

There are innumerable stalls everywhere from which to buy a snack: **falaafil** (small deep-fried chickpea fritters), **shawarma** (thin slices of lamb cut from meat roasted on a spit), **sfiiha** (delicious little pizzas). Depending on the season, they will sell oranges, strawberries, pomegranates, prickly pears, mangoes, dates and figs. An impressive selection of grains or roasted and salted nuts – delicious and flavoursome pistachios from Aleppo, chickpeas, sunflower seeds – is available all year round.

## Sweets

There are some dozen or so different kinds of *baklava* worth trying, and most are sold in special patisseries. The true **baklava** and **kulushkuur** that resembles it, are cut into diamond-shaped pieces and presented on large brass trays. Fundamental to both is the melt-in-the-mouth puff pastry dowsed in syrup or honey, and finely ground or chopped pistachios. The **asaabiyya** earn their name from their finger-like shape, containing powdered pistachio (or hazel) nuts. **Burma** look like small bobbins of fine crunchy threads made of caramelised *vermicelli* wound round whole pistachios. Vermicelli *(knafeh)* is also used to coat the **balluurieh** – pistachio-filled cases dribbled with syrup and delicately flavoured with orange-flower water. Anyone who does not like honey and sugar should try the delicious dry cakes made of pistachios called **brazés**. Some of the **ma'muuls**, small round short-crust cakes, are filled with a date purée. Rice with milk **(ruzz bi haliib)** or with maize starch **(muhallabiyya)** are particularly nourishing desserts.

Fast food, syrian-style

P. Meunier

## Non-alcoholic drinks

Fizzy drinks are enormously popular. All the main American brands can be found in Jordan but in Syria, where Coca-Cola and McDonald's are banned, there are substitutes (such as Kola). Water **(mayy)** is on sale everywhere. But it would be a shame to miss the delicious, fresh fruit juices *(asiir)* made with freshly squeezed seasonal fruits. Milk is called *haliib* when fresh and *labneh* or *ayran* when fermented.

## Alcoholic drinks

**Arak** is the most popular alcoholic drink in the Middle East. This aniseed drink is a variation on Turkish raki and Greek ouzo and, like its counterparts, it turns milky white when it is diluted with water. Beer *(biira)* is widely available in restaurants, either locally brewed or imported (though in the latter case it is considerably more expensive). In Jordan, there are wines *(nabiid)* from the Latroun or Château estates, whilst in Syria local wines such as al-Faysal, al-Mimas and al-Rayyan figure prominently on menus. These are modest wines available in red, white and rosé which feature alongside Lebanese wines (such as *ksara*).

## Hot drinks

**Tea** *(cha)* is the main drink, and is always served to welcome visitors or at any other opportunity: by a trader in the souk, a hotelier, and in the home in town and in the desert. Rather than the more familiar black or green teas, red tea is used here and flavoured with mint *(na'na')* or sage *(mirmiyya)*.

**Coffee** is its main rival. When it is **Turkish**, it is boiled three times very fast before being served. The sediment has to be allowed to sink to the bottom of the cup before the coffee is drunk. When it is **Arab**, it is very strong and served in tiny glasses. It is often flavoured with cardamom, which has a very pungent effect on its aroma.

For a change, why not try the **flower infusions** *(zuhuur)* made using camomile *(baabuunj)*, mixed flowers *(ward)* or verbena *(melisseh)*.

**Mateh** is mainly drunk through curious little metal pipes by the Druze and Alawites in the Tartus region of Syria. The use of this South American plant was introduced by Syrian and Lebanese émigrés from South American at the end of the 19C, where they were called "Turcos".

# LANGUAGE

## Language differences

The Middle East – as its name implies – has been a crossroads for people from many lands, and this heritage is reflected in the broad range of languages still in use there. The lingua franca is **Arabic**. And the form spoken across Syria and Jordan conforms with the dialects in common usage across the whole of the Middle East (*see the lexicon on p 104*). Having said this, there are fairly noticeable regional differences that betray a person's origins and education. Nevertheless, Arabic speakers are able to understand each other whether they are from Aleppo or Aqaba, and can make themselves understood in Egypt (where a more classical form is used) or North Africa. The literary form, which is markedly different from spoken Arabic, is used in newspapers, on television and for the drafting of legal documents.

In addition to Arabic, many people will be fluent in an additional language: **Kurdish**, an Indo-European language, is spoken by the Kurds in and around Aleppo in the northeast of Syria. **Aramaic** (Semitic language like Arabic), which was once the official language of the Persian Empire, is spoken by small pockets of people, notably at Maalula. **Syriac**, another Aramaic derivative, is used in the liturgy of several Eastern churches. **Armenian** is widespread among the Armenians, especially in Aleppo. **English** is the language used for international business dealings and for tourism: many Jordanians in particular, have studied in Britain or the United States and speak fluent English. In Syria, classical **French** is still spoken by the older generations as a hangover from the 25 years under French mandate, especially in Christian families that once attended Jesuit schools.

## Arabic: one language, many dialects

The Arabic language became widespread in the south and east Mediterranean countries in 7C as a result of Arab conquests and the diffusion of Islam. For centuries, the language has been the common link between communities scattered across the Arab world. An Arab is defined as a speaker of Arabic. Classical Arabic is the language of the Koran, and heavily codified variants have evolved for use in literature, the press or on television. There are, however, strong national dialects, and an Algerian might have trouble understanding a Syrian. The differences affect the vocabulary as much as the grammar, even if many roots are common to both. They are particularly noticeable in expressions used in daily life. The Arabic spoken in Egypt is the most universal because of the large audiences for Egyptian cinema, television and song.

The **Arab alphabet** – in which the language is written – is everywhere, often stylised into a calligraphy with fluid lines or geometrically square forms, for decorative effect and applied to buildings and monuments. Where the uninformed visitor might only see decoration, these are in fact the shapes of a 28-letter alphabet. Each letter has several shapes according to its position in the word: initial, medial, final or isolated. The use of these written symbols, which more often than not are transcribed from the Koran, became more widespread with the expansion of Islam. The same fundamental alphabet is used in written forms of Persian (spoken in Iran and Afghanistan), Turkish (before Mustafa Kemal opted for the Latin alphabet), Uighur in China and Urdu in Pakistan despite their disparate distance from one another.

Arabic is written from right to left and from top to bottom. For this reason, notebooks, books and magazines are bound on the right and the first page is in the place occupied by the last in English.

# SYRIA

**Official name:** Syrian Arab Republic
**Area:** 185 180sqkm
**Population:** 17 000 000
**Capital:** Damascus
**National currency:** Syrian pound

# Setting the scene

A view of Jebel
Ansariyeh

# FROM THE COAST
# TO THE DESERT

With an area equal to approximately two-thirds of that of Britain (185 180sqkm) and a population of 17 million, Syria seems enormous compared to its neighbours, Israel, Jordan and the Lebanon. The dry climate has had the effect of concentrating the population in the west of the country along the coast and on the Aleppo-Damascus axis.

Anyone fortunate enough to fly over Syria during the day and to be seated next to a window will see the main features of the country's geography take shape very speedily below. The plane will enter Syrian airspace at the latitude of Tartus on the **Mediterranean** and will immediately cross the long, mountain range, **Jebel Ansariyeh**, running north to south, as far as the **mountains of Lebanon** which are often covered with snow until May. Beyond this mountainous barrier, the great Lake Qattinah heralds the irrigated plains of the **Orontes Basin**. The great cities of Aleppo, Hama and Homs are strung out along this axis.

The air corridor passes over the **barren steppe**, which consists of a rocky plateau blocked off by an inhospitable mountain range. Beyond it, (if the aircraft does not begin a long turn toward the south to reach the oasis of Damascus) looms the long course of the **Euphrates** as it cuts across the country and the great blue stain of Lake Assad. With the capital now in sight, the desert and its cone-shaped volcanoes stretches into the distance. This is the beginning of the volcanic landscape of **Jebel al-Arab** in the south of Syria.

## Coastal plain

Syria is a Mediterranean country. With her short 183km coastline, she possesses a precious window onto the West, for which she is envied by many Arab countries. All along the coast were ancient cities, such as Latakia and Jabla which, like the nearby cities of Antioch (Turkey) and Alexandria (Egypt) looked toward Rome. The narrow coastal strip is given over to the cultivation of olives, oranges and vegetables. It holds the three **ports** of Syria, these being Latakia (the main city on the coast), Baniyas (the terminal of an oil pipeline) and Tartus, which exports Syrian phosphates. Seaside tourism is less well developed here than in Turkey.

## Mountains

They are the traditional refuge for Alawite, Christian and Ismaili minorities. In the **north**, the limestone massif of **Jebel Ansariyeh** rises to 1 510m. Situated on the wild summits of this imposing anticline, forested with oaks and pines, are the finest crusader castles. The crops, tobacco and cereals, are sparse and are traditionally cultivated on terraces. There are villages scattered across the mountainside, the highest at 1 000m. Olive trees grow on sea-facing hillsides. The rock is cut with deep fissures, canyon-like, the most impressive of which is the one connecting Qadmus to Baniyas.

At the Turkish frontier, magnificent forests extend across the slopes of Jebel al-Akra. Whilst there are no large towns in the region, the holiday resorts in the villages at Kassab, Slenfeh, Mashta al-Hilu and Safita continue to grow, popular with locals in search of a cooler and fresher climate.

In the **south**, **Mount Hermon** (2 814m) is the highest point of the **Anti-Lebanon** and of Syria. It overlooks the fertile plain of **Golan**, which has been occupied by Israel since 1967. To the north of Damascus, there are springs that feed the mountain oases (Maaloula and Seydnaya).

## The Ghab and the maamuura

In the east, the mountains drop away sharply. The Ghab depression occupies the low land formed by the long fault which stretches from Turkey to Aqaba and which constitutes the major geological feature of the Levant. Where the **Orontes** now flows, the swamps have been reclaimed and the area is now one of the richest agricultural regions of Syria. This irrigated expanse extends to the east in a limestone plateau, which never exceeds 1 000m in altitude, and then by the *maamuura* beyond, the maamuura being land on the edges of the steppe where settled peoples grow cereals. It runs from north of Aleppo to Jebel al-Arab, is a former route for caravans and contains the great cities of Syria: Aleppo, Hama, Homs and Damascus.

## The badiya – not a desert at all

The Syrian steppe (*badiya*) is a zone of transition between the *maamuura* and the true desert which makes up about half the country's territory. The landscape here is monotonous, the wide expanses of stone and sand buffeted by the winds. The little rain that there is falls only in winter. Only the nomadic or semi-nomadic Bedouins keep up the pastoral way of life in this area. In winter, the flocks move toward the interior of the desert and in summer, when there is less vegetation, they graze on the irrigated land where they can eat the stubble. Palmyra, a town made prosperous by tourism, is the main oasis of the region. Water is plentiful here making it easy to grow olive trees, pomegranate trees and date palms.

The real desert starts further south and is part of the great Arabian desert which covers most of Arabia.

## The Euphrates and the Jazira

The construction of a huge dam at Tabqa has meant that the banks of the Euphrates can now be cultivated. Once ochre and silvery in colour, the river banks have turned green. Dominating the region are the towns of Raqqa in the north and Deir ez-Zor in the south, where bridges span the river.

In the Jazira, in the northeast of the country, the Balikh and Khabur rivers bring water from the mountains of Anatolia. In autumn, when the fields turn white, it heralds the approach of the cotton harvest. The population of the Jazira is unusual in that it is made up of Kurds and settled Bedouin, as well as Christians who have come from Iraq and Turkey.

## Jebel al-Arab (Jebel Druze)

Near the Jordanian border is a volcanic massif rising to 1 800m. Of the various cone-shaped peaks the one at Salkhad is the most striking example, whilst the most impressive lava flows are to be found at Leja and Safa. These are vast, hostile stretches of lava littered with volcanic rocks which are covered in inscriptions carved in the rock by the caravaners. Since the 19C, the Druze have taken possession of the ancient Roman cities built on the slopes of the massif where the rainwater settles. To the west, the crumbling basalt has yielded fertile soil at Hauran and Golan. This soil has been Syria's traditional granary.

**From the coast to the desert**

# MODERN SYRIA

*For history prior to the First World War, see p 12*

## The French Mandate (1922-1946)

The **Emir Faisal**, who had proclaimed a great Arab kingdom at Damascus in 1920, was defeated at Khan Maisalun by the French army, to be placed on the throne of Iraq the following year. When France took control of the country it had been ravaged by war and famine. Looking to the minorities in the country for support, France went on to impose a partition of the territory, the mandate for which was confirmed by the League of Nations in 1922. Lebanon became an autonomous state in 1920, with a slight Christian majority. The other states, namely Alawite, Jebel al-Arab, Damascus and Aleppo, lasted until 1936 when they merged together to form Syria.

Of the several revolts dealt with by the mandatory power, the most important took place in Jebel al-Arab in a conflict between **Sultan al-Atrach** and French troops. Calm was restored in 1926 after which Arab nationalists further undermined political stability although no agreement on independence was reached. In 1939, France ceded the **sanjak of Alexandretta** to Turkey. This action has always been condemned by Syria: even the official maps still place the frontier to the north of Antioch.

In 1941, during the Second World War, Free French forces supported by British troops entered Syria. Independence was formally declared but took a long time to come and riots broke out once again in Damascus. The British took action to prevent French military intervention and the last foreign solder left Syria on 17 April 1946.

## Difficult beginnings of independence (1946-1956)

Syria was ill-prepared for independence and was soon confronted with the creation of the state of Israel. The war of 1948-49 led to the defeat of the Arab camp. **General Zaim** took power by force after his return from the front. It was the first in a series of coups d'état which would not end until **General Hafez al-Assad** came to power. It was during this period that Syria took on a clearly Arab character and saw the emergence of the socialist Baath Party.

## Flirting with Egypt (1956-1963)

Feeling threatened by the signature of the Turkish-Iraqi pact in Baghdad in 1956, both Syria and Egypt accepted supplies of Soviet weapons. After taking over power and the Suez crisis, Nasser became a hero in the Arab World. In 1958, Syria and Egypt founded the **United Arab Republic**, of which Syria was the northern part, although the Syrians soon became critical of the concentration of power in Cairo. The break came in 1961 after a coup d'état in Syria. In 1963, the idea of a broader agreement including Iraq was abandoned.

## Baath in power (1963-1970)

The party of Arab resurrection (Baath) is pan-Arab, socialist and secular. Whilst there were several attempts at a union, sometimes with Egypt and sometimes with Iraq, Syria began the nationalisation of the banking sector and the textile industry. It was then that the middle classes left the country.

In 1966, with the aid of the Soviet Union, Syria undertook the construction of the Euphrates dam. The following year, she went to war against Israel and lost control over the Golan plateau during the **Six-Day War**. A less dogmatic wing of the Baath then emerged, led by General Hafez al-Assad, and he assumed power on 13 November 1970.

## The Syria of General Hafez al-Assad (since 1970)

Since 1970, Syria has enjoyed a very welcome period of stability after a quarter of a century of disturbances. Although the Baath remains the dominant party, it relies heavily on the army and the security services. From the moment of his accession, President al-Assad launched a "plan for recovery", which has brought about a certain liberalisation of the economy and the creation of a large state sector. But the most important developments from an international perspective were obtained in foreign policy. Syria steadily imposed herself as an interlocutor of primary importance in any plan for peace in the Middle East. She also became the country most firmly opposed to Israel (**Yom Kippur War,** 1973) and played an active part, from 1975 on, in the war that tore Lebanon apart. Syria had a rapprochement with the United States at the time of the **Gulf War** and fought at the side of the anti-Iraqi coalition.

Within the country, Syria had to face up to a revolt by the Muslim Brothers in 1982. Since 1991, action has been taken to stimulate the economy while at the same time the country has been making steady progress towards a political settlement of the conflict with Israel. In the year 2000, the president was over 70 years old and the problem of succession remains acute following the death of his son Basil in an accident. Another son, Bashar, has been put forward as the new heir apparent.

Hafez al-Assad and his sons

P. Meunier

# The Economy

Syria has many advantages. In the past, Palmyra, Aleppo and Damascus owed their wealth to their locations at the crossroads of the great routes linking Turkey to Egypt and the East to the Mediterranean World. Although the wealth brought by the caravans has now disappeared, the varied climate and fertile soils allow the cultivation of many different crops.

## Agriculture

Approximately one third of the workforce is employed in the **agricultural sector**. The agricultural reform at the end of the 1950s brought about the redistribution of land belonging to a small landowning aristocracy (the "thirty families"). The area of land under irrigation has also been considerably increased, thanks to the dam at Tabqa. Wheat, barley, cotton, tobacco, vines and olive trees are the main crops. Sheep rearing remains the domain of the nomads.

## Industry, mines and oil

A further third of the population works in the **industrial and mining sector**. In addition to the **phosphate** mines in the Palmyra region, the **oil** from east of the Euphrates represents 40 % of total exports. The oil revenues are, however, nothing in comparison with those of the Gulf countries. Industry is essentially based on textiles and the processing of agricultural produce. Alongside these traditional activities, some **heavy industry** (metallurgy, aluminium) has developed, together with pharmaceuticals and petrochemicals, the latter being state-owned. The liberalisation laws which were introduced in 1991 have mainly affected the services sector.

## Tourism

Tourism is booming in Syria, albeit hampered by drawbacks in the Syrian economy. Two issues are particularly problematic: the inadequacy of the banking system (the absence of private banks and the existence of exchange controls) and the burden of military spending on the state budget. But if the anticipated reform to the banking system comes about and if peace is re-established in the region, Syria could very well prosper once again.

# Administration of the country

The country is divided into 14 *mouhafazats*, which take the names of the main towns in each region. Each *mouhafazat* is normally divided into *mantiqas* (47) and into *nahias* (201), which group together the towns (208) and the villages (6 454). The mukhtar is the headman of the village.

The urban landscape gives perceptible proof of the state's involvement in the development of the urban areas. The entrance of a town is often marked by a monumental arch built in cement. In the centre of the town, there is a large red and white aerial to indicate the communications centre. Further on, there will be a school, its playground and buildings concealed behind high, yellow-ochre walls. Since 56 % of the population is less than 20 years old, the classrooms are never empty.

As for the **judicial system**, French procedure provides the main model. Damascus has a supreme court of appeal (court of cassation) and there are courts of appeal in each *mouhafazat* as well as lower level courts. A system which will strike foreigners as unusual is the religious law, which rules on matters of personal status (eg. marriage or divorce) for members of the different communities. The Muslim Qadi applies a law derived from the Koran, whilst the Christian churches have their own separate courts.

# Education

With 4 million pupils (a quarter of the population), Syria is making great efforts with its education system. For example, pupils of infant school age all wear uniform: a brown overall and an orange scarf for the younger ones, khaki military dress for the older boys and girls. Except for some religious schools and those of UNWRA (United Nations Relief and Works Agency for Palestinian Refugees), which are reserved for Palestinians, all schools are run by the state. The curricula of Syrian students are strongly influenced by French models: the primary school, the middle school (collège) and the secondary school (lycée). The first experience of school often takes place when the child enters primary school, for it is not the custom to send a child to nursery school. In poorer areas, classes are combined, and there are classes in the morning as well as in the afternoon in order to overcome the lack of classrooms. Despite such developments, classes of 30 pupils are not unusual.

Nearly a third of pupils leave school at the end of primary school when compulsory attendance comes to an end. In rural areas, children prefer to keep the flocks in the fields and go to market with their father.

At the age of 13, children move up to the **middle school** for three years, where they can take up a technical subject or continue with general studies. At this level, classes are no longer mixed. The khaki uniform (which has made some specialist outfitters very rich) now becomes compulsory.

Having passed his/her baccalaureate, the student then applies to one of the **45 university faculties** located at Damascus, Aleppo, Homs and Latakia. It is a testament to the Syrian regime that women make up 40 % of the 165 000 students registered. The extracurricular activities of the Baath party have a considerable following on Fridays and in summer camps.

**Education**

# Practical Information

Souk in Aleppo

# BEFORE GOING

Some parts of this Practical Information for Syria section also apply to Jordan, so don't be surprised if information for Jordan also appears here.

## ● Time difference
Local time in Syria is two hours ahead of GMT (or UTC). When it is midday in Damascus, it will be 10am in London, 5am in New York, 4am in Chicago, 5am in Montreal, 5am in Toronto, 8pm in Sydney and 10pm in Auckland (times given are winter times, and do not take account of countries using DST). Syria does not change its clocks to DST in summer.

## ● International dialling
To telephone Syria from overseas, dial 00 + 963 + the regional code (without dialling 0) + the number you wish to call.
*For local codes in Syria, see page 90.*

## ● When to go
For a first visit to Syria, **spring** and **autumn** are without doubt the best seasons. The temperatures are moderate, and the sites free of crowds, apart from the Easter holidays. If you have the choice, opt for May, June, September or October. Having said this, it is of course possible to visit Syria during the **summer**. You won't go short of sunshine, and during heatwaves the temperature averages 40°C in the desert. Try to fit in a stay in the mountains (Slenfeh, Krac des Chevaliers) and on the Mediterranean coast if you want to get away from the heat. Choose hotels with air conditioning, at least in Damascus and Palmyra. **Winter** can be wet, and the daylight hours are short, but this can be a good time to explore the desert: the low winter sun shows up stonework in relief, in particular the ruins at Palmyra. Despite the snow-covered mountain peaks, there may be beautiful sunny days.

Whatever the season, it gets dark by 8pm at the latest. Bear this in mind when organising your voyage. It's an advantage to be an early riser! The sunrise and sunset times at Aleppo at the beginning of each season are as follows:

|              | sunrise | sunset |
|--------------|---------|--------|
| 21 March     | 5.30am  | 5.45pm |
| 21 June      | 5.15am  | 7.55pm |
| 21 September | 6.20am  | 6.30pm |
| 21 December  | 6.40am  | 4.20pm |

## ● Packing list
### Clothing
From May to October choose light, practical clothes, taking into account the hot days as well as the cool evenings (or air conditioning). On the other hand, in winter you will need the same clothes as you would at home. A winter coat or jacket will protect you from the cold spells which can descend on Syria and Jordan, and which can last until April. The nights are cool all year round, even in summer in the desert where you will experience an extreme range of temperatures. Always carry a pullover or light jacket. And don't forget your swimming costume, preferably a one-piece rather than a bikini for women. In town, women should avoid wearing shorts and low-cut necklines, and choose garments which cover their knees and shoulders. Trousers are fine, as long as

they are not too tight, or transparent. Don't forget that the best way of visiting Palmyra, Aleppo, Petra and Jarash is on foot, so be sure to bring a good pair of shoes, preferably with slightly raised sides, to avoid getting sand and grit inside them. Don't bring too many clothes, as most hotels have a rapid laundry service.

## Accessories

It's worth bringing a pair of **binoculars**, to be able to appreciate Petra's monumental tombs in detail, or to get a view of the Holy Land from Jordan's panoramic viewpoints. A **pocket torch** can prove very useful for exploring the dim underground rooms in certain castles. A **compass** will help orientate you when you get slightly lost, particularly with signs being only in Arabic. An insulated **water bottle** is a must in summer, while a **pocket calculator** will help you when bargaining. Finally, don't forget your earplugs, if you want to avoid being woken by the early morning call to prayer.

## Presents to take

Small gifts are invaluable for building friendships, whether they are postcards of your home town, paperbacks, miniature bottles of perfume, badges, key rings or other trinkets. Avoid offering food or alcohol to adults, or giving sweets or money to children. Ballpoint pens are much in demand among small children, to the point where they ask for them ("ben, ben!") every time they meet a new tourist.

## • A holiday for everyone

### Travelling with children

Both Syrians and Jordanians adore children and can't understand why anyone would want to go on holiday without them. Your family will be made to feel welcome everywhere, and travelling with children is a guaranteed way of getting to know people. Oblivious of the language barrier, your children will soon make friends, and their parents will naturally strike up conversation with you. Young children will suffer from the heat, which may make them bad tempered. Equipment for babies, such as nappies, can be found in pharmacies. Almost all hotels have suites for families, offering privacy for parents and security for children. The Mariott and Carlton hotels in Amman offer a baby-sitting service.

### Women travelling alone

Travelling alone as a woman is not always easy, and it can get irritating being stared at and being the object of remarks. To avoid these problems, try to adapt your behaviour in order not to offend local people's feelings. Clothes which avoid plunging necklines and cover the legs down to the knees should be worn in the street, which doesn't mean you have to look dowdy. At Petra, Aqaba and even in the Wadi Rum the Jordanians are used to the "eccentricities" of female tourists travelling alone. You can, of course, wear lighter clothes and swimsuits on the beach (though watch out for the sun!). Learn to ignore unwelcome advances without refusing to enter into conversation with anyone. Mentioning your 'husband' should make things clear to persistent admirers.

### Travelling as a couple

Couples who are not married can share hotel rooms without any problem.

### Elderly people

Apart from the sun, which you can avoid by keeping covered up, the hardest thing for elderly people will be visiting the sites, which can be tiring. At Palmyra, Petra and Jarash you could end up walking at least 5km, and the heat and contours make these visits exhausting. Try practising some long walks before going on holiday. If you find air-conditioning unpleasant, change the temperature to suit you or switch it off. This advice applies to everyone.

**Before going**

81

### Disabled persons
Neither Syria nor Jordan are equipped to cope with disabled tourists. However, you will find people kind and helpful. At Petra the main monuments can be visited by horse-drawn carriage.

## • Address book

### Tourist information
Ask at the embassy when you apply for your visa, or consult the following web sites.

### Web Sites
Take a look at the following sites before leaving home:
www.arab.net/syria
www.mysite.com/syria
www.syriatourism.org
www.1000traveltips.org/syria.htm
www.syriaonline.com
www.syriatel.net
www.made-in-syria.com
www.cafe-syria.com

### Embassies and consulates
**UK –** 8 Belgrave Square, London SW1X 8BH, ☎ (020) 7245 9012, Fax (020) 7235 8976
**US –** 2215 Wyoming Avenue NW, Washington DC 20008 ☎ 202 232 6313
**Canada –** 433 Laurier Avenue, Suite 3114, Ottawa, Ontario K1R 7Y1

## • Documents required
This information is given as a general guideline only and may change. Contact the Syrian embassy in your country for an update at least a month before you leave.

### ID, visas
Your **passport** must contain a visa and should be valid for at least six months after your return. The **visa** should be obtained from the Syrian consulate in your home country before you leave. It may take as little as a week (more, if you apply by post) but it is wise to allow at least two weeks. **It cannot be obtained at the Syrian border under any circumstances**. When crossing the Syrian border, your passport should not contain either an Israeli visa, or an entry stamp to Jordan or Egypt via an Israeli frontier-post. For a group of ten people or more, a collective visa is usually granted to the tour group organiser (contact your travel agent). Those who already hold an Arab passport do not need a visa.

Travellers must complete an **entry card** in duplicate when they enter Syria, and keep this document with them until they leave the country.

Your **visa application** should be accompanied by three passport photos, and a completed duplicate form, obtained from the embassy in your home country. There are two types, either a three-month single-entry visa or a six-month multiple-entry visa. Costs vary, according to your nationality. In either case, for a stay of longer than two weeks, the visa must be extended by the immigration department officials. This formality varies from place to place (in Damascus allow 24hr) and takes place in the main towns of the *mouhafazat* (regions) on the fourteenth day of your stay (or the day before, if the fourteenth day is a Friday or a public holiday). You should produce evidence of the means to support yourself (a payslip, for example). Journalists travelling either professionally or for pleasure need to make a special application. The visa extension form is also in duplicate, and should avoid any mention of "Occupied Palestine". Mentioning your religion, however, is no problem. If applying by post, you should send the cost of the visa by postal order. Include a stamped addressed envelope for sending the visa to you by recorded delivery (find out details beforehand from the embassy). Syrian visas are extremely difficult to obtain in Jordan. For access to Syria from **Lebanon**, contact the Lebanese and Syrian embassies before leaving. Some Damascus travel agents will take care of obtaining Lebanese visas for visiting Baalbek, as long as the trip is booked three days ahead.

You will have to pay a **departure tax** at the airport when leaving the country, which can only be paid in cash.

## Customs

**Imports** – You are allowed to bring in 200 cigarettes, 50 cigars or 250g of tobacco, as well as a litre of alcohol and a litre of eau de toilette. Your luggage may undergo a perfunctory search when entering the country. There is no restriction on bringing computer equipment in or out of Syria (laptops, for example).

**Currency** – The obligation to change your money into local currency at the border was abolished in 1991. Keep your exchange receipts if you want to change your Syrian pounds back into other currency. You should declare amounts higher than US$1 000.

**Driving** – The international Green Card is not recognised in Syria. An obligatory third-party insurance must be taken out at the border for US$60. The vehicle is covered for one month. A temporary import document also has to be acquired each time you enter the country, for a fee of US$40. Diesel vehicles must pay an extra tax of US$75 per week. In addition, you must obtain a customs certificate from an automobile club such as either the AA (0990 448866) or the RAC (0990 722722) in the UK. Contact them at least 3 weeks before your departure. You will be asked to pay a financial guarantee for this card, which could be about a quarter of the vehicle's current market value. This is because the issuing association could be liable for import duty on the vehicle if its exit is not registered within a year. Allow up to an hour for vehicle formalities at the border.

**Exports** – There is a limit of S£1 000 on the export of Syrian currency.

## Vaccination

No vaccinations are required for entering Syria from Europe or North America.

## Driving licence

An international driving licence is required for those wishing to hire vehicles, and may be requested by the Syrian police.

## • Local currency

Day to day expenditures should be paid for in Syrian pounds. There is one important exception to this: bills in hotels possessing more than a one-star rating will be quoted in US dollars, and should be paid in this currency by credit card (where possible) or in cash.

### Cash

The Syrian pound (marked S£ in this guide, but referred to locally as the *lira*) is divided into 100 piastres (*qirsh*). It exists in notes of 1, 5, 10, 25, 50, 100, 200, 500 and 1 000 pounds. The smaller denominations are often in a tatty condition. Small coins are increasingly rare (5, 10, 25, 50 and 100 piastres), although there are also coins worth S£1, £2, £5 and £25.

**Before going**

**Before going**

### Exchange

The official exchange rate for the Syrian pound is **S£46 to US$1.** The rate of exchange for other currencies is based on this rate, but will depend on the current rate of the dollar against other foreign currencies. The Commercial Bank of Syria is the only bank allowed to exchange currency. You will find branches in the major towns. The rate of exchange is identical everywhere. Change your last Syrian pounds before leaving the country, as you will have difficulty changing them in European countries (though you can do so in Amman).

### Travellers' cheques

These are accepted by some banks, and in a fair number of souvenir shops. You may have to pay a commission.

### Credit cards

**Important: it is not possible to withdraw money with a card in Syria.** There are no cash dispensers or banks that allow you to obtain Syrian pounds or other currencies. It is therefore vital to make sure you have enough cash or travellers' cheques to pay for meals, public transport, petrol and site entrance fees. Don't forget that quite a few of the basic hotels will expect to be paid in dollars. On the other hand, American Express, Diner's Club, Mastercard and Visa credit cards are recognised by an increasing number of hotels and tourist shops (even in the bazaars). All comfortable or luxury category hotels accept them. The amounts are always debited in dollars.

## • Spending money

With the exception of hotels, you will find the cost of living low in Syria. Train and bus fares are ridiculously cheap, and a litre of petrol costs the equivalent of UScts50. A taxi journey works out cheaper than a European bus fare. You have to go to a luxury hotel to eat before the bill exceeds US$20. On the other hand, site entrance fees are relatively very expensive (around US$8).

These **daily budgets** are calculated **per person**, based on **two people sharing** a double room and car hire. They include accommodation, meals and transport, but not site entries, drinks and souvenirs. At the most basic, you could probably get away with spending **US$25** per day per person. This would include accommodation in a cheap hotel, eating take-away meals from street vendors or in small restaurants, and getting around by public transport.

With a budget of **US$75** per person, two of you could hire a medium-priced vehicle, and stay in a hotel room with air-conditioning and private bathroom. You could also eat out in a good restaurant at least once a day.

Allowing **US$130** per day per person, you could stay in the most comfortable hotels and use the services of a chauffeur.

## • Reservations

*For details on how to telephone Syria from overseas, see p 89.*

In high season (and particularly during the Easter holidays) it is strongly advisable to reserve in advance. The easiest method from overseas is to fax, in English, giving a fax number or address for reply. Once in Syria, if you haven't already reserved ahead, your hotel proprietor should be willing to telephone to make arrangements for you. Reservations with the international car hire companies (Avis, Europcar, Hertz) can be made in advance with any of their offices worldwide. Payment is on collection of the vehicle. Reservations for the **Cham** hotel chain, as well as Cham Tour travel agents can be made direct either in Paris, ☎ (33) 142 99 98 00, Fax (33) 145 63 12 69 (there is no equivalent in London), or in the US, ☏ (202) 785 1355. You could also use the Syrian hotels reservation online service for all the major towns in Syria (www.syriaonline.com/hotelres), which is in English.

● **Travel Insurance**

Travel insurance is strongly advised. If driving, check that the countries you intend to visit are covered by your motor insurance. A general insurance is usually available from the tour operator who sells you your plane ticket or tour package.

# GETTING THERE

You are most likely to arrive in the Middle East by plane. There are, however, plenty of other alternatives. You can even arrive by boat, via the Red Sea or at Latakia in the Mediterranean, and then cycle to Amman, if you've set your heart on it (and your legs are willing!). If you are combining Syria and Jordan, you could arrive at Damascus and leave from Amman. In this case, you would cross the border between the two countries at Deraa, in the south of Syria.

● **By air**

Generally speaking, there is a much wider choice of flights to Jordan than Syria. British Airways, Syrian Arab Airlines (Syrianair) and Royal Jordanian Airlines offer direct flights from London (flight time 5hr). There are no charter flights to Syria or Jordan, but it is worth looking around at some of the other European airlines, such as Air France, Lufthansa and KLM, though you will probably have at least one stopover. Royal Jordanian also flies from New York, Chicago and Detroit, as well as from Toronto and Montreal. Travellers from North America, Australia or New Zealand should check out carriers such as Gulf Air, Emirates or Middle East Airlines, though you may be better off either flying to London to pick up a cheaper flight, or looking at more popular destinations such as Turkey, Egypt or even Greece, and then travelling overland. If you want to visit Syria, don't be tempted by a cheap flight to Israel, as you won't be allowed over the border. This could be a solution for visiting Jordan, although bear in mind the cost of additional visas and border taxes.

Combined flights (for example, arriving via Damascus and leaving via Amman) are usually sold at the same price as a straightforward return to the same destination. **British Airways** – 101/102 Cheapside, London EC2V 6DT, ☏ (0345) 222 111, Fax (020) 8562 8000. Flights daily to Amman, and daily except Fridays and Sundays to Damascus. Prices start from US$465.
**Delta Air** – US ☏ (1) 800 241 4141. Flights from New York (JFK) to Amman, via Vienna. On-line reservation www.delta-air.com
**Syrianair** – 27 Albermarle Street, London W1X 3HF, ☏ (020) 7493 2851, Fax (020) 7493 2119. Flights to Damascus on Tuesdays, Thursdays and Sundays.
**Royal Jordanian** – 32 Brook Street, London W1Y 1AG, ☏ (020) 7878 6333, Fax (020) 7629 4069. Daily flights from London. There are also offices in Manchester and Dublin, and a twice-weekly flight from Shannon. **USA:** 5 flights weekly to New York, ☏ (212) 949 0050, Fax (212) 949 0485. There are also offices in Chicago, Detroit, Los Angeles, Miami and Washington. **Australia:** (Sydney) ☏ (2) 926 26133, Fax (2) 926 26158. **New Zealand:** (Christchurch) ☏ (3) 3653910, Fax (3) 3655755.
Once in Amman, ☏ (6) 567 83 21.

Getting there

*Airports*

In Syria, you will probably land at **Damascus Airport**. The airport at **Aleppo** is accessible to international flights, but in practice the service is scant. The main airport in Jordan is **Queen Alia Airport** at Amman. The city's other airport, **Marka**, is limited to regional flights. **Aqaba** has a small airport, almost exclusively used for internal flights to and from Amman. Make sure you keep enough money aside to pay for a taxi to the airport as well as the departure tax *(see below)*.

*Flight confirmation*

It is vital to confirm your return flight by telephone at least 72 hours before departure. Ask for the local number for your airline during the outward flight.

*Airport tax*

There is no airport tax as such but there is a departure tax, both in Syria and Jordan, payable only in cash *(see "Documents required", p 82)*.

## ● By train

In theory it is possible to get to Damascus and Amman by train from London via Paris and Istanbul. In practice, once out of Europe, the service is only weekly, and connections at Istanbul and Damascus may not be the same day. You should therefore allow at least a week to get to Amman by train. This solution is far from cheap.

## ● By coach

There are weekly coaches from Paris to Istanbul during the summer (Eurolines, ☎ 0152 404511 for information on the service from London). From Istanbul there are frequent buses for Syria and Jordan. Allow a week for the journey. The journey from Paris to Damascus costs about US$140.

## ● By car

For those with time to spare. Allow at least six or seven days. The E5 international highway starts from London, reaching Turkey via Thessaloniki (to avoid the need for a Bulgarian visa). Syria can be entered at Bab al-Hawa, for Aleppo, or at Kassab, for Latakia. Contrary to widely held belief, there is no problem with bringing diesel vehicles, including camper vans, into Syria and Jordan, providing your visit does not exceed two weeks. You must possess an international driving licence. Diesel is widely available in both countries.

## ● Package deals

Syria and Jordan are now included in the catalogues of all the major tour operators. The options available range from flight only, to five-star voyages with chauffeur-driven transport. Tours for groups usually last between 6 and 21 days, with a combined trip to Syria and Jordan costing around US$2 100 for 14 days. The cheapest tours start around US$1 120. You may organise your own trip with flight, car hire and hotel reservations to suit yourself.

*Middle East specialists*

**Bales Worldwide**, Bales House, Junction Road, Dorking, Surrey RH4 3HL, ☎ (01306) 732700, Fax (01306) 740048, enquiries@balesworldwide.com, www.balesworldwide.com

**Cox & Kings**, Gordon House, 10 Greencoat Place, London SW1P 1PH, ☎ (020) 7873 5000, Fax (020) 7630 6038, cox.kings@coxandkings.co.uk

**Jasmin**, 53-55 Balham Hill, London SW12 9DR, ☎ (020) 8675 8886, Fax (020) 8673 1204, info@jasmin-tours.co.uk

**Martin Randall Travel**, 10 Barley Mow Passage, Chiswick, London W4 4PH, ☎ (020) 8742-3355, Fax (020) 8742 7766, info@martinrandall.co.uk

**Cox & Kings**, 25 Davis Blvd, Tampa, Florida, USA, ☎ (800) 999 1758, Fax (813) 258 3852, tours@coxandkings.com

*Special Interest*

**McCabe Pilgrimages**, 53-55 Balham Hill, London SW12 9DR, ☎ (020) 8675 6828, Fax (020) 8673 1204, pilgrim2000@mccabe-travel.co.uk

**Prospect Music & Art Tours**, 36 Manchester Street, London W1M 5PE, ☎ (020) 7486 5705, Fax (020) 7486 5868, sales@prospecttours.com

**The British Museum Traveller**, 46 Bloomsbury Street, London WC1B 3QQ, ☎ (020) 7323 8895, Fax (020) 7580 8677.

**Andante Travels**, The Old Telephone Exchange, Winterbourne Dauntsey, Salisbury SP4 6EH, ☎ (01980)610555, Fax (01980) 610002, andante travels @virgin.net

**Cultural Tours/Fair Winds Travel, Inc.**, 7758 Wisconsin Avenue, Bethesda, MD 20814, ☎ (1) 800 826 7995 and (301)718-7273, Fax (301)718-2851, fairwinds@fairwindtravel.com, www.fairwindtravel.com.

*Activity holidays*

**Exodus**, 9 Weir Road, London SW12 0LT, ☎ (020) 8675 5550, Fax (020) 8673 0779, sales@exodustravels.co.uk, www.exodustravels.co.uk

**Colette Pearson Travel**, 64 South Willian Street, Dublin 2, ☎ (01) 677 1029, Fax (01) 677 1390, cptravel@indigo.ie

**GAP Adventures**, 760 North Bedford Road, Suite #246, Bedford Hills, New York 10507 USA, ☎ (914) 666 4417, Fax (914) 666 4839, adventure@gap.ca

**GAP Adventures**, 266 Dupont Street, Toronto, Ontario M5R 1V7, Canada, ☎ (416) 922 8899, Fax (416) 922 0822, adventure@gap.ca

**IT Adventure**, Level 4, 46-48 York Street, Sydney, NSW 2000, Australia, ☎ (02) 9279 0491, Fax (02) 9279 0492, ita@hutch.com.au

**Destinations Adventure**, Auckland, New Zealand, ☎ (09) 309 0464, Fax (09) 377 4586, exodus@destinations-adventure.co.nz

**Explore Worldwide**, 1 Frederick Street, Aldershot, Hants GU11 1LQ, ☎ (01252) 760000, Fax (01252) 760001, www.explore.co.uk, info@explore.co.uk (*Explore works with the following agents:* **Adventure Center**, USA, ☎ (800) 227 8747, **Trek Holidays**, Canada, ☎ (1) 888 456 3522, **Adventure World**, Sydney, Australia, ☎ 9956 7766, **Adventure World**, Auckland, New Zealand, ☎ (09) 524 5118).

**Travelbag Adventures**, 15 Turk Street, Alton, Hants GU34 1AG, ☎ (01420) 541007, Fax (01420) 541022, info@travelbag-adventures.co.uk, www.travelbag -adventures.co.uk

**The Imaginative Traveller**, 14 Barley Mow Passage, Chiswick, London W4 4PH ☎ (020) 8742 8612, Fax (020) 8742 3045, info@imaginative-traveller.com, www.imaginative-traveller.com (*The Imaginative Traveller works with the following agents:* **The Adventure Travel Network**, USA ☎ (800) 467 4595, **Adventre Centre**, Toronto, Canada, ☎ (1) 800 267 3347, **Intrepidworld**, Melbourne, Australia, ☎ (1) 300 667, **Peregrine Adventures**, Melbourne, Australia ☎ (03) 9663 8611).

**Dragoman**, 99 Camp Green, Debenham, Suffolk, IP14 6LA, ☎ (01728) 861 133, Fax (01728) 861 127, info@dragoman.co.uk, www.dragoman.co.uk,

**Worldwide Adventures Abroad**, Unit HO4, Staniforth Estate, Main St, Hackenthorpe, Sheffield S12 4LB, ☎ (0114) 247 3400, Fax (0114) 251 3210, abroad@globalnet.co.uk, www.adventures-abroad.com)

**Incredible Adventures, Inc.**,6604 Midnight Pass Road, Sarasota, FL. 34242, ☎ 1-800-644-7382/941-346-2488

**Aquatours** (diving holidays), Shelletts House, Angel Road, Thames, Ditton, Surrey KT7 0AU, ☎ (020) 8398-0505, Fax (020) 8398 0570, arnie@aquatours. com, www.aquatours.com.

**Getting there**

# THE BASICS

## • Address book

### Tourist information

Each administrative region (*mouhafazat*) has a tourist office in its main town. Usually, all they have to offer is a fairly practical free map of the region. The staff are usually very friendly but cannot always answer your questions. Your hotel staff will be more accustomed to organising excursions or reserving accommodation elsewhere for you.

### Embassies and consulates

**UK –** Kurd Ali St, Kotob Building, Malki, Damascus, ☎ (11) 373 92 43, Fax (11) 371 35 92.

**USA –** Al-Mansour St, Abu Roumaneh, Damascus, ☎ (11) 333 28 14/23 15, Fax (11) 224 79 38.

**Canada –** Al-Mezzeh (near Razi Hospital), Damascus, ☎ (11) 223 68 92/05 35.

**Australia –** Farabi St, Al-Mezzeh, Damascus, ☎ (11) 666 43 17, Fax (11) 662 11 95.

## • Opening and closing times

Friday is a day of rest in Syria. Banks, government departments and the majority of businesses are closed on this day. The morning is generally the best time to get things done. During the month of Ramadan office hours are often restricted. In Syria the year is divided into two administrative seasons: summer begins on 1 April and ends on 30 September. The rest of the year is considered as winter. Shops in the Christian quarters close on Sundays instead of Fridays.

### Banks

Opening hours are 8am-2pm. It is best to be there before 12noon. Exchange bureaux are generally open from 9am-7pm and sometimes even for a few hours on Friday mornings in Damascus and Aleppo.

### Post Offices

Again, opening hours are 8am-2pm. In the main towns they are open for telephoning and sending mail until 7pm.

### Shops

9.30am-7pm (8pm in summer), sometimes with a three-hour break in the middle of the day. The bazaars are closed on Fridays.

### Restaurants

Lunch is served late, from 1.30pm onwards, and dinner from 9-11pm. Traditional cafés and fast-food restaurants stay open all day and sometimes until late at night.

### Offices

Government departments: 8am-2pm. Private sector: 10am-7pm.

### Museums and sites

Monuments and museums are sometimes closed on Tuesdays or Fridays. The major sites, such as Palmyra or Krak are open all year. Some sites close at 2pm, although most stay open until 5pm (winter) or 6pm (summer). Bosra and St Simeon are favourite venues for the Syrians on Fridays, and the rowdy atmosphere is not always conducive to a peaceful visit.

## • Museums, monuments and archaeological sites
### Entrance fees
Visitors should allow S£300 each for the majority of sites, although a few are only S£150. **Students** in possession of an international identity card may get reductions. There are plenty of sites that may be enjoyed free of charge (bazaars, small mosques, the ruins at Palmyra and the Dead Cities). Syrian mosques are open to the public, though women should cover their heads and bodies with a cape (provided at the entrance). There is no charge for photography, but cameras should be left at the entrance desk of museums.

## • Postal services
You should allow between one week and two months for mail to reach Europe, longer for further afield. Postage costs are reasonable: around S£10 for postcards and S£17 for letters. A *poste restante* service is available at Damascus and Aleppo. Sending carpets and computer material (disks or CD-Roms) by post is not allowed.

## • Telephone and fax
### International calls
Making international calls from your hotel could end up very expensive. In Damascus and Aleppo, there are plenty of blue **Easycom** card kiosks, which allow you to make calls within Syria as well as outside the country (cards of S£500 or S£1 000 are available, usually in a shop near the kiosk). Outside these two towns, the old orange telephone kiosks, which take coins or cards, are nearly always found near the main post office. A fax service is available in the main post offices of the larger towns, though you may not have your original returned to you. You might as well leave your mobile phone at home, as it will be no use to you: not only will it not work, but mobiles are not allowed in Syria!

### Local calls
You will rarely be charged by your hotel or by shops for calls made within the same town. Some shops have phone booths for local calls, which take S£1 coins. Insert the coin and close the drawer. Dial the number, then press to allow the coin to drop when your call is answered.

### Codes and charges
Syria has adopted the international system of adding 0 to the number for national calls, and 00 for international calls. Each region has a local code.

**Calling Syria from overseas**
00 + 963 + regional code (without the 0) + the number you wish to call.

**Calling the UK from Syria**
00 + 44 + the number you wish to call (without the 0)

**Calling the USA and Canada from Syria**
00 + 1 + the number you wish to call

**Calling Australia from Syria**
00 + 61 + the number you wish to call

**Calling New Zealand from Syria**
00 + 64 + the number you wish to call

**Calling Jordan from Syria**
00 + 962 + the number you wish to call (without the 0)

The basics

89

**Calling within Syria (same region)**
The number you wish to call direct (without the 0 or the local code)
**Calling within Syria (different region)**
0 + local code + the number you wish to call
**Local telephone codes**
The Syrians often omit the local code when giving their phone number.

| | | | |
|---|---|---|---|
| Aleppo | 21 | Maaloula | 12 |
| Bosra | 15 | Maarrat | 24 |
| Damascus | 11 | Palmyra | 31 |
| Deir ez-Zor | 51 | Raqqa | 22 |
| Hama | 33 | Safita | 43 |
| Homs | 31 | Slenfeh | 41 |
| Idlib | 23 | Souweida | 16 |
| Latakia | 41 | Tartus | 43 |

**Charges:**
Normal phone call rates are S£100 per minute to Europe, S£125 to America and S£115 to Australia. Hotels will normally increase these rates by 50% and may charge a minimum of 3 minutes.
*Directory enquiries*
**National –** ☎ 147 (local), 148 (inter-local). A telephone directory exists but is hard to obtain.
**International –** ☎ 149.

## ● Internet
At present there are still no Internet providers in Syria, but rumour has it that it will soon be possible to get connected at main post offices. In the meantime, the only option remains to connect to your overseas Internet provider by telephone in the larger towns, but this is hardly satisfactory, given the cost of international calls. You will need your own telephone adapter plug.

## ● Local time
*See "Time difference" (p 80).* Syria and Jordan observe the same time.

## ● Public holidays
**Fixed public holidays**
Only government offices close on secular public holidays. The bazaars stay open.
New Year: 1 January
Revolution Day: 8 March
Mothers' Day: 21 March
Evacuation Day: 17 April (Evacuation of the French, national day)
Labour Day: 1 May
Martyrs' Day: 6 May
Christmas Day: 25 December
**Changeable public holidays**
To find out the variable dates of the Muslim holidays, see the chapter on "Religions" p 48.

# GETTING AROUND

There are three main forms of transport that are ideal for visiting Syria, whilst retaining the greatest possible flexibility: air-conditioned buses or microbuses, hire car, or taxi hired by the day. The main sites can be reached by public transport, and you can always find a taxi to complete your journey from the nearest town. Discuss your plans with your hotel staff. Most things are possible in Syria and can often be organised very quickly.

You may have a little trouble finding your way around in town. The Syrians know their towns by districts rather than by street names (which are often wrongly named). They are unused to plans and maps. To be sure of finding your hotel again, ask for its address card from the reception when you go out. This will usually be both in Arabic and English, and will be vital for your taxi driver to find his way.

## • By car

An international driving licence is essential for driving in Syria.

### Rental

**Self-drive –** You should have held a national or international driving licence for more than a year, and be over 23 or 25, depending on the car hire company. Basic models from the international car hire firms (Europcar, Hertz, Avis, Rent a car) are often not much more reliable than those from local Syrian firms, whose prices are noticeably cheaper. In Damascus you will see signs advertising "Rent a car" everywhere, for the simple reason that many Syrians choose to rent a vehicle by the year to avoid paying expensive import taxes (which can double the price of a vehicle). These agencies are not always accustomed to dealing with foreigners. Under no circumstances should you sign a contract in Arabic, as you will have no idea what insurance cover is included. A deposit will be required, to be paid either by credit card or in cash. If you wish to pay in cash (you will often get a better deal this way), you will have to pay the whole amount in advance. You will have the choice between a limited or unlimited number of kilometres.

**Europcar** is one of the few companies that has a network of offices in all Syria's main towns. You can reserve in advance from the UK ☎ (020) 7387 2276. Most reservations start from Damascus. For a small car, expect to pay from US$40 with unlimited kilometres, plus US$6 insurance. There is a minimum hire period of three days (of which two days are with limited kilometres). For other firms, which are considerably cheaper (from US$25 per day before insurance, unlimited kilometres), check what cover is included. It is also important to check the condition of the vehicle, which may have a high mileage, and try it out before committing yourself.

For day trips, a taxi is preferable.

**Car hire with chauffeur –** Strange as it may seem, this method of transport hardly costs any more than hiring a self-drive car, as long as it is done through a local agency, or negotiated direct with a taxi. The hire period may be for one day only (around S£4 000 or US$90 per day), or for longer periods (around S£3 000 or US$70 per day). In the latter case, make sure that the price includes the chauffeur's meals and accommodation, as well as the petrol. Even if the chauffeur is

**Getting around**

91

not a guide, he will always be useful for getting you out of trouble, in case you run into difficulties, and may sometimes be able to act as an interpreter. Always make sure you **agree your itinerary clearly before your departure**, including its total length (and in particular the amount of time you plan to spend visiting each site) and the full price. This will ensure that there are no stressful misunderstandings, resulting in a chauffeur who is in a hurry to get home at the end.

**Borders –** Hired cars cannot cross international borders, whether it is to visit Jordan, Lebanon or Turkey. If you wish to visit Syria and Jordan, you must hire a car in each country and cross the border by taxi or by bus.

### Road network

Although the road network is generally of reasonable quality, you should be prepared for a slightly fraught driving experience: roads which suddenly narrow, the absence of road signs, potholes, unmarked verges, a lack of white lines, vehicles with faulty lights, pedestrians blithely unaware of any risk, animals ... the list of hazards is endless. Night driving is frankly dangerous, and we do not advise it. You should be aware that it gets dark early. It is a good idea to fill up with petrol long before your fuel gauge tells you to.

### Driving

Motorists drive on the right in Syria. There is a speed limit of 90kph on ordinary roads and 110kph on motorways (which have little in common with international standards). In towns there are often traffic jams, particularly at road junctions. Towns are generally small, however. If the traffic worries you, leave early in the morning (7am) while the town centres are still empty.

### Fuel

Petrol is particularly cheap in Syria, with 4-star (*moumtaz*) costing S£20 per litre, and diesel (*mazout*) even less.

### Parking in town

You will have no problem parking in town in the evening. Tourist sites always have car parks. Watch out for no parking zones, as your car may be impounded in Syria!

### In emergencies

It's usual to try and sort out the damage caused by small accidents amicably. However, if anyone is injured as a result of an accident, you should contact the police as quickly as possible, before any vehicle is moved, as well as the hire car company and your embassy. Traffic police ☎ 115.

## ● Camper vans

There are few campsites in Syria. The best solution is to stop for the night near a house or village, where you should ask permission beforehand (this is usually given without any problem).

## ● Taxis

In town, don't even bother with public transport. The municipal buses only have their destinations written in Arabic, and taxi fares are very competitive (on average around US$1). Taxis are very common in town and are easily recognised, as they are yellow. Some of them look as if they've come straight out of an automobile museum; you will recognise some vintage European and American makes which are collectors' items. Men should sit in the front seat. Don't take any notice of the "for hire" sign on the taxi's roof, it's still worth a try even if there is already a passenger, as taxis often take several different passengers at once on the same journey.

To get around the country, if you don't want to hire a car, you can hire a taxi by the day. This is a flexible service, and particularly well-suited to visiting the mountains. Ask at your hotel.

The *taxi-service* is always shared between several passengers. They leave when they are full. These taxis have their own taxi ranks, usually in the town centres. Their journey time is usually faster than by bus, although they are now losing out speed-wise since the introduction of the microbuses.

## ● By train

Syria has a good rail network which links all the main towns, from Damascus to Qamishli in the north-east. However, the trains are slow and the stations often far from the town centres. The result is that trains are little used, despite the advertising campaign by the CFS (Chemins de Fer Syrien) to improve its image. The number of connections is limited to a few trains per day, even on the main lines. It's best to reserve a couchette between Damascus and Aleppo or Deir ez-Zor (under US$10). The line through the mountains from Aleppo to Latakia is very picturesque. There is a train to Amman from Damascus which leaves every Sunday morning at 7am.

## ● By bus

There are very comfortable buses linking Syria's main towns. These are without doubt the most economic way of travelling. The journey from Damascus to Aleppo only takes five hours. The bus companies' offices are generally found grouped together in the town-centre bus stations. It is a good idea to reserve your seat a day ahead, though you will be asked for your passport when buying a ticket. There is fierce competition between the different companies but their prices do not differ greatly, so choose the one whose timetable suits you best. The main companies are: **Al Ahliah** (one of the best), **Qadmous**, **Damastour**, **Zeitouni Tour**, and **Alia**, along with the national company **Karnak**, which usually has its own bus stations.

J. F. Galmiche

**Getting around**

To reach the more isolated tourist sites, use the white microbuses. Even if they're not terribly spacious, they have the great advantage of going everywhere. They usually leave as soon as their twenty seats are full. In the bus stations the destinations are shouted out by one of the companies' agents, who will help you find the right bus. Those determined to go native can try the colourful old buses, thus saving a few pounds, but the journey won't be comfortable.

**Warning:** Microbuses are few and far between after 4pm.

**A bus journey to Homs**
The bus for Homs leaves Damascus at 3.15pm on the dot. We are scarcely out of the city before the steward, dressed in a smart sky-blue shirt embellished with the company's stripes, brings us a glass of water and some sweets. He switches on the television, which announces the weather forecast. The bus glides silently along the road as the sun sets. A video cassette is installed, and the images from Syrian television fade away, to be replaced by an eagerly-awaited Egyptian film. Lying back in our seats, we manage to follow the plot which is unfolding on the screen in Arabic without too much difficulty. A cabaret singer has decided to stitch up an honest policeman. Sadly, the journey is too short to find out how the story ends.

### • Hitch-hiking
This method of transport is hardly worthwhile, bearing in mind the cheapness of public transport, although it may be useful for reaching an isolated tourist site. You won't have to wait long for lifts, and as a tourist you will be given every possible means of help and made to feel welcome. Don't forget to carry food and water with you.

### • Domestic flights
**Syrianair** provides domestic flights from Damascus to Aleppo (about ten return flights per day), Latakia, Deir ez-Zor (quite an experience) and Qamishli. Prices around US$20 for a single flight.

### • Organised tours and excursions
**Travel agents** – Syria held its first tourist exhibition in 1996. Most Syrian travel agencies have acquired plenty of experience in the last few years (Adonis, Cham Tour), although they have little time to spare for individual tourists as they work mainly with overseas tour operators. It is best to contact the smaller agents, who have fewer resources but are much more flexible and will help you organise your visit, be it a day trip or a complete tour of Syria.

If you send a fax to one of these agents, telling them what you want to visit during your stay (from 4 to 14 days), including the main sites and towns and what standard of hotel accommodation you require (from basic to five star), they will supply an itinerary with the price including transport with chauffeur, a guide and hotel reservations. For a group of 15 people, including a minibus and driver, the cost would work out at something like US$100 per day. This system could work well for a small group or even for a couple. It would be up to you to book and pay for your plane ticket. You could add an excursion to Baalbek or extend your visit to include a stay in Jordan (agents in the two countries work together). If you haven't booked anything before you arrive in Syria, your hotel manager will be able to advise you and even organise a small tour for you, by putting you in touch with an agent that he knows.

**Guides** – You will be able to find English-speaking guides without any problem. They will be delighted to help you discover their country, and their charges are not excessive. Their knowledge of local life more than makes up for their sometimes rather vague knowledge of history. Come to a clear arrangement with them before setting off (length of time, places to be visited, means of transport). If they hold the official Ministry of Tourism card, it is a sign that they are reliable.

# BED AND BOARD

● **Where to stay**

The main tourist sites now all have a limited choice of accommodation. If you want to stay by the sea, you could opt for Chaati al-Azrak, to the north of Latakia, although the beaches are far from idyllic. In the summer the cool mountain air around Krak des Chevaliers or Slenfeh (between Latakia and Aleppo) is particularly pleasant.

● **Various categories**

Although there are no youth hostels, bed and breakfast or hostels for groups, the main tourist sites offer at least one comfortable hotel and several of a more basic quality.

*Hotels*

When staying in hotels of a two-star category or above, the bill must be paid in US dollars. You will be expected to leave your passport at reception overnight. Remember to collect it when you leave. When you book, you should be sure to state your arrival time. Hotel staff are inclined to forget your reservation if other customers arrive before you, earlier in the evening.

You will find **extremely cheap hotels** (US$10-15 for a double room) in the town centres. The standard of comfort is extremely basic (at best you will have an electric fan), the area may be noisy, but you will be sure of a friendly welcome. Dormitories are sometimes available, but only for men. Sometimes mattresses can be rented, to sleep on the roof (in summer). The shared bathrooms usually have a hot shower.

**Simple hotels**, between US$15 and US$40, have en-suite bathrooms, electric fans and television in each room. Ask to see your room before deciding, if only to choose a good sea view or to get an idea of the amount of noise or the temperature. Dinner and breakfast are almost always extra.

From US$40 upwards, you will find **comfortable** hotels. Rooms are equipped with telephones, air conditioning and towels.

Above US$70, there are **very comfortable** hotels which offer extremely good service, including satellite television. The **international class** of hotels, from around US$120 upwards, is dominated by the Cham national chain, whose hotels are of varying quality. Their luxurious decor is evocative of the Middle East, with pillars, marble and fountains. They offer all the standard services, and are mostly frequented by businessmen and tour groups. Syria also has two Meridien hotels and a Sheraton.

*Camping*

The only real campsites are found at Damascus and Aleppo. Hotels are often preferable, in view of the climate and the cheapness of accommodation.

● **Eating out**

The majority of Syria's restaurants offer local dishes; western cuisine is harder to find. Alcohol can be found in all the places frequented by tourists, and in the Christian quarters of Damascus and Aleppo. Bars are rare outside the bigger hotels and are always very discreet. Specialist shops sell wines and spirits (around Marjeh square in Damascus).

**Bed and board**

**Sports and pastimes**

### Hotels

A buffet system is found in all the bigger hotels where tour groups stay. These are a good idea for sampling some of the different dishes, which are eaten as *meze* (allow US$10-20 without alcohol). There are some western restaurants in the Cham hotel chain, and in the Meridien at Damascus.

### Restaurants

Apart from the everyday restaurants which serve good Syrian cooking, a dozen or so attractive restaurants have opened in Damascus and Aleppo in elegant former town houses. The setting and the cuisine are both refined, but the bill will still be very reasonable (under US$15 per person).

### In the street

The Syrians invented their own version of fast food long before the Americans thought of it. Sandwiches filled with *felafel* (fried balls of puréed chick peas) and *shawarma* (slices of roast lamb or chicken) can be bought at any time, sometimes from mobile vendors. You should also try *sfiha*, which are little cheese or meat pizzas, and are particularly delicious straight from the oven. Fresh fruit juice is found everywhere and is very refreshing.

# SPORTS AND PASTIMES

In Syria you will find it difficult to enjoy your favourite sports. The only place that you will find easily accessible sports facilities (swimming pools, tennis courts, gyms) will be in the main hotels. However, more interest is being shown in developing sports facilities since the Syrian heptathlon athlete Ghada Shouaa won the country's first gold medal in a major international competition in 1995.

### • Sports

**Tennis**

There are tennis courts in some of the larger hotels.

### • Water sports

Practically non-existent, apart from swimming.

***Swimming***

All the larger hotels have swimming pools. Non-residents are admitted for an entry fee of around US$10.

## • Night life

Even Damascus is not very lively in the evening.

***Concerts and live shows***

Concerts by Arab singers take place in hotel bars. Some restaurants in Damascus invite a traditional orchestra to accompany meals.

***Cinemas***

At the Cham hotel in Damascus there is a cinema showing American films in English. The majority of public cinemas show Egyptian or kung-fu films.

***Discotheques***

The only discotheques are found in the bigger hotels, and are nothing special. Sometimes they include Arab singers. The casinos are rather dubious.

# SHOPPING

Syria is a good place for finding good quality, reasonably priced arts and crafts. You should do your shopping in Damascus rather than Amman if possible, as the choice is wider and the prices lower.

## • What's on offer

*See the chapter on arts and crafts, p 58.*

***Textiles***

Wool is used to make prettily decorated **woven** objects: saddlebags which can be used as cushions, and strips of cloth which are used to decorate tents and as floor rugs can be bought in the Midhat Pacha souk in Damascus.

**Embroidered tablecloths** with interlacing gold or silver patterns make good presents. Those with plain white or cream backgrounds are better than the very bright colours. They always come with matching napkins. This is one of the specialities of Damascus.

The most beautiful textiles are without doubt the **brocades**. These are woven in silk and depict traditional themes, such as hunting scenes, carnations or ships, embellished with gold or silver. Considering the amount of work that goes into their manufacture, these luxurious fabrics are amazingly affordable at US$40-55 per metre. You will also find ready-made cushions, waistcoats and ties. These brocades are only found in specialist shops: Tony Stephan in the Hamidiyeh souk in Damascus has the widest choice of patterns.

**Silk scarves** are the speciality of Aleppo (they are found in the main street of the souk). They are not easily available in Damascus and you should beware of synthetic imitations. You should expect to pay around US$10 for a large size.

***Rugs***

Although Syria itself does not have a carpet-making tradition, it nevertheless has any number of shops where you can find old and new **rugs** from the Caucasus, Iran, Turkmenistan or Turkey, for sale at reasonable prices. In the Hamidiyeh souk in Damascus there are plenty of shops offering a restoration service for old pieces. Bartering is, of course, essential. Prices start at US$80 for a prayer rug.

### Antiques

There are plenty of fakes to be found among the Roman oil lamps, statuettes and antique coins on offer at the archaeological sites or in the shops. Occasionally you will find old 18 or 19C ceramics, but in theory it is against the law to export them.

### Copperware

The copper is rarely decorated with much skill, but the traditional **coffee pots** with their attractive curves make good decorations. Prices from US$10.

### Wood

**Marquetry** is the great speciality of Damascene cabinet makers, who create inlaid boxes, chests, chequer sets, frames, mirrors, pedestal tables and card tables which can be taken apart to make transport easier.

### Soap

The famous olive oil and laurel **Aleppo soap** can be bought near Bab al-Faraj at Aleppo. You won't find it anywhere else in Syria. An evocative souvenir of your holiday. Good quality soap costs US$5 a kilo.

### Perfumes

You will be offered imitations of the famous brands of perfume, but it would be better to stock up on the little bottles of rose, jasmine or lilac essence.

### Clothes

There are many traditional garments. Men can order a tailor-made **jellaba**, which is worn under an **abaya**. The traditional **keffieh** (the large cotton head scarf decorated with red or black checks) could be useful for the visit to Palmyra. Women might enjoy comparing the local version of Benetton fashions with those worn in Europe, in the Salihiyeh boutiques in Damascus.

### Food

Stock up on **herbs and spices**, such as thyme, oregano (*zattar*), cardamon (*hel*), nutmeg and pepper, which are to be found in the Bzouriyehé souk in Damascus. You will also find Iranian **saffron** here, which is sold in small bunches and is not dear, but which should not be confused with the paler, flavourless saffron which is sold loose. The **crystallised fruits** from the orchards of Ghouta are a treat in winter. These carefully prepared delicacies include pears, peaches, apricots, bitter oranges and even walnuts and aubergines, and are irresistible when stuffed with pistachios.

### Jewellery

Both Damascus and Aleppo offer plenty of jewellery shops selling **gold**. Jewellery is sold by weight, but bartering is not unheard of. There is little choice, however, as the chains, pendants bracelets and medallions are often based on religious motifs. Silver is increasingly rarely used, apart from in Bedouin jewellery.

## • Where to shop

### What to buy where

You will find the most choice in Damascus, although Aleppo has its own attractive specialities that can't be found anywhere else (silk scarves, soap).

### The souks

It is impossible to visit the souks without buying anything. Even the prices which are displayed are subject to bartering. Aleppo and Damascus each have a well-stocked arts and crafts souk. The antique shops are found mostly around Bab Charqi in the Christian quarter of old Damascus.

### Other shops

The hotels and modern town centres also have art and crafts shops.

- **Bartering**
*See p 100.*

- **Duty and restrictions on certain articles**
It is against the law to export antiques. Even fake items (which you will be offered everywhere) may cause problems at customs.

- **Mailing things home**
The Syrian postal system can cope with your parcel, as long as it weighs no more than 20kg (cost around US$4 per kilo). The process at the post office is extremely slow (allow about an hour). Some shopkeepers will organise sending inlaid furniture home for you.

# HEALTH AND SAFETY

- **Precautions**
Any health risks in visiting Syria and Jordan are mainly heat-related. It is sur-prisingly easy to get sunburnt in the desert, even when the sky is cloudy. Basic protective gear includes sun-screen, a hat and clothes which keep you covered. Buying a *keffieh* could be useful, as an emergency measure. Wear sunglasses if your eyes are sensitive. In case of sunstroke, lie down in a darkened room with a cold compress over the eyes, and take an aspirin. If the fever continues, see a doctor, as it could be caused by heatstroke. Although the food and water are generally safe, if you are prone to stomach upsets avoid raw food and drink bottled water. The best hotels have a water filtration system, making it safe to drink. It is important to drink plenty of liquids, because of the heat.

- **Medical kit**
As well as aspirins and sticking plasters, you should be sure to bring some kind of medication for upset stomachs. If you are following any medical treatment, don't forget to bring enough supplies. Mosquitoes can be vicious, and bringing a plug-in type of deterrent could be useful if you are staying in cheap hotels. Remember to put on mosquito repellent before going out for an evening stroll or a riverside dinner.

- **Health**
Syria's medical services can cope with the majority of minor problems which may occur. On the other hand, for more serious problems, involving hospitali-sation, repatriation would be preferable.

*First aid*
Ambulance and first aid, ☎ 110.

*Hospitals*
Hospitals are not up to European standards.

*Pharmacies*
Basic medicines are available at the chemist, though choice is limited. It is essen-tial to bring your own medicines and medical products that you are accustomed to using.

*Doctors*
Many doctors are European-trained.

- **Emergencies**
Police ☎ 112          Fire ☎ 113          Ambulance ☎ 110

**Health and safety**

# A TO Z

### • Bartering

Absolutely indispensable, and very widespread. With the exception of hotel rooms, which are paid for in US dollars, and meals and public transport, practically everything else is negotiable. It's hard to know how far to go; offering half the original price isn't always the best solution. Ask local people or other tourists if you don't know how much a service or item should cost. Beware: don't start bartering if you are not really interested in an item. A shopkeeper who accepts your price will not be pleased if you then change your mind about buying.

### • Cigarettes

International brands of cigarettes are available everywhere for US$1.50 per packet.

### • Drinking water

Tap water is supposed to be drinkable, but it is probably better to buy bottled mineral water.

### • Electricity

220V, 50Hz. The plugs are of the small diameter two-pronged type. Power failures are rare nowadays.

### • Hairdressers

There is no shortage of men's hairdressers, and these are among the few shops that stay open on Fridays (though they are closed on Mondays). S£100-200 for a good haircut.

### • Laundry

Even in the basic hotels, a 24-hour laundry service is available at a very reasonable charge (S£50 for a pair of trousers).

### • Newspapers

The **Syrian Times** is the only daily English language paper. It includes some useful information, such as exhibitions and foreign exchange rates. If you can't find it in the news kiosks in the main towns, you can ask at your hotel reception, which may also provide foreign newspapers, such as the **International Herald Tribune**.

### • Photography

Films for colour prints (Kodak, Konica) are sold in the main towns in Syria. Bearing in mind the heat, they may have already suffered some damage when you buy them. It is better to bring your own films. There are many places which offer a one-hour development service; those offering a Kodak service are reasonably priced and good quality.

### • Radio and television

*Radio*

**BBC World Service**: short wave 6195 kHz, 9410 kHz, 12095 kHz, medium wave 1323 kHz (227m)

**Voice of America**: short wave 792 kHz, 1260 kHz, 1546 kHz, 3985 kHz, 5995 kHz, 6040 kHz, 7170 kHz, 11965 kHz and 15205 kHz.

*Television*

Programme listings for the two Syrian channels are published in the *Syrian Times*. Channel 2 has many programmes in foreign languages. Syrians are particularly keen on Mexican soaps and Egyptian films. Satellite dishes are now common, giving a wider selection of channels, and are found in the bigger hotels.

● **Thefts**

Theft is rare in Syria. However, you should be careful of pickpockets when visiting the busiest tourist sites (Bosra, Palmyra, the souks).

● **Tipping**

This is a way of life. Syrians expect **bakchich** everywhere, and tipping is an important supplement to the wages of those who work in tourism. You should tip in restaurants (10% of the bill), in hotels (S£20 for small services) and everywhere you go (taxis, guides, attendants). On the other hand, you should not encourage begging, which is starting to become commonplace in the most popular spots.

Never offer money to a Syrian who helps you find your destination as a gesture of friendship, or who offers you tea, as you will cause offence.

● **Units of Measurement**

Syria uses the metric system of measuring and weighing.

Distances in this guide are given in kilometres. As a rule of thumb, one kilometre is five-eighths of a mile: 5 miles is therefore about 8 kilometres, 10 miles is about 16 kilometres and 20 miles is about 32 kilometres.

Consult the table below for useful metric equivalents:

| Degrees Celsius | 35° | 30° | 25° | 20° | 15° | 10° | 5° | 0° | -5° | -10° |
|---|---|---|---|---|---|---|---|---|---|---|
| Degrees Fahrenheit | 95° | 86° | 77° | 68° | 59° | 50° | 41° | 32° | 23° | 15° |

1 centimetre (cm) = 0.4 inch
1 metre (m) = 3.3 feet
1 metre (m) = 1.09 yards
1 litre = 1.06 quart
1 litre = 0.22 gallon
1 kilogram (kg) = 2.2 pounds

● **Weather forecasts**

These can be seen on television.

# LOOK AND LEARN

There are two excellent **bookshops** in London specialising in the Middle East: al-Saqi, 26 Westbourne Grove, London W2 5RH ☎ (020) 7221 9347, Fax (020) 7229 7492, alsaqi-books@compuserve.com, and al-Hoda, 76 Charing Cross Road, London WC2H 0BB, ☎ (020) 7240 8381, Fax (020) 7497 0180, alhoda@alhoda.com, www.alhoda.com. Both do worldwide mail order. Other helpful travel specialists include Daunts Books for Travellers, 83 Marylebone High Street, London W1M 3DE, ☎ (020) 7224 2295, Fax (020) 7224 6893. In

**Look and learn**

the US, try the Complete Traveler Bookstore, 199 Madison Avenue, New York, or Interlink Books, 99 Seventh Ave, Brooklyn, NY. For a huge selection of titles, take a look at the Internet bookstores such as Amazon.com, barnesandnoble.com and borders.com.

Reading French will be an advantage when looking for books on Syria, as much has been written on the country in this language.

## • General
### Travel writing
CHRISTIE, Agatha, *Come, tell me how you live*, Harper Collins, 1999
FLETCHER GENEISSE, Jane, *Freya Stark: Passionate nomad*, Chatto and Windus, 1999
FRIEDMAN, Thomas L. *From Beirut to Jerusalem: one man's Middle Eastern Odyssey*, Fontana
GLASS, Charles, *Tribes with flags*, Secker & Warburg/Atlantic
LAWRENCE, T.E. *The seven pillars of wisdom*, Penguin
SELBY, Bettina, *Like water in a dry land: A journey into modern Israel*, Fourt, 1998
SKINNER, Margarita, *Between despair and hope: Windows on my Middle East journey*, Radcliffe Press, 1998
SKINNER, Roy E. *Jerusalem to Baghdad, 1967-1992: selected letters*, Radcliffe Press, 1995
### Photography
FOLBERG, Neil, *In a desert land: Photographs of Israel, Egypt and Jordan*, Abbeville Press, 1998
RUTHUEN, Malise, *Freya Stark in the Levant*, Garnet
### History
HITTI, Philip K. *A history of the Arabs*, Macmillan/St Martins
HOURANI, Albert, *A history of the Arab peoples*, Faber/Warner, 1992.
JONES, Terry & ERIERA, Alan, *Crusades*, Penguin/BBC Books
LAWRENCE, T.E. *Crusader castles*, OUP (UK), Hippocrene (US).
MAALOUF, Amin, *The crusades through Arab eyes*, Al-Saqui Books
PALMER, Alan, *The decline and fall of the Ottoman empire*, John Murray
SHLAIM, Avi, *War and peace in the Middle East*, Penguin
### Art and architecture
SAKHAI, Essie, *Oriental rugs – a buyer's guide*, Parkway (UK), Moyer Bell (US)
TALBOT RICE, David, *Islamic Art*, Thames and Hudson
### Religion
AASHI, Zeidan, *Druze & Jews in Israel - a shared destiny?* Sussex Academic Press, 1997
ARBERRY, A.J. (trans), *The Koran*, OUP
GIBB, H.A.R. *Islam*, OUP
SAID, Edward, *Covering Islam*, Vintage 1997
### People and culture
FERNEA, Elizabeth Warnock and Robert A. *The Arab world: forty years of change*, Anchor
SAID, Edward, *Orientalism*, Penguin, 1995
SHAABAN, Bouthaina, *Both right and left handed*, The Women's Press (UK), Indiana University Press (US).

SLUGETT, Peter and Marion Farouk, (eds) *The Times Guide to the Middle East*, Times Books, 1996

BROOKS, Geraldine, *Nine Parts of Desire, The Hidden World of Islamic Women*, Anchor Books, 1996.

*Cuisine*

MALLOS, Tess, *The complete Middle East cookbook*, Grub Street, 1996

OSBORNE, Christine, *Middle Eastern cooking: over 100 delicious recipes*, Prion Books, 1997

UVEZIAN, Sonia, *Recipes and remembrances from an Eastern Mediterranean kitchen: a culinary journey through Syria, Lebanon and Jordan*, University of Texas Press, 1999

## ● Syria

BALL, Warwick, *Syria - an historical and architectural guide*, Melisende, UK, Infolink, US

BROWNING, Ian, *Palmyra*, Chatto and Windus

JORIS, Lieve, *The gates of Damascus*, Lonely Planet Publications

KALTER, Johannes, *The arts and crafts of Syria*, Thames and Hudson

PIPES, Daniel, *Greater Syria - the history of an ambition*, OUP

SEALE, Patrick, *The struggle for Syria*, Tauris (UK), Yale University Press (US)

SEALE, Patrick, *Liberalization between Cold War and peace,* Eberhard Kienle (ed), 1996

SMITH, A.G. *Cut and assemble a crusader castle in full colour: the Krak des Chevaliers in Syria*, 1990

TEWDWR MOSS, Robert, *Cleopatra's wedding*, Duckworth

THUBRON, Colin, *Mirror to Damascus*, Penguin

VAN DAM, Nikolaos, *The struggle for power in Syria: politics and society under Assad and the Ba'ath party*, I.B. Tauris, 1996

## ● Jordan

ALI, Wijdan, *Modern art in Jordan*, Royal Society of Fine Arts, Amman

CAULFIELD, Annie, *Kingdom of the film stars: journey into Jordan*, Lonely Planet Publications

HARDING, G. Lankester, *The antiquities of Jordan*, Jordan Distribution Agency

HOWARD, Tony, *Treks and climbs in the Wadi Rum*, Jordan, Cicerone, 1994

KHOURI, Rami G., *Petra - a guide to the capital of the Nabataeans*, Longman

MAQSOOD, Rosalyn, *Petra: a travellers' guide*, Garnet, 1996

SALIBI, Kamal, *The modern history of Jordan*, I.B. Tauris

TAYLOR, Jane, *Petra*, Hodder & Stoughton

TAYLOR, Jane, *High above Jordan*, Hodder & Stoughton

VINE, Peter, *Jewels of the Kingdom: the heritage of Jordan*, Immel

## ● Films

*Lawrence of Arabia* (1962), David Lean

## ● Music

*See the chapter "music" p 60.*

Beside the ever-popular Middle Eastern singers such as the Egyptian Oum Kalsoum, the Lebanese Fayrouz or the Druze Farid al-Atrach, there are some famous Syrian voices to be heard, such as Sabah Fakhri, Sabri Moudallal, Hamza Shakkur, Adib Dayere and Mayada al-Hennawi.

**Look and learn**

The popular songs don't last long, but can be heard everywhere while they do. Amrou Diebe and his "habibi" is the latest craze, and Georges Wassouf, from Homs, has also become popular recently. You will find recordings by these artists everywhere in Syria, but also in the world music section of western CD shops.

## ● Maps

Royal Jordanian Geographic Centre, **The Hashemite Kingdom of Jordan**, 1/175 000. The most precise road map that is available for Jordan, with town plans for the country's major towns.

Royal Jordanian Geographic Centre, **Amman**, 1/25 000. Detailed town plan of Amman with street index.

Freytag-Bendt, **Syria**, 1/1 000 000. Map of Syria, including town plans of Aleppo, Palmyra and Damascus. It is found in Syria on the bookstands in large hotels, distributed by Avicenne.

# USEFUL WORDS AND EXPRESSIONS

It is well worthwhile learning a few words of Arabic, if only for the enthusiastic reception which will meet your efforts to speak it, even if your pronunciation leaves something to be desired! Several consonants are particularly difficult. However, only three vowels are used in Arabic: a, i and u (pronounced ou), which can be long (â, î, oû) or short (a, i, ou). The transliterations of Arabic words into the Roman alphabet are necessarily approximations, and cannot convey the subtleties of pronunciation. You will also notice the wide discrepancy which exists in Roman spellings: on road signs or maps, Aleppo is sometimes called "Halab", and Damascus may be "Dimashq" or even "Cham" or "Sham", its historical name.

Don't be surprised to find a difference between the following word list and the Arabic phrase book that you may have bought. The latter will probably take its vocabulary from the literary language, which is little used in everyday life, and not from the Arab dialect. We have used the Arabic that is spoken in Damascus, and which is on the whole widely understood in Syria and Jordan.

## Pronunciation rules

All letters are pronounced. For example, **choukrân** is pronounced "choukrane", as in English. The **r** is rolled, whereas **gh** is pronounced like a normal r. The **h** is strongly pronounced, and **th** is pronounced as in English. The **kh** (as in the name Khaled) resembles the Spanish j (jota). The most difficult letter to pronounce is without doubt the **q**. It is better to under-emphasise it, and replace it with the **'**, a contraction of the larynx which creates a breath between words. When **'** is placed at the beginning of a word, it is used to emphasises the vowel which follows it. The **aî** is pronounced like the a in hay.

You will find that p and v are replaced by b, as in "barîss" for Paris, as they are unknown in the Arabic alphabet. The feminine (marked f.) gives rise to partic-ular grammatical constructions.

## Some Arabic words which you will find in this book

*Architectural terms are found on p 29.*

| | |
|---|---|
| deir | monastery |
| bab | door |
| jebel | mountain |
| hadj | a Muslim who has been on a pilgrimage to Mecca |
| hammam | public bath |
| imam | Muslim religious leader |
| madrasa | school for studying the Koran |
| medina | Arab town |
| mouhafazat | administrative region |
| muezzin | holy man who gives the prayer call |
| tell | hill |
| qalaat | castle |
| souk | bazaar |
| wadi | wadi, river |

## Numbers

You should at least learn the symbols which represent the ten numbers. As opposed to letters, numbers are written the Roman way, from left to right.

| | | | | |
|---|---|---|---|---|
| one | oûâhad ١ | seven | sab'ah ٧ |
| two | îthnân ٢ | eight | thamânïah ٨ |
| three | thalâthah ٣ | nine | tiss'ah ٩ |
| four | ârba'ah ٤ | ten | 'achrah ١٠ |
| five | khamsah ٥ | a hundred | miâah ١٠٠ |
| six | sîtah ٦ | a thousand | âlf ١٠٠٠ |

## Common expressions

| | | | |
|---|---|---|---|
| hello | marhabâ | good night | laîlah sa'îdah |
| yes | na'am, âîwa | goodbye | îlâ âl-liqâ' |
| no | lâ | there is | fî |
| please | min fadlak, fadlik (f.) | there is not | mâ fî |
| thank you | choukrân, îslamoû | perhaps | moumkan |
| that's all right | 'afoûân | I don't understand | mâ fahmit |
| good morning | sabâh âl-khîr | I speak English | âtakalam âl-înklîzîah |
| good evening | massâ' âl-khîr | French | âl-fransîah |

## Restaurant

| | | | |
|---|---|---|---|
| restaurant | mat'am | bread | khoubz |
| breakfast | foutoûr | salt | milh |
| menu | wajbah | pepper | filfil |
| water | maî | bill | hissâb, fâtoûrah |

## Hotel

| | | | |
|---|---|---|---|
| ironing | kawî | hotel | foundouq |
| laundry | ghassîl | room | ghourfah |
| passport | jawâz safar | toilet | touwâlît |
| key | mouftâh | bathroom | hamâm |
| air con'd | koûndichoun | shower | douch |
| bed | sarîr | hot water | maî soukhnah |

## Public transport

| | | | |
|---|---|---|---|
| what time is | fî âî sâ'ah | airport | matâr |
| the bus for Aleppo? | âl-bâs âlâ halab? | Plane | tâîrah |
| taxi | taksî | car | sîârah |
| train | qitâr | tyre | daoûlâb |

**Useful words and expressions**

| | | | |
|---|---|---|---|
| station | mahatah | petrol | banzîn |
| bus | bâs | four-star | moumtâz |
| microbus | mîkroû bâs | a full tank | foûl |
| bus station | karâj | shared taxi | sarfîss |

## Purchasing

| | | | |
|---|---|---|---|
| how much is it? | âdîch | money | massârî |
| give me... | â'tînî | change | frâtah |
| a little | choûîah | big | kabîr |
| a lot, too much | kathîr | little | saghîr |
| all | koul | good | koûaîas |
| more | kamân | expensive | ghâlî |
| never | âbadân | open | maftoûh |
| very well | jidân | closed | msakar |
| I would like | oûrîd, badî | gold | dahab |
| what? | choû | silver | foudah |
| why? | lîch | wool | soûf |
| that's my final price | halas | cotton | qoutoun |
| what is it? | choû hâdâ | silk | harîr |
| how many? | kam wâhad | rug | sijâdah |

## Directions and visiting

| | | | |
|---|---|---|---|
| hello | marhabâ | road | tarîq |
| where is? | waîn âl- | street | châri' |
| bank | bank | spring | 'aîn |
| customs | joumrouk | theatre | masrah |
| school | madrassah | tower | bourj |
| church | kanîssah | north | chamâl |
| bookshop | maktabah | south | janoûb |
| mosque | jâma', masjid | east | charq |
| museum | matahf | west | gharb |
| pharmacy | saîdalîah | on the right | 'alâ âl-îahmîne |
| police | chourtah | on the left | 'alâ âl-îassâr |
| bridge | jissar | beside | bijanab |
| post office | barîd | here | hoûn |

## Basic conversation

| | | | |
|---|---|---|---|
| it's a deal | mâchî | forbidden | mamnoû |
| that's all right | tafdal, tafdali (f.) | let's go | îalâ |
| too bad | ma'lîch | in other words | îa'nî |
| God willing | închâ'allah | congratulations | mabroûk |
| no problem | mâ fî mouchkilah | really? | mazboût? |

## Nature

| | | | |
|---|---|---|---|
| cold | bârad | sun | chams |
| hot | hâr | sea | bahr |
| moon | qamar | beach | châti' |

## Emergencies

| | | | | | |
|---|---|---|---|---|---|
| I am... | ânâ | cold | bardân | ill | marîd |
| thirsty | 'atchân | sleepy | na'ssân | doctor | tabîb |
| hungry | joû'ân | tired | ta'bân | hospital | moustachfâ |

## Relationship

| | | | | | |
|---|---|---|---|---|---|
| father | âb | daughter | îbnah | employee | chaghîl |
| mother | oûm | teacher | moudaras | student | tâlib, tâliba (f.) |

| brother | âkh | engineer | mouhandis | tourist | siâïh |
|---------|-----|----------|-----------|---------|-------|
| sister | oûkht | boss | mou'alam | address | 'ounwân |
| son | îbn | shopkeeper | tâjar | | |

## Time

| when? | âmtâ? | tomorrow | boukrah | week | âsboûa' |
|-------|-------|----------|---------|------|---------|
| now | halâ | day after tomorrow | ba'd boukrah | month | chahar |
| later | ba'dîn | minute | daqîqah | year | sanah |
| yesterday | âms | hour | sâ'ah | night | laïl |
| today | âl-îoûm | day | loûm | | |

## A short conversation between Imad and Frederick

| Imad | Peace be with you | âs-salâma' laïkoum |
|------|-------------------|--------------------|
| Frederick | And also with you | wa 'alîkoum âs-salâm |
| Imad | How are you? | kîf âl-hâl? |
| Frederick | Well, thanks to God | tamâm, âl-hamdoulilah |
| Imad | Where are you from? | mìn wîn ânta? |
| Frederick | I'm English | ânâ înklîzî, înklîzîah (f.) |
| | I'm American | ânâ amrîkî, amrîkîah (f.) |
| | I'm Australian | ânâ ustrâlî, ustrâlîah (f.) |
| | I'm Canadian | ânâ kanadî, kanadîah (f.) |
| Imad | Welcome, what's your name | â'lân wa sa'lân,choû îsmak? |
| Frederick | I'm Frederick, and you? | îsmî frîdîrîk, wa ânta? |
| Imad | I'm Imad, are you single? | îsmî 'imâd, ânta 'azab? |
| Frederick | No, I'm married | lâ, ânâ moutazawij |
| Imad | How many children have you? | kam walid' andath? |
| Frederick | Three boys and a girl | tlat walid' wa bintîn |
| Imad | What's your job? | choû batchtghal? |
| Frederick | I'm a teacher | ânâ moudarass |
| Imad | Goodbye | îlâ âl-l-iqâ' |
| Frederick | Goodbye | ma' âs-salamah |

## Sign language

If words fail you, you may have to resort to sign language! The Syrians and Jordanians enjoy enlivening their conversation with little gestures which will amaze you. Each one has a precise meaning:

- the right hand open, making a circular motion to the right, often indicates a question. It is used to replace the question mark.
- all five fingers pointing towards the sky is a way of asking you to wait a minute.
- the official who makes as if to draw a line on his left palm wants to examine your documents.
- the chin jerked abruptly in the air, followed by a click of the tongue, means no.
- the right hand placed on the heart after a greeting is a mark of respect. This gesture also accompanies the polite refusal of an invitation.
- the index fingers of the two hands rubbed together indicates a spouse, girl or boyfriend.
- the shopkeeper who sketches a comma with his right hand means half (a kilo, a packet ...).

**Useful words and expressions**

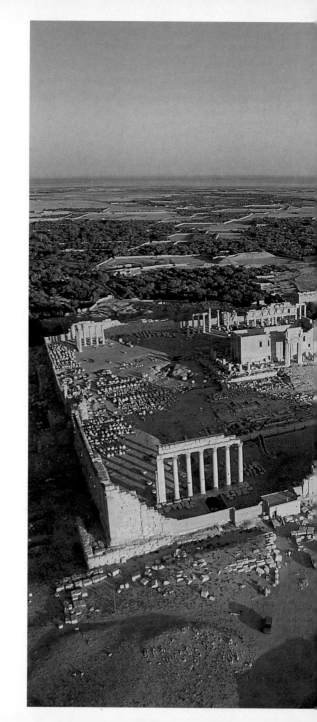

# Exploring Syria

F. Lechenet/ALTITUDE

Temple
of Bel at Palmyra

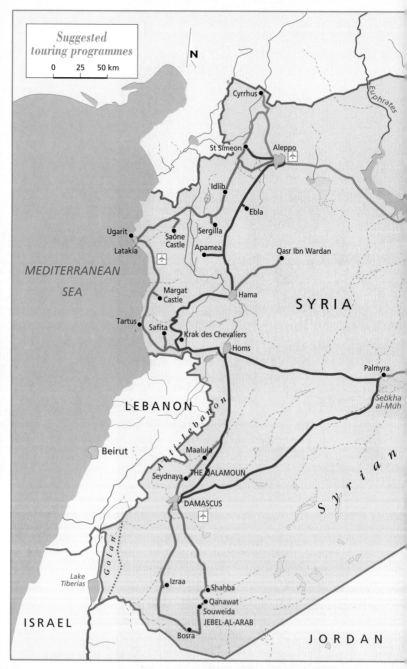

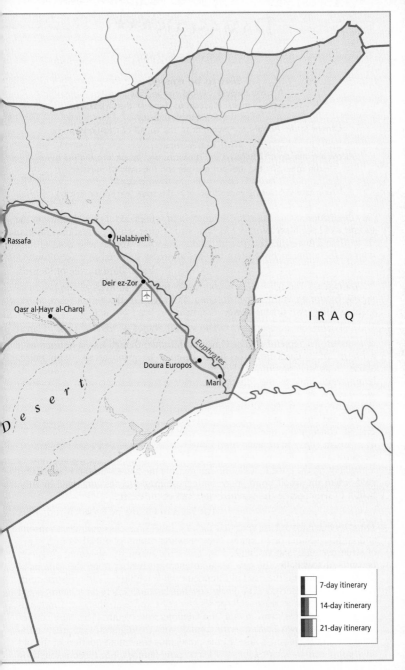

- Rassafa
- Halabiyeh
- Deir ez-Zor
- Qasr al-Hayr al-Charqi
- Doura Europos
- Mari

Euphrates

IRAQ

Desert

| | 7-day itinerary |
| | 14-day itinerary |
| | 21-day itinerary |

# DAMASCUS ★★★
Capital of Syria
Pop 1 500 000 – Alt 700m

### Not to be missed
A stroll through the old city and the souk.
A visit to the National Museum to discover the civilisations
of the Ancient Near East.
Dinner at the Aboul-Ezz restaurant to the sound of traditional music.

### And remember...
Allow a minimum of 2 full days in Damascus: one to explore the old town,
the other for the modern quarter and the national museum.
Avoid Fridays, when the town is dead.
Alternate sightseeing with shopping in the souk (except on Friday).

"My destination was Damascus, the dream of my childhood. I should follow in the footsteps of Lady Mary Wortley Montagu, Lady Hester Stanhope, and the Princesse de la Tour d'Auvergne, that trio of famous European women who lived of their own choice a thoroughly Eastern life, and of whom I looked to make a fourth."

Isabel Burton, wife of Richard.

"O Damascus! Though old as history itself, thou art as fresh as the breath of spring, blooming as thine own rosebud, as fragrant as thine own roses, as fragrant as thine own orange-flower, O Damascus, Pearl of the East!"

The Wilder Shores of Love by Lesley Blanch

"Damascus, 13 September. The Umayyad Mosque, though much restored after a fire in 1893, dates from the eighth century. Its grand arcade, with gallery above, is as well proportioned, and proceeds with as stately a rhythm, in its bare, Islamic way, as the Sansovino Library in Venice. Originally, its bareness was clothed in a glitter of mosaics. Some remain: the first landscapes of the European tradition. For all their Pompeian picturesqueness, their colonnaded palaces and crag-bound castles, they are real landscapes, more than mere decoration, concerned inside formal limits with the identity of a tree or the energy of a stream. They must have been done by the Greeks, and they foreshadow, properly enough, El Greco's landscapes of Toledo. Even now, as the sun catches a fragment on the outside wall, one can imagine the first splendour of green and gold, when the whole court shone with those magic scenes conceived by Arab fiction to recompense the parched eternities of the desert."

The Road to Oxiana by Robert Byron, 1937

These travellers have long since left the city, but Damascus continues to inspire and enthral visitors of all kinds. The sprawling capital is spread along a series of wide avenues, and dominated by the stark silhouette of Mount Qassioun beyond. Almost daily, the city seems to encroach further upon the gardens of the famous **Ghouta**, the oasis of Damascus, while within the old walls the spirit of the east is preserved. The lively covered bazaars, where fine hand-crafted goods are on sale at reasonable prices, are endowed with their own mosques and Koranic schools, caravanserai, and fabulous mausoleums. This busy, almost frenetic, part of town exists in stark contrast with the dignified tranquillity emanating from the elegant houses in the prestigious residential quarters of the old city, populated by long-established Damascene families. For those inspired by the history and atmosphere of the place, it is easy to spend hours wandering through the shaded narrow streets, maybe pausing for a tea and a smoke at a terrace café, and reflecting on how easy it is to forget that beyond Damascus lie endless miles of desert.

## A long history

**The oldest city in the world** – For nigh on three millennia, Aleppo and Damascus have disputed the claim to be the oldest continuously inhabited city in the world. Neither underestimates the fame and importance of more ancient and venerable cities in Mesopotamia, although most of these were fated to suffer such changes in fortune as to deprive them of their prosperity and population, sometimes permanently. Damascus' longevity in a hostile desert primarily relied on a constant and plentiful supply of fresh water which, in this case, is provided by a rather exceptional river that disappears into the desert before ever reaching the sea. The Barada flows straight down from the Anti-Lebanon to irrigate the orchards which, over the centuries, have intrigued travellers and delighted the people of Damascus gathered there in the shade of the apricot trees. It undoubtedly supplied the small Neolithic village on the site well before Damascus entered the history books in the 10C BC. During its time as the seat of an Aramaean principality occupied by David, Damascus succumbed to Assyrian rule; thereafter, it fell into the hands of the neo-Babylonians and Persians until, at last, Alexander the Great sent a detachment of troops there to conquer it as he headed eastwards. The town became organised on Hellenistic lines, and continued to prosper until well after the Roman conquest: the remains of the Temple of Jupiter and the course of the Straight Street immortalised by St Paul's visit are still very much in evidence. The city was raised to the rank of a Roman metropolis, then a colony, before its population converted to Christianity.

Damascus

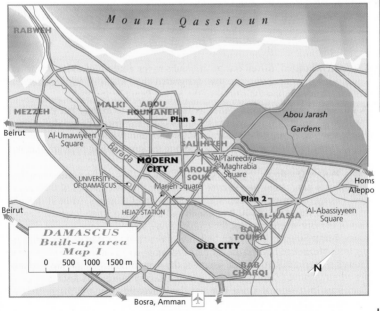

**Damascus**

**Twice a capital** – Damascus reached its apogee after the Muslim conquest. One of the few monuments to survive from these splendid times is the Great Mosque which stands as a reminder of when, in 661, the city assumed the role of capital of the great Umayyad Empire that stretched from the southern frontiers of Gaul to the Indus. It was here, at the crossroads of East and West, that men came together to debate ideas and pursue such sciences as astronomy and philosophy under the auspices of successive caliphs.

The eminence of Damascus was eclipsed by Baghdad following the Abbasids' rise to power. Thereafter, her fortunes dwindled to those of a provincial town controlled by Arab, then foreign dynasties. As the elegant buildings were plundered and defaced, the beautifully ordered streets gradually became scarred by haphazard redevelopment.

Although the Crusaders managed to occupy Jerusalem in 1099, they never succeeded in taking Damascus.

Nureddin made his entrance in 1154. Like his successor, Saladin, he erected many monuments that can still be seen today – caravanserais, *madrasa* (religious colleges), bimaristan (medical schools), hammams – and the city began to spread beyond its ancient enclosure walls.

In 1260, Baybars led a further onslaught by the Crusaders and set up a Mameluke government. The union of Syria and Egypt gave rise to a period of prosperity but it was soon to be destroyed by the Mongols' devastating raid in 1400. The artisans of Damascus were deported to Samarkand to work for the descendants of Tamerlane and the city took a long time to recover. Then in 1516, it was invaded by the Ottoman Turks who occupied the city for 400 years. The city and the surrounding region were ruled by pashas, the most famous of whom were from the al-Azem family. It became the last staging-post on the annual pilgrimage to Mecca, which took the caravans three weeks to complete, and benefited from the offshoots of the trade plied by the pilgrims. But the situation deteriorated in the 19C. The occupation of Ibrahim Pasha, followed by the inter-denominational riots in Lebanon, had grave repercussions in Damascus. 1860 was marked by Christian massacres but Ottoman Damascus was continuing to expand outside its walls at the end of the 19C. After the Ottomans departed, driven out by the Arabs in the autumn of 1918 during the Great Arab Revolt, Damascus was designated the capital of Syria under the French mandate, then the capital of the Syrian Republic in 1946.

**A sprawling city** – Ever since, the city has continued to expand but its original nucleus is miraculously well-preserved. It has absorbed the exodus of the Palestinians and that of the peasants leaving the countryside, to reach its present population of more than 3 million (including the surrounding rural area known as the *rif Dimashq*).

From **Mount Qassioun**, which rises to 1 150m further to the north, there is a magnificent panoramic **view**★★ over the city. On the lower slopes of the mountain, hastily constructed houses shelter the stream of migrants, while at the foot of the slope, the **Malki, Abou Roumaneh** and **Salihiyeh** districts form the elegant part of the city where many of the embassies are located. To the west of the old town, Beirut Street is lined with buildings more than ten storeys high, stretching from **Mezzeh** to beyond the People's Assembly, a contemporary building that crowns a nearby hill. Along the length of the main tributary of the River Barada are administrative buildings, travel agencies, luxury hotels and restaurants, the Damascus International Trade Fair and the University. The suburbs, stretching to the south behind the Hejaz railway station, include the **Yarmuk** camp, which houses a large proportion of the Palestinians living in the capital who make up 20% of the population. To the east, near **Bab Touma**, an extension of the Christian quarter of the old city, is the residential area of **al-Kassa**. Nearby are the Abou Jarash gardens, part of the Ghouta oasis, which consti-

**Out of Damascus**
The English language owes two words to jewels of Damascus artisanship, namely weaving and metal-working. Damask fabric, which is reversible, is generally made of silk: its matt pattern on a satin background is obtained by intertwining some of the threads. To damascene metal is to etch or inlay it with other metals, often with threads of gold, silver or copper.

tute one of the very few green spaces in the capital. The three minarets of the Umayyad mosque rise above the **old city** of Damascus: look out for the oval contour of its walls and the density of its buildings.

# The old city★★★
*Allow one day.*

This walk begins with the charms of old Damascus, isolated from the traffic by its walls that run the length of almost three-quarters of its perimeter. Take the time to alternate sight-seeing with shopping in the souk and just meandering. Remember that on Fridays the souk is deserted.

*Find the entrance to the Hamidiyeh souk in the centre of Damascus.*

## From the Hamidiyeh souk to the Umayyad mosque
(Map II, A1, B2)

Before entering the souk, head for the very high, heavily restored wall of the **citadel** *(on the left of the entrance, closed to the public)*, the foundations of which supported a Roman *castrum*. Near the entrance is an equestrian statue of Saladin. Behind him are Renaud de Châtillon and Guy de Lusignan who were defeated at the Battle of Hattin. Note the crown lying on the ground.

At the corner of Al-Nasr Street and Al-Thawra Street, where strains of music filter through the air, the crowds swell in the covered passage of the **Hamidiyeh souk★** (vehicles are few and far between). Sheltered from the sun, the tradespeople of the most famous market in Damascus call out to their customers. There are hundreds of stalls lining both sides of the paved street, some of them tiny. Products of local craftsmanship are displayed on inlaid wooden pedestal tables. Brightly shining copper products match the golden threads tracing arabesques on brightly-coloured tablecloths. Shop windows are crammed with robes, carpets, and gleaming sabres.

It is easy to be seduced by the vast array and variety of products on sale, egged on by adults and children who have no hesitation in approaching passers-by. They seem to know every language under the sun, from English to Russian, with a little French and Japanese thrown in. "Come to see my shop, nappes de Damas, mosaïques, change money…"

The souk owes its name to the Ottoman Sultan Abdul Hamid II, who modernised it by arranging the shops on two levels and covering it with a metal roof. On the right, 100m further on, several passages are dedicated to the sale and repair of carpets.

*250m from the entrance to the souk, turn right, where there is a gap in the metal roof. The bimaristan al-Nouri is 100m along on the left.*

The old city

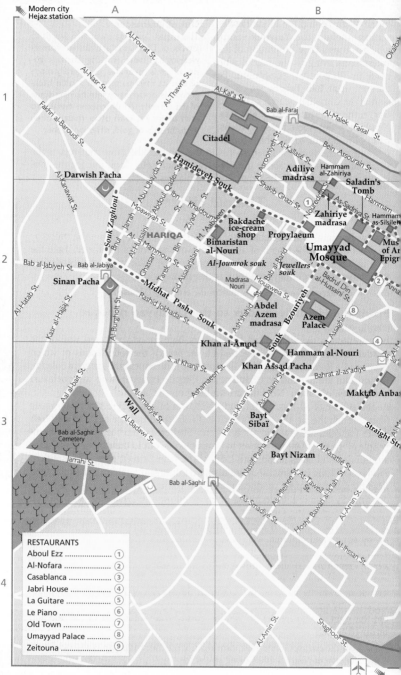

**Modern city**
**Hejaz station**

**A**        **B**

Al-Fourat St.

Al-Nasr St.

Al-Thawra St.

Fakhri al-Baroudi St.

Al-Kal'a St.

Bab al-Faraj

**Citadel**

Al-Malek Faisal St.

Bein Assourain St.

**1**

**Darwish Pacha**

Al-Kanawat St.

**Hamideyeh Souk**

Al-Astroniyeh St.

Al-Kallasé St.

Shakib Ghazi St.

**Adiliye madrasa**

Hammam al-Zahiriya

**Saladin's Tomb**

Nereddine St.

As-Sadhiya

Hammam as-Silsileh

Abu Ubayda St.

Abdul Qader St.

Ibn Khaldoumeen St.

Moawiyah St.

Zirad St.

M. Aboudeen St.

**Zahiriye madrasa**

**Bakdache ice-cream shop**

**Propylaeum**

**Mus of Ar Epigr**

**Sinan Pacha**

Bab al-Jabiyeh St.

Bab al-Jabiya

**Souk Zughloul**

Bhut Jarrah St.

Al-Husaini St.

Ghassan Mammoun St.

Tareq Bin Ziad St.

Eid Asadalalani St.

**HARIQA**

**Bimaristan al-Nouri**

*Al-Joumrok souk*

*Jewellers' souk*

Bab al-Band St.

Badrul Din al-Hussaini St.

**Umayyad Mosque**

Anna

**2**

Al-Hatab St.

Kasr al-Hajjaj St.

**Midhat Pasha Souk**

Rashid Jokhadar St.

Al-Burgholt St.

Madrasa Nouri

Ash-shahid St.

Mouaweia St.

**Bzouriyeh**

**Abdel Azem madrasa**

**Azem Palace**

M. Assaghir St.

8

2

4

**Khan al-Amod**

**Souk**

**Hammam al-Nouri**

S. al Khanji St.

Ashamaeen St.

**Khan Assad Pacha**

Bahrat al-as'adiyé

As-Saliye

**Maktab Anbar**

**Wall**

Al-al-bait St.

Al-Smadiyé St.

Al-Badawi St.

Hasan al-Kharra St.

As-Dalani St.

**Bayt Sibaï**

**Straight Stre**

Al-Kasarlié St.

**3**

**Bab al-Saghir Cemetery**

Jarrahi St.

Nassif Pasha St.

**Bayt Nizam**

As-Mehree St.

At-Taweill St.

Al-Itab St.

Hoshi Bawari St.

Al-Amin St.

Bab al-Saghir

As-Smadiyé St.

Al-Ihsan St.

Al-Amin St.

Shaghool St.

**The bimaristan al-Nouri** *(8am – 2pm; closed Fridays; entry charge)* has a fine door-way, the lintel of which is a relic of an ancient monument, the door being surmounted by an amazing honeycombed semi-dome. The hospital, founded by Nureddin in 1154, functioned until the 19C. The *bimaristan* (literally "house of patients") is built around a central courtyard; each side is occupied by an *iwan*, a sort of outside sitting room typical of Iranian architecture, which became very widespread in Arab houses. The bimaristan houses the **Museum of Arab Science and Medicine,** where instruments associated with astronomy, medicine and pharmacy are displayed.

### Arabic medicine and its teaching

At one time, Arabic medicine was one of the most advanced sciences in the world. Rather like the teaching hospitals of today, teachers, pupils and patients worked together. From the 9C onwards, it was based on translations of Greek texts by Hippocrates and Galen, on the famous "Canon of Medicine" by Ibn Sina (written in the 11C) and on the observation of clinical cases. The teacher lectured from under the iwan.

*Return to the main alley of the Hamidiyeh souk, near the narghile shops.*

On the right is the famous **Bakdache ice-cream shop** *(see "Making the most of Damascus" section)*. It is a veritable institution in Damascus and worth a stop. Whilst women and couples can savour their delicious sorbets under the trees in the courtyard, men on their own must remain in the room reserved for them! Here the elegantly-dressed townsfolk rub shoulders with the farmers in town for the day, with everybody enjoying their ice-creams.

Deep in the maze of winding alleyways is the **al-Joumrok souk** where the women, some dressed from head to foot in black, come to choose coloured fabrics trimmed with paste jewellery and gold thread.

The propylaeum

J. F. Galmiche

Damascus

Further on is the **propylaeum** (monumental gateway) of the ancient Temple of Jupiter. The gigantic columns, surviving from Antiquity, surmounted by a richly decorated pediment, used to mark the west entrance to the temenos (temple sanctuary). Housed under the portico with its columns are the vendors of religious souvenirs. As in Antiquity, the shop fronts are protected from the fierce rays of the sun by a fine canvas awning. Opposite, the long wall lined with pilasters used to demarcate the west side

**Spreading the Faith**
In order to impose a more orthodox faith, which had fallen into abeyance under the Fatimids, the Ayubbid sovereigns of the 12C, and later the Mamelukes, went to great lengths to build colleges that would spread the Sunni faith. Money left in legacy by a well-known figure was used to fund a Koranic school, built around the tomb of the dead man. The Adiliye and Zahiriye madrasas are two interesting examples of this new type of construction.

of the peribolos, the walled courtyard of the Temple of Jupiter. Today, the wall encloses the Umayyad Mosque. The door to the mosque, in the extension of the propylaeum, is the main entrance reserved for Muslims.

*Follow the wall round to the left, then head towards the domes of the two madrasas which face each other.*

**The Adiliye madrasa,** *(8am-2pm; entry free)* on the left, the oldest of the two (completed in 1222) with its portal decorated with intersecting ribs and a wedge-shaped keystone, houses a rich collection of manuscripts from the Syrian National Library. It is built around a pretty courtyard with an ornamental basin, where a medlar tree and a palm tree provide shade *(manuscript collection not open to the public)*. The funerary chamber contains the mausoleum of al-Adil, Saladin's brother.

Opposite, the **Zahiriye madrasa** (1277) *(8am-2pm; entry free; the custodian will open the door of the funerary chamber for a small tip)* houses the tomb of Baybars, the Mameluke Sultan who finished off what Saladin had begun and drove the Crusaders out of Syria once and for all. This was the first building to be erected by this dynasty in Damascus. There is a beautiful *mouqarnas* above the entrance. Three large bands of inscriptions run above the doorway. The tomb is on the right of the courtyard under a dome. The funerary chamber is decorated with mosaics reminiscent, albeit less vibrant and refined, of those of the Great Mosque.

*Follow the street that runs along the side of the Umayyad Mosque to the left. It does not take long to reach a beautiful doorway opening onto a graceful courtyard with an ornamental basin, full of flowering bougainvillaea.*

**Saladin's Tomb\*** *(8am-5pm; winter 4pm; entry free; remove shoes at the entrance)*, where the most revered adversary of the Crusaders is laid to rest, is situated in a charming garden just behind the Great Mosque. The courtyard, with its fountain from what used to be the Aziziye *madrasa* (of which there is no longer any trace), is a haven of peace and quiet. It required the intervention of Kaiser Wilhelm II of Germany, who was responsible for the German influence in the Ottoman Empire at the end of the 19C, to save the tomb from destruction. The body of Saladin now rests in an ostentatious white marble tomb, while the original wooden tomb is preserved nearby. The faience panels on the walls date from the 17C.

*Head for the first building on the left of the entrance to Saladin's Tomb.*

**The Museum of Arabic Epigraphy** *(9am-2pm; closed Tuesday; entry charge)* is housed in the Jamaqiya *madrasa* which dates from the beginning of the 15C. Its inlaid polychrome façade and doorway with honeycomb stalactite decoration are

The old city

characteristic of the last period of Mameluke architecture in Damascus. Inside is an interesting collection of calligraphy using Arabic script, along with writing instruments (reed *qalam*, ink-wells and pen-boxes), dating from the earliest times of Islam to the present day. Persian and Ottoman documents illustrate the extraordinary breadth of the Arabic script and the variety of styles used.

*The first street on the right following the museum leads to the visitors' entrance to the Umayyad Mosque.*

## The Umayyad Mosque (or Great Mosque)★★★ (Map II, B2)

*9am-9pm; entry charge. Female visitors should cover themselves with the hooded gowns provided when they buy their tickets.*

On entering the immense courtyard, the impact of the whiteness of the paving and the walls is dazzling. The effect is further enhanced by the dark gowns worn by female tourists. The courtyard used to form the peribolos or inner enclosure of the Temple of Jupiter: the propylaeum can be found at the exit to the Hamidiyeh souk. A fine example of the durability of such places of worship, this site has been successively used as a shrine to the Aramaean god Haddad (9C BC), the Roman Temple of Jupiter (3C AD), the basilica dedicated to St John the Baptist and finally a mosque. Unfortunately nothing remains of the ancient temples and the basilica. After much controversy, it is now accepted that the mosque, far from being an adaptation of the Christian basilica, was an original creation erected by the Caliph al-Walid I: the caliph wanted to give the capital of the new empire a mosque that could hold all the faithful of Damascus. Completed in 715 it took six years to build and cost a fortune. The architects planned the long prayer hall against the south wall of the peribolos and a portico on the other three sides. Despite the ravages of time, the building remains a prestigious monument for Muslims and lovers of architecture alike, drawn to the sumptuousness of the materials used, the quality of the decoration, its proportions and antiquity. It is one of the rare examples of the earliest period of Islam and the Umayyad caliphate. A prototype of Arabic mosques, its layout has served as the inspiration behind the mosques at Aleppo, Hama and Ma'arat an-Numan in Syria, as well as the one at Cordoba. It has recently been restored (*see illustration p. 27*).

Note the remarkable **mosaics**★★★ made of tiny tiles of coloured stone and glass paste on a gold background executed by Syrian and Byzantine artisans in the 8C. The first panel, just near the entrance, behind the little **kiosk** housing the ablution fountains, covers the **façade**★ of the nave. Despite extensive restoration, it gives an idea of the decoration that used to cover all the façades.

On the right-hand side of the courtyard, the domed **octagonal structure**★ (*bayt al-hal*), supported by smooth columns and beautiful ancient capitals, used to house the community's treasures. Its mosaic decoration dates from restoration carried out in the 13C or 14C.

The oldest and finest mosaic is sheltered under the portico in front of the **west wall**★★★, behind the treasury. Covering a breadth of 30 m, the sumptuous landscape decoration, dominated by gold and every shade of brown and green, covers the top part of the wall as well as the arcades and the entrance hall. In the centre, the huge panels depict two splendid palaces with columns, separated by two kiosks. In the foreground, the river has been interpreted by some as being the River Barada or the river of paradise. Above, several marble windows dating from when the mosque was built are thought to be the first examples of windows decorated with Islamic geometric motifs.

The Hamideyeh souk and the Umayyad Mosque

*Shoes must be removed before entering the prayer hall by the door on the right.*

**The prayer hall\*\***, formed of large aisles separated by columns with classical capitals, is vast. The coolness, the filtered light and the soft carpets are very inviting. Why not take the opportunity to sit down for a few minutes and contemplate the comings and goings of the faithful who come here not only to pray, but also to meditate and rest.

Above the centre of the nave, a dome rests on four robust pillars in front of the *mihrab*, the niche indicating the direction of Mecca *(qibla)* to the faithful. To the right of the *mihrab*, note the lovely *minbar*, the pulpit from which the imam preaches on Friday. To the left of the *mihrab* is the **shrine of St John the Baptist**, rebuilt by the Ottomans at the end of the 19C, which is supposed to contain the head of the saint who baptised Jesus. Numerous Muslim and Christian pilgrims come to the shrine to make their vows.

*Return to the courtyard through the door at the far end on the left of the prayer hall, then head towards the small domed kiosk.*

The dome of the **treasury\*** is supported by eight Byzantine columns. The elegant capitals with varied motifs also date from Byzantine times. Behind the treasury, at the corner of the portico, there are numerous traces of mosaic on the wall. To the right of the treasury, under the portico, are groups of women wearing the *tchador*. They are going to the **tomb of Hussein**-son of Ali, the son-in law of the Prophet, whose head is supposed to have been brought to Damascus after his defeat against the Umayyads at Karbala (680 AD).

Before leaving the courtyard, take a closer look at the **three minarets\*\*** of the mosque, each one different from the others. Above the tourists' entrance, the Minaret of the Bride dates from the 12C. It was built above the base of a Roman tower. The Minaret of Jesus, the slenderest of the three, was built in 1247, then altered by the Ottomans. Tradition has it that this is where Jesus will come down to earth to fight the Anti-Christ before the end of the world. The west minaret was built in 1488 by the Sultan Qait Bay. This elegant minaret with alternating courses of colour is characteristic of Mameluke art.

*On leaving the mosque, turn right and follow the groups of Iranian pilgrims heading towards the Rouqayya mosque (first street on the left), passing the Silsileh hammam en route.*

## From the Umayyad Mosque to Azem Palace (Map II, B2)

**The Rouqayya Mosque\*** *(entry free; female visitors should cover themselves with the gown provided at the entrance; shoes should be left at the entrance to the mausoleum)* was completely re-built in 1993 on the site of the ancient tomb of one of the daughters of Hussein, the great-granddaughter of the Prophet Muhammed.. The rebuilding project was funded by the Iranians, who come here on pilgrimages and to Saïda Zeinab in the south of the capital. It is a highly unusual example of Persian art in Syria. The funerary chamber lies beyond the small peristyle courtyard built entirely of marble. The Iranian style can be seen in the surbased arches, the mirrors and the ceramics covering the walls, and the gilded doors decorated with enamel work. The delicate whisperings of the women echoing the chanting of the men lends the place an atmosphere of profound devotion. Almost by way of reassurance, visitors may be offered some nougat from Qom or Isfahan. Notice the little brick that the Shi'ites place between their forehead and the ground when they prostrate themselves. This accessory, which is of no religious significance, simply ensures contact with pure ground.

P. Meunier

The Rouqayya Mosque

*Retrace your steps for 50m, then bear left instead of heading towards the Umayyad Mosque.*

This marks the entrance to the **Muslim quarter\*\*** of the old city. The white-washed walls of the houses, pierced only by a small low door on the ground floor, have balconies on the first floor supported by wooden beams. The *meshre-beeyehs* on the windows allow air in (as well as prying eyes access out!), without compromising the intimacy of the interior. Passages straddling the narrow streets link one house to another. Vehicles rarely venture into these small, picturesque streets and the only other noises to disturb the silence are the street vendors and the children playing, along with the bicycles zigzagging their way among the pedestrians. Visitors who have got time to spare will love strolling through this maze of little streets. Look out for the baker's oven and try one of the piping-hot wafer-thin biscuits which are piled up in front of the oven to cool.

*Visitors wishing to explore the souks still further should head for the pretty Café al-Nofara (see the "Making the most of Damascus" section), keeping to the right, and continue all the way round the Great Mosque. After a glass of tea or a narghile, keep to the south wall of the Umayyad Mosque, then turn left at the entrance to the jewellers' souk.*

The tiny shops of the **jewellers' souk** overflow with gold. Behind the counter, there are tiny electronic scales for weighing the precious metal. Remember, if tempted to buy, fierce haggling is de rigueur. Further along the same street are the perfume shops. Long lists in Arabic and French promise Chanel No. 5, Kenzo, Lancôme… These imitations of French perfumes suggest that the counterfeiters have a very good nose even though the scent evaporates very quickly.

*At the far end of the jewellers' souk, near the perfume shops, the street on the right leads to the Abdul Azem madrasa, an excellent example of a Koranic school transformed into shops selling antiques and craft products. On the left is a small square leading to the Azem Palace.*

The Azem Palace*** (9am-5.30pm, winter 3.30pm; closed Tuesdays; entry charge) was built by a governor named Assad Pasha al-Azem in the mid-18C, a time of relative stability when Damascus was under the authority of the al-Azem family. This sumptuous private residence has been exquisitely restored. Columns and marbles taken from older monuments were brought here from the Roman sites of the Hauran. The walls of the façade are formed of alternating layers of ochre and black stone. Inside, the rooms are decorated with beautiful painted wooden panelling, furniture inlaid with mother-of-pearl, beaten copper and Delft pottery. A corridor on the left of the ticket office leads to the **haremlik**, traditionally the private quarters of Arabic houses, where the pasha and his wives lived. The apartments occupy two floors, built around a charming shady courtyard with a multi-coloured pavement. Opposite the fountain, a portico of four columns sheltering two stone seats (mastaba) leads to more beautiful rooms. Each room in the haremlik, with its richly decorated floor, houses part of the Museum of Popular Arts and Traditions. Of the many small reconstructions evoking the daily life of this opulent residence and scenes from life in Damascus, one of the most memorable is the display devoted to the caravans that used to make the pilgrimage to Mecca and generated the city's fortune. There is a large **iwan** opposite the impressive rectangular pool. Beyond it is a small private **hammam**. The large **reception room** (qaa), accessed by a staircase, was the ceremonial chamber. This room, with its fountain and sumptuous decoration, furnished with fine examples of marquetry work, leads to the **salemlik**: this is the public wing of the house, with its beautiful iwan, which is separate from the rest of the house. Visitors were brought here through the winding corridor which now serves as the exit.

This part of the building was the residence of the high commissioner at the beginning of the French mandate.

## The Bzouriyeh and Midhat Pasha souks (Map II, B2, A2)

The Bzouriyeh souk* is a dream for lovers of spices and confectionery. On both sides of the covered alley, large sacks that never seem to empty are brimming with condiments that would satisfy the most demanding palace kitchen. The aromas of ground thyme (zattar) or ginger blend with the smells of peppers and curry, all sold by weight. Tiny rose-heads, camomile and various dried flowers are sold alongside delicious confectionery: pistachio nougat, preserved fruit, sugared almonds which are all produced locally. However, do not get too carried away – there is still a lot to see.

The al-Nouri hammam*, a Turkish bath founded in the 12C, was used as a soap factory at the beginning of the 20C. Thanks to an excellent restoration programme, this is now one of the most beautiful and oldest working hammams in Damascus (see the "Making the most of Damascus" section). Beyond the gorgeous candle shops is the entrance to the Assad Pasha khan (it has been closed to the public for several years, but there are plans for its restoration). The work involved in the mouqarnas and the delicate little columns at the doorway are indicative of how rich the interior decoration must be. This exceptional caravanserai, completed in 1753, which has been compared to the basilica of St Peter's in Rome, is built around a central dome. There are two floors containing 84 rooms. Opposite stands the more modest al-Amod khan.

Continue to the far end of the Bzouriyeh souk. The small paved street opens out onto Midhat Pasha Street, where the porters hang around waiting for custom.

The **Midhat Pasha souk**, which is unfortunately encumbered by heavy traffic, constitutes the western end of Straight Street. It starts with the paint shops and the dispensaries where healers using traditional medicine come for supplies. Here, the shopfronts are crammed with tortoise shells, dried reptiles and sponges with hidden properties. A few paces away, the coffee-roasting machines are grinding the coffee beans prior to cardamom being added (according to the customer's taste), the wonderful aroma wafting out to assail the nostrils of passers-by. Then there is the part of the souk specialising in the clothing traditionally worn by the Bedouin and local farmers: long *abaya* embroidered with gold thread which they wear over the *gallabia*, and which they cover in winter with a warm *karwoue* made of double-thickness woollen cloth and kouffieh. There are also groundsheets made of wool or felt for tents and houses. There are several khans (hostels and goods warehouses, these days only used for the latter) on each side of the street. At this point the souk continues in the open air, the first part being under cover. It continues on through the Hariqa quarter (meaning "fire" in Arabic), built after the French bombardments that destroyed this part of the city. These days this souk is somewhat lacking in charm, being mainly devoted to clothing.

*At the end of the souk, turn left.*

Here is the **Sinan Pasha Mosque** (1590) with its curious green-enamelled brick minaret. There may be some casual labourers at the entrance: armed with buckets, spades and mattocks they are hoping to be hired for the day. The small courtyard with its copper-nozzled basin is delightful. In front of the prayer hall is a portico with columns, two of which are twisted. The façade is composed of alternating courses of black and white stone.

*Cross the road and turn right after 200m.*

The **Darwish Pasha Mosque** (1571) was also built by one of the Ottoman rulers of Damascus. The wooden door shows signs of the passage of time. Like the Sinan Pasha Mosque, the prayer hall is crowned with a dome; the portico and the courtyard are decorated with beautiful blue-glazed faience tiles, probably made in Damascus *(see illustration p 10).*

## Straight Street and Bab Charqi* (Map II, B2, C2-3, D4)

*This itinerary may be followed in conjunction with the previous one. It can be shortened by going straight to Bab Charqi by taxi and leaving out the first part of the suggested itinerary.*

On leaving the Bzouriyeh souk, turn left into the ancient Via Recta – the Straight Street mentioned in the New Testament – which used to be the main axis (*decumanus*) of the Roman town (the colonnade has completely disappeared!). The first road on the right leads to the **Nizam** and **Sibaï Palaces**, two rich bourgeois residences dating from the 18C. Ask local children for help in finding *bayt* Nizam and *bayt* Sibaï. They will arrange for the doors to be opened.

In a street that goes off left 300m up from the Bzouriyeh souk, a small street leads to **maktab Anbar**, a beautiful late-19C house. Its stucco and marquetry decoration is quite breathtaking and the charming paved courtyards are full of flowers. The house was converted into a school by the Ottomans, then used as a barracks under the French mandate. Today it houses the Commission for the Protection of Old Damascus.

*Return to Straight Street.*

The old city

**Damascus**

**Paul at Damascus**

Paul was a Roman citizen and a Jewish Pharisee from Tarsus who had set off for Damascus to stop Christ's disciples. He lost his sight when Jesus appeared to him in a sudden vision, asking Paul to follow him. On his arrival in Damascus, Paul's sight was restored by a Christian named Ananias during his stay in Straight Street. After his conversion to Christianity Paul was baptised and preached the word of Christ alongside those whom he had wanted to persecute. However, when a Jewish plot against him was brought to his attention he had to flee Damascus by night, hidden in a basket which was lowered from the city walls. The "Apostle of the Gentiles" went on to develop his missionary activities on three long journeys which he made to Rome, where he established the basis of the Christian Church. His thoughts and his indomitable courage as he travelled throughout the Roman Empire are documented in his 14 Epistles. (cf. Acts of the Apostles, Chap.9, v. 1-25).

The street passes under a **Roman arch** which was possibly part of the tetrapyle marking the intersection with the *cardo* of the town. It then enters the Christian quarter which houses the places of worship used by the various religious persuasions in Syria. Its entrance is marked on the left by the imposing modern building of the **Greek Orthodox Patriarchate**. The right-hand side of the street used to be the Jewish quarter, but today stands empty, its inhabitants having emigrated en masse in 1991. There are a variety of shops on Straight Street selling copper, carpets and wooden furniture, before arriving at **Bab Charqi**, the Roman Gate of the Sun, which used to constitute the northern end of the *decumanus* in the old town. It probably dates from the early 3C AD. Today the quarter reflects the growth of tourism and what were once old houses are now flourishing restaurants.

The memory of St Paul is associated with two monuments in Damascus. The first, which is of no particular architectural interest, involves a detour of a kilometre (there and back) following the line of the city walls outside to **Bab Kissan**, which houses the chapel dedicated to St Paul. The building marks the spot where the saint is supposed to have been lowered from the walls in a basket. At the end of the road leading to the airport is a chapel which is dedicated to the Greek Orthodox faith. It was built into the high wall earlier this century.

*Return to Bab Charqi and continue up St Ananias Street, the last street on the left before leaving the town.*

After passing the **Nassan Palace⋆**, a delightful bourgeois residence: note the inscription on the wall inviting people to visit, and the Piano and Casablanca restaurants, there is the **St Ananias Chapel** *(9am-1pm/4-7pm; closed Tuesdays; entry free)*, right at the end of the street. This small chapel, its stone walls descending below ground level, is supposed to have been built on the site of the house inhabited by the saint who restored Paul's sight. From here to **Bab Touma**, it is a lovely walk through the maze of the **Christian quarter⋆** of the old city, along pretty little streets lined with houses whose balconies are supported by wooden beams.

# The modern city
*Allow half a day*

This itinerary, which runs from the Hamidiyeh souk to the Soulaymania complex, introduces the visitor to various features of Ottoman Damascus, albeit much altered over the years.

*The tour begins with the Historical Museum of Old Damascus, the main entrance of which is situated in a little street off Al-Thawra Street, 500m from the entrance to the Hamidiyeh souk.*

**The Historical Museum of Old Damascus**\* (Map III, C4) *(8am-2pm; closed Fridays; entry charge; allow 30min for visiting the museum)* is housed in the old quarter of Oukaibeh, in a house that once belonged to Khaled al-Azem. On the far side of the courtyard (salemlik), a corridor on the right complete with beautiful fountain leads to the ticket office and the main courtyard of the house *(haremlik)*, all the more attractive for its medlar and citron trees *(koubad)* which produce large, yellow citrus fruit. High walls muffle the noise from the road outside. Exhibits are displayed in various rooms in the house. The quality of the building work and the delicate nature of the decoration say much about the wealth of the bourgeois families of Damascus: superb painted wooden ceilings, stucco decoration above the windows, inlaid stone and wood, marble fountains *(see illustration p 58)*. In one room there is a display of scale models of the city of Damascus along with a small collection of old stamps and postcards. The hammam (very simple) and the kitchens were situated to the right.

*Head towards the Hamidiyeh souk and cross Al-Thawra Street using the raised pedestrian walkway, where the foundations of the abandoned houses descend as far as the bed of the River Barada.*

A number of little streets bustling with shoppers converge on **Marjeh Square**: the River Barada also makes an appearance here. The square used to be the city centre during the French mandate and the terminus for the tram lines. The large column in the centre commemorates the first telegraph link between Damascus and Mecca. This is a very lively part of town (especially at night) where Arab travellers come to do their last-minute shopping before going home. There are **cake shops** (among the best in the country) galore, together with confectioners, restaurants, and shops selling souvenirs and travel accessories.

*Continue as far as Al-Nasr Street, opposite the Hamidiyeh souk, via one of the little streets running slightly uphill from Marjeh Square.*

The avenue 250m to the left leads to the beautiful **Hejaz Station**\* (Map III, B4): an old locomotive adorns the square in front of the station. It serves as a sign for the jolly bar-restaurant that has been set up in one of the old wooden carriages parked on one of the platforms. Hardly any trains now use the station, built by the Ottomans to transport pilgrims from Damascus to Medina. Its ceilings and wooden ticket offices are worth a second glance.

*In the extension of Al-Nasr Street, the first street on the right leads down towards the Soulaymania complex.*

## The Soulaymania complex\*\* (Map III, A3, B3)

This complex, built in the second half of the 16C, is typical of the great Ottoman complexes comprising a mosque and a *madrasa*. Like others in the city, it was used by pilgrims setting off for Mecca.

**The artisans' souk**\*, created by the Syrian authorities to encourage local crafts, is a great success. Small shops *(see the "Making the most of Damascus" section)* line the side of a narrow street which leads to a beautiful Ottoman Koranic school: the **Soulaymania madrasa**. The craftsmen and women practice their trades (pottery, painting on fabric and wood, weaving) in the students' workshops surrounding the courtyard. Behind the ornamental basin, the little mosque *(open during the hours of prayer)* with its richly decorated façade is crowned by a dome. Don't miss the glass-blower in one of the rooms to the right of the entrance.

The modern city

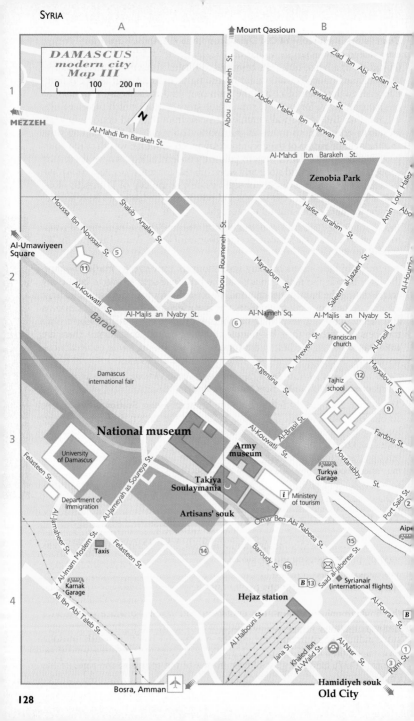

SYRIA

Mount Qassioun

## DAMASCUS
### modern city
### Map III

0    100    200 m

N

MEZZEH

Ziad Ibn Abi Sofian St.

Rawdah St.

Abdel Malek Ibn Marwan St.

Al-Mahdi Ibn Barakeh St.

Al-Mahdi Ibn Barakeh St.

Abou Roumeneh St.

Zenobia Park

Amin Louf Hafez

Abo

Al-Umawiyeen
Square

Mussa Ibn Noussair St.

Shakib Arsalan St.

⑤

⑪

Al-Kouwatli St.

Barada

Al-Majlis an Nyaby St.

Hafez Ibrahim St.

Maysaloun St.

Saleem al-Jazaeri St.

Al-Najmeh Sq.

Al-Majlis an Nyaby St.

Al-Houmra

⑥

Franciscan church

Al-Brasil St.

Damascus
international fair

Argentina St.

A. Mrewed St.

Tajhiz
school

⑫

Maysaloun St.

⑨

**National museum**

University
of Damascus

Al-Jameyah as Soureya St.

Al-Kouwatli St.

Al-Brasil St.

Moutanabby St.

Fardoss St.

**Army
museum**

🚌
Turkya
Garage

Port Said St.

②

Felasteen St.

Department of
Immigration

**Takiya
Soulaymania**

**Artisans' souk**

ℹ Ministry
of tourism

Omar Ben Abi Rabeea St.

Aïpe

Al-Jamaheer St.

Taxis

Felasteen St.

⑭

Baroudy St.

⑮

⑯

Saad al-Jaberee St.

B ⑬

✉

Syrianair
(international flights)

Al-Fourat St.

B

Al-Imam Moslem St.

Karnak
Garage

Ali Ibn Abi Taleb St.

**Hejaz station**

Al Halbouni St.

Jana St.

Khaled Ibn
Al-Walid St.

🕌 Al-Nasr St.

①

③ Rami St.

✈ Bosra, Amman

Hamidiyeh souk
**Old City**

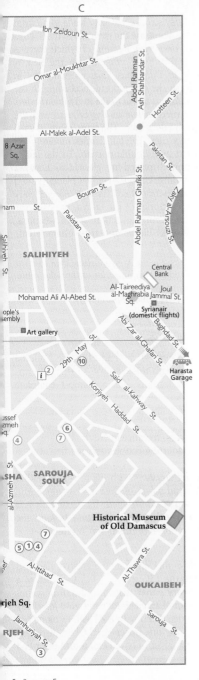

**RESTAURANTS**

| | |
|---|---|
| Al-Arabi | ① |
| Al-Kamal | ② |
| Al-Negma | ③ |
| Al-Rayess | ④ |
| Al-Souwar | ⑤ |
| Chamiat | ⑥ |
| Nadi al-Oumal | ⑦ |

**HOTELS**

| | |
|---|---|
| Alaa Tower "1" | ① |
| Alaa Tower "2" | ② |
| Alaa Tower "4" | ③ |
| Al-Haramaïn | ④ |
| Al-Iwan | ⑤ |
| Al-Majed | ⑥ |
| Al-Rabia | ⑦ |
| Cham Palace | ⑧ |
| Fardoss Tower | ⑨ |
| French Tower | ⑩ |
| Meridien | ⑪ |
| Umayyad | ⑫ |
| Orient Palace | ⑬ |
| Salam | ⑭ |
| Semiramis | ⑮ |
| Sultan | ⑯ |

**The modern city**

Further on, the hustle and bustle of this busy street eventually leads to a haven of peace and quiet, surrounded by tall trees. These are the grounds of the **Takiya Soulaymania**★★ *(open at the hours of prayer, entry free)*, in front of which there is a large ornamental basin. Completed in 1560, six years before the nearby *madrasa*, it introduced the Ottoman style to Damascus. Like its namesake in Istanbul, it was built in honour of Suleiman the Magnificent, according to the plans of the brilliant architect Sinan. Its name of *takiya* (*tekke* in Turkish) refers to a Dervish monastery. The inhabitants used to live in the cells around the basin: Syrians like to have their photograph taken here. The tympanum of each door is decorated with beautiful blue faience tiles. The tall slender minarets rise up from either side of the dome, preceded by a double portico. To the left of the mosque, the capsule of a Soyuz spaceship displayed in a glass kiosk is rather an anachronism. Don't be deterred by the strange collection of war planes parked under the trees: visit the **Army Museum** *(8am-2pm; closed Tuesdays; nominal entry charge)* which occupies the kitchens and refectories of the takiya, opposite the mosque. The first room houses a very interesting collection of old weapons, including magnificent sabres with damascened blades and their characteristic moiré pattern.

*Leave the complex by the door opposite the entrance to the Army Museum, then continue round to the right alongside the fence of the National Museum as far as the ticket office.*

# The National Museum★★ (Map III, A3)
*9am-6pm, winter 4pm; closed Tuesdays;*
*Fridays, 9am-12.30pm/2-6pm;*
*entry charge; allow 2h.*

Before embarking upon a tour of Syria, or even at the end of it, the National Museum is the perfect place to get to grips with this country, so rich in terms of history and archeology. Its priceless collections offer an almost complete panorama of Syria from Antiquity to the Ottoman period, and provide a useful complement to sites that are less exciting visually such as Mari, Ebla and Ugarit by displaying the finds from the sites. In front of the museum is a pleasant garden. Underneath the huge eucalyptus trees, the ancient basalt and limestone statues are silent witnesses to the trysts of courting couples and the fine art students at work.

Behind the ornamental basin, the imposing **façade**★★ with the towers on either side of the entrance comes from the Umayyad palace of Qasr al-Hayr al-Gharbi, whence it was brought stone by stone and re-constructed. Its decoration is a fusion of Hellenistic, Roman and Sassanid styles. The exhibition beyond the entrance hall is devoted to the Umayyad remains of this desert residence.

## Eastern Antiquities
The first room contains several masterpieces that illustrate the creative flair and skill of the artisans of **Ugarit** *(see p 182)* in the 13C and 14C BC: the **head of a man**★★ in ivory inlaid with gold, a fine **ivory panel**★ depicting hunting scenes on both sides, a **horn** (incomplete) made out of an elephant tusk, **gold jewellery** and Canaanite bronze **statuettes of Baal**★ decorated with gold leaf, to name but a few. The pride and joy of the museum is the tiny finger-sized tablet displayed behind a magnifying glass which is the first tablet to have been found inscribed with the **cuneiform alphabet**★★★.

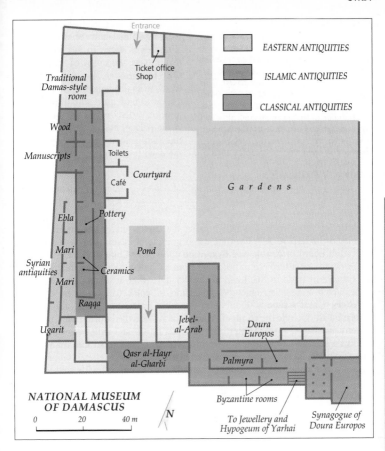

An important collection of tablets is arranged in the display cases on the left of the alphabet while, on the right, a splendid **ivory tray★** from the royal palace at Ugarit is decorated with eagles, their wings outstretched. The African ivory used in such abundance by the artisans of Ugarit was transported up the Nile. The decorative motifs are of Egyptian influence. Although less memorable, there is a second room devoted to finds from Ugarit which contains pottery, weapons and cylinder seals. The many rooms that follow contain finds from the sites of northern Syria and Amrit (dating from the 4th to the 1st millennia BC): note in particular the lovely **model of votive chariots**, the **Sfireh stele** – a treaty written in an Aramaic language – and especially the life-size basalt statue of **Haddad-Yisi★★** with an inscription in Aramaic and Assyrian carved on its robe (9C BC). Its chance discovery in 1979 was of exceptional importance because of the dual inscription in two different alphabets.

The room devoted to finds from **Ebla** (*see p 243*) begins with an interesting **cult basin** with two compartments and there are numerous tablets on display. The two rooms devoted to the **Mari** civilisation (*see p 265*) contain a fine collection

131

### The Ugarit Alphabet

It consisted of 27 consonants, sometimes completed by three additional signs, as in this case. It was read from left to right like Babylonian, although the later Semitic alphabets were read from right to left. This tablet served as a model for students practising writing. As literacy levels rose, the number of letters multiplied, although this was at the expense of the scribes, who had previously been the only ones to master the collection of complex signs.

of **statues**★★ of people at prayer, wearing animal-hair robes *(kaunakès)*. Their eyes were inlaid with lapis lazuli. Note the statue of the minstrel **Our-Nanshe**★★★, his legs crossed. Don't miss the **treasure of Ur**, a fine collection of gold and lapis lazuli jewellery discovered in the Presargonic palace, including an extraordinary lapis lazuli **pectoral**★★ decorated with an eagle.

## Islamic Antiquities

*The tour of the museum continues with the collections of Islamic antiquities. Visitors wishing to look at the exhibits chronologically should go straight to the department of classical antiquities.*

The **models** from **Raqqa,** which became the capital under Caliph Haroun al-Rachid in the late 8C AD, illustrate the beginning of Islam in Syria. There is an important hoard of **Arabic and Byzantine coins**. The **Chinese rider**★★ mounted on a dragon, a masterpiece in porcelain from a Chinese workshop, highlights the importance of trade in this town in the 9C. The room extends into a long corridor which houses an extensive collection of **coins** (displayed by dynasty), **jewellery**★★ and **weapons**. Exhibits in the other rooms to the left, also devoted to Islamic art, include the **tomb** of Prince Balakh (who died during the Crusades), a pretty jar-shaped basin, a limestone tile depicting a bearer with two ewers. There follows a splendid collection of **ceramics** and pottery. The **Arabic manuscripts** room (exhibits include copies of the Koran, scientific texts, literary commentaries) houses a rich collection of beautiful manuscripts illuminated with gold leaf, and hand-written documents dating from the first centuries of Islam. A side room contains scientific instruments such as astrolabes and compasses, and a copy of the **Book of Kings**★ by the Persian poet Ferdowsi (1592). The last room contains a display of **wooden** exhibits, some of which are painted, others bearing examples of calligraphy. The **tomb**★ of Khaled Ibn al-Walid was presented by Baybars.

## Classical Antiquities

In this section, which concentrates essentially on the Roman and Byzantine periods, the most fascinating rooms are the ones devoted to the Doura Europos Synagogue and the Hypogeum of Yarhai from Palmyra.

The first room on the left is devoted to **Jebel al-Arab** and the Hauran sites, situated to the south of Damascus. On the wall, note the large mosaic depicting an **allegorical scene** from Shahba and, in the room at the end, the **sarcophagus**★ found at Rastan (3C AD) which is decorated with an extraordinary relief of a battle scene. A hall (with a fine collection of Venuses) leads to the porticoed courtyard in front of the re-construction of the **Doura Europos Synagogue**★★ (3C AD) *(ask the custodian to open up the building itself, situated outside the main museum)*. This is one of the most remarkable examples of synagogues to survive from Antiquity, and the only one to be decorated with human forms, normally forbidden by the Jewish religion. Although the layout of the complex – a rectangular room lined with benches that could accommodate 120 worshippers – is very simple, the frescoes, miraculously well-preserved and mounted at the museum, are quite exceptional. The walls are divided into five registers, the three central ones drawing their inspiration from the Old Testament. To the right of the niche of the Torah, the best-preserved part of the frescoes, up in one of the top registers, depicts a scene from the Exodus (the hand of God guiding Moses and his people), just above a scene depicting the Temple of Solomon in Jerusalem. In a scene in a lower register, two women hold Moses, saved from the waters by the pharaoh's daughter.

The steps in the hall of mosaics lead down to the **Hypogeum of Yarhai**★★ (2C AD), a typical example of the interior of a tomb from Palmyra. In front of the tomb of the head of the family, the numerous funerary busts that sealed the loculi (shelves for sarcophagi) constitute an extraordinary portrait gallery.

To the right of the steps, the rather uninspiring **Byzantine rooms** contain fragments of wall painting (12C), Syriac manuscripts and icons, and Coptic chancels and fabrics. The **Rassafa treasure**★★, which is part of this collection, is rarely on display.

The room devoted to **Palmyra** contains some fine **statues**★★, and the **Cassiopeia mosaic**. The **Doura Europos** room contains large **frescoes** from the temple of the gods atPalmyra and a **caparison** (part of a horse's armour), not terribly well preserved.

The **jewellery room**★ situated on the first floor of the museum (*opened on request*) houses a splendid collection of jewels and a silver **box** from the Homs region.

# Making the most of Damascus

## COMING AND GOING

**By air –** The international airport at Damascus lies 30km from the town centre (30min by car).

All the taxi companies run a service from the town centre for US$20, but if you pay in local currency it will only cost you about S£400-500. Car hire is possible at the airport (Europcar and 3 local firms). There is a bank open 24 hours a day, a post office and telephone kiosks.

A blue and white bus with wooden seats and rickety windows also runs between the airport and the town centre, with departures every 30min from 6am-midnight, for S£10.

Domestic flights leave from the same terminal. To get to the airport, book a taxi the previous day if you are catching a night flight (allow around S£400), or you can get the bus from in front of the Kairouan Hotel in the town centre. Your baggage will be searched before it can be checked in, then you must buy a fiscal stamp for S£200 which you must give to the agent who deals with the police formalities. The tiny duty-free shop is worth a visit, especially for cigarettes.

**By train –** Bookings are made in the impressive Hedjaz train station in the town centre, but the majority of departures are from the Khaddam station, 4km to the south. There are daily sleeper trains with couchettes which leave at midnight for Aleppo (6hr), continuing to Deir ez-Zor and Qamishli. A train leaves for Amman every Sunday at 7am (7hr). There are also trains for Lattakia and Tartus.

**By bus –** Damascus has several bus stations:

*Harasta Garage*, near Al-Abassiyyeen Sq (Map 1), in a street parallel to the Homs road. To find it, ask for "Pullman Harasta". The majority of bus companies use this station. It is best to book your ticket at least half a day ahead. There are departures for the whole of Syria from this bus station:

Damascus Tour, Al-Ahliah and Zeitouni companies: Homs (2hr), Hama (2hr 30min), Aleppo (4hr).

Djameel, Izla and Al-Fourat companies: Palmyra (4hr), Deir ez-Zor.

Qadmous company: Tartus (3hr), Lattakia (5hr).

*Karnak Garage* (Map III A4), behind the Baramka bus station. Departures for all towns in Syria. There are also daily departures for all the major towns in the Middle East. Bus for Jordan, US$5 (7am and 3pm), but also Kuwait, Beirut, and the Gulf State capitals.

**Turkiya Garage** (Map III B3), Al-Kouwatli St, opposite the Semiramis Hotel, specialises in buses to Turkey. A bus to Istanbul costs around S£1 200 and leaves, for example, at 10pm, arriving in Istanbul at 7am two days later (33hr journey). There is a 4-hr break at Antioch on the first morning, and breakfast is included!

**By shared taxi –** The main "service taxi" station is next to the Karnak bus station. There are frequent departures all day and night, as soon as the taxi is full, for Beirut (3hr) or Amman (5hr). S£400-500 per person.

### GETTING AROUND

The main places of interest in Damascus lie close to each other, mostly within a 2km area. The microbuses (which cost between S£3-5) are very frequent but only have indications marked in Arabic. Taxis are a better idea.

**By taxi –** There are plenty of yellow taxis, which increasingly have taxi meters. A fare will rarely exceed S£25 within the city centre, or S£50 for a longer distance. When the meter is working (and if not, ask why not) it is usual to round the fare up to the nearest S£5 or S£10. A one-way trip to Mount Qassioun costs S£100.

**Car hire –** See also under travel agents. Prices are always given in dollars.

**Europcar**, at the airport, ☎ (11) 543 15 36, or the Meridien Hotel, ☎ (11) 222 92 00. Prices start from US$43 for unlimited kilometres. Add an extra US$6 for insurance. Minimum hire period of 3 days (with 2 days limited kilometres). If possible, check the condition of the vehicle before hiring it, as small cars in particular may be in poor condition.

**Chamcar**, Cham Palace Hotel, Maysaloun St, ☎ (11)223 23 00, Fax (11) 221 23 98. Prices start at US$95 for a Ford Tempo, including 250 kilometres, a chauffeur, petrol and fully compre-

hensive insurance. Allow an extra US$25 for the chauffeur's accommodation per night. Self-drive car hire, excluding petrol starts from US$46. You can also hire a chauffeur-driven car by the hour. Car hire with chauffeur: 3 days minimum.

**Marmou**, Maysaloun St, further along from the Cham Palace, ☎ (11) 333 59 59, Fax (11) 232 30 84. A fleet of Opel and Mazda cars. A chauffeur costs an extra US$100 per day, fully comprehensive insurance US$10. A Mazda 323 (the most popular car for hire in Syria) will cost around US$36 per day or US$239 per week with unlimited kilometres. A credit card can be used as a deposit, or US$1,000. Cars must be collected at and returned to Damascus.

### ADDRESS BOOK

**Tourist information** (Map III C3) – 29 May St. Plans of Damascus and Syria are available as well as some practical information. There is a second information bureau near the entrance to the craft souk.

**Travel agents – Cham Tour**, Cham Palace Hotel, (Map III C3), Maysaloun St. ☎ (11) 223 23 00, Fax (11) 221 23 98. There is a contact either in Paris, ☎ (33) 142 99 87 00 (though not in London), or in the US, ☎ (202) 785 1355. Luxury personalised tours, staying in Cham hotels, naturally. Made-to-measure tours, with or without a guide.

**Allied Tours**, Marjeh Sq. (Map III B4), ☎ (11) 222 56 73, Fax (11) 224 52 41. An agency experienced in top-of-the-range excursions for individuals or groups. Original ideas, such as a mini-cruise on the Euphrates.

**Mimosa**, town centre, 300m from the Hedjaz train station (Map III B4) along the road which follows the platforms, ☎ (11) 223 57 07, Fax (11) 222 46 27. Daily guided visits of Damascus (half or whole day, US$29), day excursion to Maaloula and Seydnaya (US$35) or Palmyra (US$39). Car hire: US$28 with 125km per day, or US$43 with unlimited kilometres, for a Renault 19. Add US$17 for a guide and US$7 for a chauffeur.

**Atlas,** Fardoss St, on the 5th floor of the building opposite the travel agent of this name (Map III B3), ☎ (11) 221 52 75, Fax (11) 222 18 07. Daily guided visit of Damascus; no minimum group size required. Various excursions.

**Syrian Holidays,** Hamra St, ☎ (11) 331 31 86, Fax (11) 332 29 68. A Syrian tour operator. Car hire, tours of Damascus by bike. Young lively team, who will reply to your faxes within 24 hours. Camel excursions around Palmyra.

**Seydnaya Travel and Tourism,** at Seydnaya, 30km from Damascus, but you can contact them by telephone ☎ (11) 595 17 02, Fax (11) 595 30 03. A small, efficiently run agency, whose director, Mr Al-Maarri, will organise made-to-measure excursions full of surprises. Small groups should not hesitate to get in touch. Reasonable prices.

**Airline companies –** Nearly all the international airline companies have offices either in Port Said St or in Fardoss St, near the Cham Palace Hotel.

**Syrian Arab Airlines** (international flights), Hedjaz Sq (Map III B4), opposite the main post office. ☎ (11) 222 90 00.

**Syrian Arab Airlines** (domestic flights) (Map III C2) ☎ (11) 222 90 00. Domestic flights can be booked in the agency opposite the central bank.

**Consulate/Embassies – Britain:** Kurd Ali St, Kotob Building, Malki, Damascus, ☎ (11) 373 92 43, Fax (11) 371 35 92

**USA:** Al-Mansour St, Abu Roumaneh, Damascus, ☎ (11) 333 28 14/23 15, Fax (11) 224 79 38

**Canada:** Al-Mezzeh (near Razi Hospital), Damascus, ☎ (11) 223 68 92/ 05 35

**Australia:** Farabi St, Al-Mezzeh, Damascus, ☎ (11) 666 43 17, Fax (11) 662 11 95

**Post/Telephone – Main Post Office** (Map III B4), Port Said St. A large building which is reached by a flight of steps, with a special counter for selling stamps. Letter box inside. Poste restante service. Parcel service in an adjoining building.

**Telephone** (Map III B4) Al-Nasr Ave, near the Hedjaz station. A dozen or so kiosks inside the building. Kiosks taking coins, outside the building, are used only for calls within the city, or within Syria. You can send and receive faxes here, Fax (11) 223 43 36.

**Express courrier, DHL,** ☎ (11) 222 76 92.

**Bank/Currency exchange – Commercial Bank of Syria,** Youssef al-Azmeh St, near the Cham Hotel. Travellers' cheques.

**Exchange bureau,** Marjeh St, on the same side as the travel agents. 9am-9pm. Cash and travellers' cheques. There is another bureau opposite the Hedjaz station, near the Orient Hotel, providing the same service, as well as at the Meridien hotel and in Youssef al-Azmeh Sq.

**American Express,** PO Box 1373, Balkis St, ☎ (11) 221 78 13, Fax (11) 221 79 38.

**Medical service –** There are several **pharmacies** in the new town. There is one in Port Said St, just before Youssef al-Azmeh Sq. Your embassy should be able to recommend a hospital or doctor, if needed.

**Visa extension –** The immigration department (Map III A3) is found behind the Syrian press agency Sanaa. Open 8.30am-1pm. A one-month extension takes 24hr to obtain. You will need 4 identity photos. There is a photography service just in front of the building, where your passport photograph can be reproduced in a few minutes.

## WHERE TO STAY

As a capital city, Damascus has a huge choice of hotels to suit all budgets, although strangely no hotels in the old city.

**Alaa Tower Hotel chain,** ☎/Fax (11) 231 12 21 for the central booking service for all the hotels in this chain, of which there are six in Damascus alone. It is on the way to becoming a more affordable version of the Cham hotel chain, with an identical standard of comfort in all its hotels. The rooms are small but well equipped, with minibar, air conditioning, telephone, television and a small but functional en-suite

**Making the most of Damascus**

**Damascus**

bathroom with shower. Impeccable room service, thanks to the many staff. All hotels provide breakfast.

### • Sarouja Souk and Basha District
(Map III B3, C4)

*Under US$20*

The Sarouja area is under threat from developers, but for the moment retains the charm of the real Damascus, with its houses with wooden balconies. The pedestrian-only streets are paved and shady, and the area is handy for the town centre and the airport bus, as well as having little shops selling *hummus* and *fuul*, and laundries – in fact everything to make life easy for the traveller. The area is so pretty and the prices so reasonable that the lack of comfort becomes bearable. Around S£300 per person, for a dormitory-type room for up to 4 people, or a single or double room.

**Al-Haramain Hotel**, Bahsa St, Sarouja, ☎ (11) 231 94 89, Fax (11) 231 42 99 – 14rm ⚊ CC There is a small patio, covered in winter. This is a favourite among those with a limited budget of all ages, because of its friendly atmosphere. Only 2 showers in the basement, but the water is always hot. Avoid the ground floor. Refrigerator. The visitors' book is an excellent means of exchanging practical information. Reservation essential all year if arriving in the evening.

**Al-Rabia Hotel**, Bahsa St, Sarouja, ☎ (11) 231 83 74, Fax (11) 231 18 75 – 17rm ⚊ ♪ CC 10m from the above. The large shady patio, with a fountain, is a haven of peace and a good place to meet other travellers, as well as the Syrians who also use the hotel. Some ground-floor rooms have a shower. The beds are being replaced, not before time. Sleeping on the roof is an option.

*From US$40-60*

☺ **Alaa Tower Hotel n° 1**, opposite the French cultural centre, ☎ (11) 231 12 21 – 34rm ⚊ 🖻 ♪ TV ✕ CC The quietest of this chain of hotels, described at the beginning of this section.

☺ **Alaa Tower Hotel n° 2**, near the airport bus terminus, ☎ (11) 231 13 88 – 35rm ⚊ 🖻 ♪ TV ✕ CC Ideal for your first night in Damascus. See description at the beginning of this section.

*From US$55-75*

**Al-Iwan Hotel**, Al-Basha St, ☎ (11) 232 14 76, Fax (11) 231 52 24 – 55rm ⚊ 🖻 ♪ TV ✕ CC Comfortable rooms in this well-sited hotel, along Al-Ittihad Ave. Generous buffet breakfast served on the mezzanine.

### • Marjeh District
(Map III C3-4)

This area has plenty of hotels, though few of them are to be recommended, unfortunately, as Marjeh is also the red light district. There are a few exceptions, but the Basha area on the other side of the Barada river is preferable, where there are several mid-priced hotels.

*From US$40-50*

**Alaa Tower Hotel n° 4**, Al-thawra St, ☎ (11) 223 81 91 – 34rm ⚊ 🖻 ♪ TV ✕ CC A favourite place to stay for Hamidiyeh souk enthusiasts. Lovely view of the Umayyad mosque from some rooms. See description at the beginning of this section.

*From US$50-65*

☺ **Al-Majed Hotel**, behind the Al-Soufara cinema, opposite the tourist office, ☎ (11) 232 33 01, Fax (11) 232 33 04 – 50rm ⚊ 🖻 ♪ TV ✕ CC This peaceful hotel is off the main streets. Comfortable, spacious rooms, some even have a small kitchen. Pretty view over the old Sarouja district and you can count the satellite dishes to get to sleep. The panoramic restaurant is open until 2am. Hearty breakfast.

**French Tower**, 29th May St., ☎ (11) 231 40 00, Fax (11) 231 40 02 233 – 16rm ⚊ 🖻 ♪ TV On the fourth floor (lift) of a small modern building. Small, well-equipped rooms, impeccably clean. From the 5th-floor terrace, you can enjoy the cool evening air with an extensive view over the city and Mount Qassioun. Friendly atmosphere.

### • Hedjaz station district
(Map III A4-B4)

*From US$25-40*

There are several simple hotels behind the post office, of which we have listed two of the more comfortable.

**Salam**, Ibin Sina St., Halbony, ☎ (11) 221 97 64, Fax (11) 231 74 57 233 – 17rm ⚊ 🖻 TV Excellent value for money. This clean, comfortable hotel has recently been renovated, and has the added advantage of being well situated, in a central yet quiet district.

**Sultan Hotel**, Baroudy St, ☎ (11) 222 57 68 – 31rm ⌁ / 🍴 ⚲ A constant stream of mainly western visitors. Between the Hedjaz station and the craft souk. Some rooms have en-suite bathrooms. Room prices vary according to the view, which is understandable, as the street side is unbearable. The pleasant receptionists will give advice and help book buses and hotels for the rest of your trip.

**Orient Palace Hotel**, Hedjaz Sq, ☎ (11) – 80rm ⌁'🍴 ⚲ 📺 Opposite Hedjaz station. Noisy and slightly shabby, but still has a certain charm. The attractive façade dates back to the days of the French mandate.

*From US$130-160*

**Semiramis Hotel**, Victoria Bridge, ☎ (11) 223 35 55, Fax (11) 221 67 97 – 116rm ⌁ 🍴 ⚲ 📺 ✕ ⚲ CC The most centrally situated of the luxuryclass hotels. Very well equipped, spacious rooms. Fitness centre. A wide range of services.

• **Cham Palace district**
(Map III B3)
This is where the really comfortable hotels are found, but still fairly close to the old town. In the evening Maysaloun St is full of activity, with restaurants, icecream parlours and pastry shops open until 11pm.

*From US$100-130*

**Umayyad Hotel**, Al-Brasil St, ☎ (11) 221 77 00, Fax (11) 221 35 16 – 80rm ⌁ 🍴 ⚲ 📺 ✕ CC A very pleasant hotel behind the Taziz school, equally suitable for businessmen and travellers alike. Rooms with balconies. Al-Andaloussia restaurant with hanging garden and lovely view over the city.

**Fardoss Tower Hotel**, Fardoss St, ☎ (11) 223 21 00, Fax (11) 223 56 02 – 99rm ⌁ 🍴 ⚲ 📺 ✕ ⚲ CC Building with metallic blue windows, not far from Cham Hotel. A little expensive but very well situated.

*Over US$160*

**Cham Palace Hotel**, Maysaloun St, ☎ (11) 223 23 00, Fax (11) 222 61 80 – 400rm ⌁ 🍴 ⚲ 📺 ✕ ⚲ CC A gigantic town-centre complex in red and gold near the Youssef al-Azmeh Sq. Much frequented by groups, although the upper floors can be cold. Lovely view of the lights of Mount Qassioun from some rooms. A collection of shops on the ground floor, among them the only Chinese restaurant in the country, and a revolving restaurant. Bowling alley, fitness centre, sauna, travel agent.

• **On the Mezzeh road**
(Map III A1-2)
Going along Al-Kouwatli Ave, the road passes beside the Damascus international fair and the Barada river.

*Over US$160*

**Meridien Hotel**, Al-Kouwatli Ave, ☎ (11) 373 87 30, Fax (11) 373 86 61 – 350rm ⌁ 🍴 ⚲ 📺 ✕ ⚲ ✗ CC Photographs on display record Jacques Chirac's visit in 1996. This hotel has every comfort, though is rather impersonal, and is situated opposite the international fair. Well-stocked library. Europcar office in the entrance hall.

• **On the Homs road**
*Under US$20*
**New Kaboun campsite**, 7km from the town centre, along the Homs motorway, ☎ (11) 512 62 35. Shade, electricity and clean toilets.

## EATING OUT

As far as restaurants are concerned, Damascus has by far the widest choice in the whole of Syria. Even though the setting is sometimes more important than the food, there are some excellent restaurants producing fine local dishes. Don't miss a visit to one of the restaurants which have opened in the traditional town houses in the Bab Charqui district.

• **Marjeh District**
(Map III B4)
The popular restaurants are found in this district, where you will find efficient service and good plain cooking. The menu is mostly limited to chicken, kebabs and

*Making the most of Damascus*

traditional *meze*. Try *fateh*, a Damascus speciality, or delicious *bamia* (okra or 'Greek horns') to accompany a meat dish.

*Under US$10*

**Al-Arabi, Al-Arabi 2**, two restaurants with the same name in a pedestrian cul-de-sac off Marjeh Sq, ☎ (11) 221 21 93. The second one is in a more agreeable setting. Simple cooking, with all the classic Syrian dishes: *frikeh*, *bamia*, kebabs, chicken, *kebbeh* and *fateh*. Breakfast is served here. Pleasant terrace.

**Al-Negma**, Rami St. A small, simple restaurant, where you can have a good Syrian breakfast (eggs, cheese, yoghurt, olives) or sample classic Middle Eastern dishes (meze, kebabs).

• **Sarouja Souk and Basha District** (Map III C3)

In this area you will find simple, good value restaurants, serving local dishes.

*Under US$10*

**Nadi al-Oumal**, opposite the Al-Majed Hotel, ☎ (11) 231 87 69. ▼ Closed at lunchtime and on Fridays. A dream setting, complete with fountain, for sampling delicately seasoned grilled fish, olive salad and a few *beurek*. This lovely old house with a porch is never empty. Simple and very good value, the "workers' club" is a meeting place for the Damascene intelligentsia.

**Al-Kamal**, 29th May St, behind the tourist office, ☎ (11) 232 35 72. Rather brash decor, but the cooking and service are impeccable. Delicious *meze*. *Saudi kabsa, makloubeh*. Rather syrupy music.

**Al-Rayess**, Youssef al-Azmeh Sq, ☎ (11) 231 72 98. ▼ Closed on Fridays. With its rather faded decor, a slightly seedy place where the locals take large swigs of arak (the smell of aniseed will hit you on entering). Perfectly good menu at S£120.

• **Hamidiyeh souk district** (Map II B2)

The old town has no hotels, but three restaurants which attract a cosmopolitan clientele of Syrians, Lebanese, expatriates and tourists. On your way there, you will notice that the Hamidiyeh souk turns into a flea market after 8pm.

*Under US$10*

**Aboul-Ezz**, the most popular restaurant in Damascus, is situated in the Hamidiyeh souk, in the last street on the left before you reach the great mosque. ☎ (11) 221 81 74. Takeaway *sfiha* on the ground floor. Several dining rooms on the first floor. Those who enjoy Arab music will be in heaven here, especially when the lights dim and the tempo increases for the whirling dervishes. There are performances every evening at around 9.30pm. The atmosphere reaches its climax when the Lebanese customers dance on the tables on Saturday evenings. Watch out for the bill, which can sometimes be incredible. Make sure you agree the price when you are ordering.

**Jabri House**, Al-Sawaf St., ☎ (11) 541 62 54. Hardly noticeable from the street, with its small wooden door and discreet sign, this splendid 18C Ottoman mansion has been converted to a restaurant. The young of Damascus come here to dine, or simply to drink tea and smoke a water pipe around the fountain, under the porch or in the attractive dining room. The menu is restricted mostly to classic meze, salads and fateh (a local speciality based on hot humus, chicken and pitta bread). Arrive early as it is often full.

*Over US$10*

**Umayyad Palace**, M. Assaghir St, ☎ (11) 222 08 26. This restaurant owes its success to its copious buffet, as well as to the musicians and dervishes who perform here. Open daily 12noon-4.30pm/8pm-12midnight. The excellent Syrian food (*meze*, hot dishes, desserts), is served on large copper trays. Antique decor.

• **Bab Charqi district** (Map II C3-4, D4)

*Over US$10*

There are several rather chic restaurants in this district, where Syrian families go to eat.

**La Guitare**, Haret al-Zaytoun St, ☎ (11) 541 98 23. ▼ CC A covered patio for candlelit dinners. Be prepared for a visit to your table by strolling singers and players. Good Italian cooking: pasta,

Damascus

minestrone, Parma ham, but no pizzas. Attractive glasswork and fountain. Romantic.

**Casablanca**, Ananias St, ☎ (11) 543 48 14. ♥ cc Very chic, near the Piano and opposite St George's church. The menu includes fish and prawns, as well as French cuisine. Smart, but open to everyone, at lunchtime as well as the evening, until midnight.

**Old Town**, Al-Ameen St, Talee al-Feddah, ☎ (11) 542 80 88. ♥ cc A tunnelled courtyard just behind the modern building of the Greek Orthodox bishop's palace. Bar under the porch and two dining rooms for the winter. A limited menu, where you will find French as well as Syrian cooking. International clientele as well as businessmen. Good value.

**Piano**, Ananias St, ☎ (11) 543 03 75. ♥ cc For couples only. Small dining room with karaoke. The photos at the entrance give an idea of the crazy atmosphere which takes over on certain evenings. Would-be singers are even filmed! In the bar there is a piano (of course) and television. Tiny but unique.

**Zeitouna**, in the same street as La Guitare, ☎ (11) 543 13 24. ♥ cc Courtyard with fountain and a first-floor ("private") dining room where there is singing and dancing every evening from 10pm. French, Italian and Syrian cuisine is served in a charming setting.

● **Maysaloun and Abu Roumaneh St** (Map III A2, B2-3)

*Under US$10*

**Chamiat**, Al-Najmeh St, Abou Roumaneh, ☎ (11) 222 72 70. Much frequented by foreign students studying in Damascus, and understandably, as here you will find a friendly welcome, and good, plain, almost family cooking. But the restaurant is tiny, so avoid coming in large groups, two at most. If fatty cooking doesn't upset you, try the *fateh*. Open 24 hours a day.

**Al-Souwar**, Moussa Ibn Noussair St, ☎ (11) 331 95 68. Don't be put off by this restaurant's façade, which looks something like a Roman temple, pediment and all. The cooking is excellent and good value. Families tend to come

here a lot. Fine white table linen and well-lit decor. A little smart, but very affordable.

*Over US$10*

**L'Etoile d'Or**, Cham Hotel. Access via a lift, on the left of the main hotel entrance. ♥ This revolving panoramic restaurant is open from 1pm-3.30pm and 8pm-12midnight. *Meze*, grills. By the time your meal is over, you will have visited the whole of Damascus without leaving your table. It almost seems a shame to come here in the evening; lunchtime is a better opportunity to appreciate the magnificent view of the city.

● **Rabweh (Map I)**

For a change of scene, take a taxi and ask to be taken to Rabweh. In 10 minutes you will be on the outskirts of Damascus (for under S£100), where the Barada river runs through a gorge. There are several open-air restaurants serving good, simple Syrian cooking, at lunchtime and in the evening. Relaxed atmosphere. Ideal in summer.

## HAVING A DRINK

### Cafés, bars, tea shops

*Nofara* (Map II B2) An extraordinary café which is sometimes enlivened by the presence of a storyteller towards the end of the afternoon. Why not go the whole way and order a water pipe and a *zourate* (herbal tea).

**Bakdache** (Map II B2), the best ice cream parlour in Syria, in the Hamidiyeh souk. As well as ice cream (*bouza*), try the rice pudding (*mouhalabiyeh*).

## OTHER THINGS TO DO

**Hammam – Hammam al-Nouri** (Map II B3), Bzouriyeh souk. A sure way to relax. This historic monument has been restored to use. Men only. Allow S$250. Open until midnight.

**Hammam al-Zahiriyya** (Map II B2), next door to the Madrassa Zahiriyya, renovated and impeccably clean. Open until midnight.

**Outdoor pursuits – Meridien Hotel swimming pool**, S£600 for non-residents.

**Making the most of Damascus**

Damascus

## SHOPPING GUIDE

You will probably want to shop either in the authentic atmosphere of the Hamidiyeh souk, or at the slightly more peaceful craft souk in the Takiya Soulaymania gardens. Avoid the Bab Charqui district, where prices tend to be excessively high.

**Craft souk** (Map III B3). Practically all the country's craft products can be found here: copperware, marquetry, Egyptian glasses, robes (*jellabas*), paintings, hand-made pottery, hand-blown glass, embroidered garments, brocades, *al-ajami* paintings on wood, textiles, reproduction antiques, cushions, dresses, tablecloths, printed cloth from Hama, jewellery. Credit cards are sometimes accepted.

**Western items** – Cornflakes, instant coffee, toothbrushes and any other items you are missing can be found in the district near Maysaloun St (Map III B2), between the Catholic church and Abu Roumaneh St, or else in Marjeh Sq (Map III C4).

**Antiques and brocades** – *Tony Stephan* (Map II B2), Hamidiyeh souk. The widest choice of brocades and some antiques.

**Local delicacies** – A small selection for the most demanding gourmets.

**Marjeh Sq** (Map III C4), a wide choice of pastries and sweets. Freshness guaranteed. Delicious baklavas (S£200 per kilo). Crystallised fruits (they should be plump, not wrinkled).

**Bzouriyeh souk** (Map II B2), for the best choice of spices. Stock up with saffron from Mechhed. A wide selection of individually wrapped pistachio nougats.

**Ghraoui** (Map III B3), Port Said St. Closed on Fridays. Damascus's famous chocolate manufacturer proudly displays the awards won in different international fairs. Nougat chocolate and cardamom-flavoured chocolate, pistachio paste and crystallised fruit chocolates (S£680 per kilo). Pretty boxes for gourmet gifts. Plain crystallised fruits as well, such as the delicious apricots with pistachios (S£400 per kilo).

**Art galleries** – *Damascus art gallery* (Map III C2), in a pretty pedestrianised street near the parliament building. A lively gallery which changes its exhibitions frequently. Syrian and other Arab artists. Paintings and sculptures, for an original souvenir.

**Clothing** – The *Adidas*, *Benetton* and *Puma* shops sell models which are not found in Europe, and which are manufactured under franchise in Syria. Worth seeing. There are several clothes shops at Salihiyeh (pedestrianised street) behind the Cham Hotel.

*Ahmad Al-Mallah* (Map II A2), Midhat Pasha souk, near the Khan al-Zeit. A clothes shop which mixes fashion and tradition. A selection of embroidered waistcoats (S£4 000), winter coats (S£8 000), but also shawls and embroidered headbands at more reasonable prices. Excellent quality.

**Photography development** – If you can't wait until you get home! *Pluto*, Maysaloun St (Map III B3), near the Cham Hotel, with a sign saying Kodak Express. Excellent results for colour prints (only) in a few hours. Development and printing, 36 exposures: S£400.

*Vahe Shahinian*, next to the Sultan Hotel (Map III B4). Fast development. Good choice of postcards.

**International bookshops** – In the bigger hotels. The Meridien has the widest choice. Guidebooks are not usually available in Syria.

**Family bookshop** (Map III B2), Al-Najmeh Sq. The biggest western bookstore, with plenty of books in English and French. Novels, history, archeology, press. Closed on Sundays.

*Avicenne* (Map III B3), next to the Umayyad Hotel. A good supply of English and French books. Magazines. Small specialised guides on Syria (Doura Europos, Krak des Chevaliers). Art and cookery books. Lebanese newspapers.

An iwan in Old Damascus

# VILLAGES OF THE QALAMOUN⋆
Tour of 119km leaving from Damascus – Allow a whole day
Perfect excursion on the way to Homs

**Not to be missed**
The Seydnaya Monastery
The village of Maalula

**And remember...**
Lunch at one of Seydnaya's large and lively restaurants

The plateaux of the Qalamoun lie north of Damascus, set before the arid eastern buttress of the Anti-Lebanon, and overlooked by towering ochre-coloured escarpments. Conditions are harsh here because of the high altitude (1000-2000m above sea level), and what few settlements there are, huddle around the rare springs and natural oases. The modern motorway from Damascus to Homs across the Qalamoun Massif provides access to three of these mountain communities namely those at Alqutayfeh, al-Nebek and Deir Attiyeh. Now linked to the capital, these places have become heavily built up over the past few years. A smaller road, meanwhile, leads west through more authentic villages such as Attal, Mnin and Seydnaya - which has an important Greek Orthodox convent, and Maalula where the houses are painted a pretty blue. Remote and isolated for such a long time, this area retains its distinctive character, and villages predominantly populated with Christians have developed into major pilgrimage centres. The inhabitants of Maalula still speak Aramaic, the language spoken by Christ. Both Syrians and Lebanese flock in their droves to Maalula and to Seydnaya in particular, to celebrate holy days and religious festivals. As a result, several restaurants have sprung up to cater for pilgrims, which have contracted Lebanese celebrities to come and entertain the crowds, who are only too happy to get up and dance after a few swigs of arak. Even on the hottest summer days, the light-hearted atmosphere and the cool shade provide a welcome escape from the torrid heat of the towns.

*Leave Damascus along the road left opposite the entrance to the Hamidiyeh souk. Continue through the suburbs of Barzeh and, 12km further on, is the village of Attal, picturesquely situated in a little valley which is not dissimilar to the Barada Valley. 5km before Seydnaya, several restaurants much frequented by Damascenes on public holidays, herald the village of Seydnaya itself.*

■ **Seydnaya —** The village stretches to the foot of the rocky mound on which the convent is built.

*Turn off the main road, drive through the village and around the right-hand side of the mound to the car park, which is located at the foot of the stairs leading up to the convent.*

The **Convent of Our Lady of Seydnaya**⋆ *(No charge)* might well be taken for a fortress if it were not for the domes and bell-towers towering above its high walls. The Greek Orthodox convent is said to be the second most-visited pilgrimage site in the Middle East after Jerusalem: an assertion confirmed by the affluence of Syrian and Lebanese Christians and Muslims alike, who pour into the region at weekends to pray before the holy image. It is said that the "Chaghoura" is a replica of one of the icons painted by St Luke the Evangelist. It is housed in the little **Chapel of Our Lady**⋆ *(at the far end of the courtyard on the right near the entrance to the convent; shoes should be removed at the entrance).* Inside, the air is heavy with incense and the atmosphere conducive to

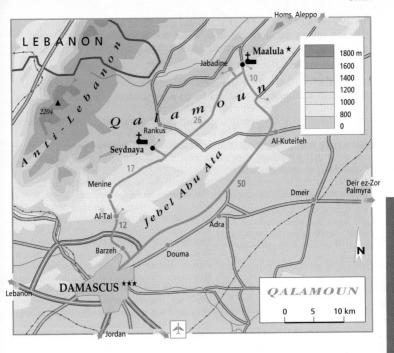

meditation. Holy oil burns in front of the icon where visitors fall to their knees: take care not to disturb those at prayer. It is difficult to make out the arrangement of the **convent** interior what with the proliferation of intercommunicating churches, courtyards and covered passageways on several levels. The convent is home to a community of 30 nuns *(hajjé)*, attired in black from top to toe, who run an orphanage.

On the way back down from the convent, you will notice the **Cave of Idols** 200m below the car park, with its carved frontispiece. At the intersection below the convent lie the ruins of the **Church of St Peter**, the earliest Roman stone building in Seydnaya.

Additional pilgrim shrines are dotted around Seydnaya, some erected on the foundations of ancient Roman buildings. The **Monastery of St Thomas** lies 2km away on a hill dominating the town. The **Cherubim Monastery** *(7km north of Seydnaya)*, rebuilt in 1982 near the summit of Mount Qalamoun (1 910m), sits on the site of an ancient monastery destroyed in the 16C: it is cool up there (freezing more like) all year round and the **view**★★ stretches for miles.

**St Luke, patron saint of painters**
Tradition attributes three icons of the Virgin Mary to St Luke, author of the third Gospel and the Acts of the Apostles. Painted from life, the spiritual power of Mary is supposed to be transmitted to all the copies that faithfully reproduce her features. One of these icons, acquired by the wife of Theodosius II in Palestine (in the 5C) was responsible for popularising the image of the Virgin and Child in Constantinople. Before long, St Luke was adopted as the patron saint of painters, giving his name to several guilds and artistic academies in places like Venice. In the 15C, the subject of "St Luke painting the Virgin Mary" is thought to have founded the tradition of the self-portrait with the painter portraying himself with the features of the Evangelist.

*Return to the main road and head north.* The road skirts some extraordinary rock faces and crosses the vineyards from which the famous local wine is made. In September, the fig trees are weighed down with luscious yellow or purple fruit.

*At the junction, turn left towards Maalula (26km from the monastery).*

■ **Maalula★** – As the road approaches the entrance to the actual village, the landscape is harmoniously ordered by terraced gardens planted with elegant poplars and apricot trees. On entering the narrow gorge, the characteristic blue and white fronted houses begin to pop into view, fitted tightly into the hillside one on top of the other, linked by a series of staircases and ladders. Each house has a terrace with a large stack of wooden logs. Two streams run around the great rock on which the village is perched, providing irrigation to the local gardens. Maalula has five churches, a convent and a monastery, and all the inhabitants still speak Aramaic.

*Turn right after the roundabout and head towards the convent of St Thekla, the silver dome of which is sheltered by the cliff. The small restaurants on the way lay on wine tastings and offer a selection of Syrian wines.*

The Greek Orthodox **St Thekla Convent** (Mar Takla) is dedicated to the saint encountered by St Paul at Iconium (modern Konya, in Turkey), who miraculously escaped martyrdom by fleeing to a remote cave, where she led a life of virtue for 72 years. Her tomb *(up the steps on the right leading into the convent)* is situated in the cave where she is supposed to have lived, sustained by a sacred spring. In the little marble funerary chapel outside, zealous believers deposit offerings of watches and bracelets.

**Aramaic, the language spoken by Christ**
The Aramaic spoken in Maalula is a vestige of a very ancient language that was first discovered in its written form at Tell Halaf (early 1st Millennium BC). It shows similarities with Hebrew and Phoenician and borrows a number of words from Arabic. Aramaic was the second language of the Assyrian Empire and the official language of the Persian Empire until it was replaced by Greek, following the conquest of the region by Alexander the Great. Thereafter it survived in its oral form, gradually being corrupted by the common people into different dialects (Palmyrian, Nabataean, Samaritan and Syriac) that lasted until the Roman occupation. Aramaic would have been spoken by Christ, and was used to transcribe the original versions of certain books of the Old Testament. With the spread of Islam (7C), Aramaic was progressively replaced in Syria by Arabic.

*Take the road that runs left of the convent of St Thekla, and along the stream that follows the attractively picturesque gorge. On emerging from the valley, turn left to the Hotel Safir and on to the Monastery of St Sergius (20min by car).*

The Greek Catholic **St Sergius Monastery★** (Mar Sarkis) *(variable opening hours)* contains a very special church, said to be the longest-serving church dedicated to the same cult in the world. Inside the bare stone walls stands a marble **altar-table★** with a 7cm-wide rim: unlike the pagan sacrificial tables, this stone slab has no hole for draining the blood. The church houses a fine collection of icons, some of which were painted in the early 19C by Michael of Crete. The priest on duty in the shop, who is liable to encourage visitors to return to the faith and uphold Christian values, often asks people to join him for a coffee or a small glass of very fruity Maalula wine (here the grapes are dried for about two weeks before being pressed). Among the souvenirs and artefacts on sale, there are tapes of the Lord's Prayer in Aramaic.

On the way back down, follow the second road running to the right of the monastery and look out for the numerous caves cut out of the rock.

*Rejoin the main road and continue to Damascus (60km) or Homs.*

**Villages of the Qalamoun**

# Making the most of the Qalamoun region

## COMING AND GOING

**By bus –** Minibuses run regularly to the sites in the Qalamoun region from the Zablatani bus station, near Al-Abassiyyeen square, in the eastern suburb of Damascus. Allow 45min. There is no public transport between Maalula and Seydnaya, although they are only 26km apart, but taxis can be hired for S£350. For an additional S£300 you can be taken to the convent of St Thomas and the Cherubim monastery on the outskirts of Seydnaya.

## WHERE TO STAY

This excursion can easily be done in a day from Damascus, but the cool air of the Qalamoun hills might be a good reason to stay overnight.

### • Seydnaya
*Under US$20*
**Seydnaya monastery.** The nuns will offer accommodation to genuine pilgrims. The level of comfort is basic, but the setting is inspiring for meditation and prayer. You will find yourself among orphan children and Arab pilgrims. No prices are listed but contributions are welcome.

*From US$20-40*
**Seydnaya Hotel**, on the edge of the village, 1km from the Damascus road, ☎ (11) 595 03 58 – 27rm ⌖ ♪ ✕ ⌁ At present this is the only hotel, but presumably not for long, as it is full every Saturday evening. With its small open-air swimming pool and simple rooms with balconies, this is a favourite place among Lebanese pilgrims. Breakfast and dinner are served in the main dining room or on the terrace. Lovely view of the snow-covered Mount Hermon in the spring. Clean, peaceful and welcoming.

### • Maalula
*From US$100-130*
**Safir Hotel**, on the rocky outcrop which dominates Maaloula, near the convent of St Serge, ☎ (12) 777 02 50, Fax (12) 777 02 55 – 38rm ⌖ ♪ ⓣⓥ ✕ ⌁ ✗ ⒸⒸ A very peaceful and pleasant

setting. View over the village. Each room has a sitting area separated by an archway. Sauna. Rather expensive.

## EATING OUT

Several restaurants have become popular meeting places for the inhabitants of Damascus and the Lebanese. They are at their busiest on Thursday and Saturday evenings, around 9pm, and at lunchtime on Fridays and Sundays, around 2.30pm. Family atmosphere.

### • Seydnaya
There are several restaurants on the outskirts of the town, where the main road forks (**Merry Land, Rihab Palace**). Avoid the hotels and restaurants 're-served' for Saudi Arabians near al-Tal.
*Under US$10*
**Al-Mazar al-Siyahi**, Damascus road, just before the turning for Seydnaya, ☎ (11) 595 03 30. ♟ A simple but well-run establishment. Large light dining room and terrace offering 600 places. At weekends there is an orchestra, for an additional S£100 per person. Bar.
*Al-Tilal*, Damascus road, 1km after the turning for Seydnaya, ☎ (11) 595 00 01. ♟ The biggest restaurant in Syria and something of a curiosity. It can serve up to 1 000 people in its sumptuous dining rooms and beneath its huge glazed open-air rotunda. Marble is everywhere. It is also famous for its crowd-pulling concerts and Lebanese singers. Diners travel from as far away as Aleppo as well as from the Lebanon to sample the excellent Middle Eastern, Italian and French cuisine.

### • Maalula
**Family**, a simple but pleasant restaurant near the Monastery of St Thecla, where you can sample local wine.
**Safir**, at the Safir Hotel (see Where to stay). ♟ Maaloula's main hotel provides a choice of two restaurants. The **al-Basteen** offers European and Middle Eastern specialities. Its large Friday lunchtime open-air buffet is famous for its grills and the wide choice of *meze*. The **al-Reef Terrace**, which overlooks the village, does grills and *meze*.

A young Druze girl

# SOUTH OF DAMASCUS

The volcanic regions of Hauran and Jebel Druze – now known as Jebel al-Arab – lie southeast of Damascus and stretch to the Jordanian border. Like the villages south of Aleppo, many of these towns were founded in early Antiquity although here the vestiges are all the more dramatic for being constructed in black basalt. Perhaps the most impressive of such monuments is the great theatre at Bosra, preserved for centuries under the sand: a powerful reminder of the area's one-time prosperity as one of the great wheat-producing areas of Syria.

The population here is predominantly Druze (*see p 42*): often strikingly blond in appearance, with piercing light-coloured eyes. The Druze also dress quite distinctively. The women do not wear veils and the men wear *saroual* (special trousers gathered at the waste and narrow at the ankle), black jackets and white turbans.

# JEBEL AL-ARAB★
## (FORMERLY KNOWN AS JEBEL DRUZE)

317km circuit from Damascus - Allow 2 days,
with an overnight stay at Bosra or Souweida.

**Not to be missed**
Bosra and its marvellous Roman theatre.
The mosaics at Shahba.

**And remember...**
Avoid Fridays and public holidays.

The proposed itinerary explores the **Hauran** and Jebel al-Arab: soon after leaving the capital, the landscape changes to one interrupted by volcanic relief. Before long, you cross the jagged basalt flow or Lejja (meaning refuge in Arabic) and reach the striking Church of St George at Izraa. The circuit also provides an opportunity of taking in the Hauran's rich urban past: most notably the fine Roman remains at Bosra. Additional artefacts – sculptures and mosaics – are on display at the museum in Souweida, and scattered in the ruins of Qanawat and Shahba among the green oaks and vines.

*Take the road out of Damascus on the right of the Hejaz railway station, following signs for Jordan (and Deraa). The motorway begins 11km beyond the station, on the edge of the capital, beside a horse-riding centre.*

It is not long before the road has climbed up through the volcanic hills near the town of Kissoueh and begun its way across the Lejja lava fields, which extend eastwards as far as the eye can see.

*80km from Damascus, leave the motorway and follow signs for Izraa. Pass in front of the large silo and across the railway before turning left 200m further on at the roundabout before the town mosque. Follow the main road, lined with attractive lamp-posts, for 3km to the Church of St George (known as Kenissat al-Khider in Arabic).*

■ **Izraa★** – The town is proud of its two remarkable churches, among the oldest and best preserved in Syria *(If the churches are closed, enquire at the houses nearby. Donations confer the right to visit.)*

The Greek Orthodox **Church of St George**★★ (Mar Georgis) was founded in 515 according to the inscription on the lintel above the central eastern doorway. The same Greek text states that "What was once the home of demons has become a House of God" which implies the church replaces an ancient pagan temple. Entry is through the south door. Unlike the Byzantine churches in the north of Syria, which are built on a basilica plan, this church conforms to an octagon within a square, with the four corners contained by exedras. The modern dome (built of wood and covered with metal as opposed to stone) rests on massive piers; the basalt-tiled deambulatory meanwhile is remarkable both for its economy and precision. The apse, screened by an iconostasis, is considered by locals to contain the **tomb** of St George.

On retracing your steps from the church of St George, you will notice the remains of a mosque prayer hall on the left. 200m further on, turn left before the primary school and follow the street up to the nearby Church of St Elias. The Greek Catholic **Church of St Elias** dates from 542. The nave extends beneath a newly built cupola to an apse at the east end.

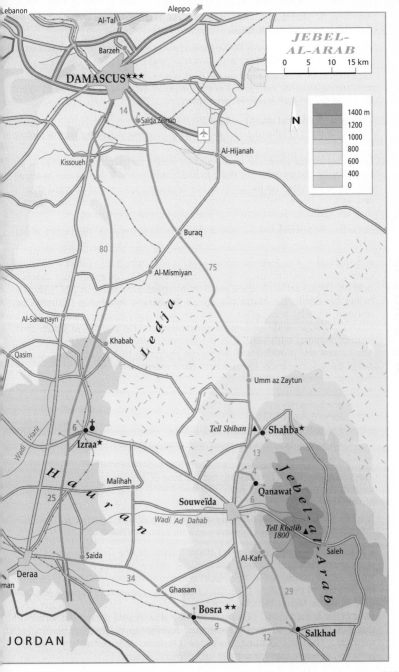

JEBEL–AL–ARAB

0    5    10    15 km

N

1400 m
1200
1000
800
600
400
0

Lebanon

Aleppo

Al-Tal

Barzeh

DAMASCUS ★★★

14

Saïda Zeïnab

Al-Hijanah

Kissoueh

Buraq

80

Al-Mismiyan

75

Al-Sanamayn

L e d j a

Khabab

Qasim

Umm az Zaytun

Tell Shihan ▲ Shahba ★

Wadi Harir

6    †

Izraa ★

13

4

J e b e l - a l - A r a b

Malihah

H   a   u   r   a   n

Qanawat

25

Souweïda

6

Wadi Ad Dahab

Tell Khalib
1800 ▲

Saleh

Saïda

Al-Kafr

Deraa

man

34

Ghassam

29

Bosra ★★

9

Salkhad

12

JORDAN

149

*Return to the Damascus-Amman motorway and head south; turn off at the exit for Assayidah some 25km after Izraa.*

The road heads east towards Bosra, passing along seamless olive groves and vineyards with vines propped up with concrete posts.

*Turn right at the entrance to the ancient town of Bosra before the monumental gateway, and continue along the walls for 500m until you reach the entrance to the citadel. Leave the car in the car park beside the large square.*

■ **Bosra**★★ (Bosral'sham) – *See p 156*
*Head out of Bosra by following signs for the Cham Hotel and then taking the first turning on the left.*

Soon after leaving town, the road gradually climbs up towards the Jebel al-Arab, providing a distant view of the Salkhad castle perched high on a volcanic outcrop, silhouetted on the skyline. The landscape is now more rugged than it was west of Bosra, and low drystone walls that have been painstakingly built over the centuries now enclose the sparsely planted olive groves.

*Just before the Salkhad, which nestles at the foot of the fortress, take the road on the left for Souweida.*

■ **Salkhad** – The **fortress** (*closed to the public*), which is built in a volcanic crater, was erected by the Ayubbids in the early 13C as an advance defence post for Damascus while the Crusaders occupied Jerusalem. In 1277, shortly before his death, the Mameluke sultan **Baybars** ordered that it should be restored, thereby sealing his reputation as an indefatigable builder after a reign that began with his famous proclamation: "Do not fail to watch over frontier outposts with zeal."

The fortress was provided with additional protection by a massive ditch carved out of the volcanic rock. The northern flank preserves the remains of the glacis that once covered the moat.

As the fortress remains inaccessible to the public – currently occupied by the Syrian army, visitors can walk around the village cobbled together with ancient and modern materials, like so many others in this remote area. Among the inhabitants, you will see the seemingly ageless Druze, traditionally attired in a turban and black *saroual* belted at the waist with a white cummerbund.

*The road heads north of Salkhad towards Souweida, some 29km away.*

The village of Al-Kafr huddles around the base of Tell Khalib (1 800m), on the western flank of the Jebel al-Arab. The land here is given over to the cultivation of vines and apple trees.

*Head for the town centre of Souweida – marked by a tall red and white telecommunications tower, and park near the square with the equestrian statue of Sultan al-Atrach.*

■ **Souweida** – Pop 22 000. Alt 1 000m. Souweida, the Druze capital of Syria, lacks charm but it is the only town in the vicinity to have a hotel. Its name which literally translates as "the black" refers to the colour of the stone used in the building of the ancient town stretching across the western flank of Jebel al-Arab opposite Mount Hermon, which is visible in the distance on a clear day. Most of the Roman town of Dionysus has now disappeared under modern buildings but recovered artefacts are collected together in the local archaeological museum. The neighbouring towns of Qanawat and particularly Shahba, however, preserve many important architectural remains.

The streets of Souweida, a small but well-to-do town, are populated with young people dressed in Western clothes and older inhabitants in more traditional attire: the women wear white headscarves and the men a black waistcoat with buttons. After a short tour of the town centre, enquire after the road to Qanawat along which the museum is situated, on the outskirts of the town.

The **Souweida Museum**\* (*Open 9am-6pm in summer, 9am-4pm in winter, during the month of Ramadan 9am-3pm. Closed Tuesdays. Entry charge. Allow 30min*) houses a remarkable collection of archaeological finds retrieved from the Jebel area. The exhibits are well arranged and excellent display boards provide useful explanations on the distribution of settlements in the region and the architecture of the massif.

### The al-Atrach dynasty

At the end of the 19C, the al-Atrach family began playing an increasingly important role in the Syrian Druze community that was to have major consequence on its future, rather like the Jumblatt family in Lebanon. During the First World War, Sultan al-Atrach took part in the offensive against the Turks, leading his troops into Damascus. In 1925, the same Sultan al-Atrach clashed swords with French Mandatory power, and thereby earned a reputation as the hero of independence in Syria. A progeny of this famous family, the singer Farid al-Atrach, settled in Egypt and became an idol of musical comedies in the Arab world (with 24 films to his credit between 1940 and 1960). The al-Atrach family still enjoys great prestige in the Syrian Druze community.

The first three rooms are devoted to prehistory, ancient sculpture and Byzantine art respectively; the central hall contains several 3C mosaics depicting scenes from mythology, including a fine **Artemis (Diana) surprised while bathing**\*\*, and a **Birth and Toilet of Venus**\*\*. The first floor concentrates on popular arts and traditions, with plaster figures used to show daily rituals from Druze life.

Birth and Toilet of Venus

P. Meunier

**Jebel al-Arab**

*Continue along the road, past the Souweida Museum, that heads northeast. The road winds its way slowly up the hillside cloaked with shrubby vegetation and small oaks. A cluster of luxury villas heralds the beginning of the village of Qanawat (5km). At the roundabout, turn right uphill taking you some 400m further on to a seraglio fronted by a large paved square.*

■ **Qanawat** – It is hard to believe that at one time, this small village in the Jebel al-Arab was one of the towns of the Decapolis, on a par with Jarash and Damascus. Today, most of the site has disappeared beneath modern housing, completing the devastation initiated by invasive plants and weeds. The complex known by locals as "the Seraglio", together with the Temple of Helios, testify to the importance of this town during the Roman and Byzantine periods when it was the seat of a bishopric. Other buildings from Antiquity (nymphaeum and odeon) have also been recovered on the far bank of the Wadi al-Ghar, which once cut through the ancient town.

The **Seraglio**★ *(8am-2.30pm, entry charge)*, which overlooks the small square now used as a car park, consists of two basilicas that were adapted for use by an Early Christian community in the 5C-6C from Roman buildings that were constructed in the 2C AD. The ground plan, therefore is confusing. Access to the first building (probably the *praetorium* or Roman governor's residence) is through a finely carved doorway decorated with vine leaves, tendrils and juicy bunches of grapes. The same motif is echoed in the two side windows. The three niches on the right of the nave probably served as a martyrium. Off to one side lies a huge court-yard (atrium with columns), the south part of which was altered in the 4C or 5C to create a church. The main doorway off the atrium is beautifully carved with elements that again allude to the importance of wine-making in the region since Roman times. The main apse is filled with a broad baptismal font and three sarcophagi stand behind the altar.

The magnificent if precarious-looking tower situated northeast of the seraglio allegedly formed part of the monastic or episcopal complex that stood alongside the churches.

**Mount Hermon**

The mountains of the Anti-Lebanon culminate with Mount Hermon (2 814m) and, as such, the snow-capped peak has served as an important point of reference since Antiquity. There are at least 15 references to it in the Bible, and the Arabs call it "Jebel al-Sheikh" likening it to an Islamic sage with a white turban until the snows melt at the end of June. It also marks the frontier between Syria and Lebanon.

*Go back to the main roundabout and take the first road on the right.*

Some 400m from the junction, a series of columns come into view on the left. These belong to the **Helios Temple**: a monument raised on a platform with well-defined edges, surmounted with a regular line of pedestals bearing smooth-shafted columns crowned with elegant Corinthian capitals that would have surrounded the cella. A flight of steps at the east end leads up to the platform from which, on a clear day, there is a magnificent view of Mount Hermon.

*To avoid returning via Souweida, go back to the main roundabout in Qanawat and turn down the little road running downhill, sign-posted for Shahba. After 3km, rejoin the Souweida-Damascus road and continue for 6.5km until you see signs for Shahba, which is dominated by the volcano of Tell Sihan.*

■ **Shahba**★ – The town owes its wealth of ruins to its most illustrious son: the Roman Emperor **Philip the Arab**. Soon after being crowned emperor (244), Philip set about rebuilding his native Chechebe on the lines of a Roman town which he renamed Philippopolis. But this city was not to survive for long, as the place seems to have been sparsely inhabited at the time of Philip's death and devoid of any Christian monuments, suggesting the town was abandoned in the 5C. In the 19C various Druze moved in to live among the ruins; since then the main buildings have been vacated to allow access to visitors.

The road from Souweida leads into the old town through the heavily restored **south gate** which was one of four gateways in the rectangular perimeter walls of Philippopolis that covered an estimated area of 1sqkm.

*Continue along the main road for 500m to the intersection with the decumanus, marked at one time by a tetrapylon. This square usually bustles with life; park the car here and continue on foot.*

The western section of the *decumanus* – which leads off to the left – is lined on the right by four columns of a hexastyle temple. The large paved space on the left was once the

**An Arab emperor in Rome**

In 248 AD, Rome celebrated the millennium of its foundation with sumptuous feasts lasting for three days and nights. The emperor responsible for organising the ceremonies was originally from Syria, and known as Philip the Arab. Philip was born in 204 into an Arab tribe that had settled in what is now known as Jebel al-Arab, and brought up in the camps of the army of the Eastern Roman Empire. As was common practice during these troubled times, Philip murdered the prefect of the praetorium, had the Emperor Gordien III assassinated, and eventually succeeded in forcing the Senate to grant him – then aged 40 years – the imperial titles. Philip the Arab ceded Mesopotamia to the Sassanids in exchange for peace, and fought the Scythians before pursuing his struggle against the Barbarian bands on the Danubian frontier. Decius, an officer sent to subdue the usurpers in the highly turbulent eastern provinces, was proclaimed emperor by his soldiers. Philip the Arab was killed in 249 near Verona.

**Jebel al-Arab**

**forum**. A strange building, probably a 3C palace, with a 30m long façade, extends across the west side of the square; before it stands a 1m high platform, ornamented with niches and alcoves. The central room, closed off by a large exedra covered with a semicircular vault, is supposed to have served as an **imperial sanctuary**. On the left stands a small square and rather austere temple fronted with a flight of some ten or so steps: the **Philippeion**, as this is referred to by archaeologists, is believed to have been a monumental tomb for a member of the imperial family. The consoles on either side of the doorway bear Greek inscriptions to Marinus, Philip the Arab's father. The niches inside used to contain sarcophagi.

A footpath along the left side of the Philippeion leads to the nearby **theatre***: a relatively small building (a mere 42.5m in diameter) furnished with two tiers of seats separated into blocks by three flights of stairs. Only nine steps of the first tier survive. The proscenium wall has three doorways and four niches. The only other form of decoration consists of small fish carved into the stone of the vaulted passages directing the spectators in and out of their seats.

*Walk back to the main square in Shahba and continue 200m towards the south gate, turning sharply left so as to reach the dramatic ruins of the baths complex on the left and, on the other side of the road, the aqueduct that supplied the town with water. Turn down the street past the baths frontage. The little Shahba museum is situated 200m further on, on the right.*

The **Shahba mosaic museum*** *(Open 8am-2pm, closed Tuesdays. Entrance fee. Allow 15min)* has been built over the exceptionally well-preserved floor of a villa. The mosaics on view date from the Constantinian Renaissance (4C AD) and illustrate subjects taken from Classical mythology. The main attractions are the four panels *in situ*. The one representing the sea-nymph **Thetis\*\*** shows the mother of Achilles with long free-flowing hair tangled with fish and an expression conveying the mystery of the depths. In the **Marriage of Dionysus (Bacchus) and Ariadne\***, Ariadne is pictured in all her finery accompanied by Bacchus who holds a thyrsus (a rod wreathed with ivy and vines symbolising fertility) and a group of thoughtful characters; in stark contrast with the serious attitude of those gathered, Heracles (Hercules) stretches out in the foreground, apparently drunk. **Orpheus among the animals\*\*\*** shows Orpheus wearing a Phrygian hat, playing his lyre in a state of ecstasy; the animals, however, are somewhat uneasy about the sound of his singing and playing. The power and sensitivity of this composition make this mosaic one of the most striking to survive from late Roman Antiquity. The **Passion of Aphrodite (Venus) and Ares (Mars)** illustrates the God of War with his beloved consort Aphrodite, half nude, surrounded by playful cupids.

*To return to Damascus, leave Shahba by the north gate.*

The road back leaves the tall mound of Tell Sihan (1 140m) on the left before skirting around the east side of Lejja. 14km from the capital, you will see the golden dome of the **Shiite mausoleum of Saida Zeinab**, a most important pilgrimage site for Iranian visitors, containing the tomb of one of Muhammad's granddaughters *(open to the public)*. Those too pressed for time to make the detour to see this monument can visit another Shiite sanctuary in Damascus, the Rouqayya Mosque.

## Making the most of the Jebel al-Arab region

### COMING AND GOING

The proposed circuit can be done in one extremely full day by car (a taxi hired for the day for S£3 500), but is better spread over two days. By public transport two days are essential without visiting Izraa. The first day can be devoted to Bosra, and the second to Souweida and the neighbouring towns of Qanawat and Shahba. There is no bus service between Souweida and Bosra, but taxis will do the journey for S£350.

### • Bosra

The Syrian name is Bosral'sham. There is a daily minibus service from Damascus (90min) with the first departure at 9.30am. The last bus leaves Bosra at 5pm. It is advisable to confirm your return journey on arrival at Bosra. Reserve your place from Damascus the day before at the **Damas Tour company** office, situated at the **Harasta garage**.

The **Challal Tour** and **Fahrat Tour** companies also run a service to Bosra. It is also possible to follow this circuit when coming from (or going to) Jordan. There is a regular bus service to Bosra from the border town of Deraa.

### • Souweida

Minibuses leave from the **Harasta garage** in Damascus. The bus station at Souweida is found on the northern edge of the town (not near the centre). Take a taxi to the town centre and museum.

### WHERE TO STAY

The choice of accommodation is extremely limited in the Jebel al-Arab. At Bosra, the possibilities are limited to the luxurious Cham Palace hotel, or basic dormitory accommodation in the Roman theatre. The lack of any other alternative means that it is best to visit Bosra on a day trip from Damascus. It can also be pretty boring being stuck there after nightfall. Another solution would be to stay at Souweida, which has two basic hotels. Avoid staying at the border town of Deraa, which offers three mediocre mosquito-infested hotels.

● **Bosra**

*Under US$20*

**Theatre Hostel**, in Bosra's Roman theatre. Apply to the restaurant at the citadel. A unique opportunity to sleep in a Roman theatre, but with Spartan comfort and questionable cleanliness! A mattress is available for a few hundred S£. Bring your own bedding. The theatre closes at 7pm, and you will be shut in for the night, which is rather dull.

*From US$130-150*

**Bosra Cham Palace Hotel**, opposite the theatre, ☎ (15) 790 488, Fax (15) 790 996 – 75rm ◢ 🗉 ♪ 📺 ✗ 🛁 ❦ ᴄᴄ The smallest and most charming in this large Syrian chain of hotels, built in the local black stone. Its entrance hall is decorated with fine examples of Druze wickerwork. The third floor rooms have views of the theatre.

● **Souweida**

*From US$25-40*

**Shooting Club Hotel**, on the outskirts of Souweida on the Qanawat road, ☎ (15) 231 929, Fax (15) 237 233 – 6rm ◢ ♪ ✗ For lack of anything better, this rather tired-looking modern building lacks charm, and prices are high given the standard of service.

**EATING OUT**

● **Bosra**

Apart from the Cham Hotel's two restaurants (the **Patio** serves sandwiches and hamburgers all day), you could eat in one of the snack bars opposite the entrance to the citadel.

**The Old City**, at the end of a lane just before the theatre entrance, ☎ (15) 790 966. The best place to go in Bosra. Attractive vaulted stone dining room, decorated with antiques, where you will find generous portions of good local family-style cooking. Friendly welcome. You can eat (and sleep) on the roof.

Reasonable meals are also sometimes available inside the theatre. In the old town, several shops have opened in the ruins since the local population has been rehoused, where tea and cold drinks are served. The atmosphere is friendly, it's a good place to meet people and the prices are lower than at the theatre. In the main square several shops sell trinkets of little value.

● **Souweida**

The town has two specialities: grapes and apples, from which delicious fruit juices are made in the autumn. The rest of the year locally made wines are available.

*Under US$10*

**Al-Amir**, in the town centre, first left when descending the road which runs beside the post office, ☎ (15) 224 992. ❢ The restaurant is on the first floor of a modern building and is without doubt the best in the town. Open from 9am-11pm, it even serves breakfast. Middle Eastern specialities: kebab, *chiche taouk*, but also European food: *chateaubriand*, pizza. Welcoming atmosphere.

**Al-Bourj**, Sultan Al-Atrach Sq ☎ (15) 222 291. ❢ A pleasant first-floor cafeteria opposite the sultan's statue. Small but well-ventilated dining room. Sandwiches. Ideal for a snack before visiting the Museum.

**Making the most of Jebel al-Arab**

# BOSRA ★★
## (BOSRAL'SHAM)
Mouhafazat of Deraa – Alt 800m
For information about access, accommodation and restaurants, see p 154
See route and map for Jebel al-Arab

**Not to be missed**
The Roman theatre.

**And remember...**
Allow at least 30min for visiting the theatre
2hr for exploring the whole site.
Watch out for pick-pockets.

Bosra, which is set deep in Druze country, is one of the less-renowned large Middle Eastern cities from Antiquity, but justifies a special journey of its own. Unlike Petra and Palmyra, Bosra continued to prosper well after the end of Antiquity and into medieval times. Indeed, the exceptional variety of forces that have precipitated the local heritage are the same as those that have fashioned history in Syria. Instead of the dynasties being eclipsed one by another, they each bequeathed a legacy to Bosra before gradually dying out. There are over 30 different monuments testifying to the glory of each age including a Nabataean arch, Roman baths, Byzantine cathedrals and palaces, an Ayubbid citadel, mosques, huge cisterns... The cathedral was used as a model for Haghia Sofia in Constantinople, the citadel is a masterpiece of Arab military art and the Manjak Hammam is a very elaborate example of a Mameluke bath. The single constant in all these great works is the black basalt which, when caught by the summer sun, stands out against its golden surrounds.

The theatre, Bosra

G Degeorge

South of Damascus

Besides the architectural heritage, the area has been home, since the 19C, to a substantial Druze community. Here, you might pick out an Ancient Greek inscription running along the lintel of a window; there you might spot a child reading a comic beside a column erected two millennia ago, before running off to kick a football with friends on a stretch of Roman road.

It is not clear who stands to gain the most – Bosra's inhabitants or teams of avid archeologists – but the Syrian Department of Antiquities has conceived a vast programme for the population of old Bosra, relocating it to more modern and more comfortable accommodation on the outskirts of town.

**Petra's rival becomes the capital of Roman Arabia** – The Nabataeans were already well-entrenched at "Bosora" living in harmony with the small Jewish communities there when **Judas Maccabaeus** came to defend them in the 2C BC at the end of the bloody expedition described in the Bible (I Maccabees, Chap5, v26). In the following century, Bosra's strategic proximity to the Hellenistic cities of Syria helped to make it the northern capital of the Nabataean Kingdom. Then, exploiting a lull in the caravan trade in Arabia, it took Petra's place as capital of the prestigious kingdom. In 106 AD, the Nabataean Kingdom was annexed under the orders of Trajan and Bosra was promoted to capital of the new Roman province of Arabia. Its governor established his offices (*scrinia*) there and headquarters were built for the 3rd Cyrenaica Legion. This army counted soldiers from all four corners of the Empire among its ranks. Archeologists have even found evidence of a legionary from Brittany at Bosra!

Boosted by its new-found status and the presence of an important garrison, the town was rapidly transformed into a beautiful eastern city: the main axes were laid out, and a forum, gallery of shops, temples, monumental arches and villas extended the Nabataean town to the west. Additional public facilities were provided for satisfying leisure pursuits and entertainment: several sets of baths were built as well as a magnificent theatre. The surrounding territory – particularly fertile – was transformed into a great breadbasket capable of supplying grain to the outlying kingdoms for years after the decline of Antiquity.

**The monk and the Prophet**
According to tradition Muhammad left Mecca with his uncle bound for Syria with a caravan of merchants when still a child. During a halt at Bosra along the way, they met a Christian monk named Bahira. The monk noticed that a small cloud perpetually followed the child wherever he went, protecting him from the burning sun. Being a learned man, the monk recalled a manuscript that predicted that a prophet would be sent to the Arabs. To verify that the hour had come he invited the members of the caravan to a meal in order to have a closer look at the child. Convinced that this was the child mentioned in the prophecy, the monk then announced the child's prophetic destiny. Some years later, Muhammad received from the Angel Gabriel the sayings of the sacred text known as the Koran.

Bosra

From the 3C, the Christian community of Bosra actively participated in the wrangling and quarrels between the various factions of the Church. Bosra was made a bishopric then the seat of an archbishop, and a magnificent cathedral was erected in the 6C.

**On the road to Mecca** – The story recounting the recognition of the Prophet **Muhammad** by the Christian monk **Bahira** to some extent marks the point at which the Byzantine era becomes eclipsed by Islam. A number of similar legends reinforce Bosra's considerable importance at the dawn of Islam: according to some, a hadith (deed from the life of the Prophet) describes how "when Amina conceived the Prophet, she saw a light radiating from her and illuminating the palace of Bosra". This is translated into history by the fact that the city was the first of modern Syria to be conquered by the Arabs (653), three years after the death of the Prophet. For years thereafter, it remained the grainstore of Damascus, an important commercial transit point for caravans from the east and a major port of call on the pilgrim route to Mecca with – it is said – some 36 mosques. During the Crusades, the citadel played a key role in defending Damascus from troops despatched by Jerusalem. Following various devastating raids by Hulagu and his Mongol hordes, the city was eventually taken by the Mamelukes, and having lost its strategic importance it became a modest Ottoman garrison town. Meanwhile, the pilgrimage route had shifted about 40km west and the trading caravans now operated alternative routes that were safer and more direct.

# Tour

*No charge for any of the sights other than the theatre. Allow 2hr.*

## Theatre**

One of the most elegant monuments of Syrian archeology, though sadly not well cared for, Bosra's Roman theatre *(10am-6pm in summer, 9am-4pm in winter. Entrance fee)* is enclosed within imposing fortifications. From the outside, there is little to suggest just what lies in store behind the straight high walls of dark stone, and yet things would have been very different if the theatre had not been trans-formed into a citadel. This large-scale initiative began shortly after the Islamic conquest, was continued by the Fatimid dynasty, and completed by the Ayubbids in the 13C. The resulting citadel* remains a marvellous example of Islamic military architecture, echoing the semicircular shape of the underlying theatre now completely enclosed within great walls and reinforced by nine towers. In the early 13C a drawbridge spanned the moat: this has long since been replaced by a small bridge.

*Enter into the dark corridors on the left between the steps and the fortifications, fol-lowing the intermittent signs.* A double flight of stairs leads up and out into the dazzling sunshine bathing the immense **semicircle***** of the theatre. The complex dates from the mid-2C AD and accommodated some 8 000 spectators. The seating is arranged in three tiers of 35 rows and accessed by a series of vom-itoria and immaculately constructed stone galleries. The fact that this theatre at Bosra bears a striking resemblance to the one at Orange (in Provence, France) on the other side of the Mediterranean is proof of the extraordinary uniformity of Roman civil engineering. From the top, a splendid view extends over the ancient city and the surrounding countryside. With luck, your visit may coin-cide with that of a group of schoolchildren who delight in testing the excellent acoustics with an impromptu dance or an improvised chorus. The sumptuous Corinthian capitals on the **proscenium wall**, although heavily restored, provide some idea of the sumptuous decoration ornamenting the stage backdrop studded with three rows of windows, statues and friezes. Every two years, these ancient stones recover their original purpose and host a famous music festival.

The **Ethnographic Museum** in the southwest tower *(left section of the semicircle)* houses a series of displays illustrating domestic scenes and the interior of a tra-ditional home. The south tower meanwhile, shelters the **Archeological Museum** including a mosaic of fish and birds from the Ayubbid palace. The **Sculpture Garden** *(situated next to the restaurant)* accommodates a selection of works in basalt – carved in the ancient Hauran tradition. A large mosaic dated 621 AD from Jebel al-Arab, depicts scenes from daily life: a caravan of camels, the date harvest and catching birds. The staircase in front of the restaurant leads down to the **foyer** and the wings backstage.

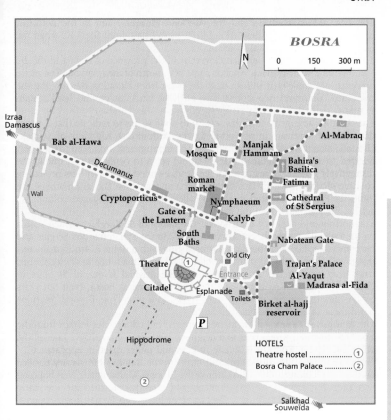

The theatre was not the only leisure facility in Bosra. Archeologists have found evidence of a **hippodrome** between the citadel and the site of the Cham Hotel (now covered in part by a modern road). Further west, a large pool is thought to have been used to host naumachia (mock sea battles).

## Bosra's eastern quarter*

Parts of the old town continue to be excavated by archeologists, and the buildings so far recovered date from throughout Bosra's long history. The following circuit takes in the main monuments.

*Start from the square before the theatre, and head down the street lined with small restaurants to the pool (walk up the steps).*

This first rectangular **reservoir*** is huge (155m by 122m, 8m deep) and has a capacity of 150 000cubic meters for collecting water from the nearby wadis. Its Arabic name "*birket al-haj*" recalls the distant past when Bosra was on the pilgrim route to Mecca for "*al-haj*" meaning "pilgrimage". A second, slightly smaller pool situated some 500m northeast of the first was built in Roman times. Both reservoirs are situated a few metres above the ancient town so as to facilitate the flow of water through a system of ducts. Their exact location is usually heralded by the sound of excited children playing and splashing about.

The **Abu al-Fida Madrasa** and the **Al-Yakut Mosque** stand in the northeast corner of "*birket al-haj*": these *(closed to the public)* date from the 13C when the Islamic town suddenly mushroomed.

The former palace of the Roman Governor of the province of Arabia in the 2C – known as **Trajan's palace** – stands some 50m north of the reservoir. The ruins, however, are somewhat uninspiring: the main front elevation overlooking the courtyard comprised two storeys, but only the vaults at ground level remain standing.

The complex arrangement of this section of town seems to indicate that it might date from Nabataean times, prior to the widespread adoption of (Greek) Hippodamian town planning principles. The monumental arch 50m to the right, referred to as the **Nabataean Gate***, would seem to confirm this. Among the distinctively Nabataean features are the double-ended capital with its projecting concave section between. This detail, which appears time and again among the tombs at Petra, is repeated in the so called "Nabataean" engaged column set against the wall 30m from the gate.

The northbound alleyway leads to the **Cathedral of St Sergius***, which stands on the right. This church, consecrated in 512 to the Syrian martyrs Sergius and Bacchus *(see p 253)*, was built on a square plan with a dome (24m in diameter) that once sat on a ring of piers, the base of which remain in situ (two columns have been re-erected). This conforms to the original layout of St Sofia in Constantinople, and so it is likely that the cathedral at Bosra, built ten years earlier than the church in Byzantium, served as a prototype. Beyond the ruins stand those of an ecclesiastical residence.

The **Mosque of Fatima**, a few metres from the cathedral, dates in part from the 11C. The minaret, which rises to a height of 19m, dates from 1306. Like all the other minarets in Bosra, it is square in plan and rather rustic in appearance.

Continue some 100m along the same street to the **Bahira's Monastery basilica** used by the famous monk who tutored the Prophet Muhammad. This building was probably erected by the Romans and later transformed by the Early Christians for use as a church. The façade includes two Roman Ionic capitals. The only section of the original roof is preserved over the semicircular apse.

By forking to the right and walking about 200m, you come to another place linked with the Prophet Muhammad: the **Al-Mabraq Mosque** which is supposed to have been built on the spot where the Prophet dismounted from his camel and first set foot in Bosra. Others, meanwhile, claim that it was in fact where the Koran was first unloaded from the camel caravan.

The small oratory from the 12C-13C has a narrow doorway sealed with a heavy slab of basalt. Inside, resides a stone bearing the imprint of a camel's hoof. This is situated where the *mihrab* would be. The mosque, together with its adjacent buildings, at one time probably formed part of a madrasa, which is considered to be one of the oldest surviving religious Islamic schools in Syria.

### Bosra's western quarter*

*Take the main thoroughfare past the mosque, and turn left down a street leading to the Manjak Hammam.*

A small **museum** *(with custodian; access to the baths after visiting the museum)* devoted to the town's Islamic monuments (plans, photographs and interesting commentaries in English and Arabic) precedes the entrance to the baths. The **Manjak Hammam** (1372), the most significant building to survive from Mameluke times was destined to serve both the local population and any pilgrims bound for the holy cities of Arabia. The complex is sub-divided into three separate sections: the domed reception hall arranged around a large central pool, complete with niches for storing shoes; the actual baths comprising 11 *maqsoura* (small steam rooms); the boiler-room and pump-room housing the equipment to heat the water and the system for diffusing it through the ducting (from where the custodian starts his tour). These baths have undergone considerable amounts of restoration.

Opposite the baths stands the **Mosque of Umar*** *(open at prayer time. No charge)*, fronted by a portico with columns topped with Ionic capitals that once lined the Roman road. For a long time it was thought to be one of the earliest mosques of Islam, and is named after the second Muslim Caliph, Umar ibn al-Khattab (634-644): recent findings seems to suggest that it is later in date, and was probably built during Ayubbid rule (13C). The minaret dates from 1221, and proves to have been constructed using building materials taken from elsewhere: the columns and capitals for example, were pillaged from the nearby theatre. The ceiling is supported on solid basalt crossbeams, as is common in the Hauran region where timber was hard to come by. Today this constitutes the town's main mosque.

The rest of the tour concentrates on the town's Roman remains. The street running between the Manjak Hammam and the Mosque of Umar leads straight to the **Roman market** where goods were bought and sold, at the very heart of the commercial quarter. All along the street, behind the wall on the right, are the remains of the vaulted storerooms where merchandise was stockpiled.

*Continue along the street to the intersection with the main Roman road linking the Nabataean Arch with the Bab al-Hawa.*

The four gigantic columns standing by the crossroads once fronted the **nymphaeum**. These are crowned with superb Corinthian capitals and are thought to have formed part of what is considered by archeologists to be a *kalybe* (open-fronted shrine with niches for statuary).

Opposite the nymphaeum stand the **South Baths** faced with 28 columns. These are well preserved and have their roof-covering still partially intact. Originally, a porch with eight columns would have preceded the complex. Bathers would then proceed into the octagonal vestibule to undress before entering the frigidarium (cold room), tepidarium (warm room) and caldarium (hot room).

*Walk along the forum towards the Bab al-Hawa.* The imposing **Gate of the Lantern** (Bab al-Qandil) is in fact a triumphal arch erected in honour of the legion stationed at Bosra. The central arch rises to a height of 13m.

On the right, a huge underground chamber – the **cryptoporticus**** – extends 65m in line with the street. This was no doubt built in the 2C as a warehouse for goods sold in the nearby market. Skylights at street level provided natural light. The remains of a tetrapylon a few metres from the cryptoporticus mark the intersection of the decumanus with the cardo (the second most important street of ancient Roman towns).

The paved street leading to the "Gate of the Wind", or **Bab al-Hawa** in Arabic, is lined with Ionic columns, some still standing, some lying on the ground, for a distance of more than 200m. The façades of the houses are a hotchpotch of re-used building stones. The Bab al-Hawa marks the entrance to the town in Antiquity, punctuating the walls that remain very much in evidence around the west quarter. The gateway is well-preserved, despite the loss of the statuary that once filled its niches, and the second vault spanning the main archway. This dates from the 2C when the Roman town was at its zenith.

**Bosra**

Margat Castle (Qalaat al Marquab)

# CRUSADER CASTLES AND THE COAST

The contrast can be quite astounding between conditions in Damascus and the coast. When stifling heat pervades the capital, a few hours' drive away at Krak des Chevaliers the landscape is shrouded in heavy mist, and temperatures drop to such levels that will have you reaching for jumpers and windcheaters.

The Jebel Ansariyeh, which rises to a height of 1510m near Slenfeh, is well served by a network of minor roads. These provide access to scenery that one might not normally associate with Syria, peppered with stretches of oak forest, pine woods, waterfalls, deep gorges and tiny villages. It was in this pleasant countryside that the Crusaders engineered their finest defensive masterpieces like Krak des Chevaliers, the fortified castle at Margat and Saône Castle at Sahyun (Qalaat Salahuddin).

The hinterland is separated from the coast by a magnificent range of mountains planted with orchards of citrus and olive groves. The only towns of any significance in the area are the harbours such as Tartus and Latakia that have a cosmopolitan trading history, and life there is far more relaxed than in the towns of the interior.

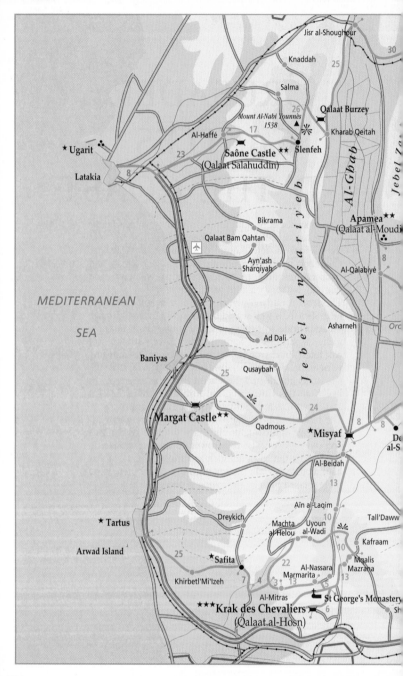

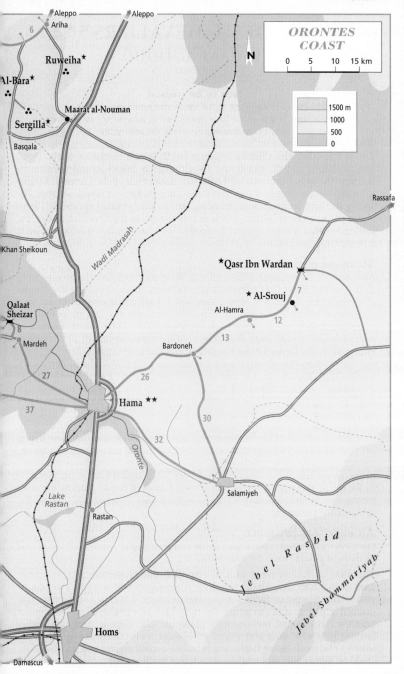

# KRAK DES CHEVALIERS★★★
## (QALAAT AL-HOSN)
### Alt 650m

**Not to be missed**
The best views are to be had from beyond the castle.
Stay the night at one of the local hotels, and in summer try to get there
early in the morning or late in the afternoon.

The fortress Krak des Chevaliers cannot fail to inspire memories of childhood history lessons and the chapter on the Crusade to defend Jerusalem from the Infidels. The most impressive of the fortress castles built by the Christian knights to ensure the protection of the Latin states sits proudly on a raised outcrop, surveying the land around and dominating the skyline, whether approached from Homs or from Hama. Although it is not the largest of the Crusader castles, the meticulous way it was engineered, together with its superb condition, makes it a remarkable monument.

## Strategic position

Krak was ideally situated at the southern tip of the Jebel Ansariyeh range so as to control the Homs Gap, a strategic pass between the coast and the large towns of the interior. From here it was easy to fend off any enemy incursion into Christian territory. However, the Crusaders were not the first to exploit this exceptional position, for records show that back in 1110 Prince Tancred of Antioch seized a small castle from a band of Kurdish warriors. In 1142 this was entrusted to the **Order of the Knights Hospitallers,** who proceeded to enlarge and fortify it so that it might accommodate up to 2 000 soldiers. Three local villages were requisitioned to provide food for the men and their mounts. In 1183 Krak successfully resisted an onslaught by Saladin. Six months after the death of King Louis IX (St Louis) of France off the coast of Tunis – an incident that sealed the fate of the 8th Crusade – **Baybars** besieged the fortress in March 1271. Five weeks later, the weakened garrison of about 60 knights succumbed, stranded as a result of the Franks suffering several defeats and divisions among the Crusader princes. Although restored by Baybars and his successor Qalawun, the strategic value of the castle was of little consequence during the ensuing centuries. At the end of the 19C a community of 500 Alawites lived in the precincts of the castle; these people were transferred to modern housing below the walls during the French Mandate to allow archeologists to clear and restore the complex for public view.

## An excellent prospect

*For a view of the whole complex (and for the best photographs), continue along the road on the right past the castle for some 400m.*

This view of the fortress is without precedent (see illustration p 000). Unlike most of the other Crusader castles, Krak is a compact unit with no lower courtyard – as at Margat or Saône – to weaken defences. It is easy to determine two distinctive phases of construction: the early-12C trapeze-shaped fort was rather primitive, so a second wall was built in the late 12C. This, in turn, was further fortified by a wide moat and a third set of outer walls punctuated by 13 round towers. The south-facing flank, which has no natural escarpment and therefore could be vulnerable, was reinforced by heavy fortifications, including a massive

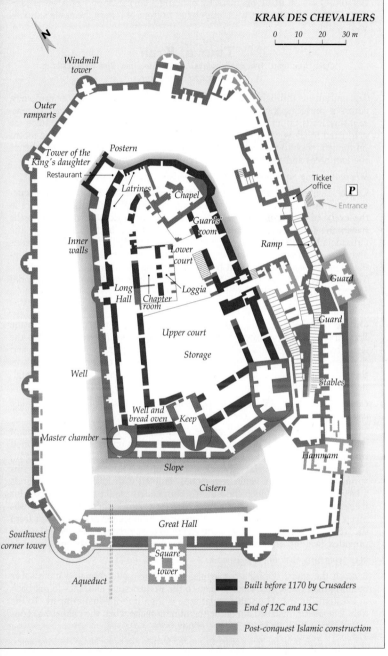

**KRAK DES CHEVALIERS**

0   10   20   30 m

- Windmill tower
- Outer ramparts
- Postern
- Tower of the King's daughter
- Restaurant
- Latrines
- Chapel
- Guards' room
- Inner walls
- Lower court
- Ramp
- Long Hall
- Loggia
- Chapter room
- Guard
- Upper court
- Guard
- Storage
- Well
- Stables
- Well and bread oven
- Keep
- Master chamber
- Hammam
- Slope
- Cistern
- Southwest corner tower
- Great Hall
- Square tower
- Aqueduct
- Ticket office
- P
- Entrance

Built before 1170 by Crusaders

End of 12C and 13C

Post-conquest Islamic construction

donjon. Qalawun made his mark by building a large bastion in the outer ramparts. The small aqueduct with four arches in front of it kept the castle supplied with water.

## Tour of Krak

*Open 9am-6pm, 4pm on Tuesdays, winter 9am-4pm, 2pm on Tuesdays.*
*Entrance fee. Allow 1hr.*

The entrance is through a **gateway** that stands proud from the **outer ramparts**, across a bridge spanning the moat. Beyond the ticket office, a vaulted **passageway** leads up and round towards the inner castle: note how the steps are graduated to allow the horses to negotiate their way to safety inside. The rooms on the left, set into the eastern flank, were used for defensive purposes – hence the loopholes and machicolations – and for stabling the animals.

*Where the ramp turns sharply to the left, continue straight on out into the open air.*

On the right sits a large 72m long **cistern**, fed from the outside by the aqueduct and by a series of ducts, which channelled the rainwater off the terraces in the event of a siege. To the left rise a succession of domes belonging to the **hammam** *(accessible by a series of stairways)* installed in the castle after the Crusaders had left. Next you come to the **Great Hall** (60m long) which extends along the south side, enclosed within walls that are 8m thick in places. The original central tower was replaced by the square one by Sultan Qalawun in 1285. The **southeast corner tower\*** at the far end of the great hall has a splendid central pier bearing a long Arabic inscription.

*Follow the wide ditch between the two enclosure walls.*

On the right below a wall sit the castle **wells** which were accessible from the floor above: note the exceptional lower section of the innermost **wall** on the right, reinforced with massive earthworks to withstand earthquake tremors and the enemy tunnelling from the outside. The rectangular tower on the right was the old **postern** of the first fort, complete with three substantial arches engineered to provide a system of battlements.

*Continue around the outside of the fortress until you find yourself back by the main ramp and climb the steps into the inner courtyard.*

The **inner precinct** consists of an open area enclosed by the early ramparts of the primitive fortress. The large chamber opening out on the left and supported by large piers was used for **storage**. Opposite the entrance, slightly to the right, stretches an elegant **loggia\*\*** reminiscent of Gothic cloisters: complete with ribs springing up to form a vault from stones sculpted with foliage. Beyond stands a **large chamber,** in which the Knights Hospitallers would have assembled for meetings, and this leads into the **long room\*\*** (120m) where the garrison was billeted. At the far end, on the left, there were facilities for drawing water from the well and an oven, which was connected to the storerooms below and which provided heating; on the right stood a row of a dozen or so **latrines**.

*Make your way back to the courtyard.*

Beneath the stairs, opposite the loggia, stands the castle **chapel**: a more sober building than the loggia, closely allied to the Romanesque churches found back in Western Europe. The semicircular apse is inset into the first rampart. To the right is a *minbar*, installed alongside the mihrab niche when the chapel was converted into a mosque by its Islamic conquerors.

*Mount the steps from the inner courtyard to the terrace extending above the storerooms.*

Crusader castles and the coast

Three huge round towers, built between the first and second sets of defences, used to defend the south flank, instead of a powerful donjon. The perfectly round northwest tower, across the curtain wall, shelters an elegant **Master chamber\*** on the first floor, decorated with a continuous frieze of five-petalled flowers, presumed to be the living quarters of the castle commander. The **view\*\*** from the top is amazingly far-reaching: in spring, the snow-capped peaks of the mountains of Lebanon are visible across the Homs Gap.

*Return to the terrace above the storerooms.*

The narrow passageway running along the west wall leads to the **Tower of the King's Daughter**, which now houses the castle restaurant.

*Follow the ramp by which you entered down and out to the car park below.*

# Making the most of Krak des Chevaliers

## COMING AND GOING

**By taxi –** From Hama

**By bus –** From Homs. Take a microbus from the main bus station for Qalaat al-Hosn, which will drop you right at the castle (the journey takes about an hour). Check the time of the last bus for the return journey, as there are few departures after 4pm.

## WHERE TO STAY

*Under US$20*
**La Table Ronde Hotel**, 200m from the car park, ☏ (31) 74 02 80 – 4rm ⌁ ✗ Modest accommodation which stands a good chance of being full, as it only has 4 rooms. You can also camp here (tents provided). The hotel has the advantage of being the only one near the castle, and is a particularly useful place to stay for those without transport. The pleasant dining room overlooks the valley, with views of the Krak.

*From US$20-40*
**Pepars Hotel,** ☏ (31) 741 201 – 16rm ⌁ A brand new hotel, whose elevated situation means that you can enjoy one of the best views of the Krak. Functional, clean rooms with private balconies. The hotel is due to expand with the addition of 14 new rooms.
**Al-Riad Hotel**, at the turn-off for Al-Nassara, near St George's church, ☏ (31) 730 402, Fax (31) 730 000 – 15rm ⌁ ⚖ ℘ ✗ The building is rather tatty, and, although the entrance hall has been done up, the rooms sometimes smell musty. Friendly and good value. Some rooms have balconies with a view of the Krak.

*From US$40-60*
**Amar Tourist Resort Hotel**, 4km down the road past the castle, ☏ (31) 730 512, Fax (31) 730 648 – 40rm ⌁ 🖹 TV ✗ ⚓ A little off the beaten track (transport is vital), but the setting makes it worthwhile. Spacious, though slightly shabby rooms, some with kitchenette and balcony. The Syrians book full board by the week. Unfortunately, the hotel is only open from May to September. Booking essential in July and August.

*From US$55-70*
🐾 **Al-Wadi Hotel**, 1.5km from the monastery of St George, ☏ (31) 730 456, Fax (31) 730 399 – 55rm ⌁ ℘ TV ✗ ⚓ ⚘ An excellent place to stay, with spacious rooms and views of the Krak. Open all year. Don't miss the strange dusk concert of animals in the valley. Large dining room and lovely terrace around the pool. The newer rooms have air-conditioning.

## EATING OUT

*Under US$10*
**Les Chevaliers (Assad al-Kurdi)**, by the Krak car park, ☏ (31) 740 411. ♟ A good place to eat, where the menu includes *meze*, chicken and kebabs, as well as steak and veal. Groups welcome. The terrace is pleasant, though the view is less spectacular than that of the Table Ronde.
**Filles du Roi**, inside the Krak. ♟ For lunch at the castle. The restaurant is found in the north tower. Lovely stone dining room with frescoes from the chapel. Local menu: *hummus, tabbouleh*, roast chicken and kebabs cooked outdoors.

# KRAK TO TARTUS
## VIA SAFITA
63km circuit – Allow half a day.
See regional map p 164

### And remember...
This route is delightful in fine weather, but if it is raining or foggy
it is better to take the more direct route to Safita.

This excursion takes in the Monastery of St George before continuing to Safita along a small, and somewhat bumpy, winding mountain road. Furthermore, the route is further complicated by a number of small tracks branching off towards various scattered villages, but the wild countryside, dominated by olives and oaks, is quite beautiful.

Alternatively, take the Homs road to where it connects with the motorway to Tartus and follow directions for Safita.

*From Krak go back to the junction with the main road below the village of Qalaat al-Hosn, 4km away. Turn left, passing before the Riald and Al-Wadi hotels, and continue a further 4km, looking out for a view of the monastery.*

■ **St George's Monastery** (Deir Mar Georgis) – *Guided tours conducted by a monk. No charge for entry, but donations welcome. Allow 20min.*

The monastery, perched up on a hillside opposite Krak, shields its tiny community of Greek Orthodox monks from the outside world behind tall bare walls of ochre-coloured stone. The complex was founded in the 6C sometime during the reign of Justinian and includes two superimposed chapels. The **new church** - on the right of the main courtyard - dates from the 19C and houses a sophisticated neo-Baroque iconostasis made of walnut. The icons produced by the School of Jerusalem are signed and dated 1870. The Virgin Mary and Christ are depicted either side of the holy doors.

The **old church** is situated off the second courtyard below, accessible down a flight of stairs. Inside this 13C chapel stands a superb ebony altar screen carved with flowers and scenes from the life of St George. The 18C icons here are by the School of Antioch. The curtains covering the base or predella of the iconostasis cover a set of beautiful faience panels made in Damascus.

*Head back towards Krak, but 2.5km from the monastery and before the turning for the castle, turn left towards Al-Nassara. Do not enter the town but continue along the main road.*

The road offers fine views of Krak and the sea beyond before entering the large and sprawling town of **Marmarita** stretched out on either side. Eventually, you will pass below a spectacularly situated villa, just as the impressive donjon of Safita appears in the west, rising tall above the gently rolling countryside. As the road dips between low dry-stone walls, the landscape becomes sharper, tamed in part by man into terraces of olive groves. At last, you descend into a valley to rejoin the road from Safita to Machta al-Helou, 16km from Marmarita.

*At this junction turn left; then after 4km fork right along a good road that leads to the outskirts of Safita (6km) and a roundabout with numerous signs. Continue towards the town centre (one-way), looking out for a small street on the right leading up to the donjon (al-Bourj), which runs up through the ruined gateway to the castle.*

**Crusader castles and the coast**

■ **Safita★** — The town looks down onto a series of undulating hills covered with olive trees. The houses of the old town are stacked up against the tallest hill, which rises to a height of 400m. At the top sits an imposing keep, the last remaining feature of the Crusader castle known as the "Chastel blanc". This region was seized by the Crusaders in 1112, snatched by Nureddin in 1167 and 1171 and finally restored to the Knights Templar. An earthquake in 1202 made it necessary for the complex to be rebuilt, and many of the surviving buildings date from this period. In 1271, Baybars captured the fortress on his way to Krak.

The great rectangular **donjon★★** *(Open daily, 8am-1pm, 4pm-7.30pm in summer, 3pm-6pm in winter. No charge, although it is customary to make a donation to the church. Park down below the donjon)* was originally encircled by two sets of walls that have provided the inhabitants of Safita with a ready supply of cut building stone since the 19C. Standing 27m high, this keep is one of the largest to have been built by the Crusaders. The ground floor continues to be used for religious functions. The old castle **chapel★★**, meanwhile, now shelters the Greek Orthodox Church of St Michael. As this was built principally for military purposes, the interior is feebly lit by five narrow slits that resemble loopholes rather more than windows. The nave extends to a semicircular apse, flanked by two smaller apses. The vast underground cistern, hewn from the base rock, is not open to the public. To the right of the entrance, a staircase leads up to the elegant **guard-room★** on the first floor: the three massive piers bisecting the room were implanted to support the upper sections of the keep. The thick walls are pierced with loopholes. From the open terrace at the top there is a marvellous **view★★★** over old Safita and the surrounding countryside.

To reach the town centre, walk down the alleyway that picks its way between various attractive houses.

*To continue to Tartus, take the main road (one-way) through Safita past the Hotel Cham.*

# Making the most of Safita

## COMING AND GOING

**By bus** – Take a minibus from Tartus bus station (45min), departures every 30min. You will be dropped on the eastern side of the town, not far from the citadel. There is also a bus service from Homs (90min). There is no public transport between Safita and Krak des Chevaliers.

## WHERE TO STAY

There is only one mediocre hotel, apart from the Safita Cham Palace.

*From US$20-30*
**Burj Safita Hotel**, 500m from the main roundabout to the east of the town, ☎ (43) 521 932 – 12rm. Prices excessive for a basic hotel. The owner is barely civil and only speaks Arabic.

*From US$80-100*
**Safita Cham Palace Hotel**, ☎ (43) 525 980, Fax (43) 525 984 – 67rm 🛎 🗏 🖉 📺 ✕ 🏊 🖭 This hill-side hotel overlooks the road that approaches Safita from the west. A lovely place to stay in summer, in this cooler region, with swimming pool and solarium open May to mid-October, and country views from all rooms. Reserve at least 10 days ahead. Off-peak reductions.

## EATING OUT

*Under US$10*
**Al-Bourj**, in the square near the tower, ☎ (43) 521 773. ♟ The large dining room overlooking olive groves is good for families and groups. Roast chicken and cold *meze*.

**Al-Kanatir**, in a street off the main street (500m from the turning for the tower), ☎ (43) 524 097. ♟ The restaurant with attractive archways occupies the former seraglio under the French mandate. View over the valley gardens. Rustic setting where you can eat kebabs and grilled chicken. Bar.

# TARTUS ★
Capital of the Mouhafazat
Pop 70 000

**Not to be missed**
The cathedral.
Margat Castle (32km away).
**And remember...**
Try one of the local fish restaurants.

Tartus is the most endearing of Syria's seaside towns nestling along the shores of the Mediterranean. Its heart is contained, unusually, within the confines of a Crusader citadel. The short seafront – glamorously named the "corniche" – is lined with cafés and restaurants that offer up freshly cooked fish bought at the nearby market, a stone's throw from the fishing-harbour. What makes this little town a particular favourite are the jostling lines of building – frontages, unchanged since the Middle Ages, and the splendid Frankish cathedral in their midst (although beach-lovers may prefer Latakia). The people here are also friendly and apparently unaffected by tourism.

Various locals use their small boats to run visitors to the adjacent island of Arwad, which makes for a highly enjoyable excursion.

## Tortosa to the Crusaders

The name Tartus is a corruption of Antartus, which in turn derived from "Ante-Aradus" – the place opposite Arwad Island, which, according to the Bible, was the place of origin of a band of celebrated Phoenician sailors.. The first fortified stronghold to be built there was erected by the Knights Templar; this was destroyed in 1291, the same year that a similar castle at Acre fell, marking the final stage in the eviction of the Crusaders from Syria.

Tartus was radically transformed with the advent of a railway that linked the then sleepy seaside hamlet to Homs and Latakia, and vindicated the development of a major new harbour (Syria's second largest). The local preference for large, spacious houses has meant that new residential areas have mushroomed inland, thereby preserving the seafront. For some years now, the citadel has been undergoing restoration.

## Tour of Tartus
*Allow 2hr.*

*Start out from the fishing harbour, where the main street meets the corniche.*

The **old port** (A2) hosts a lively fish market where freshly caught sea bream, mullet and tuna fish goes on sale to passing trade, although prices are surprisingly high.

The tower-cum-windmill opposite marks the southern limit of the town's 12C **outer defences**. A few yards northwards along the seafront, it is possible to make out the line of the old ramparts facing out towards the sea, now overtaken by modern buildings; until quite recently, the waves used to break onto the walls. The break in the continuous line of buildings (after some 200m, beyond the Cave restaurant) marks the beginning of the horse-shoe-shaped citadel.

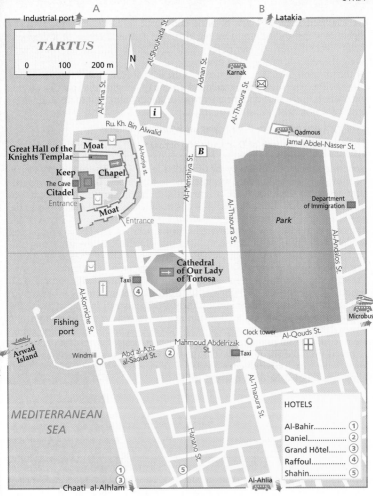

Continue along the base of the keep and round the north-western corner of the citadel to see where the moat once encircled the stronghold.

Walk past the mosque and up a passageway that runs beneath the **Great Hall of the Knights Templar** to reach the gateway into the **citadel**★ (A1). The inner yard of the fortified precinct has long since served as the central square of the old town. An alley on the left leads to the **chapel** fronted by a heavily restored vaulted entrance. Little of the four vaulted bays of the nave remains intact and the two sets of steps leading up to private houses have turned the space into a kind of front yard! The upper section of the massive **donjon**★, rusticated to emphasise its impenetrability, has been converted into residential quarters, but it is still possible to admire the base through one of the window openings. The narrow streets, lined with ancient stone buildings scuffed and fashioned by time, are insulated from all kinds of noise and bustle, occasionally interrupted by flights of steps leading up to an old door, by a shaded recess or a dead-end street. To find your way out of the citadel and its labyrinthine alleyways, walk along the left side of the inner mosque.

At the junction, turn down the street on the left (Al-Horiya Street) to the **moat**: there before you stretches a medley of dwellings clinging like parasites to the old walls, eclipsed here and there by rows of laundry hung out to dry and forests of television aerials.

*Turn right and head down to the square set before the cathedral.*

The **Cathedral Church of Our Lady of Tortosa★** (A2) (*Open 9am-6pm in summer, 9am-4pm in winter; closed Tuesdays. Entrance fee*) was built of shell-encrusted limestone with lovely ochre hues by the Crusaders in the 12C. The cathedral's austere exterior suggests the building was intended to have a defensive role, but its true fame rested on the importance attached to the ancient shrine within, dedicated to the Virgin Mary, that attracted pilgrims from far and wide. Alterations in the course of the 13C explain the presence of Gothic features.

The nave comprises four bays covered with four-part vaults. The second pier on the left rests on a cube of masonry. It is thought that the low vault was connected to the Byzantine chapel, which is supposed to have housed one of the first icons bearing a portrait of the Virgin Mary, painted by St Luke.

The cathedral now houses a **museum** devoted to antiquities found in the coastal region. In the aisles on the right are displayed fragments from Ugarit as well as various Hellenistic and Roman sites; there is also a small Islamic section. The **Roman sarcophagus★** (2C AD) in the apse is carved with a scene from the Oriental myth of Tammuz (equivalent to the Greek Adonis). To its left is a fragment of fresco from Krak des Chevaliers. The north aisle is given over to artefacts retrieved from the site of Amrit. On the way out there is a group of ten, probably Phoenician, **sarcophagi★★** made of terracotta or stone, adorned with representations of the dead interred within.

*Make your way back to the seafront down the street opposite the cathedral.*

# Arwad Island

*2hr excursion, including the crossing.*

Like many a little Greek island, Arwad Island is dotted with blue and white houses and populated by weather-beaten fishermen mending their nets or patiently building boats in the small boatyard. But the spell is soon broken after you set foot on the island and venture into the narrow alleyways of the town. For the island – which you can walk right around in 30min – is overpopulated. Local children have little to do other than hassle visitors; piles of putrefying rubbish line the streets and fill the air with evil smells as the daytime temperature rises.

Having said this, the boat ride across the few kilometres of sea separating the island from the mainland is nonetheless refreshing and highly pleasurable. And once you get there, it is good to take up position at one of the restaurants overlooking the harbour and watch the little boats coming and going, unloading their cargoes of passengers and provisions. Otherwise, you can walk up the main street (*beyond the jetty and slightly to the right*) to the **castle** and local **museum** (*Open 9am-5pm in summer, 9am-2pm in winter; closed Tuesdays. Entrance fee*) housed within its walls, displaying a very modest display of objects recovered from the sea (shells and amphorae). The castle testifies to the strategic importance of Arwad, the only inhabited island off what was once known as the Levantine

J F Galmiche

Cathedral Church of Our Lady of Tortosa (Tartus)

coast, stretching from Syria to Egypt. In ancient times, this Phoenician outpost rivalled the great maritime cities of Tyre, Sidon and Byblos, and the Arwad mentioned in the Bible suggests many of the best seamen came from here. But only a few lonely fragments of the high walls to the south and west of the harbour now survive from this brilliant period of its history.

## — Making the most of Tartus —

### COMING AND GOING

**By train –** There is a night train from Damascus, which goes via Homs (5hr). The station is to the southeast of the town.

**By bus –** Preferably reserve the previous day.

From Damascus to Tartus (3hr): take a bus from the Harasta bus station in Damascus.

From Tartus:

**Karnak** (B1), 600m north from the belfry. Daily departure for Homs (1hr) and Damascus (3hr).

**Al-Ahlia** office and bus station are 700m south of the clock tower (B2). Excellent air-conditioned buses. Daily departure for Aleppo (3hr). At least two departures per day for Latakia (90min), Hama (90min), Homs (1hr) and Damascus (3hr).

**Qadmous** (B1), at the northwest corner of the public gardens. Frequent service to Baniyas and Latakia by minibus.

**Minibus bus station**, out of the town centre, in front of the station. Several departures per day for Safita (45min) and Baniyas (30min), as well as Latakia, Homs and Damascus.

**By shared taxi –** Several departures per day from near the clock tower, for Homs and Latakia.

### • Arwad

**By boat –** The only means of transport to the island is the boat which leaves every 30min from the small fishing port, between sunrise and sunset. The journey takes 20min in calm weather. Payment on return journey only. Nice view of Tartus seafront at sunset.

### ADDRESS BOOK

**Tourist information** (A1) – to the north of the citadel.

**Main post office** (B1) – Behind the Al-Kindi cinema. Kiosks for phone cards inside.

**Telephone –** Inside the post office.

**Bank/Currency exchange – Commercial Bank of Syria** (A1), Al-Menshiya St, near the tourist office. Changes travellers' cheques and cash. Mornings only.

**Visa extensions –** in a small street behind the public gardens. Formalities dealt with on the spot. 8am-2pm.

### WHERE TO STAY

Tartus has no luxury hotels, being a more popular seaside resort than Latakia. Warning: the town undergoes a transformation in July and August with the influx of Syrian tourists, and it is wise to reserve hotels. Prices drop noticeably outside this period.

*Under US$20*

Three modest hotels near the main street and the fishing port.

**Daniel Hotel**, Abid al-Aziz al-Saoud St, ☎ (43) 220 581, Fax (43) 316 555 – 35rm ⁂ ⌁ Rooms of varying quality on several different floors, but peaceful. Second-floor reception accustomed to tourists. Furniture has seen better days.

**Raffoul Hotel**, Menchieh Sq (opposite the cathedral), ☎ (43) 220 616 – 9rm ⁂ ⌁ On the second floor of a small building, the bedrooms lead off a corridor which serves as a lounge and kitchenette. Rather basic, but clean. If you find the door locked, you will find the jolly, friendly owner in his grocery store, on the street corner. Cheaper than the above.

*From US$20-35*

**Al-Bahir Hotel**, Al-Korniche St, ☎/Fax (43) 221 687 – 53rm ⁂ ✉ ✗ This large sea-front building has unpretentious, clean rooms. Choose one with a sea view from its balcony. Electric fans and television in some rooms.

*From US$35-50*

**Shahin Hotel**, in the small street parallel to the coast road, ☎ (43) 315 290, Fax (43) 315 002 – 53rm ⚉ 🍴 ≣ ℓ 📺 ✗ CC  Very good value, for a hotel which provides air-conditioning and minibar service, even if the balconies don't have sea views. However, the seafood restaurant has splendid panoramic views of the Med.

🏨 **Grand Hotel**, Al-Korniche St, 500m south of windmill, ☎ (43) 315 681, Fax (43) 315 683 – 100rm ⚉ ≣ ℓ 📺 ✗ CC  This is the best hotel in town, offering comfortable rooms. Half have sea views, with balconies for enjoying the sunset.

## EATING OUT

For fast food (pizza, kebabs, shawarma, fresh fruit juice), you will find plenty of delicious snacks in the town centre, especially in the street near the Shahin Hotel.

Tartus is the best place in Syria to enjoy fresh fish. You can choose from mullet, sea bream or tuna, served grilled or fried, always accompanied· by grilled Arab bread and often with a salad. You will be invited to choose your fish. The best restaurants are found along the coast road and around the harbour. Even in Tartus, fish is expensive compared to other dishes. Prices are around S£1 000 per kilo. There are two restaurants on the island of Arwad.

*Under US$10*

**Al-Nabil**, Al-Korniche St, just behind the windmill. A popular restaurant where good family cooking is served. Don't be put off by the chickens roasting outside; they also serve fish. You can even buy your own at the market and ask the restaurant to cook it for you.

**Sari**, Abd al-Aziz al-Saoud St, almost opposite the Daniel Hotel If the thought of fish doesn't tempt you, this is an air-conditioned fast-food restaurant, where pizzas, hot-dogs and hamburgers are cooked to order. On your way out, through the shopping arcade, sample a *qara*, a delicious sweetmeat made from marrow.

*Over US$10*

🏨 **The Cave**, Al-Korniche St (in front of the citadel). ⚑ The most picturesque spot in town, with its lovely cool medieval stone vaults. The house speciality is excellent fish, seasoned with fresh thyme and garlic. Attractive presentation. Terrace.

## OTHER THINGS TO DO

**Swimming –** For those determined to swim (understandable in the summer), the town beach lies 1.5km south of Tartus at Chaati al-Ahlam, where there are bungalows. The amount of rubbish on the beach may put you off swimming, however.

**Cafés –** There are several pleasant little cafés along the coast road. The one opposite the windmill is the best place to watch the comings and goings of the port or the sunset. The local clientele will probably be relaxing by smoking hookahs or playing tric-trac.

**Making the most of Tartus**

# MARGAT CASTLE★★

(QALAAT AL-MARQAB)
Situated 10km from Baniyas,
between Tartus (32km) and Latakia (60km)

## And remember...
For an overview of the castle, follow the road
uphill as far as you can to the gates of the military camp.

*From Tartus: drive along the motorway towards Latakia, whichthreads its way between the mountains and the sea. 28km from Tartus, you will see the castle walls in the distance; take the next road on the right just before an isolated tower rising tall above the highway. The road climbs steeply for 4km up to the castle.*

*By bus: services both from Tartus and Latakia to Baniyas bus station and then taxi or minibus to the castle that lies some 10km further south.*

The dark silhouette of Margat (Marqab) Castle, situated on the westernmost buttresses of Jebel Ansariyeh, stand high (360m) above the sea, 7km from Baniyas (*see illustration p 162*). Although this stronghold is less well preserved than Krak des Chevaliers, its location and the scale of its fortifications make it exceptional. Its position enabled movements off the coastal strip of land to be monitored at close range, especially at times when enemy troops might be rallying prior to mounting an attack.

The castle was built by an obscure Crusader family (the Mazoyers) that hailed from an unknown region of France. The fact that a descendant of the family later married the daughter of the Count of Tripoli substantiates the considerable esteem generated by the Crusades. The building proved to be a considerable financial burden, so in 1186 it was ceded to the Knights Hospitallers who already occupied Krak des Chevaliers. They turned it into the greatest stronghold in Syria. After the battle of Hattin the following year, Saladin managed to secure control of the coast and the northern regions of Syria, while choosing to avoid attacking the castle. In 1285, when Krak had already fallen, the Mameluke Sultan Qalawun laid siege to Margat. For five weeks the troops interned in the fortress waited in vain for reinforcements before giving themselves up to the sappers entrenched all around. It was not long before restoration was begun under the orders of the sultan.

## Tour
*(Open 9am-6pm in summer, 9am-4pm in winter; closed Tuesdays. Entrance fee. Allow 45min)*

Climb the steps from the car park that lead up and around the outer walls, cross the moat and continue to the **tower** located in the middle of the west front. Below the vestibule on the left a huge lower courtyard opens out, from where a circuit of the battlement walkway can be made, affording panoramic views over Baniyas and the sea, but entailing additional time and effort. Proceed some 30m between the two sets of walls to the **gate** (1270) on the right that provides access to an inner courtyard, which for many is the most interesting part of the complex. The platform on the right scattered with pier-bases and broken keystones, is all that survives from the vaulted **great hall** of the Knights Hospitallers. To the right stands the **Diwan al-Malik**, or **king's**

Crusader castles and the coast

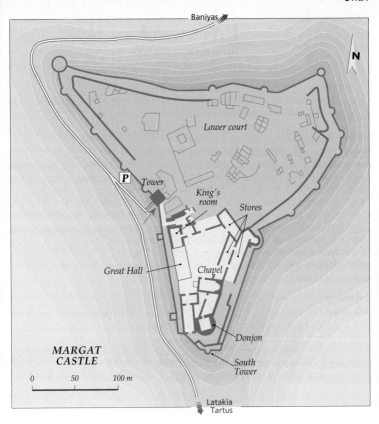

Baniyas

N

Lower court

P Tower

King's room

Stores

Great Hall

Chapel

Donjon

South Tower

*MARGAT CASTLE*

0    50    100 m

Latakia
Tartus

**room** (now occupied by the custodian), whose name is thought to allude to Isaac Comnenus who was imprisoned and died at Margat. Chroniclers recount how this Byzantine prince wore chains of gold and silver after being captured in Cyprus by Richard the LionHeart. The northern flank of the courtyard is taken up by the **chapel⋆** (1186). The austerity of the nave is somewhat relieved by two four-part vaults, before terminating in an apse. A small chamber abutting the left side of the choir preserves traces of fresco paintings representing the twelve Apostles. Walk around the right side of the building (noting the fine doorway) to reach a collection of huge halls. The one nearest the chapel is connected to the **donjon⋆** by a flight of stairs. This **circular tower⋆**, which measures 22m in diameter, comprises two superimposed square rooms. The **view⋆⋆** from the terrace is superb. From here it is also possible to see the inside of the precinct, complete with the **South Tower⋆** set into the enclosure walls that once ran right around the stronghold. The course of white stones in the upper section (which, together with the tower, can be seen from several hundred metres away from the road leading towards the castle from the south) bears a long Arabic inscription describing the repairs carried out by Sultan Qalawun.

# LATAKIA ★
Capital of the mouhafazat
Pop 260 000

**And remember...**
Have a meal at the Spiro restaurant, a veritable institution in Latakia.
For a swim, go to the beaches at Ras Ibn Hani.

In recent years, Syria's largest commercial harbour has developed here, swallowing up the picturesque old fishing port and stripping the seafront of its former charm. So, rather than walk along the industrial docks, you may prefer to go for a swim off the beaches along the **Ras Ibn Hani** peninsula, north of the town, where two large modern hotels have been built (Chaati al-Azraq or Blue Beach quarter). Latakia, despite its rich past, presents little of great interest. It is nonetheless a pleasant place and far less oppressive than the traditional cities of Aleppo and Damascus: indeed, people liken Latakia to a Lebanese resort largely because of its modern attitude. Few women wear veils, as the majority of the local population is Alawite or Christian. Latakia also provides a convenient place to stay for visiting the sites of Ugarit and Saône Castle at Sahyun (Qalaat Salahuddin).

## History
The town of Latakia goes back to Seleucid times when **Seleucus I Nicator** set about designing an elegant city on Classical principles named Laodicea after his mother. Then came the Romans, although little remains from this period, save for the odd column re-erected here and there and the interesting tetrapylon testifying to the importance of the ancient maritime trade centre. In the hands of Arabs, then Crusaders between 1098-1187, when it was known as La Liche, Latakia gradually declined as Alexandretta and Tripoli grew. The town recovered some of its status after being designated capital of the Alawite State during the French Mandate, and more commercial eminence when the port of Alexandretta was ceded to Turkey in 1939. Today, several million tonnes of imported merchandise pass through the port of Latakia every year.

## Tour of the town
*Allow 2hr.*

The **Latakia museum** (*Open 8am-2pm; closed Tuesdays. Entrance fee*), situated at the southern end of the seafront near the casino, is housed in an old restored caravanserai (16C) converted for use as the official residence of the Alawite State Governor. Fragments of the old building lie scattered beneath the palm trees, mimosas and monkey-puzzle trees in the garden. In the five vaulted rooms are displayed a variety of artefacts recovered during the excavation of Ugarit. These include a stone statue of the **god El** (13C BC) found in 1988 and, in the Islamic section, a hoard of gold coins alongside a fine coat of chain mail.

It is a short walk from the museum, along the **seafront** (400m), to the Spiro and Al-Assafari restaurants, both of which have gardens.

On the opposite side of town stands the **tetrapylon★** that probably marked the intersection of the two main streets of the Roman town. Miraculously, its vault flanked by four bays survives intact. A little further along the same street, a collection of Corinthian columns marks where the **Temple of Adonis** once stood.

Crusader castles and the coast

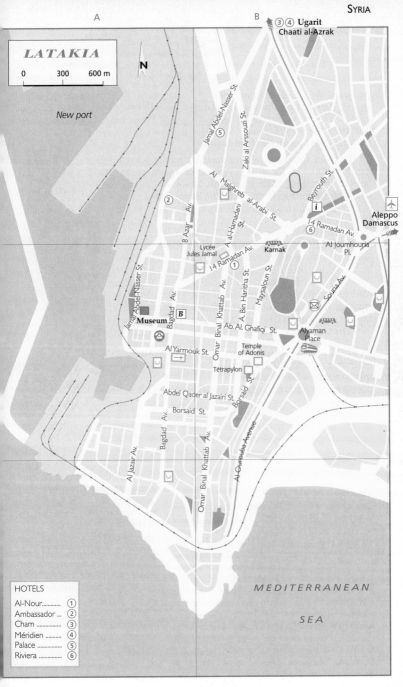

SYRIA

③ ④ **Ugarit**
Chaati al-Azrak

LATAKIA

0    300    600 m

N

*New port*

Jamal Abdel-Nasser St.

Zaki al Arssouzi St.

⑤

Al Maghreb al-Arabi St.

Beyrouth St.

*i*

**Aleppo**
**Damascus**

8 Azar Av.

A. al-Hamadani St.

14 Ramadan Av.

⑥

② 

Lycée
Jules Jamal

14 Ramadan Av.

①

Karnak

Al Joumhouria Pl.

Jamal Abdel-Nasser St.

Bagdad Av.

*B*

**Museum**

Omar Binal Khattab Av.

A. Bin Haritha St.

Maysaloun St.

Souria Av.

Ab. Al. Ghafiqi St.

Al Yarmouk St.

Temple
of Adonis

Alyaman
Place

Tétrapylon

Borsaid St.

Abdel Qader al Jazairi St.

Borsaid St.

Bagdad Av.

Al Qurouba Avenue

Al Jazair Av.

Omar Binal Khattab Av.

*MEDITERRANEAN*

*SEA*

HOTELS

| | |
|---|---|
| Al-Nour............ | ① |
| Ambassador ... | ② |
| Cham ............... | ③ |
| Méridien .......... | ④ |
| Palace .............. | ⑤ |
| Riviera ............. | ⑥ |

# Ugarit★
## (Ras Shamra)
*Open 8am-6pm in summer, 8am-5pm in winter; closed Tuesdays.*
*Entrance fee. Allow 1hr.*

*On leaving the Latakia Museum, follow the coast road north for 2km before turning off towards Kassab. After 5km, turn left along a road flanked by groves of orange trees, and continue 2km before turning left again. The site of Ugarit lies just over 1km from the junction (100m from the road). Independent travellers without use of a vehicle should take a taxi from Latakia.*

J P Garcin/DIAF

All the main museums in Syria have collections testifying to the importance of the Bronze Age site at Ugarit, a city that boasted flourishing trade links with Mesopotamia and the whole Mediterranean basin, including Egypt, making it one of the leading international harbours in the ancient world. But although the town was built of stone, which, in theory, should have been more durable than the brick used for the cities of Mesopotamia, the site is somewhat disappointing. Only a metre or so of the palace, temple and house walls remain standing, often obscured by grass (much to the delight of the local goats), and so it is quite hard to imagine how the site might have looked, let alone envisage the cosmopolitan atmosphere of the place in its heyday. Excavations have been in progress since 1929 under the direction of the French archeologist Claude Schaeffer.

Head from Ugarit

## Widespread usage of the Ugarit alphabet
Following a rather turbulent early history, the Canaanites – who were a Semitic tribe – established themselves in Syria and Palestine and grew to become the dominant people in the region throughout the 2nd millennium BC. During those times, the successive ruling dynasties worked hard at maintaining good relations with neighbouring peoples and rival powers: Egyptians, Hittites, Babylonians and Mitannians. The kingdom of Ugarit was never very extensive but its lands were fertile. The territory extended east as far as the nearby range of mountains, and south to include Latakia and Jableh. In the 14C BC Ugarit was hit by a violent earthquake, most of the city had to be rebuilt and its golden age began. It is at this time that the Ugarit alphabet is thought to have been invented: an important event that was to help formulate the Hebrew, Greek and Arabic alphabets. The new written language spread quickly to the Aegean in the 13C BC, largely as a result of the long-standing trade links with the northern part of the Mediterranean. Ugarit's commercial prosperity was suddenly interrupted with the arrival of the "Sea Peoples" in about 1200 BC.

**The birth of the alphabet**
One sign, one sound. From this fundamental, but ingenious concept, the idea of an alphabet and a written form of language was formulated. About 30 signs proved sufficient. This prodigious advance, which was widely diffused if not actually invented by the inhabitants of Ugarit, radically upset the old system of Mesopotamian ideograms that conveyed meaning with symbols. Eventually this written language became accessible to all and vital for all kinds of trade. The signs or letters, which to us appear so far removed from the Latin alphabet, despite being derived from the Ugarit alphabet, were inscribed on tablets using the old cuneiform technique. Their T-shaped marks on the tablets resemble the imprints of little tacks.

*For more information about the alphabet, see p 132.*

Crusader castles and the coast

## Tour of the site

*The ticket office has a little shop selling guidebooks and souvenirs. There are two drinks stalls opposite the ruins.*

Before reaching the ticket office, you pass through the remains of the ancient town's defences complete with **postern\***. The concealed doorway was once surmounted by what was probably a fortified tower with walls more than 5m thick. Added protection was provided outside the city walls by a steep glacis (substantial earthworks).

The ruins on the site date mainly from the 13C-14C BC. Just below the ticket office, on the right, lie the vestiges of the **Royal Palace\*\***, the best preserved building at Ugarit. At ground level, you can make out the base of two columns that marked the threshold of a paved vestibule that opened out onto a square. Once inside the palace, there are several rooms that served as archives. On the right was situated the main courtyard of the palace, paved and furnished with a well, surrounded on all sides by a series of 100 rooms that stretch over some 6 500sqm. The remains of steps seem to suggest that the palace comprised at least two floors. One particularly attractive little courtyard among the maze of rooms provides some insight into the sophistication of Ugarit society, as confirmed by the ivory artefacts on display in the National Museum in Damascus.

*Make your way out of the palace and follow the narrow street running alongside the palace wall.*

To the left stand the ruins of the **North Palace**, complete with the upright markers coated with bitumen defining the central courtyard. To the right stretched a **residential quarter** made up of large, spacious town houses owned by the wealthier inhabitants of Ugarit and criss-crossed by a network of narrow alleyways. As at the palace, family life was enacted upstairs on the first floor. On exploring the site, you may chance upon the vaulted **underground burial chamber\*\*** beneath the house of Rapanou (the most elegant) fronted by a short flight of steps. The vault is absolutely typical, for it was standard practice for the

**Ugarit**

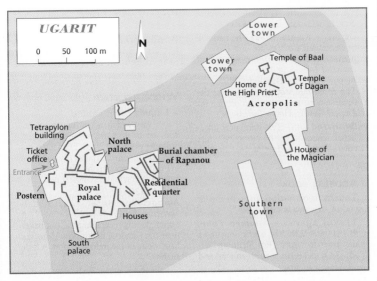

people of Ugarit to inter their ancestors under the family home. Further down the street, the path leads away from the residential quarters towards the **acropolis**, in front of which archeologists have cut a substantial trench. It was up here that the great temples of Baal and Dagan once stood (now almost indiscernible), and the **view**\* across to Mount Cassius in the north (Djebel al-Akra, 1728m) marking the border with Turkey is quite special. Mount Cassius was thought by the ancients to be where the god Baal lived. If the number of bronze statuettes covered with gold leaf found hereabouts is anything to go by, his cult enjoyed widespread popularity.

North of the acropolis lay the **lower town**; from the path downhill, the view stretches out towards the coast concealed by a screen of cypresses and orange trees. It was here that the ancient harbour of Ugarit, Minet el-Beida, was situated.

# Making the most of Latakia

## COMING AND GOING

**By car** – Latakia is accessible from Tartus, Homs and Damascus by motorway, and from Aleppo by a narrow road which follows the Nahr al-Kebir valley.

**By air** – Latakia's airport lies to the south of the town, near the turning for Al-Qardaha. There are infrequent flights to Damascus.

**By train** – The new Aleppo-Latakia line is very picturesque, with a 3-4hr-journey through rugged countryside, including impressive contours crossed by viaducts. The **station** (B2) is 1km from the town centre, near the new post office. Night train for Damascus.

**By bus** – **Karnak** (B1-2), the national bus company's offices are near the telephone exchange (on the opposite side of Baghdad Ave). 1 or 2 buses per day for Aleppo (3hr) and Damascus (5hr).
**The main bus station** (B2) is near the train station. Regular return service for Aleppo, Tartus, Homs, Damascus.

**By shared taxi** – Taxi stand near Jules-Jamal school (B2), the attractive white colonial-style building at 14 Ramadan Ave.

## ADDRESS BOOK

**Tourist information** (B1) – At the far end of 14 Ramadan Ave.

**Travel agents** – **Shamra Tour**, ☎ (41) 464 236. The agency organises day trips to Ugarit (Ras Shamra), Saladin's Citadel (Qala'at Salah ah-Din) and

Slenfeh (with views over the Ghab plain). S£3 500 per person, including entrance fees to sites, lunch and transport. Reductions for groups. Reserve at least 12hr in advance at one of the hotels (eg Riviera).

**Airline companies** – **Syria Arab Airlines** office is in Baghdad Ave (A2).

**Main post office** (B2) – The new post office is near the train station. 8am-6pm.

**Telephone** (A2) – Behind the museum. 8am-8pm. Kiosk with phone card outside.

**Express mail** – **DHL**, opposite the telephone exchange, ☎ (41) 226 066.

**Bank/Currency exchange** – **Exchange bureau** (A2), Baghdad Ave, near Al-Boustan café. 8am-7.30pm; closed Fridays.

## WHERE TO STAY

• **Latakia town centre**
Prices vary widely according to season, with up to 40 % reductions in winter. Summer prices are listed. Even if the hotel is on the seafront (Jamal Abdel-Nasser St) don't expect to be able to swim: Latakia is first and foremost a port.

*From US$20-40*
**Ambassador Hotel**, Jamal Abdel-Nasser St, ☎ (41) 477 725 – 40rm 🛉 A rather gloomy reception area, but better than the Gandool next door. 15 rooms have views of the industrial port. A little shabby.

**Al-Nour Hotel**, 14 Ramadan St, ☎ (41) 423 980 – 30rm ⌀ ⌇ This hotel represents the best value for money in town, even though it lacks charm. Not always very friendly. A little more expensive than the above, but the difference in price is justified.

*From US$35-50*

**Palace Hotel**, Jamal Abdel-Nasser St, ☎ (41) 469 250, Fax (41) 470 170 – 50rm ⌀ ▤ ✗ TV ✗ CC Without doubt the best hotel in town. Sea views, spacious, light, well-equipped rooms. The only problem is that the hotel is often reserved for tour groups, and individual travellers may have trouble finding a room. Breakfast included.

*From US$65-80*

**Cham Residence Hotel**, see the description of Cham Côte d'Azur Hotel below.

*From US$80-100*

**Riviera Hotel**, 14 Ramadan Ave, ☎ (41) 421 803, Fax (41) 418 287 – 48rm ⌀ ▤ ✗ TV ✗ CC Spotless bedding and pretty decor. A pity that the hotel is in a noisy town centre street. On the garden side the proximity of neighbours means that the shutters will have to stay closed if you want any privacy!

● **Chaati al-Azrak region**

10km north of the town is the largest seaside resort in Syria, comprising the Cham and Meridien hotels.

*Over US$130*

**Cham Côte d'Azur Hotel**, ☎ (41) 428 700 – 1 053rm ⌀ ▤ ✗ TV ✗ ⌇ ⌘ ⌘ CC A huge complex (Resort) of 3 000 beds in all, comprising both bedrooms and two- and three-floor apartments. 50 % reduction for a room without sea view. Modern, spacious rooms. Corridors rather chilly. The fine private beach is over 500m long.

Next door is a less-luxurious hotel (Residence) belonging to the same chain, which offers rooms from US$65. Access to the beach is via an underpass.

**Meridien Hotel**, Queen Zein St, ☎ (41) 428 736, Fax (41) 428 732 – 274rm ⌀ ▤ ✗ TV ✗ ⌇ ⌘ CC Comfortable rooms with views of the sea or

of the unspoilt Ras Ibn Hani peninsula. Bank open 8am-8pm. Balconies, beach and pool.

**EATING OUT**

As with Tartus, the town's speciality is fish.

● **Latakia town centre**

*Under US$10*

**Casino**, Jamal Abdel-Nasser St, near the museum. ▼ An excellent, good-value restaurant in an old colonial-style building. You might feel rather lost in the high-ceilinged dining room where there is sometimes an orchestra, but the terrace is very pleasant. Delicious *meze*. Try the cheese *beureks*. Fish and kebabs.

**Shallal**, the Palace Hotel's restaurant. ▼ Artificial waterfalls decorate the large basement dining room, with its lovely white tablecloths. Kebabs, *chiche taouk* and *meze*. No fish. Ground floor coffee shop.

*Over US$10*

**Spiro**, Jamal Abdel-Nasser St, 500m from the Palace Hotel, ☎ (41) 238 238. ▼ Closed Fridays. The in-place, but still a friendly welcome. Long dining room. Excellent grilled sea bream, as well as prawns, whiting and mullet, to be accompanied by *meze*. Fish around S£1 400 per kilo.

**Al-Assafari**, Jamal Abdel-Nasser St. ▼ Another restaurant specialising in fish, opposite Spiro. Simpler, but just as good. Hookahs, *arak* and wine.

● **Chaati al-Azrak region**

The Cham and Meridien hotels each offer a variety of excellent restaurants. The clientele tends to be either groups or on the smart side.

**HAVING A DRINK**

**Cafés, bars, tea rooms** – The best places for a drink are the cafés on Baghdad Ave (A2) or on the sea front.

**OTHER THINGS TO DO**

**Outdoor pursuits** – Swimming is possible at Chaati al-Azrak. The hotels will allow non-residents to use the beaches in return for a fee.

**Making the most of Latakia**

# LATAKIA TO ALEPPO★
## VIA SAÔNE CASTLE
191km circuit – A whole day.
See map p 164

**Not to be missed**
The view of the castle from Al-Alhaffeh
or the panoramic restaurant.

**And remember...**
Have lunch near the castle or at Slenfeh.
A visit to the dead cities of Al-Bara and Sergilla
can also be included in this itinerary (p 248).

This route avoids the main highway from Latakia to Aleppo, with its the heavily laden trucks that lumber slowly up the Nahr al-Kebir valley. It also offers the opportunity of enjoying a Crusader castle set in its landscape of green oaks before crossing the Ghab plain along a wonderful brand new road beyond Slenfeh. After visiting Saône Castle at Sahyun (Qalaat Salahuddin), the road should only be negotiated in fine weather as heavy fog can make conditions extremely treacherous. Those intending to break their journey at Slenfeh to enjoy the fresh mountain air should book their accommodation several days in advance in summer.

*Follow signs to Tartus out of Latakia. On the outskirts of town after some 8km, continue over the railway line and pick up directions for Al-Alhaffeh, but avoiding the rather dull route sign-posted on the right along the way. Continue for 23km to the edge of Al-Alhaffeh, and turn right towards Saladin Castle. After 1.5km, turn left and take care when stopping 2.5km later to admire the view of the castle in the distance.*

## ■ Saône Castle at Sahyun★★
(Qalaat Salahuddin)

Saône Castle and its surrounding mountains that extend to Slenfeh make a non-sense of images normally associated with Syria. For here there is no arid desert to be seen; instead the folds of Jebel Ansariyeh are carpeted with forests of oaks until, at last, the landscape merges with the Mediterranean in the distance. It was here, against this remarkably green backdrop reminiscent of their homes in Europe that the Crusaders set about building the grandest fortress in Syria. To this day, the magnificent ruins are one of Syria's great highlights.

### Noble castle
Unlike Krak des Chevaliers and Marqab, the stronghold at Sahyun was never occupied by the military and religious orders such as the Knights Templar or Knights Hospitallers defending the Holy Land. Victorious Byzantine troops erected the first fortress here after regaining control of Syria in the 10C. During the early Crusades (1108), this passed into the hands of a mysterious "master of Sahyun", namely a certain **Robert de Saône.** First he, then his son William, set about building the present castle which remained thereafter the property of the family until taken by **Saladin** in 1188. In more recent times, the Syrian government named the castle after its conqueror Salahuddin, maybe in honour of the mosque and baths he erected there after his conquest.

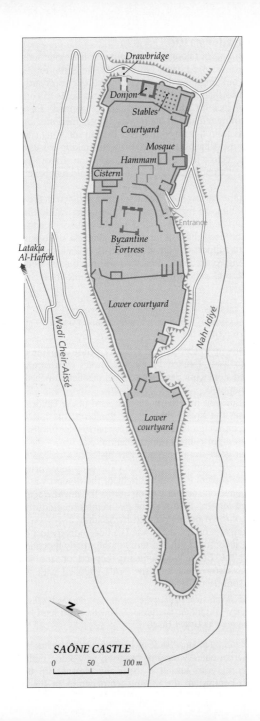

Drawbridge

Donjon

Stables

Courtyard

Mosque

Hammam

Cistern

Byzantine
Fortress

Entrance

Lower courtyard

Latakia
Al-Haffeh

Wadi Cheir-Aïssé

Nahr Idiyé

Lower
courtyard

N

**SAÔNE CASTLE**

0    50    100 m

Saône Castle

## Largest Crusader castle

Perched high on a ridge (alongside a restaurant), the castle suddenly looms into sight on the far side of a ravine. On the left stands the fortified citadel and a number of fine buildings. To the right sits the lower courtyard enclosed by less imposing defences that extend gently downwards so as to continue the line of the long spur of rock on which the complex is founded. The internal area lies in ruins and nothing remains of the modest houses inhabited by the castle farm-labourers. It was from this angle that Saladin and his army came, attacking the castle from its most vulnerable flank, shortly after taking possession of Jerusalem. The castle walls enclose a vast area of 5ha, twice the size of Krak, making it the largest of all the Crusader castles. No modern buildings have been allowed to spoil the site.

Continue down the narrow road into the ravine and across the broad bed of the river before climbing up the other side to the rather extraordinary **moat★★** cut into the mountain bedrock so as to provide the castle with added protection. In the middle of the deep ditch, a single 25m **pinnacle of rock** was left standing by the builder to support the drawbridge. It is difficult to imagine how such a feat of engineering could be accomplished without the use of dynamite. On the right, the natural rock echoes the same rounded contours as those of the towers it supports.

## Tour of the castle

*Open 9am-6pm in summer, 9am-4pm in winter; closed Tuesdays. Entrance fee. Park at the foot of the steps. Allow 1hr.*

A long ramp leads up to the modern entrance before levelling out and reaching across the south front, flanked by elegant towers with carefully dressed and heavily rusticated stonework designed to repel missiles launched by enemy man-gonels (large catapults).

Beyond the bastion you find the main courtyard of the citadel.

To the right, rises the square mass of the **donjon★★** that towers to a height of 23m. The room on the ground floor is lit by narrow loopholes and would have been screened by a portcullis. From the central pier spring the ribs of the vault, divided into four great sections. A stairway provides access to the better lit first floor and the terrace from which to survey the deep moat below.

The large, almost square, hall on the right of the donjon was used as **stables**; the narrow entrance on the left leading out to the **drawbridge** provided a side door for lone messengers. Return to the main entrance and turn right before the square minaret of the **mosque** founded by Saladin.

A little further on, also on the right, stands a fine doorway to a **hammam,** richly decorated in stark contrast to the austerity of the strictly functional military complexes built by the Crusaders. Someway beyond on the same side is the remarkably large **cistern** that kept the castle supplied with water, measuring 36m long and 16m deep.

*Return to Al-Alhaffeh and turn right at the junction. As the road picks its way to Slenfeh 17km away, scrubby oaks fill the landscape. Follow the street lined with lampposts into the centre of town and the Grand Hotel.*

■ **Slenfeh –** Standing at an altitude of 1 100m, this town has become a holiday resort for the Syrian élite. A mass of beautiful new stone buildings have been put up over recent years and it is especially pleasant up here in summer. Conditions – in contrast to the soaring temperatures in the plains – remain balmy and fresh, perfect for going out walking and enjoying the extensive views to the Mediterranean and across the Ghab. The cheap eating-houses make this a convenient place to stop for a quick bite on your way.

*Follow the high street, opposite the Grand Hotel, that slopes gently uphill for some 500m and turn left; then after 200m turn left again. For 5.5km the road climbs up to the ridge before levelling out for 2km before heading down into the valley.*

The road curves around the left-hand side of the tallest land mass in the Jebel Ansariyeh, Mount Al-Nabi Younès (1 538m). On a clear day, one particular lay-by (9km from Slenfeh) provides an extraordinary **view\*\*\*** over the **Ghab plain** 600m below: a veritable patchwork of small green, yellow or ochre fields, irrigated by the Orontes Canal, that changes with every season. The hills in the west beyond the Ghab form part of the limestone massif of Jebel Zawiyeh (rising to 935m), the southern flank of the ancient Belus relief peppered with innumerable dead cities from Roman and Byzantine times.

The road meanders through a series of hairpin bends for 17km through oaks, cypresses, broom and pines before emerging at the bottom before the village of Kharab Qeitah. At the junction, fork left so as to contour the outlying hills of the Jebel Ansariyeh. Some 3km beyond the junction, overlooking a stretch of water on the left, sit the impressive but fairly inaccessible castle ruins of **Qalaat Burzey**, an ancient fort occupied by the Crusaders in the 12C.

*At Jisrsh al-Shughour (22km), in the northernmost corner of the Ghab, the road links up with the main Latakia-Aleppo highway. Cross the bridge over the Orontes on the outskirts of the town and climb up again into the limestone massif planted with olive trees. 30km after Jisrsh a small road forking right leads to the dead cities of Al-Bara and Sergilla (see p 248). The road widens out after 6km near Ariha and then joins the motorway to Aleppo (46km).*

Saône Castle

A noria on the Orontes river

J. - F. Galmiche

# THE ORONTES VALLEY

The very name of this green and fertile valley inspires pictures of lushness and the distinctive sound of the turning norias (water-wheels). Although some will say that much of the charm has disappeared with the onset of industrialisation and advanced crude oil extraction, the Orontes Valley continues to be central to the national economy. The name of the river – Nahr Al-Asi – translates from the Arabic as the Rebellious River, probably because it flows from south to north, unlike the other rivers in Syria. It rises in the hills of the Anti-Lebanon, north of the Bekaa Valley, and crosses into Syria near Mando (Kadesh), where the armies of Egypt confronted the Hittites, south of Qattina Lake (Buhayrat Qattinah). Since the river was dammed this natural lake, southwest of Homs, has become the second-largest in the country. The river is highly valued by the locals, not only for its beauty in fine weather, but as a source of water for irrigating the land. To the south of Homs, the water is supplied by the Jebel Ansariyeh and collected behind a second dam near Rastan. In the region around Hama, the river drives the magnificent norias that tip the water up into the irrigation channels, before flowing through the marshy, but otherwise lovely, plain of Ghab at the foot of the mountains overlooking the ancient city of Apamea. The Orontes concludes its long journey in Turkey, meeting the Mediterranean coast near Antioch after travelling approximately 570km.

*See regional map p 164.*

# HOMS

Capital of the Mouhafazat.
Pop 500 000 – Alt 500m.

### And remember...
Spend the night at Hama (45km further north);
not only is it more picturesque, it offers a better selection of hotels.

At the point where the roads from Damascus, Aleppo, Palmyra and Tartus meet, less than 200km from the three main cities of Syria, sits Homs: in some ways, the guardian of Syria's crossroads. It is a pity, therefore, that little of this city's rich past is to be found in the somewhat soulless and unattractive town centre, save for an old souk that is a shadow of its former self. The Orontes River could have been made into an attractive feature in the town, but it runs some way away. The restaurants that line the banks, however, provide an excellent lunch-stop for anyone continuing to Hama or Krak des Chevaliers.

## The cradle of the Severus family

The citadel stands southwest of the main town, on a tall tell incorporating the ancient city that was never really to rival its larger neighbours Hama and Kadesh. In 145 BC, an Arab dynasty established itself in Homs and ardently defended the city's independence from Rome. Eventually, in 78 AD, the city succumbed to Imperial domination, took the name of Emesa and was forced to supply the Roman army with horsemen with a reputation for being fearless in conflict. Throughout the 2C and 3C AD, Homs served as an important transit post for caravans bound for Palmyra. The town earned particular notoriety when the Roman Emperor **Septimius Severus** married Julia Domna, the daughter of a high priest at the temple of the sun-god Baal. Four of their descendants would later wear the imperial purple.

Homs was among the first Syrian cities to embrace Christianity; this is reinforced by the martyrdom of St Elian and the excavation of substantial catacombs *(sadly inaccessible)*. In fact Homs was the seat of a bishopric when it fell into Muslim hands in 637 and subsequently became the capital of one of five military areas of Syria. In turn, the city succumbed to the rule of Byzantines, Crusaders and rival Muslim dynasties that successively managed to obliterate all vestiges of the ancient city. During the Middle Ages the city's fortune relied on its presses, mills and the silk-weaving workshops.

### The Severus family: Syrians in Rome

In 193, the army of the Danube installed its African leader Septimius Severus at the head of the Roman Empire. His consort was Julia Domna, the beautiful and ambitious daughter of the high priest of Emesa.. After the death of Septimius, she placed her son Caracalla on the imperial throne. Meanwhile, her sister Julia Maesa, an able schemer herself, conspired to get her two grandsons, who had been raised in Antioch and at Emesa, on the throne. The older of the two, Elagabalus, was eventually proclaimed emperor by his army in 218. He made a considerable impact on his entry into Rome and introduced a number of Eastern cults to the Sacred City and insisted that the black stone from the temple at Emesa be brought there. His moral laxity, childish pranks and political excesses filled the chronicles of the time. In exasperation, the praetorians decided to give preference to his German cousin. In 222 Elagabalus was assassinated in Rome, along with his mother, and his body was thrown into the Tiber. So it was that Alexander Severus claimed the imperial throne and ruled for 13 years.

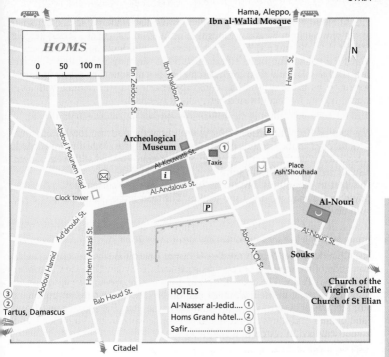

Today, Homs is the capital of a mouhafazat that stretches beyond Palmyra and yet still it maintains a low profile. Over the last 30 years the town has witnessed increased economic and commercial success. This has precipitated the need for greater housing as Christians and Alawites have flocked from the outlying villages in Jebel Ansariyeh. Sprawling suburbs now make Homs the third-largest town in the land, providing manpower to a major oil refinery (west of the town, near the Tartus motorway interchange), spinning-mills and flour-mills.

## Tour
*On foot, allow 2hr (maximum).*

*Head for the town centre and the post office standing opposite the clock tower; park on Al-Kouwatli Street where the smaller restaurants and cheaper hotels are concentrated. Opposite the tourist office is a large building housing the Archeological Museum.*

The **Archeological Museum** (*open 8am-2pm; closed Fridays. Entrance fee*) comprises a central block flanked by wings that are of limited interest. The galleries on the left concentrate on prehistoric artefacts and oriental antiquities (flints, tablets and fine vases in the shape of animals), whereas those on the right display Classical and Islamic antiquities (oil lamps, an iridescent glass bottle, marble urn, ceramics and an elegant vase with floral decoration).

*Continue along Al-Kouwatli Street for 300m and turn right at the main crossroads towards the tall, black minaret. Enter the covered souk from Al-Nouri Street and turn left down the alley leading to the mosque.*

The **Al-Nouri Mosque** *(no charge)* is the town's main mosque. Like other such places of worship in Syria it is thought to be built on the site of a former temple dedicated to the sun-god Baal. In this case, the building could be the one at which the young Elagabalus officiated before it was transformed into a church dedicated to John, and then converted for use as a mosque. The prayer hall supported by its massive piers has a mihrab ornamented with mosaic with vine motifs, framed by small twisted barley-sugar columns.

*Head down the main street of the souk directly opposite the entrance to the mosque.*

The **souk** of Homs is patronised by women from the outlying countryside with faces tattooed in the traditional way. Most, if not all, are clothed in long, black dresses and wear their hair heaped up on their head, covered with a batik-dyed (usually red and black) silk scarf.

This part of the souk is devoted to jewellery (note the current gold price displayed in the shop window) and textiles. The food section is further on, in the open air.

*Make your way back to Al-Nouri Street and turn right down Habi al-Hawl Street. 300m further on fork left at the intersection and continue for 200m.*

The **Church of the Virgin's Girdle** (Al Zunnar Church) is situated on the right-hand side of the street, between a mosque and the Syrian Orthodox (Jacobite) Archbishop's Palace. The church *(if closed, enquire at the orphanage for the custodian)* is of little interest in itself, although one of the chapels contains an important relic that was discovered in 1953, concealed in the altar. The 74cm-long, narrow band of linen and silk is considered to be a girdle worn by the Virgin Mary and is kept wrapped in cotton in a gold reliquary.

*Walk the length of the alley Qasr al-Cheikh (600m) and turn right. For access, ring the bell in the rather flamboyant doorway.*

The **Church of St Elian**\* is more interesting, for it shelters a fine cycle of frescoes that probably date from the 12C, but which were only discovered in 1970 during restoration. Originally they would have ornamented the crypt containing the body of St Elian.

*Walk up the nave painted with brightly-coloured frescoes, executed by Romanian artists in 1973, to behind the carved wooden iconostasis (on the right).* The frescoes here are dominated by the figure of Christ Pantocrator (top centre), flanked by the Virgin Mary and Mary Magdalene on the right and John the Baptist on the left, possibly with St Elian. In the niches nestle the figures of the four Evangelists, while the medallions are filled with a selection of Prophets and Apostles.

**St Elian**

The story of St Elian's life illustrates the conflicts that prevailed during the Early Christian era. The martyr was condemned to death in 285 by his father, a notable member of Homs society allied to the Roman authorities, for refusing to renounce his faith. Just 28 years later, Constantine I approved the Edict of Milan which put an end to the persecution of Christians.

*Make your way back to the town centre.*

As you leave Homs and head for Hama (left at the main crossroads before the souk), you will pass before the **Ibn al-Walid Mosque** 500m on the right. Here, beneath the silvery grey dome, lies the tomb of Khaled Ibn al-Walid, the commander in charge of the Islamic conquest of Syria. The late-Ottoman mosque dates from the dawn of the 20C.

# Making the most of Homs

## COMING AND GOING

**By train** – The modern station is remarkable for its monumental portico and lies 2km to the southwest of the town. Trains for Damascus and Aleppo. Using the bus is easier.

**By bus** – *The main bus station* is on the Hama road, on the northern edge of town. Good regional service (Hama 30min, Damascus 90min, Aleppo 3hr, Tartus 1hr), less frequent service for Palmyra (2hr). The *Karnak* buses are inside the garage.

*Other coach companies*, in the street parallel to the Hama road, 200m south of the bus station. Very comfortable coaches.

## ADDRESS BOOK

**Tourist information** – opposite the post office. Often seems to be closed.

**Main post office** – Al-Kouwatli St.

**Telephone** – At the main post office. International kiosks with phone card outside.

**Bank/Currency exchange** – *Exchange bureau* near the souks. Cash and travellers' cheques.

## WHERE TO STAY

The choice is limited. The town centre hotels are mediocre, or there are two luxury hotels on the outskirts of Homs.

*Under US$20*

**Al-Nasser al-Jedid Hotel**, Hamman Al-Tal St, ☎ (31) 227 423 – 15rm. The only friendly hotel in town. In the large corner lounge you will be welcomed formally but helpfully by the owner. Rooms rather tatty, but clean. Extra charge for first-floor showers.

*From US$90-100*

**Homs Grand Hotel**, on the southern outskirts of the town, 2km from the tetrapylon (group of 4 pillars), ☎ (31) 412 600, Fax (31) 423 021 –

60rm 📶 🍽 🔗 📺 ✖ 🆑 Some rooms have a view of the remains of ancient Homs. Comfortable hotel, 24hr service, marble entrance hall. Car hire (Europcar). Tastefully furnished rooms.

*From US$140-150*

**Safir Hotel**, 1km from town centre on the Tartus road, ☎ (31) 412 400, Fax (31) 433 420 – 60rm 📶 🍽 🔗 📺 ✖ 🛝 🍴 🆑 Unlike its competitor, it has the advantage of an open-air pool. Slightly off the main road, it is also fairly peaceful. Spacious, light rooms. Several shops and amenities on the ground floor.

## EATING OUT

There are good restaurants at the Safir and Homs Grand hotels. Lunch is better eaten in one of the restaurants along the river Orontes.

### • Town centre

There are several nice little cafés in the pedestrian streets off Al-Kouwatli St (opposite the museum). Fresh fruit juice.

**Al-Raouda al-Siyahi**, Al-Kouwatli St, next to the museum. A pleasant, large café, where you can sit outside under the cypress and eucalyptus trees. Open from 10am. Tric-trac and hookahs. Snack bar just inside.

### • Along the Orontes

**Dik al-Jinn**, 2km from the Ibn al-Walid mosque. ♟ To reach the restaurant, go through the gardens of the mosque and take the first street on the left. The leafy, tree-lined boulevard turns right, near the river. The restaurant is in a garden, and its long glazed terrace overlooks the river. Local menu.

**Nadi al-Douwar**, on the Homs al-Jedid road. ♟ At lunchtime the imposing rotunda is a discreet meeting place for lovers. Local menu in the first-floor restaurant, while the ground-floor bar has river-water fountains to keep it cool.

**Making the most of Homs**

195

# HAMA★★
Capital of the mouhafazat
Pop 340 000 – Alt 280m

**Not to be missed**
A stroll along the banks of the Orontes to admire the norias.
A visit to the Azem Palace.
**And remember...**
Have a meal at one of the restaurants situated on the left bank of the Orontes River.
The norias only function from June to September.

Hama is perhaps the most provincial and traditional of all the Syrian cities, tucked away in a bend of the Orontes River. What is more, despite the radical changes implemented in recent years, its charms remain intact. All along the river, the grinding sound of the norias may be heard as the huge wheels relentlessly turn, collecting the water and depositing it into irrigation channels stretching out to the fields. As the wooden buckets shake their way to the top, water spills out in a fine mist that refreshes the tables on the café and restaurant terraces judiciously located nearby. A short distance from here is the souk al-Khadir, where women come from the surrounding countryside to buy provisions, dressed in the most splendid arrays of traditional Syrian garb.

Everything conspires to make the place pleasantly peaceful and tranquil, and its proximity to many and diverse historic sites makes Hama an ideal base for exploring Apamea, Qasr Ibn Wardan and even Krak des Chevaliers.

## From Hamath to Hama

The excavations undertaken on the ancient tell above the town have provided conclusive evidence of the fact that the site has been occupied continuously since Neolithic times. Few actual monuments survive the eventful history that this area has witnessed over time, having been demolished by successive civilisations of which little may be said here. In the 11C BC, the town – then named Hamath – became the capital of a Syro-Hittite principality, as mentioned in the Bible. Later, the Seleucids changed the name to Epiphania, under which it prospered during Roman and Byzantine occupation and submitted to the Muslim armies in 636. After an unsuccessful siege in 1177, Raymond III's crusade was forced to renounce Hama. The town was restored to Saladin. The gigantic norias were erected when the Ayubbids were in power. During this period of great prosperity and expansion, Hama comprised an upper town (around the citadel), a lower town (near the river) and numerous khans that were visited by the Arab traveller Ibn Jubayr at the end of the 12C. Following the raids by Tamerlane, the city was restored by the Mamelukes. In the 14C, the famous writer **Abou al-Fida** became sultan, and during the 18C, it was attached to the Ottoman Pachalik of Damascus.

The fertile countryside surrounding Hama provided a limited number of large landowners with the means for building luxurious residences in town until major agricultural reforms were implemented in the 1960s. Then, in February 1982, the city suffered great violence during the popular uprisings that form one of the bloodiest episodes in Syria's recent history (a topic best avoided in Hama): nearly a quarter of the town centre was razed and had to be painstakingly rebuilt. Today, the city continues to be the main commercial centre of

The Orontes Valley

J. F. Galmiche

Norias on the Orontes

Hama

the area where the Bedouin and other rural people come to shop. Industrial processes are gradually replacing cottage-industry practices, notably in the production of textiles, while the steel and engineering sectors are developing fast.

## The town of the norias

Norias were built in rural areas where plantations could not be sustained by the natural rainfall alone. The principle is simple: the millstream is sufficient to drive the noria, as it does the wheels of a water-mill, only instead of having paddles, the norias have wooden buckets that are filled with water as they emerge from the river. When the buckets reach the top of the wheel, the water is tipped into a stone cistern from where it is then conveyed, by aqueduct, to the distant fields. During the Ayubbid period, Hama is documented as having 32 norias and one is represented in a mosaic panel at Apamea, dating from 469. This highly efficient mechanism was introduced into Southern Spain and Europe by the Arabs, but examples there have long since disappeared, having

197

been replaced by simple, and relatively maintenance-free, water-pumps. The 17 surviving wheels at Hama now only turn in the summer, much to the delight of locals and visitors. Each noria has its own nickname. There are several norias in old Hama, but the most famous group of **four norias★★** is to be found slightly further upstream.

# Tour of old Hama★ on foot
### *Allow 2hr*

The town centre is enclosed by a great loop in the Orontes River, and the two **norias★★** there overlooking the public park are known as al-Jisriyeh and al-Mamouriyeh.

In the town centre a pontoon has been built over the river, to accommodate tables from a nearby café. To the left sits the last surviving part of old Hama where a hint of the traditional character still prevails.

*Turn down the road on the left, running parallel to the river, and then fork right following the small street passing under the arches of the stone aqueduct. On the left stands the al-Osmaniyeh Hammam (see Making the most of Hama). The entrance to the Azem Palace is some 100m further on the right.*

The **Azem Palace★★** (A1) *(9am-4pm. Closed Tuesdays. Entrance fee)* was built in 1740 by the then Pasha Assad al-Azem. Nine years later, when serving as the governor of Damascus, he embarked on the construction of the Azem Palace in Damascus, which he conceived on a far grander scale. The palace in Hama mean-

**The Orontes Valley**

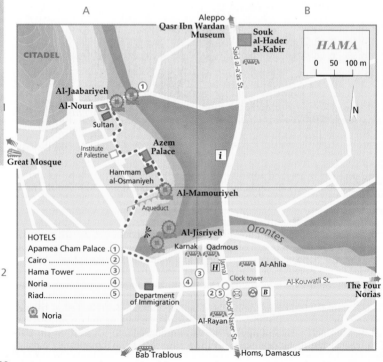

while remained in the dynasty's hands until 1920, when it came to be converted into a school. In 1956 the buildings were adapted into a provincial museum. Just inside the main entrance, on the right, opens the main courtyard of the **haremlik\***: the south wall is recessed so as to accommodate a large iwan with a fountain in front of it. The ground floor was probably used by the palace personnel and for storing the household provisions. The large room opposite the entrance is used as an exhibition area.

On the first floor a very elegant, four-columned **portico\*** leads into a large, exquisitely decorated domed chamber flanked by three raised rooms. *Go back to the entrance of the salemlik and seek out the door in the north wall leading to the hammam.* The **small hammam** comprises four rooms and provides access to the **salemlik** (reception room) built around a courtyard. The marble inlay work is best viewed from the first floor. Restoration work has yet to recapture the original beauty of this wing with bays and balconies facing out over the banks of the Orontes.

The jewel of the palace, the beautifully crafted **mosaic of the musicians\*\*\***, has been installed in a new **museum** (to the north of the town, on the Aleppo road), due to open in 2000. Dating from the late 4C AD, and in excellent condition, this remarkable artefact was found near Hama, and provides a rare insight into the instruments played in Roman times. The *emblema*, a panel surrounded by garlands of acanthus leaves depicting a hunting scene, features six young women. From left to right you can make out ancient cymbals, an organ with pipes (being supplied with air from leather goatskins by two little boys disguised as Eros), the double flute, metal bowls (on the table), a cithara and castanets.

*Turn right out of the Azem Palace, then right again in front of the Palestine Institute. The pretty little street running along the river passes before the Sultan restaurant before continuing through a vaulted passage below the al-Nouri Mosque, the entrance to which is on the left.*

The **Al-Nouri Mosque** (A1) *(please be discreet when visiting during hours of prayer)* was founded by Nureddin in 1172 as the main mosque in the lower town. The river is visible both from the prayer hall and the courtyard before it. In the northwest corner rises a square minaret, with alternating bands of black basalt and white limestone.

*Go back to the main road and head for the hill on the edge of town.*

The **ancient tell** marks the site of where the citadel once stood. Despite there being no ruin, the views from the top more than compensates for the short walk uphill.

*For the Great Mosque, walk around the tell towards the imposing Greek Orthodox Church. At the crossroads, turn left, then right and continue for 200m.*

The ground plan of the **Great Mosque** (A1) in Hama echoes that of the one in Damascus. During the intervening years of occupation by the Byzantines, the mosque was burnt down by Nicephorus II Phocas (968); in 1982 it was completely destroyed a second time and painstakingly rebuilt according to the ancient plans ready for use in 1995. The main street entrance is flanked by a tall minaret built in the Mameluke style. In the square courtyard sits a domed construction ringed with eight columns: this is the treasury in which members of the community might deposit their wealth (also modelled on the one in Damascus). The prayer hall still reflects the buildings on the site before it was made into a mosque (namely a pagan temple transformed into a Christian basilica). The second black and white striped minaret, on the left of the prayer hall, dates from 1135. Nearby, look out for the beautiful ancient lintel set into the wall of the mosque.

**Hama**

The souk in the town centre is not the most picturesque. For more local colour, cross the bridge opposite the clock tower and visit the **Souk al-Hader al-Khabir**⋆ (B1) (*on the Aleppo road, 400m up on the right*). It is here that the country people from the outlying villages come in the early morning to sell their produce (wonderful balls of cheese, fresh vegetables), while the boutiques nestling beneath the crumbling vaults try to cater for the bare necessities of life (animal fat in metal containers, tinned food, gas stoves and cylinders, ropes). The women tend also to be dressed in colourful attire, to complement their traditional hand-painted henna tattoos charged with symbolic meanings. The triangle worn on their foreheads is a kind of amulet warding off the Evil Eye. The lower lip is marked with a life line (a straight line) while the chin is often inscribed with mysterious little blue signs. On their hands is a symbol of good luck: a comb.

## Making the most of Hama

**The Orontes Valley**

### COMING AND GOING

**By train –** As with most Syrian towns, the train station is on the outskirts. There are 2 trains per day for Aleppo and the same number for Damascus.

**By bus – Karnak** (A1), near the town centre *norias*. 3 or 4 buses per day for Aleppo, Damascus and Homs.

**Al-Ahlia** (A2), 200m from the bridge, going towards the Four Norias restaurant. This excellent company provides a service for Aleppo (90min), Damascus (2hr30min), Homs (30min), Latakia (3hr) and Tartus (2hr) with several departures per day.

**Bab Trablous,** 1.5km from the town centre (take a taxi). Minibus for Al-Suqelbiyeh and Apamea (ask for Afamia). Frequent minibuses for Homs. There is another bus station behind the al-Khadir souk. Several morning departures for Al-Hamra (take the bus for Qasr Ibn Wardan).

**Qadmous**, next door to Karnak (A1). 5 buses for Latakia and Tartus.

### ADDRESS BOOK

**Tourist information** (A2) – In the town centre public gardens on the left bank of the Oronte.

**Main post office** (B1) – In the clock tower square.

**Telephone –** Public kiosks behind the post office. Fax at the post office.

**Bank/Currency exchange – Commercial Bank of Syria** (B2), in Al-Kouwatli St, next to the post office. 8am-12.30pm; closed Fridays. Travellers' cheques and cash.

### WHERE TO STAY

Some of Hama's good medium-priced hotels are very well run. They are found in Al-Kouwatli St, near the town centre and the clock tower (too bad for those counting on a good night's sleep). These hotels are a good place for meeting people and exchanging information on other places. Well organised, they offer good value day trips, among other things (for small groups), to Apamea or Krak des Chevaliers.

*Under US$20*

🏨 **Riad Hotel**, Al-Kouwatli St., ☎/Fax (33) 517 776 – 26rm ⁂ ⤬ / 🍽 ✎ TV ✗ CC An excellent place to stay, where the majority of rooms have been recently renovated. Simple but comfortable, and impeccably clean. Helpful and friendly staff. A restaurant offering local cooking is due to open on the top floor.

**Cairo Hotel**, Al-Kouwatli St, ☎ (33) 222 280, Fax (33) 237 206 – 30rm ⁂ ⤬ / 🍽 ✎ TV ✗ CC Next door to the Riad, this hotel seems to have been planned along the same lines. The standard of comfort and service is similar, although prices are slightly higher and the atmosphere slightly more commercial. Mattresses can be hired to sleep on the terrace.

*From US$25-40*

**Noria Hotel**, Al-Kouwatli St, entrance via a passageway to 2nd floor (lift), ☎ (33) 512 414, Fax (33) 511 715 – 47rm ⁂ 🍽 ✎ ✗ TV CC The rooms are arranged around a long carpeted corridor. Well organised. Cafeteria. Reservation advisable. An excellent idea: fans are available for those who don't like air-conditioning. More luxurious rooms and another restaurant are due to be completed shortly.

**Hama Tower Hotel**,Al-Assi Sq, (Burg Al-Azem), ☎ (33) 226 864, Fax (33) 521 523 – 50rm 🛏️ 🖥️ 🏊 📺 ✖️ 💳 The hotel occupies the top two floors of a modern building. Ask for a room with a view over the Orontes. Balconies. Panoramic top-floor restaurant. Satisfactory, but lacking in atmosphere.

*FromUS$130-145*

**Apamea Cham Palace Hotel**, ☎ (33) 525 335, Fax (33) 511 626 – 160rm 🛏️ 🖥️ 🏊 📺 ✖️ 🏊 💳 A short distance from the town centre, this luxurious establishment has comfortable, though ordinary, rooms. Its café-terrace (across the road), with a lovely view of the Orontes and its water-wheels, is particularly pleasant.

### EATING OUT

Al-Kouwatli St offers several small kebab restaurants, but it would be a shame not to eat in one of the restaurants over-looking the Orontes.

• **Town centre**

*Under US$10*

🍴 **Sultan** (A1), in old Hama, beside the river, between the Azem palace and the al-Nouri mosque, ☎ (33) 235 104. Lovely setting, with old stones walls, pretty fountain and the sound of the *norias*. The menu includes Hama specialities: *tartour*, puréed garlic with herbs; *maria*, a lamb pancake; *bartouche*, a kind of lasagne with minced beef, yoghurt and tomato. The bill will come as a pleasant surprise.

• **The Homs road**

**Family Club (Nadi Al-Aïli)**, Al-Medine St, near St George's church (800m from the town centre). 🍷 A good place to eat, even if a little far from the centre. Colourful decor, slightly lacking in atmosphere, but impeccably run. Good local cooking.

• **The four norias area**

*Under US$10*

It's a pleasant experience to eat lunch or dinner in one of these two restaurants on the banks of the Orontes. There is a constant shower of water falling from the top of the two pairs of water-wheels.

Children are carried up to the top of the biggest wheel by its movement and dive off the top, at the risk of life and limb. A pity that music rather spoils this charming spot.

🍴 **Al-Boustan**, the first restaurant you reach when coming from Hama. A restaurant with a shady terrace and the best view of the four wheels. Dishes are served on enormous trays. Local menu and hookahs. Dining room under the rotunda.

**Four Norias**, next to the Al-Boustan. 🍷 The rotunda smells of arak, so you might prefer the terrace. Busy on Friday.

### OTHER THINGS TO DO

**Cafés** – Hama encourages laziness. Go with the flow, and watch the sun set over the Orontes from one of the town centre cafés: **Jisser al-Marakebe** and **Nadi al-Mouhafazat** on the quayside, or **al-Rawda**, tucked away under the trees which overhang the river.

**Hammam – Hamman al-Osmaniyeh** (Ottaman Turkish bath), in the old town, near to the Azem palace. This slightly dilapidated bath has remained very traditional. Open to women 12noon-5pm, in theory, and to men the rest of the time, until midnight.

**Pastry shops** – The local speciality is halawat al-jibna, a sort of pancake stuffed with cream cheese and topped with honey syrup. Several pastry shops in Al-Kouwatli St serve this sweetmeat.

### SHOPPING GUIDE

**Textiles – Al-Madani**, ☎ (33) 516 009. If you like unusual household linen, take a taxi to Al-Madani, in the upper town, 5 minutes from the town centre (ask your hotel proprietor to write down the address in Arabic for the taxi driver). You will be able to watch weavers working on traditional looms. Their meticulous work creates masterpieces which are exported as far as Europe, but which are nowhere to be found in Syria. Cotton and silk bath towels, tablecloths, towelling dressing gowns, but also cotton embellished with silk. Superb and unique. From S£900.

*Making the most of Hama*

# AROUND HAMA

Excursions from Hama
For details of hotels and restaurants, see "Making the most of Hama"

## Excursion to Qasr Ibn Wardan

*116km there and back - Allow half a day.*
*See map p 164*

To the east of Hama lies the *Maamoura*: a semi-arid steppe and buffer zone between a sedentary way of life and a nomadic existence. The fact that peasant farmers have managed over time to cultivate this land despite the lack of rainfall is a great achievement, even if their choice of crops is limited to wheat, chickpeas and lentils, to complement a small herd of sheep. The land appears lush and green in springtime, but with the onset of summer, the soil is parched. Beyond the sprawling urban conglomerations made up of hastily constructed buildings, stand remote collections of traditional beehive mud-brick houses with conical roofs. But the main objective of this excursion is the elegant stronghold reminiscent of the ancient limes of Rome and Byzantium: Qasr Ibn Wardan.

*Start out from the clocktower in Hama and cross the Orontes. After 1.5km, turn right towards Al-Hamra, cutting through a region where villagers continue to wear the traditional costume of keffiehs and gallabias. On the far side of Al-Hamra (39km from Hama), the scenery becomes even more desert-like. Continue an additional 12km to the picturesque village of Al-Srouj.*

A distinctive beehive house

B Brillon/MICHELIN

■ **Al-Srouj** – At one time, all the dwellings in the region conformed to this traditional beehive format, comprising two or more domed cells joined together. The standard configuration of a double unit would have consisted of a living/sleeping area and a kitchen-cum-stable for the animals. Inside, the mud brick of the conical roof is left exposed, whereas on the outside it is roughcast with straw and mud, punctuated by a spiral of protruding stone to allow repairs to be undertaken after heavy rain. If you are given the opportunity of visiting such a house, you will be struck by the spacious-

The Orontes Valley

ness of the interior. Nowadays, the locals prefer to opt for more modern breeze-block houses equipped with running water, in favour of the traditional mud-brick variety that is abandoned or used to stable animals, store provisions and agricultural implements.

*Drive the remaining 7km to the ruins of the stronghold Qasr Ibn Wardan and park near the custodian's house.*

■ **Qasr Ibn Wardan**★ — *(9am-6pm, 4pm in winter. Entrance fee)* The black and yellow ruins of Qasr Ibn Wardan stand some 100m from the road, in a somewhat exposed and isolated position, 58km from Hama, that can be only be justified in this flat and bleak landscape as a defence post. Qasr Ibn Wardan was one of the many fortifications built at Justinian's behest in 564 to reinforce the frontiers of his Byzantine Empire.

Little of the original fortress remains apart from the palace (the first building) and the church (50m on the left); the outer walls and soldiers' barracks have all but disappeared. The distinctive arrangement of the complex, together with the fact that it was built of baked brick, suggest it was modelled on prototypes found in Constantinople rather than being devised by local civil engineers employed on building the Dead Cities at that time.

The **palace** was probably intended to house the military governor of the province. The main doorway leads into a dark vestibule covered by a beautifully contrived brick dome. The stairway on the right provides access to the first floor (now in ruins), from which there is a good overview of the complex with its central courtyard, flanked by stables and schoolroom.

The **church**, built on a square plan, would have had a 20m-tall brick dome rising from the piers that still point skywards. The south door into the nave has a solid basalt beam as a lintel, which bears an inscription. An apse opens out on the right with, on the first floor, two standing columns: all that remains of the gallery that would have run the length of the nave, up the stairs nestling in the northwest corner of the church.

*Follow the same itinerary in reverse to Hama.*

## Excursion to Krak des Chevaliers★

*110km circuit – Allow half a day.*
*See map p 164.*

This itinerary provides an alternative way of reaching Krak des Chevaliers, bypassing the rather lacklustre city of Homs. The wild scenery is unspoilt and there is scope for exploring some unusual sights, namely a forgotten Byzantine basilica on the edge of a village, a mysterious fortress once held by the Assassins and a scenic drive along a wooded ridge. Beyond Misyaf, the roads are potholed and broken so it is best to drive slowly. This route is not recommended in bad weather.

*From Hama, leave the Great Mosque on your left and take the road uphill, forking sharply left, following signs for Latakia. Across the railway, turn left towards Misyaf.*

After 8km, a mountain looms up ahead, rising tall above the undulating landscape that is beautifully green only in spring. 37km from Hama fork left and head for Deir al-Salib some 5km further on. The church stands on the left, before the entrance to the village.

**Around Hama**

J L Dugast/HOA QUI

The fortified citadel at Misyaf

**The Orontes Valley**

■ **Church at Deir al-Salib** – The Byzantine church (5C-6C), surrounded by fig trees, preserves a good proportion of its beige and ochre stone walls standing, notably, around the atrium that precedes the narthex and the eastern apse. The door on the right of the main entrance leads into the baptistery in which the cruciform baptism pool still survives intact. Five standing columns denote the arrangement of the aisles. The gallery on the first floor was set aside for female members of the congregation. Alongside the baptistery stands a small **mausoleum** containing three stone sarcophagi bearing medallions inscribed with a cross.

*Go back down towards the main road, taking time to enjoy the magnificent view of the plain and mountain beyond. At the junction turn left; 8km further on, you will see the citadel of Misyaf sitting proudly on the horizon, dramatically perched on a rocky outcrop. Follow the wide avenue through the outskirts of Misyaf and turn right shortly after entering town and forking right again up towards the castle.*

■ **Citadel at Misyaf★** – *(8am-5pm. Entrance fee).* The most famous Assassin castle nestles at the foot of the eastern flank of Jebel Ansariyeh. However, its origins predate the arrival of the Ismaili sect, for the defensive stronghold served the Seleucids, Romans, Byzantines and Arabs before being taken by the Crusaders in 1103. Its remote position vis-à-vis the other Frankish fortified outposts along the coast made it difficult for them to take charge of it, so the princes of Sheizar took up residence there before it was seized by the Ismailis in 1140. Only then did the place become the headquarters for "terrorist" operations. Saladin attempted to besiege Misyaf with little success, so the Assassins remained there until Baybars mounted his campaign (circa 1270) and flushed them out.

The citadel occupies a rocky spur in the middle of the village and rectangular outcrops reinforce the imposing walls. Alas, the interior is less well preserved than the exterior walls, with a series of stairways leading from inside the main entrance (note the reuse of Antique capitals) to the heart of the fortress. As you pick your way through the mass of fallen stones and broken masonry of collapsed buildings, it is not difficult to imagine how the place must have looked in its heyday. From the battlements there is a fine **view** of the nearby mountain and the surrounding countryside.

### The Assassins

This Ismaili sect with origins rooted in northern Persia came to Syria in the 11C. The apparent ease with which they managed to secure the network of some ten or so strongholds in the heart of the Jebel Ansariyeh relied essentially on their exploiting the rivalry preoccupying the great Muslim dynasties and the threat posed by the Crusaders at that time. These Assassins are reputed to be the inspiration of modern terrorists for, like their latter-day counterparts, they were highly-trained in the art of stealth and killing, unhesitant in mounting attacks on prominent Christians or Sunnis. Their undisputed leader, the famous Rachid al-Din Sinan (1163-1193) who was described as the "Old Man of the Mountains" by Frankish chroniclers, directed operations from the safety of his citadels. Their name probably derives from the fact that members of the sect habitually used hashish ("Hachichin" in Arabic) as part of their training. Since then, the word has passed into common usage in every language to refer to premeditated murder.

From Misyaf it is possible to drive to Baniyas (49km) across the Jebel Ansariyeh mountain range. This **route**\*\* affords a succession of spectacular views as the road climbs gradually up a narrow valley to reach the wind-blown ridge at the top (16km) and the town of Qadmus (another old town built around an Assassin fortress). From there the road runs along a steep-sided valley, terraced with densely cultivated plots, to a fine **viewpoint**\*\* 35km from Misyaf (*see illustration p 70*).

*To continue to Krak des Chevaliers, head back to the junction with the broad avenue out of town and turn right towards the mountain. At the roundabout turn left. Rather than following the Homs road on the left, this route takes you through the village of Al-Beidah (3km away) and up the side of the mountain. After 13km ignore the sign for Safita on the right and drive through the village of Aïn al-Laqim. 23km further on you will reach a crossroads with an array of 15 signs or more: turn left.*

From the ridge at the top, great sweeping **views**\* extend over the plain below. Eventually the road passes a large cross: a sign heralding the proximity of the Christian enclave of villages in the Wadi al-Nassara.

*Continue for an additional 10km to the junction and fork right off the Sheen road, which runs opposite from the road to Kafraam.* This leads downhill through various villages dotted with churches and crosses (Mqallis, Mazrana). 8km or so after turning off the Sheen road, just before crossing the river, you will notice Krak des Chevaliers sitting majestically on its rise above the plain. *A short way beyond the bridge turn left; continue (5km) to the fork and turn right to the Monastery of St George. At the intersection 2km further on branch left and follow the road through the village of Qalaat al-Hosn and the entrance of Krak 4km beyond it.*

■ **Krak des Chevaliers**\*\*\* - *See p 166.*

# Excursion to Apamea via Sheizar

*62km – Allow 2hr to include a visit to Sheizar Castle.*
*See map p 164.*

This drive takes you across the plain of the Orontes river stretching to the northwest of Hama, to where the river meets the Jebel Ansariyeh, taking in Sheizar Castle which sits majestically on a rocky outcrop on the way. But the highlight of this excursion must surely be the ruins of Apamea, which include a striking colonnade, lost in an otherwise rural landscape.

*Head out of Hama along the road bound for Latakia (across the railway line). Continue through Mardeh (27km from Hama) to a major crossroads: leave the Tell Salhab road and turn right towards Al-Qalibiyeh. After 7km, you will see the castle of Sheizar crowning a rocky spur. Turn right off the main road in front of the modern minaret and turn left through the entrance to the castle.*

■ **Sheizar Citadel** (Qalaat Sheizar) – *(Unguarded site. Allow 30mins).* The jagged and somewhat sinister silhouette of the ruined Castle of Sheizar sits below the large town of Sheizar. Below its eastern flank runs the Orontes River, providing the fortress with a natural moat before flowing into the Ghab through a deep limestone gorge.

The Arab Banu Munqidh clan took possession of the Fatimid castle at Sheizar in 1081. During the Crusades, the stronghold was presided over by the Emir Usamah Ibn Munqidh, a man reputed for his love and knowledge of fine literature, and ardent defender of Islam intent of resisting the Frankish incursions mounted from the east. Two major earthquakes in 1157 and 1170 devastated the complex, which subsequently fell into the hands of the Mongol hordes in 1260. What may be seen today is largely the work of the Mamelukes. The main gateway into the castle is on the northern side. The stepped ramp across the moat, supported by a bridge with two arches, leads to a fortified entrance dating from 1290. The heavily rusticated front incorporates several Antique column shafts, probably derived from the Roman town of Caesara (midway between Apamea and Hama), after which the stronghold was named. The bastion incorporating the main gateway abuts the northern corner of the citadel (on the right): note the superb glacis below that dates from the period of the Mameluke occupation. Go through the gateway and cross the flat area (200m), covered with ruined sections of various vaulted rooms, to reach the south keep (fine views over the deep gorges of the Orontes to the left). Although the original donjon would have been constructed by the Ayyubids (1233), the present one was probably rebuilt by the Mamelukes at the close of the 13C. As there is no access to the tower itself, visitors must be content to admire the exterior, notably the heavy rustication.

*Return to the main road.*

Just outside Sheizar the road to Apamea passes a noria on the left before entering the Ghab Plain,

**The Emir of Sheizar's memoirs**
The castle at Sheizar is rather less renowned for its architecture than for its inhabitant Prince Usamah Ibn Munqidh (1088-1183), whose memoirs provide an Arab's point of view on the Crusades. Unlike Frankish chronicles which emphasise the military aspect of the Crusades, the emir's often subtle and humorous account describes how the Franks lived and related to their Muslim cousins. It is the emir who reveals that, during periods of peace, Muslims and Franks would socialise quite happily and rub shoulders in the hammams!

**The Orontes Valley**

which in ancient times consisted of marshland. Since it was drained, the region has become a highly fertile agricultural area. The road passes through Al-Qalibiyeh and carries on to the citadel of Qalaat al-Moudiq (26km after Sheizar). Eventually, it passes before a striking wall that encloses the famous caravanserai at Apamea (on the right at the entrance to the town).

*Continue past the citadel and turn right towards Afamia (Arabic name for the castle). Park in front of the café (1.5km after the junction).*

■ **Apamea**★★ – *See p 208.*

Around Hama

# APAMEA★★
## (QALAAT AL-MOUDIQ)
### Mouhafazat of Hama

**And remember...**
Avoid accepting the services of a guide who does not speak English.
Politely decline the "antiques" offered by the local souvenir sellers.
Drink in the bucolic atmosphere of the site.

*From Hama take a minibus for Qalaat al-Moudiq, then climb up to the site on foot, passing the citadel (allow 90min). You could ask the driver to drop you at Qalaat Sheizar. By taxi, allow around S£1 000-2 000 for a half-day excursion. Hotels in Hama will organise this excursion for you (the price depends on the number in the group).*

To find the ancient city of Apamaea, look out for a long line of columns rising above the flat landscape, set against the steep flank of Jebel Ansariyeh. The impact and splendour of these ruins are heightened by their setting, as are those at Palmyra, only here the broken monuments are surrounded by green fields (especially in spring) rather than arid desert, and a timeless quality is sustained by the sheep and goats grazing among the fallen stones. For the site of this 2 000-year old town provides local farmers with high-quality forage as it has since time immemorial, with little regard for the possible treasures lying hidden below ground. Modern day visitors can walk along the broad, paved streets that once were trod by the likes of Cleopatra, Septimius Severus and many other such illustrious persons, and admire the majestic avenue of columns that gradually have been re-erected along the 2km-long Cardo Maximus. The town seems to extend over a vast area, peppered with reconstituted buildings that once harboured a nymphaeum, an agora and public baths. Other ruins have revealed floors paved with marvellous mosaics, now housed in the attractive caravanserai (now a museum) at the foot of the nearby medieval citadel of Qalaat al-Mudiq.

## A populous city

The origins of Apamea are hidden beneath the tell on which the modern village of Qalaat al-Mudiq is built. Despite this, research shows that the town began to prosper and expand after being conquered by Alexander the Great. It was then re-founded by **Seleucus I Nicator** around 300 BC and renamed Apamea after his Persian wife. Over the ensuing centuries, Apamea became an important strategic Seleucid stronghold until 63 BC when Pompey destroyed the citadel. At the dawn of the Christian era, the city is thought to have had a population of 500 000 (although some scholars cite a figure of 117 000 "free inhabitants"). It was certainly a thriving intellectual centre, for it was here that Iamblichus founded the breakaway neo-Platonic school of philosophy. During Byzantine times it continued to exert considerable influence. In the 6C the region was struck by a series of violent earthquakes, followed by a succession of Persian incursions, until the area was conquered by the Arabs. Apamea constituted a bone of contention between Byzantines and Muslims, and was eventually seized from the Crusaders by Nureddin. Earth tremors continued to rumble and the large town, which had extended its acropolis towards the west, was gradually abandoned in favour of a more compact settlement on the ancient tell nearby. During Ottoman times a caravanserai and mosque were built there. Since 1930 a Belgian team has been excavating the site, and the Osman Aïdi Foundation has undertaken to re-erect the columns.

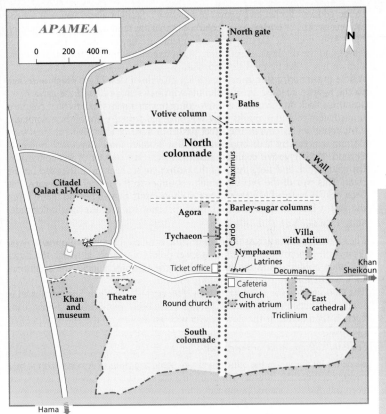

APAMEA

0    200    400 m

North gate

Baths

Votive column

North
colonnade

Maximus

Wall

Citadel
Qalaat al-Moudiq

Barley-sugar columns

Agora

Cardo

Villa
with atrium

Tychaeon

Nymphaeum

Latrines

Decumanus

Khan
Sheikoun

Ticket office

Cafeteria

Church
with atrium

East
cathedral

Khan
and
museum

Theatre

Round church

Triclinium

South
colonnade

Hama

## The Apamea of Antiquity
### Allow 2hr.

*A walk along the length of the colonnade (a total of 4km there and back) can be debil-
itating under the hot sun, so don a hat and sunglasses to avert sunstroke and pack plenty
of water to quench thirst. You can shelter from the sun in the cafeteria at the southern
entrance to the site, where you will find cold drinks and a few postcards on sale. The
site is not fenced off, but visitors should apply for an entry permit from the ticket office
opposite the café. To save on the walking, turn right below the citadel and drive up to
the north gate: the road runs along the outside of the ramparts and provides a view of
the massive scale and sophistication of the fortifications.*

The ticket office stands at the bottom of the **north colonnade\*\*\*** comprising
two parallel rows of columns stretching, it would seem, to infinity. Across the
main axis are the remains of a **nymphaeum** with a pink and green paved floor:
the exedra that opens out onto the street would have been ornamented with
statuary representing various divinities. The ramp on the right leads to the public
latrines. To the left of the cardo, level with the first group of raised columns,
stand the ruins of an **agora**, before which stood a **tychaeon** (a temple dedicated

209

to the goddess Tyche, and patron of the town). Straight ahead you will see the famous twisted or **barley-sugar columns**\*\* that are used as a symbol of the city. Note how both the capitals and the entablature are encrusted with acanthus leaves and the rhythmic effect of the 20 alternated columns on the left and right, thrown into relief by the light and shade.

A little further on, a side-street on the left provides a view of the **north entrance to the agora**\*, marked by six columns with bases shaped liked the calyx of an acanthus. Back on the cardo, a votive column with a pair of tall twisted columns immediately behind it, marks what was once the central point of the colonnade. As it continues its course, the street passes in front of four high columns supporting a pediment that once would have fronted some important building. Beyond another **votive column**\* that marks the last quarter of the colonnade, the paltry brick and stone ruins of the **baths**\* are set back from the road on the right. This part of the avenue, which continues to the town's **north gate**, has been heavily restored as have the row of shop-fronts aligned behind them. From the gate a fine view extends back over the ramparts and the long colonnade.

*Make your way back to the ticket office.*

The cardo continues across the road in what is called the **south colonnade** (*right of the café*). This part of the site holds fewer points of interest, although the views of Qalaat al-Mudiq and the full length of the colonnade make the additional walk worthwhile.

The **Church Quarter** (*300m to the right of the café*) off the Khan Sheikoun road is somewhat uninspiring because it is often completely overgrown; the only justification for a detour is the Roman **villa with an atrium** on the left-hand side of the road.

*Leave the café and head for the citadel.*

Some 600m ahead, on the left of the road, stand the ruins of Apamea's imposing **theatre** set into the hillside. These are in a parlous state as they have long since been pillaged as a source of cut stone for building the citadel and caravanserai. Despite this, the theatre remains nonetheless impressive on account of its enormous size, with a diameter of 139m (as compared with the one at Orange, in southern France, which measures 103m in diameter).

Before going to the museum, it is worth paying a brief visit to the ancient **citadel,** in which a picturesque village now nestles. From the ridge the view takes in the gate of Qalaat al-Mudiq and the Ghab Plain beyond, and the former caravanserai that now houses the Apamea museum.

*Head right around the citadel and down to the Hama road. Turn left and continue 1.3km to the museum on the left. Park the car in front of the entrance, some 20m from the main road.*

The **Apamea Museum**\*\* (*Open 8am-2.30pm; closed Tuesdays. Entrance fee. Allow 30min*) is housed in the precincts of a 17C **khan**\*\* or caravanserai used by pilgrims and traders travelling between Aleppo and Damascus.

The rooms off the central courtyard display collections composed largely of mosaics. The first room on the left after the main entrance contains the **mosaic of Socrates and the Sages**\*\*. This shows the great Greek philosopher surrounded by six bearded thinkers in an arrangement reminiscent of Paleo-Christian paintings of Christ with the Apostles. This particular panel, which was integrated into a series of other pagan floor mosaics with geometric patterns, was recovered from beneath the cathedral. In the eastern wing there is an unusual interpretation of the **Judgement of the Nereids★** with, on the right, Cassiopeia being crowned with glory. This mosaic was found in the same place as the one with Socrates and dates from the same period (4C AD). Against the wall sits a fine **altar-table★**, identical in kind to the one in the Church of St Sergius at Maalula.

The splendid **collection of capitals** includes examples of the Classical orders (Ionic and Corinthian) as well as a number of Byzantine counterparts of a type known as "basket capitals". Opposite a series of mosaics illustrate scenes with animals. The courtyard, meanwhile, contains a selection of funerary stelae. Continue left past the cistern to the fine **mosaic of the funeral procession★★** (dated 487 AD) which was found in a church at Huarté. Last, but not least, you come to a large and highly expressive mosaic depicting **fighting animals**.

*From here, head 30km east to Khan Sheikoun and join the Aleppo-Damascus motorway.*

## Making the most of Apamea

### COMING AND GOING

**By bus –** In two stages from Hama: minibus to Al-Qalabiya, then bus to Qalaat al-Moudiq. From the main road it's an uphill walk, following the citadel in the direction of Apamea. Allow 90min for the journey. You could ask to be taken to Qalaat Sheizar either on the outward or return journey.

**By taxi –** Book by the half-day at one of Hama's hotels, preferably in the group, or direct with one of the taxi services (in which case allow S£1 300 return).

### EATING OUT

**Apamea Cham Cafeteria**, on the outskirts of the ruins at Apamea. Limited selection of fast food, drinks, souvenirs, postcards, toilets. A good chance to get out of the sun after visiting the site.

The Great Mosque, Aleppo

# THE ALEPPO REGION

The limestone hills around Aleppo conceal an astonishing concentration of Byzantine remains: eerily deserted Dead Cities and ruined monasteries imbued with the ardent faith of the early Christians who lived so long ago. It is an unspoilt landscape terraced with fruit and almond trees that can be explored in the course of three different excursions.

But the jewel in the crown is Aleppo, a beautiful and a thriving commercial metropolis that has captured the imagination of countless travellers through the centuries. To this day, the traditional bustle and colour of the covered souks continue to enthral visitors, as do the countless shops in the old medina, brimming with Bedouin scarves made of soft silk, printed fabrics and jewellery. Besides these, Aleppo boasts a number of major monuments, including an impressive citadel, various caravanserais and museums.

# ALEPPO ★★★
## (HALAB)
Capital of the mouhafazat.
Pop 1 300 000 – Alt 380m.

### Not to be missed
The citadel and the archeological museum.
A few hours exploring the souks and shopping.
A meal at the Sissi Restaurant in a converted traditional home.

### And remember...
Allow at least 2 days to visit Aleppo and the Church of St Simeon,
with a few extra days for visiting the Dead Cities.
The souks are closed on Fridays.

Two things may strike first-time visitors to Aleppo: the Arab citadel that crowns the highest point at the very heart of the city and the constant hum of traffic – both motorised vehicles and human – reverberating through the souks and streets. For here Arabs, Kurds and Armenians have co-existed for generations and thrived on commercial competition, relying on their natural flair for trade instilled in the genes by their forefathers who first animated this outpost on the ancient caravan routes between East and West. Today, the same medieval covered souks continue to abound with goods that have been manufactured in far-flung places like China and Taiwan. The main traders, however, are from the young breakaway republics of the former Soviet Union (Armenia, Uzbekistan), who come to Syria in caravans of buses and trucks in search of cheap clothing, thereby sustaining the traditional prosperity and way of life of the community. In addition to a buoyant local economy, Aleppo boasts a rich and vibrant cultural heritage. For years, Oriental influences were imported by the caravans, along with the finest silks, the sheerest muslin, exotic spices and fragrant coffee, and exchanged with Venetian merchants acquainted with the fads and fashions promoted in the princely courts of Europe. No wonder Aleppo became such a major player in the Ottoman Empire and endowed her streets with palaces furnished to reflect the refined tastes of its wealthier patrons.

Nevertheless, the capital of northern Syria does not flaunt her true personality; only after nightfall, when people emerge from their homes to socialise among themselves or in restaurants, can a stranger get a true impression of the quality of life in Aleppo. The local cuisine, considered by many to be the finest in Syria, vaunts no less than 25 different recipes for making *kebbeh* (savoury burghul and minced meatballs).

Music also plays a vital role in celebrating religious festivals and marking momentous events (circumcisions, weddings, pilgrimages to Mecca), which provide opportunities for reviving ancient musical traditions. Even the Egyptian singer Abd al-Ahab, and the great Umm Kalthum have performed in Aleppo, where audiences are notorious for making and breaking reputations. The people of Aleppo all tend to be affiliated to different communities that protectively defend their own traditions and respect those of friends and neighbours; but having rubbed shoulders with foreigners for centuries they tend to be xenophiles.

On several occasions during its long history, Aleppo tottered on the edge of oblivion after being pillaged, shaken by earthquakes and bankrupted. Each time, the city managed to bounce back with new-found determination. As the poet

**Aleppo**

Abu al-Fath Kashajim wrote "No city has succeeded in beguiling its inhabitants more than Aleppo. It offers everything that anyone could possibly desire. So visit it, for those who have visited Aleppo come away enriched by the experience."

## Centuries of bartering

**Antiquity** – Aleppo claims to be the oldest continuously inhabited city in the world. Around 1780 BC it was the capital of the Amorite kingdom of Yamkhad. As the seat of a powerful confederation, it enjoyed considerable trade links with several other cities in northern Syria. But, like Ebla, it gradually was forced into becoming a vassal state of its powerful Akkadian, Hittite and Egyptian neighbours. In 1200 BC the region suffered devastating raids at the hands of the Peoples of the Sea. When Aleppo eventually recovered, it became the capital of a neo-Hittite state. By the end of the 1st millennium BC, Aleppo had been absorbed into the Assyrian, then Persian empires.

After the campaign of Alexander the Great, the Seleucus Nicator founded the town of Beroea below the tell on which the ancient town (now the citadel) was built. As expected, the new town was laid out on Classical Greek lines, in accordance with the ordered street-system established by Hippodamus of Miletus, the same principles that dictate the layout of the modern-day souks. In the course of the 1st millennium AD, Aleppo enjoyed a close rapport, first with Rome and then with Constantinople, and people fleeing from persecution flocked to the remote limestone hills to found innumerable villages where they might live in complete safety (the famous "Dead Cities").

**The Arabs** – In 611 Aleppo was burnt by Chosroes; in 637 it surrendered to the Arab infidels. Under the ephemeral but dynamic **Hamdanid** dynasty (944-1003), the capital regained its prowess, especially when the art-loving **Emir Sayf al-Dawla** encouraged the leading Arab poets of the time, including Al-Moutannabi and Abou Firas, to attend his court. In 962, the Byzantine Emperor Nicephorus Phocas mounted an attack on Aleppo that left the city devastated, but the citadel unbroken. During the ensuing years, the rulers paid tribute to the Crusader princes in Antioch, but repelled the Christian army when it set up camp outside the city in 1098 and resisted the siege laid by Baldwin in 1124. A substantial earthquake provoked further destruction in 1170 making major reconstruction work necessary during the rule of the Zengids (Zengi and his more famous son Nureddin).

Meanwhile, the orthodox Sunnis, having been threatened by schism, rallied themselves and launched an expensive campaign to retrieve their image, building Sufi *madrasas* and monasteries as centres of propaganda. In the late 12C, the Ayyubid Governor al-Zahir Ghazi applied himself to unifying Syria and Egypt – a project initiated by his predecessor Saladin, and restorers began work on the citadel.

In 1260 and 1280 Aleppo was sacked by the Mongols; in 1400, directed by Tamerlane, they struck again but while the hordes

**Aleppo**

### Capitulation Treaties

As Aleppo stands at the head of an important land route to India, Europeans flocked to the city in the hope of competing with local merchants. In 1536, Suleyman the Magnificent signed the first of what came to be known as "Capitulation Treaties", which permitted Europeans to trade in the Ottoman Empire, live under the protection of their consul and enjoy immunity from the Turkish law. To further facilitate things, merchants used the caravanserais (khans) set up by their respective homelands. Until the 19C, the trading ports of the Eastern Mediterranean operating under the capitulation system included Istanbul, Alexandretta, Latakia and Beirut.

ALEPPO

0   150   300 m

N

216

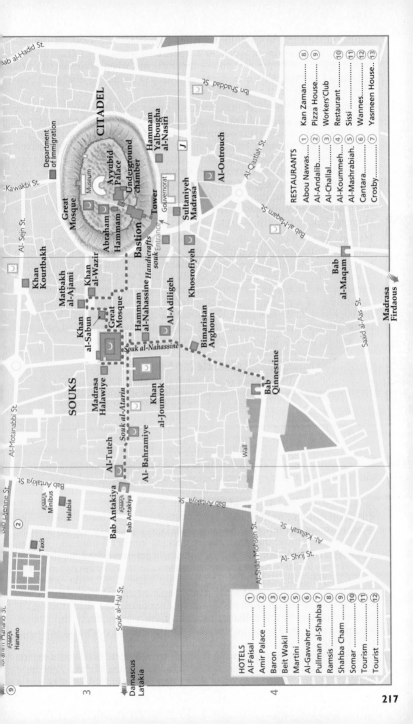

CITADEL

SOUKS

**Great Mosque**
**Khan Kourtbakh**
Matbakh al-Ajami
Khan al-Wazir
Khan al-Sabun
**Great Mosque**
Abraham Hammam
Ayyubid Palace
Museum
Underground chamber
Hammam Yalbougha al-Nasiri
Bastion
Tower
Entrance
Gouvernorat
Sultaniyeh Madrasa
Khosrofiyeh
Al-Outrouch
Bab al-Maqam

Hammam al-Nahassine *Handicrafts souk*
Al-Adiligeh
Bimaristan Arghoun
Souk al-Nahassine
Madrasa Halawiye
Souk al-Atarin
Khan al-Joumrok
Bab Qinnesrine

Al-Tuteh
Al-Bahramiye
Bab Antakiya
Halabia
Taxis
Minibus

Wall

Madrasa Firdaous

Department of Immigration

Ibn Shaddad St.
Bab al-Hadid St.
Al-Kawakbi St.
Al-Sejn St.
Al-Motanabbi St.
Bab al-Mahan St.
Al-Qastlah St.
Saaid al-Aas St.
Bab Antakiya St.
Bab Antakiya St.
Al-Shikh Mohsen St.
Al-Kallash St.
Al-Shrij St.
Souk al-Hal St.
Bab Djenine St.

Hanano
Damascus
Latakia

217

rampaged through the land, the merchants rerouted their caravans through Aleppo to avert the risk of attack. As a result, a succession of substantial khans were constructed in the city during the 15C, and when Ottoman rule was established in 1516, Aleppo came into its own and secured its hold and developed a monopoly on the silk trade with Persia.

**The Ottomans** – The capitulation treaties ensured Aleppo's importance as the prime European source of oriental goods in the Levant. Meanwhile, officials developed and encouraged commercial trade links with all the other provinces of the immense Ottoman Empire and established Aleppo as the third-largest Ottoman city after Istanbul and Cairo. Souks were built in the heart of the fortified city, in the area now known as the medina. As business flourished and peace continued to reign (briefly interrupted by unrest motivated by the Janissaries and an earthquake in 1822), the wealthier traders began building sumptuous residences outside the city walls. Even after the demise of the Ottoman Empire in 1918, stability prevailed until well into the 20C.

**Modern Syria** – Following the First World War, Aleppo faced a serious economic crisis: the new political frontiers imposed by the creation of modern Syria severed links with the cities Aleppo had traded with for centuries. Furthermore, when the city was relegated to second place after Damascus, it had no option but to review its role as a commercial transit-point for goods and rehabilitate the viability of agricultural concerns spread across a wide area that extends to the Euphrates. At the same time, the entrepreneurial spirit breathed life into new textile (mainly cotton), processed food and engineering industries. As active as ever before, the city is now the seat of an important university.

# Citadel★★★ (C3)

*Access by taxi (ask to be taken to Qalaat Halab).*
*Open 9am-6pm in summer; 9am-4pm in winter; closed Tuesdays.*
*Entrance fee. Allow 90min.*

The 38m tell covering the Antique city that grew up around an ancient acropolis is partly natural, partly man-made and is crowned by a citadel that was built principally during Ayyubid and Mameluke times (12-13C); at its foot nestles the modern city. The tell's elliptical form is echoed in the shape of the stronghold outer walls punctuated by towers and bastions. The tall walls (12m) are further fortified by a steep glacis, that survives only in part to the left of the monumental entrance, and a moat which could be flooded at will.

The main entrance to the citadel is accommodated in a fortified **tower**★. The original drawbridge however, has long since been replaced by a flight of steps. This crenellated tower shielded by heavy wrought-iron doors from the 13C now harbours the ticket office. The bridge to the main **gatehouse**★★★ comprises eight tall and thin archways. Above the loopholes runs a long Arabic inscription (dated 1292) glorifying the memory of the Mameluke Sultan Khalil, who carried out extensive repairs to the citadel. The forbiddingly austere exterior of this defensive complex, although reinforced by the six machicolations aligned along the front, is relieved by the delicate treatment of the window above the gateway (complete with small columns, *mouqarnas*, and alternating courses of black and yellow stone). Once past the gateway, there is no doubt as to the defensive purpose of this bastion, equipped as it is with an assortment of devices designed to confound any assailant. These include the successive use of sharp right-angle corners that prevent the import of a battering ram, various loopholes and a

Aleppo

The Citadel, Aleppo

ceiling pierced by openings on different levels through which arrows could be shot. On each side of the groin-vaulted passageway open out rooms that would have been used as stables and guardrooms.

The doorway flanked by two lions (note how the one on the right appears to be laughing) beyond the altar to St George leads up to the citadel's inner parade ground. The passageway on the right provides access to a vast Byzantine **underground vaulted chamber**★ that is partly excavated from the bedrock: this was devised to store water, although it has also served as a prison and as a sinister oubliette (*stairs to left of the room with piers*). The next block on the left contains a small **hammam**, and the one after that consists of the **Mosque of Abraham,** attributed to Nureddin (1168). The reason it is so called rests on a popular local legend that claims the Patriarch milked his russet-coloured cow here on his way from Ur to Canaan.

On the left, just before the Egyptian barracks built by Ibrahim Pasha (*drinks stall*) in 1834, stands the citadel's **Great Mosque**★ (1213). This comprises a domed prayer hall, which gives onto a harmoniously proportioned, if a little austere, shaded courtyard. The square minaret is contemporary with the mosque.

The walkway along the citadel ramparts provides some splendid **views**★★ over the city of Aleppo and the countryside beyond. A patchwork of flat roofs in the medina shelters private apartments and the souks, punctuated by tall, elegantly slender Ottoman minarets and a host of satellite dishes.The Ottoman barracks now accommodates a museum (*Entrance fee*) devoted to the archeology of the citadel. The area of fallow land opposite is used as an **open-air theatre**. It must be said however, that this part of the complex never really recovered from the devastation caused by the Mongols.

*Go back the way you have come, turning left immediately after the Mosque of Abraham.*

The **door**★ up ahead leads into the **Ayyubid Palace**, the west front of which is ornamented with *mouqarnas* and alternating courses of basalt and yellow limestone. It also provides access to the **hammam** (1367) situated off a courtyard furnished with four *iwans* (alcoves) and a fountain. From the hammam make your way up to the first floor of the main gateway and into the unusually large **throne room**★★★ (24x27m) built over the ramp into the citadel. This reflects Mameluke taste (15C) and would have been covered with domes; the present richly decorated painted wood ceiling is the work of contemporary Syrian craftsmen.

*Go down the cleverly concealed stairway in the throne room floor to the main entrance.*

## Below the citadel

The terrace cafes aligned outside the entrance to the citadel provide the perfect opportunity for a drink and a pause. Then head on to the nearby **handicraft souk**. Albeit less picturesque than the medina, this collection of shops offers a selection of locally made quality goods (silk, soap, leather, jewellery).

There are several well-preserved monuments of interest in the vicinity of the citadel: the striped building between the new palace and the law courts on the right houses the 14C **Hammam Yalbougha al-Nasiri**★. This has been beautifully restored to full working order and is now open to the public (*see* Making the most of Aleppo). The vast "changing area" is one of the largest in Syria.

Inside the souk

P. Meunier

Some 50m down the road opposite the entrance to the citadel is the **Khosrofiyeh Mosque** (1537) designed by the celebrated 16C Ottoman architect Sinan. The impressive **Sultaniyeh Madrasa** (1225) beyond contains the tomb of one of Saladin's sons. *Neither of these mosques is open to the public.* Directly opposite, on the far side of the square, rises the exceptionally fine, early 15C front of the **al-Outrouch Mosque,** above which towers a minaret with a double balcony and a great dome.

# Souks★★★

*Open 10am-7pm; closed Fridays and religious festivals.*
*Allow half a day.*

The souks of Aleppo are considered to be the busiest in the Middle East. There are some 12km of narrow passageways in all, crammed with thousands of little shops offering innumerable varieties of handcrafted and industrially manufactured merchandise. Retailers and craftsmen are arranged according to the goods in which they deal: gold and silver, leather, shoes, ironmongery and hardware each have their own bazaar bearing its own name (al-Nahassine for coppersmiths; al-Hammam for perfumers). Although fiercely competitive, the traders remain respectful of each other on the understanding that one good turn deserves another. It is not unusual, therefore, for one tradesman to recommend you buy from a competitor. The souk is more than a marketplace, for it operates as an entity, incorporating workshops (where goods are made up) and khans (where goods are stored prior to being sold wholesale and transported elsewhere). In the olden days (19C), foreign businessmen were represented by their consuls; they lived in enclaves screened off by huge wooden doors that protected both men and merchandise and when night fell, only a small door would be left unbolted. The atmosphere in the stone vaulted souks is timeless: the alleyways are too narrow for trucks to pass, so transport continues to be provided by tireless donkeys. So, in the early part of this 21C, the souks of Aleppo offer nothing short of a remarkably poignant experience.

## The Citadel to the Great Mosque (B3)

The entrance to the souk is some 200m to the left from that of the citadel and consists of a simple doorway from which extends the main avenue. This, in fact, is the old decumanus of the Hellenistic town that runs from east to west across the whole souk (500m).

The first "shops" specialise in Bedouin necessities (clothing, tents and the like). Where the light dims, shut out by the stone vaulting, the central avenue intersects with a street that branches right, past the **Khan Khairbeg** and the **Khan al-Kattan** (presently occupied by the Belgian consulate) to the Khan al-Wazir. The **Khan al-Wazir★** (17C) is one of the most remarkable caravanserais in the city. It has an impressive gateway with alternating courses of yellow and black stone: look back and up at the inward side to note the two delicate windows with small, slender columns.

On re-emerging, you will see the **Matbakh al-Ajami** on the right: a Mameluke palace from the 14C with a dome of 90sqm. Cross the square, passing the **al-Foustoq Mosque** (1349) on the left, and continue along the walls of the Khan al-Sabun until you reach the souk once more.

The **Khan al-Sabun★**, or soap caravanserai, has been severely truncated by the insertion of a new street. Despite this, it preserves its original, highly decorative façade from 1479, the date when the khan was founded by the Mameluke ruler Azdemir.

**Aleppo**

The street dives deeper into the souk, past a succession of tiny shops crammed with sparkling gold and silver jewellery, antique glassware, leather goods, carpets from the Caucasus and Iran, garishly bright costume jewellery and, finally, arrays of flounced long dresses and feminine underwear, displayed up against the eastern wall of the Great Mosque. Proceed along this street as it continues towards the main artery of the Souk al-Attarin (spice bazaar), through a section devoted entirely to textiles sold by the length.

The **Souk al-Attarin**, in the heart of the Souk al-Medina, is the ideal place for haggling over one of those distinctive batik silk scarves worn by the Bedouin. The best choice is probably to be had at one of the seven shops owned by the Akkad brothers.

*Walk right around the Great Mosque to its entrance.*

The **Great Mosque of Aleppo**★★ (Jami Zakariya) *(custodian. Long gowns provided for female visitors)* was founded around 715, at the end of the reign of the Umayyad Caliph al-Walid I, and completely rebuilt by Nureddin after the fire of 1169, very probably according to the original plans. The square, polychrome stone paved courtyard is enclosed within a triple row of arcading screening several doorways to the souk. The prayer hall takes up the southern block. Once inside, note the exceptional, late 13C carved wooden **minbar** with geometric motifs defined by inlaid panels of ivory and mother-of-pearl. The mosque is known by two names: Jami al-Kebir or Jami Zakariya. The latter title honours Zachary, the father of John the Baptist, whose head is said to be contained in the shrine there. The **minaret**★★, rising through four registers to a height of 50m, is a fine example of Seljuk artistry (1095).

The **Madrasa Halawiye**★, opposite the entrance to the Great Mosque, incorporates the remains of the ancient Byzantine cathedral (6C). This was dedicated to St Helena, the mother of the Emperor Constantine, and continued to be used by Christians until 1124 when the governor of Aleppo requisitioned it in retaliation for the atrocities committed by the Crusaders. A single room holds all that remains of the original quatrefoil church - six columns surmounted by superb Byzantine capitals. In the adjacent room note the splendid 13C carved wooden **mihrab** surrounded by a long calligraphy inscription.

*Return to the Souk al-Attarin.*

## Souk al-Attarin to Bab Qinnesrine (B3, C3)

The alley (Souk al-Nahassine) running perpendicular to the Souk al-Attarin leads to the **Hammam al-Nahassine** *(see Making the most of Aleppo)* opposite the khan of the same name. The baths have been rather over-restored but the main hall, visible from the street, remains beautifully proportioned (12-13C). Continue along the same street until, 10m or so from the hammam, you reach an open alleyway on the left leading to the al-Adiliyeh Mosque.

The **Al-Adiliyeh Mosque**★ was built in 1556 by the governor of Aleppo, Muhammad Pasha, and stands as a perfect embodiment of the Ottoman style. The double portico opening onto the courtyard is probably the earliest to survive from the Empire of the Sublime Porte. It has six small domes. The windows are ornamented with splendid ceramic decorations. The domed, square prayer hall is flanked by an elegant minaret. As with the Khosrofiyeh Mosque, this building formed part of a religious complex *(waqf)* spread over three hectares, with a community that administered several hundred shops, three khans and four *qaysaria*.

The exposed alleyway extends to Bab Qinnesrine, past various, successive khans, including the Khan al-Obi, and the smaller Khan Fansah (18C, wrought iron) overlooking the intersection. 50m further on the left stands the *Bimaristan* Arghoun.

The **Bimaristan Arghoun★★** (*it is customary to tip the custodian*) was founded by the Mameluke Governor Arghoun al-Kamili in 1354 as a hospital and lunatic asylum. This wholly original building was erected on the site of an old palace and must have been a

**The famous soap of Aleppo**
Beneath their yellow skin, the crudely cut square blocks of olive and laurel soap are green. More importantly, the outside is stamped with the distinctive trademark of the maker as a mark of its quality. Traditional methods are still used in its preparation, with the thick molten mixture being poured onto the soap-works floor and left to harden over several months. Only then are the crude bars left in the open air to dry. It is at this stage that the crust is formed, sealing in the oils and preventing the soap from becoming too hard.

rather fearful place in its time, filled with the anguished sounds of its incarcerated subjects echoing through the narrow vaulted corridors and small inner courtyards.

A fine doorway ornamented with *mouqarnas* opens out onto a courtyard with a large pool. Beyond the two arcaded galleries are disposed five small rooms. To the left of the main *iwan*, a corridor provides access to three further rooms with narrow vaults. On the far left, five cells are clustered around a tiny square courtyard. The ward comprising 11 cells around the octagonal courtyard was said to have been reserved for the most dangerous patients. A third rectangular room with a dome contains seven more cells.

As you continue down the street, a pungent smell coming from somewhere on the right leads you to the traditional **soap-works** (*visits by prior arrangement*) that have supplied endless hammams for generations. Here, the soap continues to be made by hand, using traditional techniques that date back to Antiquity. Those wishing to take some back home will find it stacked in pyramids in countless shops around Bab al-Faraj, near the clock tower (B2).

Complete the last 200m to the **Bab Qinnesrine★**, the best preserved of Aleppo's ancient city gates, dating back to the 12C, flanked by a 300m section of the old (restored) city walls.

*Retrace your steps back to the Souk al-Attarin.*

## Souk al-Attarin to Bab Antakia (B3)
*Head into the Souk al-Attarin until you reach the Khan al-Joumruk on the left.*

The **Khan al-Joumruk★** (1574), the largest khan in Aleppo, covers an area of 6 400sqm. In its heyday it operated 350 shops in the nearby streets and accommodated the British, Dutch and French consulates within its walls. The main porch is most striking: surmounted on the inside by a beautifully decorated window. In the middle of the central courtyard stands a small mosque.

The **Al-Bahramiye Mosque★** was once part of a *waqf* founded in 1583 by Bahram Pasha, a governor of Aleppo. The outer gallery had to be rebuilt in 1700 after a minaret collapsed on top of it. The square prayer hall extends into an apse with five lateral bays occupied by the mihrab. The original dome was also destroyed by the minaret and replaced with a smaller one resting on four piers. The overall design is Ottoman, although certain features – like the two *iwans* in the gallery – are Syrian in derivation.

**Aleppo**

223

This part of the street is open to the sky, as it picks its way between stalls heaped with spices, dried fruit (pistachios are a special delicacy in these parts), before reaching the coppersmiths' souk and the **Bab Antakia**★ (Antioch Gate). The twin hexagonal bastions were erected by the Ayyubids (13C) and restored two centuries later by the Mamelukes.

The main building, incorporating an interesting assortment of antique stones and overlooking the small square before the gate, is the **Al-Tuteh Mosque** (Mulberry Mosque); beyond the gate stretches the modern city.

## Jedaideh: the Christian quarter★ (B2)

*It is best to visit Bayt Ghazale and the Armenian Museum in the morning.*
*Allow 1hr.*

A quick tour of the Jedaideh quarter dotted with churches and luxurious residences provides a view of a markedly different part of Aleppo. The first Christians moved out of the walled city in the 17C after accumulating considerable fortunes dealing in textiles. This northern suburb is gradually being restored.

Start from the **Clock Tower**, erected in 1899 to mark the boundary between the medina and the new town, and make your way down the pedestrianised street (Al-Tilal) lined with numerous shops selling clothing destined for the Russian market (note the shop signs in the Cyrillic alphabet). Turn down the first major street on the right, largely given over to Armenian jewellers' shops, which leads to a statue of Germanus Fahrat (1770-1832) and the **Maronite Cathedral** (1872-1923) behind.

*Walk left around the cathedral, following the course of a street specialising in handbags.*

The little street on the left (Sissi Street) before Al-Hatab Square leads to the **Sissi Restaurant** (it's worth entering this antique shop on the square for a glimpse of the lovely courtyard inside). Walk right round the square and take the street running slightly downhill (past the road leading to the Al-Macharabiya Restaurant, the **Bayt Ghazale** – a fine town house now undergoing restoration – and the narrow Al-Kayali cul-de-sac where the Yasmeen Restaurant is situated), to the arch marking the entrance to Haret al-Yasmeen Street. On the same corner stands the Achiqbash House-Museum. The paved alleyway between the high stone walls is typical of this quarter: from the outside, the town houses of Aleppo betray none of the finery within. Only the balconies screened off with wooden blinds betray any sign of human habitation.

Achiqbash House contains the **Museum of Popular Arts and Traditions**★★ *(Open 8am-2pm; closed Tuesdays. Entrance fee)*. Here, within this luxuriously comfortable domestic interior, isolated from the tumult of the city, the family enjoyed peace and privacy. The courtyard (the heart of the traditional Arab home, often compared with earthly paradise) is furnished with an ornamental pool of water and a few trees. A deeply recessed *iwan* provided residents with a shaded spot in which to rest during the hottest hours of the day and receive visitors. The rooms overlooking the courtyard all have beautifully decorated stucco window frames. Carved stone gargoyles collect the rainwater. A cool cellar excavated from the bedrock has been perfectly adapted for storing foodstuffs. The room interiors recreated by the museum evoke scenes from daily life in the mid-18C.

On stepping out of the museum, turn right and follow the same little street through the old wool bazaar, taking in the rich diversity of the different Christian communities on the way. In addition to the churches serving the Syrian Catholic and Greek Orthodox congregations, there is the Armenian Cathedral for the adherents of the **Gregorian Church**. Attached to this third establishment, dedicated to the Forty Martyrs, is a small **museum** *(Open 9am-1pm; closed Saturdays. Entrance fee)*. The cathedral has three chapels, one more than a thousand years old. Inside, there are a series of beautiful Armenian crosses, a wooden Bishop's throne and a few paintings. The custodian has even been known to sing an Armenian hymn for visitors.

*To get to the Maronite Cathedral, retrace your steps and take the first little street on the left (Aidah Street), which runs before the imposing Greek Catholic church (1849).*

# Archeological Museum★★★ (A2)

*Open 9am-6pm in summer; 9am-4pm in winter; 9am-3pm during Ramadan; closed Tuesdays. Entrance fee.*
*Allow 90min for a thorough visit.*

A visit to the Aleppo Archeological Museum is like journeying through Syria's long history from the Palaeolithic to the Islamic period. The museum is pleasantly compact, but it is best to allow plenty of time for studying some of the remarkable and often stirring artefacts recovered from the ancient sites at Mari, Ugarit, Ebla and Tell Halaf. As soon as you enter the museum, you are confronted with a fine reconstruction of the **entrance to the palace-temple at Tell Halaf★★** with its basalt statues of three divinities being carried by their animal attributes. The two sphinxes on each side ornamented the doorjambs.

D Thierry/DIAF

Various glass cases in the main hall display artefacts relating to the evolution of prehistoric societies from Palaeolithic to Neolithic times, from a hunting-gathering (stone axes, arrows) way of life to a more sedentary one (kernstones). The importance given to fertility symbols is evident in the various votive figurines with pendulous breasts and wide hips, whereas the significance of death is acknowledged by the funerary urn containing a child's skeleton.

Room 1, the largest and most interesting in the museum, contains finds from the excavations of sites dating from the 5th-2nd millenia BC.

The cultural sophistication of the proto-urban period among city-dwellers (Tell Halaf and Obeïd) is evident in the **decor of the Temple of the Eyes★★**, and the numerous items of **jewellery★**, cylinder seals, alabaster idols and amulets displayed. The objects from Early Dynastic **Mari** (Tell Hariri) are evidence of the remarkable Sumerian civilisation *(see p 265)*: look out for the amazing baked-terracotta cakes or bread **moulds** (19-18C BC) shaped as fish and figures (woman holding up her breasts) on the left wall. The **diorite statue of Ishtup-Ilum★★**, a rigid figure of a Mari ruler, stands opposite an extraordinary **lion★★★** portrayed as if poised to pounce. This lion, one of a pair that flanked the entrance to the temple honouring the king of the

Statue from Tell Halaf gracing the entrance to the museum.

Aleppo

country (known as Dagan), is not made of bronze but of wood covered with copper platelets; the second is in the Louvre (Paris), the site having been excavated by the French since 1933. Several **votive statues** (3rd millennium BC) with huge staring eyes inlaid with ivory are shown wearing long garments with petal-shaped tufts of wool (*kaunakes*). It is worth noting that the use of a drill to texture such details as the beard is a hallmark of Mari sculpture. The beautifully feminine life-size **goddess with the pouring vase★★★** is regarded as one of the most treasured works of Mesopotamian art: attired in a short sleeved bodice tucked into a long flowing skirt and a heavy six-stringed beaded necklace balanced by a counterweight down her back. A cunningly concealed device enabled water to pour from her vase at will.

The **tablets** in the central case from the archives at Mari have shed a vital insight on contemporary society and its relations with its neighbouring states. The **clay livers** were used in divinations, with predictions hinging on the shape of the lobes. Excavations conducted in and around **Hama** produced a superb **ivory beaker★**. The cylindrical pots were probably intended for food offerings for burning. Among the objects recovered from **Ugarit** (Ras Shamra – *see p 182*) is an extraordinary **gold cup★★★** (14C-13C BC) inscribed on the outside with three concentric bands of animals (ibex, bulls and lions) and flowers, palmettes and pomegranates. This was discovered in 1933 alongside a patera (the one exhibited is a copy) bearing a hunting scene that reflects Egyptian influences. Several cast **bronze statues of Baal** covered with gold leaf are shown next to animal-shaped weights. Two stone moulds indicate how jewellery elements could be mass-produced, while Egyptian scarabs and carved ivories from the Aegean reveal the extent to which commerce and taste in Ugarit were fashioned by foreign forces.

Room 2 of the museum contains examples of Aramaean and Assyrian monumental art (1st millennium BC), including a number of replicas of statues, discovered for the main part at **Tell Halaf** by Baron Oppenheim, and transferred to Berlin only to be destroyed during the Second World War. On the right is displayed a group comprising two striking seated female figures with cups separated by a **panel★** (9C BC) illustrating two bull-headed genii and a bearded figure carrying a winged disk, representing a scene from the Epic of Gilgamesh. Among the artefacts from **Arslan Tash**, which formed part of the Assyrian Empire, are an exceptional collection of small Phoenician **ivory plaques★★★** (9C BC) that once decorated a ceremonial bed destined for King Haza'l of Damascus. The woman at the window and the sphinxes betray the impact of Egypt. The cow suckling its calf – a favourite Mesopotamian subject – is treated with great sensitivity.

### Epic of Gilgamesh

The Epic of Gilgamesh (3rd millennium BC), which has been pieced together from fragments found in the library at Nineveh, relates the adventures of an ancient Sumerian king who set out with his friend Enkidu to fight the giant Humbaba. After vanquishing the giant guardian of the cedar forest, they beat the Heavenly Bull sent by Ishtar and basked in glory. Meanwhile, the goddess Inanna (Ishtar by another name), piqued by Gilgamesh's rejection, decided to avenge her unrequited love by killing Enkidu. In despair, Gilgamesh set about solving the mystery of eternal life.

The two **basalt lions** guarding the entrance to the city of Hadatu have six legs (four visible from the side and two from the front).

The Assyrian palace at **Tell Barsip** revealed several **frescoes★** (mid-8C BC), as well as funerary ware from the 3rd millennium BC, including some delicate ostrich-shaped **pottery★**.

Room 3 is devoted to more recent finds principally recovered during the excavation of **Ain Dara** (*see p 237*): orthostats from the cella, stelae of the goddess Ishtar (Inanna), and from **Ebla** (*see*

**Aleppo**

*p 243)*. The two large basalt **sacrificial altars★★** from the sanctuary dedicated to the cult of royal ancestors in Ebla were used in sacrificial rites and for making offerings of the victims' blood. The **steatite hairstyle★★** (circa 2300 BC) that once graced a female head was found in the royal palace with the remains of a lovely piece of **wooden furniture★**. The **tablets** inscribed with Eblaite characters formed part of the royal archives.

On the first floor are displayed various maps and photographs charting the excavations undertaken since 1970 by various international archeological teams on the banks of the Euphrates, before being submerged as a result of the Al-Assad dam. Digging in this northern part of Syria (near the Iraqi border) has revealed traces of continuous occupation from Neolithic to Islamic times.

### Tell Brak

Tell Brak is situated by the Khabur River, equidistant from the upper reaches of the Tigris and the Euphrates, south of the Armenian uplands. The 108-acre site, which revealed the famous Eye Temple (3000 BC) and numerous idols with outsized eyes, was found by the British archeologist Sir Max Mallowan in 1937 (life on the dig is humorously related by Mallowan's wife Agatha Christie in her light-hearted book "Come Tell Me How You Live"). Other important finds include various gold and ivory imports from the Middle Uruk period. Recent research by the McDonald Institute at Cambridge University has revealed that a walled city existed at Tell Brak as early as 3800 BC, predating other Mesopotamian cities by several centuries, and that a precursor of writing was present there by 3500 BC. Some tablets bear early pictograms and a number imply the inhabitants were numerate. Having said this, current excavations suggest the origins of the world's first cities go back further than hitherto thought.

The **Hellenistic**, **Roman** and **Byzantine collections** in Room 1, although less impressive than those in Damascus, still contain some pleasant surprises (Greek pottery, basalt stele of the goddess Allat riding a dromedary, Roman lamps). The white limestone **funerary stele of Marta★★** was found at Membij (ancient Hierapolis): the Greek inscription names the dead woman, who is portrayed seated in a niche, draped in a beautifully rendered gown. The left wall is given over to various **funerary busts from Palmyra**. The two Roman tomb **reliquaries** in the centre of the room were used to store holy oil that had been touched by the bodies of martyrs from the dawn of Christianity.

The **Islamic section** includes a modest selection of objects from Umayyad to Mameluke times, mainly from Raqqa, Qalaat Djabar and Maskane on the Euphrates. Notice the large **jars** *(to the right of the doorway)*, filters and large **anthropomorphous sun dish★** among the pottery and gourds emblazoned with the Mameluke insignia.

The **model of Aleppo★** provides an interesting overview of the medina.

## Aziziyeh: "Little Beirut" (A1)

At the beginning of the 20C an important new quarter was developed near the public park in the northwest of Aleppo. As the economy grew, boosted by the completion of the railway, the wealthy set migrated from the cramped Jedaideh district to the outer suburbs of Aziziyeh overlooking the Quweiq River. This residential area became particularly popular under the French Mandate (and again after independence), as luxury town houses and spacious apartment blocks were built among various good hospitals and schools, managed by religious (Jesuit) orders. This area has its own select meeting-place, the **Aleppo Club** *(members only)*. This continues to be frequented by the city's elite (politicians and wealthy traders), although the nationalisation of industry (1963) led quite a number of Aleppo's middle class to move to Beirut. This rather sleepy district – nicknamed "little Beirut" – has retained its old-fashioned charm and is still a favourite place for locals to meet. The best restaurants line the long avenue that spans the Quweiq and the large and beautifully maintained **park** is a favourite haunt of families in search of a patch of greenery.

## Firdaus Madrasa★
*Best reached by taxi.*

This Koranic school, located in the popular quarter of Bab al-Maqam in the south of the city (C4), was founded in 1235 by Dayfa Khatun, the daughter-in-law and niece of Saladin. The pure use of line and complex forms make this is one of the most admired buildings of Aleppo. The fine dressed stone blocks are disposed around a rectangular courtyard, along three sides of which runs a gallery. Note how the arches spring from wooden dosserets inserted above the stone capitals: an ingenious device designed to absorb the vibrations caused by earth tremors and minimise the risk of damage. Opposite the large *iwan* is a small prayer area contained by three domes. Wide ribbon-like bands emanate from the *mihrab* to cover the wall of the *qibla* with interwoven decoration.

Some 300m further on, stands the **Madrasa al-Zahiriyeh**, another establishment founded posthumously in 1213 to commemorate Saladin's son El-Malek-ez-Zahir.

**Aleppo**

## Making the most of Aleppo

### COMING AND GOING

**By air** – Aleppo's international airport is 10km from the town centre, on the road to Deir ez-Zor. Some European flights. Daily flights for Damascus (around 8am) returning around 6pm in the evening. Flight time 1hr.

**By train** – *Aleppo station* (known as Baghdad station) (A1), where Agatha Christie set the opening scenes of "Murder on the Orient Express", is just to the north of the park. Daily service to Damascus (night train), Latakia and Deir ez-Zor, weekly train to Istanbul.

**By bus** – *Hanano Garage* (A3), Ibrahim Hanano St. This new bus station serves the whole of Syria with the best of the private bus companies: Damascus (5hr), Hama (90min), Homs (2hr), Latakia (3hr), Deir ez-Zor (4hr30min). Each company has its own office, where you should buy your ticket at least half a day in advance.

*Karnak* (A2), Baron St. The national bus company's agency is opposite the Ramsis Hotel. Catch the buses near the agency, opposite the tourist office.

*International* (A2), Al-Maarri St. The buses for Turkey and Lebanon use the same parking area as Karnak.

*Bab Antakiya Garage* (A3), Bab Antakiya St. This is the microbus station for Harim and Daret-Azze (St Simeon).

**By shared taxi** – The main taxi rank is just behind the Amir Hotel (A3).

### GETTING AROUND

Traffic is heavy in the town centre and traffic jams are frequent. It's often easier to walk.

**By taxi** – There are plenty of yellow taxis to be found in the new town, but none will venture into the maze of souks. It is particularly hard to find a free taxi during the rush hour and you may have to be prepared to share with other customers, which may prolong your journey. Hang on tight, as driving in Aleppo is on the brisk side.

**By taxi with chauffeur** – The best way of exploring the Dead Cities. Allow S£3 500 per day. Book the previous day through your hotel. To avoid arguments with your driver, make sure you agree your itinerary and the time you intend to spend visiting each site with him, before setting off.

**Car hire –** There is less choice of car hire firms than in Damascus.

**Europcar**, at the Pullman Hotel, on the first floor next to the Neptune travel agents, in the street opposite the post office. It is possible to hire a car in Aleppo and return it in Damascus (and vice versa).

## ADDRESS BOOK

**Tourist information –** Opposite the entrance to the archeological museum in the small park. The tourist office will provide you with a plan of Aleppo and the surrounding region, but not much practical information.

**Travel agents –** These are found in Baron St (A2).

**Halabia** (A3), behind the hotel Amir, on the first floor of a building which overlooks a busy square, full of taxis and minibuses. ☎ (21) 222 65 51, Fax (21) 221 96 57. The agency specialises in organising tours in Syria and Jordan, but will also arrange day excursions (S£2 000 for 4 people by microbus, or S£2 500 by car), or half-day trips, for example to visit the Dead Cities. Tell them what you'd like to do, with at least 24 hours' notice, even if it's unusual.

**Airline companies –** The offices of the main airline companies are found in the Baron St district (A2). To reserve domestic flights, the Syrianair office is found 100m from the main post office (A2), in the direction of the park.

**British Consulate –** Al-Sabil St, next to the law syndicate, ☎ (21) 268 05 02/3, Fax (21) 268 05 01.

**Main post office –** The main post office (A2) is near the park, at the foot of the huge red and white aerial mast. There is a *poste restante* service. Parcels must be sent from the building next door.

**Telephone –** At the main post office (A2). There are a dozen or so kiosks which take cards outside the building. You can send and receive faxes here.

**Express post – DHL**, Boustan Koulab, near Samraa restaurant, ☎ (21) 225 04 63.

**Bank/Currency exchange – Commercial Bank of Syria**, Al-Azmeh St (A2). Counters 2 and 6 will change travellers' cheques and cash.

**Exchange bureau** (B2), on the corner of Al-Kouwatli St and Bab al-Faraj St. Cash only. 8am-8pm.

**Visa renewal –** At the immigration department (C3), to the north of the citadel. Open 8.30am-1pm. Visa extension takes about an hour, with endless formalities to be gone through.

## WHERE TO STAY

Even though Aleppo doesn't have a wide choice of medium-price hotels, it can claim the distinction of having Syria's most famous hotel, the Baron.

### • Boustan Koulab district (A2-3)

*Under US$25*

The Boustan Koulab district, near the archeological museum, offers a good selection of reasonable hotels (**Yarmouk**, **Syria**, **Eshbilia**, **Al-Raouda**). What they lack in comfort they make up for in the convenience of their situation. Their clientele is not always very salubrious.

**Al-Gawaher Hotel**, Bab al-Faraj (near the clock tower), ☎/Fax (21) 223 95 54 – 15rm ⌂ ⍭ / ▤ 🖊 A pleasant, clean and friendly hotel. The rooftop has been converted into a terrace, where you can eat breakfast (included in the price of the room) or enjoy the evening air, with views as far as the citadel.

**Tourist Hotel**, Boustan Koulab, ☎ (21) 221 65 83 – 16rm ⍭ Not to be confused with the Tourism Hotel, this family hotel is impeccably kept by Madame Olga and her son. Comfortable and spotlessly clean rooms, half of which have their own bathrooms. The down side of its success is that the personal, friendly welcome seems to have been sacrificed at the expense of a more commercial approach. Reservation is essential, and even so you may find your room given away if another guest arrives before you. Still a good place to stay.

*From US$25-40*

**Somar Hotel**, Al-Yarmouk St, ☎ (21) 221 21 98 – 33rm ⍭ / ▤ 🖊 The majority of rooms have en-suite bathrooms and some have television. The simple but reasonably comfortable rooms overlook a small interior courtyard. Quiet and pleasant, with a friendly atmosphere.

**Al-Faisal Hotel**, Al-Yarmouk St, ☎ (21) 221 77 68, Fax (21) 221 37 19 – 33rm 📶 🗐 🎤 One of the newest hotels in the district, with clean, comfortable rooms, if a little stark.

*From US$40-60*

**Baron Hotel**, Baron St, ☎ (21) 221 08 80, Fax (21) 221 81 64 – 36rm ⤬/🗐 🎤 ✗ Most rooms have en suite bathrooms and television. Lawrence of Arabia, Agatha Christie and General de Gaulle were among the travellers who stayed at this legendary hotel while in search of exotic adventures in the early 20th century. Today it looks a little worn and could do with a facelift, but is still worth a stay, even if the electricity, plumbing and beds would seem to date from its early days.

**Ramsis Hotel**, Baron St, ☎ (21) 221 67 00 – 41rm ⤬ / 🗐 🎤 📺 The majority of rooms have en-suite bathrooms and some have balconies. Opposite the Baron, and also due for a facelift. Prices fairly high, given the quality of the rooms.

**Tourism Hotel**, Saad Alla al-Jabri St ☎ (21) 225 16 02, Fax (21) 225 16 06 – 100rm 📶 🗐 🎤 📺 ✗ Much frequented by tour groups. Opposite the main post office. Rooms in good condition. A copious buffet-style breakfast is served on the ground floor. Open to non-residents (S£150).

*From US$120-130*

🏨 **Amir Palace Hotel**, Bab Djenine St, ☎ (21) 221 48 00, Fax (21) 221 57 00 – 131rm 📶 🗐 🎤 📺 ✗ 🆑 Very central situation, practical for visiting Aleppo. Good standard of comfort and lovely views over the old city and the citadel from some rooms. Bookshop. The best value in this category.

• **Jedaideh district** (B2)

*From US$115-130*

🏨 **Beit Wakil Hotel**, Sissi St, Jedaideh, ☎ (21) 221 71 69, Fax (21) 224 70 82 – 16rm 📶 🗐 🎤 📺 ✗ 🆑 A charming hotel, in a restored 16C mansion in the heart of the Christian quarter. The rooms are tastefully furnished and decorated and arranged on two floors around an attractive patio with fountain. Very peaceful.

**Martini Hotel**, Jedaideh, ☎ (21) 636 100, Fax (21) 632 333 – 14rm 📶 🗐 🎤 📺 ✗ 🆑 A former mansion in the Christian quarter, with small but comfortable first-floor rooms. A pity that they are separated from the attractive restaurant patio by glazing. Seven new, larger rooms are due to be added shortly.

• **Away from the centre** (A2)

*From US$85-100*

**Pullman al-Shahba Hotel**, University St, ☎ (21) 266 72 00, Fax (21) 266 72 13 – 100rm 📶 🗐 🎤 📺 ✗ 🆑 Situated behind Aleppo's university in a pleasant residential district. Comfortable, but a little far from the town centre. Shops, hairdresser, car hire.

*Over US$160*

**Shahba Cham Palace Hotel**, Damascus Rd, ☎ (21) 227 01 00, Fax (21) 227 01 50 – 250rm 📶 🗐 🎤 📺 ✗🛋 🍽 🆑 Aleppo's most luxurious hotel, with a high standard of comfort. Two huge pillars in the entrance hall represent a reproduction of the minaret from the city's al-Qadi mosque. Uninterrupted view over the city. Set in a quiet district, but away from the town centre. Shops, discotheque from midnight onwards, sometimes lively.

• **Outside the town**

*Under US$10*

**Al-Kaddour campsite**, ☎ (21) 224 84 97, Fax (21) 221 96 57. 30km from Aleppo, near Kafr Amme on the road to St Simeon. The site consists of chalets set in an olive grove. Ideal setting for exploring the Dead Cities. Family cooking. Information from Halabia travel agency (A3).

## EATING OUT

Aleppo is the gastronomic capital of Syria and you will find the country's best restaurants here, often in magnificent settings, without necessarily being more expensive than elsewhere.

• **Boustan Koulab district** (A2-3)

The restaurants found in this area are popular and serve simple dishes. The menu is generally limited to chicken, kebabs and traditional hors d'oeuvres. There is a good choice of these small restaurants on Tarik bin Zyad St. One block further along, in the direction of

Bab al-Faraj, there are several stalls which serve delicious fresh fruit-juices.

### Under US$10

**Al-Koummeh**, Tarik bin Zyad St. Like all the other restaurants in this street, the Al-Koummeh has a first-floor dining room for more peaceful meals. Good, plain cooking.

**Abou Nawas**, Rachid St, near the Tourist Hotel. An ideal place for a good breakfast, complete with egg, cheese and the traditional apricot jam. Open for lunch and dinner. Large, peaceful dining room with subdued lighting. Air-conditioning.

**Al-Andalib**, Baron St, ☎ (21) 222 40 30. ♟ A very pleasant terrace, which is reached by a staircase on the corner of the Baron Hotel. A popular restaurant with varied family cooking. Delicious *basterma* (an Armenian speciality, consisting of dried meat coated in spices), and *lahme bseniye* (meat baked with tomato sauce).

**Workers' Club restaurant**, ☎ (21) 221 70 04. ♟ Open-air service in a small town-centre garden with a fountain. Roast chicken and kebabs. Very pleasant in the evening when the aromatic tobacco of the hookah smokers perfumes the air. Dining room. It is worth going here more for the setting than for the quality of the food.

### Over US$10

⊛ **Top of the Top**, Bab Djenine St. For dinner on the top floor of the Amir Palace Hotel. ♟ Refined local dishes and an extensive menu, where western dishes (*filet au roquefort, confit de canard*) rub shoulders with Syrian: salad with green thyme, mortadella with garlic and pistachios, minced lamb grilled with lemon (*ras nanaa*). Delicious puddings. Exceptional view of the citadel. Allow S£600. Bar, piano, air-conditioning. At lunchtime the Amir also offers a very generous buffet on the first floor.

### • Jedaideh district (B2)

Several restaurants have opened in impeccably restored stately old town houses, a good way of bringing this historic quarter of Aleppo back to life. The locals like to come in large family groups or with friends as soon as the last tourists have left (around 10.30pm). The price of this success is that a table should be reserved the previous day.

### Under US$20

⊛ **Sissi House**, Al-Harab Sq, ☎ (21) 221 94 11. ♟ The best restaurant in Aleppo, if not in the whole of Syria. Lovely stone bourgeois town house, which has been tastefully restored. You can choose to eat in the attractive patio (air-conditioned in summer, heated in winter), unless you prefer the subdued lighting and more intimate atmosphere of the first-floor dining rooms. Traditional musicians play discreetly in the evening. If you only want a drink, there is a pleasant cellar bar. The patron is devoted to promoting fine local cuisine. Try a selection of the particularly original starters before the equally delicious main dishes. Seasonal dishes: fresh thyme salad, aubergine purée with chopped walnuts and pomegranate juice, kebabs with truffles, mutton with black cherries. There's only one drawback: after a meal here you'll want to come back every day! – especially as it isn't expensive.

⊛ **Beit Wakil**, Sissi St, Jedaideh, ☎ (21) 221 71 69. ♟ (See also Where to stay). A magnificent setting: old patio, with porch, fountain and plants. Refined and tasty cooking; what more could you ask?

**Cantara**, ☎ (21) 225 33 55. ♟ The owner of the Amir Palace and Top of the Top has converted this old house into a restaurant specialising in Italian cooking. If you are tired of Middle Eastern food, try a pizza, pasta or veal steak. Leave room for a pistachio or cherry ice cream, though. Mostly local clientele.

**Kan Zaman**, ☎ (21) 331 12 99. ♟ Slightly over-restored, perhaps, this former house has several dining rooms for winter and a pleasant courtyard and terrace for the summer, where you can admire the view over the rooftops of the old town. Carefully prepared local specialities.

**Martini** (see Where to stay). ♟ Another good restaurant in the Christian quarter. Lovely patio with porch and fountain, decorated with antique nick-nacks and plants. You could also choose to eat in one of the small dining rooms, which have been tastefully restored, or even on the roof, where you have a superb view of the city and the floodlit citadel.

**Yasmeen House**, Al-Kayali St, ☎ (21) 222 44 62. ♟ This restaurant is hidden away at the end of a cul-de-sac near the

**Aleppo**

Bayt Ghazale. Small lounges and large dining room. Mostly patronised by the locals, it only gets busy after 10pm. Brunch is served on Fridays and Sundays.

*Al-Mashrabiah*, Fahrat St, ☎ (21) 240 249. Smaller than the other restaurants in the district. Family atmosphere with rustic decor: stone walls, woodwork and red-checked tablecloths. Chops, *chahraat* (steak), *chiche taouk*. Reasonably priced.

• *Azizyeh* (A1)

There are a dozen or so restaurants with terraces along George and Mathilda Salem St, near the park (Ebla, Al-Karam, Cordoba, Al-Challal, Pizzeria Reef and Wannes).

*Under US$10*

*Crosby*, ☎ (21) 224 83 50. This tiny snack bar, on the corner of two streets, sells the best sandwiches in town. These grilled "panini" are served hot and have all kinds of fillings, from cheese to chicken curry to brains in breadcrumbs (a speciality of Aleppo). Ideal for a quick lunchtime treat.

*Wannes* (pronounced "wannesse"), Omar Abou Richa St, ☎ (21) 222 43 53. ♟ The best-known restaurant in this district. You have the choice between a shady roadside terrace or a dining room inside with subdued lighting. Varied Syrian cuisine, with a good reputation and justifiably so. Smart clientele. Air-conditioning.

*Al-Challal*, Omar Abou Richa St, ☎ (21) 224 33 44. A more relaxed atmosphere than Wannes with good family cooking.

*Pizza House*, Aziziyeh, near Wannes. The young of Aleppo come here for a complete change from local cuisine. Crisp pizzas and bistro-style decor.

### HAVING A DRINK

**Cafés, bars, tearooms** – There are some pleasant cafés near the citadel, but Aleppo is desperately short of bars where tourists can have a drink in the evening.

*Baron Hotel bar* (A2), a nostalgic setting for a drink at the end of a busy day, where you can relax in a leather armchair and imagine yourself back in the days of early 20C travel. ♟

### Night life/spots

*Bimaristan Arghoun* (B4). Whirling dervishes accompanied by tambourines can be seen in the vaulted rooms here some evenings during the tourist season. An enthralling experience. Book tickets in khan al-Wazir.

*Cotton Club*. Jazz concerts organised by the French consulate take place every Monday from 7.30-9.30pm in the Amir Palace hotel's panoramic restaurant (A3).

*Shaba Cham Palace Hotel*. For the past few years the local self-taught musician As'ad Chatere has played at the Shaba Cham every evening except Wednesday, 7-10pm. He has played the lute since he was 12 and has accompanied such famous musicians as Sabah Fakhri and Mayada al-Hennawi. When the Arab audience joins in with Oum Kalsoum's well-known songs, it is a memorable experience. Drinks cost around S£100. Ice creams.

### OTHER THINGS TO DO

**Hammam – Hammam Yalbougha** (C3), near the citadel, 200m from the entrance. ☎ (21) 262 31 54. These are the only old baths in the country which are open to women, on Mondays, Thursdays and Saturdays, 10am-5pm. Open to men the rest of the time, until 2 in the morning. S£415 including sauna, a wash with a horsehair flannel and a massage. There is a cafeteria near the entrance in the summer.

*Hammam al-Nahassine* (B3), in the middle of the souks. Men only. Less luxurious than the Yalbougha but more popular. Open every day from 6am to midnight.

**Festival** – Euro-Syrian Jazz Festival, early September, entry free. Syrian and European jazz groups play in the floodlit citadel each year.

### SHOPPING GUIDE

For those with little time to spare, the craft souk near the citadel groups together most of Aleppo's local products in a single space: decorated copperware, silk, soap, marquetry, painted wood and jewellery. For better bargains (and bartering is essential) go to the old souks.

**Textiles** – Silk is sold mostly in the form of Bedouin scarves decorated with various patterns: water-wheels, camel prints, birds of paradise. Watch out for cheap imitations in synthetic fabrics. Small scarves sell for around S£250, (for large ones double this sum). There are plenty of tablecloths to choose from, woven in cotton and silk (S£300).

**Aladine**, al-Altarin souk (B3), on the main street of the souk. A stall with a friendly welcome. By far the most varied of Aleppo's shops, with the widest choice of silk scarves.

**Soap** – There are several shops near the clock tower in Al-Maarri St (A2). The soap is sold by weight and costs S£170 for the best quality.

**Local delicacies** – Aleppo is famous for its pistachios, which rival those of Iran. They are sold in the al-Altarin souk. They are particularly delicious when they are just grilled. S£350 per kilo. In the autumn they are sold fresh, with their pretty mauve skin.

**Azrak** (A2), Youssef Al-Azmeh St, opposite the Ugarit cinema. Delicious marzipan bars stuffed with pistachios (from Aleppo). S£400 per kilo. This speciality has made a fortune for this company, which now has outlets in Paris, Montreal and Beirut. Try their almond biscuits too.

**Sabbagh** (A2), Al-Abbarah St. Individually wrapped crystallised fruits, practical when travelling.

**Somar** (B1), Jebel Al-Nahr St, 100m from the Pizza Avenue. Specialities include marzipan, coconut cakes, and cinnamon and walnut macaroons. Slightly cheaper than the two cake shops mentioned above.

**Rugs** – There are several shops selling rugs in the souks, near khan al-Saboun, although the choice is more limited than in Damascus.

**Antiques** – **Hajj Hashem Mshalah**, khan al-Wazir (B3). Rugs, Iranian vases, textiles, coins. A friendly welcome. Mr Mshalah organises the concerts at the bimaristan Arghoun.

**Abou Aaref** – **Orient House**, Al-Hatab Sq (B2). You can't miss the façade of this building, next to the restaurant Sissi. On the first floor is a bric-a-brac of objects of diverse origins, ranging from an untransportable Byzantine press to a thimble, not to mention cigar boxes and fake antiques.

**International bookshops** – In the bigger hotels. The shop in the Amir Palace (A3) has a fairly well-stocked section on Syria.

**Cassettes** – Cassettes of Arab music can be bought in the street.

**Shadows** (B1). Shop selling good-quality cassettes. A good choice of Eastern and Western music, with a helpful owner.

## DAY TRIPS AROUND ALEPPO

On the following pages you will find descriptions of several circuits around Aleppo. The practical details for these excursions follow.

### • North of Aleppo to St Simeon

**Taxi** – A half-day excursion (allow S£1 500 for St Simeon and Ain Dara) or a whole day (as above, but including Cyrrhus, allow S£3 000). Book through your hotel or through the tourist office.

**Bus** – Take a minibus from for Daret-Azze (1hr) from the Bab Antakia bus station (A3), then a taxi or minibus from Daret-Azze to St Simeon. Ain Dara and Cyrrhus are much more difficult to reach by public transport. Taxi is a better option.

### • To the west of Aleppo: Harim and Qalb Lozeh

**Taxi** – A whole-day excursion, together with a visit to St Simeon (around S£3 500). Book through your hotel or through the tourist office.

**Bus** – It's fairly easy to get to Harim by taking a minibus from the Bab Antakia bus station (A3). A taxi is best for visiting the Dead Cities.

### • Ebla and the southern Dead Cities

**Taxi** – Again, the simplest option is to do a day excursion by taxi. Book through your hotel or through the tourist office.

**Bus** – There are several buses a day to Harim, Maarrat and Idlib from the Bab Antakia bus station (A3). However, these are not the most interesting sites to be visited in the region and you will have to take a taxi to complete the circuit. For Ebla, you could ask the bus diver to drop you on the Homs motorway at the turning for Ebla, so you can complete the journey to the site on foot (3km). For the return, flag down a passing bus to continue your journey.

**Making the most of Aleppo**

Aleppo

# NORTH OF ALEPPO★
## VIA ST SIMEON'S MONASTERY
183km circuit from Aleppo – Allow a whole day
No places to stay overnight and few restaurants available
For transport, see p 233

### And remember...
St Simeon is one of many places of interest so it is well worth spending a whole day
exploring a number of sites and enjoying the magnificent scenery.
For a visit to St Simeon alone allocate 3hr (80km round trip).

This excursion, through a beautiful landscape of gently undulating limestone
hills and valleys north of Aleppo, takes in various Byzantine Dead Cities
– including the marvellous monastery-church of St Simeon Stylites, as well as
the neo-Hittite site of Ain Dara and the Roman ruins of Cyrrhus. Beyond this
region, which is populated by Kurds, lies Turkey.

*From the Archeological Museum in Aleppo, follow the extension to Al-Maari Street for
4km signposted for Damascus. At the roundabout with the fountain turn right. After 1km
turn right again, marked up for Qalaat Samaan ("Samaan Castle").*

The road picks its way through the outskirts of Aleppo bristling with modern
architect-designed ochre-coloured buildings, before cutting through a limestone
plain covered with intensely-cultivated market gardens on its way to the magnificent Jebel Shaikh Barakat, the highest peak of Jebel Samaan (870m).
Some 28km from Aleppo, the church of Mushabbak built on a hill on the left
marks the gateway to the "Dead Cities": the deserted remains of several hundred
Byzantine towns, villages and monastic complexes scattered between Aleppo and
ancient Antioch.

### ■ Basilica at Mushabbak★ – *Turn left along the dirt track up to the site. The
custodian's house sits on the left side of the car park, in front of the north façade. No
charge.*
The basilica, which is virtually intact save for the missing wooden rafters, is a well-
preserved example of late-5C Christian architecture. A door in the north side provides access to the nave and aisles separated by two rows of five columns with
**capitals★**: these are all different and com-
prise one of the rare decorative features.
The clerestory above has nine windows.
These, together with the proliferation of
windows in the main front, suggest a de-
liberate attempt to make the building
light and airy. The side apse flanked by
two lateral chapels, off the north side,
preserves its roof and two small windows.
Two doorways breach the south side.
The haphazard paving stones a few metres away conceal various water cisterns
and the hollow before the plain church
front was presumably where the stone
was quarried.

### The rise of St Simeon Stylite
St Simeon took up residence on the top
of the hill, on a rock that he surrounded
with a fence (mandra). A few years
later, he built a column about four cubits high (equivalent to 2m) and had a
platform placed on top of the shaft
("stylos" in Greek, hence his name).
After five or seven years – sources vary
– the saint moved to another pillar
30 cubits high, followed by one
40 cubits high. In all he spent 40 years
on the top of this hill, completely exposed to the elements, attracting increasingly large crowds of visitors.

*Return to the main road and head for the village of Daret-Azzeh (4km, bus for Aleppo) below Jebel Shaikh Barakat. On the far side of the village turn right and head for the beautifully fertile plain of Deir Samaan.*

*Sitting 4km beyond Daret-Azzeh, on the left, are the ruins of the Dead Cities of Qatura (rock-cut tombs), Sitt ar-Rum and Refada, set before the hill of Qalaat Samaan. To reach the monastery of St Simeon, head up the hill on the right (leaving the junction for the village of Deir Samaan on the left), and park near the entrance to the site (custodian).*

## St Simeon** (Qalaat Samaan)

### St Simeon the Elder, known as the Stylite

The history of the site is closely linked to the life of St Simeon, who was born in about 389 somewhere between Syria and Cilicia. He received divine grace at a young age, while listening to the Gospels, and from then on he dedicated his life to deprivation, choosing to live in various monasteries until 417, when he decided to take up residence on his pillar. He died on 24 July 459 and his remains were borne with great ceremony to Antioch for burial. The 5C martyrium was erected here by the Byzantine Emperor Zeno, a great admirer of the stylite Daniel. Within a few years, architects were drafted from as far as Constantinople and craftsmen came from all four corners of the empire to build this major centre of pilgrimage. Throughout the 6C the city flourished, then declined after the Arab conquest, and was later fortified after being recaptured by the Byzantines in the 10C.

### Monastic buildings

*Open daily, 9am-6pm in summer; 9am-4pm in winter. Entrance fee. Refreshments stall, bookshop and toilets inside the site. Allow 1hr. Avoid Fridays and public holidays as the site is popular among locals for picnics. A restaurant 300m below the monastery benefits from a shaded terrace with a marvellous view over Deir Samaan and the surrounding countryside. The menu includes meze and kebabs.*

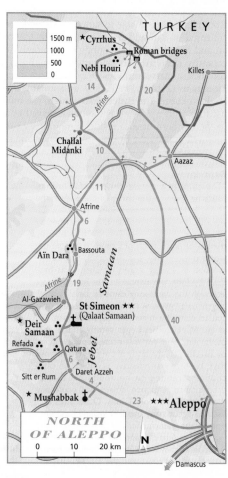

**St Simeon**

235

From the ticket office a steep shady path leads up to the terrace and the basilica complex (right) and baptistery (left). In the distant past pilgrims used to walk from the village of Telanissos (Deir Samaan) up the same hill path, through an arch that marked the beginning of the processional way to the baptistery.

The sumptuous **basilica\*\*\***, the greatest paleo-Christian monument in Northern Syria, was erected between 476 and 490 (see illustration p 24). In fact, it comprises four hall churches radiating the octagonal courtyard, with at its centre, the remains of St Simeon's famous pillar.

At first sight, the visitor will be struck by the elegance of the front elevation, articulated by three arches surmounted by a triangular pediment. Each pediment is supported by an upright element crowned with a Corinthian capital, harking back to Roman influences. The central axis runs from the main archway into the narthex, through the doors into the nave and out of the other end to the octagonal courtyard and the stump of the Saint's pillar. Little remains of this, because scores of pilgrims have removed small fragments as keepsakes through the ages. The octagonal courtyard was probably covered with a wooden roof, as the piers would have been unable to support a stone dome. Alternatively, this might have collapsed as a result of substantial earth tremors in the mid 6C. The arches around the central stump spring from superb Corinthian capitals crowning the columns clustered around heavy piers. From the westernmost part of the complex, a marvellous **view\*\*** extends on a clear day across to the Nur Daglari Mountains (2 200m) in Turkey, a mountainous barrier blocking the way to the Mediterranean. The eastern hall church, the only one with a domed apse, was used for worship, whereas the others served as assembly halls for the pilgrims. In the northern basilica resides a **monastery tomb**, set back against the enclosure wall built by the Byzantines. The crypt and sarcophagi cut from the bedrock were the preserve of monastery dignitaries.

Walk round the outside of the martyrium to look at the **chevet\*** of the main basilica lined with two tiers of small, slender columns, many lying on the ground waiting to be put back in place. This composite east end with radiating chapels was to serve as a prototype for endless Christian pilgrim churches over the ensuing centuries.

On your way back to the main entrance of the martyrium, take note of the two-storey front of a hostelry.

The **baptistery\*\*** stands at the southern end of the complex and comprises an octagon enclosed within a square building, like the martyrium. Note the remains in the eastern section, the water cistern and steps leading down into the immersion pool. The south-

## Baptism

"Therefore go and make disciples of all nations, baptising them in the name of the Father and of the Son and of the Holy Spirit" (Matthew Ch XXVIII, v19). The rite of baptism prescribed by Christ continues an ancient tradition echoing the act of purification practised by people the world over. Ideally, baptism involves total immersion in flowing water, as Christ was baptised by John the Baptist in the River Jordan, although the ceremony came to be simplified, largely as a result of running water being difficult to come by in remote desert regions.

In the 6C, churches began setting aside a self-contained room for this ritual, separate from, or attached to, the body of the church. In those days, baptism was a matter of choice, so catechumens tended to be adults capable of promising to renounce idolatry and professing their faith in the Holy Trinity. Other rites that used to accompany baptism included the unction of the catechumens with holy oil mixed with a balm (chrism) and the wearing of white. As soon as they had been baptised, the participants were administered the Holy Eucharist.

ernmost hall church next door, now in ruins, completed the baptistery complex. From the enclosure wall there is a lovely view over the village of Deir Samaan dotted with its many Byzantine buildings.

*Go back down to the bottom of the hill, turn right at the junction (towards Afrine) and continue 250m to the village of Deir Samaan. Park the car and walk into the town.*

■ **Deir Samaan**★ – A quick visit to the ancient village of Telanissos (on the road from Cyrrhus to Apamea) provides a rare insight into buildings with commercial uses. For many of the Dead Cities were simple farming villages with lively economies hinging solely on agriculture. The inhabitants of Deir Samaan, however, depended on the huge numbers of pilgrims visiting St Simeon from the late 5C onwards for their livelihoods. To cater for these visitors, a bazaar was built off the *via sacra*, as were a collection of hostelries; the remains of one may be seen standing along the right-hand side of the road to Afrine (just before the village), with its upright piers and monolithic lintels. The primitive retreat attended by St Simeon from 412 is in the actual village where various other monasteries sprang up in the 6C; one in the southwest of the old town preserves its small **church**★.

*The road to Ain Dara follows the western contours of the hill of St Simeon. After a short descent, keep right to avoid entering the village of Al-Gazawieh.*

The majority of people living in this region are Kurds, and so it is not unusual to see peasant women dressed in traditional attire working in the cotton fields, laid out on either side of the road. The road climbs steadily upwards to provide a good view of the Afrine River below.

*After 16km (3km before Ain Dara), you come to the large village of Bassuta, bisected by a cool stream that somehow imparts a refreshing breeze to the pretty open-air restaurant nearby.*

*Continue to Ain Dara and from the far side of the village take a rough track left downhill to the ancient tell; at the junction, stands a pleasant little restaurant on the edge of a pool.*

■ **Neo-Hittite site of Ain Dara** – *Park the car in the shade in front of the mission house used by the archeological team. Entrance fee.*

The ancient tell has been somewhat marred by the construction of a modern domed covering. However, it is still worth climbing the tell in order to see the scarce remains of the neo-Hittite city within and enjoy the view from the top of the town of Afrine and the river below. The history of the site spans a particularly long period, from the beginning of the 1st millennium BC to the medieval Islamic era.

A path leads left up the side of the tell to the excavations, round the top, once crowned by an acropolis, to the statue of a crouching **lion**★. This basalt sculpture is not unlike its contemporaries discovered at Tell Halaf, and now displayed at the entrance of the archeological Museum in Aleppo. Several concrete posts (intended as supports for a temporary roof) a short way further on mark the scant vestiges of a **temple**★ dating from the 10C BC. Its walls were decorated with a row of panels depicting lions facing sphinxes, surmounted by a series of huge lions of which only the claws remain.

The entrance to the temple (facing southeast towards the mission house) is framed by winged sphinxes. Note the stones paving the area in front of the cella, bearing a giant footprint. A similar imprint (the right foot in this instance) is repeated at the entrance to the vestibule. These must have had some ritual significance or symbolic meaning alluding to a divine presence, although

**Ain Dara**

archeologists are reluctant to commit themselves to a definitive interpretation. The temple was probably dedicated to Ishtar, the Semitic goddess of Fertility, who was often represented by a lion.

When walking back downhill, look out for the pool set aside for ablutions.

*From Ain Dara, continue onwards towards and beyond Afrine (leaving it behind you on the right bank of the river).*

Beyond Afrine, the Kurdish "capital" of the Aleppo region, the road to Cyrrhus threads its way up near to the Turkish border, through the attractive scenery, climbing up to an undulating range of hills covered with olive groves.

■ **Midanki Falls** (Challal Midanki) – In winter and spring, after the winter thaw, the beautiful waterfalls are full of water and provide Syrians with a popular place for an outing and a meal in the country (cafés and restaurants). Photographs of these falls are often found pinned up in public places all round Syria.

*Continue 19km north to the remarkable tomb of Nebi Houri, a few kilometres from the Turkish border. Park nearby. The sanctuary is usually open.*

■ **Tomb of Nebi Houri** – The former Roman or Byzantine tomb was transformed in the 14C into a hexagonal mausoleum for the relics of a Muslim Saint (Nebi Houri) and converted into a mosque. The host of little votive ribbons attached to the shrine grills (and nearby bushes) attest to the high devotion offered up to this revered saint. A few rickety steps lead up to the platform bearing the hexagonal sepulchre.

*To continue to Cyrrhus, fork left beyond the tomb and follow it to the site entrance.*

■ **Roman site of Cyrrhus**★ – *(Unguarded site)* Cyrrhus was founded by Seleucus I Nicator in the early 3C BC. Its vocation as a garrison town was reaffirmed after the surrounding region was annexed by the Roman Empire in 64 AD and during the Armenian assaults mounted in the 2C. In Byzantine times, Cyrrhus was renamed Hagiopolis (City of Saints) and provided with a shrine to St Cosmas and St Damian. In the 5C, the bishopric was governed by Theodoret (one of the Fathers of the Church). During the Persian invasions Justinian reinforced the fortifications. In 637 it fell into Arab hands. After being later taken by the Crusaders, it was seized back by Nureddin and finally abandoned.

Ruins – The Antique city of Cyrrhus sits in a magnificent setting at the foot of the Turkish mountains, sprawled below a somewhat isolated citadel that safeguarded its defences. Today it is a peaceful place, populated occasionally by Bedouins who graze their sheep and goats there when the grass is plentiful. At one time, the city was encircled with fortifications, which, on the east side, rose tall above a ravine containing the Sabun Suyu river; the scant remains of which may be seen on the west side of town.

The main entrance into the city is through the South Gate, from which a faint path extends along the approximate line of the ancient **cardo maximus** to the 2C **theatre**★★, one of the few monuments on site to have been excavated. Only the first 14 rows of seating built into the hill are still visible but they still give a good idea of the imposing proportions of the building. With a diameter of 115m, it outranks Bosra in the scale of Syrian theatres. Sadly, the proscenium wall is in ruins and the orchestra is now hard to differentiate from the underparts of the stage. The panoramic **view**★★ from the top of the amphitheatre pans across the olive groves that stretch away for miles.

Countryside near Cyrrhus

Follow the *cardo maximus* for a further 400m to the ruins of a **basilica** *(on the right)* before arriving at the North Gate.

Proceed along the road to Aazaz *(20km)* over two fine **Roman humpback bridges** without parapets, dating from the 2C: one with six arches, the other – less restored but taller than the first – with three.

*Take the left fork in the road 10km after the second Roman bridge. Drive through Aazaz and, after crossing the railway (the line to Istanbul), turn left onto the main road that heads south to Aleppo (40km).*

# WEST OF ALEPPO
## VIA HARIM AND QALB LOZEH
170km circuit from Aleppo - Allow half a day
No accommodation available; simple restaurant facilities at Harim
For transport, see p 233

**Not to be missed**
The exceptional Byzantine church at Qalb Lozeh.

**And remember...**
to take a picnic lunch.

This excursion into the limestone massif west of Aleppo touches upon the rich agricultural, religious and military heritage of the region that is intertwined with the history of Antioch (at one time the third city of the Roman Empire) now in Turkey. After a walk along a stretch of Roman road, this itinerary takes you on to Baqira and Dar Qita, two of the more important Dead Cities, to visit the Arab castle at Harim that towers over the green plain of Amouq and, finally, to the Byzantine church of Qalb Lozeh.

*Head out of Aleppo along the Damascus road. 7km from the town centre deviate off the main road, following signs to Bab al-Hawa (to the Turkish border) and continue through the hilly countryside, covered with fields of cereals. After 40km, where the road bends round on its approach to Tell al-Karaneh, it crosses over a well-preserved length of Roman road.*

■ **A stretch of Roman road** – *(Unguarded site. Park by the side of the road)*
This exposed fragment of Roman road, extending for more than a kilometre, survives remarkably intact, with large blocks of quarried limestone paving a 5m-wide roadway. It is thought to date from the 2C and bears witness to the enormous effort invested by the Romans in building roads and monuments in the eastern provinces of the Empire, in this case providing Antioch with a link to Aleppo and Qinnesrin (Chalcis).

*After 42km, ignoring the road to Daret-Azzeh and St-Simeon on the right, the road crosses the great fertile Dana plain. 46km from Aleppo (major crossroads) leave the road leading to the Turkish border (signed for Bab al-Hawa in the direction of Antioch) and turn left towards Harim.*

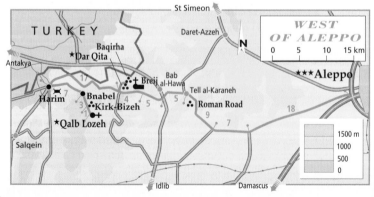

51km further on, at the foot of a hill on the right, stands the **Monastery of Breij** (*accessible on foot across the fields*) dedicated to St Daniel – follower of St Simeon and a stylite. As the road gains height, a fine view opens out over the surrounding **scenery\***. Continue for 55km and branch right towards two more Dead Cities: Baqhira and Dar Qita.

■ **Dead Cities of Baqhira and Dar Qita** – These two settlements nestle against the flanks of Jebel Barisha, which dominates a vast plain alongside the Turkish border. The ruins of a small **pagan temple\*** dedicated to Zeus (161 AD) appear on the right-hand side of the road (*1km*), keeping guard, almost, over the last vestiges - the façade and narthex - of the **west church** (546).

The road eventually descends gently towards the plain (*1km*), where an important group of ruins overgrown with vegetation may be seen on the left: this is **Dar Qita\***. This Dead City prospered during the 5C and 6C, as the three churches might testify. The ones in the east and west parts of town (*by the side of the road*) were dedicated to the Holy Trinity and St Sergius, whereas the Church of St Paul and Moses in the north (*set back 200m from the road, access on foot*) has a square baptistery in its south courtyard.

*Go back to the main road and turn right towards Harim.*

Over some 10km, the road to Harim provides a good view of the well-irrigated Amouq Plain in Turkish territory - a region once administered by Alexandretta, ceded by France to Turkey in 1939. In the distance rise the Amanus Mountains, blocking the view to the Mediterranean coast, which lies less than 50km further west as the crow flies. From here, the road heads downhill, round a few bends and arrives at the large village of Harim.

■ **Harim Castle** – *Drive through the village to the castle and park below the glacis. Ignore the road on the left running alongside the enormous ditch dug from the bedrock and walk around the castle to the right and up the steep path to the castle entrance.*

The first fort was built here in Byzantine times when Nicephorus Phocas was endeavouring to retake Northern Syria. This was then successively occupied by the Seljuks and, before the fall of Antioch (1097), by the Crusaders. In 1164 it was seized by Nureddin and rebuilt by the governor of Aleppo in 1199. The interior, for so long in a parlous state, is presently undergoing restoration, although the renovation work on the interesting **hammam** and somewhat sombre vaulted entrance passageway has been completed. From the top there is a fine **view\*** over Harim and its pretty blue houses tucked into the hillside, rather like those at Maalula.

A pleasant little restaurant by the river, down by the car park, sells cold drinks and kebabs.

*A good road passes below the castle before heading out of Harim, bound for Salqein (attractive Mediterranean scenery) and south to Idlib 54km away (see p 000). However, we recommend going back to the roundabout at the beginning of the village and taking the road on the right signposted for Qalb Lozeh.*

This more minor road climbs rapidly up and into the heart of the Jebel al-Ala. The village of **Bnabel**, after 7km, has numerous buildings erected reusing old stone and masonry. 3km further on, the road passes the village of **Kirk-Bizeh** (three ruined churches, presses, villas from the 3C-5C) on the left, perched up above the Self Plain, not far (1km) from Qalb Lozeh.

■ **Church of Qalb Lozeh★** – The church stands in the centre of the village, inhabited predominantly by Druze, so do not be surprised if your arrival solicits a greeting party of blond-haired children. The custodian will then appear as if from nowhere and open the gate of the north door *(it is customary to leave a tip)*. The Church of Qalb Lozeh (late 5C) is regarded as one of the most important in Syria, as a result of the architectural features innovated here and their excellent state of preservation. Only the north wall of the hall church and the enclosure wall have been removed. Unlike its predecessors, the nave of this church is separated from the aisles by three broad arches that spring from solid square piers, rather than columns, as would be expected. Although the nave would have had a wooden roof, the south aisle preserves its covering of thick, interlocking limestone slabs. The paved floor, meanwhile, still shows signs of the horse-shoe-shaped *bema* where the priest stood to read the Gospels. The back wall, leading into in a domed apse, is treated to look like an elegant triumphal arch, thereby continuing the rhythm set by the arches of the nave. On the outside, the east end apse is articulated with a series of engaged columns interrupted by window openings. The south flank is pierced by three richly ornamented doorways and at the west end, the door into the nave is framed by two three-storey towers.

*Return to Aleppo by the same route.*

The church at Qalb Lozeh

Y Traynard

# SOUTH OF ALEPPO★
## EBLA AND THE DEAD CITIES
213km circuit – Allow a whole (and very full) day
For transport, see p 233

**Not to be missed**
Ebla: because of its historical importance.
The Dead Cities of Sergilla and Al-Bara.
**And remember...**
It is possible to visit Al-Bara and Sergilla from Latakia or Hama.

*If coming from Aleppo, head south along the motorway towards Damascus for 51km, passing through the suburbs of Aleppo and past the turning for Latakia. Follow signs for Ebla (on the right), but take care crossing the motorway. The site of Ebla is 3km from the junction, on the far side of the village of Tell Mardikh.*

## ■ Ebla★ (Tell Mardikh)
*Allow 1hr.*

Ebla lies in the middle of the countryside, wrapped by an impressive circular wall. The remains of this city, which dates from the 3rd-2nd millennia BC, are far from representative of its historical importance, for most of the finest artefacts, recovered from the trenches seen here, are now conserved in the museums of Aleppo, Idlib and Damascus.

### Solution to an enigma

For years, scholars argued about the whereabouts of Ebla, a city repeatedly cited on numerous tablets. Then, in 1968, an Akkadian inscription on a statue dedicated to the goddess Ishtar provided the missing link and Tell Mardikh was identified as being synonymous with the Ebla of Antiquity. From then on, Paolo Matthiae's team of archeologists from an Italian university decided to investigate the site they had been working on for the past five years with even greater thoroughness. In 1974 the discovery of a large library from the 3rd millennium BC shed new light on a region and period that hitherto had been somewhat underestimated.

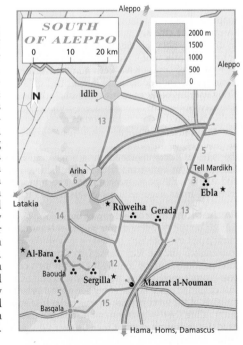

*South of Aleppo* map — Scale: 0 10 20 km. Elevation legend: 2000 m, 1500, 1000, 500, 0. Locations shown: Aleppo, Idlib, Ariha, Latakia, Tell Mardikh, Ebla★, Ruweiha, Gerada, Al-Bara★, Baouda, Sergilla★, Maarrat al-Nouman, Basqala, Hama, Homs, Damascus.

**South of Aleppo**

243

For here, it became apparent, a highly original culture had developed independently from the distant sites in Southern Mesopotamia, considered then to be the primordial cradle of civilisation. Henceforth, Ebla became one of Syria's most prestigious sites, ranking on a par with Mari.

## Two periods of intensive development

Ebla was founded sometime during the 3rd millennium BC shortly after people began to live sedentary lives in urban communities in Southern Mesopotamia. The site itself was particularly well chosen as it had ready access to good pasture (to the east), fertile land suited to cultivation (to the west), and a plentiful supply of water for irrigation and domestic use from the River Quweiq (which flows here from Aleppo). In the 24C BC, Ebla ruled over a vast territory that stretched from the foothills of the Taurus Mountains to Homs, from the Euphrates to Jebel Ansariyeh.

Where possible, peace and stability across this vast area were ensured by marriages arranged between the ruling dynasties – as at Mari and Nagar (Tell Brak). The mace bearing the emblem of Pepi I (found interred in a tomb) is the most ancient synchronic statement of the economic and political relations between Ebla and Egypt under the pharaohs found to date in the Ancient East. Much of the city's wealth was derived from its control over the supply and demand for highly prized commodities like precious stones, metals and more notably wood, which was rare in Mesopotamia, exotic unguents and perfumes from Egypt and lapis lazuli from Afghanistan.

In 2300 BC Ebla was sacked and obliterated by Sargon, the king of Sumer and Akkad who founded the Akkadian dynasty, for undermining the success of his own kingdom, even though the prosperous city lay more than 1 000km away. For ages Ebla remained abandoned; in the 20C BC it began to flourish once more. Subjugated first to the Akkad Dynasty and then to the Yamkhads (Aleppo), the city was rebuilt on a grand scale and the acropolis was fortified. In 1600 BC, Ebla was destroyed again ("shattered like a vase" in the words of a chronicler of the time), probably by the Hittite sovereign Mursilis I. But the ruins that were left must have been impressive, because 150 years later Pharaoh Tutmosis III had the name Ebla inscribed on a pillar at the Temple of Karnak, along with his other conquests. Although the site was successively occupied (by Aramaeans, Persians, Romans and Byzantines) at various intervals, the city never really recovered its former importance.

The **Ebla Museum** (*Open daily, 9am-4pm. Entrance fee includes access to the site. Park in front of the museum entrance*), situated a few hundred metres from the site, is accommodated in a small red-brick building modelled on a Mesopotamian construction. Although it does not rival the museums of Idlib and Aleppo, the photographs, plans and minor artefacts (tablets, vases) document the main stages in the excavation of Ebla.

**Archeological site –** *To reach the site, drive up past the museum and through the markers around the tell to the car park area below the acropolis. Then walk up the path running past the custodian's hut and on towards the acropolis.*

Immediately on the left, marked by three rows of lovely stones, once stood a monumental complex comprising a 15m high **ceremonial platform** destined to bear Ishtar's sacred lions, backed by a second temple, dedicated to the goddess, that extended northwards, alongside a great palace. *Walk back to the footpath.* Little remains of the **west palace**, in which the heir apparent lived, apart from for an outbuilding (*on the right*) with a fine collection of eight extant basalt **millstones**★ used for grinding corn. *Climb another 20m, veering slightly right.* The most important ruins scattered across the west flank of the acropolis include those of the **royal palace**★ dating from the pre-Sargon period. To protect the fragile mud-brick structures from the elements, a protective coating is applied after the spring rains; unfortunately, this makes the walls look as though they have been moulded out of putty. The **central stairway** (22m long) used to link the palace administrative quarters with the residential area. The broad **courtyard**★ at the bottom, surrounded by a portico supported on wooden posts (note the five post-holes in the ground), was used for audiences and to receive dignitaries. The royal podium was positioned in the centre of the left gallery. To get there, the sovereign would use the royal staircase in the corner tower leading down from his apartments, through a door and into the courtyard. The administrative area to the right of the stairway consisted largely of warehouses, a small courtyard and a throne room that was probably used in winter. The **library**★ and its fa-mous state archive, comprising many thousands of cuneiform tablets, also opened onto the courtyard. Although desolately empty now, its walls still bear the imprint of shelving.

### The Royal Archives

Long the subject of speculation, the 17 000 cuneiform tablets from Ebla are a particularly rich source of information on the ancient Near East during the half-century preceding the city's first deci-mation. Although the majority of the texts relate to administrative matters (legal and commercial issues), certain letters, literary and religious documents provide an insight into the economy and daily life of Ebla. Lists of words in two languages have also shed light on the lo-cal language ("Eblaite"), an archaic Semitic language. The museums at Idlib and Aleppo have numerous tablets from the royal archives of Ebla on display.

The buildings south of the palace pre-sumably accommodated officials and administrative staff. Several princely sepulchres uncovered beneath them have divulged some sumptuous jew-ellery (finely crafted gold necklaces and bracelets), as well as a rich collection of grave goods (vases and objects of Egyp-tian origin).

*The main stairway is closed to the public, so walk around the administrative block to the acropolis.*

The **great temple of Ishtar**★ overlook-ing the administrative buildings is the largest temple at Ebla. It contained three rooms, two of which can be made out by looking at the marks in the ground: namely a vestibule with a small ante-cella attached. Beyond stood the cella. The niche in the north wall would have contained a votive statue.

Excavation of the huge **royal palace** continues northeast of the acropolis, where a number of rooms have been identified arranged around a courtyard, but whose use remains unsure.

From the top of the acropolis there is a good view of the town's oval outer walls, interrupted by four gates, that echo the distinctive layout of the tell of Ebla.

*Come down off the acropolis and follow the path running past the custodian's hut towards the southwest gate.*

This area between the acropolis and the city walls comprises the lower town. The residential area on the left is made up of private dwellings with rooms dis-posed around a courtyard. This layout is also typical of the cities in Southern Mesopotamia. The **southwest gate**★, the largest and most imposing of the city, has been cleared to reveal its bastions dressed with basalt and limestone. This dates from the beginning of the 20C BC.

*Having completed your tour of the site, go back through the village of Tell Mardikh which still preserves a few of its ancient bee-hive houses, and then turn left to rejoin the motorway.*

**Ebla**

If you are visiting Maarat on your way to Damascus and are pressed for time, you could omit the Dead Cities Al-Bara and Sergilla and visit Ruweiha instead (detour of 22km).

*If proceeding to Ruweiha: come off the main road 13km south of Ebla and turn right following directions for Babila and Gerada. Continue through the first village and on towards the hill.* After 3km you will come to the village of **Gerada**, built up against the flank of the hill, standing among the ruins of the Dead City that include two rather remarkable square towers. The road then continues for a further 2km to arrive at a stolid-looking tomb before the entrance to the Dead City of Ruweiha.

■ **Ruweiha★** – This Dead City is somewhat overlooked, despite it having several buildings that continue to be inhabited. For a quick tour of the village *(30min)*, follow the path on the right for some 100m to the first **church**, built in the 5C on a basilica plan. To the right of the apse stands an aedicule known as **Qasr al-Benat** with eight columns that probably constituted part of a tower in which an ascetic lived.

The path heading north towards the imposing front of a church passes alongside the remains of a small country **agora** (divided up into shops by the pillars). The **Church of Bissos★**, set back 500m from the road, is impressive on account of its sheer size: certainly ranking among the largest in northern Syria. Despite their condition, the huge arches articulating the nave and aisles are magnificent. The nave itself, however, is inaccessible. If you walk left round the church to the apse, you will pass **two tombs★**; one with an astonishing distyle Greek temple front; the other with the dome contains the mortal remains of Bissos, the founder of the church.

*From here, the drive to Maarat is west across country. 4km beyond Ruweiha turn left.*

The landscape in these parts is arid and punctuated with barren hills dotted with blocks of limestone. At last the road arrives before the small citadel of Maarat, which stands at the entrance to the town (on the right).

### Abu al-Ala al-Maari, the blind poet

Abu al-Ala al-Maari was born in Maarat in 979 and became blind at an early age. To overcome this impediment, he developed a prodigious memory and set about devoting his life to study, only leaving his home town for a brief stay in Baghdad. An ascetic and a vegetarian, he came to devise an independent philosophy, in part as a result of fasting well beyond the demands of the Koran; this made certain Muslims regard him as an outspoken free-thinker. However, many of the misanthrope's ideas and sayings ("Away from other men, I can cure myself of their evils; near them, reason and religion suffer") survive largely because they encapsulated much of the scepticism and pessimism of the period resulting from the political in-fighting and backbiting prevalent at that time. For the same reasons, the Crusades were managing to secure so much territory. The man who wrote "If you meet a blind man, pity him, in the certainty that you also are blind, even if you can see," died at the age of 80. His tomb is in the main street of Maarat.

■ **Maarat al-Nouman** – From the outside, there is nothing to redeem Maarat: the Aleppo-Damascus road now runs only a few hundred metres from the town and trailer-parks have proliferated along town's periphery, stripping it of its former charms (and all the hotels have closed down). However, the Antique columns built into the local mosque hint at the importance of the city in Roman and Byzantine times. In the 10C, Abu al-Ala al-Maari, the great Arab poet and thinker, was born here. But the place is perhaps better known for a more sinister reason, relating to an episode from the First Crusade. The

Franks were besieging the town when a particularly rigorous winter set in (1098); there was no food to be found anywhere, so eventually the people, racked by starvation, were driven to eating dead bodies: an act that horrified the Muslim world only months before the fall of Jerusalem.

The **citadel** is a fine – if miniature – example of military architecture that has been colonised by domestic dwellings. It only merits a quick visit.

*At the roundabout on the left, 600m from the citadel, turn down the main street into Maarat.* If you arrive during the morning "rush hour", you will have to contend with the stream of merchants driving their carts laden with fresh fruit and vegetables the 500m to the austere walls of a caravanserai. *Park in the square.*

The **Maarat an-Numan Museum** (*Open 9am-6pm in summer; 9am-4pm in winter; closed Tuesdays and occasionally over lunch between 12noon-2pm. Entrance fee*), which boasts a collection of splendid mosaics, is housed in the superb Mourad Pasha caravanserai (1563): the largest surviving khan in Syria. A vaulted gateway leads into a large courtyard with a mosque in the centre. Unlike the caravanserais built in towns, the buildings of this one – like those at Apamea – are all one-storey. Turn right after the ticket office towards an assortment of Roman and Byzantine **basalt doors** that once graced various private dwellings. The glass cases surrounding the model of the caravanserai display a variety of objects dating to the 4th millennium BC including two superb **model wagons**⋆ and 100 or so Roman oil lamps. Much of the wall and floor-space, meanwhile, is given over to **mosaics** depicting animal subjects, in the main, like the she-wolf suckling Romulus and Remus (511 AD). The second room is devoted to Islamic things (pottery, large jars, wheel-turned and moulded receptacles) and a large mosaic with animals (lion, peacock). On the right before the exit, behind a pair of sarcophagi, the curators have reconstructed an **underground tomb** with a heavy basalt door. The finest mosaics, however, are exhibited in the last room on the right before the exit: among the assorted works (figurative and geometric) sits the outstanding 3C AD **mosaic of Hercules**⋆⋆ found at Homs and modelled with particular delicacy. On the far side of the square, opposite the museum, stands another caravanserai (*no access*). To reach the souk, head down the second street on the right and make your way towards the square minaret of the mosque (300m).

The huge courtyard of the **Great Mosque of Maarat an-Numan** is ornamented with a **bayt al-mal**, a small aedicule with columns resembling the one at the mosque in Damascus, a covered **area for ablutions** and a well. All three structures incorporate ancient columns and capitals. On Fridays, prayer mats are unrolled in the courtyard to supplement the two **prayer-halls** with huge piers situated on either side of the courtyard. The elegant **minaret**⋆, in the same style as the one at Aleppo (12C), rises through five decorative tiers. Note the window in the highest register sealed with a stone bearing a Greek cross.

When walking back to the khan, take a look up at the elegant houses fronting the main street: many of the windows are ornamented with motifs derived and blended from Classical and Islamic sources.

*Follow the high street out of Maarat to the junction (500m beyond the khan) and instead of proceeding towards the citadel, turn left.*

*Continue for 3km through the village of Kafer Rouma, then through Kafer Nabil, where you turn right at the main roundabout and right again in front of a green-domed mosque on the edge of the village.*

If you gaze over the undulating scenery stretched before you, you may make out the occasional fragment of a wall denoting the ruins of one of the Dead Cities. 19km beyond Maarat, and 1km before turning right towards Sergilla, nestles one set of ruins long since overgrown by a series of fig trees. The narrow road crosses a desolate plateau, passing the Dead City of Baouda on the right, before reaching Sergilla.

■ **Sergilla★** – The ruins of Sergilla, the most evocative and atmospheric of all the Dead Cities, stand at the end of the road, lost, it would seem, in the middle of nowhere. Life here seems caught in a time warp; a few shepherds continue to haunt the rubble that appears to have been suddenly deserted.

The path leading down towards the main buildings is lined with sarcophagi from a substantial necropolis. On the way it passes a **bath complex★★** dated 473 with a cistern before it covered by flagstones; the main hall measures some 120sqm. The small apses projecting from the central space betray signs of their intended purpose *(calidarium, frigidarium)*. The area surrounded by a double portico on the right is the **andron★★** (where men could meet and relax). Both buildings, providing facilities that were extremely rare in these parts, suggest the community was hugely prosperous. 50m east of the andron, stands a ruined church tucked into the side of the small valley. In its crypt there are three sarcophagi. The fronts of several ancient houses remain largely intact. The foundations of one, situated south of the church, have recently been excavated, revealing presses and pits dug from the bedrock.

*Head back to the main road below Al-Bara (4km), turn right and continue 300m to the village of Al-Bara. The ancient town sits opposite the modern village, on the other side of the wadi. Take a little street on the left just inside the village and follow it down and over the wadi.*

■ **Al-Bara★** – In the absence of any historical documentation, the origins of this Dead City – like so many others – remain shrouded in mystery. The exceptional length of Al-Bara (some 2km) together with its five churches and monastery seem to indicate it was more of a small town than a village. Furthermore, life continued to throng its streets long after many other Dead Cities, for Al-Bara was still the seat of a bishop when the Count of Toulouse, Raymond de Saint-Gilles, took possession of the town in 1098.

The Dead City of Sergilla

In view of the number of its walls (albeit low) and olive groves, Al-Bara is more physically demanding than Sergilla. Those defeated by such a prospect may be content to restrict themselves to the ruins along the side of the road crossing the site on a south-north axis.

First point of call: **Deir Sobat**\* (*100m left of the main road, crouched on the side of the hill*). Here there is a perfectly preserved 6C monastery and, 200m to its right, an enormous **pyramid tomb**\* decorated with Corinthian pilasters at the corners and a frieze of acanthus leaves ornamenting the lintel and base, containing five sarcophagi. Scattered all around are various villas, and 200m to the east sit the ruins of a church, the oldest of the group. The road picks its way around a second pyramid tomb, passing the Church of Al-Hosn on the left, before reaching the northern entrance of the modern town. The site also boasts a number of large farm holdings dating back to Byzantine times.

*Head north out of Al-Bara to join the main Latakia-Aleppo highway (14km). Turn right following signs for Ariha, then left on reaching it to continue to Idlib (13km away). To get to Aleppo (1hr), keep to the highway.*

■ **Idlib** – In an attempt to contain the power and influence of Aleppo's flourishing local economy, the Syrian State Department upgraded the status of Idlib to that of mouhafazat capital. Since when, the city has not ceased to expand: the present population stands at 90 000 and the white stone suburbs have encroached upon the surrounding hills.

But the place has little appeal for visitors as the old town has completely disappeared and there is no decent hotel accommodation to speak of. The only redeeming feature is the local museum housing a small collection of treasures from Ebla that appeals to few but the most ardent enthusiasts.

*The museum is located on Al-Thawra Square, on the eastern section of the main boulevard, near the town centre).*

**Idlib Museum** (*Open 9am-6pm in summer; 9am-4pm in winter; closed Tuesdays. Entrance fee*), together with its larger sister-museums at Suweida and Deir ez-Zor, is charged with presenting and promoting the region's heritage. The modern premises, surrounded by a small garden (mosaics, capitals), display an assortment of objects; antiquities of Classical, Islamic and ethnological derivation are presented on the ground floor, with, to one side, a small section devoted to ornithology. On the first floor, to the right of the stairs, is arranged a selection of artefacts dating from prehistory to the dawn of Islam, recovered during the excavations of the 190 tells or more in the Mouhafazat (Dahis, Tell Afis, Khan Sheikoun Saraqeb). The galleries to the left of the stairs are devoted to the most famous of all the tells in the region: Ebla. Among the exhibits of particular interest look out for the **frieze** depicting soldiers celebrating a triumph (18C BC) and a **talisman** decorated with a funerary banqueting scene. A **reconstruction of the library** helps to recreate a picture of the famous State archives with its shelves of carefully arranged tablets, including a number of the actual original ones found there.

Those who enjoy sampling local delicacies might like to visit the cake-shop across the road from the museum, on the far side of the roundabout.

*From Idlib, you can return to Aleppo (60km) via the back roads through the fertile countryside. Near a leisure park, 7km before Aleppo, the Idlib road links up with the motorway to Damascus. Once on the motorway, switch to the left-hand lane almost immediately (after about 200m).*

**Idlib**

The citadel, Qalaat Jaabar

R. Tixador/TOP

# THE EUPHRATES

The Euphrates, a long and tranquil river, has sometimes been compared to the Nile. Like its Egyptian counterpart, man has managed to transform the arid land along its banks into fruitful gardens by drawing on its precious water. Like the Nile, the Euphrates has been dammed to provide a large reservoir – Lake al-Assad. But there are no feluccas cruising its length, as in Egypt, and little or no commercial traffic to ruffle its surface. Furthermore, the historical sites – precious though they are in archeological terms - lack the monumental grandeur of those instigated by the pharaohs. The Euphrates, which has its source in Turkey, enters Syria at Jarablos, a few kilometres from ancient Carchemish (now part of Turkey) where TE Lawrence first became smitten by archeology and Arabia. The red bricks of the fortress of Qalaat Jaabar reflected in Lake al-Assad evoke comparison with the huge walls of the ancient Abbasid city of Raqqa, downstream from the dam. On the edge of the cultivated land on the other side of the river, sits the Byzantine city of Rassafa with its three churches shielded by high walls. At Raqqa, the river slows its progress to Deir ez-Zor, the capital of the Syrian Euphrates and home to a colourful Bedouin market. Further south lie the prestigious sites of Doura Europos and Mari, a few kilometres from Albukamal. On the other side of the frontier post, the river flows through Iraq, merges with the Tigris – its Mesopotamian twin – and concludes its 2 700km journey at the Persian Gulf.

# ALEPPO TO DEIR EZ-ZOR
## VIA RAQQA
466km circuit on good roads – Allow a whole (very full) day

**Not to be missed**
The Romantic ruins of Rassafa.
The fortress of Qalaat Jaabar.
The souk at Deir ez-Zor.

**And remember...**
Be sure to make an early start from Aleppo in order to complete the whole tour.
Stop for lunch by the lake (the fish is quite delicious!)
looking out over the reflection of the castle at Qalaat Jaabar.

This excursion from Aleppo joins up with the Euphrates near Lake al-Assad, before heading on to the isolated ruins of the Byzantine city at Rassafa, across the al-Thawra Dam to Qalaat Jaabar overlooking the lake (opportunity for a delicious fish lunch). In the afternoon, it provides the opportunity of diverting to Raqqa for a quick visit of the museum and walls before continuing down the Euphrates to Halabiyeh and Deir ez-Zor as evening approaches.

*If you are relying on public transport, make your way to Raqqa and share a collective taxi for a visit to Rassafa and Qalaat Jaabar.*
*From Aleppo, take the airport road east and continue towards Raqqa.*

A good highway runs out towards the airport (9km) and on through the vast and unremittingly monotonous Jabul flatlands transformed into green fields of cereals by networks of small concrete irrigation channels. In autumn and winter the bleak fields of stubble are stalked by sheep and their solitary shepherds muffled in thick wool-lined cloaks.

*149km after leaving Aleppo, a road forks left to Al-Thawra (try to make it in time for lunch). 20km further on, turn right in the village of Almansura and continue to Rassafa (25km) across an increasingly arid and empty desert landscape. At last the walls of Rassafa appear in the distance.*

## ■ Rassafa★ (Arrasafeh)
*Entrance fee. Allow 45min.*

Rassafa is a bewitching place: its remoteness in a deserted land, its dilapidated ruins surrounded by imposing walls haunted by memories of the martyr St Sergius, to whom its beautiful basilica is consecrated, all combine to lend Rassafa a melancholic air. And then, as if by magic, children will suddenly appear from nowhere selling "ancient" coins (swearing that they were found on the site!) and encouraging visitors to go and look at the site.

### St Sergius's town
This frontier post of the Roman Empire built in the 1C AD underwent rapid expansion during the Byzantine period (particularly in the 6C), sparked off by popularity for the cult of St Sergius. The saint's burial place was quick to draw large bands of pilgrims. During the first half of the 8C the Umayyad Caliph Hisham established his official residence there. For years, the city continued to be a transit post for caravans and a place of pilgrimage until the first Mongols invaded the region in the 13C, which in turn provoked its final ruin.

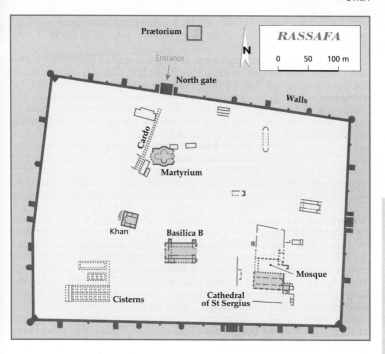

## Tour

The site is entered through the **north gate\*\*\*** framed by two bastions. The three-bay gateway modelled on a type normally found abutting a Christian basilica does much to reinforce the city's religious importance. Each opening is set into a graceful arch decorated with vine tendrils, supported by six columns with Corinthian capitals to produce one of the most harmonious and sumptuous Byzantine city gates in Syria. The standing ruins scattered over the rectangular site, approximately 550m by 400m, and enclosed by the remarkable **city walls\*\*** are surprisingly extensive. The walls are built with large blocks of gypsum brought from a quarry about 10km from Rassafa, and fortified by rectangular towers with rounded corners. Defences

### St Sergius and St Bacchus

Sergius and Bacchus were Roman officers billeted with the army on the frontiers of the Eastern limes of the Roman Empire. Both Christians came to be victimised for refusing to make sacrifices to the pagan god Jupiter; Maximian even made them walk through the streets dressed as women. They were transferred to Rassafa, and yet more punishment and torture ensued. Eventually Bacchus died from his wounds and Sergius was put to death by decapitation (303). Before long the martyrs came to be venerated by the Early Christian Church. In 431, the church built over Sergius's tomb was restored by Alexander, Archbishop of Hierapolis (present-day Membij). A century later, Justinian renamed Rassafa Sergiopolis, an act that did much to revive the cult of St Sergius in the Eastern Empire and encourage pilgrims to flock there. For his part, Bacchus was made the patron saint of the Byzantine armies.

were further reinforced in 400 AD by a continuous moat (now in-filled) which ran along the outside of the walls; this was restored in the 6C by the Emperor Justinian.

From the north gate extends the **cardo**, now marked out by a few column shafts. 100m further from the gate on the left stands the first of Rassafa's five churches. The pink stone paved floor of this building – which once incorporated the **martyrium** of St Sergius – is now littered with column shafts and capitals. The domed apse at the east end, pierced with three window openings, is flanked by two sacristies. Continue 100m along the *cardo*: on the right by the wall, nestle an intriguing group of **cisterns\*\*** – approach the edge with care – built of stone and lined with brick. The largest measures some 57m long, 21m wide and 15m deep. When full of collected rainwater, this complex of cisterns would have had a combined capacity of 20 000cu m, enough to supply 2 000 inhabitants with drinking water. From here, head out towards the most impressive ruins *(to the left of the cardo)*, taking care when crossing ground that has been potholed as much by clandestine excavations as by erosion. First come the ruins of a church that archaeologists have somewhat prosaically called **Basilica B**. Next in line is the **Cathedral of St Sergius\*\***: a basilica consecrated in 559 that may have sheltered the martyr's tomb at one time or other. At the outset, three large arches divided the nave from the aisles; but this rather daring feature was not resilient enough to withstand earthquakes so a subordinate arcade was inserted, with rather distinctive capitals. The bema (dais used by the clergy while reading the Gospels) is visible in the middle of the nave. The northern part of the church has been incorporated into a **mosque**, hence the mihrab.

Outside the North Gate, to the right as you leave the site, stands a square building: a **brick palace** built by the Ghassanids, a Christian Arab tribe. In the 6C, the Byzantines formed an alliance with this people, so that caravans might enjoy some protection from incursions mounted by other desert tribes and Sassanid invasions.

*Return to the main road and go back the way you have come for some 20km: turn right at the fork to Al-Thawra and drive through the town along the main lamp-lit road to the dam. 8km from the fork, stop at the guard-post just before the dam.*

■ **Lake Al-Assad** – All vehicles approaching the dam are stopped and summarily searched by the armed military guards; do not take photographs or stop when crossing the barrage. The bridge (4km) is unremarkable apart from the view of the downstream section of the Euphrates twisting and turning through the landscape. Work on the dam began in the late 1960s, financed in part with money from the Soviet Union. Its purpose was to transform a large area of desert – uninhabited for almost a thousand years - into a thriving agricultural region sustained by irrigation. The dam was inaugurated in 1973, although construction work continued until 1977. Although the most ambitious objectives have not been achieved, the region has become one of the most dynamic in Syria. When the dam was being built, extensive archeological digs were carried out with the help of UNESCO before the cities were flooded. One of the most important projects was the reinforcement of Qalaat Jaabar between 1968 and 1975.

*3km from the dam, turn left down the single track road to Qalaat Jaabar that terminates below the citadel some 13km away.*

■ **Qalaat Jaabar** – *Entrance fee. Parking in front of gate. Allow 30min.*
The castle of Qalaat Jaabar, which once stood high above the banks of the Euphrates looks completely different now that the valley has been flooded. Today, the fine red brick citadel stands on a promontory surrounded by blue

water shimmering with turquoise reflections of the sky from a height of 50m or so. Removed from all forms of habitation, the place is enveloped by a lingering sense of silence and quietude. When the sun goes down, the 12C walls are set aglow and shadows play over the brickwork, throwing the typically Mesopotamian decoration into high relief. Despite having been somewhat over restored, the **façade**★ overlooking the lake is quite the loveliest.

Through the newly built gate into Qalaat Jaabar, you come to a courtyard with the **museum** on the right *(key available from the restaurant. No charge)*. The first room on the ground floor is devoted to a fine collection of Islamic tableware. A low (mind your head!) and narrow doorway leads into the basement area where pottery from the 2nd and 3rd millennia are displayed together with two burial chambers from a Roman hypogeum discovered at the north end of the lake, of which only the basic structure survives.

The main **ramp** cut from the bedrock and lined with brick leads into the heart of the fortress from where it is possible to walk up to the battlements running between the two sets of defences punctuated with well-restored towers. The number of special long flat bricks (30cm) required for such a construction defies imagination! The best place from which to survey the lake is the fortress platform: although little survives of the original apart from the remarkable brick **minaret** reminiscent of the one at Raqqa. The round building rising from the square base dates from when Nureddin carried out extensive re-building works on the citadel in the 12C.

A pause down by the lakeside is highly recommended: the little restaurant by the car park serves a deliciously spiced fresh carp, grilled or fried. The more intrepid might even go so far as to swim off one of the beaches.

*Head back over the dam to the main junction. Turn left to Raqqa.*

The road passes through fields irrigated by concrete irrigation channels that draw water from the large canal. 52km from Qalaat Jaabar, the road arrives at Raqqa.

# ■ Raqqa (Ar'raqqa)
*Allow 90min.*
*For transport, hotels and restaurants, see p 259.*

The rather sleepy modern town made up of small tower blocks set back *(1km)* from the Euphrates, has absorbed the paltry ruins of the summer capital favoured by the great Abbasid Caliph Haroun al-Rachid. Despite its size and population (in excess of 100 000 inhabitants), the town remains unaccustomed to catering for tourists so there is not one single decent hotel in the place. The centre of town is marked by a roundabout with the clock tower, opposite a telephone signal station overshadowed with great pylons. A quick tour in the car is sufficient to glean an idea of the last few vestiges leftover from Abbasid times.

## The city of Haroun al-Rachid
Raqqa was founded by the Seleucids in the mid 3C BC, and prospered under successive occupiers including the Greeks, Romans, Byzantines and Arabs, benefiting throughout from its privileged position on the Silk Route. In 722 it experienced a brilliant if short-lived apogee when Caliph al-Mansour decided to make it the second capital of the Abbasid Empire. It was then that the magnificent enclosure walls were erected, modelled on the ones encircling the circular city of Baghdad. At the turn of the 9C his grandson, Haroun al-Rachid, began building a summer palace outside the walls *(no access)*. Then, in the course of the 12C, the city became famous for its distinctive ceramic ware. After the Mongols passed through the city in 1258, Raqqa fell into rapid decline.

Raqqa

**255**

*From the clock in the town centre, head east past the souk. The local museum is some 300m from the roundabout on the left and the first ramparts, with the Baghdad Gate, 500m beyond that.*

The **Baghdad Gate**\* (Bab Baghdad), a monumental gateway to the city built entirely of brick in the 12C, has an elaborately decorated façade incorporating eight very elegant blind niches. It is worth noting in passing that the line of decorative brick arches across the top, a detail borrowed from Persian Sassanid architecture, later became integral to the early Islamic style.

*Follow the road along the walls.*

This particular section of the **city walls**\*, dating from the Abbasid period, has been very heavily restored. A hundred circular towers built at 35m intervals reinforced the enclosure wall and dictated the outline of the city, locking its citizens into a horse-shoe-shaped area closed off by the Euphrates.

*Walk along the walls for 1.2km to the north (main) gate, turning left into town opposite a large silo.*

Continue 400m to the **Great Mosque** of which little has survived save for the outer wall of the prayer-hall and a circular brick minaret. This complex dates from the great restoration programme undertaken by Nureddin (12C).

*Follow the wall of the mosque, punctuated with round towers in imitation of the old city, until you reach the centre of town. Take the main street heading east of the square with the clock tower, until you find the museum set slightly back from the road.*

Just inside the **museum**\* *(Open 8am-5pm; closed Tuesdays. Entrance fee)* sits a **replica of the treasure of Rassafa** (circa 1200): a five-piece set of silver plate found in 1982 in the courtyard of the Cathedral of St Sergius, buried perhaps when the threat of a Mongol invasion loomed. The original is displayed in the National Museum in Damascus. The other rooms are devoted to artefacts recovered from the various tells in the region. The first floor, meanwhile, is given over to a collection of stucco panels decorated with organic elements found among the ruins of Abbasid palaces, together with various oil lamps and ceramics from the Great Mosque.

*Head back to the central roundabout, turn down the tree-lined avenue running west out of Raqqa to the bridge over the Euphrates. After 6km, turn left at a major crossroads in the direction of Deir ez-Zor.*

The road winds gradually southeast between the Euphrates and a line of cliffs. The river-bank is heavily cultivated with fields of cotton, wheat and maize and villages cling to the hillside. After 70km, the road reaches a plateau and the vegetation suddenly disappears, giving way to stony desert. 20km into this arid expanse, turn left after a tall radio-mast, just before the village of al-Tabni, and continue along the valley of the Euphrates. 7km from the junction the south walls of **Halibiyeh** appear.

■ **Halabiyeh** (ancient Zenobia) – *Entrance fee. Allow 30min.* To some extent, Halabiyeh resembles the sites of Rassafa and Doura Europos: like its counterparts, a certain desolation pervades the well-preserved walls and amorphous levelled ruins. However, this site is less extensive and far less spectacular, although the view over the Euphrates is particularly lovely.

The main feature is the remarkable **fortified enclosure**\*\* that runs from the citadel at the top, down the cliffs towards the Euphrates, like a great wide ribbon, punctuated with towers undulating with every contour of the natural landscape. The eastern flank, which once sealed off the city, has been somewhat damaged

**The Euphrates**

by the Euphrates altering its route over the centuries. In the main, these double walls date from Justinian times (6C) when major works were undertaken across the expanding empire to reinforce strategic outposts, although the site had already been fortified by Zenobia, the famous Queen of Palmyra, who gave the place its name *(see p 271)*. Access was via two gates, one in the north and one in the south, through which the main road now passes. For a closer look at the walls, walk up from the north gate, past the four massive towers shadowing the cliff, to the **praetorium,** which survives relatively intact, with its brick-lined gypsum vaults. On the opposite side of the river sits Halabiyeh's twin sister, the fortified town of **Zalabiyeh**.

The ground between the governor's residence and the **citadel**, also built of gypsum, is dangerously rutted, so it is best to simply turn around and head back downhill, looking out over the ruins in the centre and identifying the two **Christian basilicas**.

The best **view** of Halabiyeh is from the other side of the river; use the floating bridge spanning the Euphrates 300m from the site. Try not to be too disconcerted by the guard-post and the precarious-looking nature of the narrow pontoon: both are quite safe.

*Visitors are advised not to continue along the left bank to Deir ez-Zor (60km) after dusk: the roads are in poor condition and there are often numerous herds of sheep wending their way along it back to their villages. The right bank is much safer.*

## ■ Deir ez-Zor

*Allow half a day for visiting the town.*
*This is the starting point for the excursions to Doura Europos and Mari.*

Many Syrians may attempt to dissuade you from visiting Deir ez-Zor. Indeed, they may find it baffling that someone should want to visit this remote and empty region of the Euphrates, populated by people they suspect of being affiliated with the desert bandits that once sacked the caravans and crossed swords with the Ottomans. Do not let this put you off; few will ever have ventured as far as Deir ez-Zor. And anyway, why not discover this part of Syria for yourself. Life here remains very rural, little affected by the profound changes sweeping through Syrian society everywhere else. In Deir ez-Zor, capital of the *mouhafazat* with a population of 140 000, a certain rhythm is imparted by the thriving souks that begin to stir with life very early in the morning (6am), as the country folk stream in from the outlying region with the fruits of their labours. A long and continuous procession of brightly clad people, the elders with time-weathered faces, snakes into town, as it might have done back in ancient Biblical times.

Since 1984, the local economy has been boosted by successful soundings for crude oil and the development of full-blown wells, identifiable in the distance by the tall flues burning off excess natural gas. It comes as a surprise, therefore, that the town streets are not crowded with geo-physicists, drilling technicians, engineers and labourers. They tend to be put up by their large multinational companies in luxury hotels on the outskirts of town or special encampments on site. Indeed, do not be surprised to find the locals – young and old – staring at foreign tourists about town; they will remain courteous towards all strangers as East meets West.

Deir ez-Zor is a must for archeology enthusiasts with a passion for ancient cities. Its new museum – a model of its kind – and the famous sites of Mari, Doura Europos and Halabiyeh merit an overnight stay at least.

Open-air market, Deir ez-Zor region

The intersection of two major arteries marks the site of the souk and the town-centre. Here, in this little square, merchants come to trade all the year round.

The **souk** (*every morning except Fridays*) is very picturesque. You cannot fail to see the local women, dressed in traditional garb, near the collective taxi stand, selling fresh coriander and other wonderful pungent-smelling herbs, not to mention cartons of cigarettes! In the morning they are the life and soul of the covered souk opposite, then, as night begins to fall, they disappear from sight. Their love of bright colours dictates the assortment of loose trousers, socks, dresses and scarves of garish hue, combined with little concern for clashing greens and reds, sometimes bristling with sequins and embroidery. The women wear a scarf at all times, from which occasionally a long lock of hennaed hair escapes, and blue, green or pink transparent plastic shoes on their stockinged feet. Perhaps contrary to expectations, these Bedouin women are able to wander about on their own, out of sight of their husbands, or with a small group of friends, occasionally with a child strapped to their back.

However, the men are never far away, usually in some café enjoying a cup of mint tea with colleagues. Their heads are kept covered at all times with a red and white checked *keffieh* or a piece of white lightweight cloth held in place with a black *agal*. Their traditional garb is the *jellaba*, which is often worn with a waistcoat. The Bedouins and country people from the outlying villages congregate in and around the covered souk, whereas the townsfolk tend to prefer to shop in one of the two main high streets in the town centre. The butchers' alley is particularly memorable, lined with skinned carcasses covered with flies and stone counters with lambs' heads that unnerve passers-by with their staring eyes.

The **banks of the Euphrates** make for a lovely place for a walk. If you head along the road west (8th March Street) you come to the river and a first bridge, spanning a body of water. However, this is not the great, mythical river, but a small canal. To discover the broad, majestic Euphrates, about which there are so many legends and stories, cross to the island (al-Jezireh) of Deir ez-Zor populated with buildings that have concealed market gardens within since time immemorial. A further ten minutes and you reach the pretty little bridge built by the French in 1924: a narrow suspension bridge supported by steel cables slung from four piers, reserved for use by pedestrians and cyclists only. Throughout the day, locals flock here to while away the hours and at night the bridge is transformed into a magical sight by garlands of lights. Along the riverbanks there are several open-air cafés that offer a selection of Syrian dishes and the opportunity of enjoying a hot cup of fragrant tea. The one and only bridge in these parts for vehicles is situated 500m downstream.

The relatively new **Deir ez-Zor museum**\* *(Open 8am-8pm in summer; 8am-6pm in winter; closed Tuesdays. Entrance fee)* nestles in an imposing building on the left of the first major crossroads on the road to Aleppo, 1km from the souk. The attractively presented collections relate to the Jezireh region between the Tigris and the Euphrates: an area that has been touched by all the great cultures of each successive occupier, from the Akkadians to the Ottomans. On passing through the ticket office, turn left. A series of information boards in English and Arabic outline the main events and rich historical heritage of the area in chronological order. A number of tableaux provide an insight into the most interesting features of the various archeological sites: living conditions from **Tell Bouqras** (stone and clay receptacles from the 7th-6th millennia BC), a large gate from **Tell Bderi** (2700 BC), the Palm-tree courtyard from **Mari** with a screen for protecting the south-facing wall paintings, a model of **Doura Europos** and a replica of the large frescoes from the Temple of Baal. A second doorway leads into the galleries exhibiting Islamic artefacts (fine 12C-13C pottery from **Raqqa**, stucco from the Abbasid palaces of Raqqa). The last room is arranged (with humour) to give an idea of life in the early 20C, and the ecological consequences of developing the desert and the banks of the Euphrates.

## Making the most of Raqqa and Deir ez-Zor

### COMING AND GOING

#### • Raqqa

**By train** – Catch a train from Aleppo. The train station is 2km to the north of the town.

**By bus** – *Karnak Company*, at the Karnak Hotel. Daily buses for Aleppo (2hr), Deir ez-Zor (2hr 30min) and Damascus.

*Minibus garage*, in the town centre next to the park. Several bus companies provide a service to Aleppo and Deir ez-Zor.

#### • Deir ez-Zor

**By air** – There is a weekly flight from Deir ez-Zor to Damascus. The airport is 7km to the south of the town.

**By train** – The train station is on the left bank of the Euphrates, 4km from the town centre. Booking office in town, behind the Raghdan Hotel. There are night trains for Aleppo and Damascus.

**By bus** – *Karnak Company* buses run to Aleppo and Damascus (via Palmyra) at least once a day. Bookings can be made in a new office on the ground floor of the administrative building behind the Raghdan Hotel (entrance via a passageway next to the Karnak cafeteria).

*Intilac Garage*, in the street which crosses the canal, 1.5km from the town centre. This bus station houses the Al-Fourat and Qadmous Tour companies, as well as all the microbuses. There are around a dozen daily departures for

Raqqa (2hr 30min), Palmyra (2hr 30min) and Damascus (5hr). There are also plenty of taxis to be found here.

**By shared taxi** – These wait for customers in the market square and will take you to Damascus (S£450) and Aleppo.

## ADDRESS BOOK

### • Raqqa

**Main post office** – In the main square, on the corner of the street leading to Baghdad gate.

**Telephone** – In the building adjoining the post office. There are telephone kiosks which accept phone cards situated outside the building.

### • Deir ez-Zor

**Tourist information** – In a street off Abou Kamal St, just after the Jamaia al-Arabia Hotel. Only Arabic spoken.

**Main post office** – 8 Azar St. Opposite the waste ground 500m from the souk, going towards the Intiliac bus station.

**Telephone** – Imam Ali St. 300m from the souk on the road to Aleppo. Card phones inside the telephone centre building.

**Bank/Currency exchange** – **Exchange bureau** at the Furat Cham Hotel, open 24hrs a day. Travellers' cheques and cash.

**Commercial Bank of Syria**, Imam Ali St. Between the souk and the museum.

**Visa extensions** – This can be done any morning, except on Fridays. Passing to the left of the museum, take the first street on the left. The immigration department is found 50m from the turning. Formalities take 30min. Bring 3 photos.

## WHERE TO STAY

### • Raqqa

There is no medium-priced category between the basic town-centre hotels and the Karnak.

*Under US$10*

**Ammar Hotel,** 50m from the clock tower, between the square and the al-Waha restaurant – 8rm. The rooms lead off a large lounge/reception area. Very basic.

*From US$20-40*

**Karnak Hotel**, 800m to the west of the town, in a street parallel to the one leading to the bridge over the Euphrates, ☏ (22) 232 265 –34rm ⌁ 🗏 🖉 📺 ✗ The only tourist-grade in the town. Spacious rooms, but rather shabby. The restaurant on the ground floor serves a Syrian-style breakfast. Parking.

### • Deir ez-Zor

There is very little choice of accommodation at Deir ez-Zor. At Easter and in the summer it may be wise to reserve.

*Under US$20*

A number of cheap but rather seedy hotels are found in the souk area, in the street leading to Abou Kamal.

**Damascus Hotel**, next to the Raghdan Hotel, near the bridge over the canal, ☏ (51) 221 481 – 10rm. Don't expect much comfort in this very basic hotel, which is frequented by travellers on a tight budget (hot showers are extra, and must be reserved in advance, and the beds are pretty uncomfortable). Very good value, nevertheless, and rooms on the right of the large entrance hall have balconies overlooking a tributary of the Euphrates. As a last resort only.

*From US$25-40*

**Raghdan Hotel**, Al-Nasr St, ☏ (51) 222 053, Fax (51) 221 169 – 23rm ⌁ 🗏 ⅄ 🖉 📺 ✗ The best place for a short stay in Deir ez-Zor at a reasonable price, especially as it is inclusive of breakfast. Pleasant lounges with fans. Some rooms have balconies with views over the canal.

**Mari Hotel**, In a street parallel to the Aleppo road, 200m from the souk, ☏ (51) 224 340, Fax (51) 218 156 – 44rm ⌁ 🗏 🖉 📺 ✗ The rooms are reached via a labyrinth of corridors (perhaps a replica of those at the Mari Palace?). Prices noticeably higher than those at the Raghdan, and not really worth it.

*Over US$160*

A price-tag of around US$160 at Deir ez-Zor's luxury hotel seems very high for a small provincial town. This is mostly due to the presence of a large expatriate community employed by the oil companies.

**Furat Cham Hotel**, on the Aleppo road, 4km from the town centre, ☎ (51) 312 800, Fax (51) 312 901 – 156rm ⌂ 🖥 🖋 TV ✗ ⌕ ✧ CC An entrance worthy of an Umayyad palace for the lovely patio with cupola. Superb views of the Euphrates for half the rooms, but no balconies. Small supermarket near the entrance, where you can buy cosmetic products, tobacco and alcohol (wine).

## EATING OUT

### • Raqqa

*Under US$10*

There are little restaurants in the town centre serving roast chicken, which, together with several patisseries, could provide a basic meal or a snack while waiting for the bus.

**Al-Waha**, in the same street as the bus station. Large dining room.

**Coffee Shop**, in the park. This large room is pleasant place for a tea, with pretty armchairs.

### • Deir ez-Zor

*Under US$10*

There are several typical open-air restaurants on the banks of the Euphrates. If you're worried about the chilly evening air or the mosquitoes by the river, you have the choice of the Raghdan Hotel or the Cham Hotel's restaurants on the edge of town. For a quick snack, there are any number of cheap restaurants in the town centre (chicken, kebabs).

**Tourist Blue Beach (Shata Azrak)**, near the suspension bridge, just after the small park. ♈ To make up for the lack of a swim from the "blue beach", you can sit back and watch the world and the ancient river go by. The tables are set under large eucalyptus trees on the terraces overlooking the river. *Meze*, kebabs and

chicken. The food is nothing special. Check the bill, which is sometimes completely wrong.

**Big Bridge Restaurant (Al Gesser)**, next to the suspension bridge. ♈ Less well-kept than the above, but the same menu.

**Engeneer (Al-Mouhan Dissi)**, on the opposite bank, next to the bridge. ♈ Similar to the previous two restaurants.

**Raghdan**, restaurant on the top floor of the Raghdan Hotel. ♈ Fine view of the canal from the large picture windows. It can be reached by a lift. Good plain cooking.

*Over US$10*

**Four Seasons**, Furat Cham Hotel. ♈ This pleasant hotel restaurant offers a generous open-air buffet with meze and grills nearly every evening in the summer (when the tour groups arrive to stay). Dinner on the terrace overlooking the river is a memorable experience.

## OTHER THINGS TO DO

### • Deir ez-Zor

**Outdoor pursuits** – The hotel **Furat Cham** has a swimming pool, which is pleasant in the summer, when the temperature reaches 40°C. Open to non-residents for a fee. 9am-sundown. Bar and snacks.

## EXCURSION TO MARI AND DOURA EUROPOS

**By taxi** – This is by far the easiest and most flexible means of getting there. Negotiate a fee with one of the taxis at the taxi-service station.

**By bus** – There are fairly frequent buses for Abou Kamal which will drop you at the turning for Doura Europos. It's up to you to find transport to Mari. Don't forget to bring something to drink!

**Making the most of Deir ez-Zor**

# DOURA EUROPOS AND MARI★
248km round trip from Deir ez-Zor - Allow 5hr

### And remember...
In summer leave very early to avoid travelling during the hottest hours of the day.
Fill up with fuel and check engine water levels the night before.
There is no accommodation, but there are restaurants at Mayadin.

This excursion runs along the right bank of the Euphrates, following what was the main road to Baghdad before the border-post at Abu Kamal (marvellous morning market) was closed in 1982. Along the way, the road passes three important sites, set back (2km) from the highway: the castle of Qalaat Rahba, Doura Europos and Mari. However, do not expect too much; time has taken its toll and so a great deal of imagination is required to conjure up the splendid past of these important sites.

*From Deir ez-Zor follow the right bank of the canal. After 4km, turn right and then immediately left, towards Abu Kamal.*

The fast, well-maintained highway runs parallel to the Euphrates, although the river is too far away to be seen until Doura Europos. On leaving the town, the road passes through a landscape dominated by fields of cotton and maize. Bundles of maize stalks may be seen stacked on the house roofs, ready for the winter months. Do drive carefully through the villages, keeping an eye out for local children and untethered livestock.

*After 47km, turn right towards the castle, silhouetted against the sky on the right. After 1km, turn left and continue around the castle to the plateau.*

■ **Qalaat Rahba** (Qalaat Arrabeh) – A drive around the castle is sufficient to provide an overview of the ruins. The more adventurous might like to scale the steep path uphill to the remains of the central donjon. The castle, built by Nureddin (second half of the 12C), occupies a strategic position high on the edge of a cliff overlooking the Euphrates, separated from the valley below by a sheer drop on the eastern flank and protected elsewhere by a deep semicircular moat cut from the bedrock. But the defences proved insufficient to repel the Mongol offensive a century later, so the castle was abandoned. When viewed from the main road, the castle dominates the skyline: mapped out (in the shape of an irregular pentagon originally) by its tall walls of stone and brick.

*Return to the road to Abu Kamal, bypassing the town of Mayadin.*

On the far side of the village of Tichreen (*30km further on*), the road begins to climb up to the semi-deserted plateau frequented by the occasional group of nomads. The contrast is startling: here the villages are few and far between in this stark white landscape.

*Continue for 15km and turn left along the road bound for the ramparts of Doura Europos. Park the car in the car park in front of the Palmyra Gate.*

## ■ Doura Europos★
*9am-6pm, winter 4pm. Entrance fee. Allow 1hr.*

### Hellenistic, Parthian and Roman in turn
The town was founded on a high cliff overlooking the Euphrates in 303 BC by Seleukos Nicator, when he was still a staff-officer in the army of Alexander the Great, long before he became the king of the Seleucid Empire. In the 2C BC,

The Euphrates

Doura Europos (midway between the two capitals of the Seleucid Empire – Antioch and Seleucia on the Tigris) became overrun by a military contingent of Macedonians and Greeks and this prompted the town transformation into a veritable city. A grid of perpendicular streets was laid out, separating identical blocks of *insulae* and an *agora* was erected. 30 years later, long before work was completed, Doura Europos was seized by the Parthians under whom it prospered, largely as a result of its agriculture and artistry than on account of the caravan trade. In 165 AD, the city fell into Roman hands and was transformed into a stronghold, designed to withstand attack by both the Parthians and Sassanids. The northern third of the city was taken over for use as a camp for legionaries. Parthians, Greeks, Macedonians and Palmyrenes lived there amicably together and erected sacred sanctuaries to their respective divinities (including temples to Bel, a synagogue and a Christian chapel). In 256 AD Doura Europos was taken by the Sassanid King Shapur I as part of his campaign against Rome; the town was sacked, the population was deported and the place disappeared into oblivion.

In 1920, a different set of soldiers set up camp among the ruins. As the British made preparations to consolidate their position, having been hounded there by King Faysal's Arab troops, the Sepoys of an Indian battalion set about erecting the machine-gun emplacements. Suddenly, as they were digging, the earth caved in and a fabulous fresco depicting life-size figures dressed in tall pointed hats was revealed. They immediately sent for an archeologist, but it was not until 1923 and peace had returned to the region that the frescoes could be identified with the Doura Europos of Antiquity. More frescoes were found in the embankments hastily constructed by the Romans during a siege. Their exceptional state of preservation prompted Doura Europos to be acclaimed as "the Pompeii of the desert".

It does not take long to visit the site; the frescoes that were salvaged from the synagogue are now on display at the National Museum in Damascus, and years of neglect following the large scale excavations by French and American teams in the 1920s and 1930s have taken their toll. Much of the excavated area has suffered from being exposed to the elements; the mud-brick has disintegrated and the gypsum is crumbling. Since 1986, a Franco-Syrian team has been engaged in retrieving what it can.

## Tour

A 700m stretch of the west **ramparts**★★ gives some idea of the original defences protecting Doura Europos. The stone wall still rises to a height of 9m and would have been punctuated by towers (26 remain). During the Roman occupation the fortifications were reinforced with a brick-faced glacis.

*Rather than entering the town by the main gate (Palmyra Gate) on the left, make your way to one of the towers.*

The site is simply huge: a mass of desolate ruins with an occasional outcrop of wall. From each tower radiated a street towards the centre of town. Follow the one leading straight into the main entrance. In the block immediately on the left a **Christian house** from 230 AD was discovered. This unique example of a building specifically intended for use by Early Christians comprised a large room, in which the faithful could assemble, and a baptistery. The wall paintings depicting scenes from the New Testament are now on display at the museum in Yale (United States). A short distance beyond the house on the left stand the remains of a brick building, one of the three **public baths** built by the Romans.

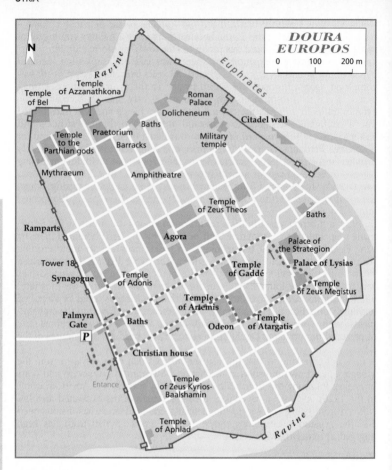

**DOURA EUROPOS**

0     100     200 m

N

Ravine

Euphrates

Temple of Bel

Temple of Azzanathkona

Roman Palace

Dolicheneum

Citadel wall

Baths

Temple to the Parthian gods

Praetorium

Barracks

Military temple

Mythraeum

Amphitheatre

Temple of Zeus Theos

Baths

Ramparts

Agora

Palace of the Strategion

Tower 18

Palace of Lysias

Synagogue

Temple of Adonis

Temple of Gaddé

Temple of Zeus Megistus

Temple of Artemis

Palmyra Gate

P

Baths

Temple of Atargatis

Odeon

Christian house

Entance

Temple of Zeus Kyrios-Baalshamin

Ravine

Temple of Aphlad

Bear right. After some 400m, you come to the vestiges of square Parthian **temples** dedicated to Artemis, Atargatis and Gaddé, flanked by a small courtyard surrounded by rooms intended for ceremonial rituals (one room built on three levels is still clearly visible).

The small **odeon** with a constricted semicircular auditorium built of stone, one block deep, and plaster has a narrow doorway with a gypsum lintel.

Turn sharply right so as to avoid the wadi, and continue to the ruins of the so-called **Palace of Lysias**. In fact, these comprised the residential quarters for the palace of the Strategion, complete with their large courtyard and central well, surrounded by a long row of interconnected rooms with gypsum doorframes that remain standing. Looking out towards the river, you get a marvellous **view★** of the Euphrates gently meandering its way through the countryside. If you follow the course of the dry wadi towards the valley, you will pass on the right the fortified front of the **Palace of the Strategion**, currently under restoration.

Lower down, the imposing wall overlooking the river, to the left of the dig-house, once formed part of the wall of the **citadel**, itself built on the site of a Greek palace.

*Retrace your steps to the main street of the town and follow it to the tall Palmyra Gate.*

On the right stands the **agora**, marked out by a series of pier bases defining the length of the *decumanus* as it extends towards the remains of the **synagogue**, before the ramparts to the right of tower 18. In the courtyard are the bases of four of the six columns supporting a portico. The doorway in the west side provided access to the assembly house, in which the exceptional frescoes – now in the museum in Damascus *(see p 132)* – were found.

The **Palmyra Gate***, at the top, was the main gateway. The tall arch rises between two bastions supported by enormous, thick walls.

*To get to Mari, go back to the car and drive out along the road to Abu Kamal. This runs steeply downhill from the plateau and into the fields around the village of Salihiyeh. Some 24km further on, you come to a slight mound on the left; this Tell Hariri (Mari).*

*A side-road leads to the dig-house where the entry tickets are sold. The tell, with its distinctive white covering, may be seen 400m up a dirt track leading off to the left. Park the car by the entrance to the sacred site.*

# ■ **Mari*** (Tell Hariri)
*Open daily. Entrance fee. Allow 45min.*

The name of this Mesopotamian city is widely known among people interested in the ancient civilisations. In this case, "Mari" evokes images of those famous statues with huge staring eyes that date from the beginning of the 3rd millennium *(see illustration on the cover).*

## The capital of the Middle Euphrates

The town of Mari was probably founded in the early 3rd millennium BC in an attempt to seize control of traffic along the caravan routes and the river, at a time when considerable developments were taking place in the valley of the Euphrates. Archeologists have uncovered the existence of a 11m broad canal, wide enough to carry barges therefore, running from the left bank of the Euphrates to the Khabur, flowing 120km away, suggesting goods were being regularly traded and exchanged.

For nigh on a century, the site was abandoned. The new settlers built a palace with a sacred precinct. The city was then incorporated into the empire of Sargon of Akkad before being suddenly destroyed. Eventually a new dynasty (Shakkanakku) took possession of the site and gradually set about establishing an independent kingdom of their own (about which little is known). A new palace was erected while reconstruction of the main palace progressed. In 1820 BC an Amorite dynasty assumed control. The last 30 years under their rule is less enigmatic following the discovery of tablets emanating from the archives of the last king, Zimrilim (1775-1761 BC). In 1760 BC Hammurabi seized the over-zealous city and crushed it a few months later. Mari declined, broken and abandoned for ever.

Although Mari is of enormous historical consequence, the excavated site itself is far less impressive. Only the walls of the sacred precinct dating from the 3rd millennium BC, thankfully preserved from the elements, provide some indication of the scale and architecture of Mari. The fragile fabric of the walls, simple bricks moulded out of dried mud, continues to disintegrate as a result of the wind and rain. The 5m walls that defined the splendid 2nd millennium palace complex at the time of the first excavations are now barely visible. The most evocative and exquisite artefacts exhumed from this rich archeological site are now to be admired in the labyrinthine museums of Damascus, Aleppo and the Louvre: only there can you piece together a picture of life here over 4000 years ago.

## Tour

Climb up from the car park to the top of the nearby **terrace** marked by a block of concrete. From up here, there is a good **view★** of the whole site. The white sheeting on the western side covers the sacred precinct and beyond it lie the remains of the Zimrilim's palace, in part destroyed during the excavations of the older palace from the 3rd millennium BC. The area in line with the burning flare in the far west was covered with residential units and continues to be investigated. It may come as some surprise that the Euphrates is not visible below the tell. Instead, the city sat on a site set back from the river, which the planners assumed might avert the risk of flooding. Imagine, therefore, a perfectly circular city with a radius of 1km, protected by a dyke, on which some ramparts were probably built. From here, a canal extended across the city on a north-south axis, enabling boats to dock in complete safety within the confines of the city. Excavations have so far concentrated on the area west of the canal, where the temples and palaces stood. Down below nestled the lower town.

The **sacred precinct★** is the best-preserved monument at Mari, thanks to its translucent protective covering supported on a metal frame. Opposite the entrance to the excavations – instigated by archeologists – stands a board bearing a plan of the site. From here, follow the narrow **corridor** with very high walls that once encircled the building (immediately to the right of the entrance). After about 20m, turn right into a rectangular room and continue to the complex's open **courtyard**. An opening in the thick wall on the right leads into the **holy of holies**: a 21m long chamber with a small room at the east end with a podium, on which idols or a statue of the deity would have stood. This sacred precinct forms part of a palace that dates from the 3rd millennium BC, and was in-filled, in order to provide stable foundations for the palace of Zimrilim, built in the early 2nd millennium. Walk back to the entrance to re-emerge outside, level with the palace of Zimrilim.

The **palace of Zimrilim, dating from the 2nd millennium BC,** has not fared so well as the sacred precinct after being left exposed to the elements all these years. This is a pity, because when it was discovered its 5m walls were in a relatively good state of preservation; today we only have the black and white photographs taken in the course of excavation to remind us of just how magnificent the residence of Zimrilim must have been. In addition to the damage caused by erosion, investigations into the nature of the earlier palace from the 3rd millennium BC have all but obliterated the ground plan layout of an extensive complex, 200m long and 100m wide, containing some 300 rooms, divided into sections.

On the way out of the sacred precinct, you will pass a brick undercroft with beautiful corbelled vaulting supported by eight piers: this was a water **cistern**. A little further on, on the left, a series of square flagstones, 30cm across, cover various **channels** designed to convey rainwater, collected from the terraces, into a tank outside the palace walls. The area beyond, on the right, comprised the reception area with a doorway and a courtyard. Wander into the section to the left of the channels, past the women's quarters on the right, and into the **courtyard of the Palm tree** (courtyard 106). This would have had an awning running along the south wall to screen it from the sun and to shade a series of wall paintings that were extremely rare in the ancient East. Beneath the

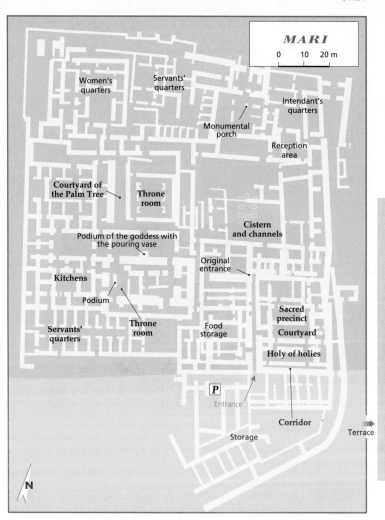

courtyard, archeologists have identified a **throne room** that formed part of the 3rd millennium complex, compete with massive mud-brick piers, ornamental niches and redans (three of which may still be seen). A decorative doorway leads south into another chamber, in which the statue of the goddess with the pouring vase (the jewel in the museum in Aleppo) was found. Today the walls are in a parlous state and the podium, on which the statue sat, is covered with rubble. Beyond, extended the **throne room** of the 2nd millennium palace, with its podium still visible on the right. This was in fact the largest room in the palace, where audiences and banquets were held, surrounded to the west by a series of rooms used as offices, kitchens and for other services and to the south by the **servants' quarters**.

Tomb of Elhabel, Palmyra

# THE DESERT

Do not imagine a desert of undulating sand dunes dotted with swaying palm trees: the Syrian desert is a bleak and stony place that extends for miles, edged with high mountain ranges. Only in spring is this barren land relieved in part with clumps of colourful flowering plants. During the rest of the year, the countryside becomes a steppe (*badiya*) rather than a real desert, scattered with occasional tufts of hardy vegetation.

The Bedouin, whose long black tents you may see camouflaged in the flat emptiness, tirelessly move their flocks through the landscape, grazing the remote quarters in winter and the fallow stubble fields in summer. This vast, hostile region holds little of interest for travellers. Visitors would probably bypass it completely were it not for Palmyra, an oasis that has attracted and fascinated people for generations.

# Palmyra ★★★
## (Tadmor)
Mouhafazat of Homs
Between Damascus (247km) and Deir ez-Zor (212km)
Very hot in summer, with temperatures rising to 42°C

### Not to be missed
Watching the sun rising (or setting) over the ruined city
from the Arab castle.
A walk along the colonnade and around the Temple of Bel.

### And remember...
In summer it is best to wander about the ruins at sunrise and visit the museums
(or snooze) during the hottest hours of the day.
Devote at least one whole day to Palmyra.

You have to drive across more than 200km of unendingly monotonous stony steppe before you see the first signs of green around the oasis and the Roman ruins emerging like a mirage from the flatness, overlooked by a square Arab fort silhouetted against the skyline.

Palmyra is the stuff of legend. Its name conjures up images of caravans, laden with spices and silks, and pictures of the mysterious if redoubtable Queen Zenobia who so bewitched many an 18C Romantic adventurer. It is now 1700 years since the place was sacked by the Roman legions of Aurelian and its proud column-fronted temples, paved streets and cyclopean complex holding the sanctuary of Bel were reduced to ruins in a silent landscape. When the sun goes down, the stones are turned a beautiful fiery golden colour in the dwindling light, the shadows lengthen and the ghosts of ancient peoples with familiar faces seem to fill the emptiness. These elusive figures might be real shepherds, herding up their flocks, or they may be fleeting illusions shaped by the portrait busts now displayed in countless archeological museums. These Palmyrenes, who dared to challenge Rome, were effective merchants and farmers that knew how to exploit to a maximum the spring nestling at the foot of Jebel Tadmor, transforming it into an oasis capable of sustaining life. Even today, the spring imparts charm to the place, feeding the tall green date palms that screen the city from the immensity of the desert and close off the southern horizon opposite the long ridge crowned with the Arab citadel.

With the advent of various modern hotels, restaurants and souvenir shops, the town has encroached upon the ruins, ever eager to harness the potential opportunities provided by tourism.

### An important transit post
The Ain Efqa spring near the Hotel Cham continues to flow profusely with sulphurous waters that surprisingly have never been deemed harmful. Quite the contrary, nomads have been

**Palm trees**

Palmyra boasts the largest production of dates in Syria. Indeed, the oasis bears the Aramaic term for the fruit (tadmor) and the date palm is now synonymous with Palmyra. A group of huge trees dominate the area around the oasis where the fruits are allowed to ripen slowly in the sun before being harvested between September and December, according to variety. Visitors to the city at that time will have the opportunity of sampling the many different kinds from stalls that spring up along the road to the site. Prices range from S£25 for the small yellow dates to S£350 for the beautiful black dates that melt in the mouth. At Palmyra they also produce a concentrate called "date honey".

The Desert

drawing its waters since Palaeolithic times and the first settlers pitched camp here in the 3rd millennium BC. A few centuries later, Palmyra is listed in tablets from Mari as **Tadmor** (meaning palm tree), the Arabic name still in use today. But the "Tadmor of the desert" mentioned in the Bible that was supposed to have been built by King Solomon has yet to be formally identified. Despite this, the city evidently enjoyed a considerable and widespread reputation from Hellenistic times onwards. Its fortune, however, was only really ensured after the Roman authorities annexed Petra in 106 AD and Antioch reached new heights in its trading with the West. From then on, all the caravans plying their wares from India, Mesopotamia, Arabia and Anatolia converged on Palmyra, which benefited handsomely from the transiting camel trains. Taxes levied on merchandise poured into the city coffers and lined the pockets of the kingdom's affluent aristocracy with gold. On retiring from their travels, the wealthy Palmyrene entrepreneurs, with Semitic names denoting tribal origins, endowed their city with splendid monuments, much as their counterparts in the West did across the Roman Empire.

## Zenobia: queen of the desert

Despite the exorbitant cost of containing troubles on the Eastern frontier, Palmyra amassed considerable wealth that solicited a desire for independence. But it was not until Rome realised that its over-stretched armies were unable to sustain the counter-offensive against the Sassanids on the far side of the Euphrates, as well as man all the remote outposts of the Empire, that the Palmyrenes were entrusted with defending the eastern frontier.

In 262 AD Odainat was named governor of the province; but his term was cut short by his death (and that of his son and heir) in 266 while fighting in Asia Minor. Many believe his murder to have been prompted by his wife Zenobia, who was in line to assume control of the kingdom as regent for her son Wahballat. Either way, the new queen, who has been described as "the noblest woman in all the Orient and the most beautiful", was devoured by ambition. By 269, **Queen Zenobia** had conquered Egypt and led her troops into Asia Minor. Three years later, she had some coins minted in Alexandria, on which she proclaimed herself *"Augusta"* and her son *"Imperator Caesar Augustus"*. This was the last straw for Emperor Aurelian, who immediately set out to defeat the Palmyrene army at Emesa (Homs), forcing the queen to retreat to Palmyra. During her attempts to win support from the Sassanids, she was captured on the banks of the Euphrates. What followed remains shrouded in mystery. Some sources claim she was made to take part in Aurelius' sumptuous triumphal entry into Rome in 274, and ended her days in a villa at Tivoli.

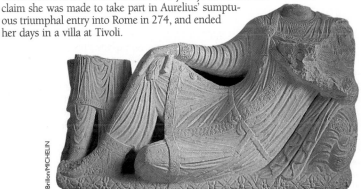

B Brillon/MICHELIN

Fragment of a Palmyrene statue

Palmyra

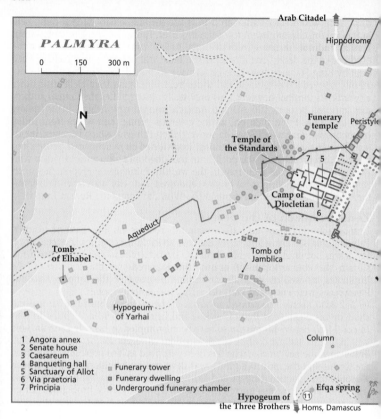

PALMYRA

0    150    300 m

N

Arab Citadel

Hippodrome

Funerary temple    Peristyle

Temple of the Standards

Camp of Diocletian

7  5

6

Tomb of Elhabel

Tomb of Jamblica

Aqueduct

Hypogeum of Yarhai

Column

1 Angora annex
2 Senate house
3 Caesareum
4 Banqueting hall
5 Sanctuary of Allot
6 Via praetoria
7 Principia

▪ Funerary tower
▪ Funerary dwelling
● Underground funerary chamber

Efqa spring

Hypogeum of the Three Brothers

Homs, Damascus

Eventually, Aurelius managed to suppress a rebellion in Palmyra, but this time, the city that had been spared at the time of conquest was sacked. Later, Diocletian posted a large garrison to Palmyra, and in the 6C its defences were reinforced by Justinian to safeguard his frontiers, just as the Christian community of Palmyra was overseeing the construction of the first churches there. But now, bypassed by the main caravan routes, the city began sliding slowly into oblivion.

In 1749 and 1750, two English travellers named Wood and Dawkins arrived to explore and document the ruins. Soon after returning home, they published a book of their findings that included a series of etchings: *The Ruins of Palmyra* caused a sensation and delivered a major impact on the Neoclassical movement sweeping Britain at that time.

During the ensuing years, the city became even more alluring, and was subsequently elevated to ever greater heights by 19C Romantic Orientalists, who were unable to visit the ruins for themselves for fear of being murdered by the local tribes. Not until the time of the French mandate were the ruins finally cleared and excavated.

The Desert

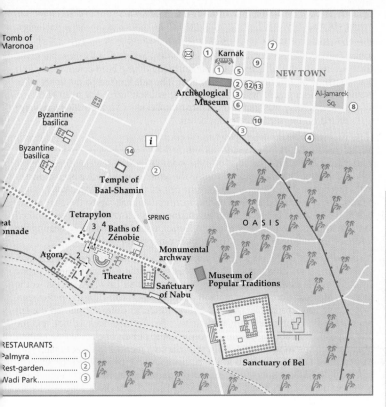

RESTAURANTS
Palmyra ...................... ①
Rest-garden............... ②
Wadi Park.................. ③

HOTELS
New Afka .................. ①
Bel .............................. ②
Citadel ...................... ③
Heliopolis .................. ④
Ishtar ........................ ⑤
Middle East .............. ⑥
Nakhil ....................... ⑦
Umayyad Palace......... ⑧
Orient ....................... ⑨
Palace ....................... ⑩
Palmyra Cham ........... ⑪
Tower ....................... ⑫
Villa Palmyra ............. ⑬
Zenobia ..................... ⑭

## The site★★★
*Allow half a day.*
*Access to the main ruins is free. Open all day.*

### Archeological Museum to the Temple of Bel

From September to December, stalls line the Damascus road over some 400m, offering local dates for sale; huge red, yellow and black bunches are hung from the poles of the shops.

Opposite the Hotel Zenobia stands the **Temple of Baal-Shamin**★, fronted with a line of six Corinthian columns, and dedicated to the god of fertility and thunderstorms. The fine decoration ornamenting the inside of the holy of holies *(adyton)*, at the far end of the cella, is visible through the grille. This formed part of a vast precinct, completed in around 150 AD, that comprised three courtyards. The bases of the columns of a peristyle, to the right of the temple, show the layout of the most important of these.

*Continue through the monumental archway and head towards the huge enclosure containing the sanctuary of Bel, set back from where the road turns through a right angle.*

The **Sanctuary of Bel**★★ *(Open daily, 8am-1pm / 4pm-6pm in summer, 8am-4pm in winter. Entrance fee)* is Palmyra's largest monument and one of the best preserved *(see illustration p 108)*. Originally, the precinct would have been contained by four walls, each measuring some 200m in length. The side flanked by the ticket office would have been graced with a monumental stairway up to the main entrance. When the sanctuary was transformed into a citadel in 1132, a **fortified gateway**★ was erected on the site of the propylaeum.

*Make your way from the ticket office into the sanctuary courtyard.* The temple stands in the centre of a vast **esplanade** surrounded by an elegant **peribole**★ (garden with statuary). Around the edge of three sides ran a wall screened by a double row of columns. During sacrificial rituals, the temenos would have been crowded with spectators. The **ramp**, visible to the left of the ticket office, with clearly defined steps, was used for leading the sacrificial animals up to the altar set up before the entrance to the temple. Attendance at such ceremonies was limited to those in possession of small tokens *(tesserae)*, issued by invitation, bearing the image of the sacrificial victims: sheep, bull, ram or other.

A special system of ducts conveyed water from a ceremonial basin on the right of the altar for washing away any blood. Set before the gigantic **temple**★ sitting squarely on its podium is a flight of broad steps that provided access to the monumental side-door. Conforming to oriental rather than Classical prototypes, this temple had two *adytons* (holy of holies) inside its cella: the one on the left honouring the Palmyrene trinity of divinities, Bel, Yarhibol and Aglibol, and the one opposite probably containing a votive statue of Bel. The carved decoration ornamenting the **monolithic ceilings**★★ of the two recesses is exceptional.

As you leave the cella, look up to the beams above the peristyle on the left. The first bears an illustration of the sanctuary, dedicated to the gods Aglibol and Malakbel on one side, and a scene showing Bel (on horseback followed by six other divinities) fighting a monster on the other. The second beam is carved with a procession that includes four women with their faces veiled.

The **Ethnological Museum** *(9am-3pm. Entrance fee)*, situated on the right as you leave the Bel complex, is housed in former living quarters built for the Ottoman governor, erected at a time when a small village was settled inside the Temple of Bel. A series of tableaux populated by plaster figures recreate scenes from Bedouin life as lived by Palmyrene villagers. Special attention is given to traditional weavings, jewellery, keeping camels and domestic interiors, local dress and basketry.

## Temple of Bel to the monumental archway

A broad street, with a few standing columns still in place, led from the propylaeum of the sanctuary of Bel to the monumental archway. This was conceived as a processional way, devised to convey great crowds of people to attend festivals in honour of Bel. Four tall Corinthian columns mark the site of a nymphaeum with a semicircular apse (just visible). At the intersection of this secondary colonnaded thoroughfare with the cardo maximus stands a **Monumental Archway**★★. In order to accommodate the corner, the monument opens out like a fan. The three arches are typical, as is the sumptuous carved ornamentation. The view from the arch along the virtually continuous curtain of columns is quite extraordinary.

The Desert

## The great colonnade

The colonnade dates from the mid 2C AD. The street, including the portico on either side, measures 23m across and would have stretched before the main buildings of the city in Antiquity.

Immediately on the left lie the ruins of the **Sanctuary of Nabu** (or Nebo), a more modest version of the Temple of Bel. The precinct extends back from the colonnade, to contain a monumental altar (clearly visible), a flight of steps and a great podium on which the peripteral temple was elevated. Such a large sanctuary honouring Nebo, who was the son of Marduk, lord of the Babylonian pantheon, testifies to Palmyra's unique position between Eastern and Western cultures, here paying tribute to an oriental deity.

A short way further on, on the right of the colonnade, stands a fine portico fronted with four granite columns standing proudly in front of the entrance to the **Baths of Zenobia**. The ground beyond the vestibule still bears the outline of the bathing pools.

A street on the left leads to the entrance to the **theatre**, which is both small – only 12 rows of seating – and heavily restored. Some claim it was never properly completed. Its somewhat baroque proscenium wall breaks with tradition by having five rather than three openings: the central one articulated by four columns and a pediment.

To the left of the stage, a door leads through to the **agora**\*: a huge rectangular area enclosed by high walls, surrounded originally on all four sides by a portico. The little brackets protruding from the columns shafts would have been used to bear statues of local dignitaries, paid for by the citizens themselves and furnished with a plaque listing their Greek, Latin and Semitic-sounding names. This part of town, nestling behind the theatre, would have been the commercial and administrative quarters; to date, archeologists have identified an **annexe** used for storing goods, a somewhat controversial **senate house**, a **Caesareum** and a **banqueting hall** flanking the *agora*.

Between the columns at Palmyra

B Brillon/MICHELIN

Palmyra

*Walk towards the tetrapylon. To the right of the colonnade you will see an exedra from the city's nymphaeum which stood before the tetrapylon.*

The **tetrapylon**★ gracing a major crossroads, comprises four large bases supporting columns. The shafts, only one of which is original, would have been from Aswan in Central Egypt! The tetrapylon marks a second break in the colonnade; this time the deviation from the Classical canon suggests that building progressed in stages.

As you walk the length of the avenue, you will pass a succession of former villas and churches (the excavations are rather disappointing) making up the residential quarter on the right.

Eventually the main thoroughfare comes to a transverse, colonnaded street before a **funerary temple**, fronted with a fine hexastyle façade and pediment that survives remarkably unscathed by the ravages of time.

To the left, the street leads to the **Sanctuary of Allat** and a quarter known as the **Camp of Diocletian**: an area of town that was developed about 30 years after the city was sacked, to meet military requirements.

The *via praetoria* branches off the transverse colonnade to run across the forum to the steps of the *principia* (seat of the military commander). Eighteen steps of this otherwise deformed monumental stairway remain in situ. The platform which stood before the main late-3C building in the middle of the military camp provided a base for the **Temple of the Standards**: a single well-preserved chamber with an apse, set aside for holding ceremonies associated with the warrior cult.

# Archeological Museum★★

*Open 8am-1pm/2pm-6pm in summer; 2pm-4pm in winter; month of Ramadan 8am-3pm; closed Tuesdays. Entrance fee.*

It is well worth visiting the Archeological Museum, (situated opposite the Karnak Bus Company offices) on the periphery of the new town and the ancient city. For here is some of the finest evidence of Palmyra's distinctive artistic heritage. The first room on the right of the entrance contains a large group of incense-burning altars and a fine set of **Palmyrene inscriptions**, an Aramaean dialect that was deciphered in 1754 by the Frenchman Abbé Jean-Jacques Barthélemy. The **scale model of the Temple of Bel** in the adjacent room recreates the astonishing proportions of the original temple. The figures displayed in the large side room represent merchants, senators and priests, among others, and would have adorned civic buildings. The more remarkable pieces include a bas-relief of a harnessed camel that would have formed part of a great caravan. The next room contains (on the right) a large door **lintel** bearing an eagle with outstretched wings symbolising Baal-Shamin. The glass cases, meanwhile, display collections of blown-glass and oil lamps, and a fine selection of **tesserae**: fired clay tokens used for gaining admission to ritual banquets. At the far end of the large room stands a huge statue of **Allat** and concludes the exhibits devoted to the desert castles (Qasr al-Hayr al-Charqi).

**Allat, goddess of the Arabs**
Allat, the great Arab goddess venerated before the dawn of Islam, is the protector of the nomads. Depicted with the features of Athena, she is sometimes shown riding a camel, as in the bas-relief in the museum at Aleppo.

The interconnected rooms leading off the left display examples of funerary art. The numerous portrait **busts**★★ would have ornamented the lid of coffins. Many recreate the face of the dead person; others bear a simple veil symbolising the curtain that separates earthly mortals from the after-life. The name of the person is generally accompanied by three letters denoting the word "Alas". The central

The Desert

spot is given over to a splendid **sarcophagus★** with some 20 or so figures bearing offerings. Various **mummies,** together with a selection of rich **textile fragments★** from the clothes they were wearing when interred, are also displayed.

# Tombs★

*The visiting hours for the four daily visits (entrance fee) are displayed at the archeological museum. After purchasing a ticket, visitors should hire a taxi (plenty wait for custom outside the museum entrance) or follow the guide when he leaves by car. The tombs of Iamlichu and the hypogeum of Artaban are generally closed to the public.*

A number of strange funerary towers, several storeys high, are to found standing west of the ruins *(see illustration p 268)*, silhouetted against the sky. Together, they comprise a wholly unique monumental necropolis. The most striking tombs are guarded. A staircase leads to the upper floors. On each level, the superimposed tombs *(loculi)* were sealed with a slab inscribed with the face of the dead person for eternity.

During the 2C, hypogeums replaced the funerary tower-tombs. A narrow stairway descended to a stone door leading into several underground rooms. During the same period, funerary temple-tombs also appeared testifying to the triumph of the Greco-Roman taste of rich aristocratic Palmyrenes.

The tour usually begins with the **Tomb of Elhabel★**, which bears an inscription (beneath the niche above the entrance) that refers to its foundation in 103 AD. The ground floor is decorated with grooved pilasters, Corinthian capitals, and coffered ceilings painted with busts on a blue background. Together with its more sombre upper floors, this family tomb would have had a capacity of about 300! From the top there is a fine view over the site, but be careful because there is no parapet!

The tour continues past the **Efqa spring** (by the Hotel Cham entrance), but warned: the pools have been dry since a landslide occurred in 1993. Ancient steps and a stele recovered there suggest the spring was used when Palmyra was at its height.

A track leads from the Hotel Cham to the **Hypogeum of the Three Brothers★** 150m away. Go down the steps and through a stone door into a long corridor that comes out before an exedra. The frescoes on the wall depict three brothers (Naamai, Male and Saadai). The two lateral tunnels were later to provide more space: in the mid 2C AD the hypogeums were known to have been a hotbed of commercial dealings.

# Arab Citadel★★ (Fakhr ud-Din ibn Ma'ani)

The angular silhouette of the castle perched on the hill above the site is particularly striking. However, although the view over the site as the sun sinks below the horizon is unforgettable, the castle itself is quite disappointing,

*If coming from the site entrance by car, drive round the post office and continue through the outskirts towards the castle, which stands some 2km away (fork left off the main road). Alternatively, you can walk to the top of the citadel in 45min: head across the ruins and take the steep path that zigzags up the side of the hill, perhaps after a tour of the Camp of Diocletian.*

A wooden bridge now spans the **moat★**, dug from the bedrock on the western flank. The first room, covered with a groin vault, is attributed to the Lebanese Emir Fakhr ud-Din (17C), although some consider it to be older (12C-13C). A passageway then leads around a bend to several more rooms and comes out on

*Palmyra*

the upper terrace, from which a breathtaking **view**★★ extends out over the mountains and ruins below; when thrown into relief by the setting sun, the monuments there seem to be rising from the past.

## Excursion to Qasr al-Hayr al-Charqi★

*240km round trip – Allow at least half a day.*
*Ask to be accompanied by a guide – Unguarded site.*

*Not to be confused with the castle of Qasr al-Hayr al-Gharbi, the front of which adorns the entrance of the museum in Damascus.*

*Visitors are strongly advised not to venture into the desert, where there are no signposts, in their own vehicles (unless suited for cross-country driving and accompanied by a guide). The best option is to hire a taxi (budget S£2 000 for a half-day excursion). Ensure that the vehicle is in good working order when booking. Abandon the excursion if it is raining: there is a risk of being washed away in a flash-flood in one of the wadis. From here, Rassafa lies due north (4hr away).*

Qasr al-Hayr al-Charqi is one of a large group of "desert castles" founded by the Umayyads between the 7C and 8C in the *badiya* (the Syrian steppe), mid-way between Palmyra and Deir ez-Zor. The most famous, however, now lie over the modern border in Jordanian territory *(see p 348)*. To arrange a visit it is best to make enquiries in Palmyra where it is reasonably easy to organise an expedition into the desert (a journey of about 120km). It is vital that you get an experienced guide, because there are few obvious landmarks and even fewer directions to follow once you get off the beaten track. As the car sets out across the track beyond Soukhneh, it throws up great clouds of dust. On the way, ask the driver to take in a Bedouin camp and keep an eye out for the shepherds with their large flocks of sheep.

The citadel Qasr al-Hayr al-Charqi

F Lechenet/ALTITUDE

The Desert

The **castle** does not take long to explore, comprising as it does two areas extending to either side of a square **minaret**. The high walls are well-preserved. The first enclosure, which is generally closed off by two beautiful semicircular brick towers and a metal gate, was used as a **caravanserai**. Around the courtyard ran two storeys (now in ruins). The second, larger section opposite, comprises a **residence**, which once was fortified by 28 towers. Among the scattered ruins, there are traces of a mosque that once complemented the minaret in the left-hand corner, and a series of apartments, where several families lived, built around a cistern.

## Making the most of Palmyra

### COMING AND GOING

There are no trains, planes or even camels to take you to Palmyra, only buses, which run between Damascus and Deir ez-Zor. There are also buses from Homs.

If you are driving, Palmyra is three hours' drive from Damascus, on a good road. You should fill up with petrol at Damascus, as there is only one filling station halfway between Damascus and Palmyra, and one at Palmyra, on the edge of the town, 3km in the direction of Damascus. You could also drive from Homs. The road from Deir ez-Zor is as good as that from Damascus and the journey takes 2hr30min. Again, fill up at Deir ez-Zor before leaving.

**By bus –** The journey to Palmyra takes 3hr from Damascus or 2hr30min from Deir ez-Zor. If you are coming from Damascus, make sure you take a bus that goes direct to Palmyra, rather than one that goes via Homs and takes two hours longer.

*Karnak*, 4 daily departures for Damascus, 2 for Homs, 7 for Deir ez-Zor. This is the simplest way of leaving Palmyra, as the booking office is in the town centre. For the other bus companies, you will need to reserve through your hotel or go to the bus station, which is 2km from the town centre (by taxi).

### ADDRESS BOOK

**Tourist information –** Just before the Zenobia Hotel, on the road to the archeological site.

**Main post office –** 50m from the roundabout at the entrance to the site.

**Bank / Currency exchange –** There are no facilities for changing money at Palmyra. Your hotel may be able to help out in an emergency.

**Telephone –** There are card phones at the post office and at the site, inside the Temple of Bel! You can also make calls from the switchboard at the Palmyra Cham Hotel.

**Visa extensions –** There are no facilities for visa extension at Palmyra. The nearest places where this can be done are Homs, Damascus or Deir ez-Zor.

### WHERE TO STAY

The ever-increasing number of tourists visiting Palmyra means that the accommodation available has also increased, to the extent where there are now about 20 hotels, making it the best-equipped town in Syria from this point of view. Each year new establishments open, or are renovated or extended, and there are no end of plans for restaurants with open-air terraces. Despite this, reservation is essential during the high season (from March to May, August to October and in December), except for the cheap hotels, where it is best to arrive early in the morning to be sure of a room for the night. Some hotels' charges increase by 20% during the season.

Palmyra's mid-price and cheap hotels are nearly all found in the main street, near the museum, which is also a good situation for visiting the site. Beware, though: the majority of these hotels don't have air-conditioning, which may be unpleasant during the summer.

*Under US$20*

🕮 **Umayyad Palace Hotel**, Al-Jamarek Sq, ☎ / Fax (31) 910 755 – 11rm 🍴 ⛤ The best place to stay in Palmyra in this category of hotel. In this former town house the rooms are arranged around a small inner courtyard. Peaceful and clean. A friendly family atmosphere. The owner should shortly have finished work on the roof, and plans to provide mattresses for sleeping there. Reductions for students sometimes.

**New Afka Hotel**, in a street near the Palmyra restaurant, ☎/ Fax (31) 910 386 – 17rm 🛏 ⛄ / 🍽 ✗ A family-run hotel providing good service. It also organises excursions around Palmyra: to the lake, or a night camping in the desert. Rooms are basic but clean. Restaurant in the basement. Keep an eye on the prices, as the owner is a bit tricky.

**Palace Hotel**, slightly set back off the main street, on the right when coming from the site, ☎/Fax (31) 911 707 – 15rm 🛏 ⛄ ♪ CC View of the site from some rooms. Spacious, light entrance hall. The rooms are small, but functional.

**Citadel Hotel**, ☎ (31) 910 537, Fax (31) 912 970 – 7rm 🛏 ⛄ ✗ CC When renovated, this hotel should have ten new air-conditioned rooms, as well as a panoramic restaurant on the roof. For the moment, only the first floor of the small building is open, with its simple rooms opening onto a small Bedouin-style salon.

*From US$20-40*

The majority of Palmyra's hotels offer rooms at around US$25, but prices tend to rise in the high season.

**Ishtar Hotel**, main street, ☎ (31) 913 073, Fax (31) 913 260 – 17rm 🛏 🍽 ♪ CC This recently built hotel offers small but reasonable rooms, though some are very noisy.

**Nakhil Hotel**, main street, ☎/ Fax (31) 910 744 – 15rm 🛏 ⛄ ♪ ✗ CC A rustic setting with a wooden staircase and an attractive dining room where all meals are available. Small rooms.

**Tower Hotel**, main street, ☎ (31) 910 116, Fax (31) 910 273 – 15rm 🛏 🍽 ♪ Some rooms are better than others. Several suites with 3 or 4 beds, ideal for small groups. Rather dreary, on the whole.

**Bel Hotel**, main street, ☎ (31) 912 096, Fax (31) 912 099 – 14rm 🛏 ⛄ ♪ CC Three rooms on each floor, not always all that clean. Friendly welcome. The owner can help you with buying souvenirs, as he has several shops in Palmyra.

**Orient Hotel**, just off the main street, ☎ (31) 910 131, Fax (31) 910 700 – 35rm 🛏 ⛄ 🍽 ♪ TV ✗ This recently

renovated hotel is idea for groups. The rooms are well kept, practical and comfortable.

*From US$30-50*

**Middle East Hotel**, ☎ (31) 913 844, Fax (31) 912 401 – 20rm 🛏 🍽 ♪ TV ✗ CC This brand new hotel provides small but comfortable rooms, though unfortunately with no views. To be able to see the archeological site, you will need to go to the top-floor restaurant. Good value for money, nevertheless.

*From US$55-75*

**Heliopolis Hotel**, ☎ (31) 913 921, Fax (31) 913 923 – 32rm 🛏 🍽 ♪ TV ✗ CC A new hotel, a little far from the site, but providing good value. Comfortable rooms, some with splendid views of the ruins and the palm groves. Panoramic restaurant on the fifth floor.

**Villa Palmyra Hotel**, main street, ☎ (31) 910 156, Fax (31) 912 554 – 42rm 🛏 🍽 ♪ TV ✗ CC A neo-Classical white façade with marble inside. Very pretty rooms decorated in blue and pink, with attractive Bedouin rugs on the floors. Soft music in the corridors. English pub in the basement.

*From US$70-90*

**Zenobia Hotel**, near the Temple of Bel, ☎ (31) 910 107, Fax (31) 912 407 – 26rm 🛏 🍽 ♪ TV ✗ CC Once run by the mysterious adventure-seeking Countess d'Andurain, the Zenobia has been recently renovated. The only hotel set inside the ruins is much in demand. The majority of rooms are on the ground floor and are equipped with minibars. Reserve at least 2 months in advance. The terrace, where you can watch the sun set, over a drink, has Corinthian capitals as tables. Camping is an option.

*Over US$190*

**Palmyra Cham Hotel**, Damascus road, ☎ (31) 912 231, Fax (31) 912 245 – 250rm 🛏 🍽 ♪ TV ✗ 🏊 ♨ CC The only hotel outside the town, near the tombs. The setting is a little worn. Spacious rooms. Rather isolated situation, far from town-centre restaurants and shops, but ideal for exploring the palm groves. The swimming pool is pleasant when it gets hot. Fine views of the ruins from some rooms. Shops and bar.

## EATING OUT

The main street of Palmyra is a mixture of small restaurants and souvenir shops. It is difficult to recommend a good restaurant in Palmyra: they all offer more or less the same menu (a selection of meze, kebabs, mensef), which are not bad but never anything special. The slightly more expensive hotel restaurants often provide a self-service buffet. There are two restaurants near the site, for those who want a break during their visit: Waha (Oasis) and Khayyam (good plain cooking).

*Under US$10*

**Wadi Park.** Hidden away in a recess near the museum, this restaurant is above all a haven of peace, in the shade of olive trees. You can eat here (meze, mensef) or simply smoke a hookah and sip a mint tea. Friendly atmosphere.

**Rest-Garden**, opposite the Zenobia hotel, ☎ (31)911 421. A peaceful place for a drink, a meal or simply a rest while visiting the site. If you are not tempted by the small, sulphurous swimming pool, sit in the garden to sample classic Eastern cooking or have a drink.

**Palmyra**, opposite the museum. ♟ A meeting place for the tour groups, with an unrivalled capacity of several hundred places. Lunch and dinner are served either in the dining room or outside in the shady garden. The cooking is good and fresh. The menu is in English, with a good choice of dishes, including a *mensef*.

*From US$10-20*

**Nakhil**, Cham Palace. ♟ The restaurant on the ground floor of the Cham Hotel, opposite the ruins, serves an assortment of *meze* (S£400) and local (kebabs, lamb chops) or western dishes (club sandwich, *salade niçoise*).

**Zenobia**, Zenobia Hotel. ♟ A small bright, air-conditioned dining room with a classic decor, where you can eat comfortably. A pity that the nearby kitchen makes rather too much noise.

**Mermoz**, Villa Palmyra Hotel. ♟ A fine view of the Temple of Bel, as long as you get here before dark. The blue and yellow decor rather competes with the subtle tones of the landscape. The tables are closely packed, to leave room for a pleasant bar at the end of this air-conditioned room.

## OTHER THINGS TO DO

**The desert festival** takes place every year at the end of April. Camel and horse races at the racecourse below the Arab castle. Folk dances from all the different regions of Syria. Visitors should have no problem finding seats in the stands during this three-day event. The troupes of Syrian dancers and singers performing among the colonnades are a lovely sight.

## SHOPPING GUIDE

There are several shops in the main street, selling all sorts of wares, notably the woven Bedouin rugs, which are more difficult to find in Damascus. Coffee-pots and other copper items, jewellery of varying quality, which should be bartered for even more than usual. Don't miss sampling the fresh dates, from September onwards.

**Making the most of Palmyra**

J. F. Galmiche

Corinthian capitals are used as tables at the Zenobia Hotel

# JORDAN

**Official Name:** The Hashemite Kingdom of Jordan
**Area:** 96 188sqkm
**Population:** 5 000 000
**Capitale:** Amman
**Monnaie:** Jordanian dinar (JD)

# Setting the scene

G. Bosio/HOA QUI

The Wadi Rum
desert

# THREE CONTRASTING REGIONS

Jordan is a small kingdom both in terms of surface area (96 188sqkm) and population (5 000 000), which stands half way between that of Lebanon and Israel. It is a nation of considerable variety with a coast famous for its seaside resorts, a major river providing water to a very fertile region, a large expanse of empty desert and high mountains. In any one day, a traveller may journey from Amman and encounter pleasant countryside dominated by fields of wheat and olive groves (north) or the dramatic scenery and fantastic mineral desert of Wadi Rum. Temperature also varies across the land mass, with three defined zones stretching from west to east dictating the conditions in three distinct sections.

## Rift Valley
The Jordan Valley is part of a major geological phenomenon known as the Rift Valley that runs south across Jordan, to form the **Dead Sea** and Wadi Araba. This gigantic furrow traces the fault-line between the two major continental tectonic plates of Europe and Africa as these have been shifted apart. Beyond the confines of Jordan, the Rift Valley stretches from Syria south across East Africa to Mozambique, a distance of almost 5 000km.

In Jordan, the fault line exposes a long depressed area that reaches 406m below sea level, filled in part by the Dead Sea, the shores of which are lowest dry land on the planet. To the north, the rift provides a course for the River Jordan, which is used to irrigate the rich soil and transform it into an important agricultural area (citrus plantations, early fruit and vegetables), whereas to the south it accommodates the more arid and stony Wadi Araba, finally reaching the Gulf of Aqaba and the Red Sea.

## Jordanian plateaux
Dominating the Rift Valley from a height of more than 1500m, the Jordanian plateaux are formed of limestone, marl and chalk in the north and splendid sandstone in the south that endows Petra with its gorgeous hue. Over time, the soft rock has been carved into valleys by the elements, and these have been transformed by man into terraced farmland appropriate for the cultivation of olives and cereals. Jordan's three largest cities, **Amman**, **Irbid** and **Zarqa**, are all situated in the north of the kingdom. In the south, the valleys crossing the King's Highway form impressive canyons (Wadi Mujib and Wadi al-Hassa), but the climate here is too dry to grow crops and only the hills can be farmed. A few trees grow on the higher ground: wild pistachios, cypresses, pines and evergreen oaks that have evolved prickly leaves around their base to safeguard them from marauding goats. It is here on the plateaux that the rare black iris, the emblem of Jordan, grows wild.

## Desert steppe
To the east, the plateau slopes gently down to the steppe and desert. The latter merges with the arid wastes of the Arabian Desert: 75 % of Jordan is desert steppe and home to the Bedouin. Little survives in the arid conditions apart from the odd scrawny herd of sheep and goats. To the north, the wide strip of land stretching towards Iraq is volcanic, the southern extension of the Djebel Druze massif in Syria. The features around **Wadi Rum** include splendid sandstone cliffs that tower above the pre-Cambrian plateau, the most ancient stratum of the earth's crust.

# MODERN JORDAN

*For history prior to the First World War, see p 12.*

Jordan's recent history has been severely affected by the repercussions of external events, but has survived as a result of the kingdom's astonishing internal stability under the rule of wise monarchs like Abdullah and Hussein.

## A Transjordanian emirate

The First World War precipitated the fall and disintegration of the Ottoman Empire and the redistribution of land to form various Middle Eastern states. In 1922, in response to a decision by the League of Nations, Great Britain inherited Palestine and Transjordan, two areas separated by the valley of the River Jordan. Until a mandate could be put into place, **Abdullah**, brother of King Faisal and descendant of the Hashemite dynasty who had reigned in Mecca since the 10C, was installed as the head of the Transjordanian emirate. The country at that time had a population of 225 000 and was designed to provide a buffer state between France (ruling over Syria and Lebanon), Ibn Saud the Arab who conquered Mecca in 1924 and thereafter seized control of the Arabian peninsula, and the expansionist-driven Jews in Palestine who were encouraged to entrench themselves there by **Lord Balfour** (1917). The British Secretary of State advocated the creation of a national Jewish homeland with the aim of reassembling the communities which, since the end of the 19C, had been clamouring for the resurrection of a Jewish state. When independence was established in 1946, Abdullah was proclaimed king.

## Arab-Israeli conflict

The Israeli declaration of independence on 14 May 1948 prompted the first Arab-Israeli war that was to draw in all the neighbouring powers and end in defeat for the Arab side. In this way, Israel secured a territory that was far more viable than that which had been suggested in proposals drawn up by the United Nations. Paradoxically, despite being on the losing side, Jordan gained the West Bank, an additional territory situated west of the River Jordan that included Jerusalem. As a result of the conflict, 100 000 Palestinians fled to Jordan. On 20 July 1951 King Abdullah was assassinated in Jerusalem by an activist linked to the Palestinian leader Hadj Amin al-Husseini, no doubt in an act of reprisal for having sided with Israel in the peace negotiations.

His grandson, the late King **Hussein**, acceded to the throne in 1953, aged 17. He rapidly gained a reputation as a skilful diplomat, a vital quality in a country the size of Jordan, and proved remarkably capable in dealing with crisis situations. The fact that he reigned for such a long time in this troubled region is quite astonishing. During his reign, he managed to survive the Suez crisis of 1956, succeeded in securing the departure of the last British contingent in 1958, supported the creation of the Palestinian Liberation Organisation in 1964 and foiled a plot to overthrow him two years later.

## 1967: Humiliation in the Six-Day War

In 1967 Egypt (an ally of Jordan) invaded Sinai and the war erupted for the third time. After a short week of action, the Hebrew state riposted by seizing control of East Jerusalem and the West Bank; 250 000 Palestinians crossed the river and fled east into Jordan, and the national boundaries reverted to those established in 1948. After this crushing defeat, the kingdom decided to provide the Palestinians with a rearguard against Israel. As the *Fedayin* became increasingly powerful they posed

*Modern Jordan*

an ever-greater threat to the reigning monarch caught in the conflict between Israel and the Palestinian resistance movement. The crisis came to a head in 1970, after the hijacking of several commercial aircraft. During the famous month known as **Black September,** the Jordanian army dismantled the Palestinian bases in the kingdom. The Hashemite dynasty continued to administer the territory occupied by the Israeli army in the West Bank and abstained from intervening in the fourth Arab-Israeli conflict (War of Yom Kippur).

In 1976 Jordan decided to improve its industry. In December 1987 the **Intifada** began to stir popular Palestinian support in the occupied territories. On 31 July 1988 King Hussein declared his kingdom's renunciation of all claims to the occupied territories in favour of the Palestinians and severed all judicial and administrative responsibilities therewith.

## Peace at last

In 1991 Jordan was one of the few Arab nations to support Iraq after the invasion of Kuwait, sparking off the **Gulf War**, and it was not long before 350 000 Jordanian Palestinians flooded back to the kingdom. This firm stand, which rallied the Palestinians, was to ensure the survival of the Hashemite kingdom, even if it was to somewhat tarnish Jordan's image in the eyes of the pro-Western powers and the oil-enriched emirates. For in so doing, Jordan was able to persuade the PLO to enter into peace negotiations with Israeli and Palestinian leaders and agree an Israeli-Palestinian pact on the autonomy of the occupied territories. This was eventually signed on 26 October 1993. Since then, the two neighbouring countries have co-operated on several projects, the most symbolic being the establishment of two frontier posts between Israel and Jordan. Other initiatives include settling the problem of managed water supply (construction of a dam, pipeline and desalination plant). Meanwhile, the kingdom continues to progress towards democratisation and maintains its commitment to economic liberalism. After an eventful 46-year reign, King Hussein named his son, Prince Abdullah, as his heir on 25 January 1999, and died on 2 February. **Abdullah II**, who was born in 1962, thus succeeded him, with his Palestinian wife, Queen Rania, at his side.

King Abdullah II and Queen Rania

M. Attar/SYGMA

# Economy

With a small population and poor subsoil, Jordan is dependent on international aid and struggles to limit its national debt. Under the supervision of the International Monetary Fund, the country has implemented major measures to ensure recovery that are bound to bear fruit as long as the area remains at peace. Significant moves have involved the privatisation of such vital industries as tourism and transport, which, it is hoped, will boost the local economy.

One in two people are employed by the state in administrative roles; one in four works in the services sector, so Jordan as a whole is heavily involved in the service rather than manufacturing or agriculture industry. Indeed, the Amman stock exchange is one of the most important in the Middle East. **Agriculture** (production of barley, wheat and tomatoes) meanwhile provides employment for only 6 % of the working population.

Although it has no oil deposits, Jordan is the second largest exporter of phosphates in the world. **Industry** is limited to a small, highly dynamic private sector. Construction and public works provide the bulk of contracts for a large section of the working population. Since 1993, Iraq has been Jordan's leading economic partner, while the United States is its second-largest supplier of goods.

Jordan employs immigrant workers mainly in the field of construction and tourism, so if the waiter in a restaurant asks you whether you have ever visited or like Egypt, you are advised to devise a diplomatic reply; this will probably prompt him to say that he comes from the Nile Delta or Cairo. Conversely, a similar proportion of Jordanians (20 %) work abroad.

# Public administration

Jordan is divided into **twelve provinces**. Most of the country's population is concentrated in the three largest provinces in the north (Amman, Zarqa and Irbid) where most of the Palestinian community are also resident. The provinces south of Wadi Mujib, meanwhile, are home to Jordanian heritage.

# Education

With 1 200 000 children of school age, the kingdom has invested great effort in providing a good system of education for its young people. The universities of Amman and Irbid are renowned.

Major reforms legislated in 1994 have transformed Jordanian schooling, ensuring that it is free and compulsory for all between the ages of 6 and 16. There follows an optional two-year programme of general or specialised teaching. All school and college students wear uniform – a souvenir of the British mandate.

The grades gained in the *Tawjihi* – the final secondary examinations – determine the right to go to university. Pupils from poorer areas and the children of certain administrations have access to a quota of places destined to favour their entry into certain faculties.

The **six** state **universities**, which lost no time in opening sites on the Internet, have beautiful campuses in Amman, Irbid and at Muta (near Kerak). Private institutions also provide higher education facilities. But many from the 100 000-strong Jordanian student population, maybe as many as a third, prefer to study abroad, preferably in Britain or the United States. The UNRWA (United Nations Relief and Works Agency for Palestinian Refugees) also plays an important role in the education of Palestinian children.

**Education**

# Practical information

Camels being
transported

# BEFORE GOING

## • Time difference

Local time in Jordan is two hours ahead of GMT (or UTC). When it is midday in Amman, it will be 10am in London, 5am in New York, 4am in Chicago, 5am in Montreal, 5am in Toronto, 8pm in Sydney and 10pm in Auckland (times given are winter times and do not take account of countries using DST). Jordan does not change its clocks to DST in summer.

## • International dialling

To telephone Jordan from overseas, dial 00 + 962 + the regional code (without dialling 0) + the number you wish to call.

*For local codes in Jordan, see p 297.*

## • When to go

You will be made to feel welcome in Jordan all year round. If you are thinking of visiting Petra, however, avoid the **summer**. The heat wave which lasts from June to September in southern Jordan, with temperatures in excess of 35°C, is not conducive to exploring the ancient Nabataean capital, even if you can be sure that it won't rain. The **spring** and **autumn** are the best seasons for appreciating Jordan's heritage, when the days are pleasantly warm and sunny. In springtime you will be able to enjoy the verdant countryside, with flowers everywhere, after the winter rains. The weeks around Easter represent the high season. At this time of year you should book your accommodation in advance (at the very latest when you arrive in Amman) and visit the sites as soon as they open and before the tour groups get there. Southern Jordan is particularly pleasant in **winter**. While it may be snowing in Amman, it is rare to have two cloudy days in a row in Aqaba. It's even possible to go swimming at Christmas in the Red Sea, with water temperatures around 20°C! At this time of year the low winter sun shows up the contours of the mountains and monuments extraordinarily well and the summer heat haze has disappeared.

Those who don't get up early will find the days very short. Night falls even earlier in Jordan than in Syria, as it is nearer the equator.

To help you organise your excursions, the sunrise and sunset times at Amman at the beginning of each season are as follows:

|  | sunrise | sunset |
|---|---|---|
| 21 March | 5.40am | 5.45pm |
| 21 June | 5.30am | 7.45pm |
| 21 September | 6.30am | 6.30pm |
| 21 December | 6.30am | 4.30pm |

## • Packing list *(see p 80)*

## • A holiday for everyone *(see p 81)*

## • Address book

*Tourist information*

**UK –** Jordan Tourist Board, 11 Blades Court, Dodar Road, London SW12 2NV
☎ (020) 8877 4524 Fax (020) 8874 4219

**USA –** Jordan Tourist Board, 3504 International Drive NW, Washington DC 20008 ☎ 202 966 2664 Fax 202 966 3110

It is also worth asking at the Royal Jordanian Airways offices worldwide for tourist information.

*Web sites*

Some sites worth taking a look at before you leave:

**Jordan on line** (www.jordan-online.com)

**Tourism** (www.accessme.com/tourism or www.arabia.com/jordan)

**UK Jordan Embassy** (www.jordanembassyuk.gov.jo)

**US Jordan Embassy** (www.jordanembassyus.org

**National Information Centre** (www.nic.gov.jo)

**Royal Jordanian Airlines** (www.rja.com.jo)

**Newsgroup** (news:soc.culture.jordan)

*Embassies and consulates*

**UK** – 6 Upper Phillimore Gardens, London W8 7HB ☎ (020) 7937 3685, Fax (020) 7937 8795

**USA** – Washington DC: 3504 International Drive NW, Washington DC 20008 ☎ (202) 966 2664 Fax (202) 686 4491

New York: 866 United Nations Plaza, Room 554, New York NY10017 ☎ (212) 752 0145 Fax (212) 826 0830

Houston: PO Box 3727, Houston, TX 77253 ☎ (713) 224 2911 Fax (713) 224 2301

Detroit: 28551 Southfield Road, Suite 203, Lathrup Village, Michigan 48076 ☎ (248) 557 4377 Fax (248) 557 4517

San Francisco: 972 Mission Street, 4th Floor, San Francisco, California 94103 ☎ (415) 546 1155 Fax (415) 546 4041

**Canada** – 100 Bronson Ave, Suite 701, Ottawa, Ontario OT K1N 6RA ☎ (613) 238 8090

**Australia** – 20 Roebuck St, Redhill, Canberra, ACT 2603 ☎ (06) 295 9951

## • Documents required

This information is given as a general guideline only and may change. Contact the Jordanian embassy in your country for an update at least a month before you leave.

*ID, visas*

Your **passport** must contain a visa and must be valid at least six months after the date of your return. The **visa** may be obtained either from the Jordanian embassy in the country of your departure, or at Amman airport or at the Syrian border when you cross into Jordan (the latter option is the simplest and cheapest). The UK and US embassies also now offer an on-line visa application service (see above for web site addresses). A single-entry visa is valid for three months from the date of issue, or one month if it is obtained at a border control post. After two weeks it must be stamped by the police authorities. This costs nothing and can be done in most of the main towns in Jordan (in Amman there are police stations at Ras al-Aïn and Abdali). There is a fine of JD1 per day if this formality is undergone late, or when you leave the country if you have not done it at all. The visa application must be accompanied by two passport photos. The cost varies according to nationality.

Groups of at least six people may be exempt from the need for a visa and exit tax (ask at the Jordanian embassy for more information). Otherwise, you must pay an **exit tax** when leaving Jordan (JD10 at the airport, JD6 at Aqaba port, JD4 by road), which is only payable in cash.

For access from Israel or Egypt, contact the embassies of these countries for information before leaving.

**Before going**

## Customs

**Imports –** You are allowed to import 200 cigarettes, 250 cigars or 200g of tobacco, as well as a bottle of wine or spirits and a reasonable quantity of perfume. There is no limit on importing currency, although large sums should be declared. If you have a video camera in your luggage, this will be mentioned on your passport. Presents are allowed up to a value of JD50 or US$150.

**Driving –** There are no particular restrictions apart from insurance, which costs around JD30 to obtain the necessary document.

**Exports –** The export of local currency is limited to JD300.

## Vaccination

No vaccinations are required for entering Jordan.

## Driving licence

An international driving licence is required for those wishing to hire vehicles, and may be asked for by the Jordanian police.

## • Local currency

Everything is paid for in dinars.

### Cash

You will need a day or two to get used to the Jordanian currency. The Jordanian dinar, which is often called the "jaydee" and is written JD, is divided not into 100 but 1 000 *fils*. Prices are usually written in dinars, followed by 3 decimals (for example 1.350), which is logical as the system is based on thousandths and not on hundredths. Just to confuse things, the Jordanians often speak of 10 *qirsh* or *piastre*, which is equal to 100 fils, or 0.1 dinar.

There are notes representing 0.5, 1, 5, 10 and 20 dinars. Those who enjoy collecting will be pleased to find at least ten different coins, five in *fils* and five more recent, of the same value, in *qirsh*. The coins in *qirsh* are easier to read and are gradually replacing the *fils*. You should always carry some small change on you for taxis, drinks and tips.

### Currency exchange

There is no black market in Jordan. Money can be changed at the many town-centre exchange bureaux or at the twenty or so different banks throughout the country. Avoid changing money at hotels, as the rates they offer are not so good. You will not need American dollars. Change all your dinars before leaving the country, as you will have difficulty changing them into other currencies elsewhere.

### Travellers' cheques

These can be useful to change money in the majority of banks, but can rarely be used to pay for goods or services. Take proof of identity with you, as well as receipts from any purchases you have made, as some banks will ask to see these. There is a charge of US$5 per transaction.

### Credit cards

American Express, Diner's Club, Mastercard and Visa are accepted by all restaurants and hotels of a reasonable standard or above, as well as by the majority of tourist shops. The cheaper hotels may accept payment by credit card, but may charge an additional commission of as much as 4%, as may certain shops. It is possible to withdraw money with a Visa card (Arab Bank, Housing Bank), although with other cards it is more difficult. There is a cash dispenser (Visa, Mastercard) in Downtown Amman (British Bank of the Middle East, withdrawal limit JD500 per week).

## • Spending money

With the exception of site entry charges, the cost of living is around 20% higher in Jordan than in Syria. Transport is cheap: a litre of petrol costs around 50 US cents, and to cross the country (330km from Amman to Aqaba) with the most luxurious bus company costs less than US$8. Taxi fares are rarely much more than US$2. As for eating out, this is also very reasonable, and a complete meal will not be much more than US$10. However, international telephone calls will rapidly increase your hotel bill.

These **daily budgets** are calculated **per person**, based on **two people sharing** a double room and car hire. They include accommodation, meals and transport, but not site entry charges, drinks and souvenirs.

You should be able to get by on a minimum of **US$35** per day per person. This includes staying in very cheap hotels, eating on the hoof or in small restaurants and visiting the sites by public transport (or sometimes by taxi). Many sites are not accessible by bus, and sometimes a taxi is the only solution for part of the journey. Even if you are on a tight budget, it's worth considering car hire if there are several of you.

Allowing **US$90** per day, you would be able to hire a mid-price vehicle and afford hotel rooms with air-conditioning and en-suite bathrooms. You would also be able to eat out in a good restaurant and hire a vehicle to visit the sites. From upwards of **US$160** per day, you would stay in hotels with every modern facility and you could hire chauffeur-driven transport.

## • Booking in advance (see p 84)
For how to telephone Jordan, see p 292.

## • Travel Insurance (see p 85)

# GETTING THERE
(see p 85)

# THE BASICS

## • Address book

*Tourist information*

The majority of tourist sites have Visitors' Centres, and the tourist police can also be helpful. Jordan has a **Ministry of Tourism**, 3rd Circle, Amman ☎ (6) 464 23 11, 8am-2pm, which is also Amman's main tourist office.

*Embassies and consulates*

It is a good idea to keep a photocopy of your passport in a separate safe place, to make its replacement easier in case the original is lost or stolen.

**UK** – Abdoun, Amman (behind the Orthodox Club) ☎ (6) 592 31 00, extensions 2245 and 2269. Open Sunday to Thursday, 8.30am-12noon, though you can telephone until 3pm. You can also ring ☎ (6) 592 65 81 or (6) 59265 86. Outside normal working hours you can call (6) 552 99 99 in an emergency and leave a message.

The basics

There is also a British consulate in Aqaba, PO Box 485, ☎ (3) 201 25 25 or 201 31 11.

**USA** – PO Box 354, Between 2nd & 3rd Circles, Jebel Amman ☎ (6) 592 01 01 or 592 32 93. Telephone calls 1.30-4pm, Sunday to Thursday. Fax (6) 592 41 02.

**Canada** – PO Box 815403, Pearl of Shmeissani Building, Amman ☎ (6) 566 61 24, Fax (6) 568 92 27. Open 8.30am-4.30pm, Sunday to Thursday.

**Australia** – Between 4th & 5th Circles, Zahran St, Jebel Amman ☎ (6) 5930246.

Syria – 4th Circle, Amman, ☎ (6) 464 19 35.

## ● Opening and closing times

Friday is a day of rest in Jordan. Banks, government departments and the majority of businesses are closed on that day. Some are also closed from Thursday afternoon onwards. The morning is the best time for getting things done. During the month of **Ramadan** office hours are generally restricted (9.30am-2pm). In Jordan the year is divided into two administrative seasons; summer begins on 1 April and ends on 30 September. The rest of the year is considered as winter.

### Banks
8.30am-12.30pm, sometimes until 3pm or 4pm. Closed Fridays and Saturdays. Currency exchange bureaux stay open until the evening, as well as on Saturdays.

### Post Offices
Open Saturday to Thursday, 7am-7pm (5pm in winter), Fridays 7am-1pm.

### Shops
Open 9.30am-7pm, sometimes closed 1.30-3.30pm.

### Restaurants
Lunch is served late, from 1.30pm onwards, and dinner from 9-11pm. Some restaurants in the centre of Amman close at 9pm. Traditional cafés and fast-food restaurants stay open all day and sometimes until late at night.

### Offices
Government departments: 8am-2pm. Private sector: 8am-1pm and 3.30-7.30pm (8.30am-1.30pm and 3-8.30pm in winter).

### Museums and sites
8am-6pm (5pm in winter). Some museums are closed on Tuesdays or Fridays. Major sites are open all year.

## ● Museums, monuments and archeological sites

### Entrance fees
Entrance fees for visiting museums and sites are usually JD1 or 2 for foreigners (as opposed to JD 0.15 for Jordanians), with the notable exception of Jerash (JD5) and above all Petra, where the prices are much higher (see p 380). It is usual to tip the Jordanian, official or otherwise, who allows you to visit a non-guarded site. Foreigners are not allowed to enter mosques.

## ● Postal services

Send your post as soon as possible if you don't want to arrive before it does! Allow between one and three weeks for Europe, and about two weeks for America and Australia. Postal charges are reasonable: JD 0.20 for postcards. There is a poste restante service at Amman.

## • Telephone and fax

All the main towns in Jordan now have telephone kiosks taking cards, for local or international calls. The two companies ALO and JPP are in fierce competition, the first being more widely found than the second. Some ALO booths take Visa cards. The cards (several different denominations) are sold at newsagents' shops or sometimes in small shops near the phone booths. You can also telephone and send faxes from your hotel, but this will work out far more expensive. Mobile phones are very popular in Jordan and can be hired from any number of companies in Amman. Mobile numbers begin with 079.

***Jordan Mobile Telephone Services*** ☎ (6) 551 20 10
***Tele Link*** ☎ (6) 586 10 55.

*Codes and charges*

Jordan has adopted the international system of adding 0 to the number for national calls, and 00 for international calls. Each region has a local code.

**Calling Jordan from overseas**
00 + 962 + regional code (without the 0) + the number you wish to call.

**Calling the UK from Jordan**
00 + 44 + the number you wish to call (without the 0)

**Calling the USA and Canada from Jordan**
00 + 1 + the number you wish to call

**Calling Australia from Jordan**
00 + 61 + the number you wish to call

**Calling New Zealand from Jordan**
00 + 64 + the number you wish to call

**Calling Syria from Jordan**
00 + 963 + the number you wish to call (without the 0)

**Calling within Jordan (same region)**
The number you wish to call direct (without the 0 or the local code)

**Calling within Jordan (different region)**
0 + local code + the number you wish to call

**Local telephone codes**

| | |
|---|---|
| Irbid, Um Qeis, Jarash, Ajlun | 2 |
| Aqaba, Petra, Maan, Kerak | 3 |
| Salt, Dea Sea, Jordan Valley, Madaba | 5 |
| Amman | 6 |
| Kan Zaman, Umm al-Amad | 7 |
| Amman airport | 8 |

**Charges –** The majority of hotels charge for a minimum of three minutes, and overcharge grossly for telephone calls, up to twice their real cost.

*Directory enquiries*

**National –** ☎ 121 for Amman, ☎ 131 for the rest of the country. A yellow pages directory is available in the main hotels.

**International –** ☎ 0132.

## • Internet

The Jordanians are fascinated by the Internet and more and more cyber-cafés are being opened. There are plenty in Amman (JD1-2 per hour), but they can also be found at Irbid, Wadi Moussa (Petra), Madaba and Aqaba (JD8 per hour!).

## • Local time

See "Time difference" *(see p 292)*. Jordan and Syria observe the same time.

## • Public holidays

Banks, offices and many shops are closed on public holidays.

**Fixed public holidays**
New Year: 1 January
Tree Day: 15 January
Arab League Day: 22 March
Labour Day: 1 May
Independence Day: 25 May
Anniversary of the Great Arab Revolt: 10 June
King Hussein's accession: 11 August
King Hussein's birthday: 14 November
Christmas Day: 25 December

**Changeable public holidays**
To find out the variable dates of the Muslim holidays, see the chapter on "Religions" *p 48.*

# GETTING AROUND

From camel to aeroplane, the choice of transport is yours for getting around Jordan. The roads are excellent and mostly fairly empty once outside Amman, which means that hiring a car is an ideal way of discovering the variety and beauty of the landscape. You will be able to reach the main tourist sites without any difficulty if you choose to travel by public transport. However, the itineraries we suggest will be more difficult to follow by this means, in particular the Kings' Highway. For the more remote sites (for example the desert castles, or Umm al-Jimal) it is essential to have your own transport (taxi or hired car). Hiring a taxi by the day is not expensive.

## • By car

An international driving licence is essential for driving in Jordan.

*Rental*
Most of the local car-hire firms are found in Amman, as well as the international companies such as Avis, Europcar and Hertz. Some companies prefer the driver to be over 25 and to have held a licence for at least a year. There is sometimes a minimum hire period of two days. Prices vary according to the category and age of the vehicle, the season, the length of the hire period and the choice of limited or unlimited kilometres. Opting for a limited number of kilometres can

J. F. Galmiche

Getting around

be more economical, as long as you don't exceed the agreed limit (which may vary between 100 and 250km per day). A mid-price vehicle (either automatic or manual, with air-conditioning) would cost around JD40 per day, for a hire period of 7-13 days (or JD25 per day for a basic vehicle) with unlimited kilometres. Make sure you understand what is covered by the insurance and the amount of the excess. Fully comprehensive insurance (optional) could make up half the hire cost. A vehicle hired in Amman can be returned in Aqaba, on payment of an additional JD25-40. To add a second driver's name to the contract, there is sometimes an extra charge of JD3 per day. The full rental price is payable on signature of the contract and a guarantee deposit will be requested, JD200-400, payable by credit card. The international car hire companies are noticeably more expensive than the Jordanian ones, however they will give a sizeable discount if the vehicle is hired direct in Jordan and not via their international representatives overseas.

You should allow JD20 per day for a chauffeur, plus his board and lodging. This service is worth considering, as it means you also have an excellent guide and interpreter with you. Four wheel drive vehicles can be hired at Aqaba.

**Borders –** Hired cars cannot cross international borders, whether it is to visit Syria or Israel. If you wish to visit both Syria and Jordan, you must hire a car in each country and cross the border by taxi or by bus.

### Road network

Jordan's roads are well kept. The proliferation of roads around Aman thins out towards the south. Road signs are good quality, and are in English as well as Arabic. Brown panels indicate tourist sites. Under no circumstances should you set off on desert tracks without a guide.

### Driving

Motorists drive on the right in Jordan. There is a speed limit of 40kph on ordinary roads and 90kph on motorways. Breaking the limit incurs heavy fines, and radar traps are common, so it is a good idea to get into the habit of driving slowly, like the Jordanians. After all, you're on holiday! In town, watch out for sudden manœuvres by Jordanian motorists who don't seem to know that indicators exist.

### Fuel

A litre of 4-star petrol (*mountaz*) costs JD0.32. A full tank will cost you around US$25.

### Parking in town

Apart from Amman, you will have no problem parking in town. Tourist sites always have good-sized car parks. The centre of Amman is much quieter after 7pm, when you will easily be able to park in one of the small side-streets (parking on the main streets is forbidden).

### In emergencies

Minor cases of damage (such as a broken rear-view mirror) are usually sorted out amicably with the other driver, if another vehicle is involved, or with the car-hire company. You will have to pay the exact amount not covered by the excess. Beware: in case of a more serious accident, the Jordanian authorities may keep you in the country until the insurance company has taken the matter in hand (3-4 days). This could be a good argument for starting your visit to Jordan with a car tour as soon as you arrive in the country, and exploring Amman and its surrounding region after you have returned your car. If you have an accident,

**Getting around**

you should contact the police as quickly as possible before any vehicle is moved, as well the car-hire company and your embassy, if anyone is injured. **Police** (in case of accident) and **traffic police:** ☎ (6) 489 63 90.

### ● Camper vans

This means of transport is very suitable for travelling in Jordan and is becoming increasingly popular. It's a wonderful experience to wake up to the wild landscape overlooking the Dead Sea. But there's a major drawback: you have to bring your own vehicle, as they are not available for hire. When you decide to stop for the night, you may find yourself surrounded by a persistent crowd of curious children.

### ● Taxis

If you don't want to hire a car, you can hire a taxi by the day. This is a very good solution for visiting the desert castles. Ask for information at your hotel, or from any taxi driver in town. In the bus stations you can find shared taxis, which take several different passengers to the same destination (usually between the main towns). There are also the **taxi-service** vehicles, which leave when all places are taken. These are used for shorter journeys, and you usually won't have to wait too long. In town, don't even bother with public transport. The municipal buses and taxis only have their destinations written in Arabic, and taxi fares are very competitive (on average around JD1 in Amman).

### ● By train

The only railway that carries passengers is the line which runs between Jordan and Syria once a week. The other line, to Aqaba, is used for transporting phosphate.

### ● By bus

The bus network links almost all the towns in Jordan, and provides the country's main means of transport. The most comfortable is the national company **Jett**, whose buses have air-conditioning and television, but they only serve the main towns (Aqaba, Petra, Amman). There are several bus stations in Amman, depending on your destination. Buses leave either when they are full, or sometimes at fixed times. They are not particularly comfortable (no air conditioning).

### ● Hitch-hiking *(see p 94)*

### ● Domestic flights

**Royal Wings** provides daily domestic flights between Amman and Aqaba (1hr). The fare is JD30 for a single. For information and reservations ☎ (6) 487 52 01, or from any **Royal Jordanian** agency in Jordan or overseas.

### ● Organised tours and excursions

There are over 200 travel agents in Jordan, which concern themselves mainly with receiving tour groups and selling plane tickets. They don't have much experience of independent travellers. In Amman, they are to be found in Al-Hussein St and above the Jabri restaurant. Your hotel will probably be of more use in helping you with your arrangements. The **Jett** bus company organises day trips from Amman to Petra, Hammamat Main and the Dead Sea. Qualified Ministry of Tourism guides are to be found at the sites of Petra, Jerash, Madaba and Amman's citadel. If they have a professional card, it is a sign that they are reliable.

*Getting around*

# BED AND BOARD

## • Where to stay

With the exception of Amman, Petra and Aqaba, you may often have difficulty finding somewhere to stay near the sites you want to visit.

## • Various categories

### Hotels

You will find **very cheap** hotels (around US$10-20) in the town centres. The level of comfort is basic (sheets that are too short, sagging mattresses, inefficient electric fans) and they may be in a noisy district, but you will be sure of a friendly welcome. The shared bathrooms always have a shower, usually hot. There are also **simple** hotels, around US$20-40, usually in the same areas of town, but which provide en-suite bathrooms, air-conditioning and television.

From US$40 upwards, you will find more **comfortable** hotels, situated in quieter districts. The rooms have their own telephone, a better standard of furnishing and towels are provided.

If you pay over US$70, you can expect a hotel with **every modern facility** and excellent service, including satellite television.

The **international class** of hotels, from US$130 upwards (Intercontinental, Marriott, Mövenpick) offer all the standard services. They are mainly frequented by businessmen.

In the basic hotels always ask to see your room before committing yourself.

Single rooms are rare. If you are travelling alone, you will be offered a double room with a reduction of around 20 %.

When booking a double room, you will be offered the choice between a "queen bed" (double bed) or twin beds.

In the hotels of a higher standard, the price of the room is supplemented by an additional 13 % government tax and 10 % service, known as "plus, plus". Breakfast is sometimes included in the room price.

J. F. Galmiche

Bed and board

New forms of accommodation making an appearance include family boarding houses (Madaba, Umm Qais) and self-catering accommodation (Dana, Azraq). *Rest houses* are exactly the same as hotels, but are run by a social organisation.

### Camping
With the exception of two camp sites with tents already pitched at Dana and Wadi Rum, Jordan has few camp sites.

### Youth hostels
There are no youth hostels in Jordan. The YWCA in Amman (3rd Circle, near the Ministry of Tourism) only accepts young women.

## • Eating out
Jordan is not known for its cuisine and in some restaurants more care is devoted to the decor than to the preparation of the food. The buffet system is very popular, particularly at the tourist sites, and provides generous helpings, if not much variety.

Alcohol is served in hotels and tourist restaurants. Bars that serve alcohol are not visible from the street and are mainly found in Amman. Alcohol can be bought in special shops or supermarkets in Amman and Aqaba. During the month of Ramadan, alcohol is only sold to non-Arab foreigners.

### Hotels
All the bigger hotels have good quality restaurants, though the cuisine on offer is often international (Italian, Mexican, French). The bill bears no relation to the price of the accommodation and will rarely exceed US$20 per person (without alcohol).

### Restaurants
There are smart restaurants offering a range of prices from US$10 to US$20 per person, again not including alcohol. Expect to pay more if you opt for fresh fish, however. There are, nevertheless, popular restaurants where you can eat well from US$5 per person.

### In the street
You will be continuously tempted by the little snack bars which serve sandwiches filled with *felafel* (fried balls of puréed chick peas) and *shawarma* (slices of roast lamb or chicken). For fast food fans, these restaurants are increasing in number (hamburger, pizza, *chilli*), and can be found in Amman, Aqaba and Petra.

# SPORTS AND PASTIMES

If you are staying for quite a long time, you may be able to take part in your favourite activities at some of the smart clubs in Amman, for a fee. As well as sport (tennis, squash, swimming), you will be able to find partners for a game of billiards, bridge or bowling (address from the Ministry of Tourism). The bigger hotels have well-equipped health clubs.

## • Sports
### Walking
Until recently there were no marked footpaths, but walking is starting to emerge as a popular activity, thanks to the **RSCN** (*see p 372*). Several kilometres of footpaths have been created around Dana and guides are available to accompany you. The Wadi Rum is a breathtaking setting for walks and you can arrange to have your luggage carried for you.

### Climbing
The Wadi Rum has some fine cliffs for climbing enthusiasts and you will find experienced guides to accompany you (*see p 400*).

### Tennis
There are tennis courts in some of the larger hotels.

### Horse riding
**Arabian Horse Club**, Amman ☎ (6) 580 12 33.

### Golf
**Golf Club**, Amman ☎ (6) 792 07 62.

## • Water sports
The Red Sea is a paradise for water-sport enthusiasts. On the other hand, don't expect to be able to do anything much in the Dead Sea, as the high level of salinity makes underwater swimming impossible.

### Swimming
All the larger hotels have swimming pools. Non-residents are admitted for a daily fee, which is often high (around US$10-20!).

### Scuba diving
Aqaba is world-famous for scuba diving. You can swim there all year round and the underwater life is spectacular.
Experienced divers should bring evidence of their level of ability.

### Glass-bottomed boats
Ideal at Aqaba, for admiring the coral and fish.

## • Night life
Amman is a city where there is always something going on, with a good choice of high quality events, such as films, exhibition openings, conferences or concerts. Both Jordanian and foreign cultural centres plan a regular programme of events. Get hold of the free monthly paper **Jordan Today** from the reception of one of the bigger hotels, as it is an excellent source of information on Jordanian cultural life. Events listings are also published in the weekly **Jordan Times**. Outside Amman it is a different matter, with few possibilities for going out.

### Concerts and live shows
Concerts are often held in hotel bars.
One of the main cultural events of the year is the festival at Jarash, held in July in the superb setting of the ancient ruins of the city of Gerasa.

### Cinemas
Foreign films are always shown in their original version with Arabic sub-titles. There are two good cinemas near the Forte Grande Hotel in Amman which show European and American films.

### Theatres
Your main problem will be the language barrier. However, for the past few years there has been an English performance by two Jordanian actors (Nabil and Hisham) of a satirical play on Jordanian society and life in general. **Nabil & Hisham Theatre**, Rainbow St, 1st Circle, Amman ☎ (6) 462 51 55.

### Discotheques
These are gradually developing and tend to attract a young clientele. They are nearly all found in the main hotels in Amman.

**Sports and pastimes**

# SHOPPING

Apart from producing cheap souvenirs, the fabrication of excellent quality arts and crafts has developed in Jordan in recent years, notably the carpets woven by the Bani Hamida. If you are planning to visit Syria as well as Jordan, buy your souvenirs in Damascus or Aleppo, with the exception of typically Jordanian items. There is more choice and the prices are lower.

## ● What's on offer

### Arts and crafts

You may be tempted by some of the many cheap items on display in the overflowing souvenir shop-windows. A fair proportion of them come from Syria (embroidered tablecloths, marquetry), Egypt (perfumes, copperware), Iran (miniatures) or Afghanistan (jewellery).

Local items include **Hebron glass**, traditionally made from sand, but now produced from recycled bottles. The vases and bottles come in shades of blue (cobalt and turquoise) and are often decorated with Arabic calligraphy.

**Jerusalem ceramic ware** consists of various sizes of plates, decorated with peacocks, fish or bunches of grapes on a white background. As their name suggests, they are Palestinian in origin. They are made in workshops at Naur, south of Amman.

You will be assured that the patterns are made up of entirely natural colours in the **bottles of sand** that are for sale at Petra. You can order one with your name in it, which will be made during your visit of the site.

**Olive wood** is used to carve figures or camels by Jordanian craftsmen.

The traditional musical instrument of the Bedouins is the **rababah**, but you will not find it easy to play.

**Copperware** is always attractive, if not always very carefully engraved.

**Miniature tents**, rather like Christmas cribs with their little figurines, make an original souvenir, though tend to be difficult to transport.

At Aqaba you will find **coral necklaces**, whose pink or turquoise colours are not entirely natural.

### Antiques

There are a few 19C pistols to be found, with ivory-inlaid butts, and plenty of imitation coins, pottery, cylindrical seals etc.

### Carpets

You won't find knotted carpets in Jordan, as these are not traditional here. On the other hand, you can buy the woven carpets made by the **Bani Hamida** tribe (see p 59), which can be found in their shops in Mukawir and Amman. Expect to pay at least US$200 for a carpet 1.3m by 1.5m. The colourful woollen **iassars** that you will see everywhere are mostly made in Iraq.

### Clothes

There is no shortage of fashion boutiques in Amman, but you will probably not find anything particularly original or cheap among the western clothes on offer, as they are mostly imported. The traditional local garments are more interesting, even if they are slightly less practical to wear. The long ceremonial robes, or **caftans**, come with or without sleeves and are richly hand-embroidered in the Jordanian and Palestinian tradition, sometimes with gold or silver thread. The traditional **keffieh**, made from red or black-checked fabric, is held in place with a cord known as an *agal*. This represents the Jordanian national head-dress for men. Female visitors may appreciate the pretty white embroidered **headscarves** worn by Jordanian women.

### Food
You can buy spices and pastries from the shops in Amman and Aqaba.

### Books
Many photographers have been inspired by Petra, Jerash and the Wadi Rum. You will find a selection of fine books depicting lovely views of Jordan.

### Dead Sea and Jordan River products
The Dead Sea is renowned for its health-giving properties, as a result of its unpolluted waters, which are rich in salt, and other minerals from the surrounding mountains. Health centres have sprung up all around it, where sea-water and mud-bath therapy is on offer. These treatments can be continued at home, thanks to the local products, which can be bought for between JD2 and JD10. The small pre-packed pots of black **mud** may have honey, jujube, beeswax or royal jelly added to them. They are used as beauty masks for the face or body and for the treatment of capillaries.

Dead Sea **salt** is rich in minerals and can be added to bath water.

**Water** from the River Jordan, where Jesus was baptised by John the Baptist, is sold in small bottles. It is a gift that is much appreciated by Christians.

## ● Where to shop
### What to buy where
You will find any number of souvenir shops near the theatre and in the bazaar in Amman, or at the entrance to the sites of Jerash and Petra, all of which offer more or less the same products. Amman is probably the best place to do your shopping, as the arts and crafts of all the different regions are found there.

### The bazaars
Only those in downtown Amman have an authentic atmosphere, but you will not find anything particularly original there.

### Other shops
Amman has a good range of high-quality art and crafts shops.

## ● Bartering (See p 100)

## ● Duty and restrictions on certain articles
It is against the law to export antiques of any value.

## ● Mailing things home
If you have succumbed to the charms of Jordanian arts and crafts, you should take a look at the baggage allowance included with your plane ticket. Even if there is a certain leeway, don't expect to be able to check in 40kg of luggage without paying a supplement. At Amman airport you will be charged JD7.50 for each excess kilo, payable by credit card. It would be better to send it by post from Amman (only from the parcel post office, in the small street behind the main post office). This will cost JD58 for 20kg by airmail (allow two weeks) or JD36 by surface mail. Sending it from Syria would be even cheaper. The parcel must be brought to the post office unsealed, for customs formalities.

**Federal Express**, Shmessani, Amman, ☎ (6) 569 54 15.

# HEALTH AND SAFETY

- **Precautions** *(see p 99)*

- **Medical kit** *(see p 99)*

- **Health**

Of all the Arab countries, Jordan is well placed in terms of medical care, with 11 000 doctors serving a population of 4 million. There are even foreign patients who come for hospital treatment, which is of a high quality and not expensive.

*Hospitals*

Aqaba and Amman have excellent hospitals.

*Pharmacies*

Most are well stocked with the usual range of medicines.

*Doctors*

Most doctors speak English.

- **Emergencies**

**Police**, ☎ 192

**Ambulance and first aid**, ☎ 193. Petra has a first aid centre.

# A TO Z

- **Cigarettes**

International brands of cigarettes are available everywhere for JD1 a packet. Cigars can be found in Amman in Safeway and near the al-Quds restaurant.

- **Drinking water**

Tap water is supposed to be drinkable, but it is probably better to buy bottled mineral water, which is available everywhere.

- **Electricity**

220V, 50 Hz. The plugs are of the small diameter two-pronged type.

- **Laundry**

The majority of hotels offer a laundry service, whereby your clothes can be washed and ironed, usually within a day, at a cost of between JD 0.50 and JD2 per garment.

- **Newspapers**

The *Jordan Times* is the main daily English language paper. As well as regional and international news, it includes useful information, such as the weather forecast, duty chemists, hospitals, flight arrival and departure times, television listings, local cultural events, exchange rates and horoscopes. Some English newspapers can be found in Amman, Petra and Aqaba.

- **Photography**

Films for colour prints (Fuji, Kodak, Konica) are sold in the main tourist centres. Films for transparencies are harder to come by. Bearing in mind the heat, films may have already suffered some damage when you buy them, and it is better to bring your own. There are many places that offer a one-hour development service, but the quality is mediocre.

A to Z

## • Radio and television

### Radio
**Radio Jordan**: 90 kHz or 96.3 kHz FM or 855 kHz AM (Amman), 98.7 kHz FM (Aqaba), transmits in Arabic and English and plays classical music from 7am-8pm.
**BBC World Service**: short wave 6195 kHz, 9410 kHz, 12095 kHz, medium wave 1323 kHz (227m).
**Voice of America**: short wave 792 kHz, 1260 kHz, 1546 kHz, 3985 kHz, 5995 kHz, 6040 kHz, 7170 kHz, 11965 kHz and 15205 kHz.

### Television
Channel 2 on Jordanian television shows programmes in English and French from 2pm to midnight, with an English news broadcast at 10pm. The majority of hotels offer international channels (CNN etc), thanks to satellite dishes.

## • Thefts
Theft is rare, even exceptional, in Jordan. However, there is no point in tempting fate. If you must leave your luggage somewhere, entrust it to a hotel receptionist or shopkeeper, where it will be perfectly safe. Don't forget to lock your car.

## • Tipping
Tips are appreciated by hotel and restaurant staff, even if a 10% service charge is included in the bill. An additional 10% will be well received. JD 0.5 is a reasonable sum for small services (doormen, porters). If you hire a chauffeur for an excursion, show your appreciation of his services. For taxi fares, you should round the total up to the nearest hundredth *fils*.

## • Units of Measurement
The metric system is officially in use, though as old habits die hard, the country still retains some vestiges of the British influence. Times are written 2pm rather than 14h and distances are still sometimes expressed in miles, yards and feet, although on signposts they are in kilometres.

Distances in this guide are given in kilometres. As a rule of thumb, one kilometre is five-eighths of a mile: 5 miles is therefore about 8 kilometres, 10 miles is about 16 kilometres and 20 miles is about 32 kilometres.

Consult the table below for useful metric equivalents:

| **Degrees Celsius** | 35° | 30° | 25° | 20° | 15° | 10° | 5° | 0° | -5° | -10° |
|---|---|---|---|---|---|---|---|---|---|---|
| **Degrees Fahrenheit** | 95° | 86° | 77° | 68° | 59° | 50° | 41° | 32° | 23° | 15° |

1 centimetre (cm) = 0.4 inch   1 metre (m) = 1.09 yards   1 litre = 0.22 gallon
1 metre (m) = 3.3 feet   1 litre = 1.06 quart   1 kilogram (kg) = 2.2 pounds

## • Weather forecasts
These can be found in the newspapers or seen on television.

# LOOK AND LEARN (see p 102)

# USEFUL WORDS AND EXPRESSIONS (see p 104)

# Exploring Jordan

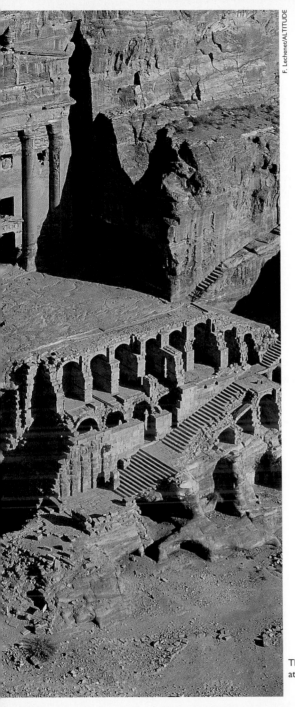

The royal tombs
at Petra

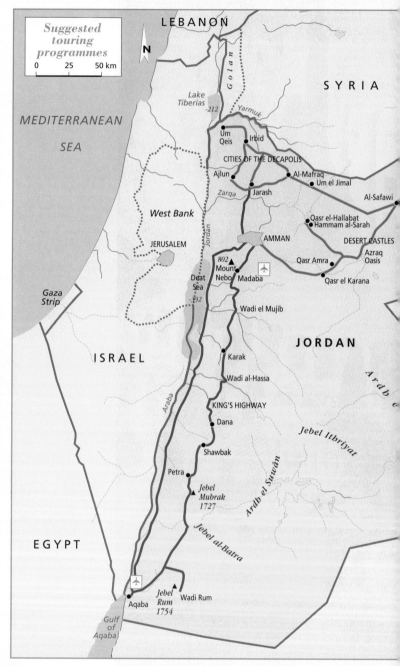

## Suggested touring programmes

0    25    50 km

LEBANON

SYRIA

MEDITERRANEAN SEA

Lake Tiberias -212

Golan

Yarmuk

Um Qeis

Irbid

CITIES OF THE DECAPOLIS

Ajlun

Al-Mafraq

Um el Jimal

Al-Safawi

West Bank

Zarqa

Jarash

Jordan

Qasr el-Hallabat
Hammam al-Sarah

JERUSALEM

AMMAN

DESERT CASTLES

Gaza Strip

802 ▲
Mount Nebo

Madaba

Qasr Amra

Azraq Oasis

Dead Sea -492

Wadi el Mujib

Qasr el Karana

ISRAEL

JORDAN

Karak

Arabe

Wadi al-Hassa

KING'S HIGHWAY

Jebel Itbriyat

Dana

Araba

Shawbak

Petra

Jebel Mubrak 1727

Ardb el Suwân

EGYPT

Jebel al-Batra

Aqaba

Jebel Rum 1754

Wadi Rum

Gulf of Aqaba

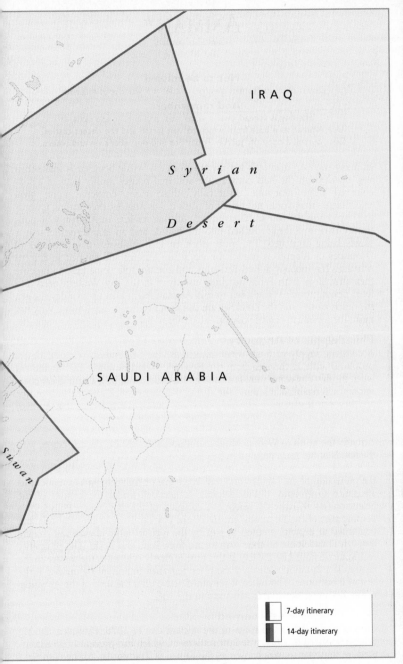

IRAQ

*Syrian*

*Desert*

SAUDI ARABIA

*Suwan*

| | 7-day itinerary |
| | 14-day itinerary |

# AMMAN★
Capital of Jordan
Pop 1 500 000 – Alt 750m

**Not to be missed**
Downtown: its Roman theatre, citadel and wonderful museum.

**And remember...**
The city is spread over a wide area, and is hilly: use taxis.
Use Amman as a base from which to visit Jarash and the desert castles.
Get yourself a copy of "Jordan Today" to find out what's on and where.

In many ways Amman feels like an American city. Wide boulevards snake their way up through the hills between the scattered houses mostly built of a soft-coloured beige limestone. Eventually, these roads converge upon great interchanges that would not be out of place in Los Angeles, ever leading towards the city centre, known as "Downtown". All that remains of Amman's fabulous history is here: a theatre tucked into the hillside and an Islamic citadel that is slowly being excavated. The souk, albeit far less impressive than the ones of Damascus or Aleppo, is one of the city's rare features still steeped in Eastern promise. Traditionally attired Bedouins and country folk come here to procure their provisions with fierce haggling; elsewhere in the city Western dress and fixed prices prevail. While a full tour of Amman might take up to a day, Jarash, the desert castles and the Dead Sea are less than two hours' drive away. Why not make the Jordanian capital your base and, when night falls, explore its night-life.

## Philadelphia of Antiquity

A constant supply of fresh water assured by the Seil Amman enabled desert people to settle in the area from the Neolithic period onwards. During the era when the first city-states were flourishing (4th millennium BC), a permanent community was established around the citadel that thrived well into the Bronze Age and beyond. It was after 1200 BC, however, during the Iron Age that Amman really began to grow in importance. Later, the place referred to in the Bible as Rabbath Ammon became the capital of a vast kingdom stretching from the River Zarqa in the north to Wadi al Mujib in the south. In 733 BC the city passed into the hands of the Assyrians and in 587 BC into those of Nebuchadnezzar II, King of Babylon. During the 5C BC, the local dynasty of Tobiads placed itself under the protection of the Lagides, and took the name of Philadelphia as a mark of its allegiance to Ptolemy II Philadelphus. It later fell under the control of the Seleucids (63 BC) shortly before the conquest of Pompey, when Philadelphia became part of the Decapolis. In AD 70 the city came under imperial rule and continued to expand, assisted in part by the regular traffic of caravans passing through Philadelphia on their way to and from Petra and Bosra. The prosperity and luxury enjoyed by the city at this time is clearly evident in the theatre in the centre. The Byzantines ensured the place remained important by making it the seat of a bishopric. Thereafter, it remained active until the time of the Abbasids, before declining slowly into obscurity in the 13C.

## How the city mushroomed

Circassians settled in the ruins of the ancient city in 1878. However, the big change occurred in 1923, when the settlement, which had previously no administrative importance, was chosen as the capital of Transjordan to the detriment

Amman

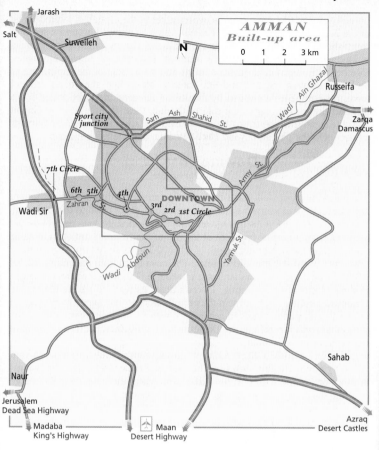

of Salt (*see p 339*) – the Ottoman capital of the region – which was deemed too unstable politically and too far away from the main Bedouin population. For some time, the town comprised around 6 000 inhabitants; in 1948, following the arrival *en masse* of displaced Palestinians, this number rocketed to an estimated population of 120 000. After the painful events of 1967, Amman reaped the benefits first from the discovery of crude oil reserves, then from the eclipse of Beirut as the pre-eminent financial centre of the Middle East. And still the city continues to evolve commercially, as it becomes increasingly westernised, and grow outwards, its sprawling suburbs extending 25km to engulf Zarqa (*northeast*), Naur (*southwest*) and Suweileh (*northwest*).

Nevertheless, the capital of the Hashemite kingdom still preserves its original kernel. The **Balad Sector**, built up around and over the Wadi Seil, occupies the central section of the city. To the north lie the smartest residential areas: **Shmeissani** and **Jebel al-Hussein** form the thriving commercial and business sectors of the city, where increasing numbers of fast-food outlets have been set up and Safeway (the most famous hypermarket in the capital) is located. West of the Balad Sector lies the **Jebel Amman**, an area arranged around a series of roundabouts or "circles" which provide locals and visitors with a convenient set of landmarks on which to set their bearings. The principal foreign embassies, together with the most prestigious hotels and restaurants of the capital, are to be found between the 2nd and 4th "circles". Meanwhile, the poorer areas of town, predominantly inhabited by Palestinian refugees, are to be found south of Balad Sector, clinging to the side of the hill; these include Jebel Al-Nadhif and Al-Ashrafiyeh, dominated by its distinctive black and white Abu Darwish mosque. On the plateau beyond lies Al-Wahdat and the refugee camp.

## Downtown★★ (C2, D2)
*Allow 2hr on foot*

The following short walk starts from the Roman theatre by Al Hashimi Square and then takes you westwards along the main axis of the town to the souk area.

The **Roman Theatre**★★ (moudarraje roumani) (D2) *(open daily, 9am–5pm. No charge)* is the most monumental fragment of the city to survive from Antiquity, cradled through time by the northern flank of Jebel Al-Taj, its slopes rippling naturally upwards beyond the last rows of seats. The *cavea* dates from the end of the 2C AD and would have held an audience of about 6 000, with spectators arranged in three blocks of tiered seating, 15 rows deep. As work to restore the theatre continues, funding and interest in the project has been maintained by the staging of recitals and performances in accordance with its original purpose. Once the proscenium wall is rebuilt by the Department of Antiquities, the theatre will have recovered its full splendour. The empty room at the top between the two niches would have contained a statue; today, it provides a wonderful vantage point from which to admire the fine **view** over the town and the citadel walls. The "wings" at either end of the stage (the *parascœnia* from where the actors used to emerge onto the stage) now accommodate the Jordan Folklore Museum (entrance side) and the Jordan Museum of Popular Traditions respectively.

The **Jordan Folklore Museum** *(9am-5pm; public holidays, 10am-4pm. Entry fee.)* houses a small collection of domestic objects and household implements used by desert nomads and people from rural communities. Visitors are welcomed by the semblance of a Circassian attired in a *sokoh*, the traditional coat worn over a red shirt, and a black cylindrical hat *(qalbaq)*. Around the walls, eight showcases display Bedouin weaponry ranging from the 17C to the 20C: various side-arms, including rapiers, daggers (some from the Yemen), pistols and rifles. One of the three rooms in the right wing is dedicated to early 20C embroidery (revolving display) that illustrates some of the wealth of colour and design in Jordanian and Palestinian traditional costume. To the left of the main entrance a few steps lead up into a vaulted room, where a camel is shown bearing the amazing litter *(ketab)* that once was used to shelter the women from the sun and the gaze of onlookers, as the extended family migrated from one place to another. At the far end of the same room, a cloth separates the section of the tent used by men and the area reserved for women and children.

The **Jordan Museum of Popular Traditions**★ *(same visiting times as Folklore Museum; separate tickets)* is almost entirely devoted to the traditional attire of women, although one section displays a number of 6C mosaics from Jarash. The dress collection, arranged with meticulous care, presents the typical costumes

Roman Theatre, Downtown Amman

found in the different parts of Jordan (Ramtha, Ma'an, Madaba, Salt, southern Sukhna). Diversity is achieved in the variable combination of fabric and stitched design using different dyed silk embroidery threads. On the whole, the jewellery *(displayed in the three rooms on the left)* is made of silver and is ornamented with Ottoman coins, coral from the Red Sea, polished agate or amber, and, in some cases, black enamel *(niello)* that was all the rage in the 1920s. Jewellery formed part of the dowry offered by the husband-to-be and became the exclusive property of the married woman. The curious characters illustrated on the tanned hides come from a shadow theatre *(karagöz)*, a highly popular form of entertainment throughout the Ottoman Empire.

*Go outside the theatre complex.*

At one time, the Roman theatre would have opened out onto a vast forum lined with a **colonnade**: now represented by the eight re-erected columns with Corinthian capitals. At the far end of the forum, by the foot of the citadel, ran the *decumanus*. Today, only a part of the ancient square survives in the form of a small public garden planted with flowering oleanders, palm and eucalyptus-trees that, in turn, provide shade for a number of souvenir shops and a restaurant with an open terrace *(see Making the most of Amman)*.

**Downtown**

315

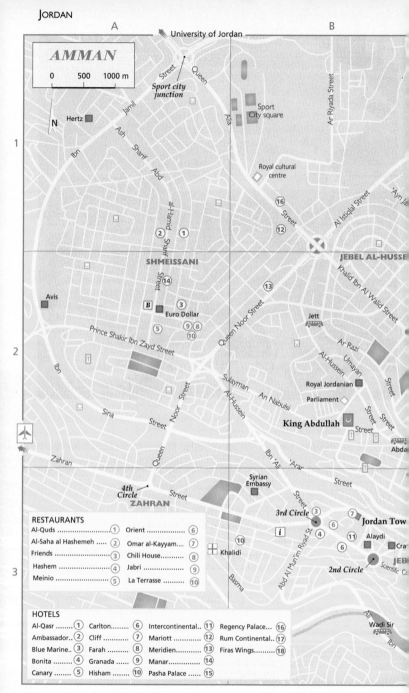

**AMMAN**

University of Jordan

Sport city junction

N

Hertz

Sport City square

Royal cultural centre

16

12

Regency Palace

SHMEISSANI

JEBEL AL-HUSSE

14

Avis

13

B

Euro Dollar

3

Jett

Prince Shakir Ibn Zayd Street

5

9 8

10

Queen Noor Street

Ar Razi

Royal Jordanian

Parliament

King Abdullah

Abda

Zahran

4th Circle

Syrian Embassy

Street

ZAHRAN

3rd Circle

3

Jordan Tow

7

i

6

11

Alaydi

Cra

10

4

JEB

6

Khalidi

2nd Circle

Scientific C

Basma

Wadi Sir

RESTAURANTS

| | | | |
|---|---|---|---|
| Al-Quds | (1) | Orient | (6) |
| Al-Saha al Hashemeh | (2) | Omar al-Kayyam | (7) |
| Friends | (3) | Chili House | (8) |
| Hashem | (4) | Jabri | (9) |
| Meinio | (5) | La Terrasse | (10) |

HOTELS

| | | | | | | | |
|---|---|---|---|---|---|---|---|
| Al-Qasr | (1) | Carlton | (6) | Intercontinental | (11) | Regency Palace | (16) |
| Ambassador | (2) | Cliff | (7) | Mariott | (12) | Rum Continental | (17) |
| Blue Marine | (3) | Farah | (8) | Meridien | (13) | Firas Wings | (18) |
| Bonita | (4) | Granada | (9) | Manar | (14) | | |
| Canary | (5) | Hisham | (10) | Pasha Palace | (15) | | |

C      D

'Abdul

**Palace complex**

Kadr

Jaza'Ari

Street

HSBC **B**

The Housing Bank **B**

al-

**Cistern**

**Archeological Museum**

**Byzantine church**

arat al-Funun

**JEBEL AL-QALAA**

Enceinte

(18)

Arab Bank **B**

ir

Muhammad St.

**Temple of Hercules**

Sha'Ban Street

(1)

(2) **Odeon**
**Al-Hashimi Square**

(4)    (8)

**DOWNTOWN**

(15)

**i**

(7)

**B**

rdan Street

Faisal

Gold souk

**Jordan Folklore Museum**

**Jordan Museum of Popular Tradition**

**BALAD**

Al-Hashimi Street

**Roman Theatre**

(17)

Basman St.

**B**

Quraish Street

**Souks**

**B**

**Souks**

**Nymphaeum**

Bani Hamida

JRP

**Al-Hussein**

0          500 m

BDALI

Al-Hussein St.

Raghadan and Bassman Palace

Marka

**JEBEL AL-WEIBDEH**

**JEBEL AL-QALAA**

Amir Muhammad St.

Al-Hashimi Street

**DOWNTOWN** **Al Hashimi Square**

MAN

Raghadan

(9) **1st Circle**

**JEBEL AL-TAJ**

King Talal St.

Quraysh St.

Talib Street

Zatari Bazar

Al Taj Street

**JEBEL AL-ACHRAFIEH**

**317**

Before you leave the theatre, note the area on the right where the **odeon** (*no charge*) has been restored. Imagine how it must have looked with its five front entrances set back from the great colonnade that extended along the eastern side of the forum. Alas, very few original features survive besides fragments of the steps from the ten or so rows inside the odeon itself and the odd decorative detail ornamenting the proscenium wall.

Behind the odeon, there are various open-air **cafés** that overlook the vast **Al Hashimi Square**. The most popular pastime here is to sit on one of the terraces bristling with parasols and watch the unending show of Egyptian films on video.

*Continue along the paved colonnade alongside the theatre.*

At the top of the steps, seated on stools, street-sellers display their wares on little mats; coins of dubious age are laid out among bundles of notes bearing the image of Saddam Hussein: although probably authentic, these are of little value. The Downtown Visitors' Centre is down on the right-hand side. Some 200m further on, the road runs past an edifice built of large stones, looking like two towers. For a long time this purported to be the south wall of a **nymphaeum** (D2), although recent research conducted by IFAPO (French Middle Eastern Institute of Archeology) has found no evidence of a water supply. It is more likely to have been an imperial sanctuary of the type found at Shahba in Syria. For a better view, turn down the first little street on the right. Through the wire fence, despite the work in progress, you can see the façade being restored to its former splendour, complete with podium, columns and niches.

*Walk on past the building site to where King Faisal Street meets Al Hashimi Street, a junction populated with all kinds of bureaux de change. Turn left into Al Hashimi Street.*

Two slender minarets mark the site of the **King Hussein Mosque** (C2) (*not generally accessible to non-Muslims*). This, the most revered mosque in the city, was rebuilt in the Ottoman style in 1924 on the site of an ancient sanctuary. Each week, on a Friday, the faithful flock here for midday prayers in such numbers as to fill the mosque and its adjoining outer courtyard.

Behind the mosque is the fruit and vegetable market and to the right, along King Talal Street, extend the **souks**. These covered markets open on Fridays, unlike those elsewhere in the Middle East. Each alley is lined on both sides with little stalls packed high with merchandise of all sorts. The main commodity for sale here is clothing, although there are a couple of boutiques selling carpets and souvenirs. Those who are familiar with the covered markets of Aleppo, Damascus, Istanbul or Cairo, however, may be disappointed by the souk in Amman.

## Jebel al-Qalaa★ (The citadel) (C1, D1)
*Allow 90min.*

*Despite it taking only 20min to walk up to the citadel, you may have trouble in zigzagging your way through the houses: by far the simplest option is to hail a taxi (ask for al-Qala'a).*

Opposite the Roman theatre stands Jebel al-Qalaa, its steep slopes covered with modest dwellings. Narrow streets, linked by steep stairways, snake their way up to the top from where extensive views open out over Amman. Although the citadel ruins in themselves may be rather unexciting, the archeological treasures displayed in the museum make the climb worthwhile. Before reaching the crest of the hill, the road makes a long detour up to the right past the modern Raghadan and Basman palaces on the hill opposite, where the late King Hussein lived.

Amman

The **enclosure wall** of the citadel, now largely ruined, was erected and maintained throughout the 1st millennium AD from the time of the Romans until the Abbasid dynasty. The citadel occupies a highly strategic position surrounded by deep wadis and, as such, has offered the people of Amman a place of sanctuary at times of impending attack. Traces of occupation have been discovered dating from the 3rd millennium BC and the ruins have been identified as the Ammonite town of Rabbath Ammon.

*Keep left of the columns of the Temple of Hercules and turn into the museum car park at the end of the road.*

## National Archeological Museum★★★ (C1)

*9am-5pm; winter 8am-4pm; public holidays, 10am-4pm. Entrance fee. Short guidebook and information on the exhibits available in English.*

The small museum traces Jordan's long past from prehistoric times until the Ottoman period. Despite its size, artefacts recovered from recent excavations are regularly being added to the collection; among the most highly prized are the statues found at Ain Ghazal in 1983 and a set of bronze pieces unearthed at Mafraq in 1986.

*Follow the arrows in the central room pointing to the right to see things presented in chronological order.*

The second showcase on the left by the entrance contains **figures from Ain Ghazal★★★**: these are considered the most ancient anthropomorphic statues ever discovered (8th to 6th millennia BC). Perhaps the most striking feature of these lime figures with highly stylised attenuated bodies sculpted around a primitive kind of armature made of reeds, are their enormous black-rimmed staring eyes *(see illustration p 13)*. Aligned against the wall on the right are a series of five **heads★★**, their skulls modelled in plaster, that were found in Jericho. These are thought to survive from an early ancestral cult in the 7th millennium BC, as does the earthenware **jar★** containing the skeleton of a child, discovered under the main room of a house dating from the 4th millennium BC.

The right wing of the museum displays the reconstruction of a grave containing 13 skeletons found in Jericho (first half of the 2nd millennium BC); the votive offerings laid out on a wooden table provide tangible evidence of a belief in the after-life. The magnificent late Bronze Age (1500-1200 BC) **carved ivory-panelled casket★★** found at Pella shows the fusion of several different influences from both east and west of the region: most notable elements being the typically Egyptian stylisation of the eyes and the solar disk, and the Asian treatment of the lions facing each other. The same Egyptian flavour determines the more recent examples of craftsmanship displayed in the central room: the **two-faced head★** from the citadel of Amman (8C BC) is reminiscent of the heads of Hator found in Egyptian temples and the statues of Yerah'Azar.

The end room, opposite the entrance to the museum, is dedicated to the art of the Nabataeans and includes discoveries made at Petra and Khirbet Tannur (between Karak and Petra), the site where the striking **relief of Atargatis** (goddess of vegetation) and other architectural fragments were excavated. Note also the lovely statue of a young woman, holding in her right hand a bearded mask of Pan, and various fine examples of the typical red Nabataean pottery – in this case decorated with floral motifs.

The annexe to the right of the last room displays an assortment of artefacts recovered from the famous site at Qumran between 1947 and 1958. These include a number of **jars** in which the Dead Sea scrolls and **passages from the Old**

**Jebel al-Qalaa**

**Testament** compiled by the Essenians were found carefully wrapped in pieces of linen for protection. Others, meanwhile, contained **copper scrolls** (68 AD) that refer to the secret hiding place of a fabulous treasure: could this be alluding to the Temple of Jerusalem? These scrolls have been cut into thin strips, in order to be deciphered. The central gallery is devoted to Greco-Roman objects discovered in Jordan (masks from Jarash, beautiful pieces of blue glass from Amman, oil lamps, gold necklaces and earrings). Miraculously, the exquisite, if fragile, collection of Byzantine **blown glass★** found at Umm al-Rassas survives intact. The section set aside for Classical antiquities in the left side-room is completed by an androgynous statue of Apollo found at Sivas (far end).

The annexe off the museum's left wing encloses five anthropomorphic, Moabite terracotta **sarcophagi★** found in Amman (13C and 7C BC) with handles that make them portable. A strange, deformed face is sketched out on the lid of some, with the arms arranged alongside the body.

The left wing is essentially reserved for Islamic antiquities. The 8C Umayyad objects found in 1986 at Mafraq are quite exceptional, particularly the bronzes. The bronze and iron **brazier★★** clearly show the predominant influences in Umayyad art; the winged griffins ornamenting the feet are of Persian Sassanid origin and the dancers have Coptic features, whereas the arcades and niches, sheltering six love scenes illustrating Dionysiac rites, are reminiscent of late Roman – rather than Byzantine – art. The garlands of pomegranates are allegories of love and fertility. A collection of ceramics, most notably a number of flasks bearing the Mameluke coat-of-arms, and a broad range of coinage in use from Byzantine to Ottoman times conclude the visit to the museum.

*On leaving the museum, walk left towards the three columns belonging to the Temple of Hercules.*

## In the vicinity of the museum (C1)

The **Temple of Hercules** has one unusual feature that distinguishes it from its closest counterpart, the Temple of Artemis at Jarash. Instead of the usual deity, the cella contained a sacred rock, which may have been a vestige of an earlier cult honoured by the Ammonites. All that remains of the original temple is the podium (18mx9m), although the sheer height of the three reconstituted columns would seem to indicate the place was held in considerable esteem. The sanctuary was connected to the forum in the lower town by a monumental stairway. From the cliff-edge, a fine **view★** extends over the theatre, odeon and Al Hashimi Square.

*Some 50m to the left of the temple stand the ruins of a Byzantine church.*

The apse of the little **Byzantine church** is clearly marked out by three rows of stones. The building dates from the 6C. The nave and aisles would have been articulated by columns with fine Corinthian capitals. The tight colonnade before the church encloses a fine pavement.

*Continue along the axis of the colonnade and make for the imposing square building ahead.*

The **palace complex★** erected towards the close of the Umayyad period (8C) has recently been subjected to an ambitious Jordanian-Spanish restoration programme. Its history was short-lived having been destroyed, soon after it was built, by a violent earthquake in 749. Entry to the palace was via a monumental hall, the best-preserved section of the complex. To the right of the entrance hall stood the **baths**, situated near the enormous (and recently

**Amman**

cleared) circular **cistern★** excavated from the bedrock to hold 1 400cum of water. The cruciform entrance **hall** was probably domed. The ornate interior decoration, with niches running along the length of the internal walls, is modelled on that found in Sassanid Persia. Outside, a flight of steps in the left corner of the building leads up to the roof, from where you get an overview of the site, which helps in understanding how it all fits together.

Beyond the hall extend the remains of a **colonnade** comprising two rows of thirteen column-bases, from which a series of porticoed courtyards lead off to either side. These, in turn, would have been enclosed on all three sides by administrative offices and residential quarters. Once you had passed through all these buildings, you would have reached the palace itself (now a sad ruin). This last block was organised as an **audience chamber**.

The ramparts at the northern end of the citadel offer a wonderful view over Jebel al-Hussein and Jebel Weibdeh. The striking blue and white dome in the distance is that of the King Abdullah Mosque.

Walk down the road and turn into any one of the many tiny streets towards the theatre: note how the tall tightly packed buildings of Amman leave little room for gardens or open patches of green. Each neighbourhood has been developed in the same way, the buildings obliterating any hint of the natural landscape and its contours and concealing every entrance into the maze of tiny streets within. Lines of brightly-coloured washing dry in the sunshine, a striking contrast against the pale buildings washed in pastel shades of white and beige. The buildings rarely exceed four storeys and have large numbers of balconies.

# Jebel Weibdeh

Heading north away from the city centre, the convergence of Al-Hussein Street and Amir Muhammad Street enclose an area known as Jebel Weibdeh. This residential quarter at the top of the hill is largely populated by Christians, with several of the houses surviving from the beginning of the 20C. **Darat al-Funun** (C1) *(open 9am-7pm; closed Fridays. Access from behind the main post office. No charge)* comprises three houses. It was here that Lieutenant-Colonel Peak, a founder of the Arab Legion, once lived and entertained T E Lawrence in 1921. In the garden of the house which overlooks the city, there are the remains (albeit modest) of a 6C Byzantine church. One of the gorgeous tiled pavilions has been converted by the private foundation responsible for maintaining the property as an exhibition area for Arabic art.

Some way further up Al-Hussein Street, level with the Jordanian Parliament building, a distinctive blue and white dome, flanked by two minarets, punctuates the skyline: this belongs to the **King Abdullah Mosque★** (B2) *(accessible outside prayer times)*. The octagonal shape is reminiscent of the Dome of the Rock in Jerusalem. This fine example of contemporary Islamic design firmly draws inspiration for its decoration from traditional Islam (*muqarnas*, window-grilles and glass lamps decorated with calligraphy). Otherwise the elements are treated with a sober and dignified monumentality. The *qibla* (facing Mecca) consists of a symbolic wall that has no structural function. The traditional scattering of carpets has here been replaced by an immense expanse of wall-to-wall carpeting, representing an infinite proliferation of individual blue, gold and red prayer mats.

# Making the most of Amman

## COMING AND GOING

**By air – Queen Alia Airport** handles all the international flights into Jordan. It is situated 32km south of Amman on the edge of the desert (40min by road). Terminal 1 is reserved for Royal Jordanian flights. If travelling without a visa, it is imperative to obtain one (JD6) immediately on arrival before baggage is reclaimed. A taxi to the city centre costs approximately JD10. Buses from the airport (JD1-2) terminate at Abdali Station. The airport has a basic cafeteria, bank counters for changing money and rental car agents, which are open all night.

If flying with Royal Wings on a domestic flight, you may be given a choice between Queen Alia Airport and Marka Airport. Unless you have an onward connecting flight to catch, it is better to fly into **Marka Airport** as this is located only 5min from Amman city centre, and tends to be far less crowded. Boarding up to 20min before departure. Taxi to city centre: JD2.

**By train –** Amman railway station, often called the Hedjaz, is located at **Mahhata**, on the left of the road to the Marka Airport (JD2 by taxi from the Roman Theatre). Every Monday at 8am, a handsome diesel locomotive wearily pulls out of the station, bound for Damascus. First class tickets costing JD2.5 make this the cheapest and most adventurous way of travelling to Syria as long as time is not an issue: the journey lasts 8hr! Customs formalities are completed at Mafraq on the Jordanian side and at Deraa on the Syrian side of the border. Tickets may be acquired from the station ticket office immediately prior to departure. Really dedicated rail enthusiasts can take the train to Mafraq (72km) and return by bus (via Zarqa) or continue to Jarash.

**By bus –** The **Jett Company** (B2), Al Hussein St. Buses leave from the company headquarters, 1km north of Abdali Station. Services 4 times a day to Aqaba (4hr); Petra (3hr 30min) and Main very early in the morning; Tel-Aviv and Haifa via the King Hussein Bridge (JD5 per person).

**Abdali Station** (B2), Al-Hussein St. 2kms from city centre. Minibuses and shared taxis run regular services to the northern towns (Irbid, Ajlun, Salt, Jarash), to King Hussein Bridge and Damascus (shared taxi: JD5).

**Al-Wihdat Station**, situated a few kilometres south of the city, is the collection point for minibuses and shared taxis going to the south of Jordan (Madaba and Aqaba). Vehicles depart only when they have a full complement of passengers. Taxi from the centre: JD1.

**By shared taxi –** Large, old-fashioned American cars shuttle between all the large cities, departing only when full from the main bus stations (see above). These are a useful alternative to buses, which take longer to fill, or if it is too late, day or night. Their large boot will also take a greater amount of luggage.

## GETTING AROUND AMMAN

**By taxi –** Ensure that the driver has set his meter running at the beginning of your journey; this will save you having to argue over the fare on arrival at your destination. Check also that the meter has been reset to zero after the previous fare. Basic charges include JD 0.15 per passenger; JD 0.25 per kilometre covered. An average journey costs JD1 (Downtown to Shmeissani).

**Car rental –** There is a good choice of car-rental companies in Amman. You can return the vehicle at Petra or Aqaba for an extra charge of around JD25.

**Star Rent a car**, between Sport City Square and the Hotel Jerusalem (B1), ☎ /Fax (6) 560 49 04. This enterprising family-run firm offers the cheapest rates: JD20 per day for the most comfortable models.

**Euro Dollar** (A2), Shmeissani, ☎ (06) 569 33 99, Fax (6) 568 72 33.

**Dallah**, 6th Circle, opposite the Amra Hotel, ☎ (6) 582 77 36, Fax (6) 582 02 36; or from Queen Alia Airport ☎ (8) 551 11 12 (open 24hr).

**Avis**, King Abdullah Gardens (A2), ☎ (6) 569 94 20, Fax (6) 569 48 83; at Queen Alia Airport ☎ (8) 445 18 88.

**Europcar** has branches in three hotels: Mariott ☎ (6)560 13 50; Meridien ☎ (6) 569 65 11; Regency Palace ☎ (6) 560 13 60.

**Hertz** (A1), Hotel Middle East, ☎ (6) 553 89 89, Fax (6)553 84 06; Queen Alia Airport ☎ (8) 445 13 45.

## ADDRESS BOOK

**Tourist information** – The Ministry of Tourism is located in the 3rd Circle, some way outside the main city-centre. Open during office hours (9am-2pm) ☎ (6) 464 23 11. There is a much more central office next to the Roman theatre (D2), ☎ (6) 464 62 64. Maps, illustrated leaflets classified by region.

**Embassies and consulates – UK –** Abdoun, Amman (behind the Orthodox Club) ☎ (6) 592 31 00, extensions 2245 and 2269. Open Sunday to Thursday, 8.30am-12noon, though you can telephone until 3pm. You can also ring on ☎ (6) 592 65 81 or (6) 59265 86. Outside normal working hours you can call (6) 552 99 99 in an emergency and leave a message.

There is also a British consulate in Aqaba, PO Box 485, ☎ (3) 201 25 25 or 201 31 11.

**USA** – PO Box 354, Between 2nd & 3rd Circles, Jebel Amman ☎ (6) 592 01 01 or 592 32 93. Telephone calls 1.30-4pm, Sunday to Thursday. Fax (6) 592 41 02

**Canada** – PO Box 815403, Pearl of Shmeissani Building, Amman ☎ (6) 566 61 24, Fax (6) 568 92 27. Open 8.30am-4.30pm, Sunday to Thursday.

**Australia** – Between 4th & 5th Circles, Zahran St, Jebel Amman ☎ (6) 5930246

**Banks/currency exchange** – There is no shortage of banks in Amman, especially in the Shmeissani district and Downtown. Most provide a currency exchange service (main foreign currencies in cash, travellers' cheques, Visa and or Mastercard).

Outside banking hours, there are many currency exchange booths grouped around King Faisal St and Hashimi St (C1); these do not display current rates of exchange, however, and so a little bartering may be called for. Check the rates published daily in the Jordan Times in advance. The simplest way of obtaining local cash is by using one of the machines at the **HSBC** (C1), Al-Hussein St, which accept credit cards (Mastercard and Visa) 24hr-a-day; or try **Housing Bank** (C1), next door (Visa). Most of the large hotels will also change travellers' cheques.

**American Express** ☎ (6) 560 70 14.

**Post office** – The main post office (C1) is located on Amir Muhammad St, 100m from the junction with Al-Hussein St. It is open daily until 7pm, except Fridays when it closes at 1.30pm. PO Box service available. To send parcels, find the back office overlooking the street at the rear of the main post office (access via a passageway on the first floor).

**Telephone** – Behind the post office building (in a steep street where the white shared taxis park), 100m from the junction with Al-Hussein St, there are several telephone agencies indicated by the sign **International Communication**. A little further up the street is the public telephone exchange.

**Internet** – There are Internet cafés everywhere in Amman, especially in Shmeissani and Downtown (JD1-3 per hour).

**Express mail** – To send valuable or express packages by courier, ring the **DHL** offices in 7th Circle ☎ (6) 585 85 14 or **Federal Express (Fed Ex)**, Shmeissani ☎ (6) 569 54 15. A number of the larger hotels have collection boxes.

**Medical services** – Your embassy should be able to recommend an English-speaking hospital or doctor. Pharmacies are plentiful, well stocked and the staff often speak English.

**Airline offices** – General flight information: ☎ (8) 445 30 00.

**Royal Jordanian** (B2), Abdali. Flight information ☎ (8) 445 32 00, Reservations ☎ (6) 567 83 21.

**Royal Wings**, Marka Airport. Reservation of domestic (Aqaba) and regional (Tel-Aviv) flights ☎ (8) 487 52 01, Fax (6) 487 56 56.

**Syrian Airways,** Seikalys ☎ (6) 462 21 47.

**Amman**

## WHERE TO STAY

### • Downtown (C2, D2)

The cheaper hotels tend to be dotted around the central part of town, near the souks. Although their location makes them ideal bases for all the main sights, banks, small restaurants, it is extremely difficult to find quiet rooms, out of earshot of the noisy street-life that begins shortly after dawn. Furthermore, the lack of air-conditioning can make these hotels nigh on unbearable in the height of summer.

*From US$10-25*

**Farah Hotel**, Al-Hussein Cinema St, ☎ (6) 465 14 43, Fax (9) 465 14 37 – 24rm ⌁ Sign in Al-Hussein St. The hotel extends beyond a small Bedouin café decked out like a nomad's tent: a strange sight at the heart of the city! Tucked away slightly off the main drag, this six-floor hotel (with lift) enjoys some sense of peace. The clean, well-kept small double/twin rooms have shared bathrooms. Mattresses can also be hired to sleep on the roof. A new haunt, increasingly popular among budget-conscious visitors.

**Cliff Hotel**, Al-Hussein St, ☎ (6) 462 42 73, Fax (6) 463 80 78 – 20rm ⌁ A veritable institution, given the generations of travellers who have passed through here. Foot-worn steps lead up from the busy street, lined with thriving businesses at the far end of Al-Hussein St, to the coffee-house on the first floor, forever crowded with people smoking a hookah and playing cards. The hotel reception is on the second floor, next to a seating area where idle gossip, visitor recommendations and useful tips are exchanged with candour. The genuine atmosphere of the place more than makes up for the lack of comfort and the street noise below.

*From US$35-50*

**Rum Continental Hotel**, Bassman St, ☎ (6) 462 31 62, Fax (6) 461 19 61 – 34rm ⌁ 🗐 ♪ 📺 ✕ Fairly disparate rooms, but basically all right. The heavy stone look-alike door at street level leads into a rather dark bar. Among the brown decor sits a television that relays various sporting activities throughout the day and night. Groups of locals sit at small round tables sipping beer.

**Pasha Palace Hotel**, Shabsoah St, almost opposite the Roman Theatre, ☎ (6) 463 91 81, Fax (6) 464 53 13 – 40rm ⌁ 🗐 ♪ 📺 ✕ 📶 A number of the simply furnished rooms look out onto the Roman Theatre. Unfortunately, the rooms are noisy, because of their proximity to Hashimi St. Direct access to the international telephone network, which is somewhat rare in this price bracket. Warm welcome; lift.

### • Jebel Amman and Jebel al-Weibdeh (B3-C3)

*From US$20-40*

**Firas Wings Hotel**, Jebel Al-Weibdeh, on a hill near Danat al-Funum, ☎ (6) 462 21 03, Fax (6) 462 19 99 – 30rm ⌁ 🗐 ♪ 📺 ✕ Rooms are clean but not very cheerful. A central yet quiet district, which is a bonus in Amman.

*From US$40-55*

**Canary Hotel**, Carualy St, ☎ (6) 463 83 53, Fax (6) 465 43 53 – 20rm ⌁ ⌁ ♪ 📺 ✕ 📶 This hotel is situated on a hill, up behind the Terra Sancta College, not far from the Abdali Bus Station. Although slightly tired, the place is nice and quiet. If no rooms are available here, the receptionists will do their best to find alternative rooms at the Dove Hotel or Caravan Hotel.

*Around US$60*

**Granada Hotel**, Jebel Amman, near 1st Circle, behind Malhas hospital, ☎ (6) 463 80 31, Fax (6) 462 26 17 – 25rm ⌁ 🗐 ♪ 📺 ✕ 📶 Comfortable rooms, well-appointed and extremely well-kept, in a very quiet district. Restaurant with cosy dining room and terrace and lively pub.

*From US$70-90*

**☺ Bonita Hotel**, 3rd Circle, ☎ (6) 461 50 61, Fax (6) 461 50 60 – 6rm ⌁ 🗐 ⌁ ♪ 📺 ✕ 📶 A charming, small, welcoming hotel, complete with pleasant bar and restaurant. You are advised to make bookings for the six pretty rooms at least one week in advance. Informal, family atmosphere. The restaurant has a Spanish menu and the bar serves tapas (starting from JD1.5 for the typical tit-bits) from 9pm. Live music.

### From US$100-115

🦞 **Hisham Hotel**, 3rd Circle St, ☎ (6) 464 27 20, Fax (6) 464 75 40 – 22rm. ⌂ ▤ ℘ TV ✗ CC Situated near the embassies in a peaceful part of town. Spacious, comfortable rooms, impeccably kept. Pleasant restaurant with terrace in shady garden. Courteous welcome from staff. Substantial reductions off season.

🦞 **The Carlton Hotel**, Queen Zein St, 3rd Circle, ☎ (6) 465 42 00, Fax (6) 465 58 33 – 60rm ⌂ ▤ ℘ TV ✗ CC This hotel is not one of the famous international chain of hotels with the same name. The rooms are spacious, but rather dull. Opt for rooms not overlooking the main road.

### Over US$290

**Intercontinental Hotel**, Queen Zein St, ☎ (6) 464 13 61, Fax (6) 461 58 35 – 500rm ⌂ ▤ ℘ TV ✗ ⚟ CC Work on refurbishing this grand hotel is finally finished. Rooms exceptionally well furnished. Clientele mainly consisting of businessmen and diplomats. Several in-house shops and lovely pool. Mexican, Indian, Italian, Eastern and Asian restaurants.

### • Shmeissani Quarter (A1-A2)

Slightly removed from the centre of town (15min by taxi), this peaceful quarter has a number of comfortable places to stay, from which its own attractions may be enjoyed.

### From US$50-65

**Blue Marine Hotel**, near the Arab Investment Bank, ☎ (6) 566 71 65, Fax (6) 566 43 12 – 30rm ⌂ ▤ ℘ TV This recently built hotel offers small, but pleasant and comfortable rooms at reasonable prices. A good place to stay, near the shops and restaurants of the Shmeissani district.

**Manar Hotel**, Abdul Hamid Sharaf St., ☎ (6) 566 21 86, Fax (6) 568 43 29 – 65rm ⌂ ▤ ℘ TV ✗ CC Another well-situated hotel, near plenty of good shops and restaurants. Don't be put off by the exterior of the building, which conceals charming, perfectly clean and comfortable rooms. The swimming pool and the standard of service make this excellent value for money.

### From US$115-140

**Al-Qasr Hotel**, near Abd al-Hamid Sharif St, ☎ (6) 568 96 71, Fax (6) 568 96 73 – 70rm ⌂ ▤ ℘ TV ✗ CC Comfortable rooms. Additional facilities include a safe deposit box and car rental. The American grill restaurant is popular; piano-bar in the basement. A swimming pool should soon be open.

**Ambassador Hotel**, Abd al-Hamid Sharif St, ☎ (6) 560 51 61, Fax (6) 568 11 01 – 100rm ⌂ ▤ ℘ TV ✗ CC Style and quality expected from a grand hotel at a more reasonable price than the international chains. Light, airy rooms appropriately furnished. Breakfast buffet on ground floor. Marco Polo Restaurant offers a choice of oriental and international menus. Open terrace in summer.

### Over US$160

**Regency Palace Hotel**, Queen Alia St, ☎ (6) 560 70 00, Fax (6) 566 00 13 – 300rm ⌂ ▤ ℘ TV ✗ ⚟ CC The tall square tower of the Regency, although somewhat tired in appearance, has a number of good rooms. The indoor pool is open all year around; the gym is on the top floor.

**Mariott Hotel**, Queen Alia St, ☎ (6) 560 76 07, Fax (6) 567 01 00 – 294rm ⌂ ▤ ℘ TV ✗ ⚟ ⚘ CC Usual facilities associated with the Mariott chain of hotels: non-smoking floor; limousine service; gym; baby-sitting; food-bar serving hamburgers and salad with television switched to sporting channels.

**Meridien Hotel**, Queen Noor St, ☎ (6) 569 65 11, Fax (6) 567 42 61 – 303rm ⌂ ▤ ℘ TV ✗ ⚟ CC The outline of this hotel, among the most recent top-of-the-range hotels to open in the capital, is easily mistaken with that of the Housing Bank. Situated at the heart of the business quarter, it is the preferred option for people on business. The spacious bedrooms enjoy extensive views out over the hills of Amman. In-built into the complex is a large shopping mall and several restaurants offering specialities from the four corners of the globe.

**Amman**

## WHERE TO EAT

Given the cosmopolitan atmosphere of Amman, the city has a number of excellent restaurants specialising in foreign fare, but very few offering succulent Arab cuisine. This is particularly the case in the centre of town. Furthermore, the import of western-style fast-food places cooking up pizzas, burgers and chilli, has been especially popular among young Ammanis. During the months after MacDonald's opened its branch on 7th Circle in the autumn of 1996, great queues waited hours to be served. For comfort, convenience and choice of food at perfectly acceptable prices, the restaurants in the big hotels – although short on local colour and atmosphere – are hard to beat.

### • Downtown – around the Roman Theatre (D1)

Fast-food joints (hamburgers, shawarma, **roast chicken**) have proliferated in the area around the theatre, most notably along the al-Hashimi Boulevard, among the cake-shops, game arcades, grocers and the Raghadan Bus Station. The more salubrious restaurants, although rather more expensive, are to be found literally opposite the Roman Theatre.

#### Under US$10

**Al-Saha al-Hashemeh (Tourist)**, opposite the Roman Theatre, al-Hashimi St, ☎ (6) 461 23 30 ♥ Near the souvenir shops, with a ground-floor dining room. Classical Arab cooking (mensef, meze), kebabs, vegetarian dishes, menu in English. Open terrace above shaded by red parasols, although this can be rather dusty and noisy, as it is at street level. Alcohol must be consumed inside; hookah pipe.

### • Al-Hussein Street (C1-A2)

#### Under US$10

Three cafés have set up shop where Amir Muhamma St leads off Al-Hussein St: Jabri, Habibah and Al-Quds.

**Al-Quds**, Al-Hussein St, also known as the Jerusalem (Al-Quds being the Arabic equivalent). Faded photographs hanging on the wall provide nostalgic views of the Holy City. This family-run establishment is never empty; its food is simple and good value; the service is efficient. Taste the mensef – a Bedouin dish of rice with a choice of mutton or chicken. Eastern sweetmeats from the counter. The delicious home-made lemonade (limoun) is particularly refreshing. A first-floor table is a good choice.

**Hashem**, Amir Muhammad St. Located in the alley immediately after the fork with Hussein St. Rickety dining tables are laid out in the alleyway. Meals are served with express haste. Exhaustive menu of felafel, hummus, fool (broad beans) and tea. A meeting point for all and sundry, people out of work and insomniacs, open 24hr-a-day and always good value.

### • Jebel Amman (B3)

For somewhere rather more sophisticated, you should head upwards towards the 3rd Circle.

#### Under US$10

**FRIENDS**, 3rd Circle ☎ (6) 564 28 30 ♥ On the square by the roundabout. A mainstream restaurant with European (mainly pizzas) and Oriental menus. Delicious halabi olives (highly spiced), choice of different grilled kebabs. Attentive service without being tiresome. Lovely terrace.

#### Over US$10

**Orient (Abu Ahmad)**, 3rd Circle, ☎ (6) 464 18 79. ♥ An elegant beige and green covered terrace. Good choice of meze and salads. Mostly Eastern dishes, carefully prepared. Impeccable service; hookahs.

**Omar al-Kayyam**, Amir Muhammad St ☎ (6) 463 40 34 ♥ Commonly known as "al-burj" by the Jordanians (immediately recognised by taxi drivers), this restaurant occupies the 23rd floor of the Jordan Tower. It therefore enjoys the most superlative views over the city and the surrounding countryside – it is almost a waste to go there at night. The eight different meze, although variations on the truly traditional recipes, are a true treat. Bread is served hot, golden and puffy straight from the oven. Fish (starting at JD15) is chosen from a trolley. Those wishing merely to study the view can restrict themselves to a drink at the bar.

- ## Shmeissani (A2)

This rather mundane residential area lies just north of the 4th Circle and consists largely of modern blocks of flats. The streets provide meeting-places for highly westernised young local residents who live at home. Cosmopolitan fast-food of all kinds is available here, ranging from a **Kentucky Fried Chicken** to the **Jabri Restaurant**, including the Italianate **Mamamia** (American deep-pan pizza) and **Milano** (pasta bar), or the ice-cream parlour **Frosti**. Among the more sophisticated eating places, there is **La Terrasse**, **Ata Ali** or **Maison Verte,** which serve French food, and various informal cafés where one can have a smoke on a hookah pipe on the open terrace **(Sultan, Meinio Café)**. This neighbourhood is at its most colourful at night when all the fluorescent neon signs are alight. If going there by taxi, ask for "Shmeissani Kentucky". All the shops and restaurants are concentrated in adjoining streets, northeast of the square at the intersection of Al-Hamid Sharaf St and Prince Sharik ibn-Zayd St.

*Under US$10*
**Chili House**, next to the Jabri. Tasty chili (spicy mince) is served with or without onions, red beans, and grated cheese on a bed of spaghetti. The Chili salad comprises a warm salad, with meat and dressed with sour cream.

*Over US$10*
**The Jabri**, opposite the Citroen shopping mall. It is hard to imagine that this glass building is a restaurant. In some ways it is more like a food complex with bakeries and take-away delicatessen occupying the ground floor; the first floor offers cafeteria-style catering; the third floor has a buffet counter: choose from 4 or 5 dishes on display, a salad and a yoghurt.
**La Terrasse,** opposite The Jabri. ♥ Ideal for those who hate junk-food; an elegant setting, where good Middle Eastern cooking is perfectly complemented by a bottle of Latroum wine or something Italian from the wine list. Live lute playing from 9pm. Estimate around JD10 for a wholesome meal or JD3.75 for a chicken kebab.

**Meinio Café**, next door to Popeye's. Peaceful tea-house with terrace, a good place to watch the world go by. *Meze* and grills. Hookah pipes, good service.

- ## Outskirts of Amman

*Over US$10*
Jordanians love outings and revel in the opportunity of having dinner or lunch out of town. They think nothing of driving 20 to 30km out of Amman, usually in the direction of Queen Alia Airport. Among their favourite haunts are the **Seven Hills** and the **Pine Palace,** which, as its name suggests, nestles in a pine forest. The **Kan Zaman**, meanwhile, is more of a tourist attraction, surrounded as it is by artisan shops. Those without cars of their own will opt for Al-Boustan, which is closer to the town centre.
**Al-Boustan,** on University Rd after Sport City (A1) ♥ A long chalet-like building, with a tile roof, accommodates this very popular Lebanese restaurant. Most of the clientele is made up of extended families and businessmen (whose mobile phones give little respite). Despite its considerable size, the place is rarely deserted and the waiting staff seem to be kept busy. Standard range dishes: meze and Middle Eastern delicacies. The fish is excellent but pushes the bill up considerably (JD15). Precise opening times: 12.30pm-4pm, 7pm-11pm. Universally known to all taxi-drivers (JD2 from central Amman).

### HAVING A DRINK

**Cafés, bars and tea shops –** If you have a hankering for alcohol, try to avoid the rather insalubrious bars in the city centre. Much better to go to one of the big hotel bars in the Jebel Amman or the panoramic restaurant in the Jordan Tower. The town centre goes dead after the souks close. One option is to wander around the area by the Roman Theatre (D1-2), which begins to close down at midnight. The **Al-Saha al-Hashemieh** Restaurant, opposite the theatre, serves beer and the souvenir shops stay open until 10pm. The Shmeissani neighbourhood, meanwhile, remains animated late into the night.

## • Downtown (Al-Hussein Street) (C1-C2)

**Arab League**, Al-Hussein St. Entrance on the right, just before the Mosque. The café up on the first floor is perhaps the most popular traditional Arab coffee-house in Amman. It essentially comprises one large split-level room with yellowing walls, smoke-stained by the hookah pipes. Much card-playing. Try to sit by a window and watch the world go by: the comings-and-goings of the souks, or the arrival of the faithful to Friday prayer. Tea, fizzy drinks, hookah pipe.

**Eco-tourism Café**, Al-Hussein St. First floor. Entrance in a side street, as with all the other hotels and coffee-shops in the district. Look out for a flurry of flag-poles marking the spot. Constant music (mainly rock) broadcast on Jordanian Radio. Tea, coffee, hookah pipe. A scout around the area by the door may reveal a couple of English-language papers. The small covered terrace overlooking the street provides the perfect opportunity to watch life going on below, but it can be very noisy. This is a truly atmospheric little place in Downtown Amman, more often crowded with the young set.

## • Jebel Amman (C3)

**After Eight**, 1st Circle ▼ Entrance to the left of the Hotel Granada. Dark pub-like retreat favoured by English-expat types. Broad selection of alcohol, beer on tap.

**Night spots –** For a full listing of what's on (and a considerable of other information as well), pick up a copy of *Jordan Today*, the magazine which is distributed free in the big hotels and certain bookshops. Amman boasts a number of night-clubs, although the main action is to be found Friday nights. The discotheques in the large hotels (Meridien, Shepherd, Mariott, Regency) have had to evolve with pressure from the local youth; gone are the lute-players and belly-dancers from all venues save the **Al-Andalous** or Hotel Jerusalem beyond the Sport City Junction (A1). Atmosphere and music tastes have given the various venues their own faithful following. Access is generally open to couples and to mixed groups, although single girls are welcome.

The Hotel Al-Qasr accommodates **The Cellar** ☎ (6) 568 96 71, the longest established club to play jazz on a regular basis, occasionally hosts live performances by players from abroad. By night, **Champions** in the Mariott Hotel ☎ (6) 585 71 90 becomes an American-style "sport-bar". Also worth investigating is the off-beat **Bonita Tapas** (3rd Circle ☎ (6) 461 50 60): although beware – it may be difficult to get in on an Wednesday or Thursday evening; it is therefore advisable to book. An additional 20 % surcharge may be levied if you are not a member.

The **Stallions Nightclub** on the 7th Circle ☎ (6) 585 71 90 will not admit single-sex parties.

## OTHER THINGS TO DO

**Outdoor pursuits –** An increasing number of hotels are equipping themselves with a gym. Even if you are not staying at one such hotel, it may be possible to use their swimming-pool for a fee.

**Cultural centres – Darat al-Funun** (C1) Jebel Al-Weibdeh ☎ (6) 464 32 52. Exhibitions, conferences, concerts, private film screenings organised by the Abdul Hamid Shomad Foundation. This is perhaps the most popular and dynamic cultural organisation in Jordan. Sculpture garden and open-air café.

## SHOPPING GUIDE

**Markets –** The greatest choice of embroidered dresses and waistcoats is to be found in the souk down by the mosque, at the bottom of Al-Hussein St. As the majority of Jordanian women wear these items every day, they are come in all sizes and colours, and at very reasonable prices!

**Supermarkets –** The first superstore to open in Jordan is **Safeway** in the Sheisani district, (near the Sport City Circle). Large car park in front, open 24hr-a-day, 7-days-a-week. Two floors largely dedicated to household goods; large range of imported things from cornflakes to deodorant, as well as spirits, cigars, French wines (Medoc, Chablis, Sauternes, Champagne).

**Special purchases** – Standard, mass-produced nick-nacks in brass or wood are readily available from the small shops opposite the Roman Theatre; although these may prove to be inexpensive, the quality of craftsmanship may be questionable. These shops also sell photographic film (express 30min developing service). The variety of souvenirs in the souk is no wider, there are simply more of them, most especially off King Talal St (Al-Afghani, Al-Boukhari, Al-Sanabel, Al-Hussein, Al-Shami). Besides the usual items, so-called "antiques" (coins, weapons, jewellery) and carpets are for sale at the **Zatari Bazaar** (C3), not far from the Amman Palace Hotel. If you are looking for contemporary gold and silver jewellery (chains, charms, necklaces, earrings, bracelets), go Downtown to the **Gold Souk** (C2), where fifty or so traders are grouped on Al-Hussein St. For more up-market craftsmanship, search round the Jebels. The **Artisana Boutique** (B3), 2nd Circle, stocks a great range of exquisitely made things – embroidery, hand-blown glass, museum reproductions. Open 9am-7pm. Closed Fridays.

**Alaydi** (B3), which nestles on the ground floor of a modern house in Jebel Amman, also specialises in fine craftsmanship: gold and silver jewellery, weavings, cross-stitch and embroideries, decorative hand-blown glass, Iron Age style candelabra, ceramics. Many unique pieces. Open Saturday to Thursday, 9am-6.30pm.

**Bani Hamida,** (C2), 1st Circle, has a large choice of Hamida carpets. Traditional designs restyled to suit modern tastes. All sizes and all price categories.

**JRP** (C2). The initials stand for a charity project sponsored by the Save the Children Fund to assist destitute women in the eastern quarters of Amman in earning money. The luxurious shop sells lovely things, hand-sewn and embroidered by some 1 500 or so women managed by a handful of astute businesswomen. The outcome is quite fabulous: quilts and cushions that may be bulky to pack or send home, household linen, traditional dolls and suede handbags.

**Bookshops** – Colourful coffee-table books, maps, guidebooks and reference books are available from hotel boutiques, or from a couple of book-shops Downtown.

**Jordan Distribution Agency Bookshop** (C2), Jebel Amman Rd (guides, art books) and **Al-Ulama** (C1), 44 Amir Muhammad St (maps, trekking manuals, guides for exploring the Wadi Rum).

**Amman Bookshop** (C3), near 3rd Circle, stocks examples of Jordanian literature, social studies and regional guides, mainly in English.

**Outdoor gear** – **Tiger Stores** (C3), Jebel Amman Rd, opposite the Jordan Distribution Agency Bookshop. Special equipment for hunting, shooting, fishing, camping (gas-stove canisters), scuba-diving and snorkelling (masks, fins), trekking (compasses).

# CITIES OF THE DECAPOLIS★
287km round trip from Amman – 2 days
Overnight stay at Ajlun, Irbid or Um Qeis

**Not to be missed**
The colonnade and the sumptuous decoration of the façades at Jarash.
The wonderful site at Um Qeis.
**And remember...**
to schedule a stop up in the hills at Ajlun
with its fine castle, Qalaat Rabadh.
Do not use your camera near military installations or control points.

The most attractive countryside in Jordan is to be found in the region north of Amman. Beyond the outskirts of the capital, the hills are terraced with olive groves and vineyards, while the open spaces are divided up into wheat fields.

**The Decapolis Confederation**
The rich agricultural regions north of Amman that stretch into modern-day Syria underwent a substantial evolution during the Greco-Roman period. Classical writers such as Pliny allude to ten wealthy and cosmopolitan cities, united in a confederation and enjoying mutual benefits in commercial and political interests. It would appear, however, that in time the number of cities exceeded ten to include the Jordanian cities of Philadelphia (Amman), Gerasa (Jarash), Gedara (Um Qeis), Pella (Tabaqat Fahl), Capitolias, Abila (Quweilbeh), Damascus and Canatha (Qanawat) in Syria and Scythopolis (Beisan) in Israel.

Further on, oaks and pines overlook the broad rift valley of the River Jordan running north-south between Lake Tiberias (Sea of Galilee) and the Dead Sea. Along the banks of the river, there is intense cultivation, as glass-houses alternate with groves of orange trees and banana palms.

The itinerary outlined below enables you to explore this part of Jordan, including four of the ten cities that made up the ancient Decapolis confederation. The first day should be spent in Jarash before journeying on to Ajlun or Irbid, the modern capital of northern Jordan. The next day takes in Um Qeis (ancient Gedara) before travelling abruptly down to some way below sea-level, following the Yarmuk Gorge, passing through Pella in the Jordan Valley and stopping at Salt and Iraq el Amir on the way, before returning to Amman.

*Follow directions out of Amman towards Salt. At the main roundabout in Suweileh, follow signs for Jarash and Ajlun.*

The road climbs up into the hills offering views of the Jordan Valley and Lake King Talal. Then it makes its way down to the River Zarqa, shadows its course, crosses it and heads uphill again towards Jarash.

■ **Jarash★★★** *—See p 342*

*To continue to Ajlun, double back towards Amman and turn right.*

The road progresses steeply uphill cutting through beautiful pine forests and olive groves. After 15km, it contours the opposite side of the valley. Then, at last, up ahead on a ridge the castle of Qalaat Rabadh comes into view.

*Below the large town of Anjara, fork right towards Ajlun.*

**Cities of the Decapolis**

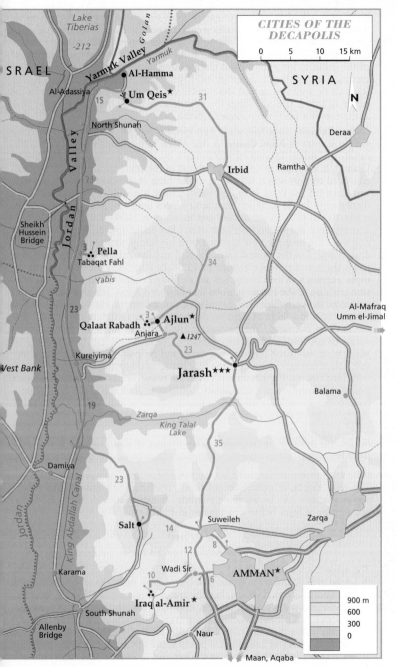

CITIES OF THE
DECAPOLIS

0   5   10   15 km

Lake
Tiberias
-212

Golan

Yarmuk

SYRIA

N

ISRAEL

Yarmuk Valley

Al-Hamma

Al-Adassiya

Um Qeis ★

15

31

Deraa

North Shunah

Ramtha

Irbid

23

34

Sheikh
Hussein
Bridge

Jordan Valley

Pella
Tabaqat Fahl

Yabis

23

Qalaat Rabadh

Ajlun ★

Anjara

▲1247

Kureiyima

23

West Bank

19

Jarash ★★★

Balama

Zarqa

King Talal
Lake

35

Damiya

23

Jordan

King Abdallah Canal

Salt

14

Suweileh

Zarqa

8

Karama

12

Wadi Sir

6

AMMAN ★

10

Iraq al-Amir ★

South Shunah

Allenby
Bridge

Naur

Maan, Aqaba

900 m
600
300
0

■ **Ajlun★** – Jordanians love to escape to this small summer resort set among wooded hills, where temperatures remain far cooler than in Amman. Although unremarkable in many ways, the town does have two hotels and one restaurant reputed for its Jordanian cuisine. As this is situated on the road to the castle, it makes for a convenient place to stop for lunch for anyone (including groups) touring the Decapolis cities. If you want to visit Qalaat Rabadh, the squat castle with fine carved stone outer-walls, turn left by the mosque in the centre of town. The road hugs the hillside until it reaches the castle car park at the top of a fairly steep slope (3.5km).

**Qalaat Rabadh★** *(8am-7pm, winter 8am-5pm. Entrance fee. Allow 30min)*, otherwise simply known as **Ajlun Castle**, is one of the rare examples of Islamic fortification in Jordan. Erected in about 1184 by a cousin of Saladin (Izz al-Din Usama), it was built to counter the threat of the crusader armies, whose most advanced outpost was at Belvoir on the far bank of the River Jordan. The castle was enlarged 30 years later, fell into Mongol hands in 1260 and was used thereafter to house local administrative offices until struck by a violent earthquake in the 19C; its restoration was initiated in 1929.

The entrance lies beyond the custodian's hut and across an impressive **moat** dug from the bedrock now spanned by a footbridge that replaces the original drawbridge. The cut stonework of the wall and two external towers dates from when the complex was extended in 1214. Pass through the wire gate to the **main entrance,** which comprises an archway decorated with birds: an allusion perhaps to the carrier pigeons that flew into Ajlun, relaying the messages couriered between Cairo and Baghdad. Continue up the ramp. Round the first sharp corner is a flight of steps on the right leading to the upstairs rooms that are lit from overhead. The passage in the corner of the first room provides access to a lovely L-shaped room.

Make your way back down to the ramp and on past several rooms to either side before emerging outside at the very kernel of this primitive, square fortress with four towers. If you climb up over the ruins on the right, you will reach a platform from where a fine **view★** extends out over the surrounding countryside. If you look out through a gap in the west wall, you will appreciate just how the castle came to dominate the Jordan Valley plain.

*Go back towards Ajlun to where the Hotel Rabadh stands. Turn down the small road on the left and follow it to the Jordan Valley (45mins of wild landscape and splendid panoramic views).*

*If you want to go on to Irbid and Um Qeis, turn left in the centre of Ajlun.*

The road climbs to quite a height before reaching the exposed ridge where the crosswinds can be alarmingly strong. It makes its way through several uninspiring villages before coming out at Irbid University (40min).

## ■ Irbid

*Pop 300 000 – Alt 530m*

The modern town of Irbid has grown very rapidly to become the third largest city in Jordan after Amman and Zarqa. The centre, built upon the foundations of the ancient Decapolis city of Arbela, has obliterated all traces of its heritage. Only its three museums and a choice of hotels, in an area where reasonable accommodation is scarce, will persuade visitors to stop over in Irbid. Head for the district south of the town where the University of Yarmuk is situated; there you will find several comfortable hotels and a selection of places where you can eat *(see Making the most of the Decapolis Cities)*. This, the most modern part of Irbid, is also the most lively.

As the road from Ajlun heads into Irbid, it runs past the campus of the **University of Yarmuk**. *Turn right after the mosque and the Station One restaurant.* The main entrance to the university is 200m further on. Its large campus, inaugurated in 1976, has an air of confidence, asserting its power over the formation of the new elite generation of Middle Eastern students.

The **Museum of Jordanian Heritage** *(10am-5pm; closed Thursdays, Fridays and public holidays. No charge.)* is to be found within the precincts of the university. The guard will direct you to the Anthropology and Archeology Departments. The museum, which competes with the one in Amman, has made great efforts to provide detailed explanations and illustrated information to accompany exhibits. Displays are arranged on two floors. The first three rooms on the ground floor are devoted to pre-Islamic archeology and include statues from Ain Ghazal and other artefacts from the excavations of the Decapolis cities, from the Bronze Age to the annexation of the area by Rome. Various trades are illustrated with displays in the last room and upstairs (the potter, the pharmacist etc).

The **Archeological Museum of Irbid** *(8am-2pm; closed Fridays and public holidays)* is to be found a short way (1km) from the university, on Al-Maamoun Street. Its collections are based upon material excavated from the area around Irbid and the Jordan Valley.

*300m beyond the main entrance to the University there is a roundabout; turn down the Amman road, then take the second left fork which goes off at a slight tangent.*

*Follow for 1km and turn right where signposted to Um Qeis. The main road bisects the town for approximately 10km, changing direction several times: keep to the directions for Um Qeis.*

On the way to Um Qeis you will pass close to the sites of two other Decapolis cities: Capitolias (Bayt Ra) and Abila (Quweilbeh). After some 18km, the road shadows the line of the ridge by means of a series of flyovers. The scenery becomes increasingly wild, scored with great ravines fronted by ragged outcrops of grey rock. At last you arrive at Um Qeis.

# ■ Um Qeis★

*Drive straight through the modern town to the site of ancient Gedara. At the foot of the hill on which the Ottoman village is perched look out for a rough track leading left. Park in the visitor car park and pay for your ticket at the hut.*

The spirit of Um Qeis, which at one time ranked among the most brilliant and intellectual cities of the Decapolis, lives on in the remains of a basalt theatre which archeologists are at pains to restore to its former, if a little mournful, glory. The exceptional view from the terrace of the rest-house embraces the Yarmuk gorge and Lake Tiberias (Sea of Galilee): this you may find to be a lot more captivating than the actual ruins. The benign and tranquil appearance of this lovely pastoral landscape in a far-flung northern corner of Jordan is quite deceptive, for Um Qeis and the foundations of the ancient city beneath it mark the convergence of contentious frontiers between three restless states, namely Israel, Jordan and Syria.

**Gedara in Antiquity** – Um Qeis occupies a strategic site at the entrance to the gorges of the River Yarmuk. It was through this valley that traders passed between the Hauran, the principal wheat-growing areas that extended south of Damascus, in order to get to the Mediterranean Sea. Gedara's unique position was reinforced by being surrounded by highly fertile land and being blessed with plentiful supplies of water all year round, enabling it to support and sustain a sizeable population and act as a defensible frontier post. The Ptolemies founded a military colony here to ward off their Seleucid rivals to the north. Many great thinkers and writers were drawn to the city that was named the "favourite of the Muses". Following Pompey's conquest in 63 BC, much of the city had to be rebuilt; then, between 30-4BC, it was entrusted to King Herod of Judea. During that time the town grew in size and importance as trade expanded across the Eastern part of the Roman Empire. The area began drawing ever larger numbers of people wishing to take the waters at the hot springs nearby at Hamat Gader that were renowned throughout the Empire for their therapeutic powers. In addition, there would always be ample opportunity to enjoy some form of entertainment at one of three theatres at Gedara. Gradually the city succumbed to Christianity, for records confirm that its bishop, one Sabinus of Gedara, was present at the Council of Nicaea. Its culture continued to flourish despite the rise of Islam until the 7C and 8C when the region was repeatedly shaken by a series of violent earthquakes, and the literati moved to safer ground. It was not until the Mameluke period that the place was revived and a community of Ottomans set down its roots among the uppermost ruins of the abandoned city of Antiquity.

## Site

*8am-7pm (winter 5pm). Entry fee. Allow 30min and an additional 30min for the Byzantine tomb*

The **north theatre** is excavated from the hill beyond the car park. Despite its dilapidated condition and the profusion of invasive vegetation, it is still possible to make out the semicircular outline of the hollow shell. It is probable that the Ottomans helped themselves to the abundant and readily available cut building stone offered by the abandoned theatre to build their village (now also deserted). *Take the path downhill running to the right of the car park.* The main track echoes the ancient **decumanus maximus**, its diagonally laid stones visible here and there, before intersecting with a road on the left. This leads to the **Byzantine church**\* and basilica terrace. At the northern end stands the **atrium**, delineated by columns with Corinthian capitals and a fine pavement laid with alternating slabs of white limestone and black basalt. The square church beyond can be dated to the 5C or 6C AD. In stark contrast with the milk-white column shafts in the atrium, eight dark basalt columns with Corinthian capitals mark out the central octagon of the original **basilica**\* which probably had a dome, forming the inner-sanctum of a second church. The slight dip within the octagon would have been where the altar stood. Beyond a kind of passageway or chancel beautifully paved with polychrome geometric tiles, symbolising the passage between the earthly and heavenly kingdoms, extends a small narthex.

*On leaving the church, make for the opening cut in the circular basalt wall. This leads straight into the underside of the west theatre.*

The **west theatre**\*\* is the best preserved of the three theatres at Gedara and preserves intact a number of rows of graduated seating arranged in three tiers. The decrepit condition of the two upper rows reveals the way the seats were attached to the vaulted gallery below. Note the wonderful seats of honour cut from a single block of basalt and polished to perfection. The proscenium wall has completely collapsed and disappeared, although the vaulted side rooms in the wings, through which the actors would have made their entrances, still stand on each side of the stage. Inevitably, this great basalt monument begs comparison with its more imposing counterpart at Bosra.

*Cross the stage and follow the track towards the decumanus.*

The main street running below the basilica was evidently the town's high street lined on the right-hand side with **17 open-fronted shops** among which are a few restored ones. Turn down the *decumanus* on the left and continue some 100m to the **nymphaeum**. Opposite, but fenced off with barbed wire, stands a series of arches built with large blocks of limestone: these formed part of a public **bath-house**.

If you have time *(30min)*, walk along the path that runs along the left side of the tarmac road *(10min)* to a group of columns set back from the pavement. Judging from the remains, this must have been a building of some importance. 200m further on the left, you will find a puzzling circular arrangement of carefully cut basalt bases: these are the foundation blocks of a tower that would have flanked the **Tiberias gate**, a free-standing barrel-vaulted archway straddling the main street. The nearby flight of steps leads down to what is perhaps the most unusual and best-preserved monument of Um Qeis: an **underground tomb** with a covered forecourt (added in the 4C), complete with four supporting columns. This Roman mausoleum with heavy basalt doors *(closed to the public)* was remodelled in the Byzantine era as a crypt for the church above. It is possible, however, to make out through the wire grille of the antechamber the ledges on which corpses were laid.

*From the baths, find your way to the rest-house overlooking the basilica.*

The restaurant terrace provides a wonderful **view★★**: on the right, a wadi reaches out towards the Yarmuk before it merges with the River Jordan which, far to the east, traces the border between Syria and Jordan. Way down in the green and fertile valley lies the village of Al Hamma. Opposite, you can make out the bleak

Vaulted shops, Gedara

G. Degeorge

Um Qeis

and barren Golan Heights, that contentious no-man's land occupied by Israel since 1967. To the north, on a clear spring day, it is possible to see the snow-capped profile of Mount Hermon. The stretch of blue water to the left is Lake Tiberias (Sea of Galilee): amazing to think of it lying at 210m below sea level!

Conclude your visit with the small **museum** (*open 8am-5pm, 4pm in winter; closed Tuesdays*) which has been installed in Bayt Russan, an old Ottoman house with black and white seating and a pretty garden planted with pomegranate trees. The statue at the entrance, swathed in the most delicate drapery, probably represents **Tyche**, the patron deity of Gedara. The enthroned figure holding a cornucopia (symbol of plenty) was discovered in the west theatre. The **Byzantine mosaic** (4C) to her left is the lid of a tomb bearing the names of three eminent Gadarenes, found in the antechamber of the Roman mausoleum. The small room opposite (on the right of the courtyard) contains artefacts recovered from local excavations. The shop stocks a wide selection of cards and books on Jordan; it also sells jars of locally produced capers.

*Exit from the car park and turn left downhill; stop at the guard post 20m further on. You may be asked to produce your passport and car-papers, and to open the boot of your vehicle. This procedure may have to be repeated at regular intervals all along the Jordan Valley road, for it is permanently under strict, although discreet, surveillance as it winds its way down to the bottom of the Yarmuk Valley.*

*At the junction some 5km further on, turn right for the village of Al-Hamma (4km).*

■ **Yarmuk Valley and Al-Hamma** – The road winds its way down through banana plantations from which emerge women with large trays on their heads, stacked high with small bunches of bananas. The vegetation is green and lush in this enclosed, humid valley that is blessed with its very own microclimate.

The **village of Al-Hamma** nestles at 150m below sea-level, at the foot of the Yarmuk gorges. Once an ancient border post safeguarding traffic to and from Syria (as indicated by the old sign), it was pushed to the actual confines of Israel when the cease-fire lines annexed the Golan Heights. The main reason for its fame in Antiquity, however, was its profusion of active thermal springs. A small **spa**, complete with self-contained apartments and a restaurant, has been built at the entrance to the village: although be warned, the facilities should not be compared too closely with those of a Western spa! The place is deserted for much of the year despite being a highly popular resort at the height of the summer season. Every two hours a bell is sounded to mark a change in the exclusive use of the bathing pools by men or women. A single large domed area encloses pools of warm and hot (50°C) water. The latter is so hot that the slightest effort quickly leaves one feeling quite exhausted. The water has a high content of sulphur and smells accordingly. The somewhat grimy blue tiles and bare mortar are reminiscent of an old-fashioned swimming pool back home. The large open-air pool, surrounded by sweet-scented jasmine and glorious bougainvillaea, is a lot more attractive, especially early in the morning when the steam hovers above the surface. A good soak does wonders for tired limbs and for a weary soul after a full day's sightseeing.

*Return to the main road and turn right towards the River Yarmuk.*

Israel lies just a few hundred metres away on the far bank of the river. As this is a politically hypersensitive area, you may have to go through several check-points. *You are strongly advised not to stop or take photographs.*

Across the landscape, you will see short stretches of the old railway line that once ran between Amman and Damascus via Haifa along the Deraa branch line into Syria. In those days it was possible to board a train at Al-Hamma and travel to the Mediterranean coast some 100km away, crossing at least 15 bridges in the Yarmuk Valley alone. The collapsed platform on the right was sabotaged in 1946 by Israeli commandos. The road curves gradually towards the left until it reaches the Jordan Valley close to the village of Al Adassiya.

■ **Jordan Valley** – The main road shadows the King Abdullah Canal, a concrete channel that extends 70km north-south parallel to the River Jordan, bearing water from the Yarmuk and draining the various streams running down to the cultivated terraces below sea-level. Without it, the Jordan Valley (the *Ghor*) would lose its sub-tropical air reminiscent of the Spanish **huerta** where the irrigated plains are covered with flourishing crops. You are advised not to make an attempt to approach the river itself that marks the cease-fire line established in 1967 between Israel and Jordan, and as such remains under strict surveillance.

### River Jordan

The River Jordan (al-Ourdon meaning "the one that descends") is fed by streams swollen with snow-melt from the heights of Mount Hermon in Lebanon. It flows through Lake Tiberias before converging with the waters of the Yarmuk, which are almost as plentiful. From here, its course meanders gradually southwards to drain into the Dead Sea completing its journey of 360km through five different countries. For obvious reasons, therefore, its waters are of primordial importance to Jordan and her future. Indeed the rift valley constitutes the principal farming region in the kingdom, and lends its name to the State. Throughout the Bible, the River Jordan is referred to as a significant land mark: it was drained to allow the Children of Israel to reach the Promised Land (Joshua V), it healed the leprosy of Naaman in accordance with Elisha's recommendations to prove the existence of a prophet of Israel (2Kings V v14), and it served in the Baptism of Christ by John the Baptist – "Then cometh Jesus from Galilee to Jordan unto Jordan, to be baptized of him" Matthew III v13.

*At the roundabout in the centre of North Shunah, turn left.*

The wonderful rubber trees growing in the gardens seem to make a mockery of their cousin *ficus elastica* that we keep in our homes. As the plain broadens outwards, the narrow pot-holed road becomes increasingly cluttered with small trucks laden with oranges and premature produce grown under glass. To the left, gentle hills divided by deep ravines stretch back into the distance. The valley is densely populated with about 140 000 inhabitants of varied ethnic extraction. The Ghoranis have tight curls and black skin inherited from their African forebears among the black slaves brought by the Mamelukes or soldiers loyal to Ibrahim Pasha, abandoned here when he retreated from the region in 1840.

*Some 10km beyond North Shunah, the sign "Jordan Valley Crossing Point" looms into view: this refers to the Sheikh Hussein Bridge which straddles the frontier with Israel built here after the signing of the 1994 peace treaty. 7km beyond the bridge, look out for a small, very steep road branching left up to Tabaqat Fahl and Pella 3km beyond that. Stop at the rest-house situated to the left of an unusually conical hill (car park at the rear of the rest-house).*

■ **Pella** – Although Pella's small theatre and Byzantine church cannot rival those of Jarash, the site and its two springs running with cool clear water is nonetheless marvellously situated high above the River Jordan, facing the hills

**The Jordan Valley**

of Palestine. Up here, watching the sun rise in the morning and set in the evening can be quite spectacular. The scarcity of available accommodation in the area is therefore all the more regrettable.

The history of the site dates back a million years. In turn, Pella has sustained stone-age hunters, Chalcolithic settlers, citizens of a fortified Iron-Age village who traded with Egypt and Cyprus, Greeks, Romans occupiers and Byzantine clansmen. Through time, people have enjoyed constant and plentiful natural supplies of water and healthy harvests of crops from the fertile land in the immediate vicinity; natural woodland provided them with fuel and, when required, there was easy access to the main overland trade routes along the rift valley. Long before Classical Antiquity the city flourished, prospering until Mameluke times. Today, the site attracts archeologists and historians intent on gleaning a rare insight into hitherto little-known periods of occupation, notably by the Abassids.

The **site** is fenced off to keep out sheep and goats. The rest-house, splendidly situated and tastefully furnished in the Ottoman style, offers the best overview of the ancient Pella against its natural and timeless backdrop. On the left, the perfectly shaped sugar-loaf hill (Tell al Hosn) once provided an opportune site for a **Byzantine citadel**, although nothing much may be seen of it from here. On the same flank as the *rest-house*, is a group of upright columns standing on a small platform; these belong to the atrium of the **eastern basilica**, a church dating from the 5C. The main centre of the ancient town is laid out directly below the rest-house. The most prominent religious building in Byzantine times was the **civic complex church**, marked out with the many columns re-erected by the Jordanian Department of Antiquities. To the left of it, next to the running water fountains, are the remains of a 400-seat **odeon** built at the end of the 1C AD. The large white building on top of the ancient tell belongs to the Australian archeological team. The exploratory trenches in the vicinity provide evidence of occupation dating back to the Bronze Age. In the distance, beyond the Jordan Valley and its patchwork of fields, lies the Israeli town of Bet She'an (the capital of the Decapolis known in Antiquity as Scythopolis), and the glistening stretches of water collected in the Nahr Jalud Valley. Up on the right stands Mount Tabor (588m), with its distinctive outline; it was here, a mere 10km from Nazareth, that the Transfiguration of Christ took place.

*Go back to the main Jordan Valley road and continue along it for 35km. At the fork, veer left up hill to Salt (23km).*

■ **Salt** – Salt has managed to preserve a little of the charm and allure of an Ottoman town. Its expansion dates from 1886 when the Governor of Damascus installed a prefect *(qaymaqam)* here in the hope of reinstating some form of order in this agitated region of the Empire. When Amman was chosen as the capital after the First World War, the wealthy gentry moved from Salt to Amman.

**Houses\*** constructed for rich merchants at the end of the 19C terrace the hillside, although many are now interspersed with more modern buildings. The narrow streets are lined with lovely mellow stone façades, articulated with bay windows, often in pairs. Here and there, a house has a red tiled roof, which is unusual in this region. A major project is underway here to preserve a unique testament to Jordan's recent history. Already, the town centre boasts

**Cities of the Decapolis**

an **Ethnographic Museum** *(open 8am-5pm; closed Fridays)*, an **Archeological Museum** *(open daily, 9am-5pm)* and the Zaman Restaurant, complete with gallery showcase for hand-made goods.

*Head towards Amman along the motorway; after Suweileh (14km), look out for and follow signs to Queen Alia Airport; after 12km, turn right at the 7th Circle in the direction of Wadi Sir. A further 10km takes you to the village of Iraq al-Amir.*

■ **Iraq el Amir**★ – The 30min drive from Amman to Iraq al-Amir brings a complete change of scenery. The great white ruins of Qasr al-Abd stand proud of the beautiful ochre-coloured cliffs behind, facing towards the enchanted valley of the Wadi es Sir. According to accounts penned by Flavius Josephus, the palace commissioned by Prince Hyrcan – a member of the local Tobiad dynasty resident in Amman since the 5C BC – was to have been surrounded by an artificial lake. Alas, soon after the project was initiated, he died and work was more or less abandoned. It is now widely acknowledged that Qasr al-Abd at Iraq al-Amir is indeed the monument described by the Jewish historian in the 1C AD.

At first sight, the most striking thing about **Qasr al-Abd**★ *(no charge as there is no access to the building interior; allow 15min)* is the sheer size of the white limestone blocks used to build the walls. Both its plan and decoration are modelled on Hellenistic prototypes, although a number of Oriental features are also integrated in keeping with the current taste and fashion prevalent in the neighbouring region during the 2C BC. As you approach the east side, you will see an iron railing protecting the carved relief of a panther, its mouth doubling as a spout from which water would flow when the basin behind was filled. The entrance to the palace was situated to the right of the animal. Two columns front the main gateway. A staircase on the left provided access to the living quarters above. Note the second panther relief completing the symmetry on the other side. The corner section overhead bears an unusual carving of a lioness attending her cub. Similar panels with animals – alternating male with female – would have ornamented the rest of the outer wall around the building.

## Making the most of the Decapolis Cities

### COMING AND GOING

It is quite easy to visit all the sites listed except Pella by bus. If you wish to limit your excursion to Al-Hamma, allow at least 2 days. The scant ruins at Pella do not really justify the effort required in getting there by public transport. What is more, the buses do not run along the Yarmuk Valley and so part of the main purpose of the excursion is lost. The most straightforward way to visit Salt and Iraq al-Amir is to arrange a trip there from Amman.

**By bus** – Before you set out by bus, it is vital that you remember to ask for the times of return services, and make a note of the last bus for it may be difficult to get back to town after 4pm. Buses to Jarash (1hr) leave Amman every 30min. The bus station at Jarash is located in the new town, in front of the eastern baths. To get to the site (500m) from here, walk along the bridge by the mosque, and turn left to the Visitors' Centre.

Buses to Ajlun (30min) depart from Jarash every 30min. Catch one of the local buses heading for Qalaat Rabadh and ask the driver to drop you off at one of the two hotels. Services to Irbid (45min) from Ajlun are by minibus.

The other way of getting to Irbid (2hr) is to catch one of the many *Hijazi* buses or minibuses leaving regularly from Amman's Abdali Station, stopping at Irbid's southern bus station. From here, take a taxi to the northern bus station.

For Um Qeis (45min): catch a minibus from the station at Irbid North.

For Al-Hamma: irregular minibus service from Um-Qeis (20min) or hitch a lift.

For Salt (45min): frequent departures from Amman Abdali Station.

For Iraq al-Amir: catch a bus from Amman Downtown leaving regularly (every 15min) for Wadi Sir. You will find a long line of green and white buses waiting on Ali Ibn Abi Taleb Street, 1.5km west of the theatre. Once there, you will find buses shuttling down to the entrance to Qasr al-Abd. Allow one hour's travelling time.

**By train –** Undoubtedly, the most picturesque way of getting to Jarash is to catch the Hedjaz train – a great diesel locomotive with 2 open-window wooden carriages – on its way north to Syria. Departures for al-Mafraq from Mahhata station at 8am every Monday. At Al-Mafraq, walk to the bus station just behind the railway station and catch a bus bound for Jarash (ETA 11am).

## ADDRESS BOOK

**Banks/currency exchange –** There are banks at Ajlun and Irbid. Visa cards are accepted.

## WHERE TO STAY

### • Jarash

Despite the importance of the archeological site, there are still no facilities at Jarash. Try and spend the night at Amman or Ajlun, and make a start early the following morning.

### • Ajlun

There are two hotels on the road to the castle worth noting. However, beds are in high demand during the summer months and so it is important to book in advance. Remember that this is one of the few places (alt 1 250m) in Jordan where people can escape from the sweltering heat.

*From US$35-50*

**Ajlun Hotel**, Rabadh Castle St, ☎ /Fax (2) 642 05 24 – 52rm 📶 𝄞 🆃🆅 ✘ 300m beyond the first. Rooms vary considerably: ask for a light room facing across to the castle and the valley rather than a room in the rather sombre extension at the rear. Warm and friendly reception.

*From US$50-65*

**Al-Rabadh Castle Hotel**, Rabadh Castle St, ☎ (2) 642 02 02, Fax (6) 463 04 14 – 22rm 📶 𝄞 🆃🆅 ✘ 🆑🆑 The first hotel on your right 200m above the road, 2km outside Ajlun. Spacious and comfortable rooms with private balcony overlooking the valley perfect for breakfast. Restaurant amenities in the garden shaded by olive trees.

### • Irbid

*Under US$10*

There are quite a few moderately priced, though basic, hotels in the centre of town *(Al-Arabia, Al-Amen)*.

*From US$55-75*

**Al-Joude Hotel**, University St, on the Ajlun road(at the end of an alley), ☎ (2) 727 55 15, Fax (2) 727 55 17 – 44rm 📶 🍽 𝄞 🆃🆅 ✘ 🆑🆑 This recently renovated hotel has comfortable rooms and has the added advantage of being very quiet, being off the main road. Terrace and Internet café.

*From US$80-100*

**Hijazi Palace Hotel**, opposite university campus on the road out of Ajlun, ☎ (2) 727 95 04, Fax (2) 727 95 20 – 80rm 📶 🍽 𝄞 🆃🆅 ✘ 🌊 🆑🆑 The best hotel in Irbid. Standard facilities. Hire car, hotel boutique, bars and open terrace in summer. Billiards table in basement. Indoor swimming pool on 3rd floor.

### • Um Qeis

*Under US$20-35*

**Um Qeis Hotel**, on the main road towards the Ottoman village, ☎ (2) 750 00 80, Fax (92) 724 23 13 – 21rm ✘ Family-run hotel offering two categories of accommodations. Empty rooms on 1st floor with use of communal bathroom, or furnished rooms with shower-room on 2nd floor. Meals are available if ordered in advance. Roof terrace with lovely view over the Jordan valley, Israel and Syria.

• **Al-Hamma**

*Under US$35*

**Recreational Area Hotel**, at the entrance to the village, ☎ (2) 750 05 10 – 40rm ⚐ ✗ Main hotel attached to the spa, overlooking the large open-air pool. Small self-contained apartments with kitchenette for people taking the waters. Two categories on offer: one with tiled concrete sleeping platform (!) and small apartments with balconies. Restaurant on the far side of bathing pool.

### WHERE TO EAT

• **Jarash**

*Under US$10*

Two pleasant restaurants specialising in local food serve meals under a trellis across the road from the Visitors' Centre: **Janat Jarash** and **Al-Kayyam**.

*Over US$10*

**Jarash Resthouse**, behind the Visitors' Centre. ♟ Large choice from the buffet (15 *meze* and 6 hot dishes). Although the quality of the food is nothing special, the restaurant's proximity to the site, its shaded terrace and air-conditioned dining room more than make up for it.

**Lebanese House**, 1km from the Arch of Hadrian along the Ajlun road. Signposted. ♟ Some consider this to be the best Lebanese restaurant in Jordan. Whether this is correct or not, the place gets crowded out with people from Amman, most especially on Fridays. Marathon menu. Covered terrace and veranda overlooking the countryside. Hookah pipes.

• **Ajlun**

*Over US$10*

⚐ **Bonita**, Rabadh Castle St, ☎ (4) 642 09 81 ♟ 200m from the castle. This place is by far your best choice in the region. It is managed by the Bonita Hotel in Amman, although Spanish food has been replaced with Eastern delights. Large choice of cold and hot meze, chops, wine from Latroum. Hookah pipe to be savoured out on the

terrace, as you contemplate the valley under the stars. Good amenities and service.

• **Irbid**

Great choice of informal eating places along the Ajlun road, opposite the university (**Pizza Hut**, **Quick Burger**). The Hijazi Hotel has a good restaurant.

*Under US$10*

**Cortina D.** Opposite the university, ☎ (2) 24 16 51. Tastefully decorated pizzeria. Attractive black benches and tables. No alcohol. Most of the regulars are students.

• **Um Qeis**

*Over US$10*

⚐ **Um Qeis Resthouse** in the Ottoman village. ♟ A new rest-house recently opened by the excellent Romero Restaurant in Amman. Italian menu with fabulous choice of pasta dishes and salads. Dining room with large windows, although the terrace is even more spectacular with splendid views. Latroum wine by the glass. No accommodation.

• **Pella**

*Under US$10*

**Pella Rest house,** overlooking the site. ♟ Six different kinds of *meze* to accompany the grilled chicken or a freshly caught fish from the River Jordan. Bar serving alcohol including a Cremisan from the Bethlehem region.

### FESTIVAL

**Jarash Annual Folklore Festival**, held in the antique theatre throughout July, brings together various country dance companies – Arab or from further afield. New life is breathed into the area as an audience of 3 000 avidly watches displays of Chinese acrobats, strutting Shakespearean players or a fabulous performance from the hugely famous Lebanese singer Fayrouz. The festival also celebrates local craftsmanship and a large exhibition, and is filmed and broadcast on television throughout the Arab world. For further information, contact the Jarash Festival Office at Amman ☎ (6) 467 51 99.

**Making the most of the Decapolis**

# JARASH ★★★

51km from Amman
See map of the Cities of the Decapolis p 331
For transport and restaurant facilities see p 340

**And remember...**
Jarash can be included in a tour
of the Decapolis cities.
If travelling in July, try to make it to the annual Folklore Festival.

Jarash is built on the banks of the Wadi Jarash, which in Antiquity was known as Chrysorhoas or the "Golden River". The modern, rather unattractive town is situated on the left bank and consists of rows of tightly packed two and three-storey buildings. Over the right bank meanwhile are scattered the glorious ruins of ancient Gerasa, a city of international fame in the 3C AD. The main monuments from Antiquity include an immense colonnade, an unusual oval precinct, no less than three theatres and many temples and churches, all built of the same harmonious limestone. The pine forests cloaking the neighbouring hills lend a pastoral Romanticism to the tranquil landscape with its almost two thousand year history.

## A great city of the ancient East

Gerasa was probably founded in the reign of Antiochus IV Epiphanes (175-164 BC). The following century saw the region benefit from the Pax Romana, implemented as a result of the Roman conquest conducted by Pompey (64 BC); Jarash began to expand. It took on its present form, however, in the 2C AD following the annexation of the Nabataean kingdom by Trajan (106 AD) and the visit of Hadrian. Soon the town was connected by a link road to the Via Nova Trajana, and thereby to Bosra and the Red Sea; later it was raised to the status of *colonia*

**The roving emperor Hadrian**
Hadrian was born in Spain in 76 AD, the son of a provincial family. He headed for Rome in pursuit of a Classical education that encompassed intellectual as well sporting disciplines. A brilliant, yet sensitive student, he became the protégé of his cousin Trajan before being appointed Governor of Syria in 117 and later succeeding to the Imperial throne. Thereafter, he rarely stayed in Rome, preferring instead to sojourn in the great cities of the Empire: Alexandria, Gerasa, Damascus and Antioch. During his long reign (21 years), he proved to be a productive head of state, assuming the role of administrator, strategist and builder of towns and walls that can still be seen across the Middle East today. Hadrian was also a great admirer of Hellenistic culture and highly aware that the Empire did not stop at Rome: at his villa at Tivoli, he had replicas of the masterpieces he had so admired in the East during his three long expeditions there. In many ways, Hadrian was the very incarnation of the spirit of Imperial Rome.

by Caracalla and the population increased to about 25 000. Parthian and Sassanid threats to the Eastern Roman Empire reverberated on Gerasa until, at last, Constantinople was established as the new capital (330) and Christianity was proclaimed to be the official religion. This in turn encouraged local Christians to build no less than 15 churches in the city, which then began to decline. Weakened by the Persian invasion (614) and the conquest of Islam (636), Gerasa was reduced to ruins by a terrible earthquake in 749. Building stones fallen from the monuments were re-used to construct a more modest range of houses, shops and workshops thus ensuring the survival of

Jarash

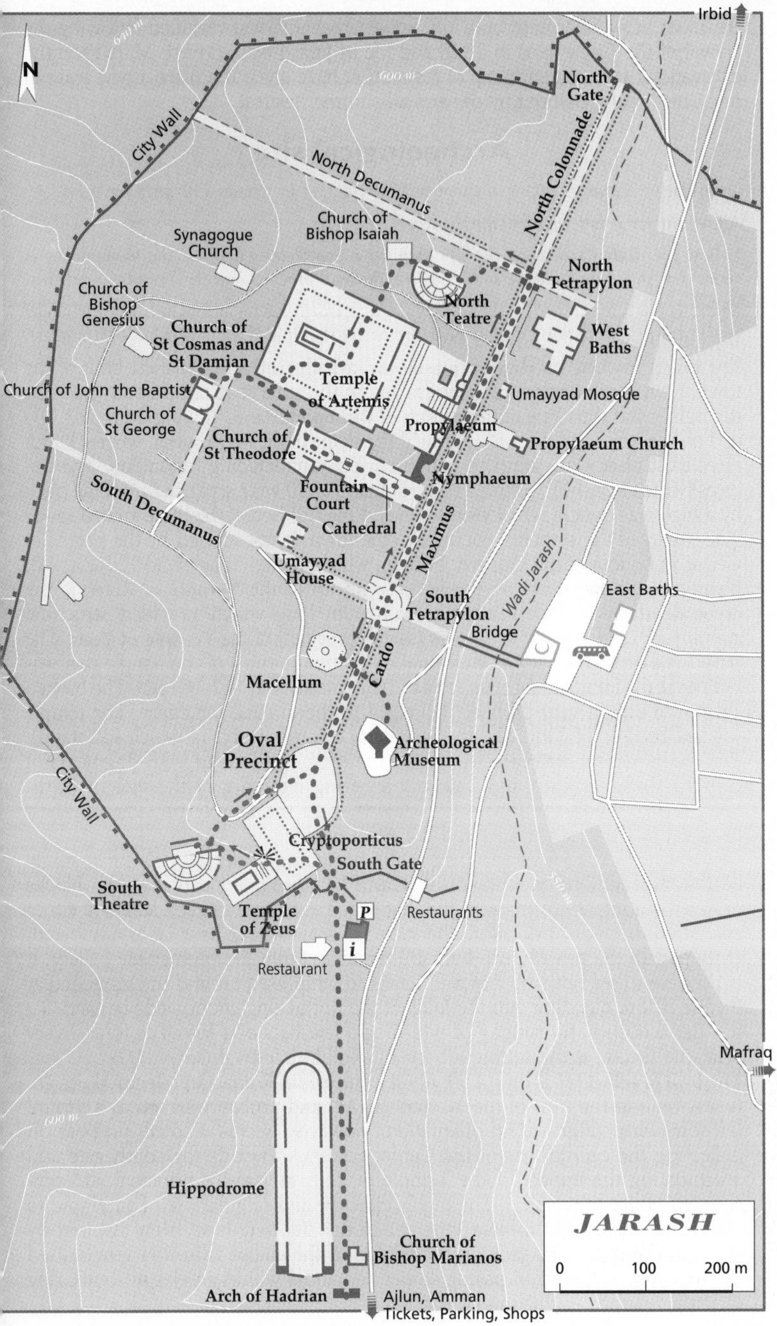

**N**

Irbid

North Gate

City Wall

North Decumanus

North Colonnade

Synagogue Church

Church of Bishop Isaiah

North Tetrapylon

Church of Bishop Genesius

North Teatre

West Baths

Church of St Cosmas and St Damian

Temple of Artemis

Church of John the Baptist

Umayyad Mosque

Church of St George

Propylaeum

Propylaeum Church

Church of St Theodore

Nymphaeum

South Decumanus

Fountain Court

Cathedral

Maximus

Umayyad House

Wadi Jarash

East Baths

South Tetrapylon

Bridge

Cardo

Macellum

Archeological Museum

Oval Precinct

City Wall

Cryptoporticus

South Gate

South Theatre

Restaurants

Temple of Zeus

**P**

**i**

Restaurant

Mafraq

Hippodrome

Church of Bishop Marianos

Arch of Hadrian

Ajlun, Amman
Tickets, Parking, Shops

**JARASH**

0    100    200 m

the town, now fallen into oblivion. Some prosperity was regained following the arrival of the Circassians in 1848 and life in Jarash was revived. More recently, excavations and a programme of restoration have given the place a new lease of life. This is now ensured by the annual summer festival.

## Archeological site

*Open daily, 7.30am-7.30pm in summer; 7.30am-5pm in winter. Entrance fee.*

*Allow 3hr for a full visit (90min, at least).*

*Follow the route marked on the site plan for a complete tour of all the monuments. A short visit should include the south theatre, the oval precinct and the Temple of Artemis.*

*Before going into the site by the south gate, it is worth having a look at the scale model of Gerasa in the Visitor's Centre near the car park. Guided tours available on request.*

The site is reached via **Hadrian's archway**, which marks the furthest limit of the town. It was built during the same era and in the same style as the south gate. On the right stand the ruins of the **church of Bishop Marianos** (dating from 570 AD) and on the left, a circular wall indicated the shape of the **racecourse**, where chariot races took place. The southern part is currently undergoing restoration. The terraces (which have been restored near Hadrian's arch) were separated from the track by a high wall, which is still visible. Beyond the rest house, the three arched **south gate**∗ marked the southern entrance to the town. It was erected by the people of Gerasa in honour of the Emperor Hadrian who wintered in Jarash in 129-130 AD. Beneath the stone ramp on the left leading up to the **Temple of Zeus**, is the **cryptoporticus**: a dark vaulted room, 100m long which provided structural support for the forecourt or *temenos* (sacred precinct) of the **Temple of Zeus**. The paved platform at the top is largely taken up by the ruins of the temple that was built over the foundations of an earlier (1C) sanctuary in 162-163 AD. The broken altar on the right very probably belonged to the original sanctuary. The temple was enclosed on all four sides by Corinthian columns (three of which still stand). The **monumental staircase** leading to the temple is littered with fragments of column shafts, capitals and lintels: a sobering reminder of the violent earthquakes that shook the town. The **view**∗∗ from the temple provides the best prospect of the oval precinct and the *decumanus*.

The **south theatre**∗∗, constructed at the beginning of the 2C AD, must surely be the most striking monument in Jarash. Its *cavea* is divided into two blocks of tiered seating, 29 rows deep. Judging from the traces of Greek letters at either end of the bottom rows before the stage, all seats would have been numbered. Only part of the proscenium wall still remains. From the promenade gallery, it is possible to see how the city wall seems to wrap itself around the semicircular theatre before blending into the folds of the undulating countryside beyond. To test the acoustics, try singing or whistling a few bars of a favourite tune. Every year, the theatre is the setting for the July folklore festival *(see p 341)*.

The **oval precinct**∗∗∗ is one of the finest examples of Roman architectural design. It was built at the turn of the 1C and 2C AD and probably served as a forum. Its somewhat unorthodox orientation, however, serves a dual purpose in deflecting the central axis of the Cardo maximus towards the south gate and accentuating the impact of the Temple of Zeus as Jarash's principal and pre-eminent house of worship. The highly effective and original use of an ellipse to resolve the planning problem inherent in the site may have been inspired by oriental examples. The pleasing roundness of the ellipse is further emphasised by the concentrically laid paving stones contained within an elegant outer ring of Ionic columns *(see illustration p 22)*.

J. F. Galmiche

The South Gate, Jarash

The **cardo maximus\*\***, which provided the main axis of the city, would have been lined with the most gracious buildings. Two tetrapylons mark the main intersections. Set back from the most monumental features and built along the flank of the hill, the avenue and its colonnade have an uncanny human dimension to their proportions: something that is often missing from other Roman sites. Altogether, the cardo runs 800m from the oval precinct to the north gate. A continuous architrave stretches from one capital to another, broken only by taller columns that once marked the entrances to the most grandiose buildings. Here and there, gaps between the enormous paving-stones laid diagonally across the street reveal an effective drainage system. The long deep ruts worn by innumerable iron wagon-wheels conjure up timeless images of laden caravans transiting through the city. The first significant monument on the left is a **macellum\***, a covered food market, dating from the early 2C AD. In the octagonal space around a central fountain were arranged a number of stalls; the four large corner exedras accommodating large stone tables would have been used by money-lenders and changers or scribes.

The **south tetrapylon**, some 20m or so beyond the market-place consists of four square plinths marking out the intersection of the cardo with the fine column-lined **south decumanus** that extends towards the Wadi Jarash before crossing into the other part of town. In the 3C AD various tradesmen and merchants set up shop around this open space, fashioning it into the elliptical place it is now. The area (100m) on the right of the *decumanus* has been excavated to reveal the ruins of simple **Umayyad houses**.

The **nymphaeum\*\***, the next feature along the *cardo*, contains a monumental and highly decorative carved fountain. A special arrangement permitted water to gush from a spout mounted in the wall into a large red granite trough added in Byzantine times.

Beyond the nymphaeum, still on the left-hand side of the cardo, sits a magnificent gateway marked by four huge Corinthian columns (1.5m in diameter). This, in turn, gives way to a monumental staircase that appears to lead up into the sky! The purpose of the **propylaeum** (entrance to a temple or sacred enclosure) was to heighten the dramatic effect of the Temple of Artemis standing further up the hill. The axis of the propylaeum in line with the gateway was extended across the other side of the cardo with an open square and a street.

Jarash

During the Byzantine era, the parallel lines of columns were enclosed to form a chamber with nave and aisles that could be used as a church (hence it is known as the **Propylaeum Church**).

Past the church, about 20m from the right-hand side of the *cardo* stood an **Umayyad mosque**, discernible from its semicircular mihrab; the ruins beyond are those of **baths** and the north tetrapylon.

Like its southerly counterpart, the **north tetrapylon** marked the intersection of the cardo with a secondary decumanus. The section of road to the right leads to an annexe to the baths. Despite the earthquakes, this square building preserves its semicircular dome built of large rectangular stones. The last and most northern section of the *cardo* leading to the city's north gate retains its original **north colonnade** of Ionic columns, the rest of the street having had its Ionic voluted capitals replaced with more ornately leafy Corinthian capitals. The **north theatre** has recently been restored. The original odeon, built in the mid 2C, was later enlarged and transformed into a theatre. The area between the two tiers of seating is backed by a wall with doorways through which spectators gained access to and from interconnected passageways. The bare wall between the entrances is further relieved by three ornamental niches. The vaulted corridors or galleries provided access to all levels of seating from behind so as to keep to a minimum the distraction and disturbance of people coming and going throughout the entertainment. Note the graceful relief ornamentation (a lyre and a bagpipe) adorning the pedestals on both sides of the orchestra.

*Climb the hill to the right of the theatre, towards the Temple of Artemis.*

The **Temple of Artemis★★★** is dedicated to the city's protective patron deity. Gigantic columns precede this immense sanctuary (the largest in Jarash) which sits grandiosely upon its podium, surrounded on all sides by a temenos (sacred precinct) contained within a large portico, 36 columns long and 26 columns wide. The most complete (restored) section of the portico is on the south side. The sacred way, leading from the left bank of the river and across the propylaeum, adds additional dramatic impact to the temple over and above the effect from the cardo. A modern stairway provides access to the cella, which lies beyond twelve 13m tall columns; only one is missing. They are so large that, at close proximity, when the wind blows, it seems as though their shafts are swaying. The central niche in the far wall of the cella would have accommodated a statue of the goddess Artemis.

*Walk down the row of columns along the left side of the temple to the group of three conjoined churches.*

The **Church of St Cosmas and St Damian**, on the right, is enclosed within a high wall. Contained within the nave is an interesting floor **mosaic★**, which, if you lean over the parapet on the right, will provide some insight into the great skill of the Byzantine mosaicists. A Greek dedication set before the apse states that the church dates from 533. The two figures on either side represent the two donors, Theodore (left) and Georgia (right). The great floor mosaic is composed of squares and lozenges containing animals and geometric figures.

The narthex, lined with columns, is shared by the churches dedicated to John the Baptist (531) and St George.

*Go back to the Temple of Artemis and make your way to the three terraces down on the right, scattered with the remains of the two churches.*

The top terrace bears vestiges of the nave of the **Church of St Theodore** clearly defined by two rows of seven columns. These predate the church's consecration in 494 AD, and so must have come from an earlier building. The original church would have been preceded by a porticoed atrium, and had two side chapels. *Follow the steps down to the right of the apse.* The **fountain court**, once the atrium of the cathedral, is graced with a fountain and a fine pavement of pink limestone. It was here that an annual festival was held to celebrate Christ's first miracle at the marriage in Cana (John II v22); the fountain was filled with water which was gradually replaced with wine, by means of a special device. The **cathedral** stands beyond the fountain court, across a pretty courtyard paved with red octagonal and small white square tiles. Judging by its central location, it was very probably the main church of Gerasa; it is certainly the oldest. On either side of the apse there are a couple of side-doors leading out to the cardo. The left one would have been reserved for women, the right one for men. Both have passageways that come out by a staircase and a wonderful great terrace at the top. The small niche dedicated to the Virgin Mary above the steps dates from Antiquity.

*Walk back to the cardo; when level with the macellum, turn left towards the museum partly concealed by vegetation.*

The **Archeological Museum** (*no charge, more restricted opening times than those of the excavations*) has a modest collection of objects found at Jarash: these range from pottery to jewellery, and are presented in chronological order from Neolithic to Mameluke times. The museum also provides a brief (but welcome) respite from the sun.

*Return to the site exit on the far side of the splendid oval precinct.*

Jordanians visiting the cardo maximus

B. Brillion/MICHELIN

Jarash

# THE DESERT CASTLES *

### 260km round trip from Amman – 2 days
(An excursion to Um el Jimal incurs an additional 108km)

### Not to be missed
Qasr al-Karana and the Umayyad frescoes at Qasr Amra.
The ghost town of Um el Jimal.

### And remember...
Make an overnight stop at Azraq and schedule a visit to Um el Jimal.
Fill up with fuel and water.
Set off southwards so as to see the architecture from the best angle.

East of Amman stretches mile upon mile of Jordanian desert. This consists of a monotonously flat expanse of dusty emptiness buffeted by winds, bisected by a mere handful of rectilinear roads. This northern extension of the Arabian Desert is extremely dry with an annual rainfall of less than 10cm. The only things on the skyline for miles around are the square profiles of the "Desert Castles" – strange buildings with windowless walls. The two most interesting ones – Qasr el Karana and Qasr Amra – date from the dawn of Islam. The first patch of green to stain the landscape pin points the oasis at Azraq (meaning blue in Arabic). As well as offering respite from the unchanging scenery, it provides a welcome excuse for a stop to stretch the legs with a walk around the castle where Lawrence of Arabia once stayed. On the return journey along the northern road that stretches northwest from Azraq lie the scant remains of two Umayyad sites, Qasr

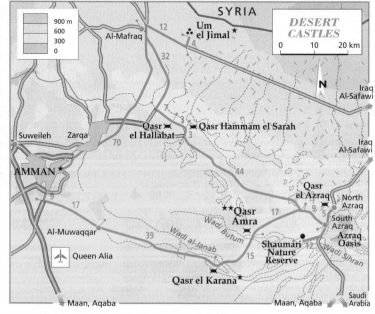

Desert Castles

el Hallabat and Qasr Hammam es Sarah. Should you have time in hand, it is well worth continuing on to Um el Jimal: although the excursion involves a considerable detour at the end of a long day, watching the shadows lengthen over the long-abandoned Romano-Byzantine town can be very moving.

*Head south out of Amman along the airport road. 9km from the centre turn left towards Azraq. Qasr el Karana lies 65km from Amman, past a telecommunications station, on the right.*

■ **Qasr el Karana**★ –
*Open daily from sunrise to sunset. Custodian. No charge. 30min. Park in front of the tent where visitors can relax on cushions with a glass of hot tea or coffee.*

### Desert strongholds

The Umayyad caliphs established their court in Damascus in 651. During their long rule, the dynasty produced a number of indefatigable builders who set about developing several dozen sites (one approximately every 15km between Amman and Azraq). These expensive residences would have served a number of purposes: their prime intention was to enhance the prestige of the reigning sovereign for whom they were built, but they also provided the prince with the perfect foil with which to secure the allegiance and co-operation of the nomadic tribes roaming the area. What better than to arrange a day's hunting followed perhaps by a lavish reception and refined entertainment in the sumptuous bathhouse: in such a way the various rival Bedouin factions were pacified and the security of the Empire was assured. They dammed the wadis so as to provide reliable sources of water to the households and their magnificent gardens. The local people were encouraged to draw supplies for themselves in the hope that they might settle in the area and spend their time cultivating the land rather than warring among themselves. Caravanserais were built as safe transit points for the great caravans laden with precious commodities, plying their way across the vast Umayyad Empire stretching from Cordova in Spain to the Indus.

The castle, whose precise function remains a mystery, is seemingly stranded in the barren landscape, its contours blurred by the glaring light of the blistering sun. The desolation is exacerbated by the high stark walls relieved only by loopholes and four corner towers. The one and only entrance is located in the south wall.

The building is arranged around a central courtyard. The apartment (*bayt*) in each wing comprised a central chamber with four lateral rooms. The rooms leading off to either side of the entrance hall on the ground floor were used as storerooms and stables.

The first floor (*up the stairs at either end of the courtyard*) is *essentially* laid out in the same way as the ground floor, with the area above the hallway being filled with a fifth and more elaborately decorated *bayt*. The most complete windows with small engaged columns, and stucco decoration survive in the apartment on the west side. The plaster over the door into the north suite bears an inked inscription in Arabic that allows the building to be dated to 712, during the caliphate of al-Walid I. The vaulted portico that encircled the courtyard on the first floor and which provided access to all four apartments has long disappeared, but it is still possible to walk through the interconnecting rooms. The flat roof terrace up an additional set of stairs provides a good view in all directions; to the south one can make out the wadi that provided water to the castle.

*Continue towards Azraq.*

Some 14km further on, a line of tall trees appears on the left. This follows the course of the Wadi Butum. What is striking about this sight, in the middle of such inhospitable scenery, is the sheer size of the trees known as turpentine

**Desert Castles**

trees *(Pistacia terebinthus)* growing in the dry wadi. As the wadi is flooded for only a few days each year, the trees must draw water from reliable underground supplies.

The unassuming building over the bridge is Qasr Amra.

*Turn left by the signpost and park in front of the entrance to the fenced site.*

■ **Qasr Amra**★★ – *Open daily from sunrise to sunset. No charge. Custodian. Toilets. Allow a good 30min for studying the frescoes.*

It is hard to imagine that this somewhat simple-looking construction, incongruously situated in the heart of the desert, once housed a fabulous hammam. The reason we know that it was so magnificent is more than evident from the frescoes that survive within. Both the subject matter and the exquisite quality of the paintings seem to qualify the importance of the complex which is thought to have been commissioned by the Umayyad prince al-Walid I in the early 8C. Originally, the existing building – a Unesco World Heritage Site – would have formed part of a larger fortified establishment equipped with spacious living quarters (now disappeared). Vestiges of the actual bathhouse comprise three elements: the noria, a buttressed enclosure wall and the baths themselves (hammam).

The **noria** *(saqqiya)* on the way into the building has been restored. A beast of burden, harnessed to a wooden device, would have been made to walk in a circle around the wheel that activated the revolving chain of pots or buckets. Water was thus collected from a depth of 15m and discharged into the large cistern above ground. From here, the precious water was distributed to the baths by means of underground pipes. To the right of the hammam rises the **buttressed wall**, re-erected to a height of 60cm, built to safeguard the complex from flooding when the water level of the wadi rose too high.

The first room or entrance hall within the hamman is divided longitudinally into three. Some consider this room to have acted as a formal audience chamber extending from a "throne room" that would have stood opposite the entrance. Adjoining it are three bathrooms.

In the middle tier of the right wall of the **hall** a woman emerges from her bath: she is depicted half naked stepping out of a blue bath below a fine arcade with Corinthian capitals. To her left is painted a

### The Qasr Amra frescoes

Together, the frescoed walls and ceilings add a new dimension to understanding the evolution of narrative painting in Islamic art, especially as they include representations of the human form which previously was thought to be forbidden by Islamic law. Instead it would seem that figurative painting was permissible outside the precincts of a mosque. Indeed, the subject matter may have been deemed appropriate for such places as a bathhouse, particularly when this was within intimate context of a private residence as at Qasr Amra. The complete prohibition on depicting the human figure was imposed later by the Abbasids who succeeded the Umayyads. As the frescoes date from a period of transition, they chart a number of changes in early Middle Eastern painting. The Hellenistic influences from Classical Greece are very strong: many of the inscriptions appear in Greek and the muses continue to provide inspiration to artists 80 years after the region was conquered by Muslims and converted to Islam. Christian and Persian elements are apparent in the figurative subject matter: in an area of 350sqm, some 250 figures and animals are portrayed for the most part engaged in such courtly pursuits as hunting, or in the practice of an applied skill, scenes from everyday life and mythology.

group taking exercise; on her right a row of figures may be discerned. According to various inscriptions recorded at the beginning of the 20C (now effaced), these probably represent the six sovereigns defeated by the Umayyads, namely Roderick, the last Visigoth king of Spain, the Persian king Chosroes, a Byzantine emperor and a king of Abyssinia. The scenes in the tier above illustrate how wild asses (onagers) were hunted by beaters bearing flaming torches herding their prey towards their nets. The sport is also celebrated on the wall to the left of the entrance, overlooking the cold-water bathing pool: the bearded figure in the centre, possibly an Umayyad prince, is shown about to slay his victim. The lower tier of paintings along the west wall depict another

G. Degeorge

A dancing girl, Qsar Amra

onager hunting expedition. Above them, to the left of the window, a woman greets a warrior with his hand poised on the hilt of his sword. The central panel shows the couple embracing. The scenes on the ceiling provide a fascinating insight into ancient practice of art and craftsmanship, with in the barrel vault, a series of eight scenes showing a coin engraver, a mason, a carpenter and a blacksmith, among others, hard at work. The same prince can be recognised on the north wall, to the left of the throne room, skinning his kill.

The fresco in the **throne room**, flanked by two shaded niches, is thought by some to be a portrait of the caliph and is modelled on the typical representations of Christ in Majesty found widely diffused across the Byzantine world.

*The doorway through the left wall of the hall leads to three small bathrooms.*

The ceiling of the changing-room or **apodyterium** (if not an additional heated room) is painted with diamond-shaped panels filled with figures and animals. Look out for the performing bear playing a lute and the man shown contemplating a reclining nude woman on the tympanum above the doorway into the hall.

The groin vault of the **tepidarium** (hot room modelled on those found in bath complexes from Antiquity) is painted with sprigs of laurel. The panels below the vault show scenes of a more intimate nature relating to domestic life in and around the hammam: a woman is shown leaving the baths carrying a child in her arms and elsewhere she may be seen bathing the child.

**Desert Castles**

**351**

The hottest public room in the complex, known as the **caldarium**, was located next door to the furnaces. In this case it has two separate bathing pools and a domed ceiling decorated with one of the earliest known representations of the heavens as the roof of the world. In the centre, you can make out the constellations of Ursa Major (the Great Bear) and Andromeda (arms open wide). The signs of the Zodiac around the edge are more difficult to discern. Note also in these last two rooms the vestiges of the *hypocaust* heating system consisting of under-floor ducting through which hot air was circulated.

*Return to the main road and continue along it for 26km.*

■ **Azraq Oasis** – A hedge of trees marking the oasis of Azraq comes into view just as the road from Amman joins the main highway running north to Iraq and south to Saudi Arabia. This junction is known as Azraq South.

*Turn right for the small Shaumari nature reserve (fork right at the junction 7km south of Azraq South or left for Azraq North, where the only two hotels of the area are located, and Azraq Castle beyond (5km).*

The terms Azraq North and Azraq South suggest a densely populated town. In fact, Azraq consists of a small agglomeration of a few thousand souls living in meagre habitations strung along the road to Syria, Iraq, Saudi Arabia and Kuwait, eking a living from the passing trade provided by long-distance truck-drivers shuttling through. A monotonous array of shops and restaurants line the main road linking the two ends of the town. The long-haul drivers halt there to buy provisions and, depending on the economic climate and the exchange rates, to purchase goods that are either expensive or unobtainable at home. Azraq has been an important crossroads for thousands of years. For more than 250 000 years, its oasis – the only one in Jordan – has allowed people to actually settle there, apparently in the middle of nowhere surrounded on all sides by miles of inhospitable desert and bleak volcanic outcrops. Below the surface, the water-table is sustained by the waters of the great Wadi Sihran, without which the trade caravans would have been unable to relay the Arabian Peninsula with the Fertile Crescent. Excessive pumping of this water to supply Amman has dried out the permanent lake that for so long used to slake the thirst of migrating birds bound for Africa and Europe. Indeed, the oasis itself is no longer as lush and plentiful as it once was, though the town is still a pleasant place on the edge of the Levant, and the green trees provide a welcome respite from the glaring sun and the surprisingly inhospitable desert landscape.

**Oryx**

The white oryx lived throughout the Sinai and Arabian peninsula before disappearing in the early 1970s. It was re-introduced in the wild in Oman in 1982 and the Jordanians are now attempting to do the same in the Shaumari Reserve. When mature, the herbivorous animal grows to a height just over a metre at the shoulder. The distinctive features of this member of the antelope family are its humped shoulders and its white fur blazed with brown on its nose, jowls and legs. Both the male and the female have long, thin, pointed and slightly curved horns. Oryx live in herds of about 20, dominated by a buck.

The **Shaumari Nature Reserve** (*24km there and back. Open daily, to sunset. Entrance fee*) is neither a zoo nor a game park, but a national park managed by the RSCN (Royal Society for the Conservation of Nature, *see page 372*). The 20sqkm area is used by the RSCN in an ambitious breeding programme in the hope of reintroducing wildlife species that once roamed freely across the Jordanian desert, but

**Desert Castles**

which long since have been hunted out of existence. Visitors are prevented from getting too close to the animals, but, with luck and patience, it may be possible to see the much coveted three onagers and 200 oryx (a kind of antelope) from the top of the four-storey observation tower. Meanwhile, there is ample opportunity to watch the blue-necked ostriches (native to Jordan) or their red-necked cousins (a gift from Israel) in the enclosure before the entrance to the reserve. The females are grey and the males are black. Do not be alarmed if you catch the males behaving strangely; they are probably performing their idiosyncratic courtship dance.

The museum *(to the right of the entrance to the reserve)* houses rather a sad display of a stuffed oryx, various types of bird and a meagre selection of photographs.

**Qasr el Azraq**, Azraq Castle *(open daily. No charge. 15min)* is more famous by reputation on account of its long history and its association with **Lawrence of Arabia** than for its actual remains. Its black, jagged silhouette sits on the left-hand side of the road, surrounded by the village. Opposite, the fallow fields are dotted with the last surviving palm trees which, not so long ago, crowded around the large water pools. On passing through the rather attractive gateway complete with machicolations and two massive basalt slabs for doorways, you may be struck by the prevailing mess and shabby construction of the courtyard. This fort probably dates from the end of the 3C, although its foundations are undoubtedly those of an earlier Roman defence outpost built to guard the Eastern extremities of the Empire. The inscription above the entrance records how the fortress was rebuilt in 1237 by the Ayyubids. It appears to have been inhabited continuously until 1917, when Lawrence of Arabia made it his winter quarters before launching his victorious offensive against Damascus in November 1918. The fortified gate and the mosque in the centre of the fort are the best-preserved parts of the building.

The road north of Azraq leading to the Iraqi border is frequented by thundering great juggernauts with green or blue registration plates, depending on whether they are from Jordan or Iraq. The landscape is marked by a succession of volcano-like forms and the ground is regularly strewn with black stones. The road continues some 40km to Al Safawi where it meets the tediously straight Highway 10, the only means of access to Iraq since the United Nations imposed its embargo in 1990.

*Go back to Azraq South and follow the same road back towards Amman. After 9km, turn right at the junction for Zarqa. The road threads its way back across desert. After 44km, follow the signs for Qsar el Hallabat. The baths are situated before the castle, 3km from the main road.*

■ **Qasr Hammam el Sarah** – *(Open daily, sunrise to sunset. Custodian. No charge)* The dome of the complex is clearly visible on the right-hand side of the road from some distance away, rising above the ruined façade. The structure of the hammam resembles that of the baths at Qasr Amra, but the frescoes have all disappeared. Walk around the left side of the building past the remains of a noria before reaching the main entrance. The bare outlines of the hall survive only at ground-level. The small door on the left leads to the two rooms with underground heating: the groin vaulted *tepidarium* and the domed *caldarium*.

*Continue for 3 km: in the next village, turn left along the road contouring the hill all the way to the custodian's tent. Subject to what mood he is in, he will allow you to drive up to the ruins or force you to go up on foot (15min).*

**Desert Castles**

■ **Qasr el Hallabat** – *(Open daily, sunrise to sunset. Custodian. No charge).* The remains of the desert complex of Qasr el Hallabat are scattered across a hillside. The extensive area, dominated by two buildings, is fenced off to prevent the goats from straying too far. The **mosque** on the left had two aisles and its apsed mihrab has been restored; the main doorway is spanned by a relieving arch decorated with ornamental gadroons (convex mouldings or fluting) and the area beyond is covered with heaps of black and beige stones. The front elevation of the building on the right, squarely set between twin towers, is pierced with the entrance to the **fort**. The building was probably constructed over the remains of a Roman fortress during the reign of the Umayyad Caliph Hisham (724-743). The hammam complex seems to be contemporary. The floor mosaics appear to suggest that the place was of some considerable importance. Access to the site, most especially the courtyards and buildings, is hampered by the fallen stone rubble. The remains of a large cistern may be discerned 400m further south.

*The main road leads to the Amman-Mafraq highway (7km): Amman is signposted to the left (40km), Mafraq(32km) to the right. For Um el Jimal, turn right towards Mafraq and drive straight through the town following directions for Al Safawi and Iraq. After 12km you come to a junction: turn left and continue. Some 4km or so further on, you will begin to make out the black ruins of Um el Jimal up ahead. Park in front of the ruins by the small white building belonging to the Department of Antiquities.*

■ **Um el Jimal**★ – *Allow 1hr (2.5km) for a thorough exploration of the site. No charge. At the height of the summer, the heat can make visiting extremely arduous: remember to take plenty to drink.*

Although far removed from the Imperial architecture of Jarash, it is easy to imagine how the narrow streets of Um el Jimal lined with sombre basalt-fronted buildings must have bustled with life, like so many other hundreds of towns and villages scattered across distant lands that together underpinned the prosperity of Rome and Byzantium. Time seems to have been suspended in this great field of ruins in which no less than 128 houses have been identified. It is as if the population of a large country town has suddenly upped-sticks and disappeared in a mass exodus – only in this case the last farmer to abandon his land left over 1 200 years ago! The sadness of the place is all the more poignant because of the lack of visitors from home or abroad, possibly because of its remote situation.

**A flourishing Byzantine city** – As the crow flies, Um el Jimal is a mere 20km from Bosra (in Syria). From the beginning of the 2C AD, when the Via Nova Trajana was built, it was linked to the towns of the Hauran. In those days, the small Roman town survived on agriculture and was protected from looters by a wall of modest proportions. Towards the end of the 3C it appears that a fort and *praetorium* were built. This change in status implies its designation by the Emperor Diocletian as a defensive military outpost of the Roman Empire. The actual ruins visible today date from Byzantine times (6C) when the town was considerably enlarged, re-organised and endowed with numerous houses and several churches for an estimated resident population of about 6 000. The town was abandoned at the end of the Umayyad period after 800 years of continued occupation.

**Site** – The best-preserved building is the tall corner tower visible from the road, opposite the Department of Antiquities. This formed part of the **barracks**★ *(castellum)* built by Pelagius in 412. The entrance into the fort is through a stone doorway with a gatehouse above. Inside, the place is rather dilapidated, with the exception of the **Byzantine corner tower**\* in which there are various long Greek inscriptions on a variety of religious subjects. The building backing onto the outside wall of the barracks (to the right as you leave) is an old chapel.

*Follow the narrow street marked out by white stones heading eastwards before veering right opposite the remains of the Church of Numerianos (first ruined building on the left of the track).*

The narrow street ahead is lined with houses; 100m further on, it turns sharply round towards the apsed east end of two **churches** on the left. The first church has a stoop (basin for holy water) jutting out from its façade. Turn your back on the east end of this church and walk on to the **house**\* with a double window on the third floor, which has come to symbolise Um el Jimal. Within, the building comprises three blocks arranged around a courtyard in the Eastern manner. Barns and stables occupied the ground floor, whereas the first floor provided the living quarters. Just try and imagine what life was like here around this farmyard, as it might have been in any one of the hundred or so examples elsewhere on the site: children chasing the hens around the courtyard, the stock-piling of the crops as the harvest comes in, and the sound of the flocks being driven home from the fields where they have been grazing all day.

*Leave the yard through the door on the right and walk left around the building.*

The alley leads to a circular **reservoir** which seems to have been the standard type at Um el Jimal. There is a second vaulted reservoir below the window in the east wall of the house. A little further on, the road conceals a drainage channel; a third tank stored water in the fenced area on the right. This ancient storage unit consists of a large rectangular **cistern**\* hollowed out of the base rock, made deeper by cement walls. The need for so many water tanks only serves to indicate that every effort was made to compensate for the lack of rainfall. Beyond the cistern but before the barracks once stood a small fort, which now is but a shapeless ruin.

*From here, cross the site from east to west and make for the rather obvious arches of the western church. Another group of houses is arranged to the north of here, just inside the town wall (traces evident at ground level) beside one of the town gates.*

A crypt sits before the four arches of the arcaded nave of the **west church**, suggesting the building might have been used for funerals. South of the church stands the **cathedral** (6C); its north wall has been removed in order to provide access to what is known as the **praetorium**\*\* *(ahead on the right)*. This is the best-built construction on the site and therefore must have fulfilled some administrative function. The stones were numbered during restoration. The steps at the front, including the six extant treads, would have led to the first floor. The basilica building on the left is now blocked off. Inside the cruciform chamber opposite is preserved the original fine roof, complete with perfectly cut basalt beams; the floor was once decorated with mosaics.

*Return to the car park via the large residential quarter in the south-western section of the site.*

*Take the road back to Mafraq and on to Amman.*

**Desert Castles**

# Making the most of the Desert Castles

## COMING AND GOING

**By taxi –** The only practical way to complete this excursion is by car. Ask your hotel reception the night before to order a taxi, confirming the overnight stops you wish to make. They may suggest an additional break at Qasr al-Mushatta near Queen Alia airport, a visit to the cave of the seven sleepers (Ahl al-Khaf: where seven persecuted Christian youths slept for hundreds of years, a legend mentioned in the Koran) and the Umayyad castle that was never completed. Lunch is usually eaten at Azraq. Several hotels in Amman offer this excursion.

**By bus –** Regular services leave Zarqa (30min from Amman Abdali bus station) stopping at Azraq South and Azraq North (75min). From Zarqa, the only way of getting to Qasr Amra and Qasr el Karana is by taxi or by hitching a lift. The meagre ruins at Qasr el Hallabat and Qasr Hammam el Sarah are only really worth making the effort to see if you have your own private means of transport.

To get to Um el Jimal you have to take three different buses: Amman to Zarqa (see above), Zarqa to Mafraq, and finally Mafraq to Um el Jimal (allow 2hr 30min).

## WHERE TO STAY

### • Azraq

Only Azraq can boast of having reasonable hotel facilities. There are plans to open a camp site near the Shaumari Reserve in the near future. The serenity of Azraq may be conducive to spending a night at one of the two hotels with a swimming pool.

*Between US$10-30*

**Al-Zoubi Hotel**, Azraq South ☎ 12 (via the operator) – 10rm 🗝 A small hotel at the entrance of town: turn right off the highway to Saudi Arabia at the traffic lights and continue 1km. The large family sitting-room sets the scene. A new hotel that is basically furnished but well cared for.

*Between US$40-60*

**Al-Sayad Hotel**, Azraq North ☎ (5) 383 40 94 – 17rm 🗝 ⚒ ✕ 🏊 400m from Azraq Castle. All the rooms are decorated with canvases painted by the owner Lydia. The two rather ugly buildings are plonked in an attractive garden. The rooms are simply but comfortably furnished.

**Azraq Resthouse and Bungalows**, Azraq North ☎ (5) 383 40 06 – 24rm 🗝 🗒 🖉 📺 ✕ 🏊 CC The oldest hotel in Azraq. Situated a good 3km from Azraq Castle and 1.5km off the main road, this government-owned guesthouse is extremely peaceful. The 24 bungalows are haphazardly arranged around the swimming pool where all meals are served. A little faded but spacious and gracious establishment.

## WHERE TO EAT

### • Azraq

A good number of snack bars and fast-food eateries have been set up around the junction at Azraq South, catering mainly for the long-distance lorry drivers. The two main hotels are open to non-residents for lunch and dinner, which might consist of an extravagant buffet if a group is expected.

*Over US$10*

**Al-Shallal al-Mountazat**, first street on the right after the castle. This place, a stone's throw from the fort, is perfect for lunch. Artificial waterfalls help to freshen the atmosphere; other tables are laid under the majestic date palms as well as on an outside terrace shaded by a trellis. Simple food, perhaps a little expensive.

The castle of Qasr el Karana

G. Antoine/HOA QUI

**Desert Castles**

# THE KING'S HIGHWAY★

## AMMAN TO AQABA

280km round trip to Petra not including excursions
(Additional 86km to Aqaba)

**Not to be missed**
The Holy Land mosaic at Madaba.
Mount Nebo, Karak Castle.

**And remember...**
Allocate a whole day to getting to Petra, stopping very briefly at Madaba,
Mount Nebo and Karak on the way.
Set aside an additional 2 or 3 days for visiting the extra sights around Madaba
and off the King's Highway.

The area south of Amman is a strange land determined by perverse geology:
the vast space in every direction is nothing but desert, arid canyon and lofty
stone cliffs. Little by little, the attraction of the historic remains is superseded
by the draw of the fascinating rock formations in the landscape.

**The royal road**

Before leaving Egypt, Moses despatched messengers to the King of Edom requesting to be allowed to take the people of Israel through southern Jordan: "Let us pass, I pray thee, through thy country (...) We will go by the king's highway, we will not turn to the right hand nor to the left, until we have passed thy borders." (Numbers XX v17). The term "royal road" (more appropriate really than "King's Highway") designated the major axes of trade and communication in the ancient Near East. From Edom, the caravans passed through the kingdoms of Moab and Ammon to the north, making their way along a route parallel to the modern King's Highway. The Nabataeans, meanwhile, used it to transport valuable spices from Persia to the Roman provinces in the west. Trajan incorporated the southernmost section into his Via Nova Trajana long before Christian (and later Muslim) pilgrims trod its path. The historic road fell from favour in the 16C when the Ottomans made the Desert Highway into a pilgrim route to Mecca reserved for the most privileged.

There are three ways of getting to Petra and the Red Sea. The **Desert Highway** provides the most direct access to the south of Jordan; use it if you are short of time as it is hassle-free. On the whole, the road to Ras al-Nabaq is unerringly dull as it cuts straight through rather uninspiring scenery; thereafter things improve as it crosses into the Wadi Rum. The **King's Highway**, on the other hand, is a truly historic road, for it echoes the route taken by the Hebrews – according to the Old Testament – which passed through several major ancient cities (Madaba, Karak and Shawbak) offering glimpses of the Dead Sea and various deep wadis along its route. When it comes to finding your way back to Amman, we suggest you take the **Dead Sea Highway** (*see p 412*). Since the final section through the Araba Valley was completed in the early 1990s, this has provided a more attractive alternative to the Desert Highway.

*From the King Hussein Mosque at the centre of Amman, follow King Talal Street for 1.5km. At the fork branch left along Al-Quds Street towards Naur. Keep to the main highway as it climbs uphill, through the suburban sprawl to the open plateau at the top.*

King's Highway

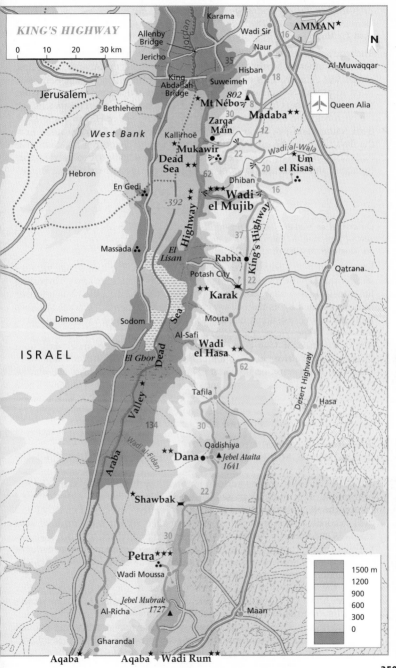

KING'S HIGHWAY

| 0 | 10 | 20 | 30 km |

Karama
AMMAN ★
Wadi Sir
Allenby
Bridge
Jericho
Naur
Al-Muwaqqar
35
Hisban
18
King
Abdallah
Bridge
Suweimeh
Queen Alia
Jerusalem
Mt Nébo ⚐ 802
Madaba ★★
Bethlehem
Zarqa
Main
West Bank
Kallirhoë
12
Mukawir ★
22
Wadi al-Wala
20
Um
el Risas
Hebron
Dead
Sea ★★
62
Dhiban
16
En Gedi
-392
★★★ Wadi
el Mujib ★
Highway
37
Massada
El
Lisan
Rabba ●
Qatrana
Potash City
22
Dimona
Sea
★★ Karak
King's Highway
Sodom
Mouta
ISRAEL
Al-Safi
Wadi
el Hasa ★★
El Ghor
62
Dead
Valley
Tafila
Araba
134
30
Wadi al-Fidan
Qadishiya
Desert Highway
Hasa
★★ Dana ● ▲ Jebel Ataita
1641
22
★ Shawbak
30
Petra ★★★
Wadi Moussa
Jebel Mubrak
1727 ▲
Al-Richa
Maan
Gharandal
Aqaba ★    Aqaba ★ Wadi Rum ★★

| | 1500 m |
| | 1200 |
| | 900 |
| | 600 |
| | 300 |
| | 0 |

359

*At 10km from the city centre, ignore the road left to the airport and continue in the direction of Naur and the Dead Sea. 17km further on, come off the motorway following signs for Madaba.*

The road shadows the undulating contours of the land of Ammon, the son of Lot and the brother of Moab, the eponymous ancestor of the Ammonites, whose capital was Amman. This part of the Transjordanian plateau is intensely cultivated to provide a livelihood for the villages scattered around the countryside; the prolific numbers of glasshouses nurture early market-garden plantations and the open fields are used to grow cereal crops. The village of **Hisban**, some 25km from Amman and just before the military college, retains its ancient name from the days when, as the capital of the Amorites, it was conquered by Moses. The ruins uncovered on the tell to the north of the village do little to evoke the Roman, Byzantine and Mameluke town of Esbus that once stood here *(of little interest)*.

# Madaba★★
*34km from Amman – Allow 90min (preferably 2-3hrs)*

*On arrival at Madaba, keep right in the direction of St George's Church. The easiest way of exploring the town centre is on foot. Then return to your car and drive to the museum and the Church of the Holy Apostles.*

From the outside, Madaba appears a sleepy little town. The King's Highway runs straight through the town providing it with a shop-lined "high street", bypassing the principal residential quarter which clusters around the Latin church further west, pinpointed by its red bell-tower on the hill. Enclosed therein is Madaba's most fascinating treasure: a rare set of mosaics illustrating a variety of subjects, uncovered in the course of the 20C.

The is a choice of four different excursions that may be undertaken from Madaba: a short drive out to Mount Nebo, or to the hot springs at Zarqa Main, the fort of Machaerus and the ghost town of Um el Risas. The last two may be visited on the way southwards and so are described below *(p 366)*. Those wanting to travel from Amman to Karak in a day should choose which option to go for; others, happy to enjoy the region at their leisure may like to stop for the night at one of Madaba's two small family-run hotels.

## The mosaic capital
In Biblical times, Madaba was conquered by the tribes of Israel before being recovered by the Moabite King Mesha in the 9C BC.

Although the town and its surrounding territory have a long and colourful history, the most eventful phases occurred in Byzantine and Abbasid times. During the 4C, archbishops began to supervise the building of churches and their decoration. This included mosaic floors laid with tesserae made of local stone. As in painting, a "school" of craftsmen was formed and together, they formulated their own particular techniques and subject matter. Their remarkable and painstaking work was gradually covered by the sands of time as Madaba was abandoned under the Mamelukes.

At last, the place was revived towards the close of the 19C by an influx of Christian Azizat tribespeople, who were originally from Karak. The new settlers moved into the ruins of the ancient city, converting the more robust constructions into houses. The mosaic floors were swept clean and forgotten until spotted by specialists. The latest initiative in the ongoing preservation of this exceptional heritage was to create a protected archeological area in 1991.

*Even if you are pressed for time, it is well worth stopping a few moments at Madaba to see the mosaic of the Holy Land.*

The Greek Orthodox **Church of St George\*** *(7am-7pm, winter 6pm. Closed during services, Fridays 7-9am, Sundays 7-10.30am. Entrance fee)* has a unique mosaic pavement that was only uncovered in 1896 when the present church was being built on the foundations of a Byzantine basilica. The floor that once would have measured 15.7m by 5.6m, would have comprised some two million or so minute pieces. Although incomplete and damaged, the section that survives shows an overview or **map of the Holy Land\*\*\***. What makes it so remarkable is that it provides a valuable insight into the urban planning and appearance of 6C Middle Eastern towns. All 127 cities – named in Greek – are orientated towards the east. Starting from the left, you can make out the fish-filled River Jordan flowing into the Dead Sea across which two boats ferry their passengers (vandalised). A group of date palms below the river delta situate the oasis at Jericho. The hills above the sea are the mountains of Moab, from which flow a number of wadis, and, beyond, the walled city of Karak *(below the pulpit)*. The oval

J. Ducange/TOP

The Holy Land mosaic

precinct on the opposite bank represents Jerusalem enclosed by walls. The Holy City is depicted with incredible attention to detail: the cardo is lined with 45 columns, in the middle sits the Church of the Holy Sepulchre – shown upside-down – with its fine yellow dome. On the right, the cardo leads out to the town of Bethlehem.

By one of the piers of the nave, you will find a tiny fragment representing Ashqelon, to the left of the major merchant town of Gaza on the eastern shores of the Mediterranean. On the far right, the Nile Delta is depicted although its orientation does not correspond to that of the rest of the map. The right tributary of the Egyptian river encircles the town of Pelusium, whose importance outweighs its modest neighbour, the town of Tanis.

Madaba

*On leaving the church, turn left up the side street for 200m.*

The Madaba Society Shop selling souvenirs fronts the entrance to the **excavations** (*no charge, mosaics covered by a protective layer of sand that is swept away on request*) *and disappointingly meagre remains* of a vast residence. Across the Roman road, behind high walls, sits the **al-Khadir Church** (*due to open to the public*) *which encloses a number of fine mosaic floor panels including* three tiers of scenes with a farmyard, a hunt, flocks of animals and a grape harvest set between friezes of acanthus leaves. Many of the figures have been conscientiously obliterated by iconoclasts.

*At the far end of the street, turn right and then immediately left. The entrance to the Archeological Park is opposite the Kan Zaman Restaurant.*

**Madaba Archeological Park**★★ (*8am -5pm, 10am-4pm Fridays and public holidays. Entrance fee inclusive of ticket for Madaba Museum and the Church of the Holy Apostles*) displays its collection of mosaics found *in situ* or in the local area. To the left of the entrance are laid out a series of mosaic fragments (719 AD) recovered from the acropolis church at Main: note how one panel depicting animals has been carefully defaced by iconoclasts and "in-filled" with decorative plants and trees. Aligned on the far side of the courtyard is an assortment of vignettes illustrating 10 townscapes, a subject that was evidently popular among the local mosaicists.

*Follow the flight of steps up to the remains of a church, enclosed by a protective roof.*

The circular **Church of the Virgin**★ (late 6C), decorated with a splendid geometric mosaic dating from the Umayyad period, is built on the site of an early-6C house. As the area below the nave was cleared, the former **hall**★★ was found to be paved with mosaic. Framed by a rich border of acanthus leaves and hunting scenes, the first section illustrates the myth of Phædra and Hippolytus. The second portrays Aphrodite and Adonis, with, above left, the Graces chasing after a roguish-looking Eros on the run. An elevated walkway straddles the **Roman road** providing access to the remains of the **Church of the Prophet Elias** (reduced to an outline of the ground-plan) and the sombre **Crypt of St Elianus** (late-6C mosaic) below. The Roman road continues along past the **Mosaic school,** which specialises in teaching the techniques for restoring antique mosaics. Before leaving the park by the ticket office, note the black and white mosaics on the right: these come from the baths at Machaerus and date from the 1C BC, which makes them the oldest mosaics so far discovered in Jordan.

*Make your way back to the intersection. Turn left towards the Latin church and then right after 300m. The museum stands at the end of a little street, 200m up on the left.*

The **Madaba Museum** (*8am-5pm; 10am-4pm Fridays and public holidays. Entrance fee*) has been somewhat eclipsed by the institution of the Archeological Park. The collections displayed in the garden and three pavilions include a considerable number of mosaics (several left as found), pieces of jewellery, costumes, pistols and guns, as well as an assortment of artefacts from nearby excavations (the great processional cross found at Mukawir (Machaerus) and three hanging lamps from Um el Risas). The displays in the small early-20C gallery on the left are dominated by a 6C Byzantine mosaic floor. In the middle sit a nude satyr and a dancing girl, surrounded by geometric designs and animal vignettes (peacocks, little lambs): all other participants of the **Bacchanalian scene** were destroyed by iconoclasts.

*Make your way along the rest of the street, and turn down the major road on the left. Continue for 400m past the Dana Restaurant.*

The 6C **Church of the Holy Apostles** *(8am-5pm, 10am-4pm Fridays and public holidays. Entrance fee)* stands at the intersection with the King's Highway. The large modern building houses a collection of mosaics found in situ or recovered from the vicinity. The main highlight is the **nave pavement** with its central medallion displaying a personification of the sea *(thalassa)*: the head and shoulders of a woman emerging from the waves surrounded by fish and sea monsters. The side chapel on the left contains different animal mosaics.

■ **Mount Nebo**★ — *20km from Madaba, round trip. Start out from the Church of the Holy Apostles and head north in the direction of Amman through the outskirts of Madaba. Keep a look out for signs pointing west to Mount Nebo (Siyagha) and fork left. Allow 1hr for visiting the Church of St Lot and St Procopius and Mount Nebo itself.*

The road quickly leaves the city sprawl behind as it eagerly stretches out towards the green and fertile countryside, but this lushness soon peters out and the scenery changes to steep and craggy desolation as it approaches the rift of the Jordan Valley. Mount Nebo is the last major outcrop before the abyss, and it was here that the Lord took the elderly patriarch Moses (aged 120 years) to show him the land of Israel that had been promised to his forefathers, Abraham, Isaac and Jacob (Deuteronomy XXIV v4). Then, as today, the views extend to the imaginary four corners of the earth and down the great valley that plunges steeply 1 000m below.

Some 6km before Madaba, a small road branches left to **Khirbet al-Moukkayyat** and the **Church of St Lot and St Procopius** *(custodian nearby. No charge)* which is also associated with the biblical town of Nebo (vestiges of a tell behind the church). The rectangular building contains a pavement **mosaic**★ from the 6C. By the altar a tree grows between two lambs. In the nave there are two series of panels: one set depicts small pastoral and hunting scenes framed with vine leaves and tendrils; the other has pairs of animals facing each other and fruit trees. Note the vivid expression captured in the features of the fisherman by the door.

**The death of Moses**

"And Moses went up from the plains of Moab unto the mountain of Nebo, to the top of Pisgah, across from Jericho. There the Lord showed him the whole land of Gilead to Dan, all of Naphtali, the territory of Ephraim and Manasseh, all the land of Judah as far as the western sea, the Negev and the whole region from the Valley of Jericho, the City of Palms, as far as Zoar. Then the Lord said to him, "This is the land I promised on oath to Abraham, Isaac and Jacob when I said, `I will give it to your descendants.' I have let you see it with your eyes, but you will not cross over into it." And Moses the servant of the Lord died there in Moab, as the Lord had said. (Deuteronomy XXXIV v1-5)

Go back to the main road lined with olive trees. The steep sides of deep wadi running parallel to the road on the right are said to conceal the Springs of Moses. Continue 2.5km to the green gate marking the entrance to the Moses Memorial Church.

The **Moses Memorial Church** *(open daily, 7am-7pm; 5pm in winter. Entrance fee. Parking outside)* is dedicated to the memory of Moses, the Patriarch who led the people of Israel to the Promised Land and then died on Mount Nebo. It is one of the most venerated sanctuaries in Jordan. The early Christians are known to have built a church in the 4C over what was claimed to be his place of burial. By the 6C, the community

**Mount Nebo**

must have grown to such numbers as to require a new baptistery to be added in 531 and the complex to be reorganised and expanded; a large **basilica** was built, incorporating all the earlier buildings and an additional number of funeral chapels, the ruins of which are to be seen today protected by a roof. Begin walking around the exterior of the east end apses and down the length of the church. Vestiges of a narthex mark the main entrance into the nave, which is marked out with columns. Down a few steps on the left, stand the ancient cruciform **baptismal fonts** and a splendid **mosaic★★**. The top section contains a long inscription in Greek that indicates the pavement was laid in the middle of the 6C. The two central sections contain hunting scenes. The fourth section depicts a peaceful pastoral scene with a shepherd overseeing his flock as it grazes among fruit trees. In the bottom panel, two figures are shown leading a procession of animals, most notably an ostrich, a zebra and a camel (with an unusual leopard-spotted coat).

Several more fragmented mosaics may be identified on the way up towards the main apse. The apse, built to contain the original 4C sanctuary, preserves several of the steps used exclusively by the clergy (*synthronon*). Mass is still celebrated here. The baptistery on the northern (right) flank of the nave dates from 597. A chapel dedicated to the Virgin Mary was added in front of the baptistery in the early 7C.

Outside the main entrance to the church stands a contemporary sculpture of **Moses with the brazen serpent** commemorating the incident described in the Old Testament when, on their arduous journey out of Egypt, the Hebrews doubted their faith in God and spoke ill of Moses (Numbers XXI v6). Beyond the excavations on the left, a Franciscan community has built a monastery south of the basilica to continue the early monastic tradition of Mount Nebo.

On a clear day, the **extensive views★★** can be quite remarkable, as they stretch from the northern shore of the Dead Sea to the green patch marking the oasis of Jericho. The pervading atmosphere is one of profound calm and serenity. How amazing it is to pause and think that it was here, in this spot, that God spoke to Moses of the land before them as Israel and advised him of his impending death.

*Go back to Madaba by the same route.*

■ **Zarqa Main** – *60km from Madaba there and back. There is only one road to Zarqa Main and that leads south out of Madaba (way marked with arrows or signposted Hammamat Maīn or Main Spa Village). Allow 2hr to include a short swim in the hot pools.*

Anyone wishing to sample the Jordanian hot spring "experience" and the drama of participating in an ancient ritual set against a stupendous backdrop, should make this detour.

The road goes straight through the village of Main to emerge on the other side, before the a great **view★** over the Dead Sea, surrounded by towering hills (1000m), rounded and bare but for the occasional tuft of grass. The first deep valley leads into the narrow gorge of the Wadi Zarqa, at the far end of which nestles the six-storey complex of **Main Spa Village**. As you approach it you can but think it would be better suited to a mountain ski resort.

The **hot springs of Zarqa Main** have been famous since Antiquity: Herod the Great came here to soothe the aches of old age in the latter years of his life. Whatever the season, hot water (up to 60°C) trickles down from the canyon's

The waterfall at Main

rocky overhang in heavy showers. The largest waterfall – opposite the Ashtar Hotel – has a drop of some 45m. The sulphurous waters are rich in minerals (potassium, calcium and magnesium) that have stained the rock-face shades of yellow, ochre and green and deposited a white coral-like crust in the pools below. Luxurious facilities are laid on at the Ashtar Hotel, whereas more basic provisions are available at the public baths beyond the mosque, on the far side of the hotel.

## From Madaba to Karak

*84km without excursions – Allow 90min*

*Mukawir is signposted right off the main road, some 12km after Madaba.*

■ **Zarqa Mukawir (Machaerus)** – *44km from the King's Highway there and back.* This two-hour detour offers the opportunity of seeing the carpets woven by hand by the Bani Hamida women and of visiting the remains of the fort of Machaerus.

The road sticks to the ridges across the plateau passing through the sparsely populated region to arrive at the most superb **view\*\*\*** over the Dead Sea (*12km after turning off the King's Highway*). The Dead Sea nestles among the limestone ridges and craggy outcrops, with the Desert of Judaea stretching out towards the horizon. On the far side of **Mukawir**, you will find a carpet shop where the **Bani Hamida** women display and sell a broad range of their amazing **rugs**. If you are lucky, you get the chance to see the women working at a loom. Although there is a sign pointing to a "rest-house", there is nowhere in fact to eat or drink in the immediate locality.

The track going downhill beyond the Bani Hamida shop leads to the strange conical hill on which the **fort of Machaerus** was once built. Park the car in the supervised plot beside the site and follow the well-marked path to the remains at the top (*20min each way. No charge. Take something to drink in summer*). Be warned, however, there is little to see other than a lonely antique column capital unearthed there, mounted on an unattractive concrete base. The **view\*** alone over the Dead Sea makes it worth the climb. The original citadel was constructed by Alexander Jannaeus in the 1C BC, destroyed by Pompey and later seized by Herod the Great. It was here in about 28 AD that Salome danced before her uncle Herod Antipas (who succeeded Herod the Great) and, on the perfidious advice of her mother, requested she be rewarded with the head of **John the Baptist** who lay imprisoned in the fort dungeons. The rest is history.

*Go back to the King's Highway.*

The road picks its way through an attractive, fairly shallow valley known as the **Wadi al-Wala**, planted with pines and eucalyptus trees, and terraces of olives and vineyards. It rapidly regains height on the other side of the plateau before arriving at **Dhiban**, the ancient capital of the kingdom of Moab, where the famous **Mesha Stela** was discovered. The original, engraved with the story of battles waged between the kings of Israel and the Moabites, is now in the Louvre in Paris, France; the one displayed in the Archeological Museum in Amman is a replica.

*To continue on to Um el Risas, turn left in the town centre after the telecommunications station (large antenna).*

King's Highway

■ **Um el Risas**★ — *32km from the King's Highway there and back. Allow 90min.*
Anyone who is drawn by the mystery surrounding an unexcavated tell should go to Um el Risas, where they will find one of the most beautiful mosaics in the country.

The narrow road leaves Dhiban and crosses a flat landscape dappled with fields that continue into the distance well beyond a place called Mezreh.

*After some 12km, you get to a small village which has a post office – a striking sight as these are few and far between in this lonely region. Turn left and continue 16km. At the crossroads, you will find the substantial but sprawling ruins of Um el Risas. Turn down the track that leads across the site and along the edge of the ruins on the right and park at the southeast corner.*

You cannot fail to be struck by the astonishing heaps of black stone at Um el Risas that date from the Kastron Mefaa **fortified encampment** built by the Romans with great 5m-high walls, of which sections still stand. But not for much longer as teams of archeologists patiently await the opportunity of excavating the area in detail! Already, preliminary searches in the southeastern corner have revealed traces of medieval churches and private houses, each with its own set of mosaic floors *(not yet open to the public)*.

Meanwhile, the true jewel of Um el Risas lies outside its walls, beyond the outer walls of the site within a yellow corrugated-iron hangar *(no charge; the custodian will open it up when he sees visitors approaching)*. The perfectly preserved **mosaic of the Church of St Stephen**★★★ is a true masterpiece and – at last – is safe from looters. The mosaic dates from 757 and indicates the great energy and vitality of the Christian community a century after the fall of Byzantium, at a time when Islam was sweeping through the Middle East. An elevated walkway enables visitors to study the mosaic in its entirety from every angle. Between the column bases separating the nave from the aisles there are 16 vignettes. These portray various large cities in a range of warm ochres and yellows. The eight along the left aisle show the towns on the left (west) bank of the Jordan including Jerusalem (up by the apse); those on the opposite side illustrate the towns on the east bank of the Jordan beginning with Um el Risas (featured in at least two of the vignettes). In addition to these, ten towns set against a striking black background relate to ten towns in the Nile Delta.

To the left of this large mosaic, yet in the same hangar, are the floors of the **Church of Bishop Sergius**. This, the oldest mosaic on the site, suffered substantial damage at the hands of the iconoclasts – most especially in the nave. The only section on display to the public is a large circular panel set between two sheep that was set before the altar. The dedicatory inscription dates the work to 587.

1.5km along the road north of the fortified camp towards the village stands a 14m-high **Byzantine tower**★ that could have served one of two purposes. It was either built as a watchtower or it provided a stylite or ascetic with a platform on which to live, at the top of a column. Scholars remain divided on the matter, although the discovery of a church at the foot of the tower would seem to validate the second theory.

*Return to Dhiban and follow the King's Highway for 3km.*

■ **Wadi el Mujib**★★★ — The terrace on the right-hand side of the road provides a truly breathtaking **view**★★★ over the Mujib rift valley, Jordan's very own "Grand Canyon". The awesome atmosphere of the place is somehow

**Um el Risas**

magnified by the lingering silence caught between the rock-faces. The space contained therein (5km from side to side as the crow flies) is empty but for jagged cliffs, dramatically eroded here and there by wind and rain, dropping precipitously down to 500m banks of discarded scree lying on the bottom. The grain and colours of the rocks are picked out by brilliant sunshine, veering from the pure opaque whites to a shimmering yellow, flicked with bronze lustre according to the time of day. The sheer faces of the canyon are deeply scored by running water. The occasional patch of greenery, encouraged and nurtured by a spring perhaps, enables the Bedouin shepherds to graze their flocks of sheep and goats. This natural rift, which cradles the biblical River Arnon, once marked out the boundary between the kingdoms of Ammon to the north and Moab in the south – the latter stretching down to Wadi el Hasa, south of Karak.

*The King's Highway continues steeply downhill before levelling off for 8km as it crosses over the river before climbing straight up the other side.* One last **viewpoint★** extends its scope over the landscape northwards. The road then embarks on its tedious route through the unchanging flatlands, in such stark contrast to the dramatic landscape containing the great rift valley so close by. Notice the proliferation of decorative low walls in this area and the imaginative use of breeze-blocks to build the modest houses. The idea of laying these diagonally to form an attractive frieze in a wall has certainly spread across the region to become a common feature right across the Transjordanian plateau. Then you reach **Rabba** with its elegant procession of columns along its main street: these come from the Rabbath Moab mentioned in the Bible or known to the Romans as Aeropolis. Look out for the front of a Roman temple with two niches to the right of the road.

*After 12km, you arrive at a major crossroads: turn right to Karak and continue as the road enters a winding gorge.*

## Karak★★
*120km from Amman*
*Pop 20 000 – Alt 950m*
*Allow 90min for visiting the castle.*

The road turns a corner and bang: you come before the Crusader castle in its full glory. To its left, yet separated from the plateau by a deep chasm, a massive square tower keeps watch over the surrounding landscape. The eastern flank is dramatically fortified by a great **glacis★★** that has been meticulously restored: this must have been a truly impregnable fortress. Its right side is protected by a moat and high perimeter walls. Further along, the ramparts are buttressed with a line of towers that extend north before encircling the modern town much as it did in the medieval city. The road contours the exterior, passing below the Baybars tower, before turning left into town.

*Fork left in the town centre rather than towards the Dead Sea and drive up to the castle entrance (car park).*

### Karak, "the obstacle that dashed all hopes"
The people living beyond the Jordan felt they required a resilient fortress if they were to withstand any attack from outsiders. In 1142 the Crusaders decided to strengthen their own defences and settled on building an extra stronghold north of Shawbak. Karak not only occupies a natural defensive

King's Highway

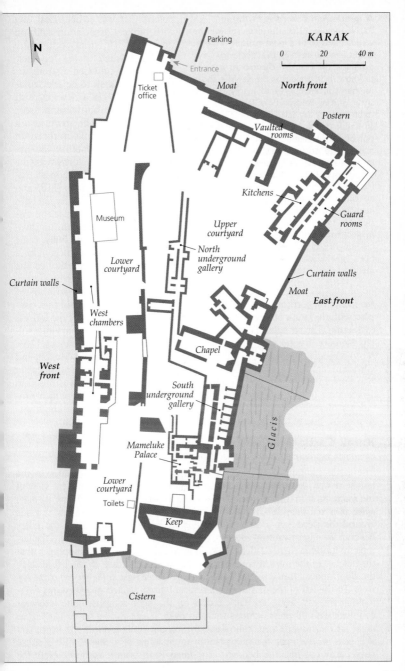

**KARAK**

0    20    40 m

**North front**

Parking

Entrance

Ticket office

*Moat*

*Postern*

*Vaulted rooms*

*Kitchens*

*Guard rooms*

Museum

*Upper courtyard*

*Lower courtyard*

North underground gallery

*Curtain walls*

*Curtain walls*

*Moat*

**East front**

*West chambers*

**West front**

*Chapel*

*South underground gallery*

*Glacis*

*Mameluke Palace*

*Lower courtyard*

Toilets

*Keep*

*Cistern*

**A gentleman's word is his bond**
22 November 1183: the date set for the wedding was to be a most inauspicious one. But Étiennette de Milly, the *"dame dou Crac"* named in the Frankish chronicles, was not to know in advance that the day she chose for her son Humphrey to marry Isabelle, sister of King Baldwin IV of Jerusalem, was to be the very day Saladin chose to lay siege to Karak. Thank heavens for the intervention of a brave gentleman named Yvain who managed to dissuade Saladin from rushing into the fortress on the heels of the wedding guests! True to his word, Saladin refrained from attacking those parts of the building where the wedding feast was being held, and Étiennette, in turn, had food carried out to her besiegers. Then, once due respect had been paid to the occasion and his integrity as an honourable Muslim had been upheld, Saladin gave the order to his men to renew hostilities.

position, it was a historical city with biblical associations and an important Christian community was established there. Together, these factors provided a strong argument for Karak to be selected as the ideal site for a new outpost. Vast defensive battlements were erected around the town and a strong castle was built on the south side. One contemporary Muslim writer described the fortress as "the obstacle that dashed all hopes". Saladin made two attempts (1183 and 1184) at besieging the city: on both occasions, the protector of the castle **Renaud de Châtillon,** the husband of **Étiennette de Milly,** came under fire from mangonels (a kind of catapult) and appealed to the King of Jerusalem for reinforcements. The Battle of Hattin sealed the fate of the territory east of Jordan which passed to the enemy and this, coupled with the death of Reynald de Châtillon, forced his wife to cede the fortress to **Saladin**. The conquerors lost no time in enlarging Karak. The Mameluke sultan **Baybars**, having seized the fort from the hands of the Ayyubids in 1264, set to remodelling the castle. The population of Karak made up of Muslim and Christian families enjoyed complete autonomy until 1893; a fact that might in part explain why there was an uproar when the price of bread was raised in 1996. Most of the buildings are built with stone from the castle, which provides a pleasing wholeness to the town; it is the fort, however, – the most impressive one in Jordan – that will most capture your imagination.

## Karak Castle★★

*8am-6pm. Entrance fee. Take a torch if you have one.*

The castle communicated with the town by a **postern**, a secret door in the northern wall *(left of the visitors' entrance)* from which there was a clear view of the **moat** cut from the bedrock. *Follow the path uphill that leads from behind the ticket office, then turn sharp left.* The scenery to the west takes in the yellow uplands around the Dead Sea, a dash of blue floating in the distant haze of the valley beyond. Two large **vaulted rooms★**, one above the other, open out onto the terreplein: it was in these draughty 60m long chambers, pierced by loopholes, that the defence of the moat was maintained in shifts. A staircase on the left leads to the floor above. *Turn down the vaulted passage on the right at the far end of the low room.* To the left of the corridor lie a series of groin-vaulted **guard-rooms** overlooking the east front; the dark rooms on the right comprised the **kitchens**, complete with oil press, various vats and oven. *Continue along the corridor and up to the top courtyard.* If you walk along the curtain walls towards the keep, you will pass on the right the subterranean foundations of a **chapel** with a single nave partly cut into the bedrock. The **keep** is an Islamic addition. Note the quality and finish of the carefully articulated limestone walls when compared to the Frankish constructions that in contrast seem to have been erected rather hurriedly. The two lower storeys of the keep are accessible and allow visitors to admire the loopholes, the glacis sloping below the east front and the subterranean vestiges of the **Mameluke Palace**.

*Go back to the upper courtyard and follow the stairway down on the west side of the chapel.* The passageway to the right runs past several small, dark rooms before emerging in a fine underground chamber. Go back to the foot of the stairway, ornamented by a stone finely carved with arabesques, and turn left down the tunnel that in part cuts straight through the solid rock to the upper courtyard. The various rooms on either side would have been used as sleeping quarters for the lord of the household and his family, as well as for billeting troops.

*Make your way back to the ticket office, and walk down left into the lower courtyard.*

This section of the castle, together with the keep, was built by the Muslims following the surrender of the Crusaders in 1188. The new fortified wing comprises two impressively large chambers (the longest is 80m long) along the west front *(entrance in the middle of the courtyard, but usually closed to visitors)*. A building at the foot of the staircase houses a **museum** devoted to the archeology of the Transjordanian plateau and the Araba Valley. Note the satellite photograph by the entrance, which clearly shows the deep wadis crisscrossing the Mountains of Moab before reaching out towards the Dead Sea. The display cabinets contain the usual assortment of tools, pottery and jewellery dating from Neolithic to Mameluke times. It is worth pausing to look at the unusually effective reconstruction of the Bab al-Dhra barrow (with two skeletons) and the oil lamps from the Byzantine monastery of St Lot, situated southeast of the Dead Sea.

## Karak to Petra

*146km – Allow 2hr.*

*From the base of Karak Castle make for the King's Highway by proceeding straight ahead towards Tafila.*

This section of the King's Highway cuts through land that is predominantly dedicated to arable farming. Rows upon rows of well-kept cereal fields are interrupted here and there by rather isolated little towns which, for the main part, are sustained by good public amenities. **Mouta,** for example, lies 10km from Karak and boasts a leading civilian and military university; it also recalls the early Byzantine defeat (albeit ephemeral) of Islam in 629. Some 9km beyond Mouta lies Wadi el Hasa.

The **Hasa rift valley (Wadi el Hasa)**\*, which is larger and less claustrophobic than Wadi el Mujib, once defined the border between the kingdoms of Moab and Edom to the south. Its more gently sloping and sun-blessed sides are dotted with groves of olive trees. Age-worn tracks contour their way up to the terraces where generations of peasant farmers have reaped meagre harvests from the small lonely patches of green dotting the arid landscape. The valley floor, meanwhile, has been claimed by Bedouins who pitch their long black and beige tents along the right bank of the wadi. Their mixed flocks of sheep and goats roam about on the lower slopes in search of the rare tuft of grass.

**Karak to Petra**

Heavy trucks shuttle their way up and down, to and from the nearby quarries, destroying the silence that otherwise reigns over the place. The road climbs steeply once more to reach a swollen tributary before passing yet more thermal springs on the right (Bourbita, Afra).

*At last, 50km from Karak, the road reaches the plateau once more.*

**Tafila** (Pop 23 000) an additional 10km further on, forms a balcony around the head of the valley. The road runs the length of the town before gaining height. The local people have a reputation among Jordanians for being uncompromising traditionalists and tight with their money, characteristics that have been forged, it is said, by the harsh climate of the region. The road continues its journey upwards until it reaches a pass where you might like to pause and admire the marvellous view. The limestone that dominated and fashioned the hills around Madaba and Karak is gone; instead, the landscape is made of sandstone that has been sculpted by time and the forces of Nature into tormented shapes and fluid forms of striated colour. The painter of this outlook must arrange his palette around a range of reds, reserving a dash of green for the occasional trees that bristle the hill tops. Beyond Rashadiya, the road climbs up to another pass in the mountains, the highest in the region. If you can manage to ignore the cement works, the scenery is quite fabulous with views stretching to the Araba Valley.

*At the entrance to the village of Qadishiya (30km from Tafila), turn right towards Dana (3km off the King's Highway).*

■ **Dana Reserve★** — *There is a bus service between the village, the entrance to the nature reserve and Rummam Camp, 12km away (see Where to stay, p 375) Guides available.* The approach to the village is spectacular. The road follows the natural direction of a wonderful canyon, then suddenly you see the flat roofs and white stone houses of a tightly packed little village precariously balanced along the edge of the precipice. The sight of such traditional villages has become such a rare phenomenon in Jordan as to arouse universal admiration. Many Jordanians united together to implore the RSCN to breathe a new lease of life into Dana and halt the emigration of its population. Eventually, when at last it took action and launched its conservation initiative, there were only five families resident in the village, whereas today there are 20, although the population figures do escalate considerably during harvest time. Both the village and its surrounding countryside – including the

**Royal Society for the Conservation of Nature (RSCN)**
The Royal Society for the Conservation of Nature was founded in 1966 under the patronage of the late King Hussein of Jordan to manage the six nature reserves in the kingdom that, together, cover an area of 1000sqkm. To help nurture the awareness of environmental issues for the future, the organisation has founded 350 youth clubs and spearheaded a number of initiatives involving rural populations in the production and distribution of quality eco-friendly handicrafts. Not only does this create new job opportunities in sparsely populated zones, it is hoped that it will encourage more urban-based people to venture out into the countryside. In due course, the RSCN hopes to open six more reserves, which, together, will cover 4.5% of the national territory. This non-governmental organisation is beginning to be respected throughout the region: it is co-operating with Syria, for example, in trying to reintroduce the oryx in a reserve near Palmyra 70 years after it disappeared. The RSCN also has links with authorities in the West Bank and the Yemen. Its magazine is called "El Reem" ☏ (6) 533 79 31.

**King's Highway**

**canyon\*\*\*** – have been formed into a reserve. Efforts to persuade residents to stay have ranged from paving the streets and laying on modern amenities such as running water and electricity. The RSCN is also hoping to allow the local population to reap benefits from tourism by launching a programme to make and distribute quality **hand-made goods** and environmentally-friendly products like jewellery inspired by the local flora and organic jams. In conjunction with its primary objective, which is to protect the natural environment, the RSCN is encouraging a different kind of tourism in this area, labelled **eco-tourism**. Various rigorous measures have been put into place so as to safeguard the 500 or so species of animals and 180 species of birds – many threatened with extinction (Nubian ibex, sand cat, Syrian wolf, spotted and imperial eagles, small raptors) – that live peaceably in their natural habitats that include some 550 or so different plants (juniper, carob and wild pistachio). The priority is not to disturb the creatures and so visits to the **reserve** are carefully controlled at all times.

*Return to the King's Highway and continue 22km, turning right at the fork signposted for Shawbak. Slow down to take a bend 1km further on and turn off the road downhill before following signs up towards a small village.*

Shawbak Castle dominates the skyline, as it grips tightly to the hillside. The blinding whiteness of the **landscape\*\*** is quite dazzling, the striated layers of folded rock having been worn bare by erosion.

*Continue along the dirt road that snakes its way around the castle walls (5km from the junction with the main road).*

■ **Shawbak Castle\*** – *(Open all year; no custodian. No charge. Allow 15min. Park opposite the souvenir shop: the man in charge will probably entice you in for a cup of tea and browse through his bric-a-brac.)*

Shawbak was the first castle to be built by the Crusaders east of the River Jordan. It was named "Montréal" (mont royal) in memory of King Baldwin I, who began its construction in 1115. Following his victory at Hattin, Saladin marched onto Shawbak. After sustaining a state of siege for eighteen months, its garrison, blind from malnutrition, surrendered in 1189. The complex was then radically remodelled by the Mamelukes, enabling Shawbak to remain independent from Ottoman power until the end of the 19C.

**A tour of the castle** is best undertaken in a clockwise direction. Go through the gateway and make for the monumental entrance; a few metres before the doorway, you will pass a vaulted room on the left that once led into the Crusader fortress **chapel**. The apse is flanked by niches; opposite, a stairway leads up to a collection of hydraulic installations and channels whose main function has not yet been ascertained.

*Go back to the main entrance.* Through the door on the right an impressive flight of 375 steps cut into the bedrock, leads down to a large **well; without** this substantial water supply, the Crusaders would have been unable to withstand such a great siege *(the steps are slippery and dangerous)*. Continue past the restored long rectangular tower to a half-vaulted passageway and the elegant round **tower** beyond, equipped with four loopholes and a lengthy inscription. At its foot are congregated a collection of traditional stone-built houses. Keep going eastwards and you will come across another vaulted passageway off to the right that leads to the ruins of an **Ayyubid Palace complex** complete with reception hall and baths. The **great hall** lined with arches at the top of the citadel echoes the

**Shawbak Castle**

foundations and form of an ancient church built by the Crusaders and later modified. From this height there is a good view of the cultivated plots that terrace the sides of the wadi. It would appear that little has changed over the centuries if one recalls the comments made by William of Tyre, a historian who was contemporary with the Crusades, who described what he saw then as it being "covered with large cultivations, pleasant vineyards and fruit trees".

*Return to the King's Highway.*

The road continues its gentle climb before beginning its descent, 34km later, towards Wadi Musa and Petra.

■ **Petra**★★★ — *See p 378.*

## Petra to Wadi Rum and Aqaba
### 71km to Rum – 86km to Aqaba

*Leave Wadi Musa and, some 500m from the town centre, turn right at the roundabout.*

The road clings to the main axis of a ridge proffering great views over Petra and the Araba Valley. Once you go beyond Taiyiba, the villages seem to peter out completely: only the occasional flock of dromedaries and sheep animate this bare wasteland. The King's Highway comes to a somewhat abrupt end some 43km further on when it joins the Desert Highway. Shortly after the junction, the road begins to spiral downwards. Jordanian and Iraqi trucks strain to climb the hill in the opposite direction. After 42km, there is a signpost for Rum (29km); Aqaba lies a further 43km away.

■ **Wadi Rum**★★ — *See p 396.*

■ **Aqaba**★ — *See p 402.*

■ **Petra**★★★ — *See p 378.* | ■ **Wadi Rum**★★ — *See p 396.* | ■ **Aqaba**★ — *See p 402.*

## Making the most of the King's Highway

The proposed itinerary would be very difficult to complete without your own independent means of transport. The most straightforward way of visiting Madaba or Zarqa Main is as an excursion from Amman. Other sights should then be undertaken by taxi.

### COMING AND GOING

• **Madaba**
Regular bus services to Madaba (30min) are operated from Amman (al-Wihdat or Raghadan).

• **Zarqa Main**
**Jett Company** (see Making the most of Amman) arranges excursions on a daily basis from Amman (2hr) leaving at 8am and returning at 4pm.

• **Mukawir**
For Mukawir, change at Madaba. Minibus shuttle depart from the bus station (1hr).

• **Karak**
Buses and minibuses operate services both from Amman and Petra to Karak. The minibus terminus is situated at the base of the castle on the side of the glacis: frequent departures for Amman (al-Wihdat, 3hr) and Ma'an (3hr 30min with ongoing services for Aqaba and Petra). Public transport services follow the more mundane route along the Desert Highway.

• **Dana and Shawbak**
Dana and Shawbak are not easily accessible by public transport: the most obvious solution would be to hitch a lift from Karak to Tafila (90min).

**By taxi –** An excursion to Mount Nebo is easily arranged from Madaba: the round trip – including a brief (15min) stop at the church of Khirbet al-Moukkatayat and at the Moses Memorial (30min) – should not cost much more than JD8. If you require any extra time to visit the sights, either get the taxi to wait (incurring a JD4 surcharge) or catch a lift with one of the group taxis ferrying farm labourers back to Madaba at the end of their day's work.

## ADDRESS BOOK

**Tourist offices – *Madaba*:** Information is available from a bureau situated by the Archeological Park or from the Madaba Society Shop nearby.
At *Karak*, next to the Towers Hotel.

**Bank/Currency exchange –** At Madaba, Arab Bank (near St George's Church). Visa card and travellers' cheques.

## WHERE TO STAY

### • Madaba
Madaba has two good family-run guesthouses. This allows visitors to enjoy the Jordanian capital of mosaics at their leisure.

*From US$25-50*
*Madaba Tourism Hotel*, midway between St George's Church and the archeological site, ☎ / Fax (5) 540 643 – 11rm ⤬ CC This former family house is gradually being converted into a hotel, without losing its friendly atmosphere. You will be warmly welcomed and will soon feel at home. Kitchen available for guests' use. Opt for a second-floor room, if possible. Simple, but comfortable and impeccably clean.

*Pension Loulou*, Mount Nebo Rd, ☎ (5) 543 678, Fax (5) 547 617 – 15rm ⤬ The majority of rooms have en-suite bathrooms. A little isolated on the outskirts of the town, this family-run pension has recently been extended. Kitchen, dining room and television lounge available for guests' use, as well as roof terrace and garden. A little more expensive than the above.

*Queen Ayola Hotel*, King Talal St (near St George's church), ☎/Fax (5) 544 087 – 8rm ⤬ CC Some rooms

have en-suite bathrooms. A new town-centre hotel, clean but lacking charm. You can choose between a small balcony on the street side, or a quieter room with a window away from the street.

### • Zaqa Main
*Over US$115*
*Main Spa Village* ☎ (5) 545 500, Fax (5)454 550 – 142rm ⤬ ▤ TV ✕ ⤬ CC The larger rooms of this luxurious hotel have views over the wild wadi. The complex boasts its own health centre (massage, hydrotherapy, mud baths, exercise facilities) which ranks among the best of its kind in the Middle East. The ground-floor restaurant overlooks the waterfalls. High season: March to May.

### • Karak
The main hotels catering for foreign visitors are situated within 5min walk from the castle.

*From US$20-40*
*Rum Hotel*, last street on the left before reaching the castle ☎ (3) 351 351, Fax (3) 351 105 – 20rm. As soon as you set foot in Karak you may be accosted by the owner of this hotel, ever eager to exalt the merits of his establishment. However, it is nothing to get excited about: the rooms are fine, but some of the bathrooms (private or shared) could do with renovating.

*Towers Hotel*, Castle St, 100m from the castle, ☎/Fax (3) 354 293 – 18rm. Same owner and standard of facilities as the above. Simple and lacking in charm, but clean and functional.

*From US$50-65*
*Karak Resthouse Hotel*, 50m from castle ☎ (3) 351 148, Fax (3) 353 148 – 16rm ⤬ ✕ ⤬ TV ✕ CC The best hotel in Karak. A few airy and spacious rooms with fabulous view of the Dead Sea.

### • Dana
Two options in this attractive little spot. Peace and quiet guaranteed after nightfall.

*Under US$20*
*Dana Hotel*, in the village itself, ☎/Fax (3) 368 537 - 5rm ✕ Very basic hotel in the main street, opposite the mosque. Rooms without views in a traditional house. Shared amenities. Three

small tents have been erected on the roof. A pleasant place to spend the evening among local residents and those enamoured with Dana. An annexe is due to open, 100m lower down in the village, comprising seven rooms with en-suite bathrooms.

**Rumman Camp**, 10km north of the village. Shuttle from Dana. Tents permanently erected along the edge of the canyon from 1 March to 30 November. No access after 8pm. Mattress and storm light provided. Bring your own food, although the custodian can come up with a barbecue and charcoal on request. The camp site is closed Tuesdays. JD12 per person, including entrance to the nature reserve.

**Feinan Camp**, Widland. Situated at the other end of the Dana reserve, in a much warmer area near the Dead Sea, this camp site is open all year. More modern than the above, with electricity and running water, though the setting is less spectacular.

*From US$50-65*

**Dana Guesthouse**, down a street on the left on entering the village. It is advised that you book in advance, ☎ (3)368 497, Fax (3) 368 499 – 9rm ✗ Lovely self-catering hostel with a large kitchen where you can make a cup of tea at any time of the day and night. Down to earth decor with a natural finish: bare stone, wrought-iron armchairs with caned seats, coarsely woven woollen fabrics. Each room is comfortable, if rather basic, with traditional rug and private balcony providing breathtaking views of the canyon. Shared amenities. Room prices vary according to season and size of room. Nourishing breakfast. A definite success, which should encourage the setting up of similar facilities elsewhere.

### WHERE TO EAT

• **Madaba**

The location of Madaba makes it a favourite lunch-time stop for groups.

*Under US$20*

**Dana**, Al-Nuzha St ☎ (5) 545 749 ♆ A stone's throw from the museum in the direction of the Church of the Holy Apostles. A clean dining area without much character. Do try the house speciality: *sadjiyeh* with unleavened bread. Buffets at lunchtime available when groups are expected, otherwise à la carte menu in the evening.

**Madaba Resthouse**, at the crossroads, near St George's Church ☎ (5) 544 069 ♆ *Meze*, *kefte* and kebabs on offer from the buffet await the arrival of groups. Eating area consigned to a large, dull room or the terrace outside.

**Haret Jdoudna**, ☎ (5) 548 650. ♆ This former stone house has recently been transformed into a restaurant. You have the choice of eating on the patio, on the little terraces that overlook it, or in the airy, elegant dining room. The menu includes good pizzas, a wide choice of hot and cold meze and other mainly Eastern dishes, of surprisingly varying quality. Traditional music on some evenings. The best place to eat in Madaba, although a little expensive. Craft shops. Luxury rooms are planned.

• **Karak**

*Under US$10*

Several rather ordinary, unpretentious restaurants line the road, particularly between the Towers and Rum hotels.

*Over US$10*

**Karak Resthouse**, in the basement of the hotel ♆ Fabulous view over the Dead Sea from the large dining room, which offers buffets for groups accommodated in the hotel. Good selection of alcoholic drinks from the bar.

### THINGS TO DO

**Great outdoors** – Rock-climbers may dream of scaling the sandstone cliffs (as others have already done) in order to abseil down the sheer rock-faces, whereas the majority will be happy to walk in and around the Dana nature Reserve.

**Dana**: visitors who are pressed for time will want to make straight for the village (preferably leaving their car in the designated car park and waiting for a bus to collect them) so that they can explore the traditional houses and survey the wonderful scenery spread out

King's Highway

below. The more intrepid may undertake a walk in the nature reserve (JD5 entrance fee; half price for students) along one or more of the well-marked trails. The services of a local English-speaking guide may also be hired (additional JD6 for 2hr or JD30 for the day). Further details, advice and information are available from the RSCN bureau at the entrance to the village. The busiest days are Wednesdays and Thursdays although the number of visitors falls during July and August as temperatures in the canyon rise to extremes.

## SHOPPING GUIDE

**Souvenirs and handicrafts** – Dana only really has two shops offering quality goods for sale: notably pieces of silver jewellery set with local polished stones typical of the region, traditional ceramics and weavings.

Hamida carpets

Y. Traynard

# PETRA ★★★
260km from Amman
Pop 10 000 – Alt 1 000 m

**Not to be missed**
*The Siq, the narrow defile leading to Petra.
The façades of the Treasury and the Monastery
(Khazneh and el-Deir)*
**And remember...**
*Savour Petra in the light, stillness and cool of early morning.
Set aside a second day for going up Jebel al-Madhbah
or climbing to the summit of Mount Harun.*

"Recall every memory of the desert as you make your way towards the great rift."
Adonis

The white desert provides little variety for mile after mile. Then suddenly, the road speeds past the King's Way Inn, slows round a corner and wow! The earth's crust breaks out in a chaotic complex of red, jagged cliffs. Indeed the most striking thing about Petra is its extraordinary geology. For this great wonder of the world is as much a phenomenon of nature as of man. No human hand could have fashioned such a combination of layered sandstone flecked with white, mottled pink cliffs and sharp needles of black granite, and no lifetime could have spanned the time required for the water, sand and wind to sculpt such a dramatic landscape on such a magnificent scale. Only the final detail, like icing on a cake, can be claimed to be the work of man. One can but wonder at how the Nabataeans – an Arab people still steeped in mystery – came to choose this secluded place for their capital, protected by ready-made ramparts. What we have inherited at Petra is a remarkable rock-hewn necropolis containing more than 800 tombs, so delicately chiselled as to provide us with one of the most fabulous sites in the Middle East.

Rock detail, Petra

C. Pavard /HOA QUI

## The workings of Nature...
Petra takes its name from the Greek word for "rock", either because it appropriately described the mountain that the Nabataeans used to squirrel away their precious merchandise, or perhaps because it understated the distinctive beauty of the stone in its natural

state that so impressed them as it does visitors today. The Jordanian plateau is predominantly covered with a coarse textured secondary limestone, formed in the Mesozoic period. At Petra, however, this layer is interrupted by an outcrop of primary sandstone (dating from the Palaeozoic period) extruded as a result of and in parallel with the great rift that exposed the crystal-rich igneous rock lining the Araba Valley. The layered strata that ranges through a panoply of whites and reds, and provides Petra with such an exceptional backdrop, was forced into folds as a consequence of major tectonic plate movements – sometimes called the continental waltz. The profile of the landscape, meanwhile, has been determined by time; with extreme changes in temperature, minute fissures in the strata become cracks that, in turn, are worn away by winds laden with sand (the Siq is the finest example of this double process of corrosion and erosion) or by rainwater seeping through the pervious rock, dissolving soluble salts on its way before chemically eating away at exposed cavities or stone ledges. This same ongoing process that has lent such haunting forms to the natural landscape and constituted its fundamental beauty also causes the most exposed parts of the majestic man-made monuments to deteriorate and melt into the sand.

## ...and of the Nabataeans

The proximity of natural fresh-water springs encouraged people to settle at Petra as far back as Neolithic times. Between the 8th and 7th millennia BC, hunter-gatherers settled at nearby al-Beidah. Later, the area was taken over by the **Edomites**, a Semitic people that had settled the region southeast of the Dead Sea and had been conquered by David. In the 6C BC, the **Nabataeans** – another Semitic tribe this time of Arab origin – arrived and gradually, despite their nomadic lifestyle, began to take control of and develop caravanserais and relay stations along the major trade routes. Before long, Petra's defensive position guaranteed a certain security for valuable consignments of prized commodities like incense, myrrh and spices to be sold before being shipped out to important markets in Greece and Rome. In her role as gateway to both the East and the West, Petra was much coveted by rival factions like the Ptolemies and the Seleucids, but the Nabataeans managed to repulse the sometimes bloody incursions and retain control of their land. Their territories became a kingdom (which at one time extended as far as Damascus) and a succession of dynasties ruled it effectively – the most famous being the Aretas. Petra reached its greatest prosperity during the reign of Aretas IV (contemporary with the life of Christ and the dawn of the

### The re-discovery of Petra

The Swiss Johann Ludwig Burckhardt arrived in Wadi Musa disguised as an Arab in 1812 after spending three years in Aleppo. Fluent in Arabic, a convert to Islam and renamed Ibrahim Ibn Abd Allah, Burckhardt finally secured permission to visit the site on the pretext of having taken a vow to sacrifice a goat on Mount Haroun. On his way through the Siq and past Qasr al-Bint, accompanied by a suspecting guide at his heels, he promptly turned round and retraced his steps, apparently after owning up to his true intent. Excited by what he had seen, he announced that he had located what he thought to be the site of Petra, which, at the time, was only known from ancient texts. Six years later, the British commanders Laborde and Linant de Bellefonds managed to spend a week at Petra, when an outbreak of the plague was declared in Wadi Musa, giving them just enough time to sketch the façades of the main monuments. These drawings were later made into detailed engravings and published in an album. Archeological excavations began in 1929.

Petra

379

modern era), and it is then that the city was endowed with its sumptuous monuments. The way of life, religious practices and cultural values the Nabataeans had inherited from their ancestors were gently reassessed to reflect the ethics, tastes and aspirations of other prestigious dynasties with whom they vied for business. They preserved their independence from the Romans until 106 AD, when the Emperor Trajan annexed the Nabataean kingdom and created the Roman province of Arabia. Petra briefly recovered her lustre before going into a slow decline. The city had its own bishop under Byzantine rule, but was completely bypassed by the Muslims; two fortresses were built by the Crusaders. The chronicles of the Mameluke sultan Baybars make one final reference to Petra in 1276 and then nothing until the 19C when **JL Burckhardt** broke the spell and rescued the legendary city from oblivion.

## The Nabataean genius

If the Nabataeans proved their ingenuity and shrewdness in matters of trade, this was little by comparison to their supremacy in the diverse fields of hydrology and civil engineering, writing and religion. In a region where water is scarce, the local population learnt how to dig channels, cisterns, and reservoirs to ensure that sufficient supplies were collected to last them all year. In order to preserve their language – an Aramaic dialect – the Nabataeans developed a written script that now is considered to be the precursor of Arabic. But it is perhaps their religion that is the most original aspect of their culture: the Nabataean pantheon, which was originally Semitic, associates the divinities of Syria and Palestine with those of the Greek and Roman world. The patron or protector of the Nabataean people and their state was Dushara who was identified both with Jupiter and Dionysus; the goddess Allat was associated with the Greek deity Athena and Al-Uzza corresponds with Aphrodite and the Egyptian goddess Isis. Worship was offered up to the gods through betyls (upright stones usually without figurative features) notably in the lower town where there were several important temples dedicated to them. However it is the cult of the dead that has left us with the most spectacular reflections of their faith in the form of splendid tombs and triclinia (where funeral banquets were held) that comprise the principal monuments of Petra. Each dead person's soul is represented by a rectangular stone (*nefesh*).

## Planning your visit

*Petra's monuments are separated from the town of Wadi Musa – where the numerous hotels and restaurants are situated – by a tall sandstone outcrop. Access is through a narrow passage known as the "Siq". The site is open from sunrise to sunset. Entrances charges are exorbitant: a single-day pass costs JD20, while those valid for two days (JD25) or three days (JD30) are more reasonable. There are no reductions or concessions. Tickets may be purchased from the office at the Visitors' Centre. There are no accommodation facilities on the site itself and sleeping rough is prohibited; there are, however, plenty of restaurants and cafés.*

*Petra is well worth a visit, but be warned – the monuments are scattered over a vast area and their exploration must entail some degree of walking, even if horse-drawn carriages are laid on for doing the Siq, and camels can be hired thereafter. It is advisable to follow certain basic recommendations to avoid suffering from heat exhaustion. Early morning temperatures may be deceptively cool given the altitude, so apply sunscreen in advance before things get too sticky, take sunglasses for protection from the glare, stop regularly for a short rest and keep hydrated by drinking plenty of water (sweetened drinks may be reviving after consumption, but can leave you feeling drained as blood-sugar levels fall).*

**Day 1** – Your first day in Petra is best spent exploring the most famous monuments. Set out from the **Gaïa necropolis**, walk down the **Siq\*\*\*** to the treasury (al Khazneh) that stands at the entrance to the **great necropolis\*\*\***. Go past the theatre and continue into the **lower town**. Stop to visit the small museum perhaps, then pause for lunch to allow the midday heat to subside a little before embarking on the path to the monastery or **Deir\*\***. On the way back, take a look at the **royal tombs\*\*** lit by the setting sun and make your way out along the Siq. This full – though not overly demanding – itinerary (apart from rather a long climb up to the Deir) will provide you with an initial overview of Petra if you are restricted to spending only one day there.

**Additional days** – Petra deserves at least one extra day's visiting. Make a plan around what you want to see without forgetting to take your own physical stamina into consideration: save on the effort of walking up and down the Siq by taking advantage of the transport provided by the local Bedouins. Herewith are listed a selection of options, but there are plenty of others for the discerning and adventurers. It may be useful to purchase the 1/5 000 map of Petra and check on information available from the Visitors' Centre before setting out.

**Jebel al-Madhbah\*\*** (*3hr round trip starting from the Khazneh; medium difficulty*) alone justifies spending a second day at Petra. This excursion combines splendid views over Petra with the opportunity of visiting some of the more unusual monuments so brilliantly conceived by the Nabataeans (high point, fountain, obelisks). Try to complete the short but steep ascent (200m uneven track) in the early morning when it benefits from some shade.

*The following itineraries are not described in great detail here but can be easily followed using the map provided.*

**Al Habis Crusader Castle** (*45min from Qasr al Bint; medium difficulty*): the ruined fortress occupies a prime position above Qasr al Bint. Fine views over Petra.

**Wadi Siyagh** (*45min from Qasr al Bint; very easy*): pleasant walk along the stream bed past lovely flowering oleanders up to its source Aïn al-Siyagh.

**Umm al Biyara** (*4hr round trip from Qasr al Bint; guide recommended as the going is difficult and dangerous*): a good hike including a most amazing ramp cut into the bedrock up to various Edomite ruins and cisterns at the top. Superb panoramic views from the summit.

**Mount Harun\*\*** (*5hr round trip from Qasr al Bint; guide recommended; medium difficulty involving a steep climb*): a long walk around Umm al Biyara that takes you on and up to 1 400m and a small white mausoleum dedicated to Moses' elder brother Aaron, who, according to tradition, is supposed to have rested here. Breathtaking **views\*\*** and the opportunity of getting away from the crowds provide the incentives to this excursion.

**Heights of Jebel al Khubtha** (*2hr from the Urn Tomb and back; guide recommended; medium difficulty*): beyond the royal necropolis there are a number of triclinia, dams and cisterns.

**Al Madras** (*90min from the obelisks tomb and back; guide recommended; medium difficulty*): a high point cut into the white sandstone near to a collection of tombs, cisterns and triclinia.

**Al Wueira Crusader Castle** (*2hr round trip from the Visitors' Centre or take a taxi to the foot of the fort; easy*): the small Crusader castle at al Wueira or Moses Valley collapsed into ruins as a result of seismic activity and destruction wrought by Saladin in 1188. Fine northeast tower.

**Petra**

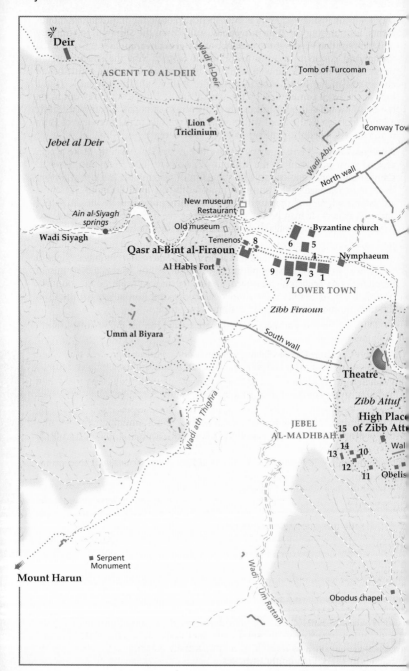

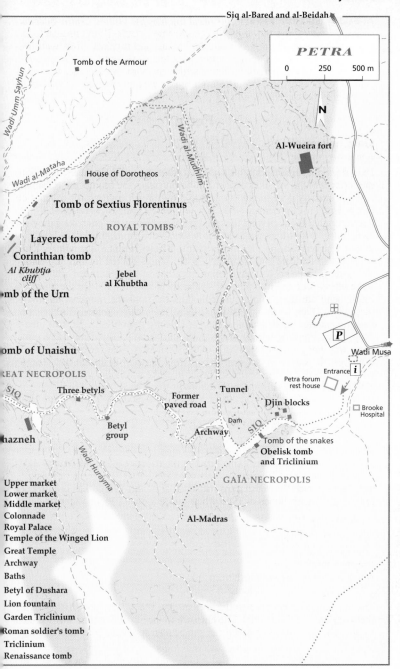

Siq al-Bared and al-Beidah

**PETRA**

0          250          500 m

N

Tomb of the Armour

Al-Wueira fort

Wadi Umm Sayhun

Wadi al-Mudhlim

Wadi al-Mataha

House of Dorotheos

**Tomb of Sextius Florentinus**

ROYAL TOMBS

Jebel
al Khubtha

**Layered tomb**

**Corinthian tomb**

*Al Khubtja
cliff*

mb of the Urn

P

Wadi Musa

Entrance          i

omb of Unaishu

Petra forum
rest house

REAT NECROPOLIS

Brooke
Hospital

SIQ          **Three betyls**

Former
paved road          Tunnel

Djin blocks

**Betyl
group**          Dam

Archway          SIQ

hazneh          Tomb of the snakes

**Obelisk tomb
and Triclinium**

Wadi Hurayma

GAÏA NECROPOLIS

Upper market
Lower market
Middle market
Colonnade
Royal Palace
Temple of the Winged Lion          **Al-Madras**

Great Temple

Archway

Baths

Betyl of Dushara

Lion fountain

Garden Triclinium

Roman soldier's tomb

Triclinium

Renaissance tomb

**Al-Beidah** and **Little Petra★★** *(2hr round trip from the Visitors' Centre, guide recommended; easy)*, the Siq al-Bared is nicknamed "Little Petra" because of its similarity to Petra. Numerous interesting tombs and tricilinia – one with frescoes – in a quiet spot with few visitors. The site of al-Beidah nearby preserves the remains of an important Neolithic settlement. Visit the Crusader Fort of al-Wueira on the way there *(see above)*. These last two itineraries do not necessitate the purchase of the entrance ticket to Petra.

# Petra

## Gaïa necropolis
*20min, easy walking*

Petra does not present itself on a plate: it takes a good 20 minutes to walk to the entrance of the Siq and a further half-hour to reach the heart of the Nabataean city. The scenery is so spectacular that it is well worth covering the distance on foot at least once *(preferably on the way in when the going is gently downhill)*.

Pass through the gate beyond the ticket office and follow the path along the right bank of the Wadi Musa, which is nearly always dry. At the foot of the hills, cultivated with terraces, on the left, stands the Brooke Hospital, a veterinary clinic dedicated to the care and well-being of the horses offered for hire to visitors. The wide path enters a strange lunar landscape of large, humped white sandstone blocks sculpted into unusual shapes by Mother Nature. On the right of a broad bend are three enormous monoliths cut from the humpbacked rocks: these three **Djinn blocks** are strange hollow multi-storey tombs. The first two have no external decoration and contain funerary chambers. A pit, two metres deep, hewn from the terrace of the third must have sheltered mortal remains. Some way along, on the other bank of the Wadi Musa, stand two superimposed frontages; the top level, set further back into the cliff, is the **Obelisk Tomb★** with its four tall tapering obelisks – hence its name – standing proud from stone cliff-face (called nefesh). Although the lower tier is badly eroded, it is still possible to make out the rich ornamentation of the **Bab al-Siq Triclinium** (broken pediments, central arch, pilasters and six engaged columns). The 50sqm rectangular chamber hewn from the cliff was used for hosting funeral banquets; the guests, seated along the three stone benches, would share the wine from the libations and the flesh of the sacrificial animals.

The valley widens out near a small dam at the entrance to the Siq; on the right, runs a **tunnel** that was dug by the Nabataeans to divert the water from the wadi. The dam – which the Nabataeans had built to protect Petra – has been rebuilt following the flash-floods of 1963 which swept away 22 French tourists.

## The Siq★★★
*30min; easy walking.*

"The siq is a single body
stretched into two parts
which may never be re-united."
                    Adonis

The Siq, the main entrance to the ancient city, is a 1.3km long, narrow defile (between 3m and 11m wide). The entrance to the Siq at one time was spanned by an arch, the remains of which can still be seen springing from each side high

The Obelisk Tomb

above the track. The rock-hewn channel running along the foot of the left wall to the far end of the Siq was, at one time, used to convey fresh water from a spring to the city centre. As if to entice you inwards, the colour of the sandstone changes from white to bloodshot with veins of red, ochre, yellow and black.

Deeper into the Siq, the scenery becomes increasingly fabulous: the high walls enclosing the narrow defile rise to more than 100m. Here and there, ledges (or *tafonis*) overhang the path, eroded by the rain and wind, meanwhile, at head height, the rock disintegrates into great flakes. The sound of footsteps falling on sand or grating on gravel and the shrill voices of tourists are a poor substitute for the slow, rhythmic procession of laden caravans that once would have resounded through the narrow rock corridor. The odd stunted tree clings to a rock-face deprived of sunlight. Elsewhere, an intriguing series of small niches seem to punctuate the rock: these are **betyls**, which would have harboured tangible representations of deities sacred to the Nabataean religion, often devoid of distinctive features. The vestiges of the old flagstones that once paved the road are clearly evident in two places more than a metre above the present level of the Siq. The passageway widens out, then narrows again several times before revealing, between two dark walls, the rose-red façade of a monument which, at first sight, looks like a temple, but which is called the Khazneh (or "Treasury"), at the entrance to the great necropolis of Petra.

## The great necropolis★★★
*30min, easy walking*

It is difficult enough to remain indifferent before the **Khazneh★★★** today, but imagine its impact on unsuspecting travellers in Antiquity: after crossing endless miles of desert and entering the Siq itself – beautiful and yet soulless as it is – to be suddenly confronted with the Treasury, a grandiose and breathtaking embodiment of the gates of civilisation on such a dramatic scale. Such a perfect combination of line and harmonious form, the delicate colour of the stone and subtlety of the relief inherent in the Treasury façade combine to make this monument Petra's most highly prized. It earned its name from an old legend that recounts how the huge urn at the top of the building once contained a rare treasure (*khazneh* in Arabic), placed there by a pharaoh. Through time, many a Bedouin has tried to smash open the urn by shooting at it with their rifles in the hope of being showered with gold, but in so doing have only succeeded in damaging the stonework. One peculiar aspect of Petra's monuments is that the tombs are hewn from the rock rather than constructed. The front of the Treasury, a large-scale sculpture, reaches some 40m in height. Its design is profoundly Hellenistic. At ground-floor level, it imitates a hexastyle temple, with two completely free-standing columns, surmounted by Corinthian capitals with double rows of acanthus leaves supporting a triangular pediment. The *tholos* (small round shrine) is surmounted by the urn, which possibly denotes the funerary function of the building. Raised on a pedestal stands Tyche holding a cornucopia in her left hand; behind her one can just make out some attendant winged Victories and two dancing Amazons brandishing axes above their heads. In stark contrast with the elegant exterior, the inside of the Treasury is rather austere. Three chambers lead off the main vestibule, all hewn from the bedrock and therefore gloriously textured with the naturally marbled stone walls.

The actual function and date of the monument are still subject to debate: perhaps the most plausible is the theory that it was the early-1C tomb of Aretas IV.

*Follow the widening course of the wadi on the right of the Treasury.*

The path picks its way between a multitude of tombs hollowed out of the rock, arranged in two rows, often aligned one above the other. The entrances to these are sometimes hidden by rock falls. Others, sunk below ground level, have been subjected to repeated flooding.

On the left, there are a further four bare-fronted **monumental tombs**, which seem especially spacious in comparison with their narrow entrances. In each case, decoration is limited to a single or double line of merlons (triangular indentations). Another important collection of tombs is situated a little further down, on the opposite side. Perhaps the most refined is the **Tomb of Unaishu**\* which is preceded by a forecourt and has, above the doorway, two monumental semi-notches of a kind found at Hegra in Arabia. The incumbent of this tomb is thought to have been a minister at the court of the Nabataean Queen Shuqailat II, who reigned during the early part of the 1C AD.

The various refreshment stalls on hand proffer a brew of sage tea *(mirmiya)*. A short way past the sign indicating the path up to the High Place *(see p 390)* in the rock-face on the left of the theatre is a multitude of small hollow tombs aligned in rows, sometimes four thick. In this section of the necropolis, the predominant type of tomb is known as a multi-storey or **tower-tomb**: each has a small forecourt and a rectangular façade with a narrow opening surmounted by one or two lines of crenallated indentations or merlons.

As with the tombs, Petra's **theatre**\* was not built as such but carved out of the rock sometime during the reign of Augustus (1C AD) and badly damaged by an earthquake in 363. The cavea, which had a seating capacity of 6 000, encroaches upon the necropolis. The proscenium wall has in places been restored. It is worth noting here, that there was another theatre in the lower town. As you continue along the Wadi Musa, you will notice many additional tombs opposite – some more remarkable than others – before the riverbed broadens out.

*Follow the track as it turns left towards a large tree, thereby turning your back on the splendid Royal Tombs, which will be treated in detail on the way back.*

## The lower city
*20min, easy walking.*

The path comes to a large pistachio tree that marks the site of the **nymphaeum** at the entrance to the lower city. The built-up section of the city, which at one time dominated the actual kernel or epicentre of Petra, has not withstood the repercussions of two violent earthquakes. Its full extent is gradually being recovered by the painstaking efforts of archeologists, although a precise idea of size and scale is still a good way off. It is highly probable that it consisted of a Hellenistic style city compete with public markets, baths, temples and a selection of private villas. The Nabataeans did not reside in troglodyte dwellings: all rock-hewn chambers were exclusively used for entombing the dead or for celebrating religious rituals allied therewith. Instead they lived among the culturally diverse local population in the streets of Petra and rubbed shoulders with traders from all four corners of the world.

Opposite the nymphaeum, amid the many piles of rubble that characterise this part of the city currently undergoing excavations, stood the **Upper Market** with its flight of steps to the first floor. To the right, traces of two adjacent market-buildings evidently extended the town's commercial sector further; these have been labelled by archeologists as the **Middle Market** and **Lower Market** (yet to

**Petra**

be excavated). Behind the **colonnade**, which in part has been rebuilt, one can discern the lines of shops. The huge area given over to traders and merchants only serves to reinforce the considerable role played by the city – and her fortunes – as a transit point for caravans. On the right, before the arch, stood two buildings straddling the wadi: a **"Royal Palace"** (yet to be excavated) and a **Temple of the Winged Lions** – the remains of which can be seen on the side of the right bank *(closed to the public)*. The square double portico of this Nabataean temple built at the dawn of our times featured griffins for decoration. On the hillside behind, a shelter protects the priceless collection of **mosaics\*\***, which cover the floor of the **Byzantine church** (access is sometimes prohibited). Their medallions represent symbolic portraits of the seasons and of animals, some mythological, such as a camel with a giraffe's skin. Opposite the temple of the winged lions rose two flights of steps to the **Great Temple** which initial excavations have revealed to be a monument of exceptional significance. The **archway** reassembled to the right of the **baths** marks the entrance to another sanctuary and the far end of the city's principal thoroughfare. This layout completely contradicts the tenets of Hellenistic town planning, which was organised around and relative to the *cardo maximus*.

*Head towards the imposing stone building.*

The large paved courtyard consisted of the **temenos**: the sacred precinct of the large temple and best-preserved building in the city, known as **Qasr al-Bint al-Firaoun\***. In modern Arabic, the name translates as "the palace of the Pharaoh's Daughter" in accordance with the Bedouin wont of attributing the construction of all the mysterious buildings in Petra to Egyptian sovereigns. The square temple would have been fronted by a grand stairway. Four columns articulate the main façade, screening the cella, which reflects an Oriental style in that it comprises three rooms. In the central room stood a platform-cum-plinth on which rested the betyl of the deity. The temple is generally considered to be from 1C BC.

At the far end of the area beyond the temenos, past the numerous covered refreshment stalls, there is a staircase leading up to a former tomb that now houses the **old museum** *(closed Fridays; no charge; allow 15min)*. This contains the remains recovered from the site (sculpted architectural fragments and fine Nabataean pottery).

The modern building sheltering under the trees on the opposite side of the wadi contains the Basin Restaurant and the **New or Forum Basin Museum** *(no charge; allow 30min)*. Room 1 displays a cross-section of the site showing its geological make-up together with a variety of rock-samples and a fine rectangular **stele\*\*** dedicated to the goddess of Hayyan with stylised facial features. Room 2 collects together the artefacts (flint) found during excavations at al-Beidah and from the Temple of the Winged Lions. A large black and white marble **basin\*** with two lion-shaped handles was discovered in the Byzantine church. In Room 3, off to one side, are arranged a fine series of 25 oil lamps that throw light on how this object evolved and changed over a period of twelve centuries, as well as some fine examples of **Nabataean pottery** described as "egg-shell ware" because of its distinctive delicacy. In the centre are displayed a dozen Nabataean **coins** dating from the 1C BC to 106 AD. Even after Rome had annexed the region, local workshops continued to mint coins bearing the head of the emperors (Trajan and Hadrian) until Imperial coinage began to be traded during the reign of Elagabal.

## The ascent to al-Deir (the "Monastery")**

*2hr 30min round trip, medium difficulty* The climb up to the Monastery (al-Deir) takes about an hour. At the top, not only is the actual monument itself of great interest and on a par with the Treasury, there are also exceptional views to be enjoyed stretching out over the Araba Valley.

*On leaving the new museum, follow the bed of the Wadi al-Deir.*

After the first few flights of steps, the gradient becomes steeper and a path branches off to the left towards the **Lion Triclinium** so called because its doorway, now eroded into the shape of a keyhole, is guarded by carved lions. Note in passing the two heads of Medusa at either end of the pediment. Continue along the path, passing beneath the fallen boulder, and on up to the left. As you rise up the side of the hill, magnificent **views**** open out over the Petra basin. Suddenly the square outline of the **Monastery (al-Deir)**** comes into view, sitting on its platform in all its majesty, carved out of an outcrop of yellow sandstone. Despite the many similarities with the Treasury, (the tholos surmounted by an urn, and its two storeys), the Monastery is more austere, designed on a grander scale, with ornament that is more restrained than that of its counterpart. Its façade measures 48m across, making it one of the largest monuments in Petra. The single urn alone measures 10m in height *(access possible but dangerous along a path leading up the left-hand side of the Monastery)*. The interior does not seem to have had a loculus upon which the dead would have been laid in state prior to burial. The stone benches cut from the sandstone around the edge of the room suggest this monument was conceived as a biclinium in the early part of the 2C AD. Later on, the building was used as a church.

*Follow the edge of the cliff for some distance until you reach the western side of the platform (15mins).*

Down on the right extends a tongue of land etched with the outline of a building; 50m below, sits a **High Place** carved out of the stone. The **view**** over Wadi Araba is superb. In the distance, a wadi shadowed with green trees winds through a ravine of black rocks glistening with quartz. Up on the top of Mount Haroun on the left sits a white aedicule.

*Go back down to the lower city, cutting through the colonnade to head towards the series of tombs in the cliff opposite, accessible by means of the stairs by the Bedouin stall-holders.*

## The Royal Tombs**

*1hr from the new museum, easy walking.*

The great mass of Jebel al-Khubtha segregates Petra from Wadi Musa. Its west-facing façade incorporates several monumental tombs, which bear the attribute "Royal" rather because of their monumentality than the rank of their occupants *(see p 308)*.

The tour is accomplished from right to left.

The first is described as the **Tomb of the Urn**** and may be reached by walking up the steps through the two vaulted passageways before it. Its forecourt would have been lined with two porticoes, although only the left one retains its five Doric columns. An urn crowns the pediment. During Byzantine times, the building is thought to have been transformed into a cathedral.

Several modest tower-tombs separate the Tomb of the Urn from the **Corinthian Tomb*** which reflects the style of the Treasury (possibly dating from the late 1C AD) but which, alas, has been badly damaged by erosion. On its left, you

**Petra**

will see the **Layered Tomb**✶✶: the grandest and most original of the complex as it consists of five superimposed storeys. The first floor above the four doorways is articulated by 18 engaged columns. The **Tomb of Sextius Florentinus**✶✶ (200m further north along the colonnade), belonging to a Roman Governor of the Province of Arabia, was built posthumously in the most suitable place by his son, in about 130 AD. Its unusual tympanum, although badly worn, is decorated with a dancing female figure and surmounted by an Imperial eagle.

*From here, the main entrance to the site of Petra is about a 60min walk. Return by the same route along the Siq.*

## Jebel al-Madhbah
*3hr there and back to the Treasury; medium difficulty.*

*400m beyond the Treasury there are a series of steps leading up towards the theatre. Follow the sign for "High Place".*

The fairly steep ancient steps, which in places are covered by a layer of fine red sand, lead into the Wadi al-Mahfour. The path zigzags its winding way through the oleanders, becoming gradually narrower, to arrive at a small café (30mins)

*Turn right before the drinks stall.*

Before long, you come across first one, then two **obelisks** rising from a platform on the left. Both stand proud from the bedrock. From here, the path picks its way through the rubble from a collapsed section of the high stone wall. If you keep to the ridge, you will eventually reach the summit of Jebel al-Madhbah where the main **High Place**✶ of Petra is sited, complete with vestiges, at ground level, of two pools and series of steps. Here, in the open air, the Nabataeans followed certain rituals derived from ancient Semitic practices involving libations (offering up wine) and animal sacrifices. A raised dais would have served to accommodate the betyls carried up from below. The animals would have been sacrificed on the left, alongside a stone with a hollowed bowl in which the blood was collected. The celebrants would have gathered around the large rectangular pool (14x6m), hewn from the bedrock, before the steps up to the dais.

*Continue along the promontory for about 100m.*

From here the **view**✶✶✶ over Petra is quite extraordinary: to the left, you see the white aedicule perched on the summit of Mount Haroun; before it rises the Jebel Umm al-Biyyara where Petra's earliest human settlements are situated. In the broad valley below, the ancient city thrived. Slightly northwest, you can perhaps make out the urn of the Monastery.

*Retrace your steps and pass between the obelisks and the café.*

The path follows a wide loop before starting downhill along Wadi al-Farassa. On the right, a platform bears a strange-looking mushroom-shaped stone, weathered by erosion, in which sits a **betyl**. The Nabataean god Dushara is represented both by the stone and by his effigy in a medallion above. The bust of a youth crowned with vineleaves is often equated with the Greek god Dionysus (or the Roman god of wine, Bacchus). A little further down on the left, a **lion fountain** fronts a small terrace: its larger-than-life outline carved into the rock-face is obvious, although the head is badly worn. The water spouting from the animal's mouth was fed from a special channel, possibly to refresh the throng engaged in the long procession up to the High Place. A beautiful ancient set of steps takes one down into a small valley that once sheltered what was probably a fabulous garden. Beside the large stone cistern on the right is the **Garden Triclinium** fronted by a pair of columns, possibly intended as a tomb. The same funerary complex continues below to include the two carved temple-fronted tombs opposite each other across the wadi. The façade of the fine **Roman Soldier Tomb** on the left is a standard arrangement of four columns and three niches containing figures – possibly representing the deceased interred within, although these are badly worn. The central statue wears a short tunic and a breast-plate. Opposite, beyond what would have been a column-lined courtyard, sits a **triclinium** containing a truly wonderful interior decor complete with engaged columns that are fluted in their upper sections. The niches would probably have contained receptacles used in cult rituals. A well-worn stone bench runs along three sides of the chamber. 100m further down on the right you will find the elegant **Renaissance Tomb**.

*Walk round the Zibb Attuf to emerge by the theatre. On the way, you can marvel at the fine view over the Royal Tombs. The hollows on the right are sometimes used by the local Bedouins to garage their pick-up trucks! It is also possible to reach Qasr al-Bint by cutting across the valley.*

# Making the most of Petra

Wadi Musa, the commercial centre outside Petra, has mushroomed along the sides of the main road. The King's Way Inn is the first establishment on the edge of the **upper town** overlooking two rather more modest hotels. The road goes steeply downhill past the Aqaba road on the left and into the **town centre** marked by a major roundabout (2.5km from the King's Way Inn). The basic and medium-standard hotels are found nearby, as are the shops, Internet cafés and several simple restaurants. The main road will then take you to the **lower town** (1.5km), which is more touristy, and where most of the souvenir shops, as well as the more comfortable hotels, are concentrated, closest to the entrance to Petra.

## COMING AND GOING

**By bus –** The **Jett Bus Company** operates a daily service that leaves Amman at 6am (6.30am in winter) and departs back at 3.30pm (3pm in winter). Departures from outside the Jett headquarters at Abdali station (see Making the most of Amman). Day-trip ticket including a meal in Petra, but excluding entrance to the site. Dull journey (3hr 30min) along the Desert Highway. Tickets for the return leg back to Amman may be purchased from the paper shop behind the Visitors' Centre.

**Minibuses** operate services very early each morning to Aqaba (3 times daily), Wadi Rum (once daily) and Amman. More frequent services along the Desert Highway to Maan. Collection points at various stages along the town's main thoroughfare. Timetables are displayed in the Visitors' Centre.

**By shared taxi –** Aqaba JD25, Rum JD30.

## GETTING AROUND PETRA

**By taxi –** If your hotel is a long way from the site, they may offer to ferry you there. If not, it is worth knowing that a ride in a taxi between the upper and lower town should not be much more than JD1, and that they cruise up and down the main street all day long. To get to Little Petra, reckon on a fare of about JD10.

**On horseback –** It costs JD7 to hire a horse and ride the length of the Siq (3km); for a seat in a carriage, estimate JD8.

Making the most of Petra

## ADDRESS BOOK

**Tourist Information** – The *Visitors' Centre* (open all day) is situated by the main car park, next to the entrance to the site. It provides basic information on what to see and a set of "approved" rates for guides, who they will be happy to book for you. Budget JD35 for a guide to accompany you on a day's excursion to Mount Harun, for example.

**Banks/currency exchange** – There are several banks in Wadi Musa. Housing Bank (with Visa cash dispenser), a little way before the roundabout when coming from the upper town; Arab Bank (with Visa cash dispenser), just after the roundabout when descending towards Petra. In Petra you will find a branch of the *Arab Bank* in the same building as the Visitors' Centre. Cash may be withdrawn by credit card or exchanged for foreign currency and travellers' cheques. The *Cairo Amman Bank* is on the ground floor of the Mövenpick Hotel.

**Post office** – In Wadi Musa, near the roundabout. At Petra, in the Visitors' Centre.

**Medical services** – A small self-contained *Emergency Clinic* is to be found near to the Petra Forum Hotel. A qualified doctor is available day and night for treating ailments such as sunstroke, stomach upsets, fractures and other accidental injuries. There are two dispensing chemists in the centre of town.

## WHERE TO STAY

It is no longer possible to sleep in the actual site under the stars like many an adventurer did in times past. Since the boom in tourism, the nearby town of Wadi Musa has become overrun with hotel facilities. It is still wise, however, to make reservations in advance of arrival, especially in the high season. The establishments located nearest to the entrance to Petra are preferable to those facing onto the busy, and therefore noisy, main thoroughfare. The higher the situation of the hotel, the more comfortable the temperatures are likely to be at night.

### • Wadi Musa

Breakfast is nearly always included in the price of the room. Prices can fall 20-50% during the low season (November to February; July and August).

*Under US$35*

**Musa Spring Hotel**, upper town, opposite the King's Way Inn ☎ (3) 215 63 10, Fax (3) 215 69 10 – 22rm ⚏ ℘ ✗ For nigh on 10 years now, this has been the popular choice of travellers on a tight budget. Situated at the entrance to Wadi Musa (free transport to Petra); first floor comprises basic but clean rooms; the two upper floors have simple rooms with bathroom facilities and brand new furniture. The ultimate experience is to opt for a mattress on the roof, beneath the stars, and pay JD2.5. Water from Moses' Spring runs beneath the hotel reception.

**Orient Gate Hotel**, indicated on the right of the main street when returning from Petra, ☎/Fax (3) 215 70 20 – 10rm ✗ A popular meeting place for backpackers from all over the world, this small hotel proposes several prices. There are basic rooms, with or without bathrooms, or mattresses on the roof for the really hard up. Youthful atmosphere.

☕ **Twaissi Inn**, indicated on the right when going towards Petra from the Wadi Musa roundabout, ☎ (3) 215 64 23 – 10rm ℘ ✗ Some rooms have bathrooms. Probably the quietest hotel in Wadi Musa, set back off the road. Unpretentious but friendly and well kept. The Bedouin tent and tables outside make for a convivial atmosphere. Good buffet in the evening. You may be able to sleep on the roof. Free transport to and from Petra.

**Al-Anbat 2 Hotel**, first street on the left after the Wadi Musa roundabout in the direction of Petra, ☎ (3) 215 72 00, Fax (3) 215 68 88 – 20rm ⚏ ⚏ ℘ ⟨TV⟩ ✗ ⟨CC⟩ In a quiet side-street. This modern hotel represents excellent value for money; what it lacks in charm it makes up for in comfort and cleanliness. Some rooms have small balconies with view. Free transport to and from Petra.

**Sunset Hotel**, lower town, on the main street, ☎ (3) 215 65 79, Fax (3) 215 69 50 – 50rm ℘ ⟨TV⟩ ✗ Cheap hotel nearest to Petra. Shared bathroom for rooms on the first floor; those on the other floors have private facilities. Large comfortable lounge area opposite the reception area is a good place to meet other travellers.

**Peace Way Hotel**, just before the roundabout when coming from the upper town, ☎/Fax (3) 215 69 63 – 19rm ⌸ ✈ ⌂ TV ✗ A friendly welcome. Some rooms are more spacious than others, but all are clean. Avoid those overlooking the street, which are noisy.

*From US$35-50*

**Al-Rashid Hotel**, next to the Wadi Musa roundabout, ☎ (3) 215 68 00, Fax (3) 215 68 01 – 40rm Carefully decorated in pastel tones, with a hushed atmosphere. Very reasonable prices, taking into account the standard of comfort and quality of service. A very good place to stay in this category of hotel.

**Elgee Hotel**, first street on the right after the Wadi Musa roundabout, going towards Petra, ☎ (3) 215 67 01, Fax (3) 215 70 02 – 13rm ⌸ ✈ ⌂ TV ✗ CC Fairly small but functional and well-kept rooms. The small first-floor pub is one of the few places in Wadi Musa which serves alcohol.

**Petra Moon Hotel**, lower town, 100m up the Al Beidah road, ☎/Fax (3) 215 62 20 – 17rm ⌸ TV ✗ CC Staff at this remarkably inexpensive hotel provide a professional service. Pleasant rooms in which the colour blue predominates. Room prices inclusive of breakfast.

**Flowers Hotel**, lower town, in the street near the Mövenpick, ☎ (3) 215 67 71, Fax (3) 215 67 70 – 30rm ⌸ ⌂ TV ✗ CC The rooms of this hotel are decorated in blue and white. Wonderful panoramic views over Petra, even at breakfast time. Half board.

**Candles Hotel**, lower town, down a street next to the Sunset Hotel ☎ (3) 215 69 54, Fax (3) 215 73 11 – 31rm ⌸ ⌂ TV ✗ CC Several rooms have balconies facing onto the site. Comfortable and welcoming place with a family feel to it.

*From US$50-65*

**Petra Palace Hotel**, lower town, 300m before the Visitors' Centre, ☎ (3) 215 67 23, Fax (3) 215 67 24 –

83rm ⌸ ⫘ ⌂ TV ✗ ⌚ CC Although situated on the main road, this hotel is a mere 10min walk from the entrance to the site and is effectively arranged around a swimming pool. Attractive, if rather sober decor, attractive furniture, newly refurbished throughout and intimate in feel. 30% reduction in prices in low season.

*From US$115-150*

**Petra Forum Guesthouse**, lower town, near to the Visitors' Centre, ☎ (3) 215 60 14, Fax (3) 215 66 86 – 72rm ⌸ ⫘ ⌂ TV ✗ CC This hotel is built so close to the site as to have its own Nabataean tomb on the premises. Affiliated to the Intercontinental chain of hotels. Only the most exceptional rooms have a view over the site. Buffet breakfast for less than JD8 will set you up for the day.

**King's Way Inn**, upper town, at the entrance to Wadi Musa, ☎ (3) 215 67 99, Fax (3) 215 67 96 – 81rm ⌸ ⫘ ⌂ TV ✗ ⌚ CC Opposite Moses' Spring, strikingly capped with white domes. Spacious and restful rooms, soberly decorated but tastefully so. Generous buffet in the ground-floor dining room.

**Petra Forum Hotel**, lower town, on the right of the main road, 300m past the Mövenpick Hotel, ☎ (3) 215 62 66, Fax (3) 215 69 77 – 188rm ⌸ ⫘ ⌂ TV ✗ ⌚ ⌑ CC Situated beyond the resthouse on the road to al Beidah by the whitish sandstone outcrop. This is the most isolated of the Petra hotels and yet remains reasonably close to the site. Request a room with a view. The panoramic view from the Olive Tree Restaurant is nothing short of spellbinding.

*Over US$240*

**Mövenpick Hotel**, lower town, at the intersection of the main road with the road to Al Beidah, ☎ (3) 215 71 11, Fax (3) 215 71 12 – 183rm ⌸ ⫘ ⌂ TV ✗ ⌚ ⌑ CC Fabulous facilities but can one really make best use of them? Extremely comfortable rooms, although it is the communal areas such as the lounges and restaurants that are especially sumptuous with painted wooden ceilings and Damascene marble floors, hand-turned wooden screens in the

**Making the most of Petra**

windows, wonderful great copper lights from Egypt and original engravings on the walls.

• **Taybet** (12km from Petra along the road to Aqaba)

*Over US$240*

🍽️**Taybet Zaman Hotel** ☎ (3) 215 01 11, Fax (3) 215 01 01 – 106rm 🛏️ 📧 ♪ 📺 ✕ ⛱️ 🆑 This hotel is in fact part of a large-scale tourist complex that has been set up in the small stone-built village of Taybet, 10km from Wadi Musa. It even has its own souk, with 10 or so boutiques selling Jordanian artefacts and travel accessories, and a hammam (JD12). Each room is accommodated within its very own stone cottage and is furnished to meet the needs of every comfort with country-style furniture. Excellent restaurant. The only thing missing is a view of Petra.

### WHERE TO EAT

• **Petra**

There is an assortment of refreshment stands and tents dotted around Petra, manned by Bedouins offering a choice of chilled soft drinks (water, fizzy drinks, sage tea), sandwiches and sweet biscuits. Some hotels may be happy to prepare a picnic lunch on request.

*Over US$10*

**Basin**, in the lower town of Petra itself. The only proper restaurant on site (owned by the Petra Forum Resthouse) is situated on the far side of the *wadi*, towards the Deir, opposite Qasr al-Bint. Buffet with good selection of *meze*, limited choice of hot dishes and fruit. Eat in the enclosed dining room or outside on the shaded terrace.

• **Wadi Musa**

In the high season all the hotels produce great buffets that are open to all. The restaurant at the Mövenpick Hotel is undoubtedly the most refined, although rather expensive at the same time. The Petra Forum dining room (not to be confused with that of the Petra Forum Resthouse) is lovely. Otherwise there are plenty of informal places – including one serving chicken tikka – in the centre of town.

*Under US$10*

🍽️**The Garden**, the restaurant at the Peace Way Hotel, just before the roundabout coming from the upper town. Pleasant, shady terrace away from the road. A good menu, where the usual Middle Eastern dishes (meze, kebabs) are mixed with some fairly spicy local dishes (maklouba, kalaya), which are less frequently found in restaurants.

### OTHER THINGS TO DO

**Hammam** – For a long time the traditional hammam declined and died out in Jordan. In an attempt to make amends, the Silk Road Hotel at the entrance to Petra has installed an old-fashioned style hammam on the first floor. The outcome is effective and the experience is to be recommended, especially after a long exhausting day spent in the heat and dust. The owner went to Syria to study the steam baths still in use there before he set to designing and building his own, complete with marble surfaces and small lockers at the entrance for bathers to store their personal effects. The only compromise is that this hammam serves both men and women – in keeping with modern needs. The JD12 fee includes a massage, towels, dressing-gown, soap – well just about everything! A second hammam has opened at the Taybet Zamam.

### SHOPPING GUIDE

There are several shops between the Visitors' centre and the Petra Forum Resthouse, selling postcards, books, kefiehs, bottles of coloured sand, T-shirts ... The Visitors' Centre shop displays Bani Hamida carpets and various quality hand-crafted luxury items for sale. They also stock the large scale 1:5 000 map of Petra.

Bottles of
Petra sand

JE. Valentin/HOA QUI

Making the most of Petra

# WADI RUM★★
Alt 950m – Pop 600 in village of Rum

**Not to be missed**
Watching the cliffs ablaze at the sunset.
Sleeping out under the stars.
**And remember...**
Spend a few hours beyond the village of Rum exploring the desert.
Be careful of the sun: drink plenty, wear a hat and apply sunscreen.

"Landscapes, in childhood's dream, were so vast and silent."
TE Lawrence

The stone cliffs of the Wadi Rum seem like tall ships' prows riding the shifting desert sands. The sheer rock-faces, carved from the stunningly beautiful ochre sandstone by the wind, tower above the bleak expanses of sandy plain *(see illustration p 284)*. The area takes its name from the wadi that crosses it. This strangely fascinating yet inhospitable land attracts only the hardiest of the kingdom's Bedouin people worthy of that name, and they continue to ply the same routes across the giant labyrinth, stretching some 400sqkm, that their forebears used. Like their forefathers, these nomadic people journey from well to water-hole, pitching their black goat-skin tents as they go, grazing their hardy flocks along the way. Every crevice and crack is accentuated by the sun with each hour as it passes across the marbled stone and coloured sands. The heavy silence blanketing the majestic landscape which, in places, rises to 1 754m, confers an alluring atmosphere to the place.

The best guides to the area are undoubtedly the local Bedouins who handle their 4WDs across the rough terrain with great expertise. This is certainly the most hassle-free option, although some people may prefer to explore the Wadi Rum by dromedary or on foot. Those pressed for time are unlikely to spend more than a day in the region before continuing their travels through Jordan: there may only be time to watch the sun setting. Others enamoured by the desert will want to spend a week here, whiling away the hours among fellow enthusiasts camping out under the stars in different places, each more wonderful and exciting than the last. Encounters with local Bedouin nomads in these remote places are likely to become one of life's special memories, for such experiences bring home the true meaning of hospitality. Following the sharing of a pot of sweetened black coffee flavoured with cardamom, the Bedouin might invite one to sleep with the family inside their tent.

## The principal sights
*Allow at least half a day.*

The gateway to the Wadi Rum is through a gap in a tall stone wall named the **Seven Pillars of Wisdom**, after the famous book written by Colonel TE Lawrence, that endowed the region with legendary status. It was here that Lawrence set up camp with the Arab Revolutionaries in September and October 1917.

At the entrance to the **village of Rum**, the coaches disgorge their parties of tourists outside the local *rest-house*, the only available accommodation *(access to the village of Rum is subject to an entry charge of JD1 per person, including a free*

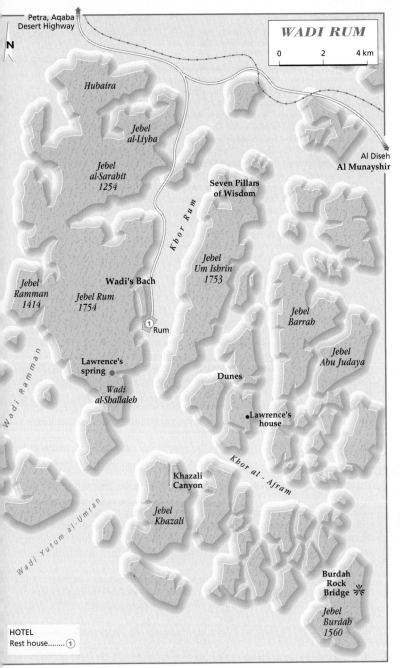

Petra, Aqaba
Desert Highway

N

0    2    4 km

Al Diseh
**Al Munayshir**

*Hubaira*

*Jebel
al-Liyba*

*Jebel
al-Sarabit*
1254

**Seven Pillars
of Wisdom**

*K b o r   R u m*

*Jebel
Um Ishrin*
1753

*Jebel
Ramman*
1414

**Wadi's Bach**

*Jebel Rum*
1754

*Jebel
Barrah*

*Jebel
Abu Judaya*

*W a d i   R a m m a n*

**Lawrence's
spring**

*Wadi
al-Shallaleh*

**Dunes**

•**Lawrence's
house**

*K b o r   a l - A j r a m*

**Khazali
Canyon**

*Jebel
Khazali*

*W a d i   Y u t u m   a l - U m r a n*

**Burdah
Rock
Bridge** ✳

*Jebel
Burdah*
1560

① Rum

HOTEL
Rest house........①

## "El Aurens"

Inspired by an ardent interest in archeology, TE Lawrence managed to contrive two trips to the Levant, between 1909 and 1914, during which time he was able to perfect his Arabic. Noticed by the British Secret Service, this complex figure became a liaison officer to Faisal, son of the Emir of Mecca. By rallying the Arabs against the Turks, he became associated with the era which saw the Bedouin armies of Al-Ouedj (Arabia) enter Damascus in 1917 and 1918. His cavalier behaviour together with his passion for the cause won him the friendship and deep respect of the Bedouin, who called him "El Aurens". All of this and more is retold in his *"Seven Pillars of Wisdom"*. After the eventual collapse of the Ottoman Empire, separate mandates were negotiated and Lawrence was mortified to find the British had reneged on their promise for an independent Arab kingdom. Disheartened, he returned to Dorset and retreated into anonymity. In 1922 he enlisted in the Royal Air Force under an assumed name. He died in a motor-cycle accident in 1935 and went down in history as "Lawrence of Arabia", made famous by David Lean's epic film (1962).

*tea or coffee at the rest-house).* Here, people live simply, for there are no hotel facilities as such, only a modest camp site with lines of small tents implanted on the sand and an open-air restaurant. The village of Rum itself, populated by Bedouins, is not very alluring, consisting as it does of ugly rubble-stone squat houses with a small, untidy and neglected courtyard at the front. Yet another reason for quickly setting off into the desert. Only the attractive little **fort** (1933) that houses the desert camel patrol garrison is worthy of a detour. The smart uniform of the camel corps manages to combine pomp with Bedouin tradition and the soldier on duty will graciously agree to be photographed.

**Excursions cross-country** – *The tour in 4WD vehicles takes in all the sites in the vicinity of Rum (for details on opening times and charges, turn to Making the most of Wadi Rum). Allow a total time of 4hr, although the actual time spent in the vehicles amounts to about 90min; this leaves plenty of time to admire the extraordinary landscape.*

The circuit begins at **Lawrence's Spring** which is where water, collected further up, is piped to a dreadful concrete reservoir and drinking trough (water undrinkable). Far better to admire the beautiful Arabian acacia, which has succeeded in withstanding both the drought and the appetite of hungry flocks, or the palm trees clinging to the rock, imparting lovely patches of green to the red stone cliffs.

The actual pools in which the British officer bathed are located further south, in Wadi al-Shallaleh. A Nabataean channel and temple stood nearby. You are then taken across the wadi and into a *Jebel* lined with beautiful natural pillars and a defile known as **Khazali Canyon**. Venture a few metres into this cool *siq*, in which the sound of footsteps echoes about you, to discover on each parapet a series of **rock paintings** (animals and footprints) and Thamudic or Nabataean inscriptions.

The long crossing of Khor al-Ajram, the valley perpendicular to Wadi Rum, leads to the foot of the natural arch known as the **Burdah Rock Bridge** apparently suspended in mid-air. The arduous climb (*3km there and back*) to the top is rewarded with a magnificent **view**\*\*.

The last attraction of the tour is **Lawrence's house**, which consists of little more than a stone wall and is of little interest, before venturing further in and among the fabulous **red sand dunes** (Dune Sand).

The rock paintings in the Khazali Canyon

**On foot –** One idea for a short and easy walk (1hr there and back) is to head out across the tented camp beside the *rest-house* and then right towards the two mountains, and beyond into **Wadi S'Bach**. From there, a path leads on to a grove of palm trees in which you will find a small spring (where the water oozes out of between the rocks). From here, a lovely **view** extends over the Wadi Rum. If travelling independently by car, you can complete the circuit by driving around the northern limits of the Wadi Rum mountain range and out towards **Al-Munayshir** where the scenery turns into a lunar landscape. *To undertake this 72km round-trip from Rum, go back 12km to the railway. At the fork, turn right towards Al-Diseh. The road into the desert eventually peters out into a dead end.*

## Making the most of Wadi Rum

### COMING AND GOING

**By bus –** There are around 2 buses a day: one to and from Petra, the other to and from Aqaba. The minibuses park on the forecourt of the rest-house.

### HOW TO GET ABOUT IN WADI RUM

**On foot –** Ensure you take good comfortable, thick-soled walking shoes or boots that provide sufficient insulation from the burning heat of the sands. To hike to Lawrence's Spring, allow 2hr there

and back. Be sure to follow the appropriate precautions against heat-exhaustion – see the section on Health, p 306.

**Hiring a vehicle –** The nearest agents for hiring out a 4WD vehicle are located at Aqaba.

### ADDRESS BOOK

**Tourist Information –** The offices of the tourism police are situated in the rest-house; it is well worth dropping in on them before you embark upon negotiations with the Bedouins.

**Wadi Rum**

## WHERE TO STAY

The only available place to stay is the rest-house. You can camp out in the desert if you arrange to be dropped off there in the evening and collected the next morning. Arrangements and equipment through the rest-house.

### • Rum

*Under US$20*

**Camping Wadi Rum Rest House**, Rum ☎ (3) 201 88 61, Fax (3) 201 23 83. This establishment is located just outside the village and as such is impossible to miss. Apart from providing a full range of information, the rest-house is an ideal spot for pairing up with other travellers intent on undertaking an excursion. The (Canadian) tents are to be found at the back of the rest-house. Mattresses and blankets are provided (temperatures can fall dramatically at night). Hot, if somewhat Spartan, shower facilities. Alternative options include sleeping in a large tent or on in the open air on the roof. Half-board tariff of JD13 per person.

## WHERE TO EAT

If you do not fancy eating at the rest-house, there is a cheap and cheerful eating -place and a grocery shop in the village.

### • Rum

*Under US$10*

**Wadi Rum Rest House** ♇ Breakfast, lunch and dinner. The restaurant offers a choice of *meze* and traditional *mensef*, which they can serve outside on the shaded terrace or inside the dining room. Buffet for groups.

## OTHER THINGS TO DO

Before undertaking any activity in the Wadi Rum, visitors are strongly advised to report to the tourism police (on the right as you enter the rest-house). An officer will then give you a detailed map of the area and make recommendations on how best to spend a day there; he will also advise you of the official charges

and rates you must reckon to pay. These are also listed inside the rest-house alongside the detailed maps of the region. Equipped with this information, it is up to you to pick a local guide from the group of Bedouins loitering thereabouts and negotiate with him an acceptable package-price. Remember that these men may not speak English very well and so it is important to clearly establish the price, the duration and the main attractions included in the proposed excursion. Once you get on your way, do not fear: you will be in very safe hands – these guys are more than capable.

**Excursions –** The cost of an outing in a **4WD** is usually all inclusive and calculated on the basis of parties of 6 people. These rates vary considerably between JD6 (Lawrence's Spring, 30min) and JD45 (for a whole day). Should you wish to visit the places we recommend here, allow JD32 (Burdah Rock Bridge, 4hr).

If you want to experience the genuine thing and travel into the desert by **camel** – and be prepared to endure the after-effects – the cost of riding to Lawrence's Spring and back is JD7 (2hr). For a two-day trip with overnight stop at Burdah, allow JD40. Prices given are per head.

**More energetic pastimes –** A different kind of attraction is the great scope for serious hiking and **rock-climbing** (challengingly sheer cliffs, canyons) in a grandiose setting and suitable weather conditions at a time when the climbing season in Europe is over. The infrastructure for this sport is basic, although relations with the Bedouins are good and so help with transport and access is forthcoming. Two local trained guides are on hand for further advice, although if you do choose to go out with them it is vital that you check their equipment before setting out. For additional information, consult Tony Howard's special handbook on the Wadi Rum (*see* *p 103*).

A member of the Desert Camel Patrol beneath the inscription: "Allah, the nation, the king".

# AQABA
Red Sea coast – Pop 63 000

**Not to be missed**
A swim in the warm waters of the Red Sea among the multi-coloured fish.
A walk along the parade of pavement cafés to the fishing port
at the close of day.
**And remember...**
Hire a mask and snorkel and dive into the water: the sight is mind-blowing.
Buy a small underwater camera and capture
your submarine experience on film.

The last few kilometres of the Desert Highway pass alongside a series of strikingly purple rock-faces down towards the sea – hence the name *Aqaba*, which means "slope" in Arabic. Amazingly enough, the first town to be seen on the right is in fact the Israeli town of Eilat, with its terraces of buildings arranged around the sweeping curve of the bay, sandwiched between the deep blue sea and the dark blue of the bare mountains of Sinaï behind. At last, as the road approaches the coast, Aqaba can be seen directly opposite, huddled against an escarpment, set ablaze by the setting sun.

Given that January temperatures here average out at 20°C, the sky is almost always cloudless, the sea is full of exceptional ranges of marine life and the town is ideally situated for a variety of day trips inland, Aqaba is the most popular and renowned seaside resort in Jordan. Unlike Eilat, however, it appears rather a sleepy place while cannily masking its vital commercial significance not only to the economy of Jordan, but of Iraq as well. Only the constant stream of trucks ploughing up and down the Desert Highway and the ships moored offshore might discreetly intimate the underlying importance of the city as a trading post.

## A much-coveted maritime outlet

Eilat and Aqaba are modern reconstructions of the ancient coastal towns of Eilath and Ezion-Geber, where **King Solomon** built his fleet of ships that were to return laden with back gold, sandalwood and precious stones from a mysterious land called Ofir. The strategic connotations associated with accessing the Gulf of Aqaba have meant that the outpost has been highly coveted throughout history. Over time, Aila was controlled by the Nabataeans; under the Romans it became Ailana; during the Byzantine era, it was the seat of a bishop; at the dawn of Islam, the medieval town was fortified by walls (still extant in places around the town centre). Thereafter, the city was a meeting place for pilgrims destined for Mecca. At last, it fell to the Crusaders; shortly after, **Renaud de Châtillon** had boats carried there overland and audaciously threatened to destroy the holy Muslim city. **Saladin** responded this scheming by sending in the Egyptian fleet. In defence, the Mamelukes erected their fort near where the modern museum stands. A small Ottoman garrison was stationed there when Arab troops seized it in 1917 to cries of "To Aqaba!", the echoes of which resounded in the first sequences of the film *Lawrence of Arabia*.

To the west, the small village of Eilat was the last Israeli conquest (1948), after which it grew into a large holiday resort. Among the initial schemes to materialise out of the peace treaty signed on 8 August 1994, a frontier-post was finally opened between the twin towns of Eilat and Aqaba, with their shared waters offshore set to be transformed into a bi-lateral marine national park.

**Aqaba**

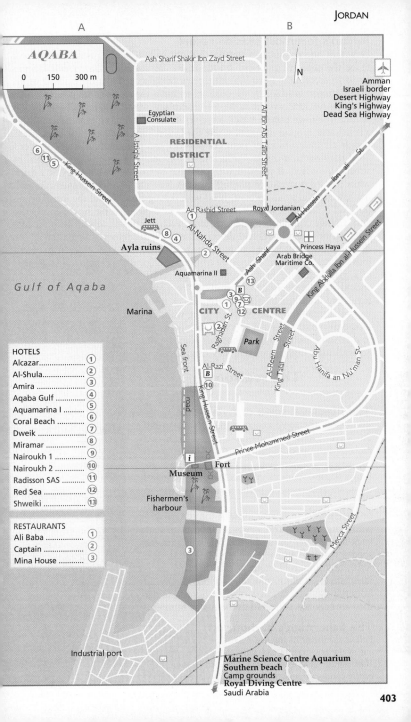

## AQABA

0    150    300 m

Ash Sharif Shakir Ibn Zayd Street

N

Amman
Israeli border
Desert Highway
King's Highway
Dead Sea Highway

Egyptian
Consulate

RESIDENTIAL

DISTRICT

A
B

Ali Ibn Abi Talib Street

Al-Istiqlal Street

King Hussein Street

Ar Rashid Street

Royal Jordanian

Al-Hussein

King Abdulla Ibn al-Hussein Street

Jett

Al-Nahda Street

Princess Haya

Ayla ruins

Ash Sharif

Arab Bridge
Maritime Co.

Gulf of Aqaba

Aquamarina II

Marina

CITY    CENTRE

Raghadan St.

Sea front road

Park

Al-Razi Street

Al-Reem Street

King Talal Street

Abu Hanifa an Nu'man St.

Prince Mohammed Street

King Hussein Street

Fort

Museum

Fishermen's
harbour

Mecca Street

Industrial port

Marine Science Centre Aquarium
Southern beach
Camp grounds
Royal Diving Centre
Saudi Arabia

### HOTELS
Alcazar...................... ①
Al-Shula.................... ②
Amira ....................... ③
Aqaba Gulf ............... ④
Aquamarina I .......... ⑤
Coral Beach ............. ⑥
Dweik ....................... ⑦
Miramar ................... ⑧
Nairoukh 1 ............... ⑨
Nairoukh 2 ............... ⑩
Radisson SAS ........... ⑪
Red Sea .................... ⑫
Shweiki .................... ⑬

### RESTAURANTS
Ali Baba ................... ①
Captain ................... ②
Mina House ............ ③

## Jordan's foremost seaside resort

Now that Aqaba can claim to have thirty or so hotels, it is justified in claiming to be the country's principal seaside resort, far outpacing the modest facilities available around the Dead Sea. Jordanians prefer to frequent the place in winter when Amman is seized by the cold. In summer, the ambient temperature rarely drops below 30°C, even at night, which explains why this is regarded as the low season. The **town centre**, which preserves its intimate quality, is contained within a small area, around the point where the Desert Highway meets the coast. Here, people are happy to loiter along the seafront and pass the time haggling over a coral necklace or a carpet. Further south lies the popular beach overlooked by street cafés which, at nightfall, are populated by local residents enjoying a drink while sharing a smoke or playing cards. A little further on, a promenade leads out towards the small harbour, filled with fishing-smacks, and the fort. Then as the road heads in the direction of Saudi Arabia, it passes along the coral reef lined with a range of facilities (aquarium, long beach, camp site, Royal Diving Centre) catering for beach lovers and divers. Those who are reluctant (even though no danger is involved) to set foot in water that is swarming with exotic fish – fabulous in form and colour – might be tempted to enjoy the spectacle from the safety of a glass-bottomed boat; several boatmen will not fail to offer their services should they be given the opportunity. The luxury hotels are clustered on the western side of town, beyond a small shopping centre bristling with fast-food outlets and ice-cream parlours. All have access to a private beach until the ambitious plans for the national marine park are eventually completed.

The public beach at Aqaba

## The seafront
*Allow 2hr.*

### The medieval town of Ayla (A1-2)

Just before the town centre, some 700m beyond the large hotels overlooking the esplanade and more or less opposite the Aqaba Gulf Hotel, stand the vestiges of old Ayla. Trenches cut into the rough ground mark out the rectangular outline of the town (140mx170m). The Syrian Gate, further along the road, is now thought by archeologists to be the entrance to a **great mosque** (on site marked with "large enclosure") – which appears to date back to the early years of Islam. Walk around the solid stone wall to the **Egyptian Gate**: this gate, Ayla's best preserved, stood astride the main shop-lined street heading into town. Finds recovered from the site that, probably, was abandoned under the Fatimids, are preserved in the Aqaba Museum.

### The fishermen's harbour (A3)

*Follow the broad Al-Hussein Avenue on the left leading out of the town centre and walk along the seafront for 1km. Amble gently below the palm trees towards the beach, cutting through the small popular pavement cafés.*

**Aqaba**

## The Red Sea is... blue!

The Gulf of Aqaba forms one of the two northernmost protrusions of the Red Sea that flank the Sinaï peninsula. The western section is connected to the Mediterranean by the Suez Canal. Beyond the Tiran Strait, where the coral islands leave only a narrow passage for shipping, the waters of the Red Sea wash the southern tip of Sinai to lap the eastern shores of Egypt, Sudan and Eritrea, and the western coast of Saudi Arabia. Between Djibouti and the Yemen, the water flows south to reach the Indian Ocean. What is exceptional about this narrow stretch of sea between the two continents is its depth (1 828m); despite this, the surface water temperature in summer reaches 30°C and only barely falls below 20°C in winter. It apparently owes its name to a very occasional proliferation of an alga, which turns red when it dies.

At the far end, you come to the pretty little **harbour** where, as night begins to fall, fishermen sell their day's catch. On the cement quayside, large tuna and perhaps the odd small shark are unceremoniously laid out and haggled over.

In the distance, a line of green palm trees separates the harbour from the barren and rocky *jebels* beyond. In the dwindling light of the setting sun, the *glass-bottomed boats* return to anchor, and a delightful serenity descends upon the scene.

The Visitors' Centre and the **Aqaba Museum** (A2) (*7.30am-6.30pm, winter 5.30pm. Entrance fee*) occupy a fine house right on the esplanade, overlooking the sea; this once belonged to the grandfather of the late

The seafront

J. L. Dugast/HOA QUI

King Hussein. The first room, opposite the tourist information desk, is devoted to Jordanian folklore (traditional dress, utensils and tools) and the second to the archeology of Aqaba. The fragments of the Arabic inscription once surmounted the Egyptian Gate of the medieval town: interestingly, this verse taken from the Koran is more usually applied to homes as an incitement of protection. Many of the objects on display confirm the role of the town as an important crossroads; among the more remarkable artefacts, there is a capital carved out of coral. The milestone discovered in Aqaba is the first of many that once lined the Via Nova Trajana that stretched all the way to Bosra.

Behind the museum nestles the entrance to the small **fort** (B2) (*open daily, sunrise to sunset; no charge*) framed between two semicircular towers with machicolations. In the vaulted vestibule there is a long elegant inscription, touched here and there with red pigment, that assigns the building of the fort to the last Mamelukes (early 16C). The courtyard within is graced by an immense eucalyptus tree and lined with rooms that, at one time, accommodated pilgrims bound for Mecca. Their state of devastation is largely due to bombing by the British during the First World War.

# The south coast
*25km – Allow 45min excluding time for a swim.*

The road south heads past the fort and down to Aqaba's **industrial port** (A3). This deep dock is easily navigable by the large container ships that come in to collect the country's two principal valuable mineral exports: phosphates and potash. A little further on, the steamer bound for Egypt waits at its mooring for passengers to embark.

The coast road makes its way along a long ledge of bare rock and yellow sand which garishly clashes in the glaring sunshine with the pale azure blue and turquoise waters of the Red Sea.

**Coral reefs**

Coral is literally constructed by a series of microscopic creatures that are hyper-sensitive to ambient temperature. Most types of this organism live in warm waters, banded into restricted areas by a combination of light and available food supply; never do the colonies venture very deep. Amassed together in large numbers, these organisms attach themselves to hard surfaces to be found in the shallows close to the shore. Where there is a bank of rock, the colony might proliferate, gradually encrusting it with an accumulation of shed skeletons to form treacherously sharp reefs and barriers. Coral varies considerably in terms of colour and texture. However, its vivid colour is usually imparted by the living layer of organisms, which, when taken out of the water, dries and fades: there is absolutely no point, therefore, in plundering the submerged coral reefs that already struggle to survive under threat from industrial pollution.

10km from the town centre it encounters a small huddle of white buildings on the right that houses the **Marine Science Centre**, which is dedicated to researching, monitoring and protecting the coral reef. Its aquarium is open to the public.

■ **Marine Science Centre Aquarium**★ (*8am-6pm, winter 5pm. Entrance fee.*)
Enthusiastic scuba divers and snorkellers can come here to identify the species they have encountered underwater. Others, meanwhile, can gain an insight into the rich diversity of flora and fauna found in the Red Sea without fear of coming face to face with any dangerous species, however minute the risk. Incidentally, do not be put off by the shark at the entrance: it is

stuffed! The fish are segregated in tanks and identified by a photograph and description (in English). Some are so similar that distinguishing one species from another calls for powerful observation, and waiting for a shy specimen to emerge from its hiding-place might involve considerable patience.

Sunfish, parrot fish and lion fish owe their names to their shimmering livery and their bizarre shapes. Look out for the aptly-named butterfly fish whose fins are so slender that it seems propelled by sails, the balloon fish blown up into a taut ball, the more common moray eel which bites its prey or the awful stone-fish that camouflages itself among the rocks and causes a dangerous wound. There is also the turkey-fish, armed with fins that double as long, poisonous barbs, that resembles a strange submarine from a futurist comic-strip.

*Proceed along the road for 2km.*

■ **South Beach★** – *Entrance fee.* There is a vast sandy beach 12km out of town, strewn with branches of broken coral detached from the reef. On Fridays, Jordanian families come and picnic in the early afternoon, and the congenial atmosphere that develops means that this is a good place to make new friends. Across the water, the skyline is marked with the steep silhouette of the Egyptian Sinaï. The real spectacle, however, lies under water, and not so far from the shore at that. As you wade out from the shallows, the sea bottom becomes alive with an extraordinary array of fish. Simple goggles are more than adequate to appreciate their variety, but do keep an eye out for sea urchins, and avoid stepping on one, as their splinters can be very difficult to remove – the best option is to don plastic sandals or fins. Better still, treat yourself to an excursion aboard a glass-bottomed boat: the view through the small plexiglass panel will allow you to see a wide variety of fish, but also superb corals that cannot be seen from the beach.

A few kilometres further south, the road leads to the **Royal Diving Centre** (*see Making the most of Aqaba*), before reaching the border with Saudi Arabia. This section of coast (25km), extending parallel to the Yemenieh coral reef, was granted to Jordan under an agreement with Riyad in 1965.

## Pharaoh's Island
*A full day's excursion by boat.*

*Since this Jordanian island lies in Egyptian waters, the trip should be booked two days in advance so as to allow the necessary customs formalities to be completed in time (see* p 411*).*

An excursion to this little island consists of a mini-cruise, with stops on the way for swimming and beautiful views of the Egyptian coasts of Sinaï. The crossing from Aqaba takes about an hour, after which the boat moors in the small cove about 6km south of Taba, opposite a line of small shops and a café. A visit to the **fortress** takes approximately 45min. Although the Crusaders are known to have settled here and named the place the Island of Graye, the fine crenellated ramparts (well restored) probably date from work undertaken in the 12C by Muslims. After a short period of relaxation, passengers go back onboard before the boat moves out into deeper water and anchors offshore in time for a swim before lunch. After lunch, there is time for another swim before the boat heads home to Aqaba.

**Pharaoh's Island**

# Making the most of Aqaba

**Aqaba**

## COMING AND GOING

**By air – Royal Wings** operates one or two scheduled flights a day from Amman to Aqaba. The small airport is located 10km northwest of the city (JD4 taxi fare). ☎ (3) 201 21 11. Airport shops and currency exchange bureaux are open for business at flight-times.

Note: there is a departure tax levied on all those leaving the country. When checking in for an onward flight from Amman, remember to state whether or not you have already paid the tax due.

**By boat – Arab Bridge Maritime Co** (B2), first street on the left past the post office ☎ (3) 201 32 35, Fax (3) 201 63 13. Two ferries operate regular crossings (3hr) between Aqaba and Nuweiba el Muzeina (Egypt). Budget US$20 per head in tourist class and US$100 for a vehicle. Note that at certain times of the year the boats are packed with pilgrims doing the Jihad. There is also a fast service (1hr) by speedboat.

**By bus –** The **Jett** bus company (A1) operates 6 services daily between Amman and Aqaba (4hr) ☎ (3) 201 52 22. They also occasionally run day-trips to Petra. Departures from outside the company offices next to the Miramar Hotel. A **minibus** service shuttles to Amman several times a day and more sporadically to Petra, Wadi Rum and Karak via the Araba Valley (3hr). Departures from the central station next to the public park; departures for Karak leave from a stop 400m further south.

**By shared taxi –** Departures for Amman and Karak from the same places as the minibuses.

**To/from Israel –** A bus operates between Eilat and Aqaba, although services seem unreliable. A taxi to the border costs JD4. The formalities on the Jordanian side of the border are straightforward during the following times: Sunday to Thursday, 6.30am-11pm; Friday and Saturday, 8am-8pm.

## GETTING AROUND AQABA

The town centre is small enough to be explored on foot; however, you will require a vehicle if you intend to go to South Beach.

**By bus –** Buses leave from the fort for the Royal Diving Centre, the beach and the Aquarium. Ask local shopkeepers when they run.

**By taxi –** Taxis driving around Aqaba itself do not have meters as such but levy a set charge according to the destination. Do be advised that they will sometimes over-charge: it is as well to know that the cost of a ride from the centre of town to the luxurious seafront hotels should not exceed JD0.5.

**Car rental – Hertz**, behind the Aquamarina II (B2) ☎ (3) 201 62 06.
**Avis**, near the Nairoukh Hotel (B2) ☎ (3) 202 28 83.
**Oryx Rent a Car** in the Hotel Miramar complex (A1) ☎ (3) 201 31 33. This agent specialises in supplying new and nearly-new 4x4/4WD vehicles for the adventurous travellers seeking to explore the Wadi Rum or the Araba Valley.

## ADDRESS BOOK

**Tourist Information** (A2) – Located within the museum precinct, 1km from the town centre, near to the fishing harbour. ☎ (3) 201 33 63.

**Banks/Currency exchange –** There are several banks and currency exchange bureaux to be found in the centre of town; several are even open at weekends and holidays. The **Amman-Cairo Bank** (B2) changes travellers' cheques and cash; it also offers VISA card holders the opportunity to withdraw cash in dinars. **Housing Bank**, King Hussein St. Visa cash dispenser.

**Post Office** (B2) – The post office in the town centre is marked by its distinctive red and white-painted metal tower.
**DHL**: ☎ (3) 201 20 39.

**Medical services – Princess Haya Hospital** (B1), set back from the main roundabout on the outskirts of town, on the Desert Road, ☎ (3) 201 41 11. Special unit dedicated to fishing/diving accidents, with decompression chamber that can accommodate up to 6 people.

**Egyptian Consulate** (A1) – 600m further along the same road that runs past the Alcazar Hotel, ☎ (3) 201 86 72. Open mornings only for visa applications to Pharaoh's Island.

**Airline offices – Royal Jordanian** (A1), opposite the Princess Haya Hospital, ☎ (3) 201 44 77. Also issues tickets for internal flights on Royal Wings.

## WHERE TO STAY

Whatever category of hotel you choose, the cost of accommodation is negotiated relative to the time of year and the length of your stay. In summer, air-conditioning is almost indispensable.

### • Town centre
*From US$25-40*

The less expensive hotels are scattered, for the most part, in the melee of buildings near the post office (the **Amira**, the **Nairoukh I** and the **Red Sea**) or near the public gardens (although the facilities at the **Flower**, the **Petra** and the **Jerusalem** are pretty basic, this is reflected in the prices charged).

**Nairoukh I Hotel**, Al-Yarmouk St, ☎ (3) 201 92 84 – 15rm ⌗ 🖹 🖋 📺 This is a simple establishment offering rooms equipped with air-conditioning.

**Red Sea Hotel**, Al-Yarmouk St, ☎ (3) 201 21 565 – 22rm 🍴 / 🖹 📺 Elementary accommodation with small private balconies. Friendly reception.

**Dweik Hotel**, Al-Yarmouk St, ☎ (3) 201 29 84, Fax (3) 201 29 85 – 18rm ⌗ 🖹 🖋 📺 🆑 Situated between the two above, this hotel has small rooms, simple but comfortable. Pleasant welcome. The best value for money in the street.

**Amira Hotel**, Al-Yarmouk St, ☎ (3) 201 88 40, Fax (3) 201 25 59 – 12rm ⌗ 🖹 🖋 📺 ✗ Pleasant little

hotel, impeccably run. The upper-floor rooms have small balconies with sea views. A good place to stay in this category. Slightly more expensive than its neighbours.

*From US$40-60*

Guests at the comfortable hotels opposite the ruins of Ayla enjoy free access to one of the beaches stretching before the large resort hotels along the seafront.

**Miramar Hotel**, King Hussein St, ☎ (3) 201 43 40, Fax (3) 201 43 39 – 140rm ⌗ 🖹 🖋 📺 ✗ 🏊 🆑 The rather dowdy rooms have balconies either overlooking the swimming pool or the sea.

**Shweiki Hotel**, Ash Sharif St, not far from the town centre, ☎ (3) 202 26 57, Fax (3) 202 26 59 – 32rm ⌗ 🖹 🖋 📺 ✗ 🆑 This brand new, characterless hotel provides a good standard of comfort at a very reasonable price. Half the rooms have balconies with sea views. Unfortunately the hotel is situated in a noisy main street.

*From US$55-80*

**Nairoukh II Hotel**, King Hussein St (Corniche), ☎ (3) 201 29 80, Fax (3) 201 29 81 – 94rm ⌗ 🖹 🖋 📺 ✗ On the main seafront road, not far from the town centre. The rooms are spacious, but rather dull. Half have sea views. A good place to stay.

*From US$80-100*

**Alcazar Hotel**, Al-Nahda Street ☎ (3) 201 41 31, Fax (3) 201 41 33 – 132rm ⌗ 🖹 🖋 📺 ✗ 🏊 🆑 The Moorish-style front conceals a prison-like complex of rooms arranged around a central courtyard. Old-fashioned furniture and interior furnishings. Scuba-diving club. Disco.

*From US$100-115*

**Aqaba Gulf Hotel**, King Hussein St, ☎ (3) 33 66 36, Fax (3) 201 82 46 – 188rm ⌗ 🖹 🖋 📺 ✗ 🏊 🎾 🆑 Comfortable new hotel, by far the most expensive in the centre of town. All the rooms have their own private, and very pleasant, sitting-area; all are soberly designed and furnished.

**Making the most of Aqaba**

**• Seafront** (A1)

The most agreeable place to stay in and around Aqaba is along the seafront northwest of the main town, out on the road to Eilat. The following 3 hotels are the only ones with direct access to the beach, which is open to non-residents for a fairly high fee.

*From US$80-100*

**Aquamarina I Hotel**, King Hussein St, ☎ (3) 201 62 50, Fax (3) 201 42 71 – 64rm ⚓ 🍽 ♪ 📺 ✗ 🏊 🌴 CC This establishment is more like a leisure complex than a simple hotel, as its Sports Centre offers complete courses in scuba-diving, water-skiing and underwater photography. The rooms vary quite considerably in quality, so ask for one on the seafront if possible. Its small artificial beach is unfortunately not very pleasant.

*From US$100-115*

**Coral Beach Hotel**, King Hussein St, ☎ (3) 201 35 21, Fax (3) 201 36 14 – 99rm ⚓ 🍽 ♪ 📺 ✗ 🏊 🌴 CC Of the 3, the furthest hotel from the town centre is also the most tropical in feel, as its rooms are arranged on 3 floors overlooking a large garden area planted with palm trees. The hotel also has 8 bungalows. The hotel has been completely renovated and lays claim to the best part of Aqaba's beach.

*Over US$225*

**Radisson SAS Hotel**, Kings Bd, ☎ (3) 201 24 26, Fax (3) 201 34 26 – 244rm ⚓ 🍽 ♪ 📺 ✗ 🏊 🌴 CC An international-style hotel, in an impersonal setting but with every possible comfort. Rooms have two prices, depending on whether they overlook the sea and the pool or the car park (to be avoided, as prices are still high!). Pleasant private beach with bar.

**• Camping**
Under US$10

**National Tourist Camp**, off the road to Saudi Arabia ☎ (3) 201 76 50. The only true camp site in the vicinity of Aqaba is situated 12km from the town centre, beside the South Beach. The two shower blocks are a little basic, but the setting has remained unspoilt.

## WHERE TO EAT

**• Town centre**
*Under US$10*

A number of informal snack bars are clustered around the main square: these serve standard, perhaps rather disappointing, but inexpensive fare.

*Over US$10*

**Mina House**, King Hussein St, ☎ (3) 201 26 99 ♀ From the comfort of an attractive white vessel moored in the fishermen's harbour, you can watch the sun go down while enjoying a fresh lobster (JD35 per kilo), a plate of squid, fresh fish or prawns. The set menu also lists cheaper alternatives including *meze* and chicken. You can also savour a glass of something at the bar. Service from 10am to 12midnight.

**Captain's Restaurant**, Al-Nahda St, behind the Aquamarina II Hotel ☎ (3) 201 69 05. It is impossible to miss this restaurant as it has a distinctive prow-shaped frontage protruding into the street. Stick to fish, in which the restaurant prides itself.

**Ali Baba**, Raghadan St, ☎ (3) 201 39 01 At one time, this was considered the best restaurant in Aqaba – however the quality goes down year by year. Specialities include fish, shellfish and Eastern delicacies. Pleasant terrace, but service is rushed.

**• Seafront** (A1)

There are no truly special restaurants in Aqaba. The large hotels serve their meals in over-decorated and somewhat tired-looking empty round spaces, rotundas or great big halls. Light meals and snacks may also be eaten outside beside the swimming pool.

*Over US$10*

**Blue Lagoon**, Aquamarina I Hotel. An attractive setting for a candle-lit dinner accompanied by a live orchestra (from 10pm). Distinctive in that the restaurant appears to be floating on the water. Buffet or à la carte.

**Having a drink**

**Cafes, bars, tea rooms** – Alcohol may be drunk in all the large hotel bars. The atmospheric places along the esplanade, frequented by Jordanians and tourists alike, tend only to serve tea and fizzy soft drinks.

Aqaba

**Hani Ali**, Raghadan St (B2) Next door to the Ali Baba restaurant, this place offers delicious ice-cream and Eastern sweetmeats, to sample on the terrace.

## OTHER THINGS TO DO

**Excursions** – Aqaba is ideally situated for day-trips to Wadi Rum, Petra and even Eilat.

**Pharoah's Island**. The Aquamarina I Hotel organises excursions to the island for US$45 per head, including a meal on board and the cost of an Egyptian visa for the day. It is essential to register for this trip two days in advance, giving details of passport numbers etc, to allow custom facilities to be completed in time. Reservations may be made by telephone. Alternatively, the same format is offered by the Aqaba Gulf Hotel.

**Sporting activities** – There are a number of fabulous opportunities provided by the resort hotels ranging between scuba-diving and water-skiing. On a more modest scale, the simple hire of a mask and snorkel, or a pair of goggles even, set a great treat in store.

**Hotel Aquamarina I** . Facilities include water-skiing and night-dives for beginners and highly experienced enthusiasts alike. Allow US$24 for a deep-sea diving expedition.

**Red Sea Diving Centre.** This specialist establishment is a registered diving school offering formal training to proficiency and PADI qualifications (hence the sign on the building opposite the Aquamarina II Hotel). PADI is recognised in over 174 countries across the world.

**Royal Diving Centre**, ☎ (3) 201 70 35. 18km south of the town centre, this diving school organises its dives among the unspoilt coastal reefs and a purpose-sunk wreck at 20m lying 200m off-shore. CMAS and PADI qualifications. Full training available. Private beach, showers, cafeteria, access JD2. JD10 per dive, plus JD5 for the hire of equipment subject to presentation of recognised certificate of proficiency. A bus collects participants from their hotels each morning at 9am and drops them off at the end of the day (4pm or 5pm depending on the time of year). Introductory sessions of 1hr on application (JD25).

## SHOPPING

The best shops (for things to take home or for an excursion into the desert) are to be found in the streets of the town centre around and about the public gardens. **Naïf Store** sells carpets and a variety of antiques. You will also find express film-developers in the neighbourhood (**Agop** and **George**).

**Regional specialities** – Pink coral necklaces and bottles filled with coloured sands are among the most popular artefacts on sale besides the usual clutter of imported "fancy goods".

**Bookshops** – The two main bookshops selling a selection of international newspapers and a good range of travel publications are to be found within 50m of each other: **Yamani** (opposite the post office) and **Redwan**.

Making the most of Aqaba

# THE DEAD SEA HIGHWAY★★

310km drive from Aqaba to Amman – 5hr
See map of the King's Highway p 359

### And remember...
Tank up with fuel and top up engine oil and water levels at Aqaba
as summer temperatures can reach 50°C.

The drive, through what will probably be the wildest landscape you encounter on your travels through Jordan, takes you through the untamed and very arid countryside of the Araba Valley before heading along a splendid stretch of road shadowing the eastern shore of the Dead Sea. This relatively recent road cuts across a barren and inhospitable land with almost no outward signs of habitation for miles on end and certainly no substantial town along the way. Despite this, the extreme temperatures which prevail for much of the year in these parts can be compensated by a wonderfully soothing and therapeutic bathe in the danger-free Dead Sea – for as the water has a saline content of 30%, it is impossible to drown in it. Indeed, the incredible buoyancy prevents one from actually swimming so it is as well to just relax into it and, like so many others around you, allow the warm and mellowing water to support you. Why not cast all cares to the wind and have a photograph taken of you lying back, feet in the air, reading a newspaper.

*Head north out of Aqaba along the Desert Highway (3km) and fork left towards the airport. The road skirts the border-post with Israel, passes the airport (10km) and finally leads off into the Araba Valley.*

**Araba Valley –** *Do not take photographs of military installations.* The long deep-set corridor between the Red Sea and the Dead Sea is not, strictly speaking, a valley at all, but a dry gorge that rises 200m above the level of the Dead Sea near Gharandal before descending to 406m below sea-level by the Dead Sea. Such as the land lies, it would be impossible for a river to flow from one end to the other. Indeed the only bodies of water consist of transient wadis formed in the space of a few minutes during the rare but dramatic thunderstorms. Otherwise, it displays the classic features of a rift valley formed by the separation of two tectonic plates stretching from the Syrian Ghab, down through the Red Sea, and south to Kenya as part of the African Rift Valley.

*38km from Aqaba, a peculiarly rare "Danger Camels" sign signals the proximity of herds near a palm grove.*

The road follows the contours of the mountains rising up on the right-hand side. If you wonder how it is that such impressively large heaps of gravel have come to stack up against the cliff, you may be surprised to learn that they are the natural result of torrential rains that wash everything away from the mountainside as they pour down the rock. The water collects quickly into wadis that feed into a kind of lake, which in turn provides sustenance for a few hardy plants before the earth dries and cracks. After a few kilometres, the first sand-dunes appear. Beyond Gharandal (the 77km mark), the road passes a strange-looking small pagoda-shaped kiosk on the left, before continuing on towards the ugly hamlet of Al-Richa (85km mark) built of rubble and breeze-blocks.

As the valley broadens out, the jebels, which flanked the road as it left Aqaba, gradually recede. In the distance, lie the tall rocks that screen Petra from the outside world. Then the road begins its descent to below sea-level, crossing several dried-out wadis on its way, including the wide **Wadi al-Fidan** containing the famous Feinan copper deposits that have been exploited since Antiquity. A few kilometres from the left-hand side of the road runs the border with Israel; outside the confines of the rift valley, the landscape levels out at this point.

**Dead Sea★** – Up to this point, the landscape has been relieved by changes in the rock and sand; now, suddenly, you come upon the Dead Sea (171km mark) surrounded, in the foreground, by lush plantations of bananas and fields of tomatoes. The climate in the valley, supplemented by irrigation, allows growers in the area to produce fruit and vegetables all year round. However fresh water is a precious commodity in these parts and the cost of transporting it here would be prohibitive, so the Jordanians pump water up from the phreatic layer and collect as much rainwater as possible. At the fork, the right turning heads out to Tafila along the **Wadi al-Hassa,** which has cut its way through a splendid dark stone canyon.

The broad, almost white expanses stretching out beyond **Al-Safi** make up the southern region of the Dead Sea, separated from the northern territories by a tongue of land. The western shore, now part of Israel, is presumed to be where the Biblical town of Sodom once stood. The Bible explains the great cataclysm that engulfed Sodom along with its neighbour Gomorrah in the 19C BC as an act of God inflicted to punish the people there for being so corrupt and immoral.

*After passing the Potash City industrial plant, the road forks off to Karak (220km mark).*

From the far side of the peninsula, it is possible to make out the rock of **Masada** on a clear day standing on the opposite shore. At the top stood Herod's ancient fortress, the last bastion to be held by the Jews in their fight to resist the Romans. Finally, the road reaches the blue shores of the Dead Sea which, at its deepest point, plunges down to 793m below the level of the Mediterranean: it is sobering to think that the lowest inhabited place on the planet lies at 400m below sea-level. The concentration of salt in this immense salt-lake is 33%, precluding any form of life.

From this point on, the **panoramic road★★** becomes truly delightful as it picks its way between the Dead Sea on one side – a broad mirror-like lake glinting in the sunshine – and rugged flanks of the Moab Mountains with the hills of Judea beyond, on the other. The odd cluster of palm trees pinpoint the presence of water, perhaps a natural spring. At the 245km mark, a metal bridge spans the **Wadi Mujib**: a massive canyon crossed further east by the King's Highway is reduced here to a steep, narrow gorge plunging down between beautiful red cliffs. A favourite spot for enthusiasts to practise "canyoning" in and among the waterfalls and natural pools; the less adventurous, however, can continue 16km further on and take a swim in the stream there. A sign marked with

**The Dead Sea dies a second time**
Is the Dead Sea going to disappear? Since the 1960s, the level of the sea has continued to fall. The water provided by the River Jordan and its tributaries, diverted for irrigation, is no longer sufficient to replace the water lost in natural evaporation. With 350sqkm of sea having already vanished or been transformed into salt marshes, particularly in the south, experts have declared that, at the present rate, the sea will disappear altogether over the next four centuries. Two projects are currently being examined with the aim of increasing the flow of water into the Dead Sea. One plan put forward by the Israelis involves pumping water from the Mediterranean through underground channels. The other, proposed by the Jordanians, consists of drawing water from the Red Sea. In both cases, electrical power could be generated if the difference in height was exploited, although it will be a very long time before these very expensive projects are put into action.

**Dead Sea Highway**

"Roman Bath" indicates where the ancient springs of **Kallirhoë** are to be found, where Herod the Great once had a bath complex built. Two kilometres further on, the road crosses over **Wadi Zarqa Maïn** running through its beautiful red gorge, before arriving at the **Dead Sea Spa Hotel** (*30km from Wadi Mujib*), *the* **Mövenpick** and the **Rest House**, 5km further on, which together are the only establishments where it is possible to swim. Although the remote beaches along the route might appear extremely tempting, the salt left on the skin after immersion quickly becomes unbearable; it is therefore well worth choosing somewhere to bathe that has a shower close by!

As the road climbs back up towards Amman, swinging from bend to bend, look out for the sign "Sea-level", about 17km beyond the *Rest-House*.

## Making the most of the Dead Sea

### COMING AND GOING

The Dead Sea is readily accessible from Amman (52km).

**By bus –** The valley is sparsely populated and so only erratically served by buses. A daily service to the rest house, however, is operated out of Amman by the **Jett** Company. From Aqaba, a minibus service to Karak follows the southern section of the Araba Valley.

### WHERE TO STAY

For the present and until tourist facilities are further developed, there are only two available places offering overnight accommodation.

• **Dead Sea**

*From US$45-65*

**Dead Sea rest house**, 2.5km south of Suweimeh, ☎ (5) 546 110, Fax (5) 546 112 – 30rm ⬚⬚ 📧 𝄞 📺 ✕ ⬚ ⬚ 🆑 Small bungalows with separate lounge, a little expensive but very convenient. Two-room family maisonettes also available. Air-conditioned restaurant (much appreciated in summer!) with terrace: a buffet is served on Fridays and holidays, à la carte menu other days. The beach is nothing special and access costs JD2.5. You can use the showers outside (or inside, for around JD0.5) to wash off the salt after your swim.

*From US$ 150-160*

⬚ **Dead Sea Spa Hotel**, 5km from the rest house on the Dead Sea highway, ☎ (6) 560 15 54, Fax (6) 560 81 00 – 100rm ⬚⬚ 📧 𝄞 📺 ✕ ⬚ 🍴 ⬚ 🆑 A luxurious complex, furnished with taste.

The medical centre specialises in treating skin conditions. People also come here to relax. The somewhat small bedrooms have views over the sea (splendid sunsets) or over the mountains. Bar on the beach and by the pool. Jacuzzi, solarium, squash and tennis courts. Car hire possible. Non-residents may use the beach, for a fee.

*Over US$225*

**Mövenpick Resort and Spa**, near the Dead Sea Spa, ☎ (5) 325 20 30, Fax (5) 325 20 20 – 225rm ⬚⬚ 📧 𝄞 📺 ✕ ⬚ ⬚ 🍴 🆑 This new luxury complex is elegant without being ostentatious. The use of desert stone in the architecture is evocative of a traditional village. Magnificent garden with springs of water running among the greenery. Several restaurants and swimming pools, hammam, beauty and fitness centre.

### WHERE TO EAT

• **Dead Sea**

The only restaurants situated on this itinerary are attached to hotels.

### OTHER THINGS TO DO

**Sporting activities –** Obviously, the main attraction of these parts are the therapeutic waters of the hot springs (no charge) or, even better, of the Dead Sea at one of the recommended resorts listed above. Plans are afoot, however, for the RSCN (Royal Society for the Conservation of Nature) to sponsor facilities for hiking and canyoning in the area.

Young Jordanian girl

**Making the most of the Dead Sea**

# NOTES

# NOTES

# NOTES

# NOTES

# NOTES

# NOTES

# NOTES

# NOTES

# Index

Aleppo: place or attraction described in the text
Abbasids: term explained in the text
Calendar: practical information
*Abdullah (king)*: individual

# MAPS

*Manufacture Française des Pneumatiques Michelin*
Société en commandite par actions au capital de 2 000 000 000 de francs
Place des Carmes-Déchaux – 63000 Clermont-Ferrand (France)
R.C.S. Clermont-Fd B 855 200 507

© Michelin et Cie, Propriétaires-éditeurs, 2000
Dépôt légal avril 2000 – ISBN 2-06-855401-1 – ISSN 0763-1383
No part of this publication may be reproduced in any form without
the prior permission of the publisher.

**Printed in the EU 04-00/1**
Compograveur: Nord Compo – Villeneuve d'Ascq
Imprimeur: IME – Baume-les-Dames

**Cover illustrations:**
The funeral temple and the Arab castle at Palmyra – B. Brillion/MICHELIN
Jordanian wearing the keffieh – J. L. Dugast/HOA QUI
Mari head – F. Lamy/TOP

## Syria

| | | | |
|---|---|---|---|
| Aazaz | اعزاز | Damascus | دمشق |
| Abou Kamal | ابوكمال | Deir ez-Zor | دير الزور |
| Afrine | عفرين | Deraa | درعا |
| Ain Dara | عين دارا | Doura Europos | دورا وروبوس |
| al-Assad lake | بحيرة الاسد | Salihiyeh | الصالحية |
| al-Bara | البارة | Ebla | ايبلا |
| al-Haffe | الحفة | Tell Mardikh | تل مرديخ |
| al-Hamra | الحمرة | Halabiyeh | حلبية |
| al-Nassara | الناصرة | Hama | حماه |
| al-Qalabiyeh | صقيلبية | Harim | حاريم |
| al-Srouje | سروج | Homs | حمص |
| al-Thawra | التورة | Idlib | ادلب |
| Aleppo | حلب | Izraa | ازرع |
| Apamea | افاميا | Jisr al-Shoughour | جسر الشقور |
| Qalaat Mudiqh | قلعة المضيق | Khan Sheikoun | خان شيخون |
| Ariha | اريحا | Krak des Chevaliers | قلعة الحصن |
| Arwad | ارواد | (Qalaat al-Hosn) | |
| Baniyas | بانياس | Latakia | اللاذقية |
| Baqirha | باقرحا | Maaloula | معلولا |
| Bosra | بصرى الشام | Maarrat al-Nouman | معرة النعماب |
| Cyrrhus | سيروس | Mardeh | محرده |
| Nebi Houri | النبي هوري | | |

| Mari | ماري |
| Tell Hariri | تل الحريري |
| Marqab | قلعة المرقب |
| Meyadin | ميادين |
| Missiaf | مصياف |
| Palmyra | تدمر |
| Qalaat Jaabar | قلعة جعبر |
| Qalaat Rahba | قلعة رحبة |
| Qalb Lozeh | قلب لوزه |
| Qanawat | قنوات |
| Qasr al-Hayr al-Charqi | قصر الحير الشرقي |
| Qasr Ibn Wardan | قصر ابن وردان |
| Raqqa | الرقة |
| Rassafa | الرصافة |
| Ruweiha | رويحة |
| Safita | صافيتا |
| Saône Castle | السون |
| Saladin | قلعة صلاح الدين |
| Salkhad | صلخد |
| Sergilla | سرجلا |
| Seydnaya | صيدنايا |
| Shahba | شهبا |
| Sheizar | شيزر |
| Slenfeh | صلنفة |
| Souweida | السويداء |
| St Simeon (Qalaat Samaan) | قلعة سمعان |
| Tartus | طرطوس |
| Ugarit | اوغاريت |
| Ras Shamra | راس الشمرة |

## Jordan

| Ajlun | عجلون |
| al-Hammeh | الحمة |
| al-Mafraq | المفرق |
| Amman | عمان |
| Aqaba | العقبة |
| Azraq | الازرق |
| Dana | ضانا |
| Hammam al-Sarah | حمام الصرح |
| Irbid | اربد |
| Jarash | جرش |
| Karak | الكرك |
| Maan | معان |
| Madaba | مادبا |
| Mont Nebo | جبل نبو |
| Siyagha | صياغة |
| Petra | بتراء |
| Qasr el Hallabat | قصر الحلابات |
| Qasr Amra | قصير عمره |
| Salt | السلط |
| Shawbak | قلعة الشوبك |
| Tafila | الطفيلة |
| Um al Jimal | ام الجمل |
| Wadi Musa | وادي موسى |
| Wadi Rum | وادي رام |
| Zarqa | الزرقاء |

## Miscellaneous

| citadel | قلعة |
| hammam | جبل |
| jebel | حمام |
| mosque | جامع |
| museum | متحف |
| town | واد |
| wadi | مدينة |
| 0 | ٠ |
| 1 | ١ |
| 2 | ٢ |
| 3 | ٣ |
| 4 | ٤ |
| 5 | ٥ |
| 6 | ٦ |
| 7 | ٧ |
| 8 | ٨ |
| 9 | ٩ |

# Your opinion matters!

In order to make sure that this collection satisfies the needs of our readers, please help us by completing the following questionnaire with your comments and suggestions and return to:

**Michelin Travel Publications**   or
The Edward Hyde Building
38 Clarendon Road
Watford, UK

**Michelin Travel Publications**
P.O. Box 19008
Greenville, SC  29602-9008
USA

## ■ YOUR HOLIDAYS/VACATIONS:

**I. In general, when you go on holiday or vacation, do you tend to travel... (Choose one)**

- ☐ Independently, on your own
- ☐ Independently, as a couple
- ☐ With 1 or 2 friends
- ☐ With your family
- ☐ With a group of friends
- ☐ On organised trips

**2. How many international holidays or vacations of I week or more have you taken in the last 3 years?** _____

Last 3 destinations: _____    Month/Year: _____

_____    _____

_____    _____

**3. What do you look for most when planning a holiday or vacation?**

|  | Not at all | Sometimes | Essential |
|---|---|---|---|
| Somewhere new and exotic | ☐ | ☐ | ☐ |
| Real experience/meeting people | ☐ | ☐ | ☐ |
| Experiencing the wildlife/scenery | ☐ | ☐ | ☐ |
| Cultural insight | ☐ | ☐ | ☐ |
| Rest & relaxation | ☐ | ☐ | ☐ |
| Comfort & well-being | ☐ | ☐ | ☐ |
| Adventure & the unexpected | ☐ | ☐ | ☐ |

**4. When travelling, do you take a travel guide with you?**

☐ Always     ☐ Usually     ☐ Sometimes     ☐ Never

## ■ You and the Michelin NEOS guides

**5. About your purchase of a NEOS Guide**

How long was your holiday where you used the NEOS guide?
How many days? _____
For which country or countries? _____
How long before your departure did you buy it? How many days? _____

**6. What made you choose a NEOS Guide?**

*Highlight everything that applies.*

- ☐ Something new and interesting
- ☐ The layout
- ☐ Easy to read format
- ☐ Cultural details
- ☐ Quality of the text
- ☐ Quality of the mapping
- ☐ Practical Information
- ☐ Michelin quality

**7. Which sections did you use most during your holiday or vacation?**

*Score 1-4*           *(1 = least used)*           *(4 = most used)*

| | 1 | 2 | 3 | 4 |
|---|---|---|---|---|
| "Setting the Scene" | ☐ 1 | ☐ 2 | ☐ 3 | ☐ 4 |
| "Meeting the People" | ☐ 1 | ☐ 2 | ☐ 3 | ☐ 4 |
| "Practical Information" | ☐ 1 | ☐ 2 | ☐ 3 | ☐ 4 |
| "Exploring …" | ☐ 1 | ☐ 2 | ☐ 3 | ☐ 4 |

**8. How would you rate the following aspects of your NEOS guide?**

*Score 1-4*           *(1 = Poor)*           *(4 = Excellent)*

| | 1 | 2 | 3 | 4 |
|---|---|---|---|---|
| Cover design | ☐ 1 | ☐ 2 | ☐ 3 | ☐ 4 |
| Chapter Order | ☐ 1 | ☐ 2 | ☐ 3 | ☐ 4 |
| Layout (photos, diagrams) | ☐ 1 | ☐ 2 | ☐ 3 | ☐ 4 |
| Ease of reading (typeface) | ☐ 1 | ☐ 2 | ☐ 3 | ☐ 4 |
| Style of writing | ☐ 1 | ☐ 2 | ☐ 3 | ☐ 4 |
| Text boxes and stories | ☐ 1 | ☐ 2 | ☐ 3 | ☐ 4 |
| Plans & Maps | ☐ 1 | ☐ 2 | ☐ 3 | ☐ 4 |
| Star ratings system | ☐ 1 | ☐ 2 | ☐ 3 | ☐ 4 |
| Format | ☐ 1 | ☐ 2 | ☐ 3 | ☐ 4 |
| Weight | ☐ 1 | ☐ 2 | ☐ 3 | ☐ 4 |
| Durability | ☐ 1 | ☐ 2 | ☐ 3 | ☐ 4 |
| Price | ☐ 1 | ☐ 2 | ☐ 3 | ☐ 4 |

**9. Did you use other travel guides during your trip?**     ☐ Yes    ☐ No

If yes, which ones? _____

**10. Please give your NEOS guide a rating out of 20:** ____/20 (with 20 as top rating)

Would you use a NEOS guide for your next trip?     ☐ Yes     ☐ No

If no, why not? _____

Which other destinations would you like NEOS to cover? _____

**11. Any other comments or suggestions:** _____

_____

_____

_____

_____

_____

_____

_____

---

Surname/Last Name: _____ First Name: _____

Address: _____

Age: _____ Sex: ☐ M ☐ F

Profession: _____

Where did you purchase your NEOS Guide: What type of store?
                                  Which country?